MODERN REAL ESTATE
EIGHTH EDITION
PRACTICE IN
PENNSYLVANIA

HERBERT J. BELLAIRS

JAMES L. HELSEL, Jr.

James L. Goldsmith, Esq.

Mary Lynne Deets, **CONSULTING EDITOR**

**Real Estate
Education Company**®
A Kaplan Professional Company

This publication is designed to provide accurate and authoritative information in regard to the subject matter covered. It is sold with the understanding that the publisher is not engaged in rendering legal, accounting or other professional service. If legal advice or other expert assistance is required, the services of a competent professional person should be sought.

Vice President: Carol L. Luitjens
Executive Editor: Diana Faulhaber
Senior Development Editor: Robert A. Porché, Jr.
Managing Editor: Ronald J. Liszkowski
Art and Design Manager: Lucy Jenkins
Cover Design: DePinto Studios

Published by Real Estate Education Company®,
a division of Dearborn Financial Publishing, Inc.®
a Kaplan Professional Company
155 North Wacker Drive
Chicago, IL 60606-1719
(312) 836-4400
http://www.dearborn.com

Printed in the United States of America.

00 01 02 10 9 8 7 6 5 4 3 2

Library of Congress Cataloging-in-Publication Data

Bellairs, Herbert J.
    Modern real estate practice in Pennsylvania / Herbert J. Bellairs,
James L. Helsel, Jr., James L. Goldsmith, Esq.—8th ed.
        p.   cm.
    Includes index.
    ISBN 0-7931-3306-8
    I. Title.   II. Helsel, James L.   III. Goldsmith, James L.

KFP112.B4   1999
346.74804'37—dc21   99-045947

Contents

Section Two
REAL ESTATE PRACTICE

About the Authors

Herbert J. Bellairs, GRI, CRS, of Reading is a graduate of the Wharton School, University of Pennsylvania, where he majored in real estate. He has taught real estate courses at Penn State, Albright College and the Graduate REALTORS® Institute. Bellairs has operated his own realty firm since 1953. He is past president of the Reading-Berks Association of REALTORS®, Pennsylvania Association of REALTORS® and the Pennsylvania REALTORS® Education Foundation. In 1983, he was named Pennsylvania REALTOR®-of-the-Year. He also served as regional vice president for the National Association in 1983, treasurer in 1987 and 1988, and received the honor of being designated REALTOR® EMERITUS in 1948.

James L. Helsel, Jr., CCIM, SIOR, CPM, CRB, GRI, of Camp Hill is a graduate of Lycoming College, where he majored in Business Administration. He is president of Helsel, Incorporated REALTORS®, specialists in commercial and industrial brokerage, management and appraising. He is past president of the Greater Harrisburg Association of REALTORS®, and was the 1994 president of the Pennsylvania Association of REALTORS®. He was the 1983 REALTOR®-of-the-Year for the Harrisburg Association, and was awarded the CPM of the Year Award by the Delaware Valley Chapter of the Institute of Real Estate Management in 1987. Additionally, he is very active in the National Association of REALTORS®, serving on its Board of Directors since 1989. Helsel has taught real estate courses for both Pennsylvania State University and his local Association, and is a faculty member of the Pennsylvania REALTORS® Institute.

James L. Goldsmith, Esquire, is an attorney engaged in the private practice of law in Harrisburg. He is a corporate member of the firm of Caldwell & Kearns which serves as counsel to the Pennsylvania REALTORS®. In cooperation with the Pennsylvania Association of REALTORS®, he has co-authored the *Pennsylvania Real Estate Reporter,* which represents the first and only indexed compilation of Pennsylvania cases devoted to real estate and related issues. He teaches Real Estate Transactions at the Widener University School of Law, Harrisburg campus, and is an instructor for the Graduate REALTORS® Institute. Mr. Goldsmith and his firm are also engaged by insurers to defend insured real estate practitioners and lawyers in lawsuits in which professional negligence is claimed. He has litigated numerous cases at trial and appellate levels of the state and federal court system. He is a graduate of Washington and Jefferson College. He attended Dickinson School of Law and the Temple University School of Law, where he earned his Juris Doctor.

Mary Lynne Deets graduated from Slippery Rock University with a BS degree and from The University of Pittsburgh with a Masters Degree in Education. An elementary school teacher for many years, Deets started in Real Estate in 1982, became a manager and received her Associate Brokers License in 1988. She has been a member of the REALTORS® Association of Metropolitan Pittsburgh since 1984, is Past President of Ramp, 1994, and is currently District 8 Vice President to the Pennsylvania Association of REALTORS®, through 1999.

Mary Lynne lists and sells for Prudential Preferred Realty in Pittsburgh and is also the Training Director for Prudential Preferred Realty, coordinating the training of all new Prudential agents from all over the Pittsburgh area.

Mary Lynne teaches Fundamentals and continuing education for the REALTORS® Educational Institute.

ACKNOWLEDGMENTS   The authors express their deepest appreciation to Mary Lynne Deets, M.Ed., REALTOR®, New Agent Trainer and Fundamentals Instructor.

Thanks go to the members of the *Modern Real Estate Practice in Pennsylvania* Editorial Review Board for their gracious participation in the development of this textbook, and their valuable contributions of time, criticisms and suggestions:

    John W. Fisher, Schlicher-Kratz Institute, Lansdale, and Temple University, Philadelphia
    Elaine K. Houser, M.Ed., REALTORS® Educational Institute, Pittsburgh
    Laurel D. McAdams, consultant and real estate author
    Ruth A. Myers, Allied School of Real Estate Practice, Etters
    James J. Skindzier, DREI, Career Growth Real Estate Academy, Pittsburgh

Additional thanks go to reviewers of the seventh edition: Robert W. Corl, GRI, CSP; Lawrence J. Dellegrotto, GRI; Norman L. Fehr, Jr.; Harry H. Higgins III; Forrest E. Huffman, PhD; Barry Hoy; Harvey M. Levin, MAI; Robert M. Rowlands, Esq.; Raymond E. Rysak; Barbara G. Samet, CRS, CRB, DREI; Ben Simon and James J. Skindzier.

Finally, the authors extend their appreciation to Diana Faulhaber, Robert A. Porché, Jr. and Ronald J. Liszkowski of the Real Estate Education Company® for their assistance in the production of this eighth edition.

Preface

One of the golden opportunities in this country is the ability of people to own and control their own land. With real estate, people can plant roots for themselves and their families, influence the quality of their lives as stakeholders in the community and invest in their financial security. Just as the first immigrants discovered the tremendous value of these opportunities, still today real estate ownership is at the heart of the American dream.

Every aspect of our lives has grown more complex since the first generations settled here, and so, too, has real estate ownership. We have learned that without certain controls, the basic freedom to enjoy land is eroded. This has resulted in a long history of laws that intend to protect the rights of property owners, protect their ability to freely transfer their ownership and protect real estate owners from unscrupulous dealings. As complex as real estate ownership might seem, armed with some information and the guidance of learned professionals, no one should feel inhibited about pursuing his or her American dream.

Whether your goal is to gather information for yourself or to become one of the learned professionals, *Modern Real Estate Practice in Pennsylvania* provides a basic guide through each aspect of ownership and through a modern real estate transaction. *Modern Real Estate Practice in Pennsylvania* has provided thousands of people with valuable real estate information since its first printing in 1975 and has set the standard for contemporary information in an easy-to-read format, tailored specifically to Pennsylvania.

With this eighth edition we strive to set a new standard for providing contemporary real estate information in Pennsylvania. The real estate industry is changing more rapidly now than at any time in recent history. This challenges us to lead the reader into the 21st century with timely and authoritative information. Although the basic foundation of ownership remains the same, little else is static. We meet our challenge with revisions in this edition to reflect the latest developments in the way real estate professionals provide their services, the way consumers are protected, including disclosures and their concerns about environmental issues and the role technology plays in this dynamic industry.

Modern Real Estate Practice in Pennsylvania, 8th Edition, is divided into two sections. The first section, Real Estate Fundamentals, is devoted to the legal concepts of ownership and the laws that govern real estate; the second section, Real Estate Practice, discusses real estate brokerage and related activities, following the sequence of a real estate transaction. As with other recent editions, the chapters are presented to conform with the latest curriculum prescribed by the Pennsylvania State Real Estate Commission for *Real Estate Fundamentals* and *Real Estate Practice*, the two courses required for licensure as a real estate salesperson in Pennsylvania.

There are a number of study aids that set *Modern Real Estate Practice in Pennsylvania* apart from other books of its kind. The end-of-chapter questions are written in the style followed by the testing agency that conducts the license exam. Appendix A discusses the licensing examination and includes questions dealing with the state license law for the student to review. Appendix B provides an examination for students to review the general information from the text. A complete reprint of the latest Real Estate Licensing and Registration Act, along with the Real Estate Commission's Rules and Regulations, appears in Appendix C. A new Real Estate Math FAQs section follows.

This text is only a tool. It is intended to introduce the reader to a variety of real estate concepts, theories and specialties in practice. The instructor is encouraged to supplement the text material with classroom discussions, using practical examples and exhibits of forms and other documents common in that area. The reader is encouraged to pursue further study through additional publications and discussions with industry practitioners. Education is a continuous process in which the reader and instructor are active participants.

Real Estate Education Company®, a Kaplan Professional Company, has developed a variety of study materials to aid the learning process, including the *Study Guide for Modern Real Estate Practice* that contains additional review questions and study problems. To assist instructors, a new comprehensive Instructor's Manual, which follows the 8th edition of *Modern Real Estate Practice in Pennsylvania* is available. Contact Real Estate Education Company® for further details about any of these materials.

Comments about this text or any services the publisher provides are always appreciated, and should be directed to Editorial Assistant, Real Estate Education Company®, 155 North Wacker Drive, Chicago, IL 60606-1719.

Section One

REAL ESTATE
FUNDAMENTALS

• • • • • • • •

The ownership of real estate is more than a parcel of land. It includes rights that provide for the use, enjoyment, possession, control and transfer of the real estate. There is a complex body of law that affects every aspect of the ownership, including the government's control of its use, the way people claim and protect their rights and interests in the ownership and the way ownership is transferred. Laws also affect various aspects of a real estate transaction and the practices of real estate licensees.

Real Estate Fundamentals introduces the language, principles, legal concepts and laws that govern real estate ownership and its transfer. The concepts covered in this section and the chapters in which they are discussed are

Basic concepts	Chapter 1
Land use and development	Chapter 2
Environmental issues	Chapter 3
Legal descriptions	Chapter 4
Interest and holdings	Chapters 5, 6, 7
Transfer, liens, recording	Chapters 8, 9, 10
Principles of contracts	Chapter 11
Principles of finance	Chapter 12
License laws	Chapter 13

1 Real Property and the Law

· · · · · · ·

LAND, REAL ESTATE AND REAL PROPERTY

We begin the discussion of real property with an explanation of the terms that are commonly used. *Land*, *real estate* and *real property* are often used interchangeably, but there are subtle yet important differences in their meanings. By looking at these differences we can also understand exactly what a person owns, what is being sold or transferred to another and what a new owner is acquiring.

Land

Land is defined as *the earth's surface extending downward to the center of the earth and upward toward space, including things permanently attached by nature, such as trees and water*. (See Figure 1.1.)

The term *land* thus refers to not only the surface of the earth but also includes the underlying soil and things that are naturally attached to the land, such as boulders and plants. Land also includes the minerals and substances below the earth's surface, together with the air above the land up into space. These are known respectively as the subsurface and airspace.

Real Estate

Real estate is defined as *land at, above and below the earth's surface, and all things permanently attached to it, whether they are natural or artificial*. (See Figure 1.1.)

The term *real estate* is somewhat broader than the term *land;* it includes not only the natural components of the land but also permanent man-made improvements. An **improvement** is any artificial thing attached to land, such as a building or fence, or improvements such as streets, utilities, sewers and other additions that make it suitable for building.

Real Property

Real property is defined as *the physical land or real estate* plus *the interests, benefits and rights that are associated with its ownership*. (See Figure 1.1.)

The term *real property* is broader than either *land* or *real estate*. Property is the rights or interests a person has in the things he or she owns. **Real property** is *the legal rights of ownership (the bundle of legal rights) that attach to ownership of a parcel of real estate as well as the physical surface of the land, what*

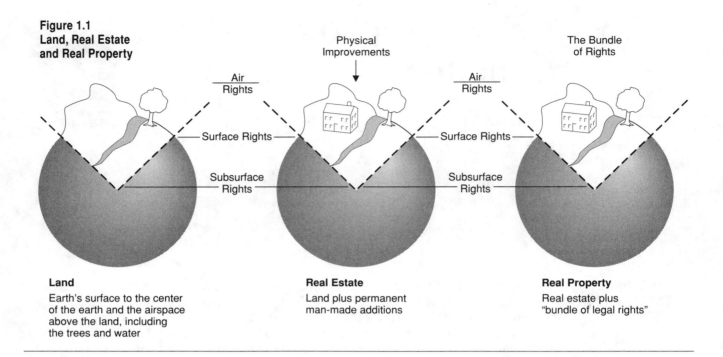

**Figure 1.1
Land, Real Estate
and Real Property**

Physical Improvements

The Bundle of Rights

Air Rights

Air Rights

Surface Rights

Surface Rights

Subsurface Rights

Subsurface Rights

Land
Earth's surface to the center of the earth and the airspace above the land, including the trees and water

Real Estate
Land plus permanent man-made additions

Real Property
Real estate plus "bundle of legal rights"

lies above and below it and what is permanently attached to it. Real property includes **appurtenances,** *which are the rights, privileges and improvements that belong to the land.* Ownership of real property thus includes not only the physical surface, subsurface and airspace, but also the rights to the surface, subsurface and airspace.

IN PRACTICE... *When people talk about buying or selling homes, office buildings, land and the like, they usually call these things real estate. For all practical purposes, the term is synonymous with real property as defined here. In everyday usage real estate includes the legal rights of ownership specified in the definition of real property. Sometimes the term* realty *is also used.*

Subsurface rights. Subsurface rights are *the rights to the natural resources lying below the earth's surface.* A transfer of **surface rights,** *the right to use the surface of the earth,* may be accomplished without transfer of subsurface rights and vice versa. For example, a landowner may sell the rights to any oil and gas found in the land to an oil company. Later the same landowner can sell the remaining interest to a purchaser and reserve the rights to all coal that may be found in the land. After these sales, three parties have ownership interests in this real estate: (1) the oil company owns all oil and gas, (2) the seller owns all coal and (3) the purchaser owns the rights to the remainder of the real estate.

The owners of any of these rights are entitled to enjoy their rights without interference from other owners. Because many parts of Pennsylvania are rich in minerals, particularly coal, it is very likely that multiple owners have interests in one parcel of real estate. The homeowner and the owner of the coal, for example, must coexist so that the homeowner can fully enjoy his or her rights while the coal-owner is free to enjoy these rights, including the ability to extract or mine the coal. A fact of life in coal-rich areas is that mining alters the land and can damage the surface or compromise the support of the surface land, resulting in mine subsidence.

The purchaser of the surface land should be aware of other owners who have interests in the real estate and whether mine subsidence is a possibility. Pennsylvania law requires the seller to provide notice to a purchaser about whether a structure on the land is entitled to support from the underlying coal. This is known as the *coal notice*. If the seller cannot certify that the structure is supported, then the seller must inform the purchaser that there is no protection to the structure against subsidence damage due to mining operations. Special insurance is available to cover damage due to mine subsidence, which is not covered in a typical homeowner's insurance policy.

Air rights. **Air rights** are *the rights to use the open space or vertical plane air above the land*. Ownership of the land includes the right to all air above the property unless the rights have been preempted by law or already sold or leased independently of the land. These rights can be an important part of real estate, particularly in cases where air rights must be purchased to construct large office buildings such as the Met-Life Building in New York City and the Merchandise Mart in Chicago. To construct such a building, the developer must purchase not only the air rights but also numerous small portions of the land's surface for the building's foundation supports, which are called *caissons*.

Before air travel was common, a property's air rights were considered to be unlimited. Today, however, the courts permit reasonable interference with these rights, such as is necessary for aircraft, as long as the owner's right to use and occupy the land is not unduly lessened. Governments and airport authorities often purchase adjacent air rights to provide approach patterns for air traffic. Pennsylvania law provides that local government authorities can obtain aviation easements (air rights) over land surrounding airports to prevent interference with takeoffs and landings.

With the continuing development of solar electric power, air rights may be redefined by the courts to include *solar access rights*. Tall buildings that block sunlight from smaller solar-powered buildings may be ruled to be interfering with the smaller buildings' sun rights.

IN PRACTICE...	*One parcel of real estate may be owned by several people, each of whom owns a separate right to a different part of the real estate. There may be (1) an owner of the surface rights, (2) an owner of the subsurface mineral rights, (3) an owner of the subsurface gas and oil rights and (4) an owner of the air rights. Any of these rights can be sold or transferred. A buyer of a home, for example, should be aware of exactly what is being purchased and whether there are any owners of other interests in the property.*

Figure 1.2
Real versus
Personal Property

Real Estate	**Personal Property**	**Fixture**	**Trade Fixture**
Land and anything permanently attached to it	Movable items not attached to real estate; items severed from real estate	Item of personal property converted to real estate by attaching it to the real estate with the intention that it become permanently a part thereof	Item of personal property attached to real estate that is owned by a tenant and is used in a business; legally removable by tenant

REAL ESTATE VERSUS PERSONAL PROPERTY

Personal property, sometimes called "personalty," is considered to be *all property that does not fit the definition of real property. An important distinction between the two is that personal property is movable.* Items of personal property, also referred to as **chattels,** include such tangibles as chairs, tables, clothing and money. (See Figure 1.2.)

The distinction between real and personal property, which is important to all real estate transactions, is not always obvious. A mobile home, for example, is generally considered to be personal property. In Pennsylvania, mobile homes are defined as motor vehicles and, as such, have been sold by licensed motor vehicle salespersons. A mobile home may, however, be considered real estate if (1) it is transferred in conjunction with and as a part of an assignment of a land lease or the transfer of an interest in land on which the mobile home is situated, (2) the mobile home is permanently attached to a foundation and (3) the registration is canceled by the owner with the Pennsylvania Bureau of Motor Vehicles. In this instance it may be sold by a licensed real estate licensee. (The Pennsylvania motor vehicle code, however, allows real estate licensees to sell used mobile homes.)

Trees and crops are generally considered in two classes. Trees, perennial bushes and grasses that do not require annual cultivation are considered real estate. Seasonal crops, such as wheat, corn, vegetables and fruit, that are produced annually through labor and industry are generally considered personal property. An individual is entitled to the annual crop that results from his or her labor. When the ownership of the land is transferred while the crop is still growing, the individual must be allowed to reenter the land to harvest the crop.

It is possible to change an item of real property to personal property by **severance.** For example, a growing tree is real estate until the owner cuts down the tree and thereby severs it from the earth. Similarly, an apple becomes personal property once it is picked from a tree, and a crop of wheat becomes personal property once it is harvested.

It is also possible to change personal property into real property. If an owner buys cement, stones and sand and constructs a concrete walk on the land, the component parts of the concrete, which were originally personal property, are converted into real estate because they have become a permanent improvement on the land. This process is called *annexation*.

Fixtures

An article that was once personal property but has been so affixed to land or to a building that the law construes it to be a part of the real estate is a **fixture.** Examples are heating plants, elevator equipment in high-rise buildings, radiators, kitchen cabinets, light fixtures and plumbing fixtures. Almost any item that has been added as a *permanent part* of a building is considered a fixture.

Legal tests of a fixture. Courts apply four basic tests to determine whether an item is a fixture (and therefore part of the real estate) or personal property.

1. Intention: Did the person who installed the item intend it to remain permanently or to be removable?

2. Method of annexation: How permanently was the item attached? Can it be removed without causing damage?

3. Adaptation to real estate: Is the item being used as real property or personal property?

4. Agreement: Have the parties agreed to treat an article as through it were personal or real property?

Although these tests seem simple, court decisions have been inconsistent. Articles that appear to be permanently affixed have sometimes been ruled to be personal property, while items that do not appear to be permanently attached have been ruled as fixtures.

Because criteria in the law is subject to court interpretation, the items that are to be included in a sale should be specifically identified rather than depend on legal interpretation. This can be done by the owner and the listing salesperson discussing which items are intended to be included when the property is listed. Then the buyer and seller should specify the articles that are to be included in the sale in their agreement, particularly if there is any doubt as to whether the items are personal property or fixtures. Articles that might be included in an agreement of sale are television antennas, satellite dishes, built-in appliances, built-in bookcases, wall-to-wall carpeting, wood stoves, chandeliers, ceiling fans and hot tubs. Landscaping is expected to remain as is.

IN PRACTICE... | *Real estate licensees need to understand the legal distinction between real estate and personal property so they can properly guide sellers and buyers. A seller, for example, may build a cabinet and expect to take it along, but the buyer may expect that the cabinet is included in the sale because it is a fixture. Although the parties to a real estate transaction can agree between themselves exactly what items are included in a sale, the licensee can help avoid controversies or misimpressions by taking the steps that are suggested in the chapter.*

Trade fixtures. *An article that is attached to a rented space or building for use in conducting a business, but is the personal property of the tenant, is a* **trade**

**Figure 1.3
The Bundle of
Legal Rights**

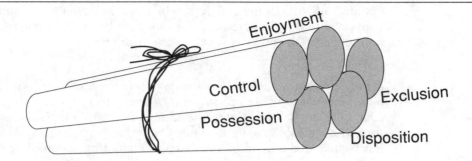

fixture, also called a *chattel fixture.* Examples of trade fixtures are bowling alleys, store shelves, bars and restaurant equipment. Agricultural fixtures such as chicken coops and tool sheds are also included in this definition.

Trade fixtures differ from fixtures generally in these ways:

- Fixtures belong to the owner of the real estate, but trade fixtures are usually owned and installed by a tenant for the tenant's use.

- Fixtures are considered a permanent part of a building, but trade fixtures are removable. Trade fixtures may be affixed to a building so as to appear to be fixtures, but the tenant has the right to remove them on or before the last day of the lease. (Otherwise, they become the real property of the landlord by accession.) The rented space must be restored to its original condition, except for reasonable wear and tear.

- Fixtures are included in a sale or mortgage of the real property, but trade fixtures are not included except by special agreement.

**OWNERSHIP OF
REAL PROPERTY**

Real property ownership is often described as a **bundle of legal rights.** In other words, a purchaser of real estate is actually buying the rights of ownership held by the seller. These rights include the right of possession, the right to control the property within the framework of the law, the right of exclusion, to keep others from using the property, the right of enjoyment, to use the property in any legal manner and the right of disposition, to sell, will or otherwise dispose of the property. (See Figure 1.3.)

The concept of a bundle of rights comes from old English law. When the populace could not commonly read and write, a seller transferred property by giving the purchaser a bundle of bound sticks from a tree on the property. This process was referred to as a *livery of seisin* (seizin). The purchaser who held the bundle also owned the tree from which the sticks came and the land to which the tree was attached. Because the rights of ownership can be separated and individually transferred, the sticks became symbolic of those rights.

A person who acquires real estate owns the property subject to any rights retained by the seller or held or acquired by other persons. As mentioned earlier, a person may sell real estate while retaining the rights to certain minerals or natural resources. Likewise, a lending institution that holds a mortgage on real estate has the right to force a sale of the property if the loan is not repaid. The various rights in real estate will be discussed in detail later in the text.

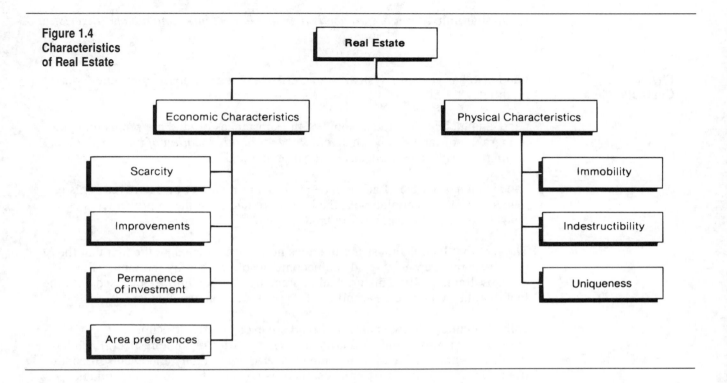

Figure 1.4
Characteristics
of Real Estate

CHARACTERISTICS OF REAL ESTATE

Real estate possesses seven basic characteristics that define its nature and affect its use. These characteristics fall into two general categories: economic and physical. (See Figure 1.4.)

Economic Characteristics

The economic characteristics of real estate affect its value as an investment.

Scarcity. Although we usually do not think of land as a rare commodity, the total supply of land is in fact fixed. Even though a considerable amount of land remains unused or uninhabited, the availability of land in a given location or of a particular quality is limited.

Improvements. Improvements such as buildings or utilities affect the usefulness of land and, consequently, its value. Building an improvement on one parcel of land also can affect the value and use of neighboring properties as well as the entire community. For example, improving a parcel of real estate by building a shopping center can change the value of land in a large area.

Permanence of investment. The capital and labor used to build the improvement represent a large fixed investment. Although even a well-built structure can be razed to make way for a newer building or other use of the land, improvements such as drainage, electricity, water and sewerage remain because they generally cannot be dismantled or removed economically. The return on such investments tends to be long-term and relatively stable.

Location preferences. This economic characteristic, sometimes called *situs,* does not refer to a geographical location but rather to people's preferences for a given area. The uniqueness of people's preferences results in different values for similar units. *Area preference is the most important economic characteristic of land.*

Physical Characteristics

Land also has certain physical characteristics that set it apart from other commodities.

Land is immobile. Although some of the substances of land are removable and topography of land can be changed, *the geographic location of any given parcel of land can never be changed.* Its location is fixed.

Land is indestructible. Land can be altered, but it cannot be destroyed. This permanence of land, coupled with the long-term nature of the improvements on it, tends to stabilize investments in land.

The fact that land is indestructible does not, however, change the fact that the improvements depreciate and can become obsolete, thereby reducing values—perhaps dramatically. This gradual depreciation should not be confused with the fact that the economic desirability of a given location can change.

Land is unique. No two parcels of land are ever exactly the same. Although there may be substantial similarity, all parcels differ in some respect. Each has its own geographic location and sun exposure, topography and even soil conditions. Because of these differences, there is no substitute for an individual parcel. The uniqueness of land is also referred to as heterogeneity or nonhomogeneity.

Characteristics Affecting Land Use

The characteristics of a parcel of real estate affect its desirability for a specific use. Although there are numerous ways a parcel of real estate could be used, some are more practical or desirable than others, depending on what is financially feasible, physically possible and economically productive. The physical and economic characteristics of a property such as its contour and elevation, the prevailing winds, transportation, public improvements and availability of natural resources such as water are factors that affect the use. Hilly, heavily wooded land, for example, would need considerable work before it could be used for industrial purposes, but would be suitable for residential use. Likewise, flat land located along a major highway network would be undesirable for residential use, but may be a desirable location for industrial or commercial use.

IN PRACTICE...

Buying or selling real estate is usually the biggest financial transaction of a person's life. The buyer typically invests more cash, undertakes more debt and has a deeper personal interest in this transaction than in any other purchase made during his or her lifetime. For the seller, it is likely to have been the biggest single investment of money and work. Although there are people for whom the sale or purchase of real estate is a routine matter, for most it is a very important, emotional and complicated affair. To ensure that the transfer of property is smooth, real estate licensees aiding in the transaction must be familiar with all applicable laws.

LAWS AFFECTING REAL ESTATE PRACTICE

The unique nature of real estate has given rise to a unique set of laws and rights. Even the simplest real estate transactions are affected by a complex body of law. The specific areas of law that are important to the real estate practitioner include *contract law, general property law, law of agency,* which covers the obligations of brokers to the people who engage their services, *fair housing law* and the *real estate license law,* all of which will be discussed in this text.

A real estate practitioner cannot be expert in all areas of real estate law but should be familiar with and understand the basic principles of the laws. Just as important is the ability to recognize issues that should be referred to a competent attorney. An attorney at law is trained and licensed to prepare documents defining or transferring rights in property and to give advice or counsel on legal matters. *Under no circumstances may a broker or salesperson act as an attorney unless separately licensed to represent a client in that capacity.*

All phases of a real estate transaction should be handled with extreme care. Carelessness in handling negotiations and the documents connected with a real estate sale can result in disputes. In many cases, expensive legal actions could have been avoided if the parties handling negotiations had exercised greater care and used competent legal counsel.

Real Estate License Laws

Because brokers and salespeople are engaged in a business that involves other people's real estate and money, the need for regulation of their activities has long been recognized. To protect the public from fraud, dishonesty or incompetence in real estate transactions, all 50 states, the District of Columbia and all Canadian provinces have passed laws that require licensure. The license laws of the various states are similar in many respects but differ in some details. In Pennsylvania, the Real Estate Licensing and Registration Act governs the activities of licensees to protect the public.

A person must obtain a license to engage in the real estate business. In most cases, applicants must possess certain stated personal and educational qualifications and must pass written examinations to prove adequate knowledge of the business for which they are seeking licensure. To continue in business, licensees must follow certain prescribed standards of conduct. Some states, including Pennsylvania, also require licensees to complete continuing education courses for license renewal. Chapter 13 more fully describes the specific provisions of the Pennsylvania law. A complete copy of the current law is printed in Appendix C.

●   ●   ●   ●   ●   ●   ●

KEY TERMS

air rights	personal property
appurtenance	real estate
bundle of legal rights	real property
chattel	severance
fixture	subsurface rights
improvement	surface rights
land	trade fixture

SUMMARY

Although most people think of land as the surface of the earth, land is the earth's surface and also the mineral deposits under the earth and the air above it. The term real estate further expands this definition to include all natural and man-made improvements attached to the land. Real property is the term used to describe real estate plus the bundle of legal rights associated with its ownership.

The different rights to the same parcel of real estate may be owned and controlled by different parties, one owning the surface rights, one owning the air rights and another owning the subsurface rights.

All property that does not fit the definition of real estate is classified as personal property or chattels. When articles of personal property are affixed to land, they may become fixtures and as such are considered a part of the real estate. However, personal property attached to real estate by a tenant for business purposes is classified as a trade, or chattel, fixture and remains personal property.

The special nature of land is apparent in both its economic and its physical characteristics. The economic characteristics consist of scarcity, improvements, permanence of investment and area preferences. Physically, land is immobile, indestructible and unique.

Even the simplest real estate transactions reflect a complex body of laws. A purchaser of real estate actually purchases from the seller the legal rights to use the land in certain ways.

Every state and Canadian province has some type of licensing requirement for real estate brokers and salespeople. Students should become familiar with the licensing requirements in Pennsylvania.

Questions

1. Which of the following best defines real estate?
   a. Land and the air above it
   b. Land and the buildings permanently affixed to it
   c. Land and all things permanently affixed to it
   d. Land and the mineral rights in the land

2. The term *nonhomogeneity* refers to
   a. scarcity.
   b. immobility.
   c. uniqueness.
   d. indestructibility.

3. The bundle of legal rights is included in the definition of
   a. land.
   b. real estate.
   c. real property.
   d. trade fixtures.

4. The bundle of legal rights includes all of the following *except* the right to
   a. possess the property.
   b. enjoy the property within the framework of the law.
   c. sell or otherwise convey the property.
   d. use the property for any purpose, legal or otherwise.

5. All of the following would be considered real estate *except*
   a. fences.
   b. buildings.
   c. growing trees.
   d. farm equipment.

6. Which of the following would *not* be a consideration when determining if an item is real property?
   a. The cost of the item when it was purchased
   b. The method of its attachment to other real property
   c. The intended use of the item by its owner
   d. The manner in which the item is actually used with other real property

7. Which of the following is not an economic characteristic of real estate?
   a. Indestructibility
   b. Permanence of investment
   c. Area preference(s)
   d. Scarcity

8. Real property can be converted into personal property through
   a. severance.
   b. accession.
   c. conversion.
   d. inference.

9. *M* is renting a single-family home under a one-year lease. Two months into the lease she installs an awning over the building's front windows to keep the sun away from some delicate hanging plants. Which of the following is true?

   a. *M* must remove the awning before the rental period is over.

   b. Because of its nature, the awning is considered personal property.

   c. The awning is considered a fixture.

   d. Because of the nature of the property, the awning is considered a trade fixture.

10. *G* purchases a parcel of land and sells the rights to minerals located in the ground to an exploration company. After selling the mineral rights, *G* no longer owns which of the following?

   a. Air rights

   b. Surface rights

   c. Subsurface rights

   d. Air and subsurface rights

2

Land-Use Controls and Development

•   •   •   •   •   •   •   •

LAND-USE CONTROLS

Broad though they may be, the rights of real estate ownership are not absolute. Although an owner is entitled to control the use of the property by virtue of the bundle of rights, this is done within certain limitations. The use of land is regulated by the government, known as public controls, and by landowners with private restrictions. Federal, state and local governments also control land by their ownership of property. Consequently, the ownership of a parcel of land is subject to these controls.

PUBLIC CONTROLS

The "police power" of the states is their inherent authority to adopt regulations necessary to protect the public health, safety and welfare. The states, in turn, delegate to counties and local municipalities the authority to enact ordinances in keeping with general laws. The largely urban population and the increasing demands placed on our limited natural resources have made it necessary for the government to increase its limitations on the private use of real estate. There are now controls over noise, air and water pollution, as well as population density.

Privately owned real estate is regulated through

- land-use planning,
- zoning ordinances,
- subdivision regulations,
- building codes and
- environmental protection legislation.

The Comprehensive Plan

Local governments establish development goals through the formulation of a **comprehensive plan**, also referred to as a *master plan*. Municipalities and counties develop plans to ensure that social and economic needs are balanced against environmental and aesthetic concerns. The plan includes the objectives of the municipality for its future development and the strategies and timing for its implementation. The **Pennsylvania Municipalities Planning Code** contains laws governing the planning process. Municipalities are authorized to establish a comprehensive plan, zoning ordinances and subdivision regulations to govern land use within their jurisdictions. The comprehensive plan, as provided for in the code, includes the following basic elements:

- *land use,* including that which may be proposed for residence, industry, business, agriculture, traffic and transit facilities, utilities, community facilities, parks and recreation, floodplains and areas of special hazards;

- *housing needs* of present and anticipated future residents, which may include rehabilitation in declining neighborhoods and accommodation of new housing in different dwelling types for households in all income levels;

- *movement of people and goods,* which may include highways and public transit, parking facilities, pedestrian and bikeway systems;

- *community facilities and utilities,* which may include education, libraries, hospitals, recreation, fire and police, water resources, sewerage and waste treatment and disposal, storm drainage and flood management;

- *energy conservation* to reduce energy consumption and promote utilization of renewable energy sources.

The preparation of a comprehensive plan involves surveys, studies and analyses of housing, demographic and economic characteristics and trends. The natural characteristics of land and the interrelationship of different kinds of land use affect the plan. The planning activities of a municipality are coordinated within the county in which it is located to achieve orderly growth and development.

Zoning

Zoning ordinances are local laws that implement the comprehensive plan and regulate and control the use of land and structures within designated land-use districts. Zoning affects such things as use of the land, lot sizes, types of structures permitted, building heights, setbacks (the minimum distance away from streets or sidewalks that structures may be built), density (the ratio of land area to structure area or population) and protection of natural resources. Ordinances cannot be static, but must remain flexible to meet the ever-changing needs of society.

Zoning powers are conferred on municipal governments by state **enabling acts.** There are no nationwide or statewide zoning ordinances. State and federal governments may, however, regulate land use through special legislation, such as scenic easement and coastal management and environmental laws.

Zoning ordinances have traditionally divided land use into residential, commercial, industrial and agricultural classifications. These land-use areas are further divided into subclasses. For example, residential areas may be subdivided to provide for detached single-family dwellings, semidetached structures containing not more than four dwelling units, walk-up apartments, high-rise apartments and so forth.

Because of the demand for housing of all types and designs and the need to encourage more efficient use of land, municipalities frequently adopt ordinances for subdivisions and Planned Residential Developments (PRDs). These ordinances provide for innovative land use by designating regulations for lot sizes, setbacks, building heights and percentages of open space that apply to these specific kinds of developments. The area and bulk regulations can stimulate efficient land-use while also controlling density and overcrowding. Ordinances for Planned Unit Developments (PUDs) allow for innovative use by incorporating a variety of land uses within a development.

Municipalities often incorporate architectural design standards or signage provisions in their ordinances or designate historic preservation districts. The goal of these regulations must be consistent with the purpose of the police powers and not based solely on societal objectives or aesthetics so they do not interfere with the private rights of ownership. Municipalities can also use **buffer zones**, such as landscaped parks and playgrounds, to screen residential from nonresidential areas and thus protect the enjoyment of the property owners.

Adoption of zoning ordinances The governing body of a municipality is responsible for enacting the comprehensive plan, zoning and subdivision ordinances in accordance with procedures in the Pennsylvania Municipalities Planning Code. The governing body may appoint a planning commission to be responsible for formulating the recommended plans and ordinances. Public hearings must be held prior to their enactment by the governing body.

The purpose of zoning ordinances is to promote and protect the public health, safety and general welfare, while providing for coordinated and practical community development. Zoning ordinances must not violate the rights of individuals and property holders (as provided under the due process provisions of the Fourteenth Amendment to the U.S. Constitution) or the various provisions of the constitution of the state in which the real estate is located. Any land-use legislation that is destructive, unreasonable, arbitrary or confiscatory is usually considered void. Tests commonly applied in determining the validity of ordinances require that:

- The power must be exercised in a reasonable manner.

- The provisions must be clear and specific.

- The ordinance must be free from discrimination.

- The ordinance must promote public health, safety and general welfare under the police power concept.

- The ordinance must apply to all property in a similar manner.

When land is taken for public use by the government's power of *eminent domain,* the owner must receive compensation. When *downzoning* occurs in an area—for instance, when land zoned for residential construction is rezoned for conservation or recreational purposes—the government ordinarily is not responsible for compensating property owners for any resulting loss of value. However, if the courts find that a "taking" has occurred, then the downzoning will be held to be an unconstitutional attempt to use eminent domain without providing fair compensation to the property owner.

Zoning laws are generally enforced by requiring that zoning permits must be obtained before property owners can begin development. A permit will not be issued unless a proposed development conforms to the permitted zoning, among other requirements. Zoning permits are prerequisite to the issuance of a building permit.

Zoning hearing board. Zoning hearing boards have been established in most communities for the specific purpose of hearing complaints about the effects of zoning ordinances on specific parcels of property. Petitions may be presented to the appeal board for variances or exceptions in the zoning law.

Nonconforming use. The use of parcels of land or the nature of improvements frequently do not conform to the zoning because they were established prior to the enactment or amendment of a zoning ordinance. Consequently, this is a **nonconforming use,** which means that it no longer conforms with current ordinances. The nonconforming use may be allowed to legally continue as long as it complies with the regulations governing nonconformities in the local ordinance or until the improvements are destroyed or torn down or the current use is abandoned. If the nonconforming use is allowed to continue indefinitely, it is considered to be "grandfathered in."

Variances and conditional-use permits. Any time a plan or zoning ordinance is enacted, owners can be inconvenienced if they want to change the use of a property. Generally, these owners may appeal for either a conditional-use permit or a variance so that they can use their properties in ways that do not meet current zoning requirements.

A **conditional-use permit** is granted to allow a property to be used for a purpose that is defined as an *allowable conditional use* within that zoning district, such as a church in a residential district. This is sometimes known as *special-use zoning.* For each conditional use there are normally certain standards that must be met.

A **variance** may be sought for a use that is expressly prohibited by current zoning laws. Variances are granted to provide relief if zoning regulations deprive an owner reasonable use of the land or building. The applicant for a variance must describe the unique circumstances that necessitate a use that is contrary to the zoning regulations and prove how the regulations harm and burden the applicant. A variance cannot alter the essential character of the locality or be contrary to the intent and the purpose of the zoning code.

Variances generally fall into two categories: dimensional variances, which cover physical dimensions such as lot or parcel sizes and setbacks; and use variances, which cover the specific uses of land. An example of a dimensional variance is one that would permit an owner to build closer to the road than the setback allows because the lot slopes too steeply to accommodate a structure within the setback requirements. An example of a use variance is one that would permit an owner to construct a multiple-unit dwelling in an area where only single-family detached homes are permitted. Use variances can be more difficult to obtain because of the burden to prove how an ordinance causes the owner harm or hardship.

Property owners can seek a *change* in the zoning classification of a general area or district which then changes the permissible use of their specific parcels of land in that area. This is done by obtaining an *amendment* to the district map or a zoning ordinance. The proposed amendment must be brought before a public hearing on the matter and approved by the governing body of the community.

IN PRACTICE...	*When the character of land use is not controlled, communities can develop in reckless or harmful ways, which can compromise the quality of life of a community's residents and threaten the enjoyment of the property owners' rights. One of the ways communities can enhance the use of land, establish a sound economic base and revitalize aging neighborhoods is with a methodical plan for using their land. In doing so, they protect the general welfare of the community, which is a fundamental use of the police powers.*

Subdivision and Land Development Ordinances

Most communities have adopted **subdivision and land development ordinances** as part of their comprehensive plan. An ordinance will include provisions for submitting and processing subdivision plats, including the charging of fees and review of plats and surveys that are submitted for approval. A major advantage of subdivision ordinances is that they encourage flexibility, economy and ingenuity in the use of land. The layout and arrangement of a subdivision or land development usually provides for

- location, grading, alignment, surfacing and widths of streets and walkways;
- location and design of curbs, gutters, streetlights and water and sewage facilities;
- easements or rights-of-way for drainage and utilities;
- minimum setback lines and lot sizes;
- renewable energy systems and energy-conserving building design;
- areas to be reserved or dedicated for public use, such as parks or recreation facilities.

A developer must submit subdivision and land development plats to the municipality for approval. This is an essential step before a subdivision plat can be filed with the recorder of deeds in the county where the proposed development is located. Subdivision ordinances include procedures for the review of the plats, including the time limits within which the governing body must respond to the application or request alterations to the plat. A public hearing may be held as part of the *preliminary approval* being granted. The installation of streets, curbs, gutters, fire hydrants, water mains and sanitary and storm sewers, as may be required by the municipality, is a major financial commitment for the developer. The *final approval* of a plat is conditioned upon the developer completing these improvements or providing some form of financial security or bonding to the municipality to ensure that they will be completed.

Providing an adequate supply of water and environmentally sound sewage disposal are major considerations in the development of land. Ordinances frequently require that water be supplied by a certificated public utility unless the individual lots within a subdivision can be properly served by private wells. Sewage disposal that does not pollute streams, rivers and underground water supplies is a major concern. The Pennsylvania Department of Environmental Protection (DEP) regulates the planning of community and individual sewerage systems. DEP may not permit septic systems where the soil's absorption or drainage capacity, as determined by a *percolation test,* may preclude their use. With the growing emphasis on environmental concerns, a developer may be required to submit an *environmental impact report* with the application for subdivision approval.

With increasing development there is a corresponding demand for municipal capital improvements. Municipalities must develop revenue sources to provide adequate transportation routes via municipal highways, roads and streets to accommodate increased traffic flow. Although the developer is responsible for installation of streets within a subdivision (an "on-site" improvement), the municipality is responsible for these "off-site" improvements.

Under the Pennsylvania Municipalities Planning Code, the governing body is authorized to establish a program to collect transportation **impact fees** at the time of approval of a new subdivision or development. These fees fund off-site public transportation improvements. Impact fees are determined on the basis of a traffic analysis of roadway capacity, deficiencies, cost of needed improvements and future impact of development on the transportation system. The municipality is responsible for making improvements to the system to correct deficiencies created from past development. Developers of new projects will be responsible for contributing the pro rata share of the cost of improvements related to the traffic they contribute to the system.

Subdividing. The process of laying out a subdivision involves identifying the raw land; analyzing its best use; studying the land with the help of a surveyor to consider natural drainage and land contours; and plotting the land into blocks, lots within the blocks, streets and other improvements and easements. The proposed development must conform to the subdivision ordinances. Close contact with municipal officials during this process provides invaluable assistance to the developer. The completed **subdivision plat,** a map of the development indicating the location and boundaries of the individual properties, is submitted to the municipality for approval.

The subdivision plat is filed with the recorder of deeds once all required approvals are obtained. Areas for streets or parks and recreation that are designated for the public are transferred or *dedicated* to the municipality when the subdivision plat is filed. Because the plat will be the basis for future conveyances, the subdivided land should be carefully measured, with all lot sizes and streets noted by the surveyor and entered accurately on the document. Subdivision plats are discussed further in the chapter about legal descriptions.

Building Codes

Most municipalities have enacted ordinances to *specify construction standards* that must be met when repairing or erecting buildings. These are called **building codes.** The purpose of these codes is to provide minimum construction standards to safeguard the public health, safety and welfare. They address such things as the design, quality of materials and standards of workmanship that must be followed. Frequently there are also specialized plumbing, electrical and fire codes. Although building codes have generally been local in nature, currently there are efforts in Harrisburg to enact a statewide building code.

Municipalities enforce building codes by issuing building permits and conducting inspections of the construction. A **building permit** is written governmental permission for the construction of a building or the substantial repair, alteration or demolition of a structure. Through the permit requirement, municipal officials are made aware of new construction or alterations and can verify compliance with building codes and zoning ordinances by examining the plans and inspecting the work. Once the completed structure has been inspected and found satisfactory, the municipal inspector issues a *certificate of occupancy*. This shows that a building is fit for occupancy and has no building code violations.

If the construction of a building or an alteration violates a deed restriction (discussed later in this chapter), the issuance of a building permit will not cure this violation. A building permit is merely evidence of the applicant's compliance with municipal regulations. Property owners should also be aware that municipalities may charge fees for these permits.

IN PRACTICE...

Land planning, zoning and other land-use restrictions have a significant impact on the use of property and a real estate transaction. A person cannot assume that the owner's current use of a property is legal, especially from a visual inspection, nor that a buyer's proposed use or alterations will be permitted. Zoning ordinances should be investigated and specific land-use questions should be addressed with a municipality's code enforcement officer or an attorney.

The State Real Estate Commission's Regulations require the disclosure of the current zoning classification for certain types of properties in an agreement of sale.

Environmental Protection Legislation

Federal and state governments, as well as some cities and counties, have passed a number of environmental protection laws in an attempt to respond to the growing public concern over the improvement and preservation of America's natural resources. For example, wetlands legislation attempts to protect wildlife; pollution control measures intend to protect the quality of air and water; and other environmental regulations govern waste disposal and provide for the cleanup of hazardous substances. Any of the environmental laws or regulations can ultimately affect builders, developers and property owners by restricting the way land is used and improvements are constructed. Some of the laws also impose significant financial burdens for the removal of environmental hazards. A builder, for example, may be prevented from constructing septic tanks or other effluence-disposal systems in certain areas, particularly where public streams, lakes and rivers are affected. See Chapter 3 for a detailed discussion of environmental issues in real estate.

PRIVATE LAND-USE CONTROLS

Certain restrictions to *control and maintain the desirable quality and character of a property or subdivision* may be created. These restrictions are separate from, and in addition to, the land-use controls exercised by the government. **Deed restrictions** are provisions placed in deeds by the owner at the time ownership is conveyed to control future use of the property. **Restrictive covenants** are declarations of conditions and restrictions that affect all of the parcels of land in a development and are included in the subdivision plat or set forth in a separate recorded instrument. The deed to a lot in a subdivision refers to the plat or declaration of restrictions, thereby incorporating these restrictions as limitations on the title conveyed by the deed and binding all future owners to the same restrictions.

Typical restrictive covenants relate to the type, height and square footage of a building that may be constructed, the size of the setbacks, the height of fences and other specific issues about the way the land can be used, such as prohibiting livestock or limiting the number of household pets. It is not uncommon to designate an architectural control committee in the subdivision that is responsible for approving building or landscape designs.

There is a distinction between restrictions on the right to *sell* and restrictions on the right to *use*. In general, a deed conveying a fee simple estate may not restrict the right of subsequent owners to sell, mortgage or convey it. Because such restrictions attempt to limit the basic right of the *free alienation (transfer) of property,* the courts consider them against public policy and therefore unenforceable. Restrictions on use are usually considered valid if they are reasonable restraints and are for the benefit of all property owners in the subdivision. If, however, the terms of the restrictions are too broad, they are construed as preventing the free transfer of property. If they are "repugnant" to the estate granted, they probably will not be enforceable. If any restrictive covenant or condition is considered ineffective by a court, the estate will then stand free from the invalid covenant or condition.

Private land-use controls may be more restrictive of an owner's use than the local zoning ordinance. The more restrictive of the two takes precedence. Restrictions may have a *time limitation,* for example, "effective for a period of 25 years from this date." After that time, they become inoperative or, in the case of covenants, may be extended by majority agreement of the owners.

Private restrictions can be enforced in court when one lot owner applies to the court for an *injunction* to prevent a neighboring lot owner from violating the recorded restrictions. If granted, the court injunction will direct the violator to stop or remove the violation. The court retains the power to punish the violator for failure to obey the court order. If adjoining lot owners stand idly by while a violation is being committed, they can *lose the right* to an injunction by their inaction. The court might claim their right was lost through *laches,* which is the loss of a right through undue delay or failure to assert it.

Land Use Laws. Section 3407 of the Uniform Condominium Act of Pennsylvania requires the seller to furnish the Buyer with a Certificate of Resale and copies of the condominium declaration, the bylaws and the rules and regulations of the association. Under the act the buyer may declare the agreement of sale void at any time before buyer's receipt of the Certificate of Resale and for five days thereafter, or until settlement, whichever occurs first. The buyer's notice declaring the agreement void must be in writing. The Act is described in more detail in Chapter 7.

Section 5407 of the Uniform Planned Community Act requires the seller to furnish the buyer with a copy of the declaration, the bylaws, the rules and regulations of the association, and a certificate containing the provisions set forth in the Act. The definition of a Planned Community is found in the Act but also is repeated in the Pennsylvania Association of REALTORS® Standard Agreement of Sale. The buyer may void this agreement of sale before or within five days after receiving these documents. This notice must also be in writing.

IN PRACTICE...	*Covenants, conditions and restrictions (CC&R) in subdivisions and deed restrictions are fairly common, but potential buyers may not know that they exist or be aware of the specific details. Because a buyer as the new owner will have to live with these covenants, conditions or restrictions, licensees should be sure that the buyer is properly informed about them before considering the purchase of a property.*

DIRECT PUBLIC OWNERSHIP

Over the years the government's general policy has been to encourage private ownership of land. It is necessary, however, for a certain amount of land to be owned by the government for such uses as municipal buildings, state legislative houses, schools and military stations. Such direct public ownership is a means of land control.

There are other examples of necessary public ownership. Urban renewal efforts, especially government-owned housing, are one way that public ownership serves the public interest. Publicly owned streets and highways serve a necessary function that benefits the entire population. In addition, public land is often used for recreational purposes such as national and state parks and forest preserves, which at the same time help to conserve our natural resources.

INTERSTATE LAND SALES FULL DISCLOSURE ACT

To protect consumers from "overenthusiastic sales promotions" in interstate land sales, Congress passed the **Interstate Land Sales Full Disclosure Act.** The law requires those engaged in the interstate sale or leasing of 25 or more lots to file a statement of record and register the details of the land with the Department of Housing and Urban Development (HUD).

The seller is also required to furnish prospective buyers with a **property report** containing all essential information about the property, such as distance over paved roads to nearby communities, number of homes currently occupied, soil conditions affecting foundations and septic systems, type of title a buyer will receive and existence of liens. The property report must be given to a prospective purchaser at least three business days before any agreement of sale is signed.

Any contract to purchase a lot covered by this act may be revoked at the purchaser's option until midnight of the seventh day following the signing of the contract. If a contract is signed for the purchase of a lot covered by the act and a property report is not given to the purchaser, an action to revoke the contract may be brought by the purchaser within two years.

If the seller misrepresents the property in any sales promotion, a buyer induced by such a promotion is entitled to sue the seller for civil damages. Failure to comply with the law may also subject a seller to criminal penalties of fines and imprisonment.

Additional laws that are specific to sales practices in Pennsylvania will be discussed in a later chapter.

•   •   •   •   •   •   •

KEY TERMS

buffer zone
building codes
building permit
comprehensive plan
conditional-use permit
deed restriction
enabling acts
impact fees
Interstate Land Sales Full
   Disclosure Act

nonconforming use
Pennsylvania Municipalities Planning
   Code
property report
restrictive covenants
subdivision and development
   ordinances
subdivision plat
variance
zoning ordinances

SUMMARY

The control of land use is exercised in three ways: through public controls, private (or nongovernmental) controls and direct public ownership.

Through power conferred by state enabling acts, local governments exercise public controls based upon the states' police powers to protect the public health, safety and welfare. The Pennsylvania Municipalities Planning Code governs the procedures to be followed by communities.

Comprehensive plans set forth the development goals and objectives for the community. Zoning ordinances carrying out the provisions of the plan control the use of land and structures within designated land-use districts. Zoning enforcement problems involve zoning hearing boards, conditional-use permits, variances and exceptions, as well as nonconforming uses. Subdivision and land development regulations are adopted to maintain control of the development of expanding community areas so that growth will be harmonious with community standards. Increased growth and development frequently necessitate additional capital improvements to provide adequate highways and roads to accommodate increased traffic. Developers may be charged impact fees relating to the increased traffic created by their developments.

Subdividing involves dividing a tract of land into lots and blocks and providing utility easements, as well as laying out street patterns. A subdivision plat is filed with the recorder of deeds once it is approved by the public officials.

In addition to land-use control on the local level, the state and federal governments have occasionally intervened when necessary to preserve natural resources through environmental legislation.

Building codes specify standards for construction, plumbing, sewers, electrical wiring and equipment.

Private land-use controls are exercised by owners through deed restrictions and restrictive covenants. These private restrictions may be enforced by obtaining a court injunction to stop a violator. Direct public ownership is a means of land-use control that provides land for such public benefits as parks, highways, schools and municipal buildings.

Interstate land sales are regulated on the federal level by the Interstate Land Sales Full Disclosure Act. This law requires developers engaged in interstate sales or leasing of 25 or more units to register the details of the land with HUD. At least three business days before any sales contract is signed, such developers must also provide prospective purchasers with a property report containing all essential information about the property. Land sales are also regulated by many states' laws.

Questions

1. A provision in a subdivision declaration used as a means of forcing the grantee to live up to the terms under which he or she holds title to the land is a
   a. restrictive covenant.
   b. reverter.
   c. laches.
   d. conditional-use clause.

2. A landowner who wants to use property in a manner that is prohibited by a local zoning ordinance but the prohibition causes a hardship for the owner can try to obtain which of the following from the municipality?
   a. Variance
   b. Downzoning
   c. Occupancy permit
   d. Dezoning

3. Public land-use controls include all of the following *except*
   a. subdivision regulations.
   b. deed restrictions.
   c. environmental protection laws.
   d. comprehensive plans.

4. The police power allows regulation of all of the following *except*
   a. the number of buildings.
   b. the size of buildings.
   c. building ownership.
   d. building occupancy.

5. The purpose of a building permit is to
   a. override a deed restriction.
   b. maintain municipal control over the volume of building.
   c. provide evidence of compliance with municipal building codes and zoning ordinances.
   d. show compliance with deed restrictions.

6. The goals of a municipal planning commission include all of the following *except*
   a. formulation of policy.
   b. determination of land uses.
   c. conservation of natural resources.
   d. preventing variances from being issued.

7. The grantor of a deed may place effective restrictions on
   a. the right to sell the land.
   b. the use of the land.
   c. who the next purchaser will be.
   d. who may occupy the property.

8. Zoning powers are conferred on municipal governments
   a. by state enabling acts.
   b. through police powers.
   c. by eminent domain.
   d. through interstate laws.

9. Zoning hearing boards are established to hear complaints about
   a. restrictive covenants.
   b. the effects of a zoning ordinance.
   c. building codes.
   d. the effects of public ownership.

10. A new zoning ordinance is enacted. A building that is permitted to continue in its former use even though that use does not comply with a new zoning ordinance is an example of
    a. nonconforming use.
    b. variance.
    c. special use.
    d. inverse condemnation.

11. To determine whether a location can be put to future use as a retail store one would examine the
    a. building codes.
    b. list of permitted nonconforming uses.
    c. housing codes.
    d. zoning ordinances.

12. Which of the following would probably *not* be included in a list of deed restrictions?
    a. Types of buildings that may be constructed
    b. Allowable ethnic origins of purchasers
    c. Activities that are not to be conducted at the site
    d. Minimum size of buildings to be constructed

13. A restriction in a seller's deed may be enforced by which of the following?
    a. Court injunction
    b. Zoning hearing board
    c. Municipal building commission
    d. State legislature

14. To control and maintain the character and quality of a subdivision a developer may establish which of the following?
    a. Easements
    b. Restrictive covenants
    c. Buffer zones
    d. Building codes

15. A map illustrating the sizes and locations of streets and lots in a subdivision is called a
    a. grid.   c. plat.
    b. survey.   d. property report.

16. Soil absorption and drainage are measured by a
    a. land survey.
    b. plat of subdivision.
    c. density test.
    d. percolation test.

17. When a development increases the traffic flow on existing streets and highways, the municipality can fund the cost of transportation improvements that are needed because of this development through
    a. fees for building permits.
    b. fees for variances.
    c. subdivision filing fees.
    d. impact fees.

18. To protect the public from fraudulent interstate land sales, a developer involved in interstate land sales of 25 or more lots must
    a. provide each purchaser with a report of the details of the land, as registered with HUD.
    b. pay the prospective buyer's expenses to see the property involved.
    c. provide preferential financing.
    d. include deed restrictions.

3

Environmental Issues in Real Estate

. . . .

ENVIRONMENTAL CONCERNS

As scientists learn more about the harmful effects of naturally-occurring and man-made substances that are common in our environment, people become more concerned about the safety of their surroundings—the air they breathe, the water they drink, the food they consume and the products they use. Health concerns have become real estate issues because building products as well as the land, water and air can contain harmful substances. People want protection from potential hazards, which means that environmental issues are becoming increasingly important in real estate. Because of the heightened awareness about the safety of our environment, the government has adopted numerous environmental laws and regulations, which also affect real estate transactions and the services licensees provide.

PROCEDURES IN REAL ESTATE TRANSACTIONS

The usability and value of real estate can be affected by environmental hazards, particularly because significant expenditures to investigate, sample, treat or remove and dispose of a substance are frequently involved. When the expenses are greater than the actual market value of the property, this has a negative effect on owners and sellers. The usability and value of a property are further affected as additional hazards are identified.

What does this mean to real estate owners and developers? How does this affect sales transactions, mortgage lenders, an appraisal or the management of real estate? While the health and safety of the user of a property are important, the burden for the discovery, disclosure and abatement or elimination of the hazard seems to arise most frequently when the ownership of property transfers.

Real estate licensees must be alert to environmental hazards and learn to protect themselves and sellers from personal injury suits and other legal liability that can arise if the user of a property contracts a health problem because of a toxic substance. Some environmental regulations make the licensee who is acting for the owner of a property responsible for certain discovery and disclosure activities. Licensees also should establish practices to ensure that prospective purchasers get authoritative information about hazardous substances so that they can make informed decisions.

3 / Environmental Issues in Real Estate

29

Discovery of Environmental Hazards

The discovery of environmental hazards begins with information. Because real estate licensees usually are more aware of possible hazards, consumers rely on their guidance, which includes knowing what to look for and how to obtain authoritative information about any conditions that affect a specific property.

What hazards are you looking for? Asbestos, carbon monoxide, lead, radon, formaldehyde and toxic substances that pollute the environment are hazards that frequently arise in real estate transactions. While these are the most common and well publicized hazards, substances that cause acute allergic reactions are hazardous or even life-threatening for some people although they may not be hazardous to others. As scientists identify environmental and chemical substances that contribute to illness and physical or emotional conditions, people with certain health problems consider these hazards, especially when they are selecting a home. Licensees must listen to the consumer's concerns as well as use the knowledge they have about common issues to assist the buyers.

How do you find the hazards? A number of resources are available. *Licensees do not need to have the technical expertise to discover hazardous substances.* First, they should ask the property owner. Who knows more about the property than the person who has owned it for a period of time? The owner may have conducted environmental tests for such things as radon, lead or carbon monoxide. This alerts the licensee to conditions that should be investigated further. Perhaps the owner has already taken steps to eliminate a hazardous condition, which is useful information for future owners and can even be an asset when marketing a property.

Scientific or technical experts are commonly used to discover environmental hazards. In fact they are the most appropriate people on whom to rely for discovery. In the case of lead-based paint, radon and asbestos, they must be certified to conduct the inspections. Inspectors can conduct air-sampling tests to detect radon, asbestos, formaldehyde, lead or other airborne hazards inside a building. In addition, tests can be performed to determine the safety of well water or contamination from malfunctioning sewage disposal systems. Although these experts can be called on at any stage in a sales transaction, frequently they are asked to conduct inspections as a condition in an agreement of sale. Inspectors can also provide guidance about how to remedy any conditions.

There are environmental auditors who conduct more comprehensive studies, which are important to land developers and to purchasers of commercial and industrial properties. An environmental audit includes a report of the history of the way a property has been used and a wide range of tests to identify detrimental conditions, including the presence or discharge of hazardous substances on the land as well as in any existing buildings.

Disclosure of Environmental Hazards

From a legal point of view, the purpose of discovery is to provide information to make accurate disclosures about environmental hazards. As will be discussed a number of times in this text, the current trend in law, which is being echoed in the courts, is to advance protections for consumers. This imposes responsibilities on the providers of goods and services to disclose information that consumers need to make prudent purchasing decisions, even when they do not ask for it. This is known as disclosure of *material facts*.

Any physical condition that substantially affects habitability and value must be disclosed to a prospective purchaser or user of a property, even if it could negatively affect a transaction. When a prospective purchaser is aware of problems, he or she can negotiate with the current owner to correct the conditions, decide to avoid the property and its problems entirely or pursue the purchase of the property with full knowledge of its condition.

Certain other disclosures are required by law. Although no federal or state laws as of this writing specifically address disclosure of substances such as radon or asbestos in residential sales transactions, there are laws concerning lead-based paint. The federal Residential Lead-Based Paint Hazard Reduction Act of 1992 and Title X, Section 1018 was implemented during the latter part of 1996. This law intends to ensure that purchasers are aware of any lead-based paint that might be present and are told about its risks and ways to avoid exposure. The law requires the seller or the seller's agent to distribute a lead-hazard pamphlet and disclose any known information about existing lead-based paint or hazards. A lead warning statement must also be included in an agreement of sale. The prospective purchaser must be given ten days to obtain an assessment or inspection before being obligated to purchase the property. Inspectors under this law must be certified.

IN PRACTICE... | *Numerous laws and regulations at all levels of government are emerging to address lead-based paint. Because these laws commonly include procedures that affect sales transactions and certain activities related to the ownership of older residential properties, real estate licensees should be aware of all prevailing legislation, including any local laws, and lead-paint disclosures that are required in sales transactions when certain types of mortgage loans are involved.*

Because complying with the volume of federal and state pollution control laws and regulations is a mammoth task and the responsibility for environmental cleanup can be even more burdensome, no prospective purchaser should unknowingly buy into these problems. Cleanup can be quite costly, and the laws create financial liability for the landowner as well as others who have an interest in the property. Consequently, future owners can be buying more than they bargained for when the real estate is contaminated or causes contamination of adjoining land. Although there are various ways for purchasers to minimize this liability, one of the best is to get an environmental assessment and make the agreement of sale conditioned on the seller remedying any problems.

Mortgage lenders are also aware of the potential problems for which they could be responsible if they have to foreclose on a loan and become the owner of the property. For this reason, lenders have as much at stake as purchasers if the property is contaminated. Although most lenders do not require tests to disclose environmental hazards for single-family residences, they usually require environmental audits for other properties.

Appraisers also have a responsibility for identifying and disclosing environmental problems. Because these conditions can affect the value of a property, they must be considered in the preparation of an appraisal report, particularly one that is ordered by a lending institution for mortgage purposes.

Treatment and Removal

One of the debates about environmental hazards is whether to treat or remove the problem. Unless removal of toxic substances is required by environmental cleanup laws, decisions about how to handle specific situations involve several considerations. Certain hazards are so serious that there is no question about whether they should be eliminated. Carbon monoxide buildup from a malfunctioning furnace, for example, can be lethal and the heating system definitely should be repaired or replaced. In cases when people feel so unsettled about the presence of any hazard, regardless of its severity, the only satisfactory course of action is removal. In either of these situations, the peace of mind is worth any cost that is involved. Decisions in other situations are not so clear-cut.

The nature of the structure and the ease with which it can be altered, the effectiveness of a method to deal with the hazard and the costs to correct a hazardous condition are all considerations that must be weighed. In some cases it is relatively easy and effective to eliminate the hazard. When dealing with radon, for example, ventilation systems are very effective and, depending on the structure, may not be expensive to install or otherwise compromise the use or enjoyment of the property.

Decisions to abate or mitigate versus remove a hazard are affected to a large degree by the risk of further contamination and the costs involved. When the hazards of asbestos, for example, were first identified, there was a rush to remove any asbestos-containing material from a building. In many cases, the effort to correct a problem only made the problem worse. In the majority of cases, asbestos-containing materials are harmless. The materials *are* hazardous when they crumble or are disturbed and then release airborne asbestos particles that can be inhaled. Asbestos removal is costly, and the removal process can further contaminate the structure. If asbestos-containing materials must be removed, only experienced, knowledgeable professionals can do this and the discarded materials must be disposed of in an environmentally safe manner. Encapsulating the material is preferred in many cases. This involves enclosing the asbestos-containing materials to prevent particles from becoming airborne.

Similar decisions are involved with lead-based paint. Not only is it costly to remove all lead-based paint in a structure, but the methods for removal can further contaminate a building. When chemicals are used to remove the paint, additional toxic conditions are created. Encapsulation by covering the lead-based paint is more practical and cost-effective and does not cause additional problems.

Lead contamination in drinking water is usually caused by the household plumbing rather than the local water supply. Remodeling over time will eliminate pipes, fittings and solder that contain lead. But a wholesale removal program is not practical and can be expensive. Lead in the drinking water can be reduced by using cold water for drinking and cooking and flushing the pipes (running the water until it is as cold as it will get) to eliminate standing water. The longer water stands in the pipes the more lead it may contain.

ENVIRONMENTAL HAZARDS

Several environmental hazards have been mentioned in this chapter. The purpose of the following discussion is to describe the hazards that commonly concern purchasers and property owners and what scientists have learned about the effect of these substances on humans. (See Figure 3.1.)

**Figure 3.1
Environmental
Issues**

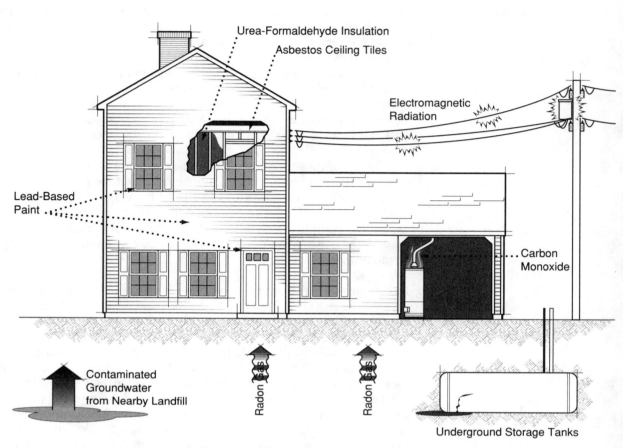

Urea-Formaldehyde Insulation

Asbestos Ceiling Tiles

Electromagnetic
Radiation

Lead-Based
Paint

Carbon
Monoxide

Contaminated
Groundwater
from Nearby Landfill

Radon Gas

Radon Gas

Underground Storage Tanks

Asbestos

Asbestos is a mineral that has been a popular component in building materials because of its fire-resistant properties and its ability to contain heat. Prior to 1978 when the Environmental Protection Agency (EPA) imposed restrictions on the use of asbestos-containing materials, asbestos was widely used in insulation, floor and ceiling materials and roofing products. Vinyl floor tiles and the mastic, acoustic ceiling and ceiling tiles and wraps covering hot water pipes, heating ducts and heating and hot water units commonly contained asbestos. It is estimated that asbestos is found in one out of every five public buildings in the country today. Asbestos was also used in residential properties.

When the EPA determined that asbestos is a health hazard, this set the stage for numerous laws and regulations. Today public school buildings, the rights of employees, indoor air quality and public, commercial and apartment buildings (with over ten units) are all affected by asbestos laws. The purpose of the various laws is to minimize the release of asbestos fibers during handling and processing during construction and removal.

Carbon Monoxide

Carbon monoxide (CO) is a colorless, odorless gas that naturally occurs as a by-product from burning oils, natural gasses and other fuels. Furnaces, space heaters or other fuel-burning appliances such as a wood stove or fireplace that function properly and efficiently, which includes proper ventilation, do not cause a problem. However, when they are inefficient or malfunction, the carbon monoxide can easily go unnoticed. CO is quickly absorbed by the body and inhibits the transport of oxygen. People often mistake dizziness, headaches, irritability and nausea for the initial signs of the flu or a cold when they may have symptoms of carbon monoxide poisoning. More serious symptoms occur as the concentrations of CO increase, and more than 200 deaths each year are attributed to carbon monoxide.

Property owners can protect themselves by having their heating systems serviced annually and installing CO detectors. A variety of detectors are available, some which sound an alarm much like smoke detectors when they sense unacceptable levels of CO.

Lead-Based Paint and Other Lead Hazards

Lead was used as a pigment and drying agent in alkyd oil-based paint. The Department of Housing and Urban Development (HUD) estimates that lead is present in about 75 percent of all the private housing that was built before 1978 or as many as 57 million homes, ranging from low-income apartments to million-dollar mansions. The paint may be found on any interior or exterior surface, particularly doors, windows and other woodwork.

Elevated levels of lead in the body can cause serious damage to the brain, kidneys, nervous system and red blood cells. The degree of harm is related to the amount of exposure and the age at which a person is exposed. Poisoning occurs when the body is exposed to high amounts that it is not capable of eliminating. In 1991 the Centers for Disease Control and Prevention lowered the threshold at which children are considered to have lead poisoning. It is estimated that as many as one in six children may have dangerously high amounts of lead in their blood.

A common misconception is that an individual must ingest paint chips to incur lead poisoning, but people are exposed to lead in a variety of other ways. The water supply may be contaminated because of lead pipes or solder that were permitted in old building codes. Lead particles from paint and varnishes and even gasoline emissions can become airborne, contaminating the air the occupants breathe.

Anyone involved in the sale, management, financing or appraisal of properties constructed before 1978, which is the time before lead-based paint was banned, must be aware of this problem. A prospective purchaser who is concerned about the presence of lead should be informed that testing is available, thereby providing information to decide about purchasing a property. (See Figure 3.2.)

Radon Gas

Radon gas is a radioactive gas produced by the natural decay of other radioactive substances. Although it can occur anywhere, some areas are known to have abnormally high amounts of radon. If it dissipates into the atmosphere, the radon is not likely to cause harm. However, when it infiltrates buildings and is trapped in high concentrations, it can cause health problems. But there is evidence that elevated levels of indoor radon may be an underestimated cause of lung cancer, particularly in children, people who smoke and those who spend a considerable amount of time indoors. The U.S. Environmental Protection

**Figure 3.2
Lead Paint
Disclosure**

Property address _____

Lead Paint Disclosure -- Housing Sales
Disclosure of Information on Lead-Based Paint and Lead-Based Paint Hazards
➲ Lead Warning Statement ☾

Every purchaser of any interest in residential real property on which a residential dwelling was built prior to 1978 is notified that such property may present exposure to lead from lead-based paint that may place young children at risk of developing lead poisoning. Lead poisoning in young children may produce permanent neurological damage, including learning disabilities, reduced intelligence quotient, behavioral problems, and impaired memory. Lead poisoning also poses a particular risk to pregnant women. The seller of any interest in residential real property is required to provide the buyer with any information on lead-based paint hazards from risk assessments or inspections in the seller's possession and notify the buyer of any known lead-based paint hazards. A risk assessment or inspection for possible lead-based paint hazards is recommended prior to purchase.

SELLER'S DISCLOSURE (initial)
_____ (a) Presence of lead-based paint and/or lead-based paint hazards (check one below):

❑ Known lead-based paint and/or lead-based paint hazards are present in the housing (explain):

_____

_____

❑ Seller has no knowledge of lead-based paint and/or lead-based paint hazards in the housing.

_____ (b) Records and reports available to the Seller (check one below):

❑ Seller has provided the Purchaser with all available records and reports pertaining to lead-based paint and/or lead-based paint hazards in the housing (list documents below).

_____

_____

❑ Seller has no reports or records pertaining to lead-based paint and/or lead-based paint hazards in the housing.

PURCHASER'S ACKNOWLEDGMENT (initial)
_____ (c) Purchaser has received copies of all information listed above.
_____ (d) Purchaser has received the pamphlet *Protect Your Family from Lead in Your Home.*
_____ (e) Purchaser has (check one below):

❑ Received a 10-day opportunity (or mutually agreed upon period) to conduct a risk assessment or inspection for the presence of lead-based paint and/or lead based paint hazards; or
❑ Waived the opportunity to conduct a risk assessment or inspection for the presence of lead-based paint and/or lead-based paint hazards.

AGENT'S ACKNOWLEDGMENT (initial)
_____ (f) Agent has informed the Seller of the Seller's obligations under 42 U.S.C. 4852(d) and is aware of his/her responsibility to ensure compliance.

CERTIFICATION OF ACCURACY
The following parties have reviewed the information above and certify, to the best of their knowledge, that the information provided by the signatory is true and accurate:

Seller	Date	Seller	Date
Agent	Date	Agent	Date
Purchaser	Date	Purchaser	Date

Agency (EPA) recommends intervention when radon levels exceed four picocuries per liter.

Radon cannot be detected without testing because it is odorless and tasteless. Tests must be done carefully because radon levels vary, depending on the amount of fresh air that circulates through a house, the weather conditions and the time of year.

ENVIRONMENTAL LAWS

Few people thought about how serious pollution-control problems could be until toxic substances were released at Love Canal, New York, as a result of the improper disposal of hazardous wastes. Local residents became ill with a variety of diseases they attributed to these toxic substances and abandoned their homes and the community, leaving thousands of undesirable properties behind.

The following discussion is a broad overview of the federal environmental laws and agencies that affect real estate. In addition, states have laws that parallel the federal laws and also address the states' specific environmental concerns. There may be local laws as well. Because of the dynamic changes in environmental law, it also is important for licensees to keep abreast of the latest developments.

Resource Conservation and Recovery Act (RCRA)

As a result of heightened awareness from Love Canal in 1976, the federal government passed the first of a series of comprehensive environmental laws, the **Resource Conservation and Recovery Act (RCRA).** This law focuses on minimizing waste and the safe treatment, storage and disposal of solid and hazardous wastes. Although the definition of a hazardous "waste" is complex, generally it is a material that is listed as a hazardous waste in the law or a material that has the characteristics of ignitability, corrosivity, reactivity or toxicity. The Hazardous and Solid Waste Amendments that were passed in 1984 added programs relating to the management of hazardous and solid wastes, including the management of landfills and underground storage tanks.

Underground storage tanks (USTs) have been used in both residential and commercial settings for many years. Three to five million USTs in the United States may contain hazardous substances, including gasoline. They are a risk as they rust and leak toxic substances into the groundwater, which then contaminates wells and pollutes the soil.

Regulation of underground storage tanks includes programs for the design, construction and operation of USTs containing petroleum or any of more than 700 other chemicals identified in RCRA. USTs are defined as tanks holding regulated substances that have more than 10 percent of their volume underground. The law generally exempts farm and residential tanks with less than 1,100 gallons of motor fuel used for noncommercial purposes, tanks storing heating oil at the premises where it is consumed and septic tanks. An important legal point is that the tank owner is financially liable for a leaking tank, even if it contaminates someone else's land.

Comprehensive Environmental Response, Compensation, and Liability Act (CERCLA)

The Comprehensive Environmental Response, Compensation, and Liability Act (CERCLA) was created in 1980. It is also known as the Superfund Law because it established a fund of $9 billion to clean up uncontrolled hazardous waste sites and to respond to spills. This is the single most important environmental law affecting real estate transactions because of the broad liability that it creates. If contamination is discovered on a property, the buyer, seller and lender may find themselves responsible for enormous cleanup costs. The responsible parties as defined by the law include present owners and operators of a landsite, past owners and operators, the parties who generated the hazardous substance and the persons who arranged for the disposal of the hazardous substance at the site.

A landowner may become liable under this act when there has been a release or a threat of release of a hazardous substance. Regardless of whether the contamination is the result of the landowner's own actions or those of others, the owner could be held responsible for cleaning up any resulting contamination. The liability includes the cleanup of the landowner's property and any neighboring property that has been contaminated.

When the Environmental Protection Agency determines that a hazardous material has been released, it has the authority to begin remedial action. Initially this includes identifying the parties responsible for the leak and then approaching the *potentially responsible parties* (PRPs) to see if they will voluntarily cooperate in the cleanup. The PRPs for a given site may include hundreds of industrial generators of waste, previous landowners and transporters. The PRPs must decide whether and on what terms they can fund the cleanup. Otherwise the EPA will begin work through its own contractors and charge the responsible parties for the cost. If a court determines liability for the cost and refusal to pay for the cleanup, the responsible parties could be required to pay triple damages.

Basically the liability provision means that all owners and transporters of hazardous waste are liable for the resulting cleanup cost without regard to fault. Therefore, the EPA need not prove wrongdoing to complete the cleanup or obtain recovery costs.

Superfund Amendments and Reauthorization Act (SARA)

Superfund Amendments and Reauthorization Act (SARA) was passed in 1986 to reauthorize the Superfund that was established by CERCLA. This law contains stronger cleanup standards for contaminated sites and five times the funding of the original Superfund.

SARA also sought to clarify the obligation of mortgage lenders. Because the liability for cleanup extends to the present and all previous owners of a contaminated site, mortgage lenders were very concerned about their liability. A lender could unwillingly or unknowingly be either the present owner or one of the previous owners of a contaminated property through foreclosure proceedings. The amendments clarified the lenders' financial liability for cleanup.

The law also created a concept called *innocent landowner immunity*. It recognized that in certain cases a landowner in the chain of ownership had been completely innocent of all wrongdoing and therefore should not be held liable. Criteria is established by which to judge if a person or business could be exempted from liability as an innocent landowner. Immunity depends on whether the pollution was caused by a third party, the landowner acquired the property after the pollution occurred, the landowner had actual or constructive knowledge of the damage, the landowner made a reasonable search when purchasing the property to determine that there was no damage and the precautions that the landowner took while exercising the ownership rights.

Water Acts

The federal government has several laws that affect water. The *Clean Water Act* (CWA) intends to restore and maintain the chemical, physical and biological integrity of the nation's water. Under this law the discharge of oil and hazardous substances into the water is governed. The *Rivers and Harbors Act* was passed in 1899 but still is used to require permits for building a wharf, pier or other structure in any water outside established harbor lines. The *Coastal Zone Management Act,* which is implemented primarily by the states, addresses coastal environmental problems.

Clean Air Act

The *Clean Air Act* regulates air pollution. It sets forth air quality standards to protect human health and safety and the environment and identifies approximately 190 different substances that are regulated. In 1993 the EPA issued final regulations that significantly affect property owners and businesses. These apply to appliances used for residential or commercial air conditioning, cold storage and refrigeration and the refrigeration chemicals that are used in these appliances.

Sewage Facilities Act

The state's Department of Environmental Protection passed the *Pennsylvania Sewage Facilities Act* in 1994. Section 7 of the law gives notice to prospective buyers that if a property is not serviced by a public sewage system and no community sewage system is available, a permit for an individual system must be obtained. The act also provides four other notices to buyers, all of which must be included in an agreement of sale if applicable:

Notice 2: THIS PROPERTY IS SERVICED BY AN INDIVIDUAL SEWAGE SYSTEM INSTALLED UNDER THE TEN-ACRE EXEMPTION.

Notice 3 : THIS PROPERTY IS SERVICED BY A HOLDING TANK (PERMANENT OR TEMPORARY) TO WHICH SEWAGE IS CONVEYED BY A WATER CARRYING SYSTEM AND WHICH IS DESIGNED AND CONSTRUCTED TO FACILITATE ULTIMATE DISPOSAL OF THE SEWAGE TO ANOTHER SITE.

Notice 4 : AN INDIVIDUAL SEWAGE SYSTEM HAS BEEN INSTALLED AT AN ISOLATION DISTANCE FROM A WELL THAT IS LESS THAN THE DISTANCE SPECIFIED BY REGULATION.

Notice 5 : THIS LOT IS WITHIN AN AREA IN WHICH PERMIT LIMITATIONS ARE IN EFFECT AND IS SUBJECT TO THOSE LIMITATIONS.

Enforcement Agencies

Federal environmental law is administered by a number of agencies such as the United States Department of Transportation (USDOT) under the Hazardous Material Transportation Act; the Occupational Safety and Health Administration (OSHA) and the United States Department of Labor, which administers the standards for all employees; and the EPA. Established in 1970, the EPA today is responsible for administering the following comprehensive environmental protection laws:

- Clean Air Act (CAA)

- Clean Water Act (CWA)

- Safe Drinking Water Act (SDWA)

- Comprehensive Environmental Response, Compensation and Liability Act (CERCLA)

- Resource Conservation and Recovery Act (RCRA)

- Toxic Substance Control Act (TSCA)

- Hazardous Solid Waste Act (HSWA)

There are also state environmental agencies responsible for administering Pennsylvania's laws.

KEY TERMS

asbestos
carbon monoxide
Comprehensive Environmental
Response, Compensation and
   Liability Act
lead

radon
Resource Conservation and
   Recovery Act
Superfund Amendments and
   Reauthorization Act

SUMMARY

Because people want protection from potentially hazardous substances, health issues are becoming increasingly important in real estate. Building products as well as the land, water and air can contain harmful substances.

The usability and value of real estate can be affected by environmental hazards, particularly because significant expenditures to investigate, sample, treat or remove and dispose of a substance are frequently involved. When the expenses are greater than the actual market value of the property, this has a negative effect on owners and sellers.

Real estate licensees must be alert to environmental hazards and learn to protect themselves and sellers from personal injury suits and other legal liability that can arise if the user of a property contracts a health problem because of a toxic substance. Licensees must also ensure that prospective buyers are protected, which includes discovery and disclosure of hazardous substances at the time purchasing decisions are made. Resources such as professional inspectors are available to conduct tests for hazardous substances and environmental assessments. Specific laws about lead-based paint require certain disclosures at the time a property is sold.

Hazardous substances can be abated or removed. In some cases environmental cleanup laws require removal. In other cases, decisions about how to remedy a hazardous condition depend on the nature of the structure and the ease with which it can be altered, the effectiveness of a method to deal with the hazard and the costs to correct a hazardous condition. The risk of causing further contamination by removing a substance must also be considered.

Asbestos, carbon monoxide, lead, radon, formaldehyde and toxic substances that pollute the environment are hazards that frequently arise in real estate transactions.

Federal environmental laws such as the Comprehensive Environmental Response, Compensation and Liability Act (CERCLA), Resource Conservation and Recovery Act (RCRA) and the Superfund Amendments and Reauthorization Act (SARA) protect the environment and provide pollution control measures.

Questions

1. Underground storage tanks are regulated by the
   a. Clean Water Act.
   b. Resource Conservation and Recovery Act.
   c. Superfund Act.
   d. Occupational Hazard Administration Act.

2. Air conditioning and refrigeration equipment contain substances that are regulated by the
   a. Resource Conservation and Recovery Act.
   b. Clean Water Act.
   c. Superfund Act.
   d. Clean Air Act.

3. The law that contains the broadest liabilities for environmental cleanup is the
   a. CERCLA.
   b. Resource Conservation and Recovery Act.
   c. Clean Air Act.
   d. Occupational Hazard Administration Act.

4. Which of the following people do not have liability under the environmental law?
   a. Real estate licensees selling property
   b. Mortgage lenders
   c. Real estate educators
   d. Appraisers

5. When attempting to discover environmental hazards in a real estate transaction, licensees can do several things to protect their professional liability. Which of the following is *not* advisable?
   a. Use licensed environmental inspectors
   b. Use environmental auditors
   c. Conduct their own environmental inspections
   d. Encourage buyers to have professional inspections conducted

6. The Residential Lead-Based Paint Hazard Reduction Act requires
   a. the seller or the seller's agent to distribute a federal lead hazard pamphlet.
   b. the seller to remove any known lead paint.
   c. the buyer to purchase the property after inspections are performed.
   d. a lead warning statement to be included in a listing agreement.

7. The most common sources of lead poisoning in a home are
   a. auto emissions.
   b. paint and plumbing.
   c. flooring and insulation.
   d. refrigeration equipment.

8. Which of the following is true regarding asbestos?
   a. All asbestos-containing materials must be removed in all commercial buildings.
   b. Asbestos causes a health problem only when ingested.
   c. The level of asbestos in a building is affected by weather conditions.
   d. The removal of asbestos can further contaminate a building.

9. One of the most common sources of carbon monoxide in a house is/are
   a. malfunctioning air conditioners.
   b. crumbling insulation.
   c. leaking heating fuel tanks.
   d. malfunctioning furnaces.

10. Which of the following is true about radon?
   a. It can be reduced in a building with proper ventilation.
   b. It is commonly found in building materials.
   c. It is easy to detect because of its odor.
   d. It is commonly found around landfills.

4 Legal Descriptions

DESCRIBING LAND

In everyday life we often refer to real estate by its street address, such as "1234 Main Street." While that information is usually adequate for the average person to find the designated house, it is not precise enough to be used on legal documents, particularly deeds. The courts have stated that a description is legally sufficient for documents if a competent surveyor can locate the parcel using it. However, *locate* in this context means to define the exact boundaries of the property. The street address would not tell anyone precisely how large the parcel of land is or where it begins and ends. Therefore several systems of identification have been developed to produce a **legal description,** that is, a precise, legally acceptable way of identifying or referring to a parcel of land so that its location may be known with certainty. A legal description may be followed by the words "commonly known as" and the street address on documents such as agreements of sale.

Typically, ownership of a parcel of property has been transferred many times. The legal description used in the documents for each transfer should be identical to the one used in prior transfers. By following this practice for each transfer of ownership, discrepancies, errors and legal problems can be minimized or avoided.

METHODS OF DESCRIBING REAL ESTATE

The methods used to describe real estate are metes and bounds, lot and block (recorded plat) and rectangular (government) survey. Although each method can be used independently, the methods may be combined in some situations.

In Pennsylvania, as well as the other states in the East, land is described by metes and bounds and lot and block, not by rectangular survey. However, all three methods of describing land are discussed so that licensees are familiar with systems used throughout the country as well as in Pennsylvania.

Metes and Bounds

A **metes-and-bounds description** uses the boundaries and measurements of the parcel in question. The description starts at a designated place on the parcel called the **point of beginning** (POB) and proceeds around the boundaries by referring to linear measurements and directions. A metes-and-bounds description always ends at the POB so that the tract being described is completely enclosed.

Monuments are fixed objects used to identify the point of beginning, the end of a boundary or the location of intersecting boundaries. Natural objects such as stones, large trees, lakes, streams and intersections of major streets or highways, as well as man-made markers placed by surveyors, are commonly used as monuments. In a metes and bounds description, the actual distance between monuments takes precedence over linear measurements set forth in the description if the two measurements differ. Measurements often include the words "more or less"; the location of the monuments is more important than the distance stated in the wording.

An example of a metes-and-bounds description of a parcel of land (pictured in Figure 4.1) follows.

"ALL THAT CERTAIN piece or parcel of land situate in Wayne Township, Clinton County, Pennsylvania, bounded and described in accordance with a survey made by H. Richard Ohl, Registered Surveyor, dated November 9, 1984, as follows:

BEGINNING at an iron pin on the Easterly line of Pennsylvania Route 18013, which iron pin is on the Boundary line between the parcel to be conveyed and land of the United States of America (United States Army Reserve Center of Lock Haven); thence along the land of the said United States of America, North 70 degrees 41 minutes 10 seconds East a distance of sixty-six and 27/100 (66.27) feet to an iron pin; thence continuing along the same, South 31 degrees 23 minutes 30 seconds East a distance of six hundred seventy-seven and 1/10 (677.1) feet to an iron pin on the Northerly line of Township Route 425, thence along the Northerly line of said Township Route 425, the following five (5) courses and distances: (1) South 70 degrees 44 minutes West a distance of fifty-one and 5/10 (51.5) feet to an iron pin, (2) South 60 degrees 06 minutes West a distance of five hundred thirty-six and 6/10 (536.6) feet to an iron pin, (3) North 29 degrees 54 minutes West a distance of thirteen and 5/10 (13.5) feet to an iron pin, (4) South 61 degrees 54 minutes West a distance of eighty and 5/10 (80.5) feet to an iron pin; (5) South 74 degrees 05 minutes West a distance of 54.00 feet to an iron pin; thence along Pennsylvania Route 18013 North 34 degrees 40 minutes West a distance of fifty-nine and 6/10 (59.6) feet to an iron pin; thence continuing along Pennsylvania Route 18013 North 17 degrees 28 minutes East a distance of eight hundred seventy-two and 8/10 (872.8) feet to an iron pin, the place of beginning, containing an area of 6.74 acres.

"BEING a portion of Tract No. 12 of the premises granted and conveyed to the Grantors herein by Deed of Betroblen Realty, Inc., dated January 6, 1986, and recorded in Clinton County Deed Book 295, Page 191."

The description must close by returning to the POB.

Metes-and-bounds descriptions may be very complex and should be handled with extreme care. When they include compass directions of the various lines and concave or convex curved lines, they can be difficult to understand. In these cases, the advice of a surveyor should be sought. Computer programs are available that convert the data of the compass directions and dimensions to a drawing that verifies that the description closes to the POB.

Figure 4.1
Metes-and-Bounds
Tract

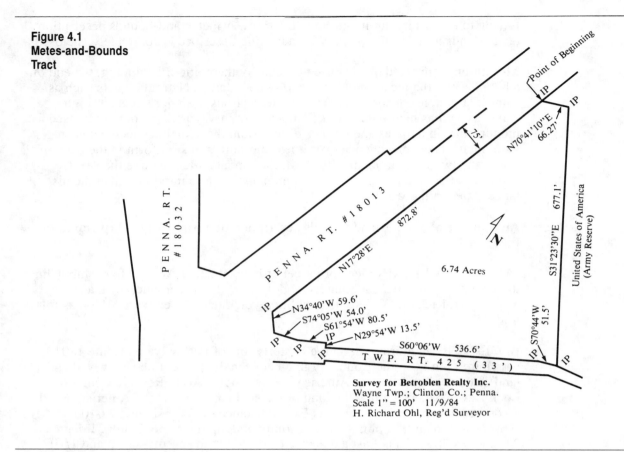

Survey for Betroblen Realty Inc.
Wayne Twp.; Clinton Co.; Penna.
Scale 1" = 100'   11/9/84
H. Richard Ohl, Reg'd Surveyor

Lot and Block

The **lot and block system** (or *recorded plat system*) uses *lot and block numbers* referred to in a **plat map** filed in the recorder of deeds office in the county where the land is located.

The first step in subdividing land is the preparation of a *survey plat* by a licensed surveyor or engineer, as illustrated in Figure 4.2. On this plat the land is divided into blocks and lots, and streets or access roads for public use are indicated. The blocks and lots are assigned numbers or letters. Lot sizes and street details must comply with all local ordinances and be indicated precisely. When properly signed and approved, the subdivision plat map is recorded. When describing a lot from a recorded subdivision plat, the lot and block numbers, name or number of the subdivision plat and the name of the municipality, county and state are used as the legal description. For example:

"Lots 2, 3 and 4 in Block 5 of L. Robinson's Subdivision of the property beginning at a point on the North side of Main Road, 175 feet east from the corner formed by the intersection of the south side of Main Road and the east side of State Route 54; thence. . ."

Some subdivided lands are further divided by a later resubdivision. For example, if Alan Roswell bought two full blocks of John Welch's subdivision and resubdivided this land into different sized lots, Roswell might convey "Lot 1 in Block A of Roswell's resubdivision of Blocks 2 and 3 and John Welch's

**Figure 4.2
Subdivision
Plat Map**

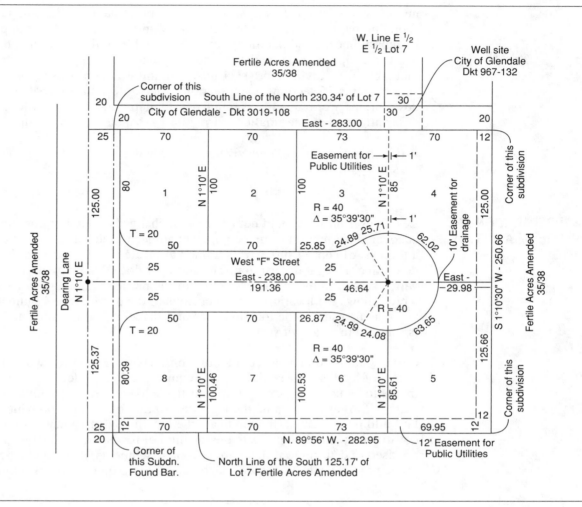

Hometown Subdivision of the property beginning at a point on the east side of State Route 33 . . ."

The lot-and-block system is used, at least in part, in all states. Some states have passed plat acts that specify the smallest parcel that may be sold without a subdivision plat map being prepared, approved and recorded. The Pennsylvania Municipalities Planning Code defines a subdivision as two or more lots, tracts or parcels, unless it is for agricultural purposes.

**Rectangular
(Government)
Survey System**

The **rectangular survey system,** sometimes called the *government survey method,* was established by Congress in 1785, soon after the federal government was organized. The system was developed as a standard method of describing all lands conveyed to or acquired by the federal government, including the extensive area of the Northwest Territory.

The rectangular survey system is based on sets of two intersecting lines: principal meridians and base lines. The **principal meridians** are north and south lines and the **base lines** are east and west lines. Both are exactly located by reference to degrees of longitude and latitude. Each principal meridian has a name or number and is crossed by a base line. Each principal meridian and its corresponding base line are used to survey a definite area of land within prescribed boundary lines. Land parallel to meridians and base lines is divided into ranges and townships, respectively, forming imaginary squares, known as **townships,** that are further divided into **sections,** then into fractions of sections. Each township contains 36 sections; each section is one mile square or 640 acres. These descriptions are frequently combined with metes and bounds or lot and block descriptions to define smaller or irregularly shaped parcels of land.

Again, remember that Pennsylvania does not describe land using the rectangular survey method.

PREPARATION AND USE OF A SURVEY

Legal descriptions should not be created, changed, altered or combined without adequate information from a competent authority, such as a surveyor or title attorney. A licensed surveyor is trained to locate a given parcel of land and to determine its legal description. The surveyor does this by preparing a *survey,* which sets forth the legal description of the property, and a *survey sketch,* which shows the location and dimensions of the parcel. (See Figure 4.3.) A survey that also shows the location, size and shape of buildings located on the lot is referred to as a *spot survey.*

Surveys are used in a variety of situations. They are required when a portion of a tract of land is conveyed. Lenders require surveys to identify the real estate that is to be used as security for a mortgage loan when the boundaries are not certain. Surveys determine the legal description of the land on which a particular building is located; they indicate the location where a new building is to be constructed; and they indicate the location of roads and highways. Surveys also are used to determine if there are any encroachments, that is, whether an improvement extends or intrudes beyond a building line or property line.

IN PRACTICE. . .

By studying the legal description or reviewing the plat plan or a survey that the landowner may have, licensees can identify the dimensions of the parcel of land to accurately represent properties to potential buyers. Otherwise a buyer may find that the dimensions of a lot do not satisfy the buyer's intended use. If the construction of a particular kind of building or other improvement cannot be accommodated or the parking or open area is insufficient according to zoning requirements, the buyer could be injured, which also creates potential liability for the licensee.

MEASURING ELEVATIONS

The owner of a parcel of land may subdivide the air above the land into **air lots.** Air lots are composed of airspace within specific boundaries located over a parcel of land. This type of description is found in titles to tall buildings located on air rights, generally over railroad tracks. Similarly a surveyor, in preparing a subdivision plat for condominium use, describes each condominium unit by reference to the elevation of the floors and ceilings on a vertical plane above the city datum.

Figure 4.3
A Survey Sketch

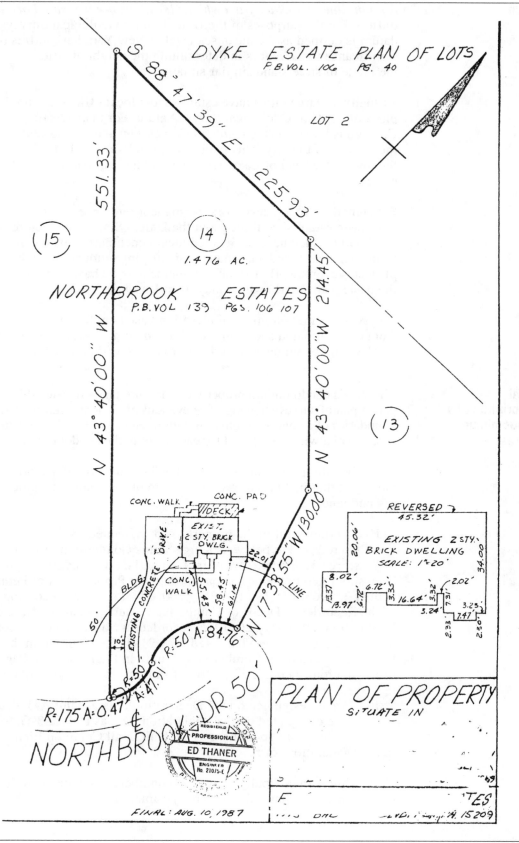

Datum

A point, line or surface from which elevations are measured or indicated is a **datum.** For the purposes of the United States Geological Survey (USGS), datum is defined as the mean sea level at New York harbor. It is of special significance to surveyors in determining the height of structures, establishing the grade of streets and similar situations.

Virtually all large cities have established a local official datum that is used in place of the U.S. Geological Survey datum. For instance, the official datum for Chicago is known as the *Chicago City Datum* and is a horizontal plane below the surface of the city. This plane was established in 1847 as corresponding to the low-water level of Lake Michigan in that year and is considered to be zero elevation.

Benchmarks. To aid surveyors, permanent reference points called **benchmarks** have been established throughout the United States (See Figure 4.4). Cities with local datums also have designated local benchmarks, which are given official status when assigned a permanent identifying number. Local benchmarks simplify surveyors' work, for measurements may be based on them rather than on the basic benchmark, which may be miles away.

A surveyor's measurement of elevation based on the USGS datum will differ from one computed according to a local datum. A surveyor can always translate an elevation based on a local datum to the elevation based on the USGS datum.

Legal Description of a Condominium Interest

The state's condominium property acts require that a registered land surveyor prepare a plat of survey showing the elevations of floor and ceiling surfaces and the boundaries of a condominium unit with reference to an official datum. Typically, a separate plat will be prepared for each floor in the condominium building.

The following is an example of the legal description of a condominium apartment unit that includes a fractional share of the common elements of the building and land:

"THAT certain Unit in the property known, named and identified in the Declaration Plan referred to below as King's Arms Condominium, situate in the Village of Westover, Hampden Township, Cumberland County, Pennsylvania, which has been submitted to the provisions of the Unit Property Act of Pennsylvania, Act of July 3, 1963, P.L. 196 (68 P.S. §700.101 et seq.), by recording in the Office of the Recorder of Deeds of Cumberland County, Pennsylvania, of a Declaration dated May 20, 1975, recorded in Miscellaneous Book 215, Page 836, and a Declaration Plan dated May 21, 1975, recorded in the Office of the Recorder of Deeds of Cumberland County in Plan Book 26, Page 70 and a Code of Regulations, being Exhibit "B" of said Declaration, described as follows:

"BEING and designated on the Declaration Plan as Unit A-3, detached garage, said garage designated on the Declaration Plan as Unit A-3-G, together with an undivided interest appurtenant to the Unit in all Common Elements (as defined in the Declaration) of 5.26%.

"THE Unit is municipally known and numbered as Three King's Arms, Village of Westover, Mechanicsburg, Pennsylvania.

**Figure 4.4
Benchmark**

"BEING the same premises which Pennsboro Homes, Inc., by Deed dated August 1, 1975, recorded in the Office of the Recorder of Deeds of Cumberland County in Deed Book E, Volume 26, Page 359, granted and conveyed unto Thomas D. Smith, Seller herein."

IN PRACTICE...	*Because legal descriptions, once recorded, affect the title to real estate, they should be prepared only by a surveyor or attorney. Real estate licensees should not attempt to draft legal descriptions and also must use great care when copying descriptions in documents. An incorrectly worded legal description may obligate a seller to convey or a buyer to purchase more or less land than is intended. The buyer also may have title problems when trying to convey the property at a future date. The licensee may be held liable for damages suffered by an injured party because of an improperly worded legal description.*

LAND UNITS AND MEASUREMENTS

It is important to know and understand land units and measurements—they are an integral part of legal descriptions. Some commonly used measurements follow:

- A *rod* is 16½ feet.
- A *chain* is 66 feet, or 100 links.
- A *mile* is 5,280 feet.
- An *acre* contains 43,560 square feet, or 160 square rods.
- A *section* of land is one square mile and contains 640 acres; a *quarter section* contains 160 acres; a *quarter of a quarter section* contains 40 acres.
- A *circle* contains 360 degrees; a *quarter segment* of a circle contains 90 degrees; a *half segment* of a circle contains 180 degrees. One *degree* (1°) can be subdivided into 60 minutes (60′), each of which contains 60 seconds (60″). One-and-a-half degrees would be written 1°30′0″.

Table 4.1 lists further land measurement units.

Table 4.1	Unit	Measurement
Units of Land	mile	5,280 feet; 320 rods; 1,760 yards
Measurement	rod	5.50 yards; 16.50 feet
	sq. mile	640 acres
	acre	4,840 sq. yards; 160 sq. rods; 43,560 sq. feet
	sq. yard	9 sq. feet
	sq. foot	144 sq. inches
	chain	66 feet or 100 links
	kilometer	0.62 mile
	hectare	2.47 acres

●   ●   ●   ●   ●   ●   ●

KEY TERMS

air lot   monument
base line   plat map
benchmark   point of beginning
datum   principal meridian
legal description   section
lot and block system   township
metes-and-bounds description

SUMMARY

Documents affecting or conveying interests in real estate must contain an accurate description of the property involved. The three methods used to legally describe land in the United States are metes and bounds, lot and block and rectangular (government) survey systems. Pennsylvania, however, does not use the rectangular survey system. A legal description is a precise method of identifying a parcel of land. A property's description should always be the same as the one used in previous documents.

A metes and bounds description uses direction and distance measurements to establish precise boundaries for a parcel. Monuments are fixed objects used to establish boundaries. The actual location of monuments takes precedence over the written linear measurement in a document. When property is being described by metes and bounds, the description must always enclose a tract of land; that is, the boundary line must end at the point at which it started.

Land in every state can be subdivided into lots and blocks by means of a recorded plat of subdivision. An approved plat of survey showing the division into blocks, giving the size, location and designation of lots and specifying the location and size of streets to be dedicated for public use is filed for record in the recorder's office of the county in which the land is located. By referring to a subdivision plat, the legal description of a property can be identified by lot, block and subdivision in a specific municipality, county and state.

The rectangular survey system involves surveys based on 35 principal meridians. Under this system each principal meridian and its corresponding base line are specifically located. This system is not used in Pennsylvania.

A survey, prepared by a licensed surveyor, is the usual method for certifying the legal description of a parcel of land. When a survey also shows the location, size and shape of the buildings located on the lot, it is referred to as a spot survey.

Air lots, condominium descriptions and other measurements of vertical elevations may be computed from the United States Geological Survey datum, which is the mean sea level in New York harbor. Most large cities have established local survey datums for surveying within the area. The elevations from these datums are further supplemented by reference points, called benchmarks, placed at fixed intervals from the datums.

Questions

1. A *monument* is used in which of the following types of legal descriptions?
   a. Lot and block
   b. Metes and bounds
   c. Rectangular survey
   d. Street address

2. The least acceptable method for identifying real property is
   a. rectangular survey.
   b. metes and bounds.
   c. street address.
   d. lot and block.

3. An *acre* contains
   a. 160 sq. ft.   c. 640 sq. ft.
   b. 43,560 sq. ft.   d. 360 degrees.

4. A *datum* is
   a. used in the description of an air lot.
   b. measured in New York only.
   c. a calendar method of measurement.
   d. All of the above

5. In describing real estate, a system that uses feet, degrees and monuments is
   a. rectangular survey.
   b. metes and bounds.
   c. government survey.
   d. lot and block.

6. A woman purchased 4.5 acres of land for which she paid $78,400. An adjoining owner wants to purchase a strip of her land measuring 150 feet by 100 feet. What should this strip cost the adjoining owner if the woman sells it for the same price she originally paid for it?
   a. $3,000   c. $7,800
   b. $6,000   d. $9,400

7. A property contained ten acres. How many 50-foot by 100-foot lots could be subdivided from the property if 26,000 square feet were dedicated for roads?
   a. 80   c. 82
   b. 81   d. 83

8. At $800 per acre, a lot that is 264 feet wide and 660 feet long would cost
   a. $1,320.   c. $3,200.
   b. $1,584.   d. $4,356.

9. A survey that shows the location, size and shape of buildings located on a lot is called a/an
   a. survey sketch.
   b. legal description.
   c. angular course.
   d. spot survey.

Answer questions 10 through 13 according to the information given on the plat of Mountain-side Manor in Figure 4.5.

10. Which of the following statements is true?
     a. Lot 9, Block A is larger than Lot 12 in the same block.
     b. The plat for the lots on the southerly side of Wolf Road between Goodrich Boulevard and Carney Street is found on Sheet 3.
     c. Lot 8, Block A has the longest road frontage.
     d. Lot 11, Block B has more frontage than Lot 2, Block A.

11. Which of the following lots has the most frontage on Jasmine Lane?
     a. Lot 10, Block B
     b. Lot 11, Block B
     c. Lot 1, Block A
     d. Lot 2, Block A

12. "Beginning at the intersection of the east line of Goodrich Boulevard and the south line of Jasmine Lane and running south along the east line of Goodrich Boulevard a distance of 230 feet; thence east parallel to the north line of Wolf Road a distance of 195 feet; thence northeasterly on a course N 22° E a distance of 135 feet; and thence northwesterly along the south line of Jasmine Lane to the point of beginning." Which lots are described here?
     a. Lots 13, 14 and 15, Block A
     b. Lots 9, 10 and 11, Block B
     c. Lots 1, 2, 3 and 15, Block A
     d. Lots 7, 8 and 9, Block A

13. On the plat, how many lots have easements?
     a. One   c. Three
     b. Two   d. Four

Figure 4.5

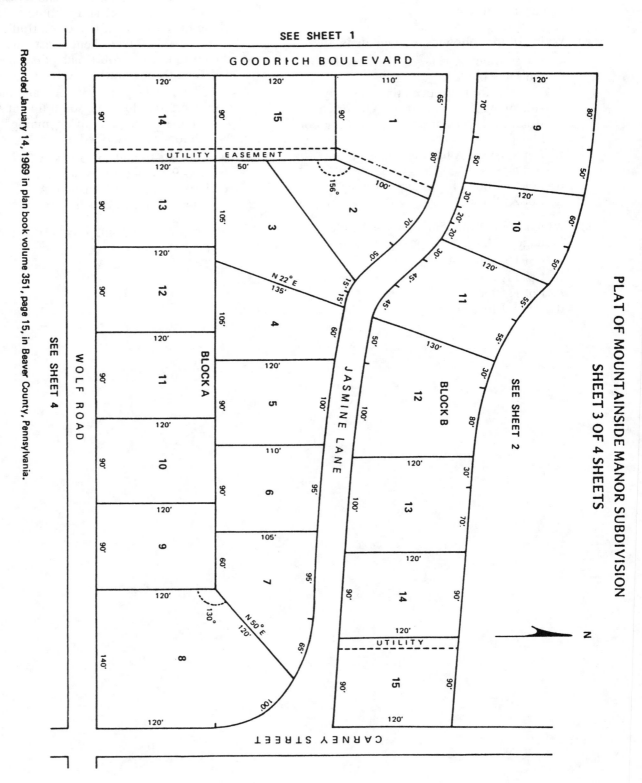

5 Interests in Real Estate

HISTORICAL BACKGROUND

According to old English common law, the government or king held title to all land, under what was known as the **feudal system** of ownership. A person was merely a tenant under this system, and the rights of use and occupancy of the real property were held at the sufferance of an overlord. In the seventeenth century, the feudal system evolved into the **allodial system** of ownership. Under this system a person was entitled to property rights, and the government or the king no longer had proprietary control.

Ownership as we know it in the United States, is held under the allodial system. In fact The Bill of Rights of the U.S. Constitution firmly establishes the private ownership of land. But as has been discussed already, the enjoyment of the entire bundle of rights associated with the ownership of real property is not absolute. Even the most complete form of ownership that the law allows is limited by public, and possibly, private restrictions. Ownership also can be viewed as a variety of interests, some of which an owner might retain for himself or herself while transferring the remainder to another owner, and interests in a person's ownership that others can claim.

For licensees selling real estate, it's important to understand exactly what a seller owns and intends to sell and ensure that a prospective buyer understands exactly what the owner is transferring. This chapter is devoted to putting all of the various interests in perspective—to understand the rights that are being conveyed and how ownership may be limited.

GOVERNMENT POWERS

Individual ownership rights are subject to certain powers, or rights, held by federal, state and local governments. These limitations on the ownership of real estate are imposed for the general welfare of the community, and therefore, supersede the rights or interests of the individual. Government powers include police power, eminent domain, taxation and escheat-PETE.

Police Power

As was discussed in Chapter 2, states have the power to enact legislation to preserve order, to protect the public health and safety and to promote the general welfare. That authority is known as the states' **police power**. The authority is passed on to municipalities and counties through legislation called *enabling acts*.

What is identified as being in the public interest will, of course, vary widely from area to area. Generally, however, a state's police power is used to enact environmental protection laws, zoning ordinances, building codes and regulations governing the use, occupancy, size, location, construction and rents of real estate—the kinds of activities discussed in Chapter 2 relating to the government's land-use controls.

Laws must be uniform and nondiscriminatory so as not to be an advantage or disadvantage to any one particular owner or owners. The community's needs and desires can be reflected in these laws. If, for example, a city deems growth to be desirable, it will exercise its police powers to encourage the purchase and improvement of land. If an area wishes to retain its current character, it may enact laws that discourage construction and the expansion of population.

Eminent Domain

Eminent domain is the right of the government to acquire privately owned real estate for public use. **Condemnation** is the process, either by judicial or administrative proceedings, by which the government exercises this right. The proposed use must be for the public good, just compensation must be paid to the owner and the rights of the property owner must be protected by due process of law. Public use has been defined very broadly by the courts to include not only public facilities but also property that is no longer fit and must be destroyed to protect the community.

The legislature empowers the state to delegate its power of eminent domain to local government, quasi-public bodies and publicly held companies responsible for various facets of public service. A public housing authority might take privately owned land to build low-income housing on it; the state's land-clearance commission or redevelopment authority could use the power of eminent domain to make way for urban renewal. If there were no other feasible way to do so, a railway, utility company or state highway department might acquire farmland to extend a railroad track, build a highway or bring electricity to a remote new development—again, as long as the purpose contributes to the public good.

Ideally, the public agency and the owner of the property in question reach agreement through direct negotiation, and the government purchases the property for a price viewed as fair by the owner. In some cases the owner even dedicates the property to the government as a site for a school, park, library or other use the owner deems worthy. When the owner's consent cannot be obtained, however, the government can initiate condemnation proceedings to acquire the property. Condemnations are presumed to be proper unless the owner objects, which is likely to occur when the owner feels the "taking" is improper or the amount of the compensation is unjust. The owner may file suit for the court to decide the matter.

Taxation

Taxation is a charge on real estate to raise funds to meet the public needs of a government. See Chapter 9 for more information on real estate taxes.

Escheat

Although escheat is not actually a limitation on ownership, it is an avenue by which the state acquires privately owned real or personal property. State laws provide for the ownership to transfer, or **escheat**, to the state when an owner dies leaving no heirs as defined by the escheat law and no will designating the disposition of the real estate. Escheat is intended to prevent property from being ownerless. In some states, real property will escheat to the county where the land is located, rather than to the state.

ESTATES IN LAND

An **estate in land** defines an owner's degree, quantity, nature and extent of interest in real property. Many different types of estates exist, but it is important to understand that not all *interests* in real estate are *estates*. To be an estate in land, an interest must allow possession (either now or in the future) and must be measurable by duration. Lesser interests such as easements (discussed later in the chapter), which allow use but not possession, are not estates. The various estates and interests in real estate are illustrated in Figure 5.1.

Historically, estates in land have been classified as freehold estates and leasehold estates. According to English common law, freehold estates were real estate, while leasehold (less-than-freehold) estates were merely contracts and thus personal property. Both then and now, the two types of estate are distinguished primarily by their duration.

Freehold estates last for an *indeterminable length of time,* such as for a lifetime or forever. These include fee simple, also called an indefeasible fee, defeasible fee and life estates. The first two of these estates continue for an indefinite period and are inheritable by the heirs of the owner. The life estate terminates upon the death of the person on whose life it is based.

Leasehold estates last *for a fixed period of time.* They include estates for years and estates from period to period. Estates at will and estates at sufferance are also leaseholds, though by their operation they are not generally viewed as being for fixed terms. Leaseholds are discussed in Chapter 6.

Fee Simple Estate

An estate in **fee simple** is the *highest quality of interest in real estate recognized by law.* Although rights of ownership can exist in various freehold estates, the fee simple estate is distinguished above all the others because the holder has absolute, complete and total rights to the ownership forever. Also known as an estate in *fee simple absolute*, it is limited only by controls imposed by public and private restrictions. In common usage, the terms *fee* and *fee simple* are used interchangeably with *fee simple absolute.* Because the estate is of unlimited duration, it is said to run forever. Upon the death of its owner it passes to the owner's heirs or as provided by will. A fee simple estate is also referred to as an *estate of inheritance.*

Fee simple defeasible. A **fee simple defeasible** (or *defeasible fee*) estate is a qualified estate, subject to the occurrence or nonoccurrence of a specified event. There are two types of defeasible estates. A fee simple estate may be qualified by a *condition subsequent.* This specifies some action or activity that the new owner must *not* perform. The former owner retains a *right of reentry,* so that if the condition is broken, the former owner can retake possession of the property.

58

Modern Real Estate Practice in Pennsylvania

**Figure 5.1
Estates and
Interests in
Real Estate**

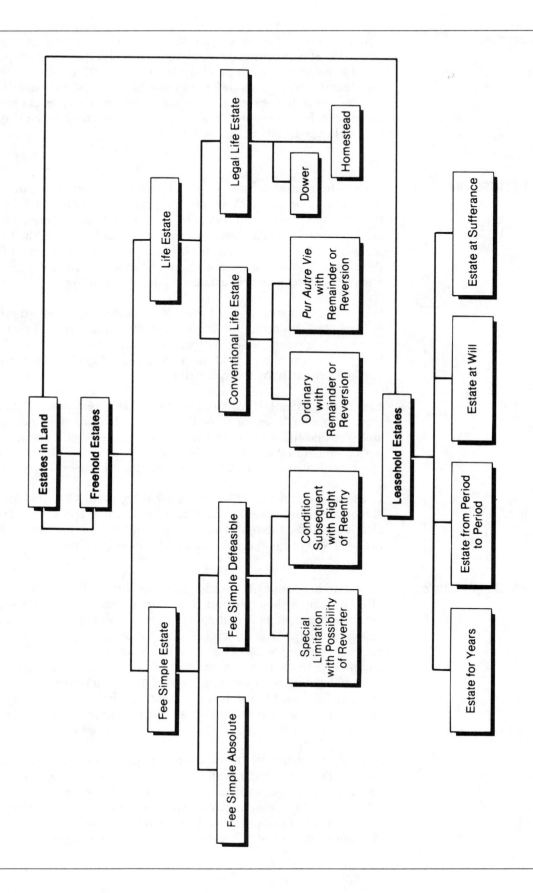

It is necessary, however, for the grantor (the person who created the condition) or the grantor's heirs or successors to go to court to assert this right.

A grant of land "on the condition that" there be no consumption of alcohol on the premises is a fee simple on condition subsequent. If alcohol is consumed on the property, the former owner has the right to reacquire full ownership. Conditions in a deed are different from restrictions or covenants because the grantor has the right to reclaim ownership, a right that does not exist under private restrictions.

A fee simple estate may be qualified by a *special limitation*. The estate ends *automatically* upon failure to comply with the limitation. The former owner (or the former owner's heirs or successors) retains a *possibility of reverter* and reacquires full ownership, with no need to reenter the land. A fee simple with a special limitation is also called a **fee simple determinable**. The language used to distinguish a special limitation—the words "so long as" or "while" or "during"—is the key to the creation of this estate. For example, a grant of land from an owner to her church "so long as" the land is used only for religious purposes is a fee simple with a special limitation. If the church uses the land for a nonreligious purpose, title reverts to the previous owner (or her heirs or successors).

The *right of entry* and *possibility of reverter* may never take effect. If they do, it will only be some time in the future. Therefore, both of these rights are considered *future interests*.

IN PRACTICE. . .	*This discussion about fee simple estates serves a very important practical purpose. The kind of fee simple estate affects the ownership and, consequently, the purchaser of a property. The seller cannot convey to the buyer an estate that is greater than what the seller owns. For example, if a seller has a defeasible fee estate, the seller cannot convey an absolute fee simple estate. It is important to know what kind of estate the seller is capable of delivering. This can be done when the seller's property is listed. If the estate is less than a fee simple absolute, the licensee should seek the guidance of legal counsel about how to proceed.*

Life Estate

A **life estate** is a freehold estate that is *limited in duration to the life of the owner or to the life or lives of some other designated person or persons*. Unlike other freehold estates, a life estate is not inheritable. It will pass to future owners according to the provisions of the life estate.

Conventional life estate. A *conventional life estate* is created by the intentional act of the owner either by deed when the ownership is transferred or by a will. The estate is conveyed to an individual known as the *life tenant*. The life tenant has full enjoyment of the ownership for the duration of the individual's life. Upon the death of the life tenant, the estate ends and the ownership will pass to another designated individual or return to the previous owner or their heirs. For example, *A,* who has a fee simple estate in Blackacre, conveys a life estate to *P* for *P*'s lifetime. *P* is the life tenant. Upon *P*'s death the life estate terminates. (See Figure 5.2.)

Figure 5.2
Conventional
Life Estate

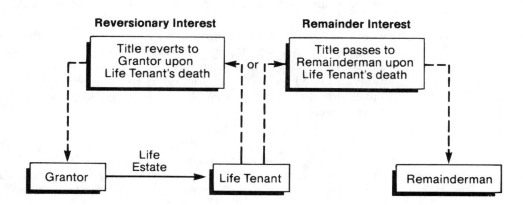

Remainder and reversion. The fee simple owner who creates a conventional life estate must plan for its future ownership. When the estate ends, it is replaced by a fee simple estate. The future owners of the fee simple estate may be designated in one of two ways:

1. **Remainder interest:** The creator of the life estate may name a *remainderman* as the person to whom the property will pass when the life estate ends. In the example, when A conveys Blackacre to P for P's lifetime, at the time the life estate is created, A can designate R to be the remainderman. While P is still alive, R owns a *remainder* interest which is a nonpossessory estate. This is a *future interest* in the fee simple estate. Upon P's death, R becomes the fee simple owner with all of the rights associated with that estate.

2. **Reversionary interest:** The creator of the life estate may choose not to name a remainderman and recapture the ownership when the life estate ends. In this case, A conveys Blackacre to P for P's lifetime. During the life of P, A has a reversionary interest, which is a nonpossessory estate. Upon P's death, the ownership reverts to A. A has a future interest in the ownership and reclaims the fee simple estate when P dies. If A dies before P, the ownership reverts to A's heirs or individuals specified in A's will when P dies.

A life estate can also be based on the lifetime of another person. This is known as an *estate pur autre vie* (for the life of another). In this case, A conveys a life estate in Blackacre to P as the life tenant for the duration of the life of D. P is still the life tenant, but the measuring life is D's. Upon D's death, the life estate ends. Although a life estate is not considered an estate of inheritance, a life estate *pur autre vie* provides for inheritance by the life tenant's heirs only until the death of the person against whose life the estate is measured. In the example, if P died while D is still alive, P's heirs could be the owners of the life estate. When D dies, the estate ends for the heirs. Life estates pur autre vie are usually created in favor of someone who is physically or mentally incapacitated in the hope of providing an incentive for someone else to care for them. (See Figure 5.3.)

A life tenant is entitled to the rights of ownership (not to be confused with the interest of a tenant in a lease). The life tenant can enjoy possession and the

Figure 5.3
Pur Autre Vie
Life Estate

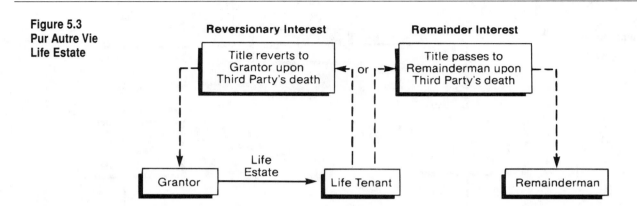

ordinary use and profits arising from the ownership, just as if the individual was a fee owner. The ownership may be sold, mortgaged or leased.

The ownership rights for a life tenant are not absolute, however. The life tenant may not injure the property, such as by destroying a building or allowing it to deteriorate. This injury is known in legal terms as *waste*. Those who will eventually own the property could seek an injunction against the life tenant or sue for damages. Because the ownership will terminate upon the death of the person against whose life the estate is measured, a purchaser, lessee or lender can be affected. The life tenant can sell, lease or mortgage only the interest that he or she has, that is ownership for a lifetime. Because the interest is less desirable than a fee simple estate, the life tenant's rights are somewhat limited in practice.

IN PRACTICE. . .	*What is the effect of conventional life estates on a real estate transaction? Because the seller cannot convey to the buyer an estate that is greater than what the seller owns, the buyer could receive ownership that terminates when the life tenant or the person on whose life the estate is based dies. Conventional life estates may be useful for specific estate-planning purposes, but it is unknown how commonly this strategy is used or how often they will arise in a real estate transaction. Again, this can be investigated when the seller's property is listed, and the licensee can seek the guidance of legal counsel about how to proceed if the estate is less than a fee simple absolute.*

Legal life estate. A *legal life estate* is one created by "operation of law" upon the occurrence of certain events, rather than voluntarily by the owner. The Pennsylvania Probate, Estates and Fiduciaries Code, which has been adopted consistent with the Uniform Probate Code, allows a surviving spouse to have a life estate in 33 percent of the deceased spouse's property at the time of death. The statute gives the surviving spouse the option to take a life estate in the specified percentage of the value of the estate of the deceased spouse in lieu of whatever the survivor would have otherwise received under the will.

If the spouse died *intestate* (without a will) the statute directs the percentage of distribution of the assets to the surviving spouse and other specified heirs.

Figure 5.4
Encumbrances

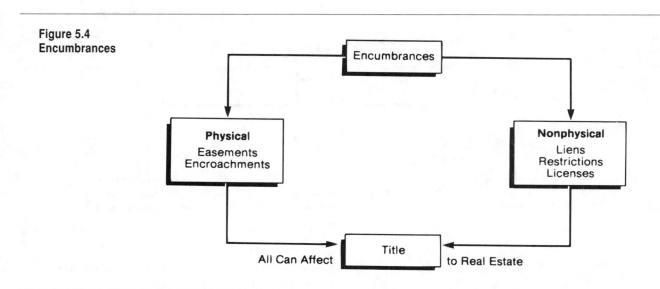

This "marital life estate" arises from the common law concept of *dower and curtesy,* which provided the nonowning spouse with a means of support after the death of the owning spouse. (*Dower* is the life estate that a wife has in the real estate of her deceased husband. *Curtesy* is a similar interest that a husband has in the real estate of his deceased wife.) Dower and curtesy provided that the nonowning spouse had a right to a one-half or one-third interest in the real estate for the rest of his or her life, even if the owning spouse willed the estate to others.

Because of the possibility that a nonowning spouse might claim an interest in the future, even where one may not exist, it was common practice for both spouses to sign the documents when real estate was conveyed. The signature of the nonowning spouse would be needed to release any potential common law interests in the property being transferred. Most states, including Pennsylvania, have abolished the common law concepts of dower and curtesy by amendment to the Uniform Probate Code. While the signature of the nonowning spouse is no longer a legal requirement in real estate documents, some financial institutions continue to demand it.

ENCUMBRANCES

An **encumbrance** is a claim, charge or liability that attaches to and is binding on real estate. Simply put, it is *anything* that affects title to real estate as a right or interest held by someone other than the fee owner of the property. An encumbrance may lessen the value or obstruct the use of the property, but it does not necessarily prevent a transfer of title.

Encumbrances may be divided into two general classifications: liens (usually monetary) and encumbrances that affect the physical condition of the property, such as easements and encroachments. (See Figure 5.4.)

Liens

A **lien** is *a financial charge against property that provides security for a debt or obligation of the property owner.* If the obligation is not repaid, the lienholder, or creditor, has the right to have it paid out of the debtor's property, usually from the proceeds of a court-ordered sale. Real estate taxes, mortgages and trust deeds, judgments and mechanics' liens (for people who have furnished labor or materials in the construction or repair of real estate) all represent possible liens against an owner's real estate. Liens will be discussed in detail in Chapter 9.

Restrictions

Deed restrictions (also referred to as *covenants, conditions* and *restrictions*) are private agreements that affect the use of land. They usually are imposed by an owner of real estate when the property is sold and are included in the seller's deed to the buyer. Typically, *restrictive covenants* are imposed by a developer or subdivider to maintain specific standards in a subdivision, and are listed in the original development plans for the subdivision filed in the public record, as discussed in a previous chapter.

Easements

An **easement** is the *right to use the land of another party for a particular purpose*. It gives the holder of an easement limited use or enjoyment of another's land. An easement may exist in any portion of the real estate, including the airspace, or represented by a right-of-way across the land.

Appurtenant easement. An **appurtenant easement** or *easement appurtenant* is annexed to the ownership of one parcel and allows this owner the use of a neighbor's land. It fulfills the need of one property at the expense of another. For such an easement to exist, there must be two adjacent parcels of land owned by two different parties. The parcel over which the easement runs is known as the *servient tenement* (meaning that it serves the other property); the neighboring parcel that benefits is known as the *dominant tenement*.

For example, if *A* and *B* own properties in a lake resort community, but only *A*'s property borders the lake, *A* may grant *B* an easement across *A*'s property to the beach. (See Figure 5.5.) *A*'s property is the servient tenement, and *B*'s property is the dominant tenement. Conversely, *B* may grant *A* an easement across *B*'s property so that *A* can have access to the road. In this situation *B*'s property is the servient tenement and *A*'s property is the dominant tenement.

An appurtenant easement is part of the dominant tenement, and if the dominant tenement is conveyed to another party, the easement transfers with the title. This type of easement is said to *run with the land*. It is an encumbrance on property, and unless the holder of the dominant tenement somehow releases that right, it will transfer with the deed of the dominant tenement forever.

Common examples of appurtenant easements include the right to travel over another's property (a right-of-way), shared driveways and party walls.

A **party wall** can be an exterior wall of a building that straddles the boundary line between two lots, with half of the wall on each lot, or it can be a commonly shared partition wall between two properties. Each lot owner owns the half of the wall on his or her lot, and each has an appurtenant easement in the other half of the wall. A written party wall agreement should be used to create the easement rights. Expenses to build and maintain the wall are usually shared. A *party driveway* shared by adjoining owners and partly on the land of each

**Figure 5.5
Easements**

The owner of Lot A has an *appurtenant easement* across Lot B to gain access to his property from the paved road. Lot A is dominant, and Lot B is servient. The owner of Lot B has an *appurtenant easement* across Lot A to gain access to the beach. In this situation Lot B is dominant and Lot A is servient. The utility company has an *easement in gross* across both parcels of land for its power lines.

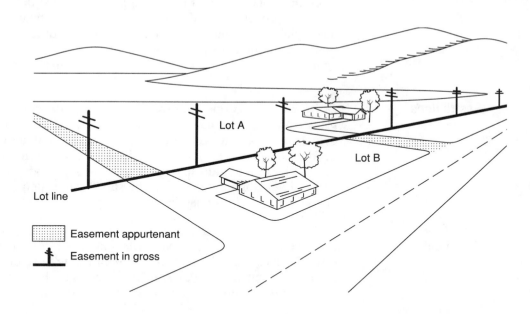

should also be created by written agreement, specifying responsibility for expenses.

A kind of appurtenant easement, which is distinguished as much by the way it is created as it is by its purpose, is an easement by necessity. An **easement by necessity** is generally created by a court of law to serve a just and necessary purpose, particularly in a landlocked situation. Because all owners are entitled to the right of ingress to and egress from the land, an easement is a necessity, not merely a convenience, when a parcel is landlocked. These easements have a common grantor, that is, the person who grants the ownership of the land is also the grantor of the easement. For example, a person who owns a tract of land and sells a part that has no street access becomes the grantor of the easement over the remaining land to provide ingress and egress to the landlocked parcel. The courts would declare an easement by necessity in this case.

Another kind of appurtenant easement is a *prescriptive easement.* An **easement by prescription** occurs when the person claiming the easement has made use of another's land for a time-period defined by state law, which is 21 years in Pennsylvania. The claimant's use must have been continuous, exclusive and without the owner's approval. The use must be visible, open and notorious so that the owner could readily learn of it. Prescriptive easements cannot usually be acquired on public land. To reach the prescriptive period and successfully establish a claim for the easement, *tacking* can be applied. This provides that successive periods of continuous occupation by different parties may be tacked or combined. The parties must have been successors in interest, such as an ancestor and his or her heir, landlord and tenant, or seller and buyer.

Easement in gross. An *individual interest* in or limited right to use the land of another is an **easement in gross.** This easement is a right granted for the benefit of a person or entity, rather than the land (as is the case in an appurtenant easement). Examples include an easement the landowner grants as a convenience to a friend to cross the property and commercial easements granted to utilities companies. Commercial easements in gross may be assigned or conveyed and may be inherited. However, personal easements in gross usually are not assignable and terminate upon the death of the easement owner. Easements in gross are often confused with the similar personal right of license, discussed later in this chapter.

Creating an easement. Easements are commonly created by written agreement between the parties establishing the easement right. They also may be created by the grantor in a deed of conveyance either *reserving* an easement over the sold land or *granting* the new owner an easement over the grantor's remaining land; by longtime usage, as in an easement by prescription; by necessity; and by *implication,* that is, the situation or the parties' actions imply that they intend to create an easement. The creation of an easement involves two separate parties, one of whom is the owner of the land over which the easement runs. It is impossible for the owner of a parcel of property to have an easement over his or her own land.

Terminating an easement. Easements may be ended

- when the purpose for which the easement was created no longer exists;
- when the owner of either the dominant or the servient tenement becomes the owner of both and the properties are merged under one legal description (termination by merger);
- by release of the right of easement to the owner of the servient tenement;
- by abandonment of the easement (the intention of the parties is the determining factor);
- by nonuse of a prescriptive easement;
- by adverse possession by the owner of the servient tenement;
- by destruction of the servient tenement, as in the demolition of a party wall;
- by lawsuit (an *action to quiet title*) against someone claiming an easement; or
- by excessive use, as when a residential use is converted to commercial purposes.

Note that an easement may not *automatically* terminate for these reasons. Certain legal steps may be required.

Easement by condemnation. An **easement by condemnation** is acquired for a public purpose, such as a highway, power line or sewage treatment facility, through the right of eminent domain. The owner of the servient tenement must be compensated for any loss in property value.

IN PRACTICE...	*Easements are common encumbrances, especially for public utilities, and can easily be taken for granted. However, they can hinder the owner's use of the property because the landowner cannot interfere with rights of an easement holder. For example, the landowner would be prevented from building a structure where it would block access to a sewer easement. Therefore, a landowner should be familiar with any easements, preferably before rather than after, he or she purchases a property or makes plans for using it.*

License

A personal privilege to enter the land of another for a specific purpose is a **license.** A license differs from an easement in that *it can be terminated or canceled by the licensor* (the person who granted the license). If a right to use another's property is given orally or informally, it will generally be considered to be a license rather than a personal easement in gross. A license ends upon the death of either party or the sale of the land by the licensor. Examples of license would include permission to park in a neighbor's driveway and the privileges that a ticket to theater or a sports event conveys.

Encroachments

An **encroachment** is the unauthorized intrusion of an improvement or other real property onto another's property. Examples include a building (or some portion of it), a fence or a driveway that illegally *extends beyond the land of its owner or beyond the legal building lines*. The wrongful invasion by a person who has no lawful right to another's property, also known as a *trespass,* can occur below the surface and in the airspace, such as overhanging tree branches, as well as on the land. Encroachments usually occur as the result of poor planning or carelessness, rather than as purposeful illegal acts.

Encroachments can be discovered by either a physical inspection of the property or a spot survey. Because a spot survey shows the location of all improvements located on a property, it is obvious whether they extend over the lot or building lines. The owner of the neighboring land can either recover money damages or secure removal of the encroachment. Long-standing encroachments (for the prescriptive period) may give rise to easements by prescription.

IN PRACTICE...	*Because an undisclosed encroachment could make a title unmarketable, an encroachment should be noted in a listing agreement and the agreement of sale. Encroachments are not disclosed by the usual title evidence provided in a real estate sale unless a survey is submitted while the title is being examined.*

WATER RIGHTS

In its natural state, water is real estate. The ownership of the water or the rights to its use and the ownership and use of adjacent land, however, are not so simply defined. When water flows in a fixed channel, such as a watercourse, or is collected in an identifiable body, such as a river or lake, this raises questions about who owns the water, how it can be used and how the ownership of the bordering land is affected. Because water in some areas is a diminishing natural

**Figure 5.6
Riparian
Rights**

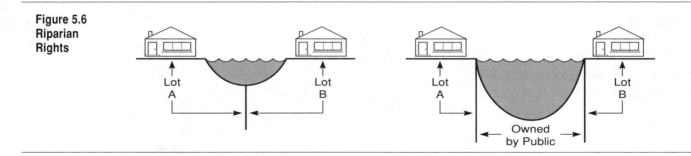

resource, its use may be significantly limited. The use and ownership of water and the adjacent land may be governed by the common law doctrines of riparian and littoral rights or the state may control all but the limited domestic use of water according to the doctrine of prior appropriation.

Riparian Rights

Riparian rights are inherent to owners of land located along the course of a river, stream or lake (*riparian* literally means riverbank). These owners have the unrestricted right to use the water, provided the use does not contaminate the water or interrupt or alter its flow. In addition, an owner of land that borders a nonnavigable waterway owns the land under the water to the exact center of the waterway. Land adjoining navigable rivers is usually owned to the water's edge, with the state holding title to the submerged land. (See Figure 5.6.) Navigable waters are considered public highways on which the public has an easement or right to travel. The laws governing and defining riparian rights differ from state to state.

Littoral Rights

Closely related to riparian rights are the **littoral rights** of owners whose land borders on large, navigable lakes and oceans. Owners with littoral rights may enjoy unrestricted use of available waters, but they own the land adjacent to the water only up to the mean high-water mark. (See Figure 5.7.) All land below this point is owned by the government.

Riparian and littoral rights are appurtenant (attached) to the land and cannot be retained when the property is sold. The right to use the water belongs to whoever owns the bordering land and cannot be retained by a former owner after the land is sold.

The quantity of land ownership can be affected by the natural action of the water. An owner is entitled to all land created through *accretion*—increases in the land resulting from the deposit of soil by the water's action. These deposits are called *alluvion or alluvium.*

Conversely, an owner may lose land through *erosion,* the gradual and impercep-tible wearing away of the land by flowing water (or other natural forces). This contrasts with *avulsion,* the sudden removal of soil by an act of nature. A ripar-ian owner generally does not lose title to land lost by avulsion—the boundary lines stay the same, no matter how much soil is lost. In contrast, a riparian owner loses title to any land washed away by erosion.

**Figure 5.7
Littoral
Rights**

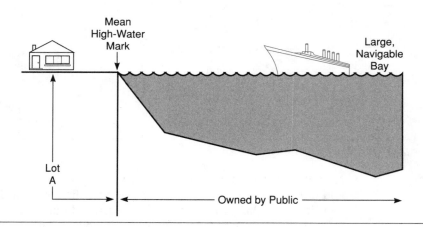

**Doctrine of Prior
Appropriation**

In states where water is scarce, the ownership and use of water are often determined by the **doctrine of prior appropriation.** Under this doctrine, *the right to use any water, with the exception of limited domestic use, is controlled by the state rather than by the adjacent landowner.* Ownership of the land bordering bodies of water in prior appropriation states is generally determined in the same way as riparian and littoral ownership.

To secure water rights, a person must show a beneficial use for the water, such as crop irrigation, and file for and obtain a permit from the proper state department. Although statutes governing prior appropriation vary from state to state, the priority of the water right is usually determined by the oldest recorded permit date.

Once granted, water rights may be perfected through the legal processes prescribed by the individual state. When the water right is perfected, it generally becomes attached to the land of the person holding the permit. The permit holder may sell such a water right to another party.

Issuance of a water permit does not grant access to the water source. All access rights-of-way over the land of another (easements) must be obtained from the property owner.

●   ●   ●   ●   ●   ●   ●

KEY TERMS

allodial system	fee simple defeasible
appurtenant easement	fee simple determinable
condemnation	feudal system
doctrine of prior appropriation	freehold estate
easement	leasehold estate
easement by condemnation	license
easement by necessity	lien
easement by prescription	life estate
easement in gross	littoral rights
eminent domain	party wall
encroachment	police power
encumbrance	remainder interest
escheat	reversionary interest
estate in land	riparian rights
fee simple	taxation

SUMMARY

An individual's ownership rights are subject to the powers held by government. These powers include the police power, by which states can enact legislation such as environmental protection laws and zoning ordinances. The government may also acquire privately owned land for public use through the power of eminent domain. Real estate taxes are imposed to raise government funds. When a property becomes ownerless, ownership of the property may revert, or escheat, to the state.

An estate is the degree, quantity, nature and extent of interest a person holds in land. Freehold estates are estates of indeterminate length. Less-than-freehold estates are called leasehold estates and they involve tenants. Freehold estates are further divided into estates of inheritance and life estates. Estates of inheritance include fee simple and defeasible fee estates. There are two types of life estates: conventional life estates, which are created by acts of the parties; and legal life estates, which are created by law.

Encumbrances against real estate may be in the form of liens, deed restrictions, easements, licenses and encroachments.

An easement is the right acquired by one person to use another's real estate. Easements are classified as interests in real estate, but are not estates in land. Appurtenant easements involve two separately owned tracts. The tract benefited is known as the dominant tenement; the tract that is subject to (or burdened by) the easement is called the servient tenement. An easement in gross is an individual right, such as that granted to utility companies to maintain poles, wires and pipelines.

Easements may be created by agreement, express grant, grant or reservation in a deed, implication, necessity, prescription or party-wall agreement. They can be terminated when the purpose of the easement no longer exists, by merger of both interests with an express intention to extinguish the easement, by release or by an intention to abandon the easement.

A license is permission to enter another's property for a specific purpose. A license is usually created orally, is of a temporary nature and can be revoked.

An encroachment is an unauthorized use of another's real estate.

Ownership of land encompasses not only the land itself but also the right to use the water on or adjacent to it. Many states subscribe to the common-law doctrine of riparian rights, which gives the owner of land adjacent to a non-navigable stream, ownership of the land to the stream's midpoint. Littoral rights are held by owners of land bordering large lakes and oceans and include rights to the water and ownership of the land up to the mean high-water mark. In states where water is scarce, water use is often decided by the doctrine of prior appropriation. Under prior appropriation, water belongs to the state and is allocated to users who have obtained permits.

Questions

1. The right of a governmental body to take ownership of real estate for public benefit is called
   a. escheat.
   b. eminent domain.
   c. condemnation.
   d. police power.

2. A purchaser of real estate learned that the ownership rights will continue forever and that no other person claims to be the owner or has any ownership control over the property. This person owns a
   a. fee simple interest.
   b. life estate.
   c. determinable fee estate.
   d. fee simple on condition.

3. *J* owned the fee simple title to a vacant lot adjacent to a hospital and was persuaded to make a gift of the lot. She wanted to have some control over its use, so her attorney prepared her deed to convey ownership of the lot to the hospital "so long as it is used for hospital purposes." After completion of the gift, the hospital will own a
   a. fee simple absolute estate.
   b. license.
   c. fee simple determinable.
   d. leasehold estate.

4. After *D* had purchased his house and moved in, he discovered that his neighbor regularly used his driveway to reach a garage located on the neighbor's property. *D*'s attorney explained that ownership of the neighbor's real estate includes an easement over the driveway. *D*'s property is properly called
   a. the dominant tenement.
   b. a freehold.
   c. a leasehold.
   d. the servient tenement.

5. A *license* is an example of
   a. easement.
   b. encroachment.
   c. encumbrance.
   d. restriction.

6. Which of the following best describes a *life estate?*
   a. An estate conveyed to *A* for the life of *Z*
   b. An estate held by lease
   c. An estate without condition
   d. A fee simple estate

7. If the owner of real estate does not take action against a trespasser before the statutory period has passed, the trespasser may acquire a/an
   a. easement by necessity.
   b. license.
   c. easement by implication of law.
   d. prescriptive easement.

8. Many states determine water use by allocating water to users who hold recorded beneficial use permits. This type of water use privilege is called
   a. riparian rights.
   b. littoral rights.
   c. the doctrine of prior appropriation.
   d. the doctrine of highest and best use.

9. All of the following are powers of the government *except*
   a. condemnation.
   b. police power.
   c. eminent domain.
   d. taxation.

10. Property deeded to a school "for educational purposes only" conveys a
   a. fee simple absolute.
   b. fee simple on condition precedent.
   c. leasehold interest.
   d. fee simple on condition subsequent.

11. *T* has the legal right to pass over the land owned by his neighbor. This is
   a. an estate in land.
   b. an easement.
   c. police power.
   d. an encroachment.

12. A father conveys ownership of his residence to his daughter but reserves for himself a life estate in the residence. The interest the daughter owns during her father's lifetime is
   a. pur autre vie.
   b. a remainder.
   c. a reversion.
   d. a leasehold.

13. *K* has fenced his property. The fence extends one foot over his lot line onto the property of a neighbor, *M*. The fence is an example of a/an
   a. license.
   b. encroachment.
   c. easement by necessity.
   d. easement by prescription.

14. *K* has permission from *X* to hike on *X*'s property during the summer. *K* has
   a. an easement by necessity.
   b. an easement by condemnation.
   c. riparian rights.
   d. a license.

15. Encumbrances on real estate
   a. include easements, encroachments and licenses.
   b. make it impossible to sell the encumbered property.
   c. must all be removed before the title can be transferred.
   d. are of no monetary value to those who own them.

16. A tenant in an apartment holds a/an
   a. easement.
   b. license.
   c. freehold interest.
   d. leasehold interest.

6 Landlord and Tenant Interests

LEASEHOLD ESTATES

Estates in land identify the extent of an interest in real property. Freehold estates, which are ownership interests, were discussed in Chapter 5. A lesser estate in land, known as a *leasehold* or *nonfreehold estate*, can also exist. This is a possessory rather than an ownership estate. The person who has a leasehold estate—the tenant—has the exclusive right to *possess and occupy* a property, and the owner of the real estate—the landlord—retains all other rights of ownership. The tenant's right of possession is personal property.

Although written contracts are not necessary to create leasehold estates, they are commonly used and even required for certain purposes. The contract, or lease agreement, transfers the possessory right of the owner's property to the tenant and states the length of time the contract is to run, the amount the tenant is to pay for the use of the property and other rights and obligations of the landlord and the tenant.

Just as there are several types of freehold estates as were discussed in Chapter 5, there are also various types of leasehold estates. (See Table 6.1.)

Estate (Tenancy) for Years

An **estate (tenancy) for years** is a leasehold estate that continues for a *definite period of time,* whether for years, months, weeks or even days. An estate for years always has a specific starting and ending time. When that period expires, the tenant is required to vacate the premises and surrender possession to the owner. No notice is required to terminate the lease agreement because the contract states a specific expiration date. If both parties agree, the estate for years may be terminated prior to the expiration date. Otherwise, neither party may terminate without showing that the contract has been breached. Any extension of the tenancy requires the negotiation of a new contract, unless the original agreement provides for the conversion to a periodic tenancy. As is characteristic of all leases, a tenancy for years gives the tenant the right to occupy and use the property according to the terms and conditions contained in the lease agreement.

Periodic Estate (Tenancy)

Periodic tenancies, sometimes called **estates (tenancies) from period to period** or from *year to year,* are created when landlord and tenant enter into an

Table 6.1 Leasehold Estates	Type of Estate	Distinguishing Characteristic
	Estate for years	For definite period of time
	Estate from period to period	Automatically renews
	Estate at will	For indefinite period of time
	Estate at sufferance	Without landlord's consent

agreement for an indefinite time without a specific expiration date. These tenancies are created initially to run for a definite amount of time—for instance, month to month, week to week, or year to year—but continue indefinitely until proper notice of termination is given. Rent is payable at definite intervals. These tenancies are characterized by continuity because they are automatically renewable under the original terms of the agreement for similar succeeding periods until one of the parties gives notice to terminate. In effect, the payment and acceptance of rent extends the lease for another period. A **month-to-month tenancy** is, for example, created when a tenant takes possession with no definite termination date and pays rent on a monthly basis. Periodic tenancy is commonly used in residential leases.

An estate from period to period can be created when a tenant with an estate for years remains in possession, or holds over, after the expiration of the lease term. If no new lease agreement has been made, a **holdover tenancy** is created. The landlord may evict the tenant or treat the holdover tenant as a periodic tenancy. The landlord's acceptance of rent usually is considered conclusive proof of the landlord's acquiescence to the periodic tenancy. The courts customarily rule that a tenant who holds over can do so for a term equal to the term of the original lease, provided the period is for one year or less. For example, a tenant with a lease for six months would be entitled to a new six-month tenancy. However, if the original lease were for five years, the holdover tenancy could not exceed one year. Some leases stipulate that in the absence of a renewal agreement, a tenant who holds over does so as a month-to-month tenant. This is usually a valid agreement.

To *terminate* a periodic estate, either the landlord or the tenant must give *proper notice*. To terminate an estate from week to week, one week's notice is required; to terminate an estate from month to month, one month's notice is required. To terminate an estate from year to year, three months' notice is required. The Pennsylvania Landlord/Tenant Act specifies the period of notice required in a variety of circumstances. The amount of time required for proper notice is stated in most written lease agreements.

Estate (Tenancy) at Will

An **estate (tenancy) at will** gives the tenant the right to possess with the *consent of the landlord* for a term of unspecified or uncertain duration. The term of an estate at will is indefinite until it is terminated by either party giving proper notice. No definite initial period is specified, as is the case in a periodic tenancy. An estate at will is automatically terminated by the death of either the landlord or the tenant. It may be created by express agreement or by operation of law and during its existence, the tenant has all the rights and obligations of a lessor-lessee relationship, including payment of rent at regular intervals.

As a practical matter, tenancy at will is rarely used in a written agreement and is viewed unfavorably by the courts. Most likely it will be interpreted as a periodic tenancy—the period being defined by the interval of rental payments.

Estate (Tenancy) at Sufferance

An **estate (tenancy) at sufferance** arises when a tenant who was lawfully in possession of real property continues in possession of the premises *without the consent of the landlord* after the rights have expired. This estate arises when a tenant for years *fails to surrender* possession at the expiration of the lease. A tenancy at sufferance also can occur *by operation of law* when a borrower, without consent of the purchaser, continues in possession after a foreclosure sale and the expiration of the redemption period.

LEASE AGREEMENTS

A **lease** is a contract between an owner of real estate, the **lessor,** and a tenant, the **lessee.** In effect the lease agreement is a combination of a conveyance of an interest in the real estate and a contract to pay rent and assume other obligations. The lessor grants the lessee the right to occupy the real estate and use it for certain stated purposes. In return, the landlord receives payment for the use of the premises and retains a reversionary right to retake possession after the lease term has expired. The lessor's interest is called a *leased fee estate plus reversionary right.*

No special wording is required to establish the landlord-tenant relationship. The lease may be written, oral or implied, depending on the circumstances. The Statute of Frauds in Pennsylvania, which requires that contracts conveying interests in real estate must be in writing to be enforceable (to force a party to perform), applies to leases for more than three years' duration. In other words, a lease for a term of more than three years *must be written.* An oral lease for three years or less is usually enforceable. A written lease, however, may be used for any period of time. An example of a typical residential lease is shown in Figure 6.1.

IN PRACTICE... | *While the Statute of Frauds requires leases of more than three years to be in writing to enforce performance on the contract, the Rules and Regulations of the Pennsylvania Real Estate Commission requires licensees to use written contracts, which includes leases for less than three years. References to the use of oral leases are relevant when no licensee is involved in the transaction. As a practical matter, written leases, provided they are specific and as inclusive as possible, clarify the intentions of the parties and thus help avoid misunderstandings and controversies.*

Requirements for a Valid Contract

The requirements for a valid lease are essentially the same as those for any other contract, as is discussed further in Chapter 11.

- *Offer and acceptance.* The parties must reach a mutual agreement on all the terms of the contract.

- *Consideration.* All leases, being contracts, must be supported by a valid consideration. *Rent* is the normal consideration given for the right to occupy the leased premises; however, the payment of rent is not essential as long as

Figure 6.1
Residential
Lease
Agreement

RESIDENTIAL LEASE   **L-R 1995**
COPYRIGHT PENNSYLVANIA ASSOCIATION OF REALTORS® 1995
This form recommended for but not restricted to use by members of the Pennsylvania Association of REALTORS®

1. DATE of Lease _____

2. TENANT: (list all Tenants)
   Name _____
   Mailing Address _____
   Phone Number(s) _____
   Name _____
   Mailing Address _____
   Phone Number(s) _____

3. LANDLORD: (list all Landlords)
   Name _____
   Mailing Address _____
   Phone Number(s) _____
   Name _____
   Mailing Address _____
   Phone Number(s) _____

4. AGENT FOR THE LANDLORD is _____
   _____

5. PROPERTY
   Landlord agrees to rent to Tenant the following Property: _____
   _____

6. STARTING AND ENDING DATES OF LEASE   (also called "Term")
   A. **Starting Date:** This Lease starts on _____, at 12 Noon.
   B. **Ending Date:** This Lease ends on _____, at 12 Noon.

7. RENEWAL TERM
   This Lease will automatically renew for a term of _____ at the Ending Date unless:
   A. Tenant gives Landlord _____ days' written notice before Ending Date or before the end of any Renewal Term, **OR**
   B. Landlord gives Tenant _____ days' written notice before Ending Date or before the end of any Renewal Term.
   C. **For Month to Month Leases Only:** Either Landlord or Tenant may end a month to month Lease by giving 30 days' written notice on or before the day the next rent is due.

8. RENT
   A. The total amount of rent due over the term of this Lease is $ _____
   B. The total rent due each month is $ _____
   C. Rent is due on or before the _____ day of the month.
   D. Tenant pays a late charge of $ _____
      if rent is more than _____ days late.
   E. Tenant makes payments to:
      address _____

9. BEFORE MOVING IN, TENANT PAYS   Paid   Due
   A. Part of a month's rent if Tenant takes possession before first regular due date $ _____ $ _____
   B. First month's rent $ _____ $ _____
   C. _____ $ _____ $ _____
   D. Security Deposit, on deposit at: _____
                                       (name of bank)
      _____ $ _____ $ _____
   Total rent and security deposit received to date $ _____
   Total amount due before Tenant moves in $ _____

10. USE OF PROPERTY
    A. Tenant will use property as a residence or _____.
    B. Not more than _____ people will live on property.

11. UTILITIES AND SERVICES
    A. Landlord will pay for
       ☐ cold water   ☐ hot water
       ☐ gas   ☐ heat
       ☐ electricity   ☐ lawn and shrubbery care
       ☐ snow removal   ☐ water cost over yearly charge
       ☐ heater maintenance contract   ☐ sewage costs and maintenance
       ☐ other _____   ☐ trash removal
    B. Tenant will pay for
       ☐ cold water   ☐ hot water
       ☐ gas   ☐ heat
       ☐ electricity   ☐ lawn and shrubbery care
       ☐ snow removal   ☐ water cost over yearly charge
       ☐ heater maintenance contract   ☐ sewage costs and maintenance
       ☐ other _____   ☐ trash removal

TENANT(S) _____   LANDLORD(S) _____
        Initials   Initials   Page 1 of 4

**Figure 6.1
(continued)**

12. **CONDITION OF PROPERTY**
Tenant understands that Landlord will make no repairs, additions, or changes to the property except as follows:

_____

13. **SPECIAL CLAUSES** (Any Special Clauses must comply with the Pennsylvania Plain Language Consumer Contract Act.)

14. **RULES AND REGULATIONS**
    A. Rules for use of the Property are attached.   ☐ Yes   ☐ No
    B. Tenant promises to obey the Rules.
    C. Landlord cannot change the Rules unless the change benefits the Tenant or improves the health, safety, or welfare of others.

15. **SECURITY DEPOSIT**
    A. Landlord cannot make Tenant pay a security deposit of more than two-months' rent the first year, and one-months' rent after the first year.   After five years, the security deposit cannot be raised, even if the rent is raised.
    B. If the security deposit is more than $100, Landlord must keep it in a special bank account (escrow account) and give Tenant the name and address of the bank.
    C. After the second year (if Tenant continues to live on Property), Landlord must keep the security deposit in an escrow account that earns interest.   Landlord may keep 1 percent of the interest.   Landlord must pay Tenant the balance of the interest once a year.
    D. Landlord can use the security deposit to pay for unpaid rent and damages (beyond normal wear and tear) that are Tenant's responsibility.
    E. When Tenant moves from the Property, Tenant will return all keys and give Landlord written notice of Tenant's mailing address where Landlord can return the security deposit.
    F. Landlord will prepare a list of charges for damages and unpaid rents.   Landlord may deduct these charges from the security deposit.   Landlord must return security deposit and interest (minus any charges to Tenant) within 30 days.

16. **POSSESSION**
    A. Tenant may move in (take possession of the Property) on the Starting Date of this Lease.
    B. If Tenant cannot move in because previous tenant is still there or because of property damage, Tenant can
        1. change the starting date of the Lease to the day when Property is available.   Tenant will not owe rent until Property is available;
           OR
        2. end the lease and have all money already paid as rent or security deposit returned.

17. **RENT INCREASES**
    A. If the Lease is for a term of more than one year, Tenant agrees to pay Tenant's share of any increase in real estate taxes and water and sewer charges.
    B. If Tenant's actions cause an increase in property insurance, Tenant will pay the amount of the increase.

18. **LANDLORD'S RIGHT TO ENTER**
    A. Tenant agrees to let Landlord or Landlord's representatives enter the Property at reasonable hours to inspect, repair, or show the Property to prospective buyers.
    B. Landlord will give Tenant 24 hours' notice of date, time, and reason for the visit.   In cases of emergency, Landlord may enter Property without notice.   If Tenant is not there, Landlord will tell Tenant who was there and why within 24 hours of the visit.

19. **TENANT'S CARE OF PROPERTY**
    Tenant, Tenant's family and guests agree to obey all laws and Rules that apply to Tenant.
    A. Tenant **will:**
        1. Keep the Property clean and safe.
        2. Get rid of all trash, garbage and any other waste materials as required by Landlord and the law.
        3. Use care when using any of the electrical, plumbing, ventilation or other facilities or appliances on the Property, including any elevators.
        4. Tell Landlord immediately of any repairs needed.   Landlord does not have to repair any damage caused by Tenant's willfull, careless, or unreasonable behavior.
    B. Tenant **will not:**
        1. Keep any flammable materials on the Property.
        2. Willfully destroy or deface any part of the Property.
        3. Disturb the peace and quiet of other tenants.
        4. Make changes to the property, such as painting or remodeling, without the written permission of Landlord.   Tenant understands that any changes or improvements will belong to Landlord.
    C. Repairs By Tenant: Tenant will pay to repair any item in or on the Property that costs less than $_____.   Tenant also will pay to repair any damage to the Property or to any item in or on the Property that Tenant or Tenant's guests cause through a lack of care.

20. **SMOKE DETECTORS**
    A. Tenant will maintain and test (monthly) any smoke detectors on the Property.
    B. Tenant will notify Agent or Landlord of any broken smoke detector(s).
    C. Tenant will pay for any damage to Property if Tenant fails to maintain smoke detectors.

TENANT(S) _____ ― LANDLORD(S)_____
Initials   Initials

**Figure 6.1
(continued)**

21. **LANDLORD WILL MAINTAIN PROPERTY**
    A. Landlord will keep the Property and common areas in reasonable condition and as required by law.
    B. Landlord will keep the structural parts of the Property in good working order, including:

ceilings	roof	doors
steps	floors	walls
porches	windows	

    C. Landlord will keep all systems, services, facilities, or appliances supplied by Landlord in safe and good working order, including:

air conditioning	sanitary	drainage
security	electrical	ventilation
heating	water heating	plumbing

    D. Landlord will keep Property reasonably free of pests, rodents and insects. **This does not apply if Property is a single-family dwelling.**
    E. Landlord will supply utilities and services listed in paragraph 11 (Utilities and Services) of this Lease, unless the service is interrupted for reasons beyond the Landlord's control.
    F. Landlord cannot increase rents, decrease services, or threaten to evict Tenant because Tenant
        1. complains to a government agency or to Landlord about a building or housing code violation.
        2. organizes or joins a Tenant's organization.
        3. uses Tenant's legal rights in a lawful manner.

22. **NO PETS**
    Tenant will not keep any pets on any part of the Property without Landlord's written permission.

23. **FIRE OR OTHER DAMAGE**
    A. If the Property is accidentally damaged (fire, flood, etc.)
        1. Tenant may continue to live on the livable part of the Property and pay a reduced rent as agreed to by Tenant and Landlord until the damages are repaired; if the law does not allow Tenant to live on the Property, then this Lease is ended; OR
        2. If it is not possible for Tenant to live on the Property, Tenant must notify Landlord immediately that Lease is ended and move out within 24 hours.
    B. If Lease is ended, Landlord will return any unused security deposit or advanced rent to Tenant.
    C. If Tenant, Tenant's family or guests cause damage by fire or by other means, this Lease will remain in effect and Tenant will continue to pay rent, even if Tenant cannot occupy the Property.

24. **AFTER NOTICE TO END LEASE**
    A. After Tenant or Landlord has given written notice to end this Lease, Landlord may show Property to possible tenants. Landlord will not show Property unless Tenant is there or has a reasonable chance to be there. Tenant does not have to allow possible tenants to enter unless they are with the Landlord or Landlord's representative, or unless they have written permission from the Landlord.
    B. Landlord may put up For Sale or For Rent signs on or near Property.
    C. Tenant agrees to move out peacefully when Lease is ended.

25. **SALE OF PROPERTY**
    A. If Property is sold, on the date of settlement, Landlord will give Tenant in writing:
        1. The name, address, and phone number of the new landlord.
        2. Where rent is to be paid.
        3. Notice that the security deposit has been given to the new landlord, who will be responsible for it.
    B. Tenant agrees that Landlord may transfer Tenant's money and advance rent to the new landlord.

26. **IF TENANT BREAKS LEASE: WAIVER OF RIGHTS**
    A. **Tenant breaks this Lease if**
        1. Tenant does not pay rent or other charges.
        2. Tenant leaves (abandons) Property before the end of this Lease.
        3. Tenant does not move out when supposed to.
        4. Tenant fails to do anything Tenant agreed to in this Lease.
    B. **Non-Payment of Rent:** If Tenant breaks Lease by not paying rent or other charges, Landlord cannot evict Tenant (force Tenant to move out) from the Property without a written notice. Tenant agrees that a written notice of FIVE DAYS is sufficient. This means that if Tenant has not moved from the Property before the sixth day after Landlord has given Tenant written notice, Landlord can file a lawsuit to evict Tenant. **TENANT IS WAIVING (GIVING UP) TENANT'S RIGHT TO A LONGER NOTICE TO MOVE OUT.**
    C. **Other Lease Violations:** If Tenant breaks any other term of this Lease, Landlord must give Tenant a written notice describing the violation and giving Tenant FIVE DAYS to correct the problem. If Tenant does not correct the problem, Landlord can then give Tenant FIVE DAYS' written notice to move from the Property. If Tenant does not move out, Landlord can file a lawsuit to evict Tenant on the sixth day. **TENANT IS WAIVING (GIVING UP) TENANT'S RIGHT TO LONGER NOTICES TO CORRECT PROBLEMS AND TO MOVE OUT.**
    D. **If Tenant Breaks Lease for any Reason, Landlord may**
        1. **Recover possession of the Property (evict Tenant).** If Landlord hires a lawyer to start eviction, Tenant agrees to pay the lawyer's fees and Landlord's reasonable costs.
        2. **File a lawsuit against Tenant** for rents and charges not paid and for rents and charges for the rest of the Lease term.
        3. **Keep Tenant's Security Deposit.**

TENANT(S) _____   LANDLORD(S)_____
Initials   Initials

**Figure 6.1
(continued)**

27. **IF GOVERNMENT TAKES PROPERTY**
    A. The government or other public authority can take private property for public use. The taking is called *condemnation*.
    B. If any part of the Property is taken by condemnation, Landlord will reduce Tenant's rent proportionately. If all the Property is taken or is no longer usable, this Lease will end and Tenant will move out. Landlord will return to Tenant any unused security deposit or advance rent.
    C. No money paid to Landlord for the condemnation of the Property will belong to Tenant.

28. **SUBLEASING AND ASSIGNMENT**
    A. Landlord may transfer this Lease to another Landlord. Tenant agrees that this Lease remains the same with the new landlord.
    B. Tenant may not transfer this Lease or *sublease* (rent to another person) this Property without Landlord's written permission. Landlord will be reasonable about giving written permission.

29. **TENANT HAS FEWER RIGHTS THAN MORTGAGE LENDER**
    Landlord may have a mortgage on the Property. If so, Landlord agrees to make the mortgage payments. The rights of the mortgage lender come before the rights of the Tenant. (Example: If Landlord fails to make mortgage payments, the mortgage lender could take the Property and end this Lease.)
    TENANT IS WAIVING (GIVING UP) TENANT'S RIGHTS. TENANT UNDERSTANDS THAT IF THERE IS A FORECLOSURE, THE NEW OWNER WILL HAVE THE RIGHT TO END THIS LEASE.

30. **MEDIATION**
    A. *Mediation* is a way of resolving disputes. A *mediator* helps the disputing parties reach an agreeable solution without having to involve the courts.
    B. Landlord and Tenant may agree to take any disputes arising from this Lease to a mediation program offered by the local association of REALTORS® or to another mediator. Landlord and Tenant can agree to mediation as a part of this Lease (by signing a mediation form to attach to this lease), or they can sign an agreement to mediate after a dispute arises.

31. **INSURANCE AND RELEASE**
    A. Tenant understands that
        1. LANDLORD'S INSURANCE DOES NOT COVER TENANT, TENANT'S PROPERTY OR GUESTS.
        2. TENANT SHOULD HAVE FIRE & LIABILITY INSURANCE TO PROTECT TENANT, TENANT'S PROPERTY AND GUESTS WHO ARE INJURED WHILE ON THE PROPERTY.
    B. Landlord is not liable or responsible for any injury or damage that occurs on the Property and Tenant agrees to pay any loss or claim, including attorney's fees, that result from the damage or injury.
    C. Landlord is responsible for any injury or damage that results from Landlord's carelessness.
    D. Tenant is responsible for any loss to Landlord that Tenant, Tenant's family or guests cause.

32. **CAPTIONS**
    The headings in this Lease are meant only to make it easier to find the paragraphs.

33. **ENTIRE AGREEMENT**
    This Lease is the entire agreement between Tenant and Landlord. No spoken or written agreements made before are a part of this Lease unless they are included in this Lease.

34. **NOTICE BEFORE SIGNING**
    THIS LEASE IS A LEGAL CONTRACT. IF TENANT HAS LEGAL QUESTIONS, TENANT IS ADVISED TO TALK TO A LAWYER BEFORE SIGNING THIS LEASE.

WITNESS _____ TENANT _____ DATE_____
WITNESS _____ TENANT _____ DATE_____
WITNESS _____ TENANT _____ DATE_____
WITNESS _____ LANDLORD _____ DATE_____
WITNESS _____ LANDLORD _____ DATE_____
WITNESS _____ LANDLORD _____ DATE_____

LANDLORD TRANSFERS LEASE TO A NEW LANDLORD

As part of payment received by Owners (Landlord) _____
(name of current Landlord)
now assigns or transfers this Lease to _____
(name of new landlord)
his heirs and estate. The new Landlord has all the rights and responsibilities of the Landlord under this Lease.

WITNESS _____ LANDLORD _____ DATE_____
WITNESS _____ LANDLORD _____ DATE_____
WITNESS _____ LANDLORD _____ DATE_____
WITNESS _____ LANDLORD _____ DATE_____

consideration was granted in creation of the lease itself. Because a lease is a contract, it is not subject to subsequent changes in the rent or other terms unless these changes are in writing, supported by additional consideration and executed in the same manner as the original lease.

- *Capacity to contract.* The parties must have the legal capacity to contract, which means they must be of legal age (18 years old in Pennsylvania) and have sufficient mental capacity to understand the nature or consequences of their actions in a contract.

- *Legal objectives.* The objectives of the lease must be legal, which means that a contract must not contemplate a purpose or action that is illegal or against public policy.

The leased premises should be clearly described. The legal description of the real estate should be used if the lease covers land, such as a ground lease. If the lease is for a part of a building, such as office space or an apartment, the space itself or the apartment designation should be described specifically. If supplemental space is to be included, the lease should clearly identify it.

Possession of Premises

Once a valid lease has been executed, the lessor, as the owner of the real estate, is usually bound by the implied *covenant of quiet possession.* Under this covenant, the lessor guarantees that the lessee may take possession of the leased premises and that the landlord will not interfere in the tenant's legal possession or use of the property or permit any other party to interfere.

In Pennsylvania, the landlord must give the tenant *actual* occupancy, or possession, of the leased premises. If the premises are occupied by a holdover tenant or adverse claimant at the beginning of the new lease period, the landlord must bring whatever action is necessary to recover possession and to bear the expense of this action.

Term of Lease

The term of a lease is the period for which the lease will run. It should be stated precisely, including the beginning and ending date together with a statement of the total period of the lease: for example, "for a term of 30 years beginning June 1, 1999 and ending May 31, 2029" or "for a term of 3 years beginning September 1, 1999 and ending August 31, 2002." Perpetual leases for an inordinate amount of time or an indefinite term will be ruled invalid unless the language of the lease and the surrounding circumstances clearly indicate that the parties intend such a term. Some states, in fact, prohibit leases that run for 100 years or more. In Pennsylvania, the law requires payment of transfer taxes on leases that run for more than a total of 30 years.

Security Deposits

Most leases require the tenant to provide some form of **security deposit** that may be held by the landlord during the lease term. If the tenant defaults on payment of rent or destroys the premises, the lessor may keep all or part of the deposit to compensate for the loss. The landlord's entitlement to recover damages from the security deposit has been subjected to various interpretations. Some assert that damage to the premises, not including damage from defaulted rent, is the intent of the security deposit and, therefore, is the only recovery the landlord can claim through this vehicle. Because of varied interpretations, the lease agreement should clearly state the purpose of the security deposit and the recovery that may be claimed by the landlord.

Other safeguards against nonpayment of rent include an advance rental payment, contracting for a lien on the tenant's property and/or requiring the tenant to have a third person guarantee payment.

IN PRACTICE...	*A lease should specify whether a payment is a security deposit or an advance rental. If it is a security deposit, the tenant is usually not entitled to apply it to the final month's rent. If it is an advance rental, the landlord must treat it as income for tax purposes.*

Pennsylvania law limits the amount that landlords may require residential tenants to pay as a security deposit. An amount equivalent to two months' rent is the maximum security deposit that a landlord may charge during the first year of tenancy. At the beginning of the second year, the landlord must return to the tenant the amount that exceeds the amount of one month's rent for the second year. The landlord may hold for security deposit the amount equivalent to one month's rent for the second through fifth years of a lease to reflect increased rents. After a lease has run five years, the landlord cannot raise the amount of security deposit.

The law also requires that the landlord hold security deposits in an escrow account, which must be in a federally or state-regulated banking or savings institution. The tenant must be notified of the name and address of the institution where the deposits are held and the amount. By law, if the amount of the security deposit exceeds $100, the landlord is responsible for depositing the funds in an interest-bearing account commencing on the second anniversary of the lease. In these cases, the interest earned on the deposit must be paid to the tenant each year on the anniversary of the lease. The landlord may retain 1 percent of the interest as administrative expenses.

The landlord must return the security deposit, including any interest owed to the tenant, within 30 days of the termination of the tenancy. If any of the money is withheld for damages, the landlord must provide the tenant with an itemized list that details the type and the amount of damages. The landlord pays to the tenant the difference between the funds deposited in escrow (including any unpaid interest) and the damages. A landlord who fails to settle the security account within the 30-day period forfeits all rights to the security deposit and is liable for double its amount. A tenant must provide a forwarding address, in writing, to the landlord or agent or forfeit any claim to a security deposit that might otherwise be returned.

Bond in lieu of escrowing. Instead of depositing such funds in a financial institution, a Pennsylvania landlord has the option of purchasing a guarantee, or surety, bond, which guarantees that the security deposit (including any required interest) less the cost of any necessary repairs will be returned to the tenant at the termination of the tenancy.

Use of Premises

A lessor may restrict a lessee's use of the premises through provisions included in the lease. Such restrictions are most important in leases for stores or commercial space. For example, a lease may provide that the leased premises are to be used *only* for the purpose of a real estate office *and for no other.* In the absence of such limitations a lessee may use the premises for any *lawful* purpose.

Improvements

Neither the landlord nor the tenant is required to make any improvements to the leased property. Unless the lease agreement specifies otherwise, the tenant may make improvements with the landlord's permission. Any such alterations generally become the property of the landlord; that is, they become fixtures. However, as discussed in Chapter 1, a tenant may install trade fixtures according to the terms of the lease. It is customary to allow the tenant to remove the trade fixtures before the lease expires as long as the tenant restores the premises to their previous condition.

Maintenance of Premises

Many states, including Pennsylvania, require a residential lessor to maintain dwelling units in a habitable condition and to make any necessary repairs to the common areas, such as hallways, stairs or elevators, and to safety features, such as fire sprinklers and smoke alarms. The tenant does not have to make any repairs, but must return the premises in the same condition they were received, with allowances for ordinary wear and tear.

Destruction of Premises

In land leases involving *agricultural land,* the courts have held that when the improvements are damaged or destroyed, even if not the tenant's fault, the tenant is not relieved from the obligation to pay rent to the end of the term. This ruling has been extended in most states to include *ground leases* on which the tenant has constructed a building. In many instances it also includes leases that give possession of an entire building to the tenant, in which case the tenant is leasing the land on which that building is located as well.

A tenant who is leasing only a part of the building, such as office or commercial space or an apartment, is *not* required to continue to pay rent upon destruction of the leased premises. In some states, if the property was destroyed as a result of the landlord's negligence, the tenant can recover damages from the landlord.

Assignment and Subleasing

Assignment and subleasing are permitted whenever the lease does not prohibit it. A tenant who transfers all of the leasehold interests *assigns* the lease. One who transfers less than all of the leasehold interests by leasing them to a new tenant **subleases** the premises. (See Figure 6.2.)

In most cases, the sublease or assignment of a lease does not relieve the original lessee of the obligation to make rental payments, unless the landlord agrees to waive such liability. Most leases prohibit the lessee from assigning or subletting without the lessor's consent. The lessor thus retains control over the occupancy of the leased premises, but must not unreasonably withhold consent. The sublessor's (original lessee's) interest in the real estate is known as a *sandwich lease.*

**Figure 6.2
Assignment
versus
subletting**

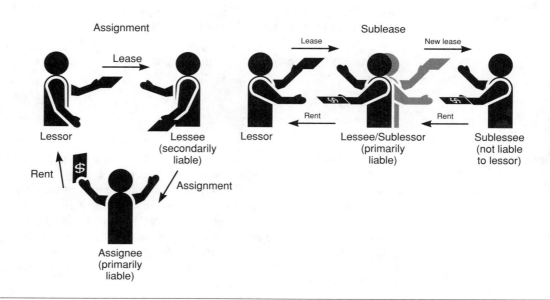

**Confession of
Judgment
Clauses**

Confession of judgment clauses are included in many leases to assist the landlord in forcing *collection of rent*. The tenant authorizes any attorney of record to appear in court in the tenant's name and to confess judgment, or to agree that a judgment be entered against the tenant in favor of the landlord for the delinquent rent, court costs and attorney's fees. Such a clause may be called a *cognovit*. Many states have now declared confession of judgment clauses illegal when used in residential leases.

Because of a federal court ruling regarding the use of confession of judgment clauses, a practice has developed in Pennsylvania for tenants who sign a confession of judgment to sign an *explanation of rights* as well. This document explains to the signer the terms of the confession of judgment.

**Recording a
Lease**

Possession of leased premises is considered constructive notice to the world of the tenant's leasehold interests, and anyone who inspects the property receives actual notice. For these reasons, recording a lease is usually considered unnecessary. However, leases can be recorded in the county where the property is located, which is more common when leases run for three years or longer, unless the contract prohibits recording. Recording a *long-term lease* serves notice to the world of the long-term rights of the lessee. Recording is usually required if the lessee intends to mortgage the leasehold interest.

In Pennsylvania only a *memorandum of lease* is filed for record. The terms of the lease are not disclosed to the public; however, the objective of giving public notice of the rights of the lessee is still accomplished. The memorandum of lease must set forth the names of the parties and a description of the property being leased.

Table 6.2 Types of Leases	Type of Lease	Lessee	Lessor
	Gross lease (residential)	Pays basic rent	Pays property charges (taxes, repairs, insurance, and the like)
	Net lease (commercial/industrial)	Pays basic rent plus all or most property charges	
	Percentage lease (commercial/industrial)	Pays basic rent plus percent of gross sales (may pay property costs)	May pay some property charges
			May pay some or all property charges

Options

A lease may contain an *option* that grants the lessee the privilege of *renewing* or *extending* the lease. The lessee must, however, give *notice* before a specific date of the intention to exercise the option. Some leases grant the lessee the *option to purchase* the leased premises. This option normally allows the tenant the right to purchase the property at a predetermined price for a certain time period, possibly the term of the lease. Although it is not required, the owner may give the tenant credit toward the purchase price for some of the rent paid. The lease agreement is a primary contract over the option to purchase. Options are discussed further in Chapter 18.

An option is not to be confused with a *lease purchase*. In a lease purchase, the tenant agrees to purchase the property but has a lease until the time that the terms in the purchase agreement are fully satisfied. This enables the tenant to use the property even though the tenant is presently unable to purchase it. Lease purchase agreements are commonly used when a purchaser is unable to obtain favorable financing or a clear title or when the tax consequences of a current purchase are unfavorable. The purchase agreement is the primary consideration over the lease.

IN PRACTICE...

Note that throughout the discussion about lease contracts, there are repeated references to the fact that the terms of the lease are controlled largely by the specific details in the written contract. A lease should be carefully prepared to ensure that it accurately reflects the intentions of the landlord and tenant. When preprinted forms are used (commonly in residential leasing), the parties must be sure that preprinted language is satisfactory to both of them. The parties to any contract are advised to have their attorneys review the contract before signing it. Real estate licensees are cautioned not to give legal advice or draft language for legal documents.

TYPES OF LEASES

The manner in which rent is determined indicates the type of lease that is in force. (See Table 6.2.)

Gross Lease

In a **gross lease,** the tenant pays a *fixed rental,* and the landlord pays all taxes, insurance, mortgage payments, repairs, utilities and the like connected with the property (usually called *operating expenses*).

MATH CONCEPT Calculating Percentage Lease Rents

Percentage leases usually call for a minimum monthly rent plus a percentage of gross sales income over a stated annual amount. For example, a lease might require minimum rent of $1,300 per month plus 5 percent of the business's sales over $160,000. On an annual sales volume of $250,000, the annual rent would be calculated as follows:

$$\$1,300 \text{ per month} \times 12 \text{ months} = \$15,600;$$

$$\$250,000 - \$160,000 = \$90,000; \$90,000 \times .05 \ (5\%) = \$4,500;$$

$$\$15,600 \text{ base rent} + \$4,500 \text{ percentage rent} = \$20,100 \text{ total rent}$$

Net Lease

In a **net lease,** the tenant pays *all or some of the operating expenses* as defined in the lease agreement in addition to the rent. The monthly rental is net income for the landlord after operating costs have been paid. Leases for entire commercial or industrial buildings and the land on which they are located, ground leases and long-term leases are usually net leases.

In a *triple net lease,* or *net-net-net lease,* the tenant pays all operating and other expenses, such as taxes, insurance, assessments, maintenance and other charges, in addition to periodic rent.

Percentage Lease

Either a gross lease or a net lease may be a **percentage lease.** The rent is based on a *percentage of the gross or net income* received by the tenant doing business on the leased property. This type of lease is usually used for retail businesses.

Under a percentage lease, the lessee pays a minimum fixed rental fee plus a percentage of that portion of the tenant's business income (usually gross sales) that exceeds a stated minimum. The percentage charged varies widely with the nature of the business, the location of the property and general economic conditions. It is negotiable between landlord and tenant. A tenant's bargaining power is determined by the volume of the business.

Other Lease Types

Variable leases. Several types of leases allow for increases in the fixed rental charge during the lease period. One of the more common is the *graduated lease,* which provides for increases in rent at set future dates in specified amounts. Another is the *index lease,* which allows rent to be increased or decreased periodically based on changes in the consumer price index or some other index agreed to by the landlord and tenant.

Ground leases. When a landowner leases unimproved land to a tenant who agrees to erect a building on it, the lease is usually referred to as a **ground lease.** Ground leases usually involve separate ownership of the land and building. These leases must be for a long enough term to make the transaction desirable to the tenant investing in the building. Ground leases are generally *net leases* that require the lessee to pay rent on the ground as well as real estate taxes, insurance, upkeep and repairs. Such leases often run for terms of 50 years or longer, and a ground lease for 99 years is common. Although such leases are considered to be personal property, certain states' laws may give leaseholders some of the rights and obligations of real property owners.

Oil and gas leases. When oil companies lease land to explore for oil and gas, a special lease agreement must be negotiated. Usually, the landowner receives a cash payment for executing the lease. If no well is drilled within a year or other period stated in the lease, the lease expires; however, most oil and gas leases permit the oil company to continue its rights for another year by paying another flat rental fee. Such rentals may be paid annually until a well is produced. If oil and/or gas is found, the landowner usually receives one-eighth of its value as a royalty. In this case, the lease will continue for as long as oil or gas is obtained in significant quantities.

DISCHARGE OF LEASES

As with any contract, a lease is discharged when the contract terminates. Termination can occur when each party fully performs the obligations defined in the agreement within the period defined by the type of leasehold estate. In addition, the landlord and tenant can mutually agree to cancel the lease. The tenant may offer to surrender the leasehold interest and if the landlord accepts, the lease is terminated. A tenant who abandons leased property, however, remains liable for the terms of the lease—including the rent. The terms of the lease will usually indicate whether the landlord is obligated to try to rerent the space. If the landlord intends to sue for unpaid rent, however, most states will require an attempt to rerent the premises to limit the amount owed (to "mitigate damages"). A tenancy may also be terminated by operation of law, as in a bankruptcy or condemnation proceeding.

The lease *does not terminate* if the parties to a lease agreement die or the property is sold. There are two exceptions: a lease from the owner of a life estate terminates on the death of that person, and the death of either party terminates a tenancy at will. Otherwise, the heirs of the deceased are bound by the terms of existing valid leases. *In addition, if a landlord sells leased real estate, the new landlord takes the property subject to the rights of the tenants.* A lease agreement may, however, state that a new landlord, after taking title, shall give the tenant a period of notice to terminate an existing lease. This is commonly known as a *sale clause.* Because the new owner has taken title subject to the rights of the tenant, the sale clause enables the new landlord to claim possession and/or negotiate new leases under his or her own terms and conditions.

Breach of Lease

When a tenant breaches or violates any lease provision, the landlord may sue the tenant to obtain a judgment for past-due rent, damages to the premises or other defaults. Likewise, when a landlord breaches any lease provision, the tenant is entitled to certain remedies.

Suit for possession—actual eviction. When a tenant breaches a lease or improperly retains possession of leased premises, the landlord may regain possession through a **suit for possession.** This process is known as **actual eviction.** Pennsylvania law requires the landlord to serve notice to the tenant at an appropriate interval before commencing the suit, which could be 15 days to three months, depending on the circumstances. Once notice has been served, the landlord files a complaint and the district justice issues a summons requiring the tenant to appear to answer the complaint. If it appears that the complaint is proven, the district justice enters a judgment against the tenant for the delivery of the property to the landlord. The judgment also can include any damages for the unjust detention of the premises, the amount of any remaining due and unpaid rent and any other costs, including reasonable attorney fees, permitted under the law or in accordance with the written lease.

When the court issues the landlord a judgment for possession, the tenant must peaceably remove himself or herself and all belongings. Otherwise the landlord can have the judgment enforced by a constable who will *forcibly* remove the tenant and his or her possessions. Until such a judgment is issued, the landlord must be careful not to harass the tenant in any manner such as by locking the tenant out of the property, impounding the tenant's possessions or making the property unusable by disconnecting services (such as electricity and natural gas).

Tenants' remedies—constructive eviction. If a landlord breaches any clause of a lease agreement, the tenant has the right to sue, claiming a judgment for damages against the landlord. If an action or omission on the landlord's part results in the leased premises becoming uninhabitable for the purpose intended in the lease, the tenant may have the right to abandon the premises. This action, called **constructive eviction,** terminates the lease agreement if the tenant can prove that the premises have become uninhabitable because of the landlord's conscious neglect. The tenant must actually remove himself or herself from the premises while the uninhabitable conditions exist to claim constructive eviction.

For example, if the landlord fails to repair a defective heating system and the leased premises become uninhabitable because of lack of heat, the tenant may abandon the property. Some leases provide that if the failure to furnish heat is accidental and not the landlord's fault, this is not grounds for constructive eviction.

Warranty of habitability. Pennsylvania courts recognize a doctrine known as **warranty of habitability** in residential leases. The theory of this warranty is that the lessor who leases residential premises warrants that the premises shall be fit for habitation. If the lessee can prove that the premises are not fit for habitation, the court can order a reduction in or cessation of rent.

Protenant Legislation

Recent consumer awareness has fostered the belief that a valid lease requires both the landlord and tenant to fulfill certain obligations, not just the tenant. The *Uniform Residential Landlord and Tenant Act,* which has been adopted in some variation by a number of states, stipulates the rights and responsibilities of both parties. This model law addresses such issues as the type of tenancy, the landlord's right to enter the property, use and maintenance of the premises, the tenant's protection against retaliation by the landlord for complaints and the disclosure of the property owners' (or manager's) names and addresses to the tenants. The act also establishes specific remedies available to both the landlord and the tenant if a breach of the lease agreement occurs.

The *Pennsylvania Landlord and Tenant Act of 1951* contains the remedies available to the landlord in the event of a lease default and rules of civil procedures for district justices to follow in these cases. The Pennsylvania Consumer Protection Law, which prohibits unfair practices in the conduct of commerce, provides remedies for tenants of residential property.

The federal *Tenants' Eviction Procedures Act,* in 1976, established standardized eviction procedures for people living in *government-subsidized housing.* It requires the landlord to have a valid reason for evicting the tenant and to give the tenant proper notice of eviction. This act does not supersede state laws; however, it does provide recourse for tenants in states that have no such laws. The act applies only to multiunit residential buildings that are owned or subsidized by the Department of Housing and Urban Development and to buildings that have government-insured mortgages.

CIVIL RIGHTS LAWS   The fair housing laws affect landlords and tenants just as they do sellers and purchasers. All persons must have access to housing of their choice under the *Pennsylvania Human Relations Act* without any differentiation in the terms and conditions because of their race, color, religion, national origin, sex, age (40 years old or older), handicap, use of guide or support animals due to a handicap or disability or familial status. Local municipalities may have their own fair housing laws that add protected classes such as sexual orientation. Withholding an apartment that is for rent, segregating certain persons in separate sections of an apartment complex or parts of a building, charging different amounts for rent or security deposits to persons in the protected classes and advertising "No Children Allowed" are examples of violations of the laws. The fair housing laws are discussed in greater detail in Chapter 16.

Landlords should be aware that changes in the laws stemming from the federal *Fair Housing Amendments Act,* followed by changes in the Pennsylvania Human Relations Act, significantly alter past practices. Families with children have had difficulty finding suitable rentals because many landlords refused to accept children. Under the current laws, if a landlord has determined that an apartment is suitable for two people, for example, then the apartment must be available to any two people—two adults or one adult and one child. The landlord cannot charge a different amount of rent or security deposit because one of the tenants is a child. While landlords have historically argued that children are noisy or destructive, a better question is "Aren't some adults noisy or destructive?" The fair housing laws require that the same tenant criteria be applied to families with children as well as to adults.

Another issue that landlords must be aware of is protections that the fair housing laws provide to people with handicaps and disabilities. The landlord must afford them the opportunity to make alterations to the property that enable them to enjoy their leased unit. People with disabilities are also entitled to access the same services or facilities in a building as other tenants. This may mean that the landlord would have to provide reasonable accommodations in accordance with the fair housing laws to offer them this opportunity.

The *Americans with Disabilities Act* (ADA, a federal law discussed in greater detail in Chapter 16) also affects leasing practices. A property in which public services and goods are provided must be free of communications and architectural barriers or accommodations must be provided so that people with disabilities can patronize those businesses or access the services. Landlords and managers of nonresidential properties should be familiar with the requirements of the ADA to ensure that their buildings comply with the law.

●   ●   ●   ●   ●   ●   ●

KEY TERMS

actual eviction
confession of judgment clause
constructive eviction
estate (tenancy) at sufferance
estate (tenancy) at will
estate (tenancy) for years
estate (tenancy) from period to period
gross lease
ground lease
holdover tenancy
lease

lessor
lessee
month-to-month tenancy
net lease
percentage lease
periodic tenancy
security deposit
sublease
suit for possession
warranty of habitability

SUMMARY

A lease is an agreement that grants one person the right to use the property of another for a certain period in return for consideration.

A leasehold estate that runs for a specific length of time creates a tenancy for years; one that runs for an indefinite period creates a periodic tenancy (year to year, month to month). An estate at will runs as long as the landlord permits, and an estate at sufferance is possession without the consent of the landlord. A leasehold estate is generally classified as personal property.

The lease agreement is a combination of a conveyance creating a leasehold interest in the property and a contract outlining the rights and obligations of the landlord and the tenant. The requirements of a valid lease include offer and acceptance, consideration, capacity to contract and legal objectives. In addition, the Pennsylvania Statute of Frauds requires that any lease of more than three years must be in writing to be enforceable. However, Pennsylvania real estate licensees are required to use written agreements. Leases also generally include clauses relating to rights and obligations of the landlord and tenant such as the use of the premises, subletting, judgments, maintenance of the premises and termination of the lease period.

There are several basic types of leases, including net leases, gross leases and percentage leases. These leases are classified according to the method used in determining the rental rate of the property.

Leases may be terminated by the expiration of the lease period, the mutual agreement of the parties or a breach of the lease by either landlord or tenant. In most cases neither the death of the tenant nor the landlord's sale of the rental property terminates the lease.

Upon a tenant's default on any of the lease provisions, a landlord may sue for a money judgment or for actual eviction in a case where a tenant has improperly retained possession of the premises. If the premises have become uninhabitable as a result of the landlord's negligence, the tenant may have the right of constructive eviction, that is, the right to abandon the premises and refuse to pay rent until the premises are repaired.

The fair housing laws protect tenants from discrimination because of race, color, religion, national origin, sex, age (40 years or older), handicap or disability, use of guide or support animals because of a handicap or disability or familial status.

The Americans with Disabilities Act provides for access to goods and services by people with disabilities.

Questions

1. A *ground lease* is usually
   a. short-term.
   b. for 100 years or longer.
   c. long-term.
   d. a gross lease.

2. A *percentage lease* is a lease that provides for a
   a. rental of a percentage of the value of a building.
   b. definite periodic rent not exceeding a stated percentage.
   c. definite monthly rent plus a percentage of the tenant's gross receipts in excess of a certain amount.
   d. graduated amount due monthly and not exceeding a stated percentage.

3. If several tenants move out of a rented store building because the building has collapsed
   a. it would be an actual eviction.
   b. the tenants would be liable for the rent until the expiration date of their leases.
   c. the landlord would have to provide substitute space.
   d. it would be a constructive eviction.

4. *R*'s written five-year lease with monthly rental payments expired last month, but *R* has remained in possession and the landlord has accepted his most recent rent payment without comment. At this point
   a. *R* is a holdover tenant.
   b. *R*'s lease has been renewed for another five years.
   c. *R*'s lease has been renewed for another month.
   d. *R* is a tenant at sufferance.

5. A lease for more than three years must be in writing because
   a. either party may forget the terms.
   b. the tenant must sign the agreement to pay rent.
   c. the Statute of Frauds requires it.
   d. it is the customary procedure to protect the tenant.

6. A tenant who transfers his or her entire rights for the remaining term of the lease to a third party is
   a. a sublessor.
   b. assigning the lease.
   c. automatically relieved of any further obligation under it.
   d. giving the third party a sandwich lease.

7. A tenant's lease has expired. The tenant has neither vacated nor negotiated a renewal lease and the landlord has declared that she does not want the tenant to remain in the building. The tenant holds a/an
   a. estate for years.
   b. periodic estate.
   c. estate at will.
   d. estate at sufferance.

8. *F* has a lease that will expire in two weeks. At that time he will move into larger quarters on the other side of town. To terminate this agreement
   a. *F* must give his landlord prior notice.
   b. the landlord must give *F* prior notice.
   c. nothing needs to be done—the agreement will terminate automatically.
   d. the agreement will terminate only after both parties renegotiate the original agreement.

9. When a tenant holds possession of a land-lord's property without a current lease agreement and without the landlord's approval

    a. the tenant is maintaining a gross lease.
    b. the landlord can file suit for possession.
    c. the tenant has no obligation to pay rent.
    d. the landlord may be subject to a constructive eviction.

10. Under the terms of a residential lease the landlord is required to maintain the water heater. If a tenant is unable to get hot water, all of the following remedies would be available to the tenant *except*

    a. sue the landlord for damages.
    b. sue the landlord for back rent.
    c. abandon the premises under constructive eviction.
    d. terminate the lease agreement.

11. The leasehold interest that automatically re-news itself at each expiration is the

    a. tenancy for years.
    b. tenancy from period to period.
    c. tenancy at will.
    d. tenancy at sufferance.

12. *K* has leased space in her shopping center to *B* for *B*'s dress store. However, *B*'s business fails and *B* sublets the space to *D*. Then *D* fails to make rental payments when they are due. The lease has been breached, therefore,

    a. *K* would have recourse against *B* only.
    b. *K* would have recourse against *D* only.
    c. *K* would have recourse against both *B* and *D*.
    d. *D* would have recourse against *B*.

13. Which of the following best describes a *net lease?*

    a. An agreement in which the tenant pays a fixed rent and the landlord pays all taxes, insurance and so forth, on the property
    b. A lease in which the tenant pays rent in addition to some or all operating expenses
    c. A lease in which the tenant pays the landlord a percentage of the monthly income derived from the property
    d. An agreement granting an individual a leasehold interest in fishing rights for shoreline properties

14. A lease calls for a minimum rent of $1,200 per month plus 4 percent of the annual gross business over $150,000. If the total rent paid at the end of one year was $19,200, how much business did the tenant do during the year?

    a. $159,800   c. $270,000
    b. $25,200   d. $169,200

15. *Holdover tenancy* is also referred to as

    a. tenancy for years.
    b. periodic tenancy.
    c. tenancy at will.
    d. tenancy at sufferance.

7

Forms of Real Estate Ownership

LEGAL FORMS OF OWNERSHIP

Chapter 5 describes the various interests in land that an owner can have. Understanding this makes it possible to identify exactly what sellers have to convey and, therefore, what buyers are acquiring. The next step is to look at the legal form of ownership, that is, the way ownership is titled and held.

Ownership in a fee simple estate can be titled as a tenancy in severalty if one person holds title in his or her name alone. If there are two or more people, they may hold title as tenants in common or as joint tenants. Married couples own real estate as tenants by the entireties in Pennsylvania, unless the deed creating the estate identifies a different form of ownership. If title is held by a third person for the benefit of another, the ownership is held by a trust. The possible legal forms of ownership are controlled by state law.

The form of ownership is important in a real estate transaction. By identifying the person(s) having interests in the property, this identifies who is entitled to make decisions about the ownership, including who must sign the various documents (listing contracts, agreements of sale and deeds). The purchaser(s) of a property must decide the form of ownership in which to take title. Although real estate licensees must understand the fundamentals of the forms of ownership, specific questions and guidance about ownership decisions should be referred to legal counsel.

OWNERSHIP IN SEVERALTY

Ownership in **severalty** is *vested in,* or presently owned by, one individual or one legal entity. The term comes from the fact that the *sole owner* is "severed" or "cut off" from other owners. A severalty owner has sole rights to the ownership and sole discretion over the transfer of it.

CO-OWNERSHIP

When title to a parcel of real estate is vested in two or more persons or entities, these parties are said to be *co-owners,* or *concurrent owners,* of the property. Concurrent ownership means that title is vested in two or more owners at the same time, each sharing in the rights of ownership, possession, and so forth. There are several forms of *co-ownership,* each having unique legal

**Figure 7.1
Tenancy in
Common**

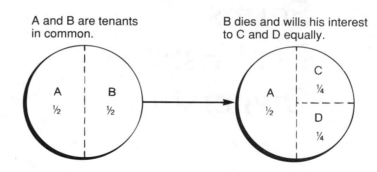

characteristics. The forms commonly recognized in the various states are tenancy in common, joint tenancy, tenancy by the entirety, community property and partnership property.

**Tenancy in
Common**

A parcel of real estate may be owned by two or more people as **tenants in common.** Each tenant holds an *undivided fractional interest* in the property. A tenant in common may hold, say a one-half or one-third interest in a property. The physical property, however, is not divided into a specific half or third. It is the *ownership* interest and not the property that is divided. The co-owners have *unity of possession,* that is, they are entitled to possession of the whole property. The deed creating a tenancy in common may or may not state the fractional interest held by each co-owner. If no fractions are stated, the tenants are presumed to hold equal shares. For example, if two people hold title to the property, each has an undivided one-half interest. Likewise, if five people held title, each would own an undivided one-fifth interest.

Each owner holds his or her undivided interest in severalty and can sell, convey, mortgage or transfer that interest without consent of the other co-owners. However, no individual tenant may transfer ownership of the entire property. Upon the death of a co-owner, that tenant's undivided interest passes to his or her heirs or devisees according to the will. The interest of a deceased tenant in common does not pass to another tenant in common unless the surviving co-owner is an heir, devisee or purchaser. (See Figure 7.1.)

When two or more new owners acquire title to a parcel of real estate and the deed does not stipulate the tenancy, by operation or rules of law, they acquire title as tenants in common. In Pennsylvania, if the conveyance is made to a husband and wife with no further explanation (as will be detailed later), a tenancy by the entirety is created.

Joint Tenancy

Most states recognize some form of **joint tenancy** in property owned by two or more people. The feature that distinguishes a joint tenancy from a tenancy in common is *unity of ownership.* Title is held as though all owners collectively constitute one unit. The death of one of the joint tenants does not destroy the ownership unit; it only reduces by one the number of people who make up the unit. This occurs because of the **right of survivorship.** The joint tenancy continues until there is only one owner, who then holds title in severalty. The right of survivorship applies to the co-owners of the joint tenancy, not to their

**Figure 7.2
Joint Tenancy
with Right of
Survivorship**

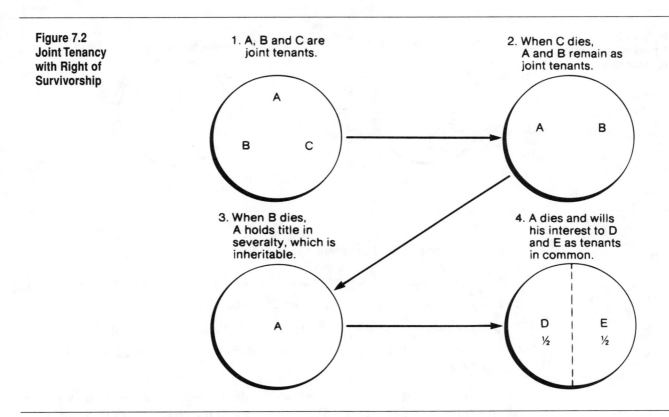

1. A, B and C are
   joint tenants.

2. When C dies,
   A and B remain as
   joint tenants.

3. When B dies,
   A holds title in
   severalty, which is
   inheritable.

4. A dies and wills
   his interest to D
   and E as tenants
   in common.

heirs. As each successive joint tenant dies, the surviving joint tenant(s) ac-
quire(s) the interest of the deceased joint tenant. The last survivor takes title
in severalty and then has all of the rights of sole ownership, including the
right to have the property pass to his or her heirs. (See Figure 7.2.)

Right of survivorship is an alternative to ownership passing through a will or
inheritance upon death. As such, it has come to be known as the "poor man's
will," though it can be a dangerous substitute for a will.

A Pennsylvania statute passed in 1812 provides that the interest of a joint tenant
who dies shall not accrue automatically to the surviving tenant. Although this
law does not prevent the creation of the right of survivorship, it does require
that the conveyance include language to specify survivorship if it is desired. For
example, the conveyance might be made "to *A* and *B* as joint tenants with right
of survivorship and not as tenants in common." Without this language, a joint
tenancy would not have the characteristic of survivorship. A joint tenancy without the right of survivorship is similar to a tenancy in common, even though the
co-owners are known as joint tenants. The distinction between such a joint tenancy and a tenancy in common is more technical than actual.

Creating joint tenancies. A joint tenancy can be created only by the intentional
act of conveying a deed or giving the property by will (known as a devise). It
cannot be implied or created by operation of law. The deed must specifically
state the parties' intention to create a joint tenancy. The parties must be
explicitly identified as joint tenants, and if they intend to create right of survivorship, that must be clearly stated as well.

**Figure 7.3
Combination
of Tenancies**

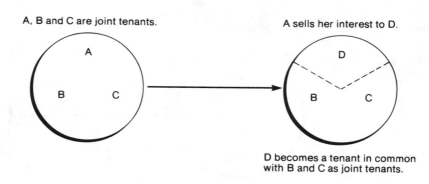

A, B and C are joint tenants.

A sells her interest to D.

D becomes a tenant in common
with B and C as joint tenants.

Four unities are required to create a joint tenancy:

1. Unity of *possession*—all joint tenants hold an undivided right to possession.

2. Unity of *interest*—all joint tenants hold equal ownership interests.

3. Unity of *time*—all joint tenants acquire their interest at the same time.

4. Unity of *title*—all joint tenants acquire their interest by the same instrument of conveyance.

These four unities (PITT) are present when title is acquired by *one deed, executed and delivered at one time and conveying equal interests to all of the parties, who hold undivided possession of the property as joint tenants.*

Terminating joint tenancies. A joint tenancy is destroyed when any one of the four unities of joint tenancy is terminated. A joint tenant is free to convey his or her interest in the jointly held property, but doing so will destroy the unity of interest. The new owner does not become a joint tenant. Rights of other joint tenants, however, will be unaffected. For example, if *A, B* and *C* hold title as joint tenants and *A* conveys her interest to *D,* then *D* will own an undivided fractional interest as a tenant in common with *B* and *C,* who will continue to own their undivided interest as joint tenants. The tenant in common may be presumed to have a one-third interest unless otherwise stated. (See Figure 7.3.)

Joint tenancies also may be terminated by operation of law, such as in bankruptcy or foreclosure sale proceedings. In addition, in states where a mortgage on real property is held to be a conveyance of land, a joint tenant who mortgages his or her property without the other tenants joining in the mortgage will also destroy the joint tenancy.

**Termination of
Co-Ownership by
Partition Suit**

Cotenants who wish to terminate their co-ownership may file a suit in court to *partition* the land. Partition is a legal way to dissolve the relationship when the parties do not voluntarily agree to its termination. If the court determines that the land cannot be divided physically into parts, it will order the real estate sold. The court will then divide the proceeds of the sale among the co-owners according to their fractional interests.

Tenancy by the Entirety

A **tenancy by the entirety** is a *special joint tenancy between husband and wife in Pennsylvania.* Each spouse has an equal, undivided interest in the property; each, in essence, owns the entire estate. The term *entirety* refers to the fact the owners are considered one indivisible unit because early common law viewed a married couple as one legal person. During the owners' lives, title can be encumbered or conveyed *only by both parties.* One party cannot encumber or convey a one-half interest, and generally there is no right to partition.

A husband and wife who are tenants by the entirety have rights of survivorship. Upon the death of one spouse the surviving spouse automatically becomes sole owner. Married couples often take title as tenants by the entirety so that the surviving spouse can enjoy the benefits of ownership without waiting for the conclusion of probate proceedings.

Like a joint tenancy, a tenancy by the entirety must be created by deed or devise. In Pennsylvania, the intention to create a tenancy by the entirety does not need to be stated in the deed. Any conveyance to a husband and wife that does not designate a specific tenancy automatically creates a tenancy by the entirety.

Tenancy by the entirety may be terminated by the death of either spouse, which leaves the survivor as owner in severalty. It can be ended by divorce, which leaves the parties as tenants in common. Both spouses can agree to end it. If the court has rendered a judgment against the husband and wife as joint debtors, the tenancy is dissolved so that the property can be sold to pay the judgment.

IN PRACTICE...	*The form of ownership under which title is to be taken should always be discussed with an attorney. One form may be more advantageous than another depending on individual circumstances, but these are situations about which only an attorney should advise. Also note that personal property such as stocks and bonds can be held under these various forms of ownership.*

Community Property Rights

The concept of community property originated in Spanish law rather than in English common law. Community property laws are based on the idea that a husband and wife, rather than merging into one entity, are equal partners in the marriage. Any property acquired during a marriage is considered to be obtained by mutual effort.

While Pennsylvania is *not* a community property state, it's important to realize that the community property laws of the states vary widely. Essentially they recognize two kinds of property. **Separate property** is owned solely by either spouse before the marriage or acquired by gift or inheritance after the marriage. It also includes any property purchased with separate funds after the marriage. Any income earned from a person's separate property generally remains part of the separate property. **Community property** consists of all other real and personal property acquired by either spouse during the marriage. Any conveyance or encumbrance of community property requires the signatures of both spouses. Upon the death of one spouse, the survivor automatically owns one-half of the community property. The other half is distributed according to the deceased's will. If the deceased died without a will, the other half is inherited by the surviving spouse or by the deceased's other heirs, depending upon state law.

In the event of a no-fault divorce, the nonowning spouse may be entitled to claim assets of the other spouse in a property settlement. Married persons are advised to seek legal counsel for complete estate planning.

Examples of Co-Ownership

To clarify the concepts of co-ownership, here are some examples of co-ownership arrangements:

- A deed conveys title to *A* and *B*. The intention of the parties is not stated, so generally ownership as tenants in common is created. If *A* dies, her one-half interest will pass to her heirs or according to her will.

- A deed conveying title one-third to *C* and two-thirds to *D* creates a tenancy in common, with each owner having the fractional interest specified.

- A deed to *H* and *W* as husband and wife creates a tenancy by the entirety.

- A conveyance of real estate to two people (not husband and wife) by such wordings as "to *Y* and *Z,* as joint tenants with rights of survivorship and not as tenants in common," creates a joint tenancy ownership with the right of survivorship. Upon the death of *Y,* his share of the title to the property will pass to *Z* automatically. In Pennsylvania, unless the right of survivorship is specifically stated, that portion of the title will pass to *Y*'s heirs, rather than to *Z.*

A combination of interests can exist in one parcel of real estate. For example, when *M* and *M*'s spouse hold title to an undivided one-half as joint tenants and *S* and *S*'s spouse hold title to the other undivided one-half as joint tenants, the relationship among the owners of the two half interests is that of tenants in common.

TRUSTS

A **trust** is a vehicle by which an individual can transfer ownership of property to another individual to hold or manage for the benefit of yet another person. Perhaps a grandfather wishes to ensure the college education of his granddaughter, so he transfers the oil field he owns to the grandchild's mother. He instructs the mother to use its income to pay for the grandchild's college tuition. In this case the grandfather is the *trustor* (known as a *settlor* in Pennsylvania)—the individual who creates the trust and who originally owned the property. The granddaughter is the *beneficiary,* the person who reaps the benefits of the trust. The mother is the *trustee,* the party who holds legal title to the property and is entrusted with carrying out the instructions regarding the benefit the granddaughter is to receive. The trustee is a *fiduciary,* who acts in confidence or trust and has a special legal relationship with the beneficiary. (See Figure 7.4.)

This example is, of course, oversimplified. Trusts can be created for myriad reasons: to prevent an heir from using bequeathed property unwisely, to provide funds for a specific anticipated need when that need arises; to preserve the anonymity of a purchaser of real estate, to enable a group to invest in property that individually they could not afford; to give a settlor (trustor) tax benefits, etc. The legal and tax implications are complex and vary widely from state to state, so attorneys and tax experts should always be consulted.

**Figure 7.4
Trust
Ownership**

Depending on the type of trust and its purpose, the settlor (trustor), trustee and beneficiary can all be either people or legal entities such as corporations. Trustees often are corporations set up for this specific purpose called trust companies. The trustee has only as much power and authority as the settlor gives through a trust agreement, will, trust deed or deed in trust. Ownership can be held under a living or testamentary trust or a land trust. In addition, real estate may be held by a number of people in a *real estate investment trust.*

**Living and
Testamentary
Trusts**

Property owners may provide for their own financial care and/or that of their families by establishing a trust. Such trusts may be created by agreement during a property owner's lifetime (*living trust*) or established by will after his or her death (*testamentary trust*).

The settlor (trustor) conveys real or personal property to a trustee (usually a corporate trustee) with the understanding that the trustee will perform certain duties. Those duties may include the care and investment of the trust assets to produce an income. After payment of operating expenses and trustee's fees, the income is paid to or used for the benefit of the beneficiary. The trust may continue for the lifetime of the beneficiary, or the assets can be distributed when the beneficiary reaches a predetermined age or when other conditions of the trust agreement are met.

Land Trusts

A few states, including Pennsylvania, permit the creation of *land trusts,* in which real estate is the only asset. As in all trusts, the legal title to the property is conveyed to a trustee, and the beneficial interest belongs to the beneficiary. In cases of land trusts, however, the beneficiary is usually also the trustor. While the beneficial interest is *personal property*, the beneficiary retains management and control of the real property and has the right of possession and the right to any income or proceeds from its sale.

One of the distinguishing characteristics of a land trust is that the *public records do not name the beneficiary.* A land trust may be used for secrecy when assembling separate parcels. There are other benefits as well. A beneficial interest can be transferred by assignment, making the formalities of a deed unnecessary. The property can be pledged as security for a loan without having a mortgage recorded. Real property is subject to the laws of the state in which it is located. But since the beneficiary's interest is personal, it will pass at the beneficiary's death under the laws of the state in which the beneficiary resided. If the deceased owned property in several states, additional probate costs and inheritance taxes can thus be avoided.

Usually only individuals create land trusts, but corporations as well as individuals can be beneficiaries. A land trust generally continues for a definite term, such as 20 years. If the beneficiary does not extend the trust term when it expires, the trustee is usually obligated to sell the real estate and distribute the net proceeds to the beneficiary.

IN PRACTICE...

Licensees should exercise caution in using the term "trust deed." It can be used to mean a deed in trust (which relates to the creation of a living, testamentary or land trust) or a deed of trust (which is a financing document similar to a mortgage). Because these documents are not interchangeable, using an imprecise term can cause misunderstanding.

OWNERSHIP OF REAL ESTATE BY BUSINESS ORGANIZATIONS

A business organization is an entity that exists independently of its members. Ownership by a business organization makes it possible for a number of people to hold an interest in the same parcel of real estate. Although real estate can be owned by an individual, with this person engaging in business as a sole proprietor, when real estate is owned by a business organization, people can organize as investors to finance a real estate project. This can be done in several ways—the entity itself may own the real estate, or the investors may have direct ownership of the real estate. The formation of business entities for the purchase or sale of real estate involves complex legal questions that should be referred to legal counsel.

Partnerships

An association of two or more people who carry on a business as co-owners and share in the business's profits and losses is a **partnership.** There are general and limited partnerships. In a **general partnership,** all partners participate to some extent in the operation and management of the business and share full personal liability for business losses and obligations. A **limited partnership** consists of one or more general partners as well as limited, or silent, partners. The business is run by the general partner or partners. The limited partners do not participate, and each can be held liable for the business's losses *only* to the extent of his or her investment. The limited partnership is a popular method of organizing investors in a real estate project because it permits investors with small amounts of capital to participate in large real estate projects.

Under common law a partnership is not a legal entity and technically cannot own real estate. Title must be held by the partners as individuals in a tenancy in common or joint tenancy. However, in states that have adopted the *Uniform Partnership Act,* including Pennsylvania, realty may be held in the partnership name. The *Uniform Limited Partnership Act* establishes the legality of the limited partnership form and also provides that realty may be held in the partnership name. Profits and losses are passed through the partnership to the individual partners, whose individual tax situations determine the tax consequences.

General partnerships are dissolved and must be reorganized if one partner dies, withdraws or goes bankrupt, unless a partnership agreement makes provisions for these events. In a limited partnership, the agreement creating the partnership may provide for the continuation of the organization upon the death or withdrawal of one of the partners.

Corporations

A **corporation** is a nonnatural person, or legal entity, created under the authority of the laws of the state from which it receives its charter. Because the corporation is a legal entity, it can own real estate ownership in *severalty*. A corporation is managed and operated by its *board of directors*. The articles of incorporation set forth the nature of the business that the corporation will conduct; bylaws set forth the specific powers of the board of directors in behalf of the corporation, including its right to buy and sell real estate. Some corporations are permitted to purchase real estate for any purpose; others are limited to purchases that are needed to fulfill the entity's corporate purpose.

As a legal entity, a corporation exists in perpetuity until it is formally dissolved. The death of one of the officers or directors does not affect title to property owned by the corporation.

Individuals participate, or invest, in a corporation by purchasing stock. Because stock is *personal property,* stockholders do not have a direct ownership interest in real estate owned by a corporation. Each stockholder's liability for the corporation's losses is usually limited to the amount of the investment.

One of the main disadvantages of corporate ownership of income property is that the profits are subject to double taxation. As a legal entity, a corporation must file an income tax return and pay tax on its profits. The portion of the remaining profits distributed to stockholders as dividends is taxed again as part of the stockholders' individual incomes. An alternative that provides the benefit of a corporation as a legal entity but avoids the double taxation is known as an *S Corporation*. Only the shares of the profits passed to the stockholder as dividends are taxed.

Limited Liability Companies

A limited liability company (LLC) is a hybrid organization that falls between a partnership and a corporation. The owners are characterized as members rather than partners or stockholders. An LLC minimizes their personal liability because they are not liable for the debts and obligations of the organization as they would be in a partnership. The LLC offers tax advantages over a corporation because it is treated as a partnership under the Internal Revenue Code. For Pennsylvania taxes, however, an LLC is treated as a corporation but may be considered an S corporation if it meets the requirements for this type of an organization. Pennsylvania joined 47 other states that recognize this type of organization by enacting the Limited Liability Company Act in February 1995.

Syndicates

Generally speaking, a **syndicate** is a *joining together of two or more people or firms to make and operate a real estate investment*. A syndicate is not in itself a legal entity; however, it may be organized into a number of ownership forms, including co-ownership (tenancy in common, joint tenancy), partnership (general or limited), trust or corporation. A *joint venture* is a form of partnership in which two or more people or firms carry out a *single business project*. Joint ventures are characterized by a time limitation resulting from the fact that the joint ventures do not intend to establish a permanent relationship.

**Figure 7.5
Condominium
Ownership**

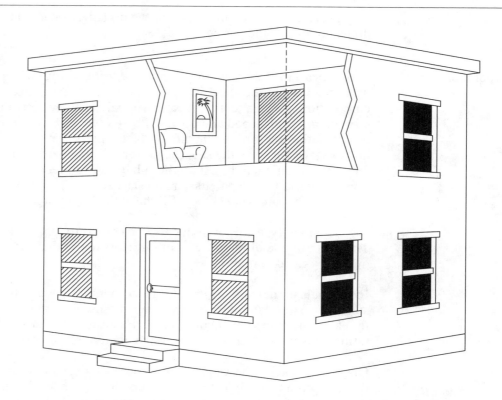

CONDOMINIUMS, COOPERATIVES AND TIME-SHARES

As the nation's population grew, the population concentrated in large urban areas. This led to multiple-unit housing. Initially these buildings were occupied by "tenants," under the traditional rental system. But the urge to "own a part of the land," together with certain tax advantages that accrue to such ownership, led to the condominium and cooperative forms of ownership.

Condominium Ownership

The **condominium** form of ownership has become increasing popular in the United States. Condominium laws, often called *horizontal property acts,* have been enacted in every state. In Pennsylvania, the law governing condominiums is known as the **Pennsylvania Uniform Condominium Act.** Under these laws, the owner of each apartment holds a *fee simple estate* to the unit and a specified share of the undivided interest in the remaining building and land, which are known as the **common elements.** (See Figure 7.5.) The individual unit owners own these common elements together as tenants in common. State law usually provides, however, that unit owners do not have the right to partition as do other tenants.

Architectural style. The condominium form of ownership can exist in a variety of *architectural styles,* ranging from single free-standing units and townhouse structures to high-rise buildings. The common elements include such items as the land, walls, hallways, elevators, stairways and roof. In some instances lawns and recreational facilities such as swimming pools, clubhouses, tennis courts and golf courses may also be considered common elements. The condominium form of ownership is also used for commercial property, office buildings or multiuse buildings that contain offices and retail shops as well as residential units.

The fact that a unit is owned as a condominium is not apparent from its architectural style. Townhouses, for example, may be condominium units or may be separately owned. In the case of separate ownership, the ownership includes the building and the land, rather than specified shares of the undivided parts of the building and land as is the case in a condominium.

Creation of a condominium. According to the provisions of the state Uniform Condominium Act, a condominium is created and established when the owner of an existing building or the developer of unimproved land executes and records a *Declaration of Condominium* in the county where the property is located. The declaration includes a legal description of the condominium units and the common elements, including the *limited* common elements—those that serve only one particular unit. The recording also includes a copy of the condominium's bylaws, drafted to govern the operation of the owners' association; a survey of the property; and an architect's drawings of the buildings, illustrating both the vertical and the horizontal boundaries of each unit. It may also include restrictive covenants controlling the use of the rights of ownership.

If the development is to be a *flexible* condominium—one in which the owner or developer leaves open the right to add or subtract units or convert units to common elements or vice versa—this must be spelled out in the declaration. In addition, the owner or developer must record a *certificate of completion* from an independent surveyor, architect or engineer, assuring that all structural components and mechanical systems have been substantially completed.

Ownership. Once the property is established as a condominium, each unit becomes a separate parcel of real estate that may be dealt with like any other parcel of real property that is *owned in fee simple and that may be held by one or more people in any type of ownership or tenancy that is recognized by state law. It can be mortgaged like any other parcel of real estate.* A condominium unit can usually be sold or transferred to whomever the owner chooses, unless the condominium association provides for a "first right of refusal." In this case the owner must first offer the unit at the same price to the other owners in the condominium or the association before accepting an offer to purchase from the public.

Real estate taxes are assessed and collected on each unit as an individual property. Default in the payment of taxes or a mortgage loan by one unit owner may result in a foreclosure sale of that owner's unit, but it does not affect the ownership of the other unit owners.

Operation and administration. The condominium property generally is administered by an association of unit owners, according to the bylaws set forth in the declaration. The association may be governed by a board of directors or other official entity; it may manage the property on its own, or it may engage a professional property manager to perform this function.

Acting through its board of directors or other officers, the association functions to enforce restrictive covenants and any rules it adopts regarding the operation and use of the property. The association is responsible for the maintenance, repair, cleaning and sanitation of the common elements and structural portions of the property. It must also maintain fire and extended-coverage insurance as well as liability insurance for these portions of the property.

Expenses incurred in fulfilling these responsibilities are paid for by the unit owners in the form of assessments or "maintenance fees" collected by the owners' association. These fees are assessed to each unit owner. They are due monthly, quarterly, semiannually or annually, depending on the provisions of the bylaws. If the assessments are not paid, the association has the right to impose a lien on the property and to seek a court-ordered judgment to have the property sold to cover the outstanding amount.

Condominium conversions. Pennsylvania law requires an owner or developer converting an existing rental property to condominium ownership to give the building's current tenants *one year's prior notice* that a conversion will occur. Tenants cannot be evicted from their rental units unless they have received one year's prior notice (unless they violate the terms of the original lease or rental agreement). This notice must inform the tenants of their rights under state law and include a copy of the owner's or developer's public offering statement (described later in this section) that details the proposed conversion and sale.

Tenants must be given a six-month option to purchase their units. If a tenant chooses not to exercise this option, the owner or developer *may not sell the unit to any other person for a higher price within one year* from the date the original notice of conversion was issued.

After receiving a notice of conversion, a tenant may, without penalty, choose to terminate the original lease within a 90-day period. The owner or developer is prohibited by law from coercing the tenant in any way to terminate his or her lease.

At least 30 days prior to issuing a conversion notice, the owner or developer is required to hold a tenant meeting, open to the public, to discuss the conversion.

Tenants who are aged 62 years or older, or who are blind or otherwise disabled, and who have lived in the building for at least two years are entitled by law to remain in possession of their units for at least *two years* after the conversion notice is issued, even if their lease is to expire within the two-year period. In addition, the owner or developer cannot raise rents for these people during this period, except to cover the costs of increased real estate taxes and/or utilities. If an existing rental building was rehabilitated using federal community development funds, the building cannot be converted to condominium ownership for a period of *ten years* after the rehabilitation has taken place.

Unit sales—newly created condominiums. An owner or developer of a new or existing condominium conversion by law must provide each prospective unit purchaser with a *public offering statement* at least 15 days before a sales contract is signed. This document must detail 22 separate categories of information, including such items as bylaws, rules and regulations, projected operating budgets for the building, liens or encumbrances on the property and so forth. If the purchaser is not provided with a copy of the statement within the prescribed period, he or she may cancel the contract without penalty within 15 days after receiving the material. In addition, the prospective buyer may recover an amount equal to 5 percent of the unit's sale price—up to a maximum of $2,000—or actual damages, whichever is greater.

Owners or developers of newly converted units are required to give purchasers a two-year warranty against structural defects in both the building's units and the common elements; this takes effect on the day the units are conveyed. In addition, purchasers must be furnished with a report prepared by an independent architect or engineer that describes the age and condition of all structural components and mechanical/electrical systems.

Unit sales—existing condominiums. When a unit owner wants to sell his or her unit, the owner by is required by law to provide the prospective purchaser with a *resale certificate,* prepared by the homeowners' association, along with a complete set of documents for review prior to the closing. In addition, the seller must furnish the buyer with a copy of the condominium declaration, the bylaws, the rules and regulations of the owners' association and a certificate containing pertinent information such as monthly assessments, capital expenditures and insurance coverage. The owners' association is permitted to charge the seller for the expense of providing this information. Buyers who receive this information after a sales agreement has been signed have the right to void the agreement within five days after receiving it, if they so choose.

Cooperative Ownership

In the usual **cooperative,** a corporation that holds title to the land and building offers shares of stock to a prospective tenant. The price set by the corporation for each apartment becomes the price of the stock. The purchaser becomes a shareholder in the corporation by virtue of stock ownership and receives a *proprietary* ("owner's") *lease* to the apartment for the life of the corporation. The cooperative tenant-owners do not own real estate as is the case in a condominium, because stock is personal property.

Operation and management. The shareholders control the property and its operation. They elect officers and directors, as provided for in the corporation bylaws, who are responsible for directing the affairs of the corporation and its real estate operation. They may engage the services of a professional property manager to assist them. The bylaws also provide for tenant use of the property (similar to the matters addressed in the restrictive covenants in a condominium) and the method of transfer of the shares in the corporation, which may include approval of prospective shareholders by the board of directors. In some cooperatives, a tenant-owner must sell the stock back to the corporation at the original purchase price so that the corporation will realize any profits when the shares are resold. Ownership in the cooperative corporation is accompanied by the individual shareholder's commitment to abide by these bylaws.

The corporation incurs costs in the operation and maintenance of the entire parcel, including the common property as well as the individual apartments. These costs include real estate taxes and any mortgage payments that the corporation may have. The corporation also budgets funds for such expenses as insurance, utilities, repairs and maintenance, janitorial and other services, replacement of equipment and reserves for capital expenditures. Funds for the budget are assessed to the individual shareholders, generally in the form of monthly fees, similar to those charged by a homeowners' association in a condominium.

Unlike a condominium association, which has the authority to impose a lien on the ownership in the event of defaulted maintenance payments, the burden of any defaulted payment in a cooperative falls on the remaining shareholders. Each shareholder is affected by the financial ability of the others, whereas in a condominium the other owners are unaffected. For this reason approval of prospective tenant-owners by the board of directors frequently involves financial evaluation. If the corporation is unable to make mortgage and tax payments because of shareholder defaults, the property might be sold by court order in a foreclosure suit. This would destroy the interests of all tenant-shareholders, including those who have paid their assessments. (Nonpayment in a condominium would result in foreclosure against only the property of the defaulting owner.)

Advantages. Cooperative ownership, despite its risks, has become more desirable in recent years for several reasons. Lending institutions view the shares of stock, although personal property, as acceptable collateral for financing, which was not always the case. The availability of financing expands the transferability of shares beyond "cash buyers." As a tenant-owner, rather than a tenant who pays rent to a landlord, the shareholder has some control over the property and realizes some income-tax advantage from the payment of property tax. Owners also enjoy freedom from maintenance.

Time-Share Ownership

Time-share permits multiple purchasers to buy interests in real estate—usually in a resort—with each purchaser having a right to use the facility for either a fixed or a variable time period. A *time-share estate* includes a real property interest in condominium ownership. A *time-share use* is a right by contract under which the developer owns the real estate.

A time-share *estate* consists of a fee simple interest. The owner's estate is limited to the period purchased, for example, the 17th complete week, Sunday through Saturday, of each calendar year. The owner is assessed for maintenance and common area expenses based on the relationship of the ownership period to the total number of ownership periods in the property. Time-share estates theoretically never end because they are real property interests. However, the physical life of the improvements is limited and must be carefully considered when making such a purchase.

The principal difference between a time-share estate and a time-share use lies in the interest transferred to an owner by the developer of the project. A time-share *use* consists of the right to occupy and use the facilities for a certain number of years; at the end of such time, any rights in the property held by the owner terminate. In effect, the developer has sold only a right of occupancy and use to the owner, not a fee simple estate.

Some time-share programs specify certain months or weeks of the year during which the owner can use the property. For example, 12 individuals could own equal, undivided interests in one condominium unit, with each owner entitled to use the premises for a specified month in each year. Others provide for a rotation system under which the owner can occupy the unit at different times of the year in different years. Time-share properties are typically used for 50 weeks each year, with the remaining time being reserved for maintenance of the improvements. Some time-share developments offer a "swapping" privilege that enables the holder of a time-share interest to trade time in the same or another development to provide convenience and variety for the owner.

Campground membership is similar to a time-share *use* in that the owner has the right to use the facilities of the developer. However, there is usually an open range area available with minimal improvements (such as camper/trailer hook-ups and restrooms). Normally the owner is not limited to a specific time for use of the property; use is limited only by weather and access.

IN PRACTICE...	*The laws governing the development and sale of time-share and campground membership are generally complex and vary from state to state. Time-share may be subject to subdivision regulations. The Pennsylvania Real Estate Licensing and Registration Act requires licensure for a time-share salesperson and a campground membership salesperson. The sales and licensing procedures for time-share and campground memberships can be found in Appendix C.*

●   ●   ●   ●   ●   ●   ●

KEY TERMS

common elements
community property
condominium
cooperative
corporation
general partnership
joint tenancy
limited partnership
partnership

Pennsylvania Uniform Condominium Act
right of survivorship
separate property
severalty
syndicate
tenancy by the entirety
tenancy in common
time-share
trust

SUMMARY

Sole ownership, or ownership in severalty, means that title is held by one person or legal entity. Under co-ownership, title can be held concurrently by more than one person in several ways.

Under tenancy in common, each party holds an undivided fractional interest in severalty. Individual owners may sell their interests. Upon death, a tenant in common's interest passes to the tenant's heirs or according to a will. There are no special requirements to create this interest. When two or more parties hold title to real estate, they will hold title as tenants in common unless another intention is expressed.

In joint tenancy, title is held by two or more owners as though all owners collectively constitute one unit. The four unities of possession, interest, time and title must be present. To establish a joint tenancy with right of survivorship, the intentions of the parties must be stated clearly.

Tenancy by the entirety resembles a joint tenancy but is between husband and wife. It gives the surviving spouse sole ownership upon the death of the other owner. During their lives, both must sign the deed for any title to pass to a purchaser. Community property rights exist only in certain states and pertain only to land owned by husband and wife.

Real estate ownership may also be held in trust. To create a trust, the trustor conveys title to the property to a trustee, who owns and manages the property. Living or testamentary trusts or a land trust can be created.

Various types of business organizations may own real estate. A corporation is a legal entity and can hold title to real estate in severalty. Although a partnership is technically not a legal entity, the Uniform Partnership Act and the Uniform Limited Partnership Act, adopted in Pennsylvania, recognizes a partnership as an entity and enables it to own property in the partnership's name. A syndicate is an association of two or more people or firms organized to make an investment in real estate. Many syndicates are joint ventures and are organized for only a single project. A syndicate may be organized as a co-ownership, trust, corporation or partnership.

In condominium ownership, an occupant/owner holds a fee simple estate to the unit plus a share of the common elements. Each owner receives an individual property tax bill and may mortgage the unit as desired. Expenses for operating the common elements are collected by an owners' association through periodic assessments. The Pennsylvania Uniform Condominium Act is the Pennsylvania law governing condominiums.

In cooperative ownership, title to real estate is held by a corporation. Shareholders in the corporation have proprietary, long-term leases entitling them to occupy their apartments. The corporation is responsible for paying taxes, mortgage interest and principal and all operating expenses. Shareholders are responsible for supporting these expenditures through periodic assessments.

Time-share enables multiple purchasers to own an estate or use an interest in real estate, with the right to use it for a part of each year.

Questions

1. The four unities of possession, interest, time and title are associated with which of the following?
   a. Tenancy by the entirety
   b. Severalty ownership
   c. Tenants in common
   d. Joint tenancy

2. A parcel of real estate was purchased by *K* and *Z*. The deed they received from the seller at the closing conveyed the property "to *K* and *Z*" without further explanation. Therefore, *K* and *Z* most likely took title as
   a. joint tenants.
   b. tenants in common.
   c. tenants by the entirety.
   d. community property owners.

3. *M, B* and *F* are joint tenants with rights of survivorship in a tract of land. *F* conveys her interest to *V*. Which of the following statements is true?
   a. *M* and *B* are joint tenants.
   b. *M, B* and *V* are joint tenants.
   c. *M, B* and *V* are tenants in common.
   d. *V* now has severalty ownership.

4. In Pennsylvania, a conveyance made "to Arnold and Julia Haber, Husband and Wife," without further elaboration, creates a
   a. joint tenancy.
   b. tenancy in common.
   c. tenancy by the entirety.
   d. partnership.

5. Individual ownership of a single unit and concurrent ownership of the common areas best describes
   a. a cooperative.
   b. a condominium.
   c. a time-share.
   d. membership camping.

6. *E, J* and *Q* were concurrent owners of a parcel of real estate. *J* died, and his interest passed according to his will to become part of his estate. *J* was a
   a. joint tenant.
   b. tenant in common.
   c. tenant by the entirety.
   d. severalty owner.

7. A legal arrangement under which the title to real property is held to protect the interest of a beneficiary is a
   a. trust.
   b. corporation.
   c. limited partnership.
   d. general partnership.

8. A condominium is created when
   a. the construction of the improvements is completed.
   b. the owner files a declaration in the public record.
   c. the condominium owners' association is established.
   d. all of the unit owners file their documents in public record.

9. Ownership that allows possession for a specific time each year is a
   a. cooperative. c. time-share.
   b. condominium. d. trust.

10. Which of the following forms of ownership may be created by operation of law?
    a. Joint tenancy
    b. Tenancy by the entirety
    c. Joint tenancy with right of survivorship
    d. Tenancy in common

11. A corporation may own real estate in all of the following manners *except* in

    a. trust.   c. partnership.
    b. severalty.   d. joint tenancy.

12. All of the following are forms of concurrent ownership *except*

    a. tenancy by the entirety.
    b. community property.
    c. tenancy in common.
    d. severalty.

13. The right of survivorship is associated with

    a. severalty ownership.
    b. community property.
    c. tenancy in common.
    d. joint tenancy.

14. All of the following involve a fee simple interest *except* a

    a. condominium.
    b. time-share use.
    c. tenancy by the entirety.
    d. tenancy in common.

15. If a property is held by two or more owners as tenants in common, the interest of a deceased cotenant will pass to the

    a. surviving owner or owners.
    b. heirs of the deceased.
    c. state by the law of escheat.
    d. trust under which the property was owned.

16. Which of the following best evidences the ownership of a cooperative?

    a. A tax bill for the individual unit
    b. The existence of a reverter clause
    c. A shareholder stock certificate
    d. A right of first refusal

17. A proprietary lease is characteristic of the ownership of a

    a. condominium unit.
    b. cooperative unit.
    c. time-share estate.
    d. membership camping interest.

18. A trust created by will after a property owner's death is called a

    a. real estate endowment trust.
    b. testamentary trust.
    c. real estate investment trust.
    d. beneficiary trust.

19. *T* owns a fee simple interest in Unit 9 and 5 percent of the common elements. *T* owns a

    a. campground membership.
    b. time-share estate.
    c. cooperative unit.
    d. condominium unit.

20. If property is held by two or more owners as joint tenants, the interest of a deceased cotenant will be passed to the

    a. surviving owner or owners.
    b. heirs of the deceased.
    c. state under the law of escheat.
    d. trust under which the property was owned.

21. An owner or developer of a newly built condominium building must provide each prospective unit purchaser with all of the following *except* a

    a. public offering statement.
    b. two-year warranty against structural defects.
    c. resale certificate.
    d. property report.

8 Transfer of Title

TITLE

The term *title* has two functions. **Title** to real estate means the right to or ownership of the land; it represents the "bundle of rights" that an owner possesses. Title also serves as *evidence of ownership;* it represents the facts that, if proven, would enable a person to recover or retain ownership or possession of a parcel of real estate.

Title is a legal concept that refers to ownership, which is not to be confused with a written document that people sometimes refer to as the "title," such as the "title" to a car. The differentiation may seem subtle but it is important because a document, whether it is the title to a car or a deed to the real estate, is used to support a person's claim to the ownership.

Title, or ownership, to real estate may be transferred in several ways. The transfer may be *voluntary* by the owner such as by a sale or a gift, or the ownership may be taken *involuntarily* by operation of law. The title may be transferred while the owner is living or by will or descent after the owner has died.

VOLUNTARY ALIENATION

Voluntary alienation is the legal term for the voluntary transfer of title. The owner may voluntarily transfer title by either making a gift or selling the property. To transfer during one's lifetime, the owner must use some form of deed of conveyance.

A **deed** is a *written instrument by which an owner of real estate intentionally conveys the owner's right, title or interest in a parcel of real estate to another.* The Statute of Frauds requires all deeds to be in writing. The owner who is transferring the title is referred to as the **grantor,** and the person who is acquiring title is called the **grantee.** A deed is executed (signed) by the grantor.

Elements of a Deed

A typical deed in Pennsylvania contains a number of elements. Certain elements are required for the document to be valid. (See Figure 8.1.) These include

* a *grantor* who has the legal capacity to execute (sign) the deed;

**Figure 8.1
Requirements
for a Valid
Deed**

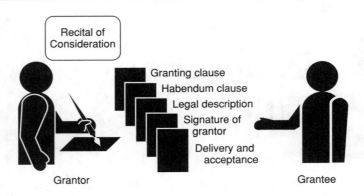

- a *date*;

- a *grantee* named with reasonable certainty to be identified;

- a recital of *consideration;*

- a *granting clause* (words of conveyance);

- a *habendum clause* (to define ownership taken by the grantee);

- an accurate *legal description* of the property conveyed;

- the *signature of the grantor,* sometimes with a seal; and

- *delivery* of the deed and *acceptance* by the grantee to pass title.

Other elements that are commonly found include the designation of any *limitations* on the conveyance of a full fee simple estate, any *exceptions* and *reservations* affecting the title ("subject to" clause) and an *acknowledgment.*

Grantor. A grantor must be of lawful age, generally at least 18 years old. As is the case with most documents, a deed executed by a *minor* (one who has not reached majority or lawful age) is considered to be *voidable.* A minor can disaffirm, or repudiate, the conveyance of real estate during minor age and within a reasonable period after reaching majority.

A grantor also must be of sound mind. Generally any grantor who can understand the action will be viewed as mentally capable of executing a valid deed. A deed executed by someone who was mentally impaired at the time will be *voidable* but not void. If, however, the grantor has been judged legally incompetent, the deed will be void. Real estate owned by one who is legally incompetent can be conveyed only with the authority of the court.

The grantor's name must be spelled correctly and consistently throughout the deed. If the grantor's name has been changed since the title was acquired, such as when a woman changes her name by marriage, both names should be shown as, for example, "Mary Smith, formerly Mary Jones."

Grantee. A deed must name a grantee and do so in such a way that the person or people who are acquiring the ownership can be readily identified. This means using proper legal names and indicating the relationship or form of ownership that multiple owners intend to hold. A sole owner, for example, would be

**Figure 8.2
Sample
Deeds**

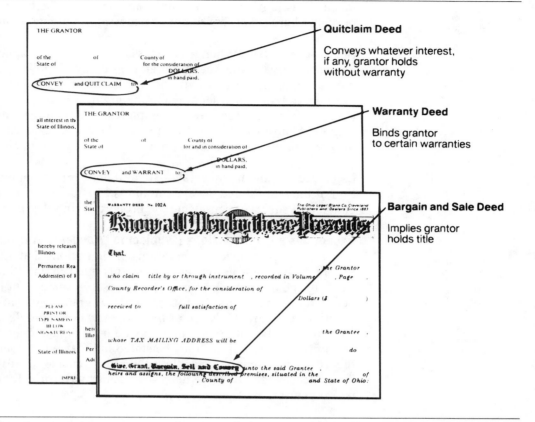

Quitclaim Deed

Conveys whatever interest,
if any, grantor holds
without warranty

Warranty Deed

Binds grantor
to certain warranties

Bargain and Sale Deed

Implies grantor
holds title

identified as "Mary J. Smith, single," or "Mary J. Smith, married." Multiple owners would be identified by their names and the tenancy they intend (refer to the discussion in Chapter 7). A deed naming a wholly fictitious person, a company that does not legally exist or a society or club that is not properly incorporated is considered void.

Consideration. A deed must contain a clause acknowledging the grantor's receipt of consideration. Generally, the amount of consideration is stated in dollars. When a deed conveys real estate as a gift to a relative, "love and affection" may be sufficient consideration, but it is customary in most states to recite a *nominal* consideration, such as "$10 and other good and valuable consideration."

Granting clause (words of conveyance). A deed must state, in the **granting clause,** the grantor's intention to convey the property. Depending on the type of deed and the obligations agreed to by the grantor, the wording is generally either "convey and warrant," "grant," "grant, bargain and sell" or "remise, release and quitclaim." (See Figure 8.2.) Deeds that convey the entire fee simple interest of the grantor usually contain wording such as "to Jacqueline Smith and to her heirs and assigns forever." If the grantor is conveying less than his or her complete interest, such as a life estate, the wording must indicate this limitation: for example, "to Jacqueline Smith for the duration of her natural life."

If more than one grantee is involved, the granting clause should specify their rights in the property. The clause might state, for example, that the grantees will take title as joint tenants or tenants in common. The wording is especially important where specific wording is necessary to create a joint tenancy.

Habendum clause. When it is necessary to define or explain the ownership to be enjoyed by the grantee, a **habendum clause** follows the granting clause. The habendum clause begins with the words "to have and to hold." Its provisions must agree with those set down in the granting clause. For example, when conveying a time-share interest or an interest less than fee simple absolute, the habendum clause specifies the rights that the owner is entitled to as well as how they are limited (time frame, prohibited activity and the like).

Legal description of real estate. A valid deed must contain an accurate description of the real estate conveyed. Land is considered adequately described if a competent surveyor can locate the property using the description.

Exceptions and reservations ("subject to" clauses). A deed should specifically note any encumbrances, reservations or limitations that affect the title being conveyed, such as restrictions and easements that run with the land. In addition to existing encumbrances, a grantor may reserve some right in the land for his or her own use (an easement, for instance). A grantor may also place certain restrictions on a grantee's use of the property. For example, a developer may restrict the number of houses that may be built on a one-acre lot in a subdivision. Such private restrictions must be stated in the deed or contained in a previously recorded document (such as the subdivider's master deed) that is expressly cited in the deed. Many of these deed restrictions have time limits, often including renewal clauses.

Signature of grantor. To be valid, a deed must be signed by *all grantors* named in the deed. A grantor's nonowning spouse may be required to sign a deed to waive any marital rights; without this signature the conveyance will be valid only if sold for "adequate" consideration. Because "adequate" is variously defined, lenders almost always require the signature of the non-owning spouse. This requirement varies according to state laws and the manner in which title is held by the conveying parties. In lieu of a nonowning spouse's signature, the owning spouse may be required to sign an affidavit that there is no pending domestic litigation. The law in Pennsylvania that governs property distribution in the event of a divorce provides for "equitable distribution" of assets. An affidavit that there is no pending domestic litigation will ensure that the title would not be clouded by claims in a property settlement.

In some states there must be witnesses to the grantor's signature. Most states, including Pennsylvania, permit an attorney-in-fact to sign for a grantor. An *attorney-in-fact* is any person who has been given *power of attorney,* the specific written authority to execute and sign one or more legal instruments for another person. The power of attorney must be recorded in the county where the property is located. Because the power of attorney terminates upon the death of the person granting such authority, adequate evidence must be submitted that the grantor was alive at the time the attorney-in-fact signed the deed.

A grantor who is unable to write is permitted to sign by *mark.* With this type of signature, two persons other than the notary public taking the acknowledgment usually must witness the grantor's execution of the deed and must sign as witnesses.

In Pennsylvania, unlike some other states, it is not necessary for a seal or the word *seal* to be written or printed after an individual grantor's signature. The use of a corporate seal by corporations, however, is always required.

Acknowledgment. An **acknowledgment** is a formal declaration that a person who is signing a written document does so *voluntarily* and that the person's *signature is genuine*. This declaration is made before a *notary public* or authorized public officer, such as a judge, district justice or recorder of deeds. An acknowledgment usually states that the person signing the deed or other document is known to the officer or has produced sufficient identification to prevent a forgery.

Although an acknowledgment is not essential to the *validity* of a deed, a deed that is not acknowledged is not a satisfactory instrument. In Pennsylvania, an unacknowledged deed is not eligible for recording. An unrecorded deed is valid between the grantor and the grantee, but it may not be a valid conveyance (to secure good title) for subsequent innocent purchasers. Therefore, the grantee should require acknowledgment of the grantor's signature to help ensure good title.

Delivery and acceptance. A title is not considered transferred until actual *delivery* of the deed by the grantor *and* either actual or implied *acceptance* by the grantee. The grantor may deliver the deed either to the grantee personally or to a third party, commonly known as an escrow agent (discussed in Chapter 21), for ultimate delivery to the grantee upon the fulfillment of certain requirements. *Title is said to "pass" when a valid deed is delivered.* The effective date of the transfer of title from the grantor to the grantee is the date of delivery of the deed itself. When a deed is delivered in escrow, the date of delivery generally "relates back" to the date that it was deposited with the escrow agent. Delivery is a very technical aspect of the validity of a deed, and real estate licensees should consult legal counsel with questions regarding delivery.

Execution of Corporate Deeds

The laws affecting corporations' rights to convey real estate are complex. Some basic rules must be followed.

- A corporation can convey real estate only by authority granted in its *bylaws* or upon a proper resolution passed by its *board of directors*. If all or a substantial portion of a corporation's real estate is being conveyed, a resolution authorizing the sale must be secured from the *stockholders*.

- Deeds to real estate can be signed *only by an authorized officer*.

- The corporate *seal* must be affixed to the conveyance.

Rules pertaining to religious corporations and not-for-profit corporations vary widely. Because the legal requirements must be followed explicitly, it is advisable to consult an attorney for all corporate conveyances.

Types of Deeds

The deed can take several forms, depending on the grantor's pledges to the grantee. Regardless of whatever guarantees the deed offers to the grantee, however, the grantee will want additional assurance that the grantor does indeed have the right to offer what the deed conveys. To obtain this protection, grantees seek evidence of title, discussed in Chapter 10. The most common deed forms are the

- general warranty deed,
- special warranty deed,
- quitclaim deed,
- bargain and sale deed,
- deed in trust,
- deed executed pursuant to a court order.

General warranty deeds. A **general warranty deed** (see Figure 8.3) provides a grantee with the *greatest estate* or *greatest protection* of any deed. It is called a *general warranty deed* because the grantor is legally bound by certain covenants or warranties. The warranties are express or implied by the use of certain words specified in state statutes. The basic warranties are:

1. *Covenant of seisin:* The grantor warrants that he or she is the owner of the property and has the right to convey title to it. The grantee may recover damages up to the full purchase price if this covenant is broken.

2. *Covenant against encumbrances:* The grantor warrants that the property is free from any liens or encumbrances except those specifically stated in the deed. Encumbrances generally include mortgages, mechanics' liens and easements. If this covenant is breached, the grantee may sue for expenses to remove the encumbrance(s).

3. *Covenant of quiet enjoyment:* The grantor guarantees that the grantee's title will be good against third parties who might bring court actions to establish superior title to the property. If the grantee's title is found to be inferior, the grantor is liable for damages.

4. *Covenant of further assurance:* The grantor promises to obtain and deliver any instrument needed to make the title good. For example, if the grantor's spouse has failed to sign away spousal rights, the grantor must deliver a quitclaim deed executed by the spouse to clear the title.

5. *Covenant of warranty forever:* The grantor guarantees to compensate the grantee for the loss sustained if the title fails any time in the future.

These covenants in a general warranty deed are not limited to matters that occurred during the time the grantor owned the property; they extend back to its origins. The grantor defends the title against himself *and against all others as predecessors in title.*

Special warranty deeds. A **special warranty deed** warrants that the grantor received title and that *the property was not encumbered during the time the grantor held title,* except as noted in the deed. The grantor defends the title against himself. Any additional warranties to be included must be specifically stated in the deed. Special warranty deeds generally contain the words "remise, release, alienate and convey" in the granting clause. In areas where a special warranty deed is more commonly used, the purchase of title insurance is viewed as providing adequate protection to the grantee in lieu of a general warranty deed.

Figure 8.3
Warranty
Deed

No. 50 — GENERAL WARRANTY DEED (With Coal Notice)

This Indenture

Made *the* *day of* *19* *,*

Between

(hereinafter called "Grantor ") and

(hereinafter called "Grantee "):

Witnesseth, *that the said Grantor in consideration of*

paid to the Grantor by the Grantee do grant, bargain, sell and convey unto the said Grantee ,
and assigns,

All

Reprinted with the permission of the P.O. Naly Co., Pittsburgh, PA.

**Figure 8.3
(continued)**

Commonwealth of Pennsylvania } ss.
County of...

On this   day of
A.D. 19   , before me
in and for said

came the above named

and acknowledged the foregoing Indenture to be
act and deed, to
the end that it may be recorded as such.

Witness my hand and   seal.

.... (SEAL)

My Commission Expires...............................

State of
County of

On this, the   day of   , 19
before me

the undersigned officer, personally appeared

known to me (or satisfactorily proven) to be the
person   whose name   subscribed to the
within instrument and acknowledged that   he
executed the same for the purposes therein contained.
In Witness Whereof, I hereunto set my hand and
official seal.

....

....
Title of Officer.

My Commission Expires...............................

Certificate of Residence

I,   do hereby certify that

precise residence is

Witness my hand this   day of   , 19   .

....

From

To

Fees, $

For Sale by P. O. Naly Co. Law Blank Publishers
427 Fourth Avenue, Pittsburgh, Pa. 15219

**Figure 8.3
(continued)**

with the appurtenances: 𝕿𝖔 𝕳𝖆𝖛𝖊 𝖆𝖓𝖉 𝕿𝖔 𝕳𝖔𝖑𝖉 *the same to and for the use of the said Grantee*

and assigns

forever, And the Grantor *for*

and assigns hereby covenant and agree that *will* WARRANT GENERALLY *the property hereby conveyed.*

NOTICE—THIS DOCUMENT $\frac{\text{MAY NOT}}{\text{DOES NOT}}$ SELL, CONVEY, TRANSFER, INCLUDE OR INSURE THE TITLE TO THE COAL AND RIGHT OF SUPPORT UNDERNEATH THE SURFACE LAND DESCRIBED OR REFERRED TO HEREIN, AND THE OWNER OR OWNERS OF SUCH COAL $\frac{\text{MAY HAVE}}{\text{HAVE}}$ THE COMPLETE LEGAL RIGHT TO RE-MOVE ALL OF SUCH COAL AND, IN THAT CONNECTION, DAMAGE MAY RESULT TO THE SURFACE OF THE LAND AND ANY HOUSE, BUILDING OR OTHER STRUCTURE ON OR IN SUCH LAND. THE INCLUSION OF THIS NOTICE DOES NOT ENLARGE, RESTRICT OR MODIFY ANY LEGAL RIGHTS OR ESTATES OTHERWISE CREATED, TRANSFERRED, EXCEPTED OR RESERVED BY THIS INSTRUMENT. [This notice is set forth in the manner provided in Section 1 of the Act of July 17, 1957, P. L. 984, as amended, and is not intended as notice of unrecorded instruments, if any.]

𝖂𝖎𝖙𝖓𝖊𝖘𝖘 *the hand* *and seal* *of the said Grantor*

𝖂𝖎𝖙𝖓𝖊𝖘𝖘: _____ (SEAL)

_____ (SEAL)

_____ (SEAL)

_____ (SEAL)

_____ (SEAL)

NOTICE THE UNDERSIGNED, AS EVIDENCED BY THE SIGNATURE(S) TO THIS NOTICE AND THE ACCEPTANCE AND RECORDING OF THIS DEED, (IS, ARE) FULLY COGNIZANT OF THE FACT THAT THE UNDERSIGNED MAY NOT BE OBTAINING THE RIGHT OF PROTECTION AGAINST SUBSIDENCE, AS TO THE PROPERTY HEREIN CONVEYED, RESULTING FROM COAL MINING OPERATIONS AND THAT THE PURCHASED PROPERTY, HEREIN CONVEYED, MAY BE PROTECTED FROM DAMAGE DUE TO MINE SUBSIDENCE BY A PRIVATE CONTRACT WITH THE OWNERS OF THE ECONOMIC INTEREST IN THE COAL. THIS NOTICE IS INSERTED HEREIN TO COMPLY WITH THE BITUMINOUS MINE SUBSIDENCE AND LAND CONSERVATION ACT OF 1966, AS AMENDED 1980, OCT. 10, P.L. 874, NO. 156 § 1.

WITNESS: _____

_____

𝕮𝖔𝖒𝖒𝖔𝖓𝖜𝖊𝖆𝖑𝖙𝖍 𝖔𝖋 𝕻𝖊𝖓𝖓𝖘𝖞𝖑𝖛𝖆𝖓𝖎𝖆 } ss.

𝕮𝖔𝖚𝖓𝖙𝖞 𝖔𝖋_____

On this the *day of* *, 19 ,*

before me *the undersigned officer, personally appeared*

known to me

(or satisfactorily proven) to be the person *whose name* *subscribed to the within instrument and acknowledged that* *executed the same for the purposes therein contained.*

𝕴𝖓 𝖂𝖎𝖙𝖓𝖊𝖘𝖘 𝖂𝖍𝖊𝖗𝖊𝖔𝖋, *I hereunto set my hand and official seal.*

_____

_____

My commission expires *(Title of Officer)*

A special warranty deed may be used by fiduciaries, such as trustees, executors and corporations, and sometimes by grantors who have acquired title at a tax sale. A fiduciary has no authority to warrant against acts of its predecessors in title. Fiduciaries may hold title for a limited time without having a personal interest in the proceeds.

Bargain and sale deeds. A **bargain and sale deed** contains no express warranties against encumbrances; however, it does *imply* that the grantor holds title and possession of the property. The words in the granting clause are usually "grant and release" or "grant, bargain and sell." Because the warranty is not specifically stated, the grantee has little legal recourse if defects later appear in the title. In some areas this deed is used in foreclosures and tax sales. The buyer should purchase title insurance for protection.

A covenant against encumbrances initiated by the grantor may be added to a standard bargain and sale deed to create a *bargain and sale deed with covenant against the grantor's acts*. This deed is roughly equivalent to a special warranty deed. Warranties used in general warranty deeds may be inserted into a bargain and sale deed to give the grantee similar protection.

Quitclaim deeds. A **quitclaim deed** provides the grantee with the least protection. It carries no covenant or warranties and generally conveys only any interest, if any, that the grantor may have when the deed is delivered. If the grantor has no interest, the grantee will acquire nothing. Nor will the grantee acquire any right of warranty claim against the grantor. A quitclaim deed can convey title as effectively as a warranty deed if the grantor has good title when he or she delivers the deed, but it provides none of the guarantees that a warranty deed does. Through a quitclaim deed, the grantor only "remises, releases and quitclaims" his or her interest in the property to the grantee.

Usually, a quitclaim deed is the only type of deed that may be used to convey less than a fee simple estate because it conveys only the grantor's right, title or interest. For example, it might convey an easement or it might convey equitable title back to a seller.

A quitclaim deed is also frequently used to cure a defect, called a "cloud on the title." For example, if the name of the grantee is misspelled on a warranty deed filed in the public record, a quitclaim deed with the correct spelling may be executed to the grantee to perfect the title.

A quitclaim deed is also used when a grantor allegedly has *inherited* property, but is not certain that the decedent's title was valid. A warranty deed in such an instance could carry with it obligations of warranty, while a quitclaim deed would convey only the grantor's interest.

Trust deed. A **trust deed** is the means by which a *trustor* conveys real estate to a *trustee* for the benefit of a *beneficiary*. The real estate is held by the trustee to fulfill the purpose of the trust as was discussed in Chapter 7.

Deeds executed pursuant to court order . This classification, also known as **judicial deed**, covers such deed forms as executors' or administrators' deeds, masters' deeds, sheriffs' deeds and many others. These statutory deed forms are used to convey title to property that is transferred by court order or by will. The forms of these deeds must conform to the laws of the state where the property is located.

One characteristic of such instruments is that the *full consideration* is usually stated in the deed. This is done because the deed is executed pursuant to a court order, and as the court has authorized the sale of the property for a given amount of consideration, this amount must be stated exactly in the document.

IN PRACTICE...	*A deed signals the end of one ownership and the beginning of another ownership. People transfer ownership for a number of reasons, the sale of a property being one of them. It is important for real estate licensees to understand the various deed forms that can be used, especially because the form of deed that will be conveyed is stated in the agreements of sale. Because of the significant legal consequences, however, licensees should not advise parties about which deed form is suitable for their situations nor should they prepare the deed. This advice should be provided by an attorney, and an attorney should also actually prepare the deed.*

Realty Transfer Tax

Most states have enacted laws that provide for a tax on conveyances of real estate, usually referred to as a **transfer tax.** The tax is usually payable when the deed is recorded and a notation is made on the deed as to the amount of tax paid.

The Pennsylvania transfer tax is currently imposed at the rate of 1 percent of the full consideration paid for the real estate. In addition, Pennsylvania law permits the local taxing districts (city, borough, township and school district) to impose an additional transfer tax. Generally this is 1 percent of the full consideration, but municipalities with a "Home Rule Charter Government" may exceed the 1 percent state-imposed limitation; for example, their tax may be 1.5 or 1.75 percent. The real estate transaction itself is taxed, not the buyer or seller. The buyer and seller usually state in the agreement of sale how the tax obligations will be paid; for example, the total tax may be divided equally.

Certain deeds normally are *exempted* from the tax: transfers between parent and child or between siblings; deeds not made in connection with a sale, such as changing joint tenants; conveyances to, from or between governmental bodies; deeds between charitable, religious or educational institutions; deeds securing debts or deeds releasing property as security for a debt; partitions; tax deeds; deeds pursuant to mergers of corporations; and deeds from subsidiary to parent corporations for cancellations of stock.

Transfer of property by ground lease is accomplished by lease assignment. As discussed in a previous chapter, transfer taxes are charged on leases in excess of 30 years.

INVOLUNTARY ALIENATION

Title to property can be transferred by **involuntary alienation,** that is, without the owner's consent. (See Figure 8.4.) Such transfers are usually carried out by operation of law, such as by condemnation or the sale of property to satisfy delinquent tax or mortgage liens. When a person dies intestate and leaves no heirs, the title to the estate passes to the state by the state's power of escheat.

**Figure 8.4
Involuntary
Alienation**

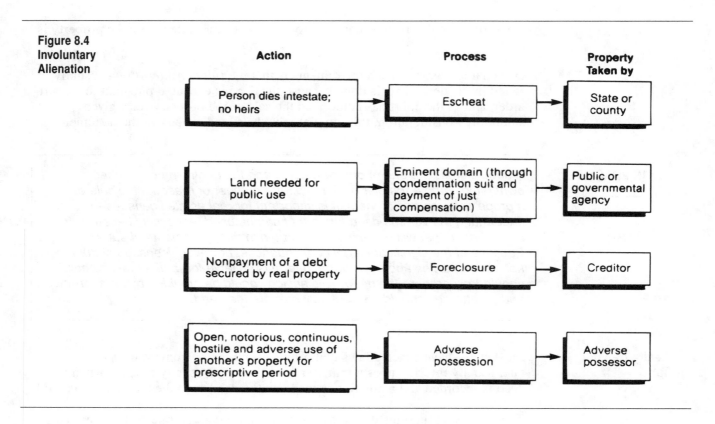

As described in Chapter 4, federal, state and local governments, school boards, some governmental agencies, and certain public and quasi-public corporations and utilities (railroads and gas and electric companies) have the right of *eminent domain.* Under this right, private property may be taken for public use through *condemnation.* Eminent domain may be exercised only when: the use is for the benefit of the public; an equitable amount of compensation will be paid to the owner; and the rights of the property owner will be protected by due process of law. Pennsylvania's Eminent Domain Code provides that the owner is entitled to just compensation or the difference between the fair market value of the entire property interest immediately before condemnation and its fair market value after condemnation.

Land may also be transferred without an owner's consent to satisfy debts contracted by the owner. In such cases, the debt is foreclosed, the property is sold at a sheriff's sale and the proceeds of the sale are applied to pay off the debt. Debts that could be foreclosed include mortgage loans, real estate taxes, mechanics' liens or general judgments against the property owner.

In addition to the involuntary transfer of land by legal processes, land may be transferred by natural forces. Owners of land bordering rivers, lakes and other bodies of water may acquire additional land through the process of *accretion,* the slow accumulation of soil, rock or other matter deposited by the movement of water on an owner's property. The opposite of accretion is *erosion,* the gradual wearing away of land by the action of water and wind. In addition, property may be lost through *avulsion,* the sudden tearing away of land by such natural means as earthquakes or tidal waves.

Adverse possession is another means of involuntary transfer. An owner who does not use the land or inspect it for a number of years may lose title to another person who has some claim to it, takes possession and, most important, uses the land. Usually the possession of the claimant must be open, notorious, hostile and uninterrupted for the number of years set by state law (21 years in Pennsylvania). Through the principle of *tacking,* successive periods of adverse possession can be combined by successive adverse possessors, enabling a person who is not in possession for the entire required time to establish a claim of adverse possession.

Through adverse possession, the law recognizes that the use of land is an important function of its ownership. In many cases, an adverse user's rights may supersede those of a fee owner. In Pennsylvania, a person claiming title to land by adverse possession can secure undisputed title by filing an action in court to quiet title. A claimant who does not receive title might acquire an easement by prescription. When a transaction involves the possibility of title by adverse possession, the parties should seek legal counsel.

TRANSFER OF A DECEASED PERSON'S PROPERTY

A person who dies **testate** has prepared a will indicating the way the property will be disposed of after the person's death. In contrast, when a person dies **intestate** (without a will), the real estate and personal property pass to the decedent's heirs according to the *statute of descent and distribution.* In effect, the state makes a will for such decedents.

Legally, when a person dies, title to the real estate immediately passes either to the heirs by descent or to the persons named in the will. Before these individuals can take possession of the property, however, the estate must be probated and all claims against it must be satisfied.

Transfer of Title by Will

A **will** *and testament* is an instrument made by an owner to voluntarily convey title to property after the owner's death. Because a will takes effect only after the death of the decedent, until that time, any property covered by the will can be conveyed by the owner and thus be removed from the owner's estate.

The gift of *real property* by will is known as a **devise;** a person who receives property by will is known as a *devisee.* Technically, an **heir** is one who takes property by the law of descent, but the term is commonly used to include devisees, as well. A gift of *personal property* is known as a *legacy* or *bequest;* the person receiving the personal property is known as a *beneficiary.*

The privilege of disposing of property by will is statutory. To be effective, a will must conform to all the statutory requirements of the state in which the real estate is located. In a case in which a will does not provide the minimum statutory inheritance, the surviving spouse has the option of informing the court that he or she will take the minimum statutory share rather than a lesser share provided in the will. This practice, called *renouncing (or taking against) the will,* is a right reserved only to a surviving spouse.

A will differs from a deed in that a deed conveys a present interest in real estate during the lifetime of the grantor, while a will conveys no interest in the property until after the death of the testator. To be valid, a deed *must* be delivered during the lifetime of the grantor. The parties named in a will have no rights or interests as long as the party who has made the will is still alive; they acquire interest or title only after the owner's death. Upon the death of a testator, the will must be filed and *probated* for title to pass to the devisees.

Legal requirements for making a will. Because a will must be valid and admitted to probate to effectively convey title to real estate, it must be executed and prepared in accordance with the laws of the state where the real estate is located. A **testator** must have legal capacity to make a will. In Pennsylvania, a person must be of *legal age* (18) and *sound mind.* There are, however, no rigid tests to determine the capacity to make a will. Generally the courts hold that to make a valid will, the testator must have sufficient mental capacity to understand the nature and extent of the property owned, the identity of natural heirs, and that at the testator's death the property will go to those named in the will. The drawing of a will must be a voluntary act, free of any undue influence by other people. A will in Pennsylvania must be signed by the testator.

The testator may alter the will. A modification of, an amendment of or an addition to a previously executed will is set forth in a separate document called a *codicil.*

In Pennsylvania, a handwritten will or *holographic will* must be signed by the testator and need not be further witnessed or acknowledged. If the testator is unable to sign the will for some reason, the person may make his or her mark (usually an "x") on the document, with the name subscribed. This mark, however, must be signed by two witnesses to be valid. Pennsylvania also recognizes the use of *nuncupative wills,* those that are given orally and put into writing by witnesses.

Transfer of Title by Descent

Title to real estate and personal property of a person who dies intestate passes to the decedent's heirs as specified by the **descent** statutes. The primary heirs of the deceased are the spouse and close blood relatives. The right to inherit varies from state to state, but could include relatives such as children, parents, brothers, sisters, grandparents, aunts, uncles and, in some cases, first cousins. The specific rights of the heirs and their shares of the estate are defined by the law and depend on which parties survive the decedent and the closeness of their relationship. When children have been legally adopted, most states, including Pennsylvania, consider them to be heirs of the adopting parents but not heirs of ancestors of the adopting parents. In Pennsylvania, illegitimate children may inherit from both the father and the mother as long as parentage has been legally established.

Probate Proceedings

Probate is the formal judicial process to determine the assets of the deceased person and the persons to whom the assets will pass. The purpose of probate is to see that the assets are distributed correctly. They must be properly accounted for and the debts of the decedent and taxes on the estate must be satisfied prior to the distribution of the assets. Assets distributed through probate are those which do not otherwise distribute themselves because of the way they are titled, such as in joint tenancy or tenancy by the entirety. Probate proceedings take place in the county in which the decedent resided. If the decedent owned real estate in another county, probate would occur in that county as well.

When a person dies *testate,* probate is necessary to prove the validity of the will before the assets can be distributed. The person who has possession of the will, normally the individual designated as the *executor or executrix* in the will, presents it for filing with the Register of Wills in the county in which the testator last resided. The will must meet the statutory requirements for its form and execution. A will is assumed to be valid unless it is challenged. The court rules on a challenge. Once the will is upheld, the assets can be distributed according to its provisions.

When a person dies *intestate*, the Pennsylvania statute known as the Intestate Act determines who will inherit the property. To initiate probate proceedings, the court will appoint an *administrator* (in lieu of an executor who would have been named in a will) to oversee the administration and distribution of the estate.

The administrator, executor or executrix has the authority to see that the assets of the estate are appraised and satisfy all debts owed by the decedent. The estate representative is also responsible for paying federal estate taxes and state inheritance taxes. Once all obligations have been satisfied, the representative distributes the remaining assets of the estate according to the person's will or the state law of descent.

IN PRACTICE...

A broker entering into a listing agreement with the executor or administrator of an estate should be aware that this person has a fiduciary duty to the estate. This duty affects all decisions about the assets as well as the amount of commission that the estate will pay for the broker's services. If the amount of commission is deemed by the court to be wasteful and, therefore, unreasonable, the court could reduce it. The commission is payable only from the proceeds of the sale, and the broker will not be able to collect a commission unless the court approves the sale.

KEY TERMS

acknowledgment
adverse possession
bargain and sale deed
deed
descent
devise
general warranty deed
grantee
granting clause
grantor
habendum clause
heir
intestate

involuntary alienation
judicial deed
probate
quitclaim deed
special warranty deed
testate
testator
title
transfer tax
trust deed
voluntary alienation
will

SUMMARY   Title to real estate is the right to and evidence of ownership of the land. It may be transferred by voluntary alienation, involuntary alienation, will and descent.

The voluntary transfer of an owner's title is made by a deed, executed (signed) by the owner as grantor to the purchaser as grantee. The form and execution of a deed must comply with the statutory requirements of the state in which the land is located.

Among the most common of these requirements are a grantor with legal capacity to contract, a readily identifiable grantee, a granting clause, a legal description of the property, a recital of consideration, exceptions and reservations on the title and the signature of the grantor. In addition, the deed should be acknowledged before a notary public or other officer to provide evidence that the signature is genuine and to allow recording. Title to the property passes when the grantor delivers a deed to the grantee and it is accepted. Deeds are subject to state transfer taxes when they are recorded.

The obligation of the grantor is determined by the form of the deed. The words of conveyance in the granting clause are important in determining the form of deed.

A general warranty deed provides the greatest protection of any deed by binding the grantor to certain covenants or warranties. A special warranty deed warrants that the grantor received title and that the grantor did not encumber the estate except as stated in the deed. A bargain and sale deed carries with it no warranties but implies that the grantor holds title to the property. A quitclaim deed carries with it no warranties whatsoever and conveys only the interest, if any, that the grantor possesses in the property.

An owner's title may be transferred without his or her permission by a court action, such as a foreclosure or judgment sale, a tax sale, condemnation under the right of eminent domain, adverse possession or escheat. Land also may be transferred by the natural forces of water and wind, which either increase property by accretion or decrease it through erosion or avulsion.

The real estate of an owner who makes a valid will (a person who dies testate) passes to the devisees through the probating of the will. The title of an owner who dies without a will (intestate) passes according to the law of descent and distribution.

Questions

1. The basic requirements for a valid conveyance are governed by

    a. state law.
    b. local custom.
    c. national law.
    d. law of descent.

2. It is essential that every deed be signed by the

    a. grantor.
    b. grantee.
    c. grantor and grantee.
    d. devisee.

3. *H,* age 15, recently inherited many parcels of real estate from his late father and has decided to sell one of them to pay inheritance taxes. If *H* enters into a deed conveying his interest in the property to a purchaser, such a conveyance would be

    a. valid.
    b. void.
    c. invalid.
    d. voidable.

4. An instrument authorizing one person to act for another is called a/an

    a. power of attorney.
    b. release deed.
    c. quitclaim deed.
    d. acknowledgment.

5. The grantee receives greatest protection with what type of deed?

    a. Quitclaim
    b. Warranty
    c. Bargain and sale
    d. Executor's

6. Determination of the type of deed used in conveying title can be made by examining the

    a. grantor's name.
    b. grantee's name.
    c. granting clause.
    d. acknowledgment.

7. Which of the following best describes the covenant of quiet enjoyment?

    a. The grantor promises to obtain and deliver any instrument needed to make the title good.
    b. The grantor guarantees that if the title fails in the future he or she will compensate the grantee.
    c. The grantor warrants that he or she is the owner and has the right to convey title to it.
    d. The grantor assures that the title will be good against the title claims of third parties.

8. Which of the following deeds would be most likely to recite the full, actual consideration paid for the property?

    a. Gift deed
    b. Trustee's deed
    c. Deed in trust
    d. Deed executed pursuant to court order

9. Which of the following deeds merely implies but does not specifically warrant that the grantor holds good title to the property?

    a. Special warranty deed
    b. Bargain and sale deed
    c. Quitclaim deed
    d. Trustee's deed

10. Title to property transfers at the moment a deed is

    a. signed.
    b. acknowledged.
    c. delivered and accepted.
    d. recorded.

11. Consideration in a deed refers to

    a. gentle handling of the document.
    b. something of value given by each party.
    c. the habendum clause.
    d. the payment of transfer taxes.

12. A declaration before a notary or other official providing evidence that a signature is genuine is an

    a. affidavit.
    b. acknowledgment.
    c. affirmation.
    d. estoppel.

13. *R* executes a deed to *P* as grantee, has it acknowledged and receives payment from the buyer. *R* holds the deed, however, and arranges to meet *P* the next morning at the courthouse to deliver the deed to her. In this situation at this time

    a. *P* owns the property because she has paid for it.
    b. title to the property will not officially pass until *P* has been given the deed the next morning.
    c. title to the property will not pass until *P* has received the deed and recorded it the next morning.
    d. *P* will own the property when she has signed the deed the next morning.

14. Title to real estate may be transferred during a person's lifetime by

    a. devise.
    b. descent.
    c. involuntary alienation.
    d. escheat.

15. *F* bought acreage in a distant county, never went to see it and did not use the ground. *H* moved his mobile home onto the land, had a water well drilled and lived there for 22 years. *H* may become the owner of the land if he has complied with the state law regarding

    a. requirements for a valid conveyance.
    b. adverse possession.
    c. avulsion.
    d. voluntary alienation.

16. Which of the following is *not* one of the ways in which title to real estate may be transferred by involuntary alienation?

    a. Eminent domain
    b. Escheat
    c. Erosion
    d. Deed

17. The acquisition of land through deposit of soil or sand washed up by water is called

    a. accretion.   c. erosion.
    b. avulsion.   d. condemnation.

18. A house is selling for $89,500. The buyer pays $50,000 cash and gives the seller a mortgage for the balance. What is the amount of state transfer tax that must be paid on this transaction?

    a. $895   c. $8,950
    b. $3,950   d. $17,900

19. A person who has died leaving a valid will is called

    a. a devisee.   c. an escrow agent.
    b. a testator.   d. intestate.

20. Title to real estate can be transferred at death by which of the following documents?

    a. Warranty deed
    b. Special warranty deed
    c. Trustee's deed
    d. Will

21. An owner of real estate who had been adjudged legally incompetent made a will during his stay at a nursing home. He later died and was survived by a wife and three children. His real estate will pass

    a. to his wife.
    b. to the heirs mentioned in his will.
    c. according to the state law of descent.
    d. to the state.

9

Real Estate Taxes and Other Liens

LIENS

An encumbrance was defined in Chapter 5 as a right or interest that someone other than the fee owner has in a property. The point was made in that discussion that one kind of an encumbrance is a lien. A **lien** is a charge or claim that is attached to the property because of a debt of the property owner. All liens are viewed as encumbrances, but not all encumbrances are liens because not all of them attach as a result of a debt. A lien provides security for the debt and thus represents an *interest in* the ownership, though it does not constitute ownership in the property. The interest gives the lienholder the right to force the sale of the property if the owner defaults on the debt. Generally, a lienholder must institute a legal action to force sale of the property to collect the debt or acquire title.

Liens can be classified in several ways, depending on how they are created. (See Figure 9.1.) A **voluntary lien** is created intentionally by the debtor's action such as when someone gets a mortgage loan, which then gives the lender the right to file a lien on the property. An **involuntary lien** is created by law without any action by the property owner. Examples include a real estate tax lien and a court-ordered judgment that requires payment of the balance on a delinquent charge account.

Liens are also classified according to the property they affect. **General liens** usually affect all property of a debtor, both real and personal, and include judgments, estate and inheritance taxes, debts of a deceased person, corporation franchise taxes and Internal Revenue Service taxes. There is a difference, however, between a lien on real and a lien on personal property: A lien attaches to real property when it is filed. In contrast, the lien does not attach to personal property until the personal property is seized. **Specific liens** are secured by a specific parcel of real estate and affect only that particular property. Specific liens on real estate include mechanics' liens, mortgage liens, taxes and liens for special assessments and utilities.

Effects of Liens on Title

The existence of a lien does not prevent the property owner from conveying title to someone else. The lien could very well reduce the value of the real estate, however, because the seller could find it difficult to locate a buyer willing to

Figure 9.1
Types of Liens

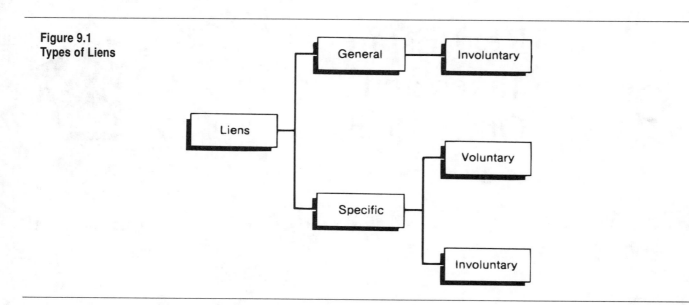

take on the risk of such a burdened property. Although a purchaser will not be personally liable for the debt of a specific lien—which attaches to the property, not to the property owner—the new owner could lose the property if the creditors take court action to enforce payment. Once properly established, liens *run with the land* and will bind all successive owners until the liens are cleared. Therefore future resales could also be jeopardized if the debt is not satisfied.

Priority of liens. *Priority of liens* establishes the order of claim against the property. Liens take priority from the *date of recording* in public records of the county where the property is located.

There are notable exceptions to this rule, however. Real estate taxes and special assessments generally take priority over all other liens. This means that if the property goes through a court sale to satisfy unpaid debts or obligations, outstanding real estate taxes and special assessments will be paid from the proceeds *first*. The remainder of the proceeds will be used to pay other outstanding liens in the order of their priority. Mechanics' liens take priority as provided by state law but never take priority over tax and special assessment liens.

Subordination agreements. Subordination agreements are written agreements by lienholders to change the priority of mortgage, judgment and other liens under certain circumstances. Recording of liens will be discussed in detail in Chapter 10.

**REAL ESTATE
TAX LIENS**

As discussed in Chapter 5, the ownership of real estate is subject to certain government powers. One of these powers is the right of state and local governments to impose **tax liens** for the support of their functions. Because the location of real estate is permanently fixed, the government can levy taxes with a high degree of certainty that the taxes will be collected. The annual taxes levied on real estate usually have priority over other previously recorded liens, so they may be enforced by a court-ordered sale.

There are two types of real estate taxes. Both are levied against specific parcels of property and automatically become liens on those properties.

**General Tax
(Ad Valorem Tax)**

The general real estate tax, or **ad valorem tax,** is made up of the taxes levied on real estate by various government agencies and municipalities. These taxes are known as *ad valorem* (Latin for "according to value") *taxes* because the amount is based on the *value of the property being taxed.*

General real estate taxes are levied for the general operation of the government body or agency authorized to impose the levy. Taxing bodies include counties, cities, boroughs and townships. Others are school districts or boards, drainage districts, water districts and sanitary districts. Municipal authorities operating recreational preserves such as forest preserves and parks are also authorized to levy real estate taxes.

Many government bodies in Pennsylvania depend to a great extent on revenue from real estate taxes to fund their operations. Although revenue is generated from other sources, real estate taxes have historically been the base for their budgets. The heavy reliance on these taxes and concerns about real estate owners bearing a disproportionate share of the burden for supporting the government's activities have become the subject of considerable debate. In many cases, real estate owners pay for services they do not personally use, such as public schools. Increasing costs to operate and maintain a home, plus increases in real estate taxes, threaten the ability of some people, particularly those on fixed incomes and the elderly, to continue their homeownership. Consequently, the state legislature is discussing tax reform that would permit local governments to shift to sales or income taxes as their base of revenue and decrease real estate taxes.

Exemptions from general taxes. In Pennsylvania, as in most other states, certain real estate is exempt from taxation. For example, property owned by cities, various municipal organizations, the state and federal governments are tax exempt; religious corporations, hospitals or educational institutions are usually tax exempt. Usually the property must be used for tax-exempt purposes by the exempted group or organization. Land that is not used for tax-exempt purposes, even though it is owned by such an organization, will be subject to tax. For example, a parking lot owned by a church and adjacent to the church building is not exempt because the purpose of the parking lot is to park cars, not to conduct religious activities.

State laws also allow special exemptions to reduce real estate tax bills for certain property owners or land users. In certain cases, homeowners and senior citizens are granted reductions or limited increases in assessed values on their homes. These exemptions are especially important for the longtime residents, particularly senior citizens, in neighborhoods where significant increases in property values would otherwise make the taxes unaffordable. Temporary reductions in real estate taxes are frequently used to attract industries, stimulate economic growth and development or encourage rehabilitation of property.

Assessment. An **assessment**, or *assessed value,* is the official value of real estate that is used for tax purposes. Real estate is valued, or assessed, for tax purposes by county assessors, evaluators or appraisers. Assessments are normally a percentage of the fair market value of a property. Depending on the type of property and the county, one value may be assigned to the real estate or separate values may be assigned to the land and building.

Property owners who claim that errors were made in determining the assessed values may appeal the assessment, usually to a local board of appeal or board of review. Appeals regarding tax assessments may ultimately be taken to court.

Equalization. In some jurisdictions, when it is necessary to correct general equalities in statewide tax assessments, uniformity may be achieved by use of an **equalization factor.** Such a factor may be provided for use in counties or districts where the assessments are to be raised or lowered. The assessed value of each property is multiplied by the equalization factor, and the tax rate is then applied to the equalized assessment. For example, the assessments in one county are determined to be 20 percent lower than the average assessments throughout the rest of the state. This underassessment can be corrected by decreeing the application of an equalization factor of 120 percent to each assessment in that county. Thus, a parcel of land assessed for tax purposes at $98,000 would be taxed on an equalized value of $117,600 ($98,000 × 1.20 = $117,600).

Tax rates. The process of arriving at a real estate tax rate begins with the *adoption of a budget* by each county, city, school board or other taxing district. Each budget covers the financial requirements of the taxing body for the coming fiscal year, which may be a January to December calendar year or some other 12-month period designated by the taxing body. The budget must include an estimate of all expenditures for the year and indicate the amount of income expected from all fees, revenue sharing and other sources. The net amount remaining to be raised from real estate taxes is then determined from these figures.

The next step is *appropriation,* the action taken by each taxing body that authorizes the expenditure of funds and provides for the sources of such monies. Appropriation generally involves the adoption of an ordinance or the passage of a law setting forth the specifics of the proposed taxation.

The amount to be raised from the general real estate tax is then imposed on property owners through a *tax levy,* which is the formal action taken by the taxing district's governing body to impose the tax.

The *tax rate* for each individual taxing body is computed separately. To arrive at a tax rate, the total monies needed for the coming fiscal year are divided by the total assessments of all real estate located within the jurisdiction of the taxing body. For example, a taxing district's budget indicates that $300,000 must be raised from real estate tax revenues, and the assessment roll (assessor's record) of all taxable real estate within this district equals $10,000,000. The tax rate is computed thus:

$$\$300,000 \div \$10,000,000 = 0.03 \ or \ 3\%$$

The tax rate may be expressed in a number of different ways. In many areas it is expressed in mills. A **mill** is *1/1,000 of a dollar, or $.001.*

The tax rate computed in the foregoing example could be expressed as

30 mills or $3 per $100 of assessed value or $30 per $1,000 of assessed value.

Tax bills. A property owner's *tax bill* is computed by applying the tax rate to the assessed valuation of the property. For example, on a property assessed for tax purposes at $90,000 at a tax rate of 3 percent, or 30 mills, the tax will be $2,700 ($90,000 × 0.03 = $2,700). If an equalization factor is used, the computation on a property with an assessed value of $120,000 and a tax rate of 4 percent with an equalization factor, say, of 120 percent would be as follows:

$$\$120,000 \times 1.20 = \$144,000; \$144,000 \times 0.040 = \$5,760 \text{ tax.}$$

Generally, one tax bill that incorporates all real estate taxes levied by the various taxing districts is prepared for each property. In some areas, however, separate bills are prepared for select taxing bodies. Sometimes the real estate taxing bodies operate on different budget years so that the taxpayer receives separate bills for various taxes at different times during the year.

Due dates for payment of taxes are usually set by statute. Taxes may be payable in 2 installments, 4 installments or 12 installments. In some areas, taxes become due during the current tax year and must be paid in advance (2000 taxes at the beginning of 2000); in others they are payable during the year after the taxes are levied (2000 taxes payable during 2000 and 2001). To encourage prompt payment of real estate taxes, some states offer discounts. Penalties in the form of monthly interest charges are added to all taxes that are not paid when due. The due date is also called the *penalty date.*

IN PRACTICE. . .

The prospective purchaser of a property needs accurate and complete information about the real estate taxes. This includes verifying the amount of the county, school and municipal taxes levied against a property, when each tax is due and the payment schedule. The information is important for computing the taxes that will be owed when the purchase is completed (at closing or settlement) and for calculating the buyer's yearly ownership costs.

Enforcement of tax liens. To be enforceable real estate taxes must be valid, which means they must be properly levied, used for a legal purpose and applied equitably to all affected property. Real estate taxes that have remained delinquent for the period of time specified by state law can be collected by the tax-collecting officer through a tax foreclosure or a **tax sale.**

Individual counties may set up tax claim bureaus. Under this system the names of real estate owners who have not paid their taxes after one year are turned over to the tax claim bureau. Such property may be sold after the second week in September of the following year. Once the property is sold, the owner usually does not have the right to redeem the interest, that is, buy back the real estate by settling all back taxes and other costs. However, there are some counties in which the county treasurer holds tax sales and a redemption period is granted. In addition, the cities of Pittsburgh and Scranton are governed by special acts regarding the sale of property to satisfy delinquent real estate taxes. Ask local authorities about the specific procedures used in your county.

**Special
Assessments
(Improvement
Taxes)**

Special assessments, the second category of real estate taxes, are special taxes levied on real estate for public improvements to that real estate. Property owners in the area of the improvements are required to pay for them because their properties benefit directly from the improvements. The installation of paved streets, curbs, gutters, sidewalks, storm sewers and street lighting increases the values of the affected properties, so the owners are, in effect, merely reimbursing the levying authority for that increase. However, dollar-for-dollar increases in value are rarely the result.

Improvements are recommended or initiated by either the property owners, who may petition for an improvement, or a proper legislative authority such as the city council or board of commissioners. Public hearings are held, for which the owners of the affected properties are given notice. After the preliminary legal steps have been taken, the government body adopts an *ordinance* that states the nature of the improvement, its cost and a description of the area to be assessed.

Typically, each property in the improvement district will be charged a prorated share of the total amount of the assessment, either on a fractional basis (four houses may share the cost of one streetlight equally) or on a cost-per-front-foot basis (wider lots will incur a greater cost than narrower lots for street paving and curb and sidewalk installation).

In most states, an assessment becomes a *lien* following the confirmation of the assessment roll (the approval of the improvements to be made). In Pennsylvania, if the assessment is determined by the front footage method, it becomes a lien from the date the lien is filed. If the assessment is determined by the benefit method, it becomes a lien from the date the taxing authority determines an assessment of benefits. Special assessments are usually due and payable in equal annual installments over a period of five to ten years. Interest is also charged each property owner on the total amount of the assessment. The first installment generally becomes due during the year following confirmation. The bill will include yearly interest on the entire assessment. As subsequent installments are billed in following years, each bill will include a year's interest on the unpaid balance. Property owners usually have the right to prepay any or all installments and thereby stop the interest charges.

IN PRACTICE...   *Although real property taxes are deductible for income-tax purposes, only the annual interest charged in connection with special assessments is deductible, not the assessments themselves. At the time an agreement of sale is negotiated, any pending or existing special assessments should be disclosed and the person who is responsible for payment should be identified.*

**OTHER LIENS ON
REAL PROPERTY**

In addition to real estate tax and special assessments liens, the following types of liens may be charged against real property.

Mortgage Lien

A **mortgage lien** is a specific, voluntary lien on real estate given to a lender by a borrower as security for a mortgage loan. It becomes a lien on real property when the lender files or records the mortgage in the recorder of deeds office in the county where the property is located. Mortgage lenders generally require a first lien, referred to as a *first mortgage lien,* meaning that, aside from real estate taxes, there are no other major liens against the property that would take priority over the mortgage lien. Mortgages will be discussed in greater detail in a later chapter.

Mechanic's Lien

The purpose of the **mechanic's lien** is to *give security to those who perform labor or furnish material to improve real property.* The right to file a mechanic's lien is based on the *enhancement of value theory;* that is, the labor performed and material furnished have enhanced the value of the real estate. Contractors, subcontractors, architects, equipment lessors, surveyors, laborers and others have the right to file a lien as security for the payment of their charges. A mechanic's lien is a specific, involuntary lien.

A person claiming a mechanic's lien must have a contract with the owner or owner's authorized representative. The lien is intended to cover situations in which the owner has not fully paid for the work or when the general contractor has been paid but has not paid the subcontractors who actually furnish the labor or materials.

Under the Pennsylvania Mechanic's Lien Law of 1963, a contractor or subcontractor can file a claim with the court of common pleas in the county in which the property is located. This must be done within four months after the work is completed. (The requirement is subject to certain exceptions and requirements regarding notice to be served on the owner of the property.) If the claim is successful, the lien takes priority as of the date of the first "visible construction" in the case of the erection or construction of an improvement or as of the date the claim is filed in the case of the alteration or repair of an improvement. A claimant must take steps to enforce a lien within two years of the date the claim is filed. Enforcement requires a court action to foreclose the lien through the sale of the real estate, thus producing money to pay the lien.

A property owner can avoid a mechanic's lien by including a *waiver of liens* in the construction contract to protect the title from liens being filed by the general contractor. Or a *stipulation against liens* can be filed in the prothonotary's office to protect the title from liens of the subcontractors. Because the general contractor is liable to the subcontractors for payment, a stipulation against liens serves notice that they cannot file liens against the property but must seek recovery from the general contractor instead.

Another way to protect against a mechanic's lien is a *release of liens.* This document is signed by everyone who has delivered material or labor to the property after work is completed. A release of liens, however, is not foolproof because there is no way to show that all subcontractors have signed the release.

Because a mechanic's lien can be filed within four months after completion of the work, there may be liens that have not yet been recorded. This can cause problems for the purchaser of real estate recently constructed, altered or repaired. Because a mortgage lender expects to be the senior lienholder, the lender may require evidence that no work has been done recently or a release of liens as evidence that there are no claims that take priority. The lender may require *mechanic's lien insurance,* which accompanies a title insurance policy, because of the failings inherent in a release.

If improvements have been ordered by a third party such as a tenant, a property owner should execute a document called a *notice of nonresponsibility* to be relieved from possible mechanic's liens. By posting this notice in a conspicuous place on the property and recording a verified copy of it in public record, the owner gives notice that he or she will not be responsible for the work done.

Judgments

A **judgment** is a *decree issued by a court*. When the decree sets forth an amount of money owed by the debtor to the creditor, the judgment is referred to as a *money judgment*.

A judgment becomes a *general, involuntary lien on both real and personal property* owned by the debtor. Usually a lien covers only property located within the county in which the judgment is issued. Notices of the lien must be filed in other counties when a creditor wishes to extend the lien coverage. A judgment differs from a mortgage in that a *specific* parcel of real estate was not given as security when the debtor-creditor relationship was created. A judgment does not become a lien against personal property until the creditor orders the sheriff to levy the property and the property is actually seized.

In Pennsylvania, judgments obtained as a result of a *court suit* take priority as of the time they are filed in the prothonotary's office. Amicable judgments are those resulting from *confessions of judgment*. These are clauses included in notes, bonds and leases that authorize any attorney to confer a judgment against the borrower or lessee for nonpayment of the debt. Because of court rulings regarding confession of judgment clauses, persons who sign a confession of judgment must also sign an explanation of rights. This document explains the rights that are waived when a party agrees to a confession of judgment and is recorded along with the judgment. The judgment takes priority from the date of that recording.

Judgments are enforced through the issuance of a *writ of execution* and the ultimate sale of the debtor's real or personal property by a sheriff to pay the debt and the expenses of the sale. When the property is sold to satisfy the debt, the debtor should receive a *satisfaction of judgment* (unless there are insufficient funds from the sale), which should be filed with the prothonotary, so that the record is cleared of the judgment.

Lis pendens. When any lawsuit is filed that affects title to a specific parcel of real estate (such as a foreclosure suit), a notice known as a **lis pendens** (Latin for "litigation pending") is recorded. A lis pendens is not a lien, but rather gives *notice of a possible future lien* to all interested parties such as prospective purchasers and lenders. Generally, there is a considerable time lag between when a lawsuit is filed and when a judgment is rendered. The date the lis pendens is filed establishes priority for the later lien.

Attachments. To prevent a debtor from conveying title to previously unsecured real estate (realty that is not mortgaged or is similarly unencumbered) while a court suit is being decided, a creditor may seek a writ of **attachment.** The court retains custody of the property by this writ until the suit is concluded. The creditor must first post a surety bond with the court or deposit sufficient money to cover any possible loss or damage to the debtor while the court has custody of the property.

Estate and Inheritance Tax Liens

Federal **estate taxes** and state **inheritance taxes** (as well as the debts of deceased persons) are *general, involuntary liens* that encumber a deceased person's real and personal property. These are normally paid or cleared in probate court proceedings, as was discussed in an earlier chapter.

Liens for Municipal Utilities

Municipalities are generally given the right to a *specific, involuntary municipal utility lien* on the property of an owner who refuses to pay bills for water or any other municipal utility services.

Commercial Real Estate Broker Lien

The Commercial Real Estate Broker Lien Act enables real estate brokers to place a specific involuntary lien against property for nonpayment of services. *This law applies only to commercial real estate transactions.* It does not include real estate zoned for one to four residential units or real estate zoned for agricultural purposes. The lien can only be recorded by the broker of record and not by associate brokers or salespeople. It may be filed against an owner or buyer client. The lien can only be placed against the owner's property when the broker has a written listing agreement, has provided real estate services, and the property is under agreement. Lien priority is based on the date of filing and will be paid in the order filed, except for mortgages and mechanic's liens. Formal proceedings must be initiated by the filing broker within two years of recording.

Domestic Support Lien

The Domestic Relations Code (also known as the "Deadbeat Parent Law") was amended in 1997 by Act 58, making overdue child support obligations a general involuntary lien on all real estate owned by the person obligated to pay support. Overdue support obligations, existing as of January 1, 1998, constitute a lien on real property of the obligor within the judicial district where the overdue support is owed. Lien priority will be determined by the date that each support payment, which makes up the lien, becomes overdue. Only that portion of a support lien that predates a creditor's judgement or mortgage will have priority over the creditor's lien. Title searchers will be required to obtain a statement of lien from the Domestic Relations Section of the county where the property to be sold is located.

Surety Bail Bond Lien

A real estate owner charged with a crime for which he or she must face trial may choose to put up real estate instead of cash as surety for bail. The execution and recording of such a *surety bail bond* creates a *specific, voluntary lien* against the owner's real estate. This lien is enforceable by the sheriff or other court officer if the accused person does not appear in court as required.

Corporation Franchise Tax Lien

State governments generally levy a *corporation franchise tax* on corporations as a condition of allowing them to do business in the state. Such a tax is a *general, involuntary* lien on all property, real and personal, owned by the corporation.

IRS Tax Lien

An *Internal Revenue Service (IRS) tax lien* results from a person's failure to pay any portion of federal taxes, such as income and withholding taxes. A federal tax lien is a *general, involuntary lien* on all real and personal property held by the delinquent taxpayer.

●   ●   ●   ●   ●   ●   ●

KEY TERMS

ad valorem tax	lis pendens
assessment	mechanic's lien
attachment	mill
equalization factor	mortgage lien
estate taxes	special assessment
general lien	specific lien
inheritance taxes	subordination agreement
involuntary lien	tax lien
judgment	tax sale
lien	voluntary lien

SUMMARY

Liens are claims of creditors or tax officials against the real and personal property of a debtor. A lien is a type of encumbrance. Liens are either general, covering all real and personal property of a debtor/owner, or specific, covering only identified property. They are also either voluntary (arising from an action of the debtor) or involuntary—created by statute.

With the exception of real estate tax liens and mechanics' liens, the priority of liens generally is determined by the order in which they are filed in the prothonotary's office of the county in which the debtor's property is located.

Real estate taxes are levied annually by local taxing authorities and are generally given priority over other liens. Payments are required before stated dates, after which penalties accrue. An owner may lose title to the property for nonpayment of taxes, because such tax-delinquent property can be sold at a tax sale. Some states allow a time period during which a defaulted owner can redeem the real estate from a tax sale.

Special assessments are levied to allocate the cost of improvements such as new sidewalks, curbs or paving to the real estate that benefits from them. Assessments are usually payable annually over a five- or ten-year period, together with interest due on the balance of the assessment.

Mortgage liens are voluntary, specific liens given to lenders to secure payment for mortgage loans.

Mechanics' liens protect general contractors, subcontractors and material suppliers whose work enhances the value of real estate.

A judgment is a court decree obtained by a creditor, usually for a money award from a debtor. The lien of a judgment can be enforced by issuance of a writ of execution and sale by the sheriff to pay the judgment amount and costs.

Attachment is a means of preventing a defendant from conveying real estate before completion of a suit in which a judgment is sought.

Lis pendens is a recorded notice of a lawsuit that is awaiting trial in court and that may result in a judgment that will affect title to a parcel of real estate.

Federal estate taxes and state inheritance taxes are general liens against a deceased owner's property.

Liens for water charges or other municipal utilities and surety bail bond liens are specific liens, while corporation franchise tax liens are general liens against a corporation's assets.

Internal Revenue Service tax liens are general liens against the property of a person who is delinquent in payment of IRS taxes.

Questions

1. Which of the following best refers to the type of lien that affects all real and personal property of a debtor?
   a. Specific lien
   b. Voluntary lien
   c. Involuntary lien
   d. General lien

2. *Priority of liens* refers to which of the following?
   a. The order in which a debtor assumes responsibility for payment of obligations
   b. The order in which liens will be paid if property is sold by court order to satisfy a debt
   c. The dates liens are filed for record; the lien with the earliest recording date will always take priority over other liens
   d. The fact that specific liens have greater priority than general liens

3. A lien on real estate made to secure payment for specific municipal improvements made to a parcel of real estate is which of the following?
   a. Mechanic's lien
   b. Special assessment
   c. Ad valorem
   d. Utility lien

4. Which of the following is classified as a general lien?
   a. Mechanic's lien
   b. Surety bail bond lien
   c. Judgment
   d. General real estate taxes

5. Which of the following liens would usually be given higher priority?
   a. A mortgage dated last year
   b. Real estate tax
   c. A mechanic's lien for work started before the mortgage was made
   d. A judgment rendered yesterday

6. A specific parcel of real estate has a market value of $80,000 and is assessed for tax purposes at 25 percent of market value. The tax rate for the county in which the property is located is 30 mills. The tax bill will be
   a. $500.
   b. $550.
   c. $600.
   d. $700.

7. Which of the following tax is used to distribute the cost of public services among real estate owners?
   a. Personal property tax
   b. Sales tax
   c. Real property tax
   d. Special assessment

8. A mechanic's lien claim arises when a general contractor has performed work or provided material to improve a parcel of real estate on the owner's order and the work has not been paid for. Such a contractor has a right to
   a. tear out his or her work.
   b. record a notice of the lien.
   c. record a notice of the lien and file a court suit within the time required by state law.
   d. have personal property of the owner sold to satisfy the lien.

9. What is the annual real estate tax on a property valued at $135,000 and assessed for tax purposes at $47,250 with an equalization factor of 125 percent, when the tax rate is 25 mills?

   a. $1,418   c. $945
   b. $1,477   d. $1,181

10. Which of the following is a voluntary, specific lien?

    a. IRS tax lien
    b. Mechanic's lien
    c. Mortgage lien
    d. Seller's lien

11. Seller *W* sold buyer *T* a parcel of real estate. Title has passed, but to date *T* has not paid the purchase price in full, as was originally agreed. If *W* does not receive payment, which of the following would she be entitled to enforce?

    a. Attachment   c. Lis pendens
    b. Buyer's lien   d. Judgment

12. A general contractor is going to sue a homeowner for nonpayment. The suit will be filed in two weeks. The contractor just learned that the homeowner has listed the property for sale with a real estate broker. In this situation, which of the following will be used by the contractor and his attorneys to protect his interest?

    a. Seller's lien   c. Assessment
    b. Buyer's lien   d. Attachment

13. Special assessment liens

    a. are general liens.
    b. are paid on a monthly basis.
    c. take priority over mechanics' liens.
    d. cannot be prepaid in full without penalty.

14. Which of the following is a lien on real estate?

    a. An easement running with the land
    b. An unpaid mortgage loan
    c. An encroachment
    d. A license

15. Both a mortgage lien and a judgment lien

    a. must be entered by the court.
    b. involve a debt.
    c. are general liens.
    d. are involuntary liens.

16. A mechanic's lien would be available to all of the following *except* a

    a. subcontractor.   c. surveyor.
    b. contractor.   d. broker.

17. Taxes levied for the operation of the government are called

    a. assessment taxes.
    b. ad valorem taxes.
    c. special assessments.
    d. improvement taxes.

18. All of the following would probably be exempt from real estate taxes *except* a/an

    a. medical research facility.
    b. public golf course.
    c. community church.
    d. apartment building.

10 Title Records

PUBLIC RECORDS

Public records are maintained to make readily available a wide variety of information about each parcel of real estate. These records are crucial in establishing official ownership, giving notice of encumbrances and establishing priority of liens, thereby protecting the interests of real estate owners, taxing bodies, creditors and the general public. The real estate recording system includes written documents that affect title such as deeds and mortgages. There are also public records regarding taxes, judgments, probate and marriage that will have a bearing on the title. In Pennsylvania, most records that affect title to real estate are kept in the office of the **recorder of deeds.** Records are also maintained by the county clerk, county treasurer, city clerk and collector and clerks of various courts of record.

Because the records are open to the public, anyone interested in a particular property can review the records to learn about the documents, claims and other interest that affect its ownership. A prospective purchaser, for example, needs to be sure that the seller can convey title to the property as well as what liens and other encumbrances exist. By examining the public records before settlement, the purchaser can ascertain that he or she will receive good title and that any debts secured by liens will be properly accounted for at the settlement.

Recording

Recording is the act of placing documents in public record. All documents affecting any estate, right, title or interest in land *must be recorded in the county where the land is located* to serve as public notice. Everyone interested in the title to a parcel of real estate can discover the various interests of all other parties. Because documents are readily available, a person can examine the *kind and condition* of the title before taking ownership, and this can be done each time the property changes hands. From a practical point of view, the recording acts give legal priority to those interests that are recorded first.

In Pennsylvania, to be *eligible for recording,* a document must be in writing, be signed by the person executing it and be acknowledged. Individuals who cannot sign by placing their signatures on a document may sign "by mark," an action that complies with statutory requirements.

Notice

Anyone who has an interest in a parcel of real estate can take certain steps, called giving *notice*, to provide information that makes that interest known to anyone who inquires. **Constructive notice** is the legal presumption that information is available, and by diligent inquiry, an individual can obtain it. Properly recording documents in public record or the physical possession of a property serves as constructive notice to the world of an individual's rights or interest. Because the information is readily available, prospective purchasers or mortgage lenders are responsible for discovering the interests that any others may have in the real estate.

In contrast, **actual notice** means the person has been given the information and actually knows it. (See Figure 10.1.) An individual who has searched the public records and seen the instruments or inspected the property has actual notice, *direct knowledge,* of the information. If an individual can be proved to have *actual knowledge* of information concerning a parcel of real estate, he or she cannot use a lack of *constructive notice,* such as an unrecorded deed or an owner who is not in possession, to justify a claim.

Priorities. Many complicated situations can arise that affect the **priority** of rights. For example, a purchaser may receive a deed and take possession of the property but not record the deed. By taking possession, the purchaser gives constructive notice of an interest in the land. His or her rights would be considered superior to the rights of a purchaser who acquired a deed from the original owner at a later date and recorded the deed. How the courts rule in any situation depends, of course, on the specific facts of the case. These are strictly legal questions that should be referred to an attorney.

Unrecorded Documents

Deeds that are not recorded cannot serve constructive notice of their existence and raise the issues previously mentioned about their impact on future owners. Pennsylvania law provides that a *deed or mortgage may not be effective as later purchasers are concerned,* unless these documents have been *recorded.* Although the condition of the title should be apparent from a search of the public records, an unrecorded deed or mortgage should not necessarily be considered void.

There are also certain types of liens that are not recorded. Real estate taxes and special assessments are direct liens on specific parcels of real estate and do not need to be recorded in the recorder's office. Other liens that are not recorded include inheritance taxes and franchise taxes. These are placed by statutory authority against all real estate owned either by a decedent at the time of death or by a corporation at the time the franchise tax became a lien.

Notice of these liens must be gained from sources other than the recorder's office. Evidence of the payment of real estate taxes, special assessments, municipal utilities and other taxes can be gathered from paid tax receipts and letters from municipalities to provide information about the likelihood of a title being encumbered by these "off the record" liens.

Chain of Title

The **chain of title** is the record of ownership of the property over a period of time. Beginning from the original source, ownership subsequently passes to many individuals. Each owner is linked to the next so that a "chain" is formed.

**Figure 10.1
Notice**

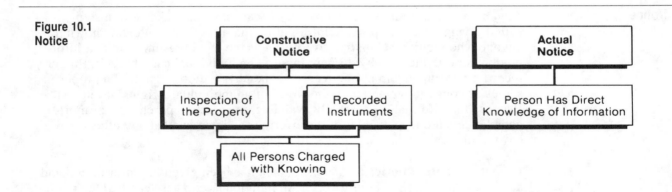

An unbroken chain of title can be traced through linking conveyances from the present owner back to its origin.

If ownership cannot be traced through an unbroken chain, it is said that there is a *gap* in the chain. In such cases it is usually necessary to establish ownership by a court action called a **suit to quiet title.** A suit to quiet title may be required when, for example, a grantor acquired title under one name and conveyed title under a different name or because of a forged deed in the chain, after which no subsequent grantee acquired legal title. All possible claimants to the ownership will be allowed to present evidence during a court proceeding, and then the court's judgment will be filed. The simpler procedure of obtaining any relevant quitclaim deeds may be used to establish ownership.

**Title Search and
Abstract of Title**

A **title search** is an examination of all public records to determine what, if any, defects exist in the chain of title. The records of conveyances of ownership are examined beginning with the present owner. The title is traced back to its origin or 40 to 60 years, depending on local custom or the requirements of a title insurer. The examination is normally performed by an abstractor who, after examining the title records in the recorder of deeds and prothonotary's offices, searches the records in other government offices, such as the tax offices and assessment offices (for sewer or special assessment liens that may be in effect).

An **abstract of title** is a condensed or brief history (in abstract or brief form) of the instruments appearing in the county record that affect title to the real estate in question. The abstractor searches all of the public records and then summarizes the various instruments and proceedings that affect the title throughout its history. The report lists the instruments in chronological order of recording, together with a statement of all recorded liens and encumbrances and their current status. A list of all of the public records that were examined is included as well. The abstract of title will not reveal such items as encroachments or forgeries or any interests or conveyances than have not been recorded.

After the abstractor has completed the abstract, it is submitted to an attorney who *examines the entire abstract.* The attorney must examine each section from the origin of the title to the present to evaluate all facts and material in order to prepare a written report on the condition of the ownership; this report is called an **attorney's opinion of title.**

Marketable Title

Under the terms of the typical real estate agreement of sale, the seller is required to deliver **marketable title** to the buyer at the closing. To be marketable, a title must

- disclose no serious defects and not depend on doubtful questions of law or fact to prove its validity.
- not expose a purchaser to the hazard of litigation or threaten the quiet enjoyment of the property.
- convince a reasonably well-informed and prudent person, acting on business principles and willful knowledge of the facts and their legal significance, that he or she could, in turn, sell or mortgage the property.

Although an unmarketable title (one that does not meet these requirements) may still be transferred, it contains *certain defects that may limit or restrict its ownership*. A buyer cannot be forced to accept a conveyance that is materially different from the one bargained for in the sales contract. Questions of marketable title must be raised by a buyer (or the buyer's attorney) prior to acceptance of the deed. Once a buyer has accepted a deed with unmarketable title, the only available legal recourse is to sue the seller under the covenants of warranty (if any) contained in the deed.

IN PRACTICE...

Normally a title search is not ordered until major contingencies in the agreement of sale have been cleared, such as after a loan commitment has been secured to satisfy a mortgage contingency. A lender will generally require a title search to ascertain the condition of the title and assure the lender that there will be no liens superior to its mortgage lien.

PROOF OF OWNERSHIP

Proper proof of ownership is evidence that title is, in fact, marketable. A deed by itself is not considered sufficient evidence of ownership. Although it conveys the interest of the grantor, even a warranty deed contains no proof of the condition of the grantor's title at the time it is conveyed. The only effective proof is based on the adequate search of the public records to ascertain the ownership interests and condition of the title. Customarily, in Pennsylvania, a buyer can be satisfied that proof of ownership exists by acquiring a certificate of title or title insurance that is based on this search.

Certificate of Title

A **certificate of title** is a statement of opinion of the title's status as of the date it is issued. The certificate is not a guarantee of ownership. Rather it certifies the condition of the title based on the title search. The certificate is prepared by *an attorney,* stating the title owner and the details of all liens and encumbrances against the title. The certificate is the attorney's opinion of the validity of the grantor's or mortgagor's title and the existence of liens and encumbrances.

Although a certificate of title can be used as evidence of ownership, it is not perfect. Based on the public records, it may appear that no other interests in the ownership or claims exist. However, unrecorded liens or rights of parties in possession cannot be discovered. Nor can hidden defects such as forged documents, incorrect marital information, transfers by incompetent parties or minors or fraud be detected. A certificate offers no defense against these defects because they are unknown. The person who prepares the certificate is only liable for negligence in preparing the certificate and only to the extent of his or her personal assets.

Title Insurance

A **title insurance** policy is a contract under which the policyholder is protected from losses arising from defects in the title. A title insurance company will determine if the title is insurable based on a review of the public records. If so, a policy will be issued. Unlike other insurance policies that insure against future losses, title insurance protects the insured from an occurrence before the policy is issued. *Title insurance is considered to be the best defense of title* because the company will defend any lawsuit that is based on an insurable defect and pay claims if the title proves to be defective.

Exactly which defects the title company will defend depends on the type of policy it issues. (See Table 10.1.) A *standard coverage policy* normally insures the title as it is known to exist from the public records plus such hidden defects as forged documents, conveyances by incompetent grantors, incorrect marital statements and improperly delivered deeds. *Extended coverage* as provided by an *American Land Title Association policy* includes the protections of a standard policy plus defects that may be discovered by inspection of the property, such as rights or parties in possession, examination of a survey and certain unrecorded liens. None of these defects are covered by a certificate of title.

Title insurance, however, will not protect against all defects. Obviously a title company will not insure a bad title or defects that can be found in a title search. The policy generally names certain uninsurable losses or *exclusions* such as zoning ordinances, restrictive covenants, easements, certain water rights and current taxes and special assessments.

There are different kinds of policies depending on who is named as the insured. An *owner's policy* is issued for the benefit of the owner and his or her heirs or devisees. A *lender's policy* is issued for the benefit of the mortgagee. In this case, the amount of the coverage is commensurate with the amount of the mortgage loan and coverage decreases as the loan balance is reduced. Because only the lender's interest is insured, it is advisable for the owner to obtain a policy as well. There are also *leasehold* policies to insure a lessee's interests and *certificate of sale* policies for purchasers in a court sale.

Upon completion of the examination, the title company usually issues what may be called a *preliminary report of title* or a *commitment* to issue a title policy. This describes the policy that will be issued and includes

• the name of the insured party;

• the legal description of the real estate;

• the estate or interest covered;

• the conditions and stipulations under which the policy is issued; and

• a schedule of all exceptions, including such items as encumbrances and defects found in the public records and unrecorded defects of which the policyholder has knowledge, rights of parties in possession and questions of survey.

Table 10.1 Owner's Title Insurance Policy	Standard Coverage	Extended Coverage	Not Covered by Either Policy
	1. Defects found in public records	Standard coverage plus defects discoverable through:	1. Defects and liens listed in policy
	2. Forged documents	1. Property inspection including unrecorded rights of persons in possession	2. Defects known to buyer
	3. Incompetent grantors		3. Changes in land use brought about by zoning ordinances
	4. Incorrect marital statements	2. Examination of survey	
	5. Improperly delivered deeds	3. Unrecorded liens not known of by policyholder	

The *premium* for the policy is paid once for the life of the policy. The maximum loss for which the company may be liable cannot exceed the face amount of the policy (unless the amount of coverage has been extended by use of an *inflation rider*). When a title company makes a payment to settle a claim covered by a policy, the company acquires the right of **subrogation** to all the remedies and rights of the insured party against anyone responsible for the settled claim.

IN PRACTICE... *When buyers depend on mortgage loans to finance their purchases, the lender normally requires the purchase of a title insurance policy. Buyers should be aware that their interests also should be insured along with the lenders'. Because title defects can be costly, title insurance provides valuable protection and should be considered even when it is not required. Title insurance is more commonly used as proof of ownership than a certificate of title.*

UNIFORM COMMERCIAL CODE

The **Uniform Commercial Code** (UCC) is a commercial law statute that has been adopted, wholly or in part, in all states to govern personal property transactions. Although this code generally does not apply directly to real estate, it does govern documents when *personal* property is used as security for a loan.

For a lender to create a security interest, including chattels that will become fixtures, the code requires the borrower to sign a **security agreement.** It must contain a complete description of the items against which the lien applies. A short notice of this agreement, called a **financing statement** or UCC-1, which includes the legal description of the real estate involved, must be filed in the recorder's office where mortgages are recorded. The recording of the financing statement constitutes notice to subsequent purchasers and lenders of the security interest in personal property and fixtures on the real estate. Many lenders require the signing of a security agreement and the recording of a financing statement when the real estate includes chattels or readily removable fixtures (washers, dryers and the like) as part of the security for the mortgage debt. If the borrower defaults, then the creditor can repossess the chattels and remove them from the property.

•   •   •   •   •   •   •

KEY TERMS
abstract of title
actual notice
attorney's opinion of title
certificate of title
chain of title
constructive notice
financing statement
marketable title
priority

recorder of deeds
recording
security agreement
subrogation
suit to quiet title
title insurance
title search
Uniform Commercial Code

SUMMARY
The purpose of the recording acts is to give legal, public and constructive notice to the world of parties' interests in real estate. The recording provisions have been adopted to create system and order in the transfer of real estate. Without them, it would be virtually impossible to transfer real estate from one party to another. The interests and rights of the various parties in a particular parcel of land must be recorded so that such rights will be legally effective against third parties who do not have knowledge or notice of the rights.

Possession of real estate is generally interpreted as notice of the rights of the person in possession. Actual notice is knowledge acquired directly and personally.

Title evidence shows whether or not a seller is conveying marketable title. A deed of conveyance is evidence that a grantor has conveyed his or her interest in land, but it is not evidence of the kind or condition of the title. The purpose of a deed is to transfer a grantor's interest in real estate to a grantee. It does not prove that the grantor has any interest at all, even if he or she conveys the interest by means of a warranty deed that carries with it the implied covenants of warranty. Marketable title is generally one that is so free from significant defects that the purchaser can be assured against having to defend the title.

There are two forms of proof of ownership commonly used in Pennsylvania: certificate of title and title insurance policy. Each form bears a date and is evidence up to and including that date. All forms of title evidence show the previous actions that affect the title.

Under the Uniform Commercial Code (UCC), security interests in chattels must be recorded using a security agreement and financing statement. The recording of a financing statement gives notice to purchasers and lenders of the security interests in chattels and fixtures on the specific parcel of real estate.

Questions

1. Public records may be inspected by
   a. anyone.
   b. attorneys and abstractors only.
   c. attorneys, abstractors and real estate licensees only.
   d. anyone who obtains a court order under the Freedom of Information Act.

2. Which of the following statements *best* explains why instruments affecting real estate are recorded?
   a. Recording gives constructive notice to the world of the rights and interests in a particular parcel of real estate.
   b. The law requires that such instruments be recorded.
   c. The instruments must be recorded to comply with the terms of the Statute of Frauds.
   d. Recording proves the execution of the instrument.

3. A purchaser checked the public records and learned that the seller was the grantee in the last recorded deed and that no mortgage was on record against the property. Thus, the purchaser may assume which of the following?
   a. All taxes are paid and no judgments are outstanding.
   b. The seller has good title.
   c. The seller did not mortgage the property.
   d. No one else is occupying the property.

4. The date and time a document was recorded establish which of the following?
   a. Priority of liens or title
   b. Chain of title
   c. Subrogation
   d. Marketable title

5. *P* bought *L*'s house, received a deed and moved into the residence but neglected to record the document. One week later *L* died, and his heirs in another city, unaware that the property had been sold, conveyed title to *M,* who recorded the deed. Who owns the property?
   a. *P*   c. *L*'s heirs
   b. *M*   d. Both *P* and *M*

6. If a property has encumbrances, it
   a. cannot be sold.
   b. can be sold only if title insurance is provided.
   c. cannot have a deed recorded without a survey.
   d. can be sold if a buyer agrees to take it subject to the encumbrances.

7. *Chain of title* refers to which of the following?
   a. A summary or history of all instruments and legal proceedings affecting a specific parcel of land
   b. A series of links measuring 7.92 inches each
   c. An instrument or document that protects the insured parties (subject to specific exceptions) against defects in the examination of the record and hidden risks such as forgeries, undisclosed heirs, errors in the public records and so forth
   d. The succession of conveyances from some starting point whereby the present owner derives title

8. Evidence of the kind of estate and all liens against a parcel of real estate can usually be proven by
   a. a recorded deed.
   b. a court suit for specific performance.
   c. one of the forms of proof of ownership.
   d. a foreclosure suit.

9. The person who prepares an abstract of title for a parcel of real estate
   a. writes a brief history of the title after inspecting the county records for documents affecting the title.
   b. insures the condition of the title.
   c. inspects the property.
   d. issues a certificate of title.

10. S is frantic because she cannot find her deed and now wants to sell the property. She
    a. may need a suit to quiet title.
    b. will have to buy title insurance.
    c. does not need the deed in order to sell if it was recorded.
    d. should execute a replacement deed to herself.

11. When a title insurance policy is being issued, the public records are searched and the title company's record of title is continued to date. When the title examination is completed, the title company notifies the parties in writing of the condition of the title. This notification is referred to as a/an
    a. chain of title.
    b. report of title or commitment for title insurance.
    c. certificate of title.
    d. abstract.

12. When a claim is settled by a title insurance company, the company acquires all rights and claims of the insured against any other person who is responsible for the loss. This is called
    a. escrow.
    b. abstract of title.
    c. subordination.
    d. subrogation.

13. A title insurance policy with standard coverage generally covers all but which of the following?
    a. Forged documents
    b. Incorrect marital statements
    c. Rights of parties in possession
    d. Incompetent grantors

14. The documents referred to as title evidence include
    a. title insurance.
    b. warranty deeds.
    c. security agreements.
    d. abstract of title.

15. To give notice of a security interest in personal property items, a lienholder must record which of the following?
    a. Security agreement
    b. Financing statement
    c. Chattel agreement
    d. Quitclaim deed

Principles of Real Estate Contracts

11

CONTRACT LAW

Many types of contracts and agreements are used in the real estate business. Although the purpose of the contracts and their specific terms and conditions vary, they all have one thing in common: they are governed by a general body of law known as *contract law*. A **contract** is a voluntary agreement or promise between legally competent parties to perform or refrain from performing some legal act, which is supported by legal consideration. Contract law sets forth certain basic rules or principles for forming a contract or agreement between the parties.

Depending on the situation and the nature or language of the agreement, a contract may be categorized in several ways.

Express and Implied Contracts

A contract may be express or implied depending on how it is created. An **express contract** exists when the parties state the terms and show their intentions in words. An express contract may be either oral or written. The majority of real estate contracts are express contracts, having been reduced to writing. According to the Statute of Frauds, contracts for conveyances of real estate must be in writing to be enforceable (to force performance) in a court of law. In an **implied contract,** the agreement of the parties is demonstrated by their acts and conduct. The restaurant patron who orders a meal has implied a promise to pay for the food.

Bilateral and Unilateral Contracts

Contracts also may be classified as either bilateral or unilateral. In a **bilateral contract,** both parties to the contract promise to do something; one promise is given in exchange for another. "I will do this, *and* you will do that." "Okay." A real estate sales contract is a bilateral contract, because the seller promises to sell a parcel of real estate and deliver title to the property to the buyer, who promises to pay a certain sum of money for the property.

A **unilateral contract,** however, is a one-sided agreement. One party makes a promise to induce a second party to do something. The second party is not legally obligated to act; however, if the second party does comply, the first party is obligated to keep the promise. "I will do this *if* you will do that." For

Table 11.1 Legal Effects of Contracts	Classification of Contract	Legal Effect	Example
	Valid	Binding and enforceable on both parties	Agreement complying with essentials of a valid contract
	Void	No legal effect	Contract for an illegal purpose
	Voidable	Valid, but may be disaffirmed by one party	Contract with a minor

example, a law enforcement agency might offer a monetary payment to anyone who can aid in the capture of a criminal. The reward is paid only if someone *does* aid in the capture. An option, which will be discussed later, is another example of a unilateral contract.

Executed and Executory Contracts

A contract may be classified as either executed or executory, depending on whether the agreement is completely performed. An **executed contract** is one in which all parties have fulfilled their promises and thus performed the contract. This usage is not to be confused with the verb, *execute*, which refers to *signing* a contract. An **executory contract** exists when something remains to be done by one or both parties. An agreement of sale is an executory contract from the time it is signed until closing, at which time it is said to be executed.

Validity of Contracts

A contract can be described as valid, void, voidable or unenforceable (see Table 11.1), depending on the circumstances.

A contract is **valid** when it meets all the essential requirements of a contract that make it legally sufficient to be enforceable.

A contract is **void** when it has no legal force or effect because it does not have all the essential elements of a contract. One of the essential requirements for a contract to be considered valid is that it be for a legal purpose; thus, a contract that violates a law is void.

A contract that is **voidable** appears on the surface to be valid but may be rescinded or disaffirmed by one of the parties (in some cases, both parties), based on some legal principle. Consider the requirement that contracts must be entered into by legally competent parties: A contract with a minor is usually voidable because legal age to contract in Pennsylvania is 18. Generally, a minor is permitted to disaffirm or negate a real estate contract at any time while under age and for a certain period of time after reaching majority age. A voidable contract will be considered by the courts to be a valid contract if the party who has the option to disaffirm the agreement does not do so within a prescribed period of time. Note that the contract is voidable only by the minor, not by a person of majority age who enters into the contract with the minor.

A contract that is **unenforceable** also seems on the surface to be valid; however, neither party can sue the other to force performance. Because of the requirements of the Statute of Frauds, oral real estate contracts are unenforceable.

**Figure 11.1
Offer and
Acceptance**

This means that if either party does not comply with the terms of the contract, the other party is unable to sue to force the defaulting party to perform. The defaulting party, however, could be sued for damages the other party suffered because of the default. Oral contracts are said to be "valid as between the parties," because once the agreement is fully performed, neither has reason to sue for performance.

ESSENTIALS OF A VALID CONTRACT

A contract must meet certain minimum requirements including a *date* to be considered legally valid. Under contract law the following are the fundamentals that are essential for a valid contract.

Offer and Acceptance

There must be an offer by one party, the *offeror,* that is accepted by the other, the *offeree*. This requirement, also called *mutual assent,* means that there must be a "meeting of the minds." Courts look to the objective intent of the parties to determine if they intended to enter into a binding agreement. In cases where the Statute of Frauds applies, the offer and acceptance must be in writing. The wording of the contract must express all the agreed-on terms and it must be clearly understood by the parties. (See Figure 11.1.)

An **offer** is a promise made by one party with the request for something that is the agreed exchange for that promise. The offer is made with the intention that the offeror will be bound to the terms if the offer is accepted. The terms of the offer must be definite and specific, and the offer must be communicated to the offeree.

An **acceptance** is the promise by the offeree to be bound to the *exact* terms proposed by the offeror. The acceptance must be communicated to the offeror. Proposing any deviation from the terms of the offer constitutes a rejection of the original offer and becomes a new offer. This is known as a **counteroffer,** which must be communicated to the original offering party and accepted for a contract to exist. (See Figure 11.2.)

Besides being terminated by a counteroffer, an offer terminates in several other ways. The offer may terminate if the offeree flatly rejects it or if the offeree fails to accept the offer within the prescribed period of time stipulated in the offer. Also, the offeror may revoke the offer at any time prior to receipt of the acceptance. This *revocation* must be communicated directly to the offeree by the

**Figure 11.2
Counteroffer and
Acceptance**

Acceptance

Counteroffer

Offer

Buyer   Seller

offeror. The offer is also revoked if the offeree learns of the revocation and observes the offeror act in a manner that indicates that the offer no longer exists.

Consideration

The contract must be based on consideration. **Consideration** is something of legal value offered by one party and accepted by another as an inducement to act or to refrain from some act. There must be a definite statement of consideration in a contract to evidence that something of value was given in exchange for the promise made. Consideration is referred to as that which is "good or valuable" between the parties. The courts do not inquire into the adequacy or kind of consideration. It does not have to be money. A promise that has been bargained for and exchanged is legally sufficient as long as there has been no undue influence or fraud.

**Legally
Competent
Parties**

All parties to the contract must have *legal capacity.* That is, they must be of legal age and have sufficient mental capacity to understand the nature or consequences of their actions in the contract. In most states, 18 is the age of contractual capacity. As previously discussed, a minor may disaffirm a contract, which would result in the contract's not being enforceable. A contract by a party who has been judged insane is void, and it may be void*able* once the individual is judged capable to contract. Mental capacity is not the same as medical sanity.

**Legality of
Object**

To be valid, a contract must not contemplate a purpose that is illegal or against public policy. A contract, or any provision in it, that violates criminal or civil law will result in all or part of the contract being unenforceable. Parties cannot "mutually agree" to acts that are contrary to law.

**Reality of
Consent**

Even when contracts have all of the basic essentials, they still may be either void or voidable. There are certain circumstances that violate *reality of consent.* A contract must be entered into as the free and voluntary act of each party. That is, each party must be able to make a prudent and knowledgeable decision without undue influence. A mistake, misrepresentation, fraud, undue influence or duress would deprive a person of that ability. If these conditions are present, the contract is voidable by the injured party. If the uninjured party were to sue for breach, the injured party could use lack of voluntary assent as a defense. In cases where unlawful force was used or the fraudulent act was so deceptive that a party entered into a contract that he or she had no intention of signing, the contract could be considered void.

Statute of Frauds

Oral contracts can be just as valid as written contracts as long as the essentials of offer and acceptance, consideration, legal capacity and legality of object are present and there is reality of consent.

In certain circumstances, however, an essential element of a contract *is* that the contract must be in writing to be enforceable. The **Statute of Frauds,** which has been passed in every state, requires that *all contracts for the sale of real estate be in writing* and signed by the seller to be enforceable in a court of law. This statute also applies to certain lease agreements, as was described in Chapter 6. The *parol evidence* rule states that a written contract takes precedence over oral agreements or promises.

The Pennsylvania Real Estate Commission's rules and regulations require that a real estate broker representing a party to a transaction ensure that all such contracts are in writing. As stated in previous chapters, this essentially means that real estate licensees must use written agreements rather than rely on oral ones. As a practical matter, the printed word, as long as it is sufficiently complete and specific, gives all parties written evidence of the rights and responsibilities to which they have agreed, and minimizes the likelihood of controversies.

DISCHARGE OF CONTRACTS

A contract is discharged upon termination of the agreement. The most desirable case is when a contract is terminated because of complete performance, with all terms carried out. This occurs when all parties fulfill the obligations they agreed to when they first entered into the contract. A less desirable way that contracts terminate is because they are breached or broken. This means that one of the parties defaults, leaving the other party to seek remedies because the contract is broken. The following discussion explains various ways contracts are discharged.

Performance of a Contract

Because each party has certain rights and duties to fulfill, it's important to know exactly *when* these acts must be performed so that it's clear precisely when the contract is fulfilled. Many contracts call for a specific time at or by which the agreed-upon acts must be completely performed. In addition, many contracts provide that **time is of the essence.** This means that the contract must be performed within the time limit specified, and any party who has not performed on time will be liable for breach of contract.

When a contract does not specify a date for performance, the acts it requires should be performed within a reasonable time. The interpretation of what constitutes a reasonable time will depend upon the situation. Generally, if the act can be done immediately, such as a payment of money, it should be performed immediately, unless the parties agree otherwise. Courts have sometimes declared contracts to be invalid because they did not contain a time or date for performance.

Assignment and Novation

After a contract has been signed, one party may want to withdraw from the contract without jeopardizing the performance of an agreement. This may be accomplished through either an assignment or a novation.

Assignment refers to a transfer of rights and/or duties under a contract. Generally, rights may be assigned to a third party, the assignee, unless the contract forbids it. Obligations may also be assigned (delegated), but the original obligor, the assignor, remains primarily liable for them unless specifically released from this responsibility. A party to a contract might elect to assign the contract obligations in lieu of defaulting or performing on a contract that is no longer in the party's best interest. Many contracts include a clause that either permits or forbids assignment.

A contract may also be performed by **novation,** the substitution of a new contract. The new agreement may be between the same parties, or a new party may be substituted for either (this is *novation of the parties*). The parties' intent must be to discharge the old obligation. For example, when a real estate purchaser assumes the seller's existing mortgage loan, the lender may choose to release the seller and substitute the buyer as the party primarily liable for the mortgage debt.

Breach of Contract

If one of the parties to a contract defaults, or fails to act, the contract is terminated because it is breached or broken. A **breach of contract** is a violation of any of the terms or conditions without legal excuse, such as when a seller fails to deliver title under the conditions stated in the agreement. The breaching or defaulting party assumes certain burdens, and the nondefaulting party has certain remedies. Normally there are provisions in the contract for these events.

Unless an agreement of sale, for example, specifies otherwise, the buyer may file a **suit for specific performance** to force the seller to convey the property or sue for damages if the seller defaults on the contract. The seller can sue for damages or sue for the purchase price (and tender the deed) if the buyer defaults. Provisions in the agreement of sale may permit the seller to retain the earnest money and all payments from the buyer as *liquidated damages.*

Statute of limitations. State law allows a specific time limit during which parties to a contract may bring legal suit to enforce their rights. In Pennsylvania, the *statute of limitations* is four years from the date the contract is breached. Any party who does not take steps to enforce his or her rights within this statute of limitations may lose them.

Contracts may also be discharged or terminated when any of the following occur:

- *Partial performance* of the terms, along with a written acceptance by the person for whom acts have not been done or to whom money has not been paid

- *Substantial performance*, in which one party has substantially performed on the contract but does not complete all the details exactly as the contract requires (Such performance may be sufficient to force payment with certain adjustments for any damages suffered by the other party.)

- *Impossibility of performance*, in which an act required by the contract cannot be legally accomplished

- *Mutual agreement* of the parties to cancel, which returns the parties to their position prior to the contract, an action requiring that any payments or deposits that were made be returned

- *Operation of law*, as in the voiding of a contract by a minor, as a result of fraud, the expiration of the statute of limitations or a contract's being altered without the written consent of all parties involved

USE OF CONTRACTS IN THE REAL ESTATE BUSINESS

The types of written agreements most commonly used by brokers and salespeople are listing agreements, agreements of sale, option agreements, contracts for deed, leases and escrow agreements. These contracts must be contracts that are written according to the rules and regulations of the Pennsylvania Real Estate Commission. Examples of some of these agreements appear in other chapters in this text.

Contracts are important in the real estate business, but how are they actually drafted? The preparation of legal documents is considered to be a practice of law, and real estate licensees are not authorized to practice law. As a practical matter, however, it is important for licensees to be able to prepare contracts during the course of a transaction. Many states address this dilemma by establishing specific guidelines, whether by agreement between lawyer and real estate associations, by court decision or by statute, regarding the authority of real estate licensees to prepare contracts for their clients and customers. Licensees must use great care in completing contract forms because they, just like attorneys, are liable for injury resulting from errors in the drafting documents.

Preprinted Forms

Preprinted forms are commonly used for real estate contracts because most transactions are basically similar in nature. In Pennsylvania, licensees are permitted to fill-in-the-blanks on certain preprinted documents such as agreements of sale contracts and leases as long as they do not charge a separate fee for completing the forms. A number of preprinted forms prepared by REALTOR® associations and/or bar associations are available, both in hard copy and on computer disk, for licensees to complete. There is no one standard form for an agreement of sale or a lease that is used throughout the state. Their use varies according to local customs and brokers' preferences.

The use of printed forms raises three problems: what to write in the blanks; what printed matter is not applicable in a particular transaction and is to be *ruled out* by drawing lines through the unwanted words; and what additional clauses or agreements (called *riders* or *addenda*) are to be added. The newer forms provide a greater number of alternate provisions, which may be used or ruled out, depending upon what the parties wish to express in their agreement. All changes and additions to the preprinted forms are usually initialed in the margin or on the rider by all parties when the contract is executed.

IN PRACTICE...	*It is essential that both parties to a contract understand exactly what they are agreeing to. Poorly drafted documents, especially those containing extensive legal language, may be subject to various interpretations and lead to litigation. The parties to a real estate transaction should be advised to have agreements of sale and other legal documents examined by their lawyers before signing, to ensure that the agreements accurately reflect their intentions. When preprinted forms do not sufficiently cover special provisions in a transaction, the parties should be encouraged to have an attorney draft a contract that properly covers such provisions.*

Plain Language Act

Many consumers, or anyone who is not trained in law, have difficulty understanding the words that are commonly used in legal documents. The Plain Language Consumer Contract Act in Pennsylvania intends to promote the writing of consumer contracts in plain language. The law is expected to help consumers know their rights and duties to protect them from making contracts they do not understand. Written agreements in which a consumer borrows money, buys, leases or rents personal property, real property or services for cash or on credit for personal, family or household purposes must be written in plain language. Deeds, mortgages, certificates of title and title insurance contracts, documents used by state or federal financial institutions, contracts to buy securities, insurance policies and commercial leases are not covered by the law.

The guidelines for plain language include using short words, sentences and paragraphs and using active verbs. Contracts should not use technical legal terms other than those that are commonly understood, Latin or foreign words and double negatives and exceptions to exceptions in sentences. Words should be defined using commonly understood meanings. There are also guidelines for the type size, spacing, headings and page layout.

Any creditor, lessor or seller who does not comply with the tests of readability defined by the law is liable to the consumer for compensation for loss caused by the violation, statutory damages of up to $100, court costs and attorney fees. Anyone drafting consumer contracts should refer to the law for the specific guidelines and may submit the contracts to the attorney general for preapproval.

● ● ● ● ● ● ● ●

KEY TERMS

acceptance
assignment
bilateral contract
breach of contract
consideration
contract
counteroffer
executed contract
executory contract
express contract
implied contract

novation
offer
Statute of Frauds
suit for specific performance
time is of the essence
unenforceable
unilateral contract
valid
void
voidable

SUMMARY

A contract is defined as a legally enforceable promise or set of promises that must be performed, and if a breach occurs, the law provides a remedy.

Contracts may be classified as express or implied, depending on how they are created. They may also be classified as bilateral, when both parties have obligated themselves to act, or unilateral, when one party is obligated to perform only if the other party acts. In addition, contracts may be classified according to their legal enforceability as valid, void, voidable or unenforceable.

The four essentials of a valid real estate contract are (1) offer and acceptance, (2) consideration, (3) legally competent parties and (4) legality of object. A valid real estate contract must include a description of the property and should be in writing and signed by both parties.

Many contracts specify a time for performance. In any case, all contracts must be performed within a reasonable time. An executed contract is one that has been fully performed. An executory contract is one in which some act remains to be performed.

In a number of circumstances, a contract may be canceled before it is fully performed. Furthermore, in many types of contracts, either of the parties may transfer his or her rights and obligations under the agreement by assignment of the contract or novation (substitution of a new contract).

If either party to a real estate agreement of sale defaults, several alternative actions are available. Contracts usually provide that the seller has the right to declare a sale canceled through forfeiture if the buyer defaults. In general, if either party has suffered a loss because of the other's default, he or she may sue for damages to cover the loss. If the buyer defaults, the seller can sue for the purchase price; if the seller defaults, the buyer can sue for specific performance.

Contracts frequently used in the real estate business include listings, agreements of sale, options, installment contracts (contracts for deed), leases and escrow agreements. Licensees are not authorized to practice law. However, they are authorized by state licensing officials, court decisions and statutes to prepare contracts for their clients and customers in certain circumstances. The use of preprinted forms, provided the licensees have adequate knowledge to understand their provisions, has become common practice. Consumer contracts, including real estate sales agreements and leases, must comply with the Plain Language Act in Pennsylvania.

Questions

1. A legally enforceable agreement under which two parties agree to do something for each other is known as a/an
   a. escrow agreement.
   b. legal promise.
   c. valid contract.
   d. option agreement.

2. *D* drives into a filling station and tops off her gas tank. She is obligated to pay for the fuel through what kind of contract?
   a. Express   c. Oral
   b. Implied   d. Voidable

3. A contract is said to be *bilateral* if
   a. one of the parties is a minor.
   b. the contract has yet to be fully performed.
   c. only one party to the agreement is bound to act.
   d. all parties to the contract are bound to act.

4. During the period of time after a real estate agreement of sale is signed but before title actually passes, the status of the contract is
   a. void.   c. unilateral.
   b. executory.   d. implied.

5. A contract for the sale of real estate that does not state the consideration to be paid for the property and is not signed by the parties is considered to be
   a. voidable.   c. void.
   b. executory.   d. enforceable.

6. The Statute of Frauds requires that a contract must be in writing to be enforceable for
   a. all real estate sales.
   b. all real estate contracts of any sort.
   c. all contracts.
   d. bilateral contracts only.

7. The buyer asked the seller to leave the washing machine. The seller said yes, but the agreement of sale said nothing about the seller's leaving the washing machine and the seller took it with her. The buyer has no right to legal recourse because of the rule of
   a. partial performance.
   b. novation.
   c. undue influence.
   d. parol evidence.

8. A suit for specific performance of a real estate contract asks for
   a. money damages.
   b. a new contract.
   c. a deficiency judgment.
   d. the conveyance of the property.

9. If a real estate sales contract states that time is of the essence and the stipulated date of transfer comes and goes without a closing, the contract is
   a. binding for only 30 more days.
   b. novated.
   c. still valid.
   d. breached.

10. In filling out a sales contract, someone crossed out several words and inserted others. To eliminate future controversy about whether the changes were made before or after the contract was signed, the usual procedure is to

   a. write a letter to each party listing the changes.
   b. have each party write a letter to the other approving the changes.
   c. redraw the entire contract.
   d. have both parties initial or sign and date the margin near each change.

11. Under the Statute of Frauds, contracts for the sale of real estate to be enforceable must be

   a. originated by a real estate broker.
   b. on preprinted forms.
   c. in writing.
   d. accompanied by earnest money deposits.

12. *T* has a contract to buy property but would rather let his friend *M* buy it instead. If the contract allows, *M* can take over *T*'s obligation by the process known as

   a. assignment.
   b. substantial performance.
   c. subordination.
   d. mutual consent.

13. Broker J has found a buyer for *G*'s home. The buyer has indicated in writing his willingness to buy the property for $1,000 less than the asking price and has deposited $5,000 earnest money with broker *J*. *G* is out of town for the weekend, and *J* has been unable to inform him of the signed document. At this point, the buyer has signed a/an

   a. voidable contract.
   b. offer.
   c. executory agreement.
   d. implied contract.

14. Which of the following is *not* one of the essential elements for a valid contract?

   a. Offer and acceptance
   b. Earnest money
   c. Legality of object
   d. Consideration

12 Principles of Real Estate Financing

THE FLOW OF MONEY

Many buyers must borrow money to finance their real estate purchases. Usually borrowers are concerned about getting a loan and making the payments, but they cannot influence the availability or cost of the money. A complex network of organizations and forces in the economy affect the supply of money, its cost and the way financial institutions lend it.

Historically, the national economy is cyclical, growing and shrinking over time. Economists typically watch the gross domestic product (GDP); it is the broadest indicator that shows the strength of the economy. An annual increase of approximately 3 percent in the GDP is generally thought to indicate sound economic growth for healthy industrialized economies. An expanding economy fueled by abnormal increases in the supply of money creates inflation, which drives up the price of goods and services. Left unchecked, inflation can eventually lead to a sharp decline in the economy and stifle growth. The country's monetary policy uses certain checks and balances to help the economy grow in controlled, nondestructive ways. These checks and balances affect the flow of money, including loan availability and interest rates.

Federal Reserve System

The role of the **Federal Reserve System** (also known as "the Fed") is to maintain sound credit conditions, help counteract inflationary and deflationary trends and create a favorable economic climate. The Federal Reserve System divides the country into 12 federal reserve districts, each served by a federal reserve bank. All nationally chartered banks must join the Federal Reserve and purchase stock in its district reserve banks.

The Federal Reserve regulates the flow of money and interest rates in the marketplace indirectly through its member banks by controlling their *reserve requirements* and *discount rates.*

Reserve requirements. The Federal Reserve requires each member bank to keep a certain amount of its assets on hand as reserve funds unavailable for loans or any other use. This requirement was designed primarily to protect customer deposits, but more important, it provides a means of manipulating the flow of cash in the money market.

By increasing its reserve requirements, the Federal Reserve in effect limits the amount of money that member banks can use to make loans, causing interest rates to rise. In this manner the government can slow an overactive economy by limiting the money available for major purchases of goods and services. The opposite is also true: by decreasing the reserve requirements, the Federal Reserve increases the amount of money available for loans, which also causes interest rates to drop.

Discount rates. Federal Reserve member banks are permitted to borrow money from the district reserve banks to expand their lending operations. The interest rate that the district banks charge for the use of this money is called the *discount rate*. This rate is the basis on which the banks determine the percentage rate of interest that they, in turn, charge their loan customers. Theoretically, when the Federal Reserve discount rate is high, bank interest rates are high; therefore fewer loans will be made and less money will circulate in the marketplace. Conversely, a lower discount rate results in lower interest rates, more bank loans and more money in circulation.

The Primary Mortgage Market

Where can a borrower get the money for a mortgage loan? The answer is the **primary mortgage market**, which is made up of the lenders who originate the loans thereby making money available directly to the borrowers. How available is the money and how expensive is it? That depends to a large degree on the what measures the Federal Reserve is instituting to stimulate or cool the economy.

Loans represent investments to lenders and a means of generating income. They gain income from finance charges collected at closing (loan origination fees and discount points) and interest on the loans. The primary investment objective for some lenders is to generate income from the fees charged to originate loans. These lenders then sell the loans to investors, thereby generating funds with which to originate additional loans.

When the Fed's monetary policies make money too expensive to attract borrowers, this disturbs the lenders' investment plans. Lenders insulate themselves by diversifying their cash-producing activities. One way is to generate income by *servicing loans* for other primary lenders or the investors who have purchased the loans. Servicing involves duties such as collecting payments (including insurance and taxes), accounting bookkeeping, preparing insurance and tax records and processing payments of taxes and insurance and following up on loan payment and delinquency. Conversely, some primary lenders look to other lenders or organizations acting as mortgage loan correspondents to service their loans so they can direct their efforts to other income-producing activities.

A number of lenders are active in the primary mortgage market.

- *Thrifts, Savings Institutions and Commercial Banks*—These institutions are also known as *fiduciary lenders* because of their fiduciary obligations to protect and preserve their depositors' funds. Mortgage loans are viewed as secure investments to generate income, which also enables them to pay interest to the depositors. A number of regulatory bodies govern the practices of the fiduciary institutions to protect the depositors' funds.

- *Insurance Companies*—Insurance companies amass large sums of money from the premiums paid by their policyholders. While a certain portion of this money is held in reserve to satisfy claims and cover operating expenses, much of it is invested in profit-earning enterprises, such as long-term real estate loans. Although insurance companies are considered primary lenders, they normally invest in large, long-term loans that finance commercial and industrial properties rather than single-family mortgage loans. Sometimes life insurance companies secure their investments by participation financing, taking equity positions (known as *equity kickers*) in the projects they finance.

- *Credit Unions*—Credit unions are cooperative organizations in which members place money in savings accounts, usually at higher interest rates than other savings institutions offer. In the past, most credit unions made only short-term consumer and home-improvement loans, but in recent years they have branched out to longer-term first and second mortgage loans.

- *Pension Funds*—Pension funds have begun to participate actively in financing real estate projects. Most of the real estate activity for pension funds is handled through mortgage bankers, mortgage brokers and life insurance companies.

- *Investment Group Financing*—Large real estate projects such as high-rise apartment buildings, office complexes and shopping centers are often financed as a joint venture through group financing arrangements such as syndicates, limited partnerships and real estate investment trusts. These complex investment agreements are discussed in a later chapter.

- *Mortgage Banking Companies*—Mortgage banking companies originate mortgage loans with money belonging to insurance companies, pension funds and individuals, as well as with funds of their own. They make loans with the intention of later selling them to investors and receiving a fee for servicing the loans. Mortgage banking companies often serve as middlemen between investors and borrowers. The companies are generally organized as stock companies and are therefore subject to considerably fewer lending restrictions than thrift and savings institutions. Mortgage bankers should not be confused with mortgage brokers.

- *Mortgage Brokers*—Mortgage brokers are not lenders but act as intermediaries in bringing borrowers and lenders together. They locate potential borrowers, process preliminary loan applications and submit the applications to lenders for final approval. Mortgage brokers do not lend money nor do they service loans. They may, however, be affiliated with mortgage banking companies.

IN PRACTICE... | *The Pennsylvania Mortgage Bankers and Brokers Act provides for the regulation and licensing of mortgage bankers and mortgage brokers. The Department of Banking of the Commonwealth issues licenses to mortgage bankers and mortgage brokers. Their activities are governed by the Department of Banking, with certain limited authority for the State Real Estate Commission, when licensed real estate brokers are involved. The Mortgage Bankers and Brokers Act includes requirements for licensure and regulates the activities of these licensees.*

The Secondary Mortgage Market

As mentioned previously, primary lenders often seek investors for the mortgage loans they originate. The **secondary mortgage market** is where loans are bought and sold only after they have been originated. A lender sometimes sells loans to raise immediate funds when it needs more money to meet the mortgage demands in its area. Secondary market activity is especially desirable when money is in short supply because it can stimulate construction as well as mortgage lending. In fact, agencies in the secondary market can play a major role in stimulating the economy when they expand the type of loans they will buy.

When a loan has been sold, the original lender continues to collect the payments from the borrower. The lender then passes the payments along to the investor who has purchased the loan and charges the investor a fee for servicing the loan.

Warehousing agencies purchase a number of mortgage loans, assemble them into packages of loans and sell securities that represent shares in these pooled mortgages to investors. Loans are eligible for sale to the secondary market only when the collateral, borrower and documentation meet certain requirements to provide a degree of safety for the investors. The following are the major warehousing agencies.

Fannie Mae. "Fannie Mae" is a quasi-governmental agency organized as a privately owned corporation that issues its own common stock and provides a secondary market for mortgage loans—conventional as well as FHA and VA loans (discussed in Chapter 20). Fannie Mae will buy a *block or pool* of mortgages from a lender in exchange for *mortgage-backed securities* that the lender may keep or sell. Fannie Mae guarantees payment of all interest and principal to the holder of the securities. (Fannie Mae was formerly known as the Federal National Mortgage Association or FNMA.)

Government National Mortgage Association. The **Government National Mortgage Association (GNMA), "Ginnie Mae,"** exists as a corporation without capital stock and is a division of the U.S. Department of Housing and Urban Development (HUD). GNMA is designed to administer special assistance programs and work with FNMA in secondary market activities. Fannie Mae and Ginnie Mae can join forces in times of tight money and high interest rates through their tandem plan. Basically, the *tandem plan* provides that FNMA can purchase high-risk, low-yield (usually FHA) loans at full market rates, with GNMA guaranteeing payment and absorbing the difference between the low yield and current market prices.

Ginnie Mae also guarantees investment securities issued by private offerors (such as banks, mortgage companies and thrift and savings institutions) and backed by pools of FHA and VA mortgage loans. The *Ginnie Mae pass-through certificate* is a security interest in a pool of mortgages that provides for a monthly "pass-through" of principal and interest payments directly to the certificate holder. These certificates are guaranteed by Ginnie Mae.

Federal Home Loan Mortgage Corporation. The **Federal Home Loan Mortgage Corporation (FHLMC), "Freddie Mac,"** provides a secondary market for mortgages, primarily conventional loans. Freddie Mac has authority to purchase mortgages, pool them and sell bonds in the open market with the mortgages as security. Note, however, that FHLMC does not guarantee payment of Freddie Mac mortgages.

Many lenders use the standardized forms and follow the guidelines issued by Fannie Mae and Freddie Mac; the use of these forms is mandatory for lenders who wish to sell mortgages in these agencies' secondary mortgage market. The standardized documents include loan applications, credit reports and appraisal forms.

MORTGAGE LAW

Mortgage loans are viewed as desirable investments because of the principles of mortgage theory. The borrower, or **mortgagor,** pledges the real estate to the lender, or **mortgagee,** as *security* for the debt. A mortgage is considered a voluntary lien on real estate. That is, the person who borrows money willingly gives the lender certain rights to the property. The lender has both the borrower's personal promise to pay the debt as well as the right to take the property if the borrower fails to meet that obligation.

Some states, known as **title theory** states, recognize that the mortgagor actually gives legal title to the mortgagee. Legal title is returned to the mortgagor only upon full payment of the debt (or performance of some other obligation). In theory, the mortgagee actually owns the real estate until the debt is paid, meanwhile allowing the borrower all the usual rights of ownership. The lender has the right to possession of the real estate and rents from the property immediately upon default by the borrower.

On the other hand, states in which the mortgage is viewed purely as a lien on real property are called **lien theory** states. The mortgage serves as security for the debt or collateral for the loan. If the mortgagor defaults, the lender must foreclose (generally through a court action) to obtain legal title. The property is offered for sale and the funds from the sale are used to pay all or part of the remaining debt. Some states protect the borrower by allowing the defaulting mortgagor to redeem the property during a certain period after the sale. A borrower who fails to redeem within this time period loses the property forever.

Today, a number of states, including Pennsylvania, have modified the strict interpretation of title and lien theories. These *intermediary theory* states allow a lender to take possession of the mortgaged real estate upon default. Pennsylvania, historically, is a title theory state but has adopted a hybrid philosophy. Title theory in Pennsylvania does not mean that the property owner automatically forfeits the real estate upon default of payment. The borrower is entitled to *notice of intention to foreclose* before the lender can file suit and proceed with foreclosure.

Regardless of whether a state follows the title or lien theory, a mortgage is a *security instrument;* the real estate is given as *security* for the payment of a debt, which is represented by a *note*. The mortgagee's interest in the real estate is legally considered *personal property*. This interest can be transferred *only* with a transfer of the debt that the mortgage secures. In reality, the differences between the rights of the parties to a mortgage loan in a lien theory state and a title theory state are more technical than actual.

SECURITY AND DEBT

Generally, any interest in real estate that may be sold may be pledged as security for a debt. The basic principle of the property law, that a person cannot convey greater rights in property than he or she actually has, applies equally to the right to mortgage. Thus, the owner of a fee simple estate can mortgage the fee, and the owner of a leasehold or subleasehold can mortgage that leasehold interest. For example, a large retail corporation renting space in a shopping center may mortgage its leasehold interest to finance some remodeling work.

The owner of a condominium unit can mortgage the fee interest in the condominium apartment. Although the owner of a cooperative interest holds personal rather than real property, it is becoming more acceptable as collateral.

Mortgage Loan Instruments

There are two parts to a *mortgage loan*—the debt itself and the security for the debt. When a property is to be mortgaged, the owner must execute, or sign, two separate instruments:

1. The **note,** or *financing instrument,* is the personal promise to repay a debt according to agreed-on terms. The note exposes all of the borrower's assets to the claim by creditors. The mortgagor executes one or more promissory notes to total the amount of the debt.

2. The **mortgage,** or *security instrument,* is the document that creates the lien on the property. The mortgage exposes the real estate to claim by the creditor and is the document on which the lender would sue for foreclosure.

Hypothecation is the term used to describe the pledging of property as security for payment of a loan without surrendering possession of the property. A pledge of security—a mortgage—cannot be legally effective unless there is a debt to secure. Both note and mortgage must be executed to create an enforceable mortgage loan.

Deeds of trust. In some areas of the country and in certain situations, lenders prefer to use a three-party instrument known as a **deed of trust,** or a *trust deed,* rather than a mortgage document. In Pennsylvania, however, deeds of trust are rarely used. A trust deed conveys "naked title" (title without the right of possession) to the real estate as security for the loan to a third party, called the *trustee.* The trustee then holds title on behalf of the lender, known as the *beneficiary,* who is the legal owner and holder of the note. The wording of the conveyance sets forth actions that the trustee may take if the borrower, usually known as the trustor, defaults on any of the terms. (See Figure 12.1 for a comparison of mortgages and trust deeds.) Foreclosure procedures for defaulted trust deeds are usually simpler and faster than those for mortgage loans.

PROVISIONS OF THE NOTE

In general, a promissory note executed by a borrower (known as the maker or payor) states the amount of the debt, the time and method of payment and the rate of interest. If the note is used with a mortgage, it names the lender (mortgagee) as the payee; if it is used with a trust deed, the note may be made payable to the bearer. The note may also refer to or repeat several of the clauses that appear in the mortgage document. The note, like the mortgage, should be signed by all parties who have an interest in the property. Figure 12.2 is an example of a note commonly used with a mortgage and is one of the standard forms used by lenders who may want to sell the loan to Fannie Mae or Freddie Mac.

A note is a **negotiable instrument,** like checks or bank drafts. The holder, the payee, may transfer the right to receive payment to a third party, either by signing the instrument over (assigning it) to the third party or, in some cases, by merely delivering the instrument to that person. Because a note is a negotiable instrument, a mortgage lender may sell or transfer it to the secondary mortgage market.

Interest

A charge for the use of money is called **interest.** Interest may be due either at the end of each payment period (known as interest in arrears) or at the beginning of each payment period (interest in advance). Whether interest is charged in arrears or in advance is specified in the note. In practice, the distinction becomes important if the property is sold before the debt is repaid in full, as will become evident when closings are discussed in a later chapter.

Usury. To protect consumers from unscrupulous lenders who charge unreasonably high interest rates, many states have enacted laws limiting the interest rate that may be charged on loans. In some states, the legal maximum rate is a fixed amount. In others, it is a floating interest rate, which is adjusted up or down at specific intervals based on a certain economic standard, such as the prime lending rate or the rate of return on government bonds.

Whichever approach is taken, charging interest in excess of the maximum rate is called **usury,** and lenders are penalized for making usurious loans. In some states, a lender who makes a usurious loan will be permitted to collect the borrowed money, but only at the legal rate of interest. In other states, a usurious lender may lose the right to collect any interest or may lose the entire amount of the loan in addition to the interest. Loans made to corporations are generally exempt from usury laws. There is a broad exemption from state usury laws for residential mortgage loans made by federally chartered institutions or insured or guaranteed by a federal agency. In effect, state usury laws apply to private lenders.

Loan origination fee. When a mortgage is originated, a **loan origination fee,** or *loan fee,* is charged by most lenders for generating the loan. Loan origination fees are not prepaid interest; they are an expense that must be paid to the lender. The typical fee is 1 percent of the loan amount. An additional service charge based on a percentage of the loan amount, termed *prepaid interest,* may also be included in the origination fee.

Prepayment

When a loan is paid in installments over a long-term, the total interest paid by the borrower can be larger than the principal of the loan. If the borrower repays the loan before the end of the term, the lender will collect less interest. For this reason, some mortgage notes contain a *prepayment clause.* This clause requires

**Figure 12.1
Mortgages**

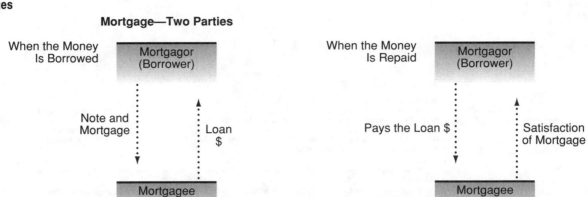

the borrower to pay a **prepayment penalty** against the unearned portion of the interest for any payments made ahead of schedule.

Pennsylvania law, however, does not permit such penalties to be charged on residential mortgage loan prepayments when the principal amount is $50,000 or less. In addition, lenders are prohibited from charging prepayment penalties on mortgage loans insured or guaranteed by the federal government.

Payment Plans

Most mortgage loans are **amortized loans.** Regular payments are made over a term of 15 to 30 years, with each payment being applied first to the interest owed and the balance to the principal amount. At the end of the term, the full amount of the principal and all interest due will be reduced to zero. Such loans are also called *direct reduction loans*. Most amortized mortgage loans are paid in monthly installments; some, however, are payable quarterly or semiannually. The payments may be computed based on a number of payment plans, which tend alternately to gain and lose favor with lenders and borrowers as the cost and availability of mortgage money fluctuates. While these are commonly referred to as "mortgages," they actually are *loans* that are secured by a mortgage.

Fully amortized loan. The most frequently used plan, the *fully amortized mortgage loan,* requires the mortgagor to pay a *constant amount,* usually monthly. This is also referred to as a *level payment* loan. The mortgagee credits each payment first to the interest due, then applies the balance to reduce the principal of the loan. Thus, while each payment is the same, the portion applied toward repayment of the principal grows, because the portion applied to interest declines as the unpaid balance of the loan is reduced. The loan can be amortized more rapidly, unless prohibited by the note (lock-in clause), by paying additional amounts that are applied directly to the principal. This results in less interest dollars being paid because the loan is paid off before the end of its term.

Figure 12.2
Note (Used with
Mortgage)

NOTE

...., 19..........   ...., ...
                                                                          [City]   [State]

....
                                          [Property Address]

1. BORROWER'S PROMISE TO PAY

In return for a loan that I have received, I promise to pay U.S. $....................................... (this amount is called
"principal"), plus interest, to the order of the Lender. The Lender is ....
.... I understand
that the Lender may transfer this Note. The Lender or anyone who takes this Note by transfer and who is entitled to
receive payments under this Note is called the "Note Holder."

2. INTEREST

Interest will be charged on unpaid principal until the full amount of principal has been paid. I will pay interest at a
yearly rate of ....%.

The interest rate required by this Section 2 is the rate I will pay both before and after any default described in
Section 6(B) of this Note.

3. PAYMENTS

(A) Time and Place of Payments

I will pay principal and interest by making payments every month.

I will make my monthly payments on the .... day of each month beginning on ....,
19......... I will make these payments every month until I have paid all of the principal and interest and any other charges
described below that I may owe under this Note. My monthly payments will be applied to interest before principal. If, on
...., ..., I still owe amounts under this Note, I will pay those amounts in full on that date,
which is called the "maturity date."

I will make my monthly payments at ....
.... or at a different place if required by the Note Holder.

(B) Amount of Monthly Payments

My monthly payment will be in the amount of U.S. $..

4. BORROWER'S RIGHT TO PREPAY

I have the right to make payments of principal at any time before they are due. A payment of principal only is
known as a "prepayment." When I make a prepayment, I will tell the Note Holder in writing that I am doing so.

I may make a full prepayment or partial prepayments without paying any prepayment charge. The Note Holder
will use all of my prepayments to reduce the amount of principal that I owe under this Note. If I make a partial
prepayment, there will be no changes in the due date or in the amount of my monthly payment unless the Note Holder
agrees in writing to those changes.

5. LOAN CHARGES

If a law, which applies to this loan and which sets maximum loan charges, is finally interpreted so that the interest
or other loan charges collected or to be collected in connection with this loan exceed the permitted limits, then: (i) any
such loan charge shall be reduced by the amount necessary to reduce the charge to the permitted limit; and (ii) any sums
already collected from me which exceeded permitted limits will be refunded to me. The Note Holder may choose to make
this refund by reducing the principal I owe under this Note or by making a direct payment to me. If a refund reduces
principal, the reduction will be treated as a partial prepayment.

6. BORROWER'S FAILURE TO PAY AS REQUIRED

(A) Late Charge for Overdue Payments

If the Note Holder has not received the full amount of any monthly payment by the end of .... calendar
days after the date it is due, I will pay a late charge to the Note Holder. The amount of the charge will be ....% of my
overdue payment of principal and interest. I will pay this late charge promptly but only once on each late payment.

(B) Default

If I do not pay the full amount of each monthly payment on the date it is due, I will be in default.

(C) Notice of Default

If I am in default, the Note Holder may send me a written notice telling me that if I do not pay the overdue amount
by a certain date, the Note Holder may require me to pay immediately the full amount of principal which has not been paid
and all the interest that I owe on that amount. That date must be at least 30 days after the date on which the notice is
delivered or mailed to me.

(D) No Waiver By Note Holder

Even if, at a time when I am in default, the Note Holder does not require me to pay immediately in full as described
above, the Note Holder will still have the right to do so if I am in default at a later time.

(E) Payment of Note Holder's Costs and Expenses

If the Note Holder has required me to pay immediately in full as described above, the Note Holder will have the
right to be paid back by me for all of its costs and expenses in enforcing this Note to the extent not prohibited by applicable
law. Those expenses include, for example, reasonable attorneys' fees.

7. GIVING OF NOTICES

Unless applicable law requires a different method, any notice that must be given to me under this Note will be given
by delivering it or by mailing it by first class mail to me at the Property Address above or at a different address if I give the
Note Holder a notice of my different address.

Any notice that must be given to the Note Holder under this Note will be given by mailing it by first class mail to the
Note Holder at the address stated in Section 3(A) above or at a different address if I am given a notice of that different
address.

MULTISTATE FIXED RATE NOTE—Single Family—FNMA/   UNIFORM INSTRUMENT   Form 3200 12/83

**Figure 12.2
(continued)**

8. OBLIGATIONS OF PERSONS UNDER THIS NOTE

If more than one person signs this Note, each person is fully and personally obligated to keep all of the promises made in this Note, including the promise to pay the full amount owed. Any person who is a guarantor, surety or endorser of this Note is also obligated to do these things. Any person who takes over these obligations, including the obligations of a guarantor, surety or endorser of this Note, is also obligated to keep all of the promises made in this Note. The Note Holder may enforce its rights under this Note against each person individually or against all of us together. This means that any one of us may be required to pay all of the amounts owed under this Note.

9. WAIVERS

I and any other person who has obligations under this Note waive the rights of presentment and notice of dishonor. "Presentment" means the right to require the Note Holder to demand payment of amounts due. "Notice of dishonor" means the right to require the Note Holder to give notice to other persons that amounts due have not been paid.

10. UNIFORM SECURED NOTE

This Note is a uniform instrument with limited variations in some jurisdictions. In addition to the protections given to the Note Holder under this Note, a Mortgage, Deed of Trust or Security Deed (the "Security Instrument"), dated the same date as this Note, protects the Note Holder from possible losses which might result if I do not keep the promises which I make in this Note. That Security Instrument describes how and under what conditions I may be required to make immediate payment in full of all amounts I owe under this Note. Some of those conditions are described as follows:

Transfer of the Property or a Beneficial Interest in Borrower. If all or any part of the Property or any interest in it is sold or transferred (or if a beneficial interest in Borrower is sold or transferred and Borrower is not a natural person) without Lender's prior written consent, Lender may, at its option, require immediate payment in full of all sums secured by this Security Instrument. However, this option shall not be exercised by Lender if exercise is prohibited by federal law as of the date of this Security Instrument.

If Lender exercises this option, Lender shall give Borrower notice of acceleration. The notice shall provide a period of not less than 30 days from the date the notice is delivered or mailed within which Borrower must pay all sums secured by this Security Instrument. If Borrower fails to pay these sums prior to the expiration of this period, Lender may invoke any remedies permitted by this Security Instrument without further notice or demand on Borrower.

WITNESS THE HAND(S) AND SEAL(S) OF THE UNDERSIGNED.

....(Seal)
-Borrower

....(Seal)
-Borrower

....(Seal)
-Borrower

[Sign Original Only]

172 Modern Real Estate Practice in Pennsylvania

MATH CONCEPT
Interest and Principal Credited from Amortized Payments

A lender charges a borrower a certain percentage of the principal, as interest, for each year the debt is outstanding. The amount of interest due on any one installment payment date is calculated by computing the total yearly interest, based on the unpaid balance, and dividing that figure by the number of payments made each year. For example, if the current outstanding loan balance is $70,000 with interest at the rate of 7½ percent per annum and constant monthly payments of $489.30, the interest and principal due on the next payment would be computed as shown:

$70,000.00		$437.50	month's interest
× .075		12)$5,250.00	
$ 5,250.00	annual interest		
$ 489.30	monthly payment	$70,000.00	principal
− 437.50	month's interest	$ −51.80	month's principal
$ 51.80	month's principal	$69,948.20	new principal balance

This process is followed to calculate the new principal balance after each monthly payment.

The constant payment is determined from a prepared mortgage factor chart. (See Table 12.1.) The chart indicates the amount of monthly payment per $1,000 of loan, depending on the term and interest rate. The factor is multiplied by the number of thousands (and fractions thereof) of the amount being borrowed. Computer programs also are available to calculate payments and show how the loan is amortized as each monthly payment is made.

Straight-line amortized loan. With *straight-line amortization* the mortgagor pays a *different amount for each installment*. Each payment consists of a fixed amount credited toward the principal plus an additional amount for the interest due on the balance of the principal since the last payment.

Straight payment loan. A *straight payment plan* calls for periodic payments of *interest only*, with the principal to be paid in full at the end of the loan term. This is known as a **straight loan,** or *term loan*. Such plans are generally used for home-improvement loans and second mortgages rather than for residential first mortgage loans. Because no principal is repaid during the loan term, the borrower must have sufficient cash to repay the debt at the end of the loan or obtain another loan for the principal.

Prior to the 1930s, the straight loan was the only form available, and the principal was paid after a relatively short-term such as three to five years. The high rate of foreclosure on these loans during the Great Depression prompted amortized loans that are now the norm.

**Table 12.1
Mortgage
Factor Chart**

EQUAL MONTHLY PAYMENT TO AMORTIZE A LOAN OF $1,000

Term Rate	10 Years	15 Years	20 Years	25 Years	30 Years
4	10.13	7.40	6.06	5.28	4.78
4⅛	10.19	7.46	6.13	5.35	4.85
4¼	10.25	7.53	6.20	5.42	4.92
4⅜	10.31	7.59	6.26	5.49	5.00
4½	10.37	7.65	6.33	5.56	5.07
4⅝	10.43	7.72	6.40	5.63	5.15
4¾	10.49	7.78	6.47	5.71	5.22
4⅞	10.55	7.85	6.54	5.78	5.30
5	10.61	7.91	6.60	5.85	5.37
5⅛	10.67	7.98	6.67	5.92	5.45
5¼	10.73	8.04	6.74	6.00	5.53
5⅜	10.80	8.11	6.81	6.07	5.60
5½	10.86	8.18	6.88	6.15	5.68
5⅝	10.92	8.24	6.95	6.22	5.76
5¾	10.98	8.31	7.03	6.30	5.84
5⅞	11.04	8.38	7.10	6.37	5.92
6	11.10	8.44	7.16	6.44	6.00
6⅛	11.16	8.51	7.24	6.52	6.08
6¼	11.23	8.57	7.31	6.60	6.16
6⅜	11.29	8.64	7.38	6.67	6.24
6½	11.35	8.71	7.46	6.75	6.32
6⅝	11.42	8.78	7.53	6.83	6.40
6¾	11.48	8.85	7.60	6.91	6.49
6⅞	11.55	8.92	7.68	6.99	6.57
7	11.61	8.98	7.75	7.06	6.65
7⅛	11.68	9.06	7.83	7.15	6.74
7¼	11.74	9.12	7.90	7.22	6.82
7⅜	11.81	9.20	7.98	7.31	6.91
7½	11.87	9.27	8.05	7.38	6.99
7⅝	11.94	9.34	8.13	7.47	7.08
7¾	12.00	9.41	8.20	7.55	7.16
7⅞	12.07	9.48	8.29	7.64	7.25
8	12.14	9.56	8.37	7.72	7.34
8⅛	12.20	9.63	8.45	7.81	7.43
8¼	12.27	9.71	8.53	7.89	7.52
8⅜	12.34	9.78	8.60	7.97	7.61
8½	12.40	9.85	8.68	8.06	7.69
8⅝	12.47	9.93	8.76	8.14	7.78
8¾	12.54	10.00	8.84	8.23	7.87
8⅞	12.61	10.07	8.92	8.31	7.96
9	12.67	10.15	9.00	8.40	8.05
9⅛	12.74	10.22	9.08	8.48	8.14
9¼	12.81	10.30	9.16	8.57	8.23
9⅜	12.88	10.37	9.24	8.66	8.32
9½	12.94	10.45	9.33	8.74	8.41
9⅝	13.01	10.52	9.41	8.83	8.50
9¾	13.08	10.60	9.49	8.92	8.60
9⅞	13.15	10.67	9.57	9.00	8.69
10	13.22	10.75	9.66	9.09	8.78
10⅛	13.29	10.83	9.74	9.18	8.87
10¼	13.36	10.90	9.82	9.27	8.97
10⅜	13.43	10.98	9.90	9.36	9.06
10½	13.50	11.06	9.99	9.45	9.15
10⅝	13.57	11.14	10.07	9.54	9.25
10¾	13.64	11.21	10.16	9.63	9.34

PROVISIONS OF THE MORTGAGE DOCUMENT

The mortgage document refers to the terms of the note and clearly establishes that the property is security for the debt. It identifies the lender and the borrower and includes an accurate legal description of the property. It should be signed by all parties who have an interest in the real estate. (Figure 12.3 is a sample mortgage.) The document shown is an example of the FNMA/FHLMC uniform instruments, which must be used for the loan to be traded in the secondary mortgage market.

Duties of the Mortgagor

The borrower is required to fulfill many obligations. These usually include the following:

- Payment of the debt in accordance with the terms of the note
- Payment of all real estate taxes on the property given as security
- Maintenance of adequate insurance to protect the lender if the property is destroyed or damaged by fire, windstorm or other hazard
- Maintenance of the property in good repair
- Lender authorization before making any major alterations on the property

Failure to meet any of these obligations—most frequent is failure to meet monthly installments—can result in a borrower's default. The loan documents may provide for a grace period (30 days, for example) during which the borrower can meet the obligation and cure the default. If the borrower does not do so, the lender has the right to foreclose the mortgage and collect on the note.

Provisions for Default

The provisions of a mortgage include an **acceleration clause,** to assist the lender in foreclosure. If a borrower defaults, the lender has the right to accelerate the maturity of the debt that is to declare the *entire* debt due and payable *immediately.* Without the acceleration clause the lender would have to sue the borrower every time a payment was overdue.

Other clauses in a mortgage enable the lender to take care of the property in the event of the borrower's negligence or default. If the borrower does not pay taxes or insurance premiums or make necessary repairs on the property, the lender may step in to protect the security (the real estate). Any money advanced by the lender to cure such defaults is either added to the unpaid debt or declared immediately due and owing from the borrower.

Assignment of the Mortgage

When a note is sold to a third party, the mortgagee will endorse the note to the third party and also execute an *assignment of mortgage*. The assignee becomes the new owner of the debt and security instrument. This assignment must be recorded. Upon payment in full, or satisfaction of the debt, the assignee is required to execute the satisfaction, or release, of the security instrument as discussed in the following section.

Release of the Mortgage Lien

When all mortgage loan payments have been made and the note has been paid in full, the mortgagor wants the public record to show that the debt has been paid and the mortgagee is divested of all rights conveyed under the mortgage.

By the provisions of the **defeasance clause** in the usual mortgage document, the mortgagee is required to execute a **satisfaction** of mortgage, also known as a *release of mortgage,* when the note has been fully paid. This document returns to the mortgagor all interest in the real estate that was conveyed to the mortgagee by the original recorded mortgage document. Entering this release in the public record shows that the mortgage lien has been removed from the property. If the mortgage has been assigned by a recorded assignment, the release must be executed by the assignee/mortgagee.

Tax and Insurance Reserves

Many lenders require borrowers to provide a reserve fund, called an *escrow account,* to meet future real estate taxes and insurance premiums. When the mortgage loan is made, the borrower starts the reserve by depositing funds to cover the amount of unpaid real estate taxes. If a new insurance policy has just been purchased, the insurance premium reserve will be started with the deposit of one-twelfth of the annual insurance premium. Thereafter, the borrower's monthly payments will include principal, interest and tax and insurance reserves (PITI—*P*rincipal, *I*nterest, *T*axes and *I*nsurance). RESPA, the federal Real Estate Settlement Procedures Act (discussed in detail in a later chapter), limits the amount of tax and insurance reserves that a lender may require.

Federal flood insurance program. Property owners in certain areas may be required to obtain flood-damage insurance when financing with loans, grants or guarantees from federal agencies and federally insured or regulated lending institutions. The federal flood insurance program authorized by Congress seeks to improve future management and planning of floodplain areas through land use and control measures.

Assignment of Rents

The borrower may provide for rents to be assigned to the lender upon the borrower's default. The assignment may be included in the mortgage or made as a separate document. In either case, language should clearly indicate that the borrower intends to assign the rents and not merely to pledge them as security for the loan.

Buying Subject to or Assuming a Seller's Mortgage

When a person purchases real estate that has an outstanding mortgage on it, the buyer may take the property *subject to* the mortgage or may *assume* it and agree to pay the debt. This technical distinction becomes important to the seller if the buyer defaults and the mortgage is foreclosed.

When the property is sold *subject to* the mortgage, the courts frequently rule that the buyer is not personally obligated to pay the debt in full. The buyer has taken title to the real estate knowing that he or she must make the payments on the existing loan. Upon default, the lender will foreclose and the property will be sold by court order to pay the debt. If the sale does not pay off the entire debt, the purchaser is not liable for the difference, though the original seller might be.

In contrast, a buyer who purchases the property and *assumes and agrees to pay* the debt becomes personally obligated for the payment of the *entire debt.* If the mortgage is foreclosed and the court sale does not bring enough money to pay the debt in full, a deficiency judgment against both the assumer and the original

**Figure 12.3
Mortgage**

——————————————————————— [Space Above This Line For Recording Data] ———————————————————————

MORTGAGE

THIS MORTGAGE ("Security Instrument") is given on .... ,
19 .... The mortgagor is ....
.... ("Borrower"). This Security Instrument is given to ....
.... , which is organized and existing
under the laws of .... , and whose address is ....
.... ("Lender").
Borrower owes Lender the principal sum of ....
.... Dollars (U.S. $ ....). This debt is evidenced by Borrower's note
dated the same date as this Security Instrument ("Note"), which provides for monthly payments, with the full debt, if not
paid earlier, due and payable on .... This Security Instrument
secures to Lender: (a) the repayment of the debt evidenced by the Note, with interest, and all renewals, extensions and
modifications of the Note; (b) the payment of all other sums, with interest, advanced under paragraph 7 to protect the security
of this Security Instrument; and (c) the performance of Borrower's covenants and agreements under this Security Instrument
and the Note. For this purpose, Borrower does hereby mortgage, grant and convey to Lender the following described property
located in .... County, Pennsylvania:

which has the address of .... , ... ,
                                                            [Street]   [City]
Pennsylvania .... ("Property Address");
                        [Zip Code]

    TOGETHER WITH all the improvements now or hereafter erected on the property, and all easements, appurtenances,
and fixtures now or hereafter a part of the property. All replacements and additions shall also be covered by this Security
Instrument. All of the foregoing is referred to in this Security Instrument as the "Property."

    BORROWER COVENANTS that Borrower is lawfully seised of the estate hereby conveyed and has the right to mortgage,
grant and convey the Property and that the Property is unencumbered, except for encumbrances of record. Borrower warrants
and will defend generally the title to the Property against all claims and demands, subject to any encumbrances of record.

PENNSYLVANIA—Single Family—**Fannie Mae/Freddie Mac UNIFORM INSTRUMENT**   Form 3039   9/90   *(page 1 of 6 pages)*

**Figure 12.3
(continued)**

THIS SECURITY INSTRUMENT combines uniform covenants for national use and non-uniform covenants with limited variations by jurisdiction to constitute a uniform security instrument covering real property.

UNIFORM COVENANTS. Borrower and Lender covenant and agree as follows:

1. Payment of Principal and Interest; Prepayment and Late Charges. Borrower shall promptly pay when due the principal of and interest on the debt evidenced by the Note and any prepayment and late charges due under the Note.

2. Funds for Taxes and Insurance. Subject to applicable law or to a written waiver by Lender, Borrower shall pay to Lender on the day monthly payments are due under the Note, until the Note is paid in full, a sum ("Funds") for: (a) yearly taxes and assessments which may attain priority over this Security Instrument as a lien on the Property; (b) yearly leasehold payments or ground rents on the Property, if any; (c) yearly hazard or property insurance premiums; (d) yearly flood insurance premiums, if any; (e) yearly mortgage insurance premiums, if any; and (f) any sums payable by Borrower to Lender, in accordance with the provisions of paragraph 8, in lieu of the payment of mortgage insurance premiums. These items are called "Escrow Items." Lender may, at any time, collect and hold Funds in an amount not to exceed the maximum amount a lender for a federally related mortgage loan may require for Borrower's escrow account under the federal Real Estate Settlement Procedures Act of 1974 as amended from time to time, 12 U.S.C. § 2601 *et seq.* ("RESPA"), unless another law that applies to the Funds sets a lesser amount. If so, Lender may, at any time, collect and hold Funds in an amount not to exceed the lesser amount. Lender may estimate the amount of Funds due on the basis of current data and reasonable estimates of expenditures of future Escrow Items or otherwise in accordance with applicable law.

The Funds shall be held in an institution whose deposits are insured by a federal agency, instrumentality, or entity (including Lender, if Lender is such an institution) or in any Federal Home Loan Bank. Lender shall apply the Funds to pay the Escrow Items. Lender may not charge Borrower for holding and applying the Funds, annually analyzing the escrow account, or verifying the Escrow Items, unless Lender pays Borrower interest on the Funds and applicable law permits Lender to make such a charge. However, Lender may require Borrower to pay a one-time charge for an independent real estate tax reporting service used by Lender in connection with this loan, unless applicable law provides otherwise. Unless an agreement is made or applicable law requires interest to be paid, Lender shall not be required to pay Borrower any interest or earnings on the Funds. Borrower and Lender may agree in writing, however, that interest shall be paid on the Funds. Lender shall give to Borrower, without charge, an annual accounting of the Funds, showing credits and debits to the Funds and the purpose for which each debit to the Funds was made. The Funds are pledged as additional security for all sums secured by this Security Instrument.

If the Funds held by Lender exceed the amounts permitted to be held by applicable law, Lender shall account to Borrower for the excess Funds in accordance with the requirements of applicable law. If the amount of the Funds held by Lender at any time is not sufficient to pay the Escrow Items when due, Lender may so notify Borrower in writing, and, in such case Borrower shall pay to Lender the amount necessary to make up the deficiency. Borrower shall make up the deficiency in no more than twelve monthly payments, at Lender's sole discretion.

Upon payment in full of all sums secured by this Security Instrument, Lender shall promptly refund to Borrower any Funds held by Lender. If, under paragraph 21, Lender shall acquire or sell the Property, Lender, prior to the acquisition or sale of the Property, shall apply any Funds held by Lender at the time of acquisition or sale as a credit against the sums secured by this Security Instrument.

3. Application of Payments. Unless applicable law provides otherwise, all payments received by Lender under paragraphs 1 and 2 shall be applied: first, to any prepayment charges due under the Note; second, to amounts payable under paragraph 2; third, to interest due; fourth, to principal due; and last, to any late charges due under the Note.

4. Charges; Liens. Borrower shall pay all taxes, assessments, charges, fines and impositions attributable to the Property which may attain priority over this Security Instrument, and leasehold payments or ground rents, if any. Borrower shall pay these obligations in the manner provided in paragraph 2, or if not paid in that manner, Borrower shall pay them on time directly to the person owed payment. Borrower shall promptly furnish to Lender all notices of amounts to be paid under this paragraph. If Borrower makes these payments directly, Borrower shall promptly furnish to Lender receipts evidencing the payments.

Borrower shall promptly discharge any lien which has priority over this Security Instrument unless Borrower: (a) agrees in writing to the payment of the obligation secured by the lien in a manner acceptable to Lender; (b) contests in good faith the lien by, or defends against enforcement of the lien in, legal proceedings which in the Lender's opinion operate to prevent the enforcement of the lien; or (c) secures from the holder of the lien an agreement satisfactory to Lender subordinating the lien to this Security Instrument. If Lender determines that any part of the Property is subject to a lien which may attain priority over this Security Instrument, Lender may give Borrower a notice identifying the lien. Borrower shall satisfy the lien or take one or more of the actions set forth above within 10 days of the giving of notice.

5. Hazard or Property Insurance. Borrower shall keep the improvements now existing or hereafter erected on the Property insured against loss by fire, hazards included within the term "extended coverage" and any other hazards, including floods or flooding, for which Lender requires insurance. This insurance shall be maintained in the amounts and

Form 3039 9/90 *(page 2 of 6 pages)*

**Figure 12.3
(continued)**

for the periods that Lender requires. The insurance carrier providing the insurance shall be chosen by Borrower subject to Lender's approval which shall not be unreasonably withheld. If Borrower fails to maintain coverage described above, Lender may, at Lender's option, obtain coverage to protect Lender's rights in the Property in accordance with paragraph 7.

All insurance policies and renewals shall be acceptable to Lender and shall include a standard mortgage clause. Lender shall have the right to hold the policies and renewals. If Lender requires, Borrower shall promptly give to Lender all receipts of paid premiums and renewal notices. In the event of loss, Borrower shall give prompt notice to the insurance carrier and Lender. Lender may make proof of loss if not made promptly by Borrower.

Unless Lender and Borrower otherwise agree in writing, insurance proceeds shall be applied to restoration or repair of the Property damaged, if the restoration or repair is economically feasible and Lender's security is not lessened. If the restoration or repair is not economically feasible or Lender's security would be lessened, the insurance proceeds shall be applied to the sums secured by this Security Instrument, whether or not then due, with any excess paid to Borrower. If Borrower abandons the Property, or does not answer within 30 days a notice from Lender that the insurance carrier has offered to settle a claim, then Lender may collect the insurance proceeds. Lender may use the proceeds to repair or restore the Property or to pay sums secured by this Security Instrument, whether or not then due. The 30-day period will begin when the notice is given.

Unless Lender and Borrower otherwise agree in writing, any application of proceeds to principal shall not extend or postpone the due date of the monthly payments referred to in paragraphs 1 and 2 or change the amount of the payments. If under paragraph 21 the Property is acquired by Lender, Borrower's right to any insurance policies and proceeds resulting from damage to the Property prior to the acquisition shall pass to Lender to the extent of the sums secured by this Security Instrument immediately prior to the acquisition.

6. Occupancy, Preservation, Maintenance and Protection of the Property; Borrower's Loan Application; Leaseholds. Borrower shall occupy, establish, and use the Property as Borrower's principal residence within sixty days after the execution of this Security Instrument and shall continue to occupy the Property as Borrower's principal residence for at least one year after the date of occupancy, unless Lender otherwise agrees in writing, which consent shall not be unreasonably withheld, or unless extenuating circumstances exist which are beyond Borrower's control. Borrower shall not destroy, damage or impair the Property, allow the Property to deteriorate, or commit waste on the Property. Borrower shall be in default if any forfeiture action or proceeding, whether civil or criminal, is begun that in Lender's good faith judgment could result in forfeiture of the Property or otherwise materially impair the lien created by this Security Instrument or Lender's security interest. Borrower may cure such a default and reinstate, as provided in paragraph 18, by causing the action or proceeding to be dismissed with a ruling that, in Lender's good faith determination, precludes forfeiture of the Borrower's interest in the Property or other material impairment of the lien created by this Security Instrument or Lender's security interest. Borrower shall also be in default if Borrower, during the loan application process, gave materially false or inaccurate information or statements to Lender (or failed to provide Lender with any material information) in connection with the loan evidenced by the Note, including, but not limited to, representations concerning Borrower's occupancy of the Property as a principal residence. If this Security Instrument is on a leasehold, Borrower shall comply with all the provisions of the lease. If Borrower acquires fee title to the Property, the leasehold and the fee title shall not merge unless Lender agrees to the merger in writing.

7. Protection of Lender's Rights in the Property. If Borrower fails to perform the covenants and agreements contained in this Security Instrument, or there is a legal proceeding that may significantly affect Lender's rights in the Property (such as a proceeding in bankruptcy, probate, for condemnation or forfeiture or to enforce laws or regulations), then Lender may do and pay for whatever is necessary to protect the value of the Property and Lender's rights in the Property. Lender's actions may include paying any sums secured by a lien which has priority over this Security Instrument, appearing in court, paying reasonable attorneys' fees and entering on the Property to make repairs. Although Lender may take action under this paragraph 7, Lender does not have to do so.

Any amounts disbursed by Lender under this paragraph 7 shall become additional debt of Borrower secured by this Security Instrument. Unless Borrower and Lender agree to other terms of payment, these amounts shall bear interest from the date of disbursement at the Note rate and shall be payable, with interest, upon notice from Lender to Borrower requesting payment.

8. Mortgage Insurance. If Lender required mortgage insurance as a condition of making the loan secured by this Security Instrument, Borrower shall pay the premiums required to maintain the mortgage insurance in effect. If, for any reason, the mortgage insurance coverage required by Lender lapses or ceases to be in effect, Borrower shall pay the premiums required to obtain coverage substantially equivalent to the mortgage insurance previously in effect, at a cost substantially equivalent to the cost to Borrower of the mortgage insurance previously in effect, from an alternate mortgage insurer approved by Lender. If substantially equivalent mortgage insurance coverage is not available, Borrower shall pay to Lender each month a sum equal to one-twelfth of the yearly mortgage insurance premium being paid by Borrower when the insurance coverage lapsed or ceased to be in effect. Lender will accept, use and retain these payments as a loss reserve in lieu of mortgage insurance. Loss reserve payments may no longer be required, at the option of Lender, if mortgage insurance coverage (in the amount and for the period that Lender requires) provided by an insurer approved by Lender again becomes available

Form 3039   9/90 *(page 3 of 6 pages)*

**Figure 12.3
(continued)**

and is obtained. Borrower shall pay the premiums required to maintain mortgage insurance in effect, or to provide a loss reserve, until the requirement for mortgage insurance ends in accordance with any written agreement between Borrower and Lender or applicable law.

9. Inspection. Lender or its agent may make reasonable entries upon and inspections of the Property. Lender shall give Borrower notice at the time of or prior to an inspection specifying reasonable cause for the inspection.

10. Condemnation. The proceeds of any award or claim for damages, direct or consequential, in connection with any condemnation or other taking of any part of the Property, or for conveyance in lieu of condemnation, are hereby assigned and shall be paid to Lender.

In the event of a total taking of the Property, the proceeds shall be applied to the sums secured by this Security Instrument, whether or not then due, with any excess paid to Borrower. In the event of a partial taking of the Property in which the fair market value of the Property immediately before the taking is equal to or greater than the amount of the sums secured by this Security Instrument immediately before the taking, unless Borrower and Lender otherwise agree in writing, the sums secured by this Security Instrument shall be reduced by the amount of the proceeds multiplied by the following fraction: (a) the total amount of the sums secured immediately before the taking, divided by (b) the fair market value of the Property immediately before the taking. Any balance shall be paid to Borrower. In the event of a partial taking of the Property in which the fair market value of the Property immediately before the taking is less than the amount of the sums secured immediately before the taking, unless Borrower and Lender otherwise agree in writing or unless applicable law otherwise provides, the proceeds shall be applied to the sums secured by this Security Instrument whether or not the sums are then due.

If the Property is abandoned by Borrower, or if, after notice by Lender to Borrower that the condemnor offers to make an award or settle a claim for damages, Borrower fails to respond to Lender within 30 days after the date the notice is given, Lender is authorized to collect and apply the proceeds, at its option, either to restoration or repair of the Property or to the sums secured by this Security Instrument, whether or not then due.

Unless Lender and Borrower otherwise agree in writing, any application of proceeds to principal shall not extend or postpone the due date of the monthly payments referred to in paragraphs 1 and 2 or change the amount of such payments.

11. Borrower Not Released; Forbearance By Lender Not a Waiver. Extension of the time for payment or modification of amortization of the sums secured by this Security Instrument granted by Lender to any successor in interest of Borrower shall not operate to release the liability of the original Borrower or Borrower's successors in interest. Lender shall not be required to commence proceedings against any successor in interest or refuse to extend time for payment or otherwise modify amortization of the sums secured by this Security Instrument by reason of any demand made by the original Borrower or Borrower's successors in interest. Any forbearance by Lender in exercising any right or remedy shall not be a waiver of or preclude the exercise of any right or remedy.

12. Successors and Assigns Bound; Joint and Several Liability; Co-signers. The covenants and agreements of this Security Instrument shall bind and benefit the successors and assigns of Lender and Borrower, subject to the provisions of paragraph 17. Borrower's covenants and agreements shall be joint and several. Any Borrower who co-signs this Security Instrument but does not execute the Note: (a) is co-signing this Security Instrument only to mortgage, grant and convey that Borrower's interest in the Property under the terms of this Security Instrument; (b) is not personally obligated to pay the sums secured by this Security Instrument; and (c) agrees that Lender and any other Borrower may agree to extend, modify, forbear or make any accommodations with regard to the terms of this Security Instrument or the Note without that Borrower's consent.

13. Loan Charges. If the loan secured by this Security Instrument is subject to a law which sets maximum loan charges, and that law is finally interpreted so that the interest or other loan charges collected or to be collected in connection with the loan exceed the permitted limits, then: (a) any such loan charge shall be reduced by the amount necessary to reduce the charge to the permitted limit; and (b) any sums already collected from Borrower which exceeded permitted limits will be refunded to Borrower. Lender may choose to make this refund by reducing the principal owed under the Note or by making a direct payment to Borrower. If a refund reduces principal, the reduction will be treated as a partial prepayment without any prepayment charge under the Note.

14. Notices. Any notice to Borrower provided for in this Security Instrument shall be given by delivering it or by mailing it by first class mail unless applicable law requires use of another method. The notice shall be directed to the Property Address or any other address Borrower designates by notice to Lender. Any notice to Lender shall be given by first class mail to Lender's address stated herein or any other address Lender designates by notice to Borrower. Any notice provided for in this Security Instrument shall be deemed to have been given to Borrower or Lender when given as provided in this paragraph.

15. Governing Law; Severability. This Security Instrument shall be governed by federal law and the law of the jurisdiction in which the Property is located. In the event that any provision or clause of this Security Instrument or the Note conflicts with applicable law, such conflict shall not affect other provisions of this Security Instrument or the Note which can be given effect without the conflicting provision. To this end the provisions of this Security Instrument and the Note are declared to be severable.

16. Borrower's Copy. Borrower shall be given one conformed copy of the Note and of this Security Instrument.

Form 3039   9/90 *(page 4 of 6 pages)*

**Figure 12.3
(continued)**

17. Transfer of the Property or a Beneficial Interest in Borrower. If all or any part of the Property or any interest in it is sold or transferred (or if a beneficial interest in Borrower is sold or transferred and Borrower is not a natural person) without Lender's prior written consent, Lender may, at its option, require immediate payment in full of all sums secured by this Security Instrument. However, this option shall not be exercised by Lender if exercise is prohibited by federal law as of the date of this Security Instrument.

If Lender exercises this option, Lender shall give Borrower notice of acceleration. The notice shall provide a period of not less than 30 days from the date the notice is delivered or mailed within which Borrower must pay all sums secured by this Security Instrument. If Borrower fails to pay these sums prior to the expiration of this period, Lender may invoke any remedies permitted by this Security Instrument without further notice or demand on Borrower.

18. Borrower's Right to Reinstate. If Borrower meets certain conditions, Borrower shall have the right to have enforcement of this Security Instrument discontinued at any time prior to the earlier of: (a) 5 days (or such other period as applicable law may specify for reinstatement) before sale of the Property pursuant to any power of sale contained in this Security Instrument; or (b) entry of a judgment enforcing this Security Instrument. Those conditions are that Borrower: (a) pays Lender all sums which then would be due under this Security Instrument and the Note as if no acceleration had occurred; (b) cures any default of any other covenants or agreements; (c) pays all expenses incurred in enforcing this Security Instrument, including, but not limited to, reasonable attorneys' fees; and (d) takes such action as Lender may reasonably require to assure that the lien of this Security Instrument, Lender's rights in the Property and Borrower's obligation to pay the sums secured by this Security Instrument shall continue unchanged. Upon reinstatement by Borrower, this Security Instrument and the obligations secured hereby shall remain fully effective as if no acceleration had occurred. However, this right to reinstate shall not apply in the case of acceleration under paragraph 17.

19. Sale of Note; Change of Loan Servicer. The Note or a partial interest in the Note (together with this Security Instrument) may be sold one or more times without prior notice to Borrower. A sale may result in a change in the entity (known as the "Loan Servicer") that collects monthly payments due under the Note and this Security Instrument. There also may be one or more changes of the Loan Servicer unrelated to a sale of the Note. If there is a change of the Loan Servicer, Borrower will be given written notice of the change in accordance with paragraph 14 above and applicable law. The notice will state the name and address of the new Loan Servicer and the address to which payments should be made. The notice will also contain any other information required by applicable law.

20. Hazardous Substances. Borrower shall not cause or permit the presence, use, disposal, storage, or release of any Hazardous Substances on or in the Property. Borrower shall not do, nor allow anyone else to do, anything affecting the Property that is in violation of any Environmental Law. The preceding two sentences shall not apply to the presence, use, or storage on the Property of small quantities of Hazardous Substances that are generally recognized to be appropriate to normal residential uses and to maintenance of the Property.

Borrower shall promptly give Lender written notice of any investigation, claim, demand, lawsuit or other action by any governmental or regulatory agency or private party involving the Property and any Hazardous Substance or Environmental Law of which Borrower has actual knowledge. If Borrower learns, or is notified by any governmental or regulatory authority, that any removal or other remediation of any Hazardous Substance affecting the Property is necessary, Borrower shall promptly take all necessary remedial actions in accordance with Environmental Law.

As used in this paragraph 20, "Hazardous Substances" are those substances defined as toxic or hazardous substances by Environmental Law and the following substances: gasoline, kerosene, other flammable or toxic petroleum products, toxic pesticides and herbicides, volatile solvents, materials containing asbestos or formaldehyde, and radioactive materials. As used in this paragraph 20, "Environmental Law" means federal laws and laws of the jurisdiction where the Property is located that relate to health, safety or environmental protection.

NON-UNIFORM COVENANTS. Borrower and Lender further covenant and agree as follows:

21. Acceleration; Remedies. Lender shall give notice to Borrower prior to acceleration following Borrower's breach of any covenant or agreement in this Security Instrument (but not prior to acceleration under paragraph 17 unless applicable law provides otherwise). Lender shall notify Borrower of, among other things: (a) the default; (b) the action required to cure the default; (c) when the default must be cured; and (d) that failure to cure the default as specified may result in acceleration of the sums secured by this Security Instrument, foreclosure by judicial proceeding and sale of the Property. Lender shall further inform Borrower of the right to reinstate after acceleration and the right to assert in the foreclosure proceeding the non-existence of a default or any other defense of Borrower to acceleration and foreclosure. If the default is not cured as specified, Lender at its option may require immediate payment in full of all sums secured by this Security Instrument without further demand and may foreclose this Security Instrument by judicial proceeding. Lender shall be entitled to collect all expenses incurred in pursuing the remedies provided in this paragraph 21, including, but not limited to, attorneys' fees and costs of title evidence to the extent permitted by applicable law.

Form 3039   9/90   *(page 5 of 6 pages)*

**Figure 12.3
(continued)**

22.   Release. Upon payment of all sums secured by this Security Instrument, this Security Instrument and the estate conveyed shall terminate and become void. After such occurrence, Lender shall discharge and satisfy this Security Instrument without charge to Borrower. Borrower shall pay any recordation costs.

23.   Waivers. Borrower, to the extent permitted by applicable law, waives and releases any error or defects in proceedings to enforce this Security Instrument, and hereby waives the benefit of any present or future laws providing for stay of execution, extension of time, exemption from attachment, levy and sale, and homestead exemption.

24.   Reinstatement Period. Borrower's time to reinstate provided in paragraph 18 shall extend to one hour prior to the commencement of bidding at a sheriff's sale or other sale pursuant to this Security Instrument.

25.   Purchase Money Mortgage. If any of the debt secured by this Security Instrument is lent to Borrower to acquire title to the Property, this Security Instrument shall be a purchase money mortgage.

26.   Interest Rate After Judgment. Borrower agrees that the interest rate payable after a judgment is entered on the Note or in an action of mortgage foreclosure shall be the rate payable from time to time under the Note.

27.   Riders to this Security Instrument. If one or more riders are executed by Borrower and recorded together with this Security Instrument, the covenants and agreements of each such rider shall be incorporated into and shall amend and supplement the covenants and agreements of this Security Instrument as if the rider(s) were a part of this Security Instrument. [Check applicable box(es)]

☐ Adjustable Rate Rider	☐ Condominium Rider	☐ 1—4 Family Rider
☐ Graduated Payment Rider	☐ Planned Unit Development Rider	☐ Biweekly Payment Rider
☐ Balloon Rider	☐ Rate Improvement Rider	☐ Second Home Rider
☐ Other(s) [specify]		

BY SIGNING BELOW, Borrower accepts and agrees to the terms and covenants contained in this Security Instrument and in any rider(s) executed by Borrower and recorded with it.

Witnesses:

....(Seal)
                                                                                                —Borrower

                                      Social Security Number..

....(Seal)
                                                                                                —Borrower

                                      Social Security Number..

———————————————— **[Space Below This Line For Acknowledgment]** ————————————————

Form 3039   9/90   *(page 6 of 6 pages)*

borrower (unless the borrower has been released) may be obtained for the unpaid balance of the note.

Before a conventional mortgage may be assumed, most lending institutions require the assumer to qualify financially and charge a transfer fee to cover the costs of changing their records. This charge is customarily borne by the purchaser.

Alienation clause. The lender may want to prevent a future purchaser of the property from being able to assume that loan, particularly at its old rate of interest. For this reason, some lenders include an **alienation clause,** also known as a *resale clause* or *due-on-sale clause,* in the note. An alienation clause provides that, upon the sale of the property, the lender can either declare the entire debt due immediately or permit the buyer to assume the loan at current market interest rates. Some kinds of loans prohibit use of alienation clauses.

Recording Mortgages

The mortgage document must be recorded in the recorder's office of the county in which the real estate is located. Recording gives constructive notice to the world of the borrower's obligations and establishes the lien's priority.

Priority of mortgages and other liens normally is determined by the order in which they were recorded. A mortgage on real estate that has no prior mortgage lien on it is a *first mortgage.* When the owner of this land later executes another loan for additional funds, the new loan becomes a *second mortgage,* or *junior lien,* when recorded. The second lien is subject to the first lien; the first has prior claim to the value of the property pledged as security. Because second loans represent a greater risk to the lender, they are usually issued at higher interest rates.

The priority of mortgage liens may be changed by the execution of a *subordination agreement,* which means that the first lender subordinates its lien to that of the second lender. A subordination agreement must be signed by both lenders to be valid.

IN PRACTICE...

As a condition of granting the mortgage loan, lenders may prohibit a prospective mortgagor from borrowing any portion of the down payment. The possibility of a prior claim on the property—a lien by the person or institution who lent the down payment—can threaten the position of the lender who intended to be the first recorded lien.

FORECLOSURE

When a borrower defaults on the payments or fails to fulfill any of the other obligations set forth in the mortgage, the lender's rights can be enforced through foreclosure. A **foreclosure** is a legal procedure whereby the property that is pledged as security in the mortgage document is sold to satisfy the debt. The foreclosure procedure brings the rights of all parties to a conclusion. It passes title in the subject property to either the person holding the mortgage document or to a third party who purchases the real estate at a *foreclosure sale.* Property is sold *free of the mortgage and all junior liens.*

Methods of Foreclosure

There are three general types of foreclosure proceedings—judicial, nonjudicial and strict foreclosure. The specific provisions of these vary from state to state.

Judicial foreclosure. Judicial foreclosure allows the property pledged as security to be sold by court order after the mortgagee has given sufficient public notice. Upon the borrower's default the lender may *accelerate* the due date of all remaining monthly payments. The lender's attorney can then file a suit to foreclose the lien after the borrower has been informed of the lender's intention. A public sale is advertised and held by the sheriff's office, and the real estate is sold to the highest bidder. This is the prevalent form of mortgage foreclosure in Pennsylvania.

Nonjudicial foreclosure. Other states allow nonjudicial foreclosure procedures to be used when the security instrument contains a *power-of-sale clause*. No court action is required. Notice of default is filed at the county recorder's office within a designated time period to give notice to the public of the intended auction. This official notice is generally accompanied by advertisements published in local newspapers that state the total amount due and the date of the public sale. The purpose of this notice is publicize the sale. After selling the property, the trustee or mortgagee may be required to file a copy of a notice of sale or affidavit of foreclosure. The trustee is generally given the power of sale when deeds of trust are used, although some states permit a similar power of sale to be used with a mortgage loan.

Strict foreclosure. Although the judicial foreclosure procedure is prevalent in Pennsylvania, in some states it is still possible for a lender to acquire the mortgaged property by a strict foreclosure process. After appropriate notice has been given to the delinquent borrower and the proper papers have been prepared and recorded, the court establishes a specific time period during which the balance of the defaulted debt must be paid in full. If this is not done, the court usually awards full legal title to the lender and no sale takes place.

Deed in Lieu of Foreclosure

As an alternative to foreclosure, the lender can accept a **deed in lieu of foreclosure** from the borrower. This is sometimes known as a *friendly foreclosure,* for it is by agreement rather than by civil action. The major disadvantage to this manner of default settlement is that the mortgagee takes the real estate subject to all junior liens, while foreclosure eliminates all such liens.

Redemption

Most states give a defaulting borrower a chance to redeem the property. Historically the right of redemption is inherited from the old common-law proceedings in which the court sale ended the **equitable right of redemption.** Carried over to statutory law, this concept provides that if, during the course of a foreclosure proceeding but *before the foreclosure sale,* the borrower or any other person who has an interest in the real estate (such as another creditor) pays the lender the amount currently due, plus costs, the debt will be reinstated as before. In Pennsylvania, a borrower may cure a default in a residential mortgage loan with an outstanding balance of $50,000 or less by merely bringing the payments up to date.

Certain states, though not Pennsylvania, also allow a defaulted borrower a period in which to redeem the real estate after the foreclosure sale. During this *statutory redemption* period (which may be as long as one year), the court may appoint a receiver to take charge of the property, collect rents, pay operating expenses and so forth. The mortgagor raises the necessary funds to redeem the property within the statutory period and pays the redemption money to the court. Because the debt was paid from the proceeds of the sale, the borrower can take possession free and clear of the former defaulted loan.

Deed to Purchaser at Sale

If redemption is not made or if the law does not provide for a redemption period, the successful bidder at the sale receives a deed to the real estate. This is a statutory form of deed that may be executed by a sheriff or master-in-chancery to convey whatever title the borrower had. The deed does not contain any warranties. Title passes as is, but is free of the former defaulted debt.

Deficiency Judgment

If the foreclosure sale does not produce a sales price sufficient to pay the loan balance in full after deducting expenses and accrued unpaid interest, the mortgagee may be entitled to a *personal judgment* against the borrower for the unpaid balance. Such a judgment is called a **deficiency judgment.** It may also be obtained against any endorsers or guarantors of the note and any owners of the mortgaged property who may have assumed the debt by written agreement. Any surplus proceeds from the foreclosure sale after the debt, all junior liens, expenses and interest are deducted and paid to the borrower after deducting.

KEY TERMS

acceleration clause
alienation clause
amortized loan
deed in lieu of foreclosure
deed of trust
defeasance clause
deficiency judgment
equitable right of redemption
Fannie Mae
Federal Home Loan Morgage Corporation (FHLMC)
Federal Reserve System
foreclosure
Freddie Mac
Ginnie Mae
Government National Mortgage Association (GNMA)

hypothecation
interest
lien theory
loan origination fee
mortgage
mortgagee
mortgagor
negotiable instrument
note
prepayment penalty
primary mortgage market
satisfaction
secondary mortgage market
straight (term) loan
title theory
usury

SUMMARY

The federal government affects real estate financing money and interest rates through the Federal Reserve Board's discount rate and reserve requirements. The primary mortgage market consists of lenders that originate the loans such as thrift and savings institutions, life insurance companies, mortgage banking companies, credit unions, pension funds and investment group financing. Mortgage brokers are instrumental in bringing borrowers and lenders together, but are not lenders themselves.

The secondary market is generally composed of the investors that ultimately purchase and hold the loans as investments. These include insurance companies, investment funds and pension plans. Fannie Mae, Ginnie Mae (Government National Mortgage Association) and Freddie Mac (Federal Home Loan Mortgage Corporation) take an active role in creating a secondary market by regularly purchasing mortgage loans from originators and retaining or warehousing them until investment purchasers are available.

Mortgage loans provide the principal sources of financing for real estate operations. Mortgage loans involve a borrower, called the mortgagor, and a lender, the mortgagee.

Some states recognize the lender as the owner of mortgaged property; these are known as title theory states. Others recognize the borrower as the owner of mortgaged property and are known as lien theory states. Intermediary theory states, such as Pennsylvania, recognize modified versions of these theories.

After a lending institution has received, investigated and approved a loan application, it issues a commitment to make the mortgage loan. The borrower is required to execute a note, agreeing to repay the debt, and a mortgage, placing a lien on the real estate to secure the note. This is recorded in the public record to give notice to the world of the lender's interest.

The note for the amount of the loan usually provides for amortization of the loan. The note also sets the rate of interest at which the loan is made and that the mortgagor must pay as a charge for borrowing the money.

If a state has a "Usury Act" for mortgages, charging more than the maximum interest rate allowed by state statute is called usury and is illegal. The mortgage document secures the debt and sets forth the obligations of the borrower and the rights of the lender. Payment in full of the note by its terms entitles the borrower to a satisfaction, or release, which is recorded to clear the lien from the public records. Default by the borrower may result in acceleration of payments, a foreclosure sale and loss of title.

Questions

1. Which of the following is *not* a participant in the secondary market?
   a. FNMA
   b. GNMA
   c. Fed
   d. FHLMC

2. The person who obtains a real estate loan by signing a note and a mortgage is called the
   a. mortgagor.
   b. beneficiary.
   c. mortgagee.
   d. vendor.

3. The borrower under a deed of trust is known as the
   a. trustor.
   b. trustee.
   c. beneficiary.
   d. vendee.

4. Which of the following is true about a second mortgage?
   a. It has priority over a first mortgage.
   b. It cannot be used as a security instrument.
   c. It is not negotiable.
   d. It is usually issued at a higher rate of interest than a first mortgage.

5. Laws that limit the amount of interest that can be charged to the borrower are
   a. established by the Federal Reserve.
   b. usury laws.
   c. established by the country's monetary policy.
   d. illegal in Pennsylvania.

6. After the foreclosure sale, a borrower who has defaulted on the loan seeks to pay off the debt plus any accrued interest and costs under the right of
   a. equitable redemption.
   b. defeasance.
   c. usury.
   d. statutory redemption.

7. The clause in a note that gives the lender the right to have all future installments become due upon default is the
   a. escalation clause.
   b. defeasance clause.
   c. alienation clause.
   d. acceleration clause.

8. What document is used by the mortgagee to show that the mortgage debt is completely repaid?
   a. A satisfaction
   b. A defeasance certificate
   c. A deed of trust
   d. A mortgage estoppel

9. Which of the following *best* defines the *secondary market?*
   a. Lenders who deal exclusively in second mortgages
   b. Where loans are bought and sold after they have been originated
   c. The major lender of residential mortgage loans
   d. The major lender of government-sponsored loans

10. With a fully amortized mortgage loan
    a. interest may be charged in arrears, meaning at the end of each period for which interest is due.
    b. the interest portion of each payment remains the same throughout the entire term of the loan.
    c. interest only is paid each period.
    d. a portion of principal will still be owed at the end of the term of the loan.

11. Freddie Mac
    a. buys mortgages that are guaranteed by the full faith and credit of the federal government.
    b. buys and pools blocks of primarily conventional mortgages, selling bonds with such mortgages as security.
    c. can tandem with GNMA to provide special assistance in times of tight money.
    d. buys and sells only VA and FHA mortgages.

12. In theory, when the Federal Reserve Board raises its discount rate, all of the following will happen *except*
    a. interest rates will rise.
    b. interest rates will fall.
    c. mortgage money will become scarce.
    d. less money will circulate in the marketplace.

13. A borrower obtains a $76,000 mortgage loan at 7½ percent interest. If the monthly payments of $531.24 are credited first on interest and then on principal, what will the balance of the principal be after the borrower makes the first payment?
    a. $75,468.76   c. $75,943.76
    b. $75,525   d. $70,300

13 Pennsylvania Real Estate Licensing Law

PENNSYLVANIA REAL ESTATE LICENSING AND REGISTRATION ACT

Pennsylvania has had legislation to regulate the real estate business since the original law was passed on May 1, 1929. That law has been amended numerous times to address changes in the industry. The current law is the **Real Estate Licensing and Registration Act,** which was adopted on February 19, 1980 and amended most recently in November of 1998. The *purpose* of the Act is to protect the public interest by defining requirements for licensure, licensed activities and standards of conduct and practice for licensees.

State Real Estate Commission

Laws passed by legislative bodies set broad standards of conduct as well as specific provisions, and establish administrative and enforcement agencies. The **State Real Estate Commission** is the agency established to administer the Act and supervise the activities of licensees. The commission is authorized to promulgate **Rules and Regulations.** They effect the Act by implementing and enforcing the law and providing detailed information on legal and illegal actions. Rules and Regulations have the same force and effect as the Act itself.

The State Real Estate Commission functions under the Bureau of Professional and Occupational Affairs within the Pennsylvania Department of State. It is comprised of eleven people: the commissioner of Professional and Occupational Affairs, the Director of the Bureau of Consumer Protection (or a designee), three members who represent the public at large (public members), five persons licensed as real estate brokers and one person licensed as a broker or cemetery broker (representing the cemetery business). The Act requires that the five commissioners licensed as brokers shall have been engaged in the real estate business for at least ten years; the commissioner representing the cemetery business shall have been engaged in selling cemetery lots for at least five years prior to appointment. All of the commissioners are appointed by the Governor and confirmed by the Senate, to serve five-year staggered terms. A Chairman is elected by the commission from its members.

The commission conducts monthly meetings that, under the state "sunshine laws," are open to the public. Normally these meetings are held in Harrisburg. A quorum of a majority of the members currently serving on the commission is necessary to conduct business. In addition to its regularly scheduled meetings, the commission conducts formal and informal hearings relating to complaints that have been filed against licensees. The commission is also required to hold *public meetings* each year in Philadelphia, Harrisburg, Pittsburgh and frequently holds these meetings elsewhere in the state. The purpose of these special meetings is to solicit suggestions, comments and objections about real estate practice in Pennsylvania from members of the public.

The commissioners are reimbursed for their expenses and compensated on a per diem basis, as the Act provides, for their time devoted to the business of the commission. The commission is supported by a staff employed through the Bureau of Professional and Occupational Affairs. Individuals who have questions regarding licensure procedures and real estate activities can obtain information from the commission at (717) 783-3658.

The major provisions of the Act and the commission's Regulations discussed in *Modern Real Estate Practice in Pennsylvania* are those in effect as of its publication date. The Act and the Regulations can be amended at any time. A complete text of the Act and Regulations appears in Appendix C. Throughout this chapter the appropriate sections in the Act and Regulations are provided for reference. Additional copies and revisions may be obtained from the State Real Estate Commission at P.O. Box 2649, Harrisburg, PA 17105-2649.

IN PRACTICE... | *Pay careful attention to the licensed activities that are described below. It's important that people have the appropriate license before engaging in any of the activities for which licensure is required. Otherwise they are in violation of the law and can be subject to disciplinary action by the commission. Unlicensed activity is one of several of the most frequent violations of the license law.*

LICENSED ACTIVITIES

The Act defines the activities relating to real estate for which licensure is required and the procedures for obtaining those licenses. *Real estate* is defined as *any interest or estate in land, freehold or nonfreehold, situated in this Commonwealth or elsewhere, including leasehold interests, time share and similarly designated interests.* The sale of mobile homes is deemed to be a transfer of a real estate interest if the sale is accompanied by the assignment of a lease or sale of the land on which the mobile home is situated.

There are currently ten separate licenses that may be issued by the Department of State. Licenses shall be granted to persons who bear a good reputation for honesty, trustworthiness, integrity and competence. In addition to meeting requirements for specific licenses, all applicants must submit to the commission, appropriate fees and details of a conviction, plea of guilty or nolo contendere to a felony or misdemeanor and the sentence imposed.

Real Estate Broker

A broker license is issued to a person, which may be an individual or an entity (corporation, partnership or association). According to Sections 201 of the Act and 35.201 of the Regulations, a **broker** is defined as an individual or entity who, for another and for a fee, commission or other valuable consideration, performs one or more of the following Acts:

- negotiates with or aids a person in locating or obtaining for purchase, lease or acquisition any interest in real estate

- undertakes to perform a comparative market analysis

- negotiates the listing, sale, purchase, exchange, lease, time-share, financing or option for real estate

- manages real estate

- represents himself or herself to be a real estate consultant, counselor, agent or house finder

- undertakes to promote the sale, exchange, purchase or rental of real estate (does not apply to an individual or entity whose main business is that of advertising, promotion or public relations)

- attempts to perform any of these Acts

The Act, as of this writing, requires individuals engaged in appraisal activities to have a broker/appraisers license, certified residential real estate appraisers license, or a certified general real estate appraisers license. The law does not require individuals who are certified appraisers to have a broker's license. All appraisal activities are certified by the State Board of Certified Appraisers.

Licensure requirements (Sections 511, 512 and 513 of the Act and 35.221, .222 and .271 of the Regulations). An applicant for a broker license must

- be at least 21 years of age.

- be a high school graduate or equivalent.

- have completed 240 hours (16 credits) of real estate instruction as prescribed by the commission within 10 years of the date of passing both portions of the licensing examination. (Instruction for the salesperson license does not qualify for broker licensure.)

- have been engaged as a licensed real estate salesperson for at least three years or have experience and/or education that the commission considers to be equivalent. (The commission has established a "point system" to evaluate the experience of an applicant.)

- pass both portions of a written examination within three years of the date of the license application. (All examinations consist of two portions: the General exam, which is general real estate information relating to the licensed practice, and the State exam, which covers the Act and the commission's Regulations.)

- submit a written application including the name and address under which the applicant will do business and recommendations attesting to the applicant's reputation for honesty, trustworthiness, integrity and competence.

Broker of record. The Regulations define the **broker of record** as the individual broker who is responsible for the real estate transactions of a partnership, association or corporation licensed as a broker. This individual assumes all responsibility for the business conducted by the firm.

Associate Broker

An **associate broker** is defined as an individual broker who is *employed by another broker.* Associate brokers may perform all of the activities of licensed brokers *except* employ other licensees or engage in the real estate business in their own name or from their own place of business. The requirements for licensure are the same as for a broker. A licensed broker who wishes to be employed by another broker surrenders the broker license and is issued an associate broker license.

Salesperson

Sections 201 of the Act and 35.201 of the Regulations define a **salesperson** as an individual who is employed by a licensed broker to do one or more of the following:

- sell or offer to sell real estate, or list real estate for sale
- buy or offer to buy real estate
- negotiate the purchase, sale or exchange of real estate
- negotiate a loan on real estate
- lease or rent real estate or offer to lease or rent real estate
- collect, offer or attempt to collect rent for the use of real estate
- *assist* a broker in managing property
- perform a comparative market analysis

The activities for which a salesperson is licensed are performed under the supervision and responsibility ultimately of the employing broker. *Employment,* as defined by the Act, includes *independent contractors.* This means that regardless of whether salespersons are employees or independent contractors for income-tax purposes, this does not affect the accountability of the salesperson to the broker under the license law.

The commission has determined that any activities that involve the public or are customary in selling real estate must be performed by licensees. These include *showing properties, preparing and presenting offers; preparing listing information, soliciting listings, hosting open houses for the public and disseminating any real estate information to the public.* Unlicensed people may host open houses that are *not* conducted for the public (for example, open house tours for other licensees), and they may communicate, but not interpret or explain, property information to the licensees.

Supervised property management activities (Section 35.287 of the Regulations). The assistance rendered by a salesperson in property management activities is directly supervised and controlled by the employing broker. The salesperson is not permitted to independently negotiate the terms of a lease or execute a lease on behalf of the lessor.

A salesperson must be at least 18 years of age, complete 60 hours of real estate as prescribed by the commission and pass both portions of the examinations prior to being issued a license (Section 521 and 522 of the Act and Sections 35.223 and 35.272 of the Regulations).

Cemetery Broker

Sections 201 of the Act and 35.201 of the Regulations define a **cemetery broker** as an individual or entity who engages in the business in the capacity of a broker, exclusively within the limited field of business that applies to cemetery lots, plots and mausoleum spaces or openings. The cemetery broker is responsible for the business activities and maintenance of an office in the same manner as a licensed broker. Sections 531, 532 and 533 of the Act and 35.224 and 35.273 of the Regulations describe the requirements and procedures for licensure. The cemetery broker must obtain 60 hours of instruction as approved by the commission, be engaged for three years (or equivalent) as a salesperson or cemetery salesperson (as determined by the commission) and pass a written examination prior to licensure.

Cemetery Associate Broker

Sections 201 of the Act and 35.201 of the Regulations define a **cemetery associate broker** as an individual cemetery broker who is employed by another cemetery broker or broker. This individual has the same relationship with the employing broker as an associate broker.

Cemetery Salesperson

Sections 201 of the Act and 35.201 of the Regulations define a **cemetery salesperson** as an individual who is employed by a broker or cemetery broker for the exclusive purpose of engaging in the specialized field of the sale of cemetery lots, as described for the cemetery broker. The cemetery salesperson must be at least 18 years of age and submit a sworn affidavit from the employing broker or cemetery broker attesting to the applicant's good reputation and that the broker will actively supervise and train the applicant. There is no education or examination requirement prior to licensure. (See Sections 541 and 542 of the Act and Section 35.225 of the Regulations.)

Builder-Owner Salesperson

Sections 201 of the Act and 35.201 of the Regulations define a **builder-owner salesperson** as an individual who is a *full-time employee* of a builder-owner of single-family and multifamily dwellings and who performs one or more of the following activities:

• List for sale, sell or offer for sale real estate of the builder-owner

• Negotiate the sale or exchange of real estate of the builder-owner

• Lease or rent real estate of the builder-owner

• Collect or offer or attempt to collect rent for the real estate of the builder-owner

The applicant must be at least 18 years of age, be employed by the builder-owner (who is not licensed) and complete a written examination prior to licensure. There is no education requirement. (See Sections 551 and 552 of the Act and 35.226 and 35.274 of the Regulations.)

Rental Listing Referral Agent

Sections 201 of the Act and 35.201 of the Regulations define a **rental listing referral agent** as an individual or entity who owns or manages a business that collects rental information for the purpose of referring prospective tenants to rental units. This licensee does not lease or show property, but rather sells lists of available rentals. Sections 35.289 and 35.335 of the Regulations describe requirements for compiling the list of rentals and verifying their availability for a prospective tenant, as well as language that must be included in a rental listing referral agreement. The agreement must include the following statement in bold print: *"We are a referral service only. We are not acting as real estate salespersons or brokers. We do not guarantee that the purchaser will find a satisfactory rental unit through our service. Our only purpose is to furnish the purchaser with lists of available rental units."*

The applicant must meet licensure requirements, which are essentially the same as for a salesperson licensee; however, the rental listing referral agent is not affiliated with a broker. A rental listing referral agent is responsible for maintaining an office under the same requirements as a broker and cemetery broker. (See Sections 561 of the Act and 35.227 and 35.275 of the Regulations.)

Campground Membership Salesperson

Sections 201 of the Act and 35.201 of the Regulations define a **campground membership salesperson** as an individual who, either as an employee or independent contractor, sells campground memberships under the supervision of a broker. **Campground memberships** are interests, other than in fee simple or by lease, that give the purchaser the right to use a unit of real property for the purpose of locating a recreational vehicle, trailer, tent, tent trailer, pickup camper or other similar device on a periodic basis under a membership contract. The applicant shall be at least 18 years of age, complete 15 hours of instruction in specific topics and complete not less than 30 days of on-site training at a campground membership facility prior to licensure. (See Sections 581 and 582 of the Act.) The broker is responsible for further training and supervising the licensee. Licensed salespersons, brokers and time share salespersons do not need a separate license to sell campground memberships.

Time-Share Salesperson

Sections 201 of the Act and 35.201 of the Regulations define a **time-share salesperson** as an individual who, either as an employee or independent contractor, sells time shares under the supervision of a broker. *Time-shares* are defined as the right, however evidenced or documented, to use or occupy one or more units on a periodic basis. A time-share salesperson must be at least 18 years of age, complete 30 hours of instruction in specific topics and complete not less than 30 days of on-site training at a time share facility prior to licensure. (See Sections 591 and 592 of the Act.) The broker is responsible for further training and supervising the licensee. Licensed salespersons and brokers do not need a separate license to sell time shares.

Exclusions

Sections 304 of the Act and 35.202 of the Regulations establish the following categories of individuals and entities that are excluded from the requirements for real estate licensure:

- Owners of real estate performing the activities associated with the ownership, lease or sale of their own property. So as not to be used as a means of circumventing licensure, the exclusion does not extend to more than five partners in a partnership or officers of a corporation nor to other employees.

- Employees of a public utility acting in the ordinary course of the utility-related business.

- Officers or employees of a partnership or corporation whose principal business involves the discovery, extraction, distribution or transmission of energy or mineral resources. This exclusion applies to the purchase, sale or lease of real estate in the course of the conduct of this business.

- An attorney-in-fact who renders services under an executed and recorded power of attorney from the owner or lessor of real estate. The power of attorney cannot be used to circumvent licensure. The commission has determined that granting a power of attorney to a property manager for the purpose of having the property managed by an individual who does not have a broker license circumvents the intent of the Act.

- An attorney-at-law who receives a fee from a client for rendering services within the scope of the attorney-client relationship and does not represent himself as a broker.

- A trustee in bankruptcy, administrator, executor, trustee or guardian who is acting under the authority of a court order, will or trust instrument.

- The elected officer or director of any banking institution, savings institution, savings bank, credit union or trust company operating under federal or state laws involving only the property owned by these institutions.

- An officer or employee of a cemetery company who, as incidental to principal duties, shows cemetery lots without compensation.

- A cemetery company or cemetery owned by a bona fide church, religious congregation or fraternal organization. (This applies to the requirement for registration.)

- An auctioneer, licensed under the Auctioneers' License Act, while performing duties at a bona fide auction.

- Any person employed by an owner of real estate for the purpose of managing or maintaining multifamily residential property. This person is not authorized to enter into leases on behalf of the owner, negotiate terms or conditions of leases, or hold money belonging to tenants other than on behalf of the owner. As long as the owner retains authority to make all such decisions, the employees may show apartments and provide information on rental amount, building rules and Regulations and leasing determinations.

- The elected officer, director or employee of any banking institution, savings institution, savings bank, credit union or trust company operating under federal or state laws, when acting on behalf of the institution in performing appraisals or other evaluations of real estate in connection with a loan transaction.

LICENSING PROCEDURES

It is the duty of the Department of State to issue licenses and registration certificates to individuals who meet the requirements established by the Act. The State Real Estate Commission has the authority to approve proprietary real estate schools, set fees subject to review under applicable Pennsylvania law and prescribe the subject matter to be tested when written examinations are required for licensure. The Department of State contracts with an independent testing agency to conduct licensing examinations; currently, Experior is under contract to provide that service.

The commission prescribes the application forms that must be completed for licensure and has the authority to investigate the accuracy of the information submitted. Inaccurate or untruthful information could result in an application's being denied or disciplinary action being taken by the commission against any license the individual currently possesses.

The license period for all real estate licenses is currently two years, beginning June 1 through the last day of May in each even-numbered year. When a license is first issued, it will expire at the end of the current license period. A license is considered to be *active* once the license is issued and remains properly renewed.

License Renewal

Prior to the end of each license period the commission will establish procedures for submitting documentation and fees to renew a license for the next two-year period. Licensed brokers and salespersons are required to satisfy a 14-hour continuing education requirement during the two-year period before the date that the license is to be renewed.

Continuing education. The purpose of continuing education is to maintain and increase competency to engage in licensed activities, keep licensees abreast of changes in laws, Regulations, practices and procedures that affect the business and better ensure that the public is protected from incompetent licensees. The continuing education requirement applies only to brokers and salespersons.

The commission's Regulations require that continuing education courses include a minimum of 3 hours in fair housing laws and practices and a minimum of 2 hours in the licensing law and Regulations. The commission may require up to 3 hours in a topic that addresses a critical issue of current relevance to licensees. The remaining six to nine hours can cover a variety of "elective" topics that the commission has determined to be acceptable. Courses may be obtained from a college, university or commission-approved real estate school.

The commission is responsible for approving courses, materials, locations and instructors for continuing education, and has the authority to waive all or part of the requirement for a salesperson or broker who shows evidence that he or she is unable to complete the requirement due to illness, emergency or hardship. (See Section 404a of the Act and subchapter H of the Rules and Regulations for more details about continuing education procedures.)

Inactive Licenses

Failure to renew a license prohibits the person from performing the activities for which the license was issued. A license may be reactivated by submitting the proper forms and fees within 5 years of the date the license became inactive. Brokers and salespersons must obtain 14 hours of continuing education before they can reactivate a license. A licensee who fails to activate a license after 5 years must retake the appropriate examination.

Out-of-State Licensees

An individual who holds a license issued by another jurisdiction and wants to engage in the real estate business in Pennsylvania may do so by complying with certain requirements. That individual must

* possess a license, issued by another jurisdiction, that has been active within five years of application in Pennsylvania.

- have scored a passing grade on the Pennsylvania portion of the licensing exam within three years prior to submitting an application.

- have obtained the prelicensure education that the commission has determined to be satisfactory, according to its Regulations.

- submit the appropriate application, which includes the license number, date of issuance and evidence of whether the license has been active within the past five years, confirmation that the applicant obtained the initial license by written examination and evidence of past disciplinary action taken against the applicant, if any. Applicants for salesperson or associate broker licensure must have an employer who is a Pennsylvania-licensed broker.

OPERATION OF A REAL ESTATE BUSINESS

According to Section 601 of the Act, each resident licensed broker, cemetery broker and rental listing referral agent shall maintain a fixed office. The current licenses of these individuals or entities, including the address of the office, and each of the licensees employed by them, shall be *prominently displayed in the office*. The Regulations (Section 35.242) require that the office be devoted to the transaction of the real estate business and be arranged to permit business to be conducted in privacy. If the office is located in a private residence, the entrance to the office shall be separate from the entrance to the residence.

Business name. The **business name** is the name under which a broker, cemetery broker license or rental listing referral agent is issued, whether it is an individual or a business entity. The business name becomes the name under which business is conducted. The name, as is designated on the license, must be displayed *prominently and in a permanent fashion outside all offices*. Any time the name of the business is represented, it must appear *exactly* as it is designated on the license.

Branch Offices

If a broker or cemetery broker intends to maintain more than one place of business, the licensee must obtain an additional license for each office. A branch office license, including its address, must be obtained before any office is opened. This license will be issued in the same name under which the brokers or cemetery brokers are licensed to conduct business at their main offices.

A branch office shall meet the same requirements as the main office. The broker is responsible for the activities of all licensees in each office. Branch offices may not be operated in a manner that permits a licensee to carry on business in the office for the person's sole benefit. If the broker delegates the duties of supervising and directing an office (as manager) to another licensee, that individual must be an *associate broker*. The broker, however, is still ultimately responsible for the activities conducted in a branch office.

In addition to the branch office license, the licenses of all individuals who work out of that office shall be displayed in a conspicuous place at the branch office. The broker shall maintain a list at the main office of licensed employees and the branch office out of which each works.

Change of Address; Change of Employment

Section 603 of the Act requires that no associate broker or other underlying licensee (associate cemetery broker, salesperson, time-share salesperson, campground membership salesperson or cemetery salesperson) shall be employed by any broker other than the broker designated on the license. Section 604 prohibits any licensee from receiving compensation from anyone other than the employing broker. A broker is prohibited from paying compensation to anyone other than a licensee employed by that broker or another licensed broker. This also means that the broker cannot pay unlicensed individuals or entities.

In case of removal of a broker's office from the designated location, all licensees at that location shall make application to the commission *before the removal or within ten days thereafter,* designating the new location of the office. A current license will be issued at the new location for the unexpired license period, provided the new location complies with the terms of the Act.

Whenever a licensee desires to change employment from one broker to another, the licensee shall notify the commission *no later than ten days after the intended date of change,* return the current license and pay the required fee. When the new broker acknowledges the employment, a new license will be issued. In the interim, a copy of the notification of the change of employment serves as the temporary license, pending receipt of the new license. The applicant is responsible for notifying the commission if the new license is not received within 30 days.

DISCIPLINARY ACTIONS

The State Real Estate Commission has the power under the Real Estate Licensing and Registration Act to enforce the Act and the commission's Rules and Regulations. Upon receipt of a complaint, the commission (or its representative) will conduct an investigation to determine if there has been a violation. The commission cannot take disciplinary action until the accused party has been afforded an opportunity to have a hearing before the commission. Section 701 of the Act sets forth the manner in which the commission will conduct these deliberations. There are a number of disciplinary actions from which the commission can choose, depending on the nature of the violation.

Section 702 of the Act limits the disciplinary action that may be taken against an employing broker because of disciplinary action against a licensee employed by that broker. If it appears from evidence presented at hearings that the employing broker had *actual knowledge of a violation,* or if there is *a course of dealing that has been followed by an employee that violates the law,* these are grounds for the commission to suspend or revoke the employing broker's license. A "course of dealing" constitutes *prima facie evidence* of knowledge on the part of the employer. If these conditions do not exist, the commission may find that the broker failed to properly supervise the licensee and take a lesser disciplinary action.

Under Act 48 of 1993, which authorizes the Commission of Professional and Occupational Affairs to adopt a Schedule of Civil penalties, the inspectors and investigators have the authority to issue citations, with accompanying civil penalties, for lesser violations of the Act and Regulations. At the time a real estate office or proprietary school is inspected or during the investigation of a complaint, the licensee can admit fault for the offense and pay a predetermined penalty. A licensee can, of course, refuse to accept the citation and pursue all rights of due process as previously described. This procedure is intended to free the Real Estate Commission's resources to concentrate on more serious offenses.

Unlicensed Activity

Section 301 of the Act stipulates that it is unlawful for any unlicensed individual or entity to be engaged in or to represent themselves to be conducting an activity for which licensure is required. They must be licensed at the time the service is offered as well as at the time the service is rendered. Because unlicensed persons are not entitled to compensation, they are prohibited from entering into a civil suit for recovery.

Any person who engages in activity for which licensure is required or employs an individual or entity that does not possess a current active license is subject to *criminal penalties* according to Section 303 of the Act. This includes situations in which a license has been suspended or revoked. The first conviction for unlicensed activity is a summary offense, which involves a sentence to pay a fine not exceeding $500 and/or imprisonment, not exceeding three months. A second or subsequent offense is a felony of the third degree, which involves a sentence to pay a fine of $2,000 to $5,000 and/or imprisonment for one to two years.

Civil Penalties

Section 305 of the Act provides that, in addition to other remedies or criminal penalties allowed for in the Act, the commission may levy a civil penalty of up to $1,000 on any current licensee who violates any provision of the Act or on any person who practices real estate without being properly licensed.

Prohibited Acts

Section 604 of the Act sets forth a list of specific activities that are prohibited in the real estate business. Some of the most common violations of this section include misrepresentations, mishandling escrow funds, paying commissions to unauthorized people and advertising complaints.

Once a written complaint is verified, the commission has the authority to hold a hearing for the suspension or revocation of a license or registration certificate, or to impose fines up to $1,000. The commission also has the power to refuse or suspend a license, or to levy fines once it is determined that a license has been obtained by a fraudulent act, or that a licensee has been found guilty of violating any of the prohibited acts.

Posting a suspension notice (Section 35.291 of the Regulations). A broker or cemetery broker whose license is suspended shall return the license to the commission and post a notice of the suspension action prominently at the public entrance of the main office and any branch offices. The commission will provide the notice that must be posted. Failure to post the notice constitutes ground for further disciplinary action.

Relicensure after revocation (Sections 501 of the Act and 35.251 of the Regulations). A revocation of a license lasts for at least five years following the date revocation begins. After the five-year period, the individual may petition the commission for relicensure. If the commission determines that relicensure is permitted, the individual shall comply with current requirements for licensure before the license is issued.

Reporting Crimes and Disciplinary Actions

Section 35.290 of the Regulations states that a licensee shall notify the commission of being convicted of, or pleading guilty or nolo contendere to, a felony or misdemeanor. The report must be made within 30 days of the verdict or plea. If a disciplinary action has been taken against a licensee by the licensing authority in another jurisdiction, the licensee must notify the commission in Pennsylvania within 30 days of that action.

REAL ESTATE RECOVERY FUND

The **Real Estate Recovery Fund** was established to provide a fund to which aggrieved persons may apply for the payment of uncollected judgments. These judgments must result from civil suits against real estate licensees for fraud, deceit or misrepresentations in a real estate transaction. The purpose of the fund is to ensure that after exhausting all other attempts to collect payment, a person injured by these actions has a means to collect the award made by the civil court.

To collect from the fund, the aggrieved person must be able to show that he or she is not a spouse or personal representative of the spouse of the licensee; that a final judgment was awarded; that all reasonable remedies have been exhausted to collect the judgment; and that the application is being made within one year after the termination of the proceedings (including appeals). The maximum amount that may be paid out of the fund for any one claim is $20,000 and $100,000 per licensee. If $100,000 is insufficient to settle the claims against a licensee, it shall be distributed according to the same ratio as the respective claims. If the Real Estate Recovery Fund is insufficient to satisfy any claim or portion thereof, the commission shall satisfy unpaid claims plus accumulated interest at the rate of 6 percent per year, once the fund is reestablished.

Monies for the fund are collected from licensees. When the fund was originally established in 1980, all licensees at the time paid $10 into the fund when they renewed their licenses. Subsequently, any person to whom a license is issued and who has not paid into the fund makes the $10 contribution. Section 802 of the Act provides that at such time as the balance of the fund is $300,000 or less, the commission has the authority to assess an additional fee, not to exceed $10 per licensee, to bring the balance of the fund to $500,000. The fees are paid into the State Treasury and are allocated exclusively for the purposes of the fund. The fund shall be invested and interest and dividends accrue to the fund.

The license of the person involved in the claim is automatically suspended as of the date of the payment from the fund. No licensee shall be granted reinstatement until repayment is made plus interest at 10 percent per year.

The Real Estate Recovery Fund does not apply to the sale of a campground or campground membership salesperson.

REAL ESTATE DOCUMENTS

Section 35.281 of the Regulations requires that a licensee who Acts in a representative capacity in a real estate transaction shall ensure that all sale or lease contracts, commitments and agreements regarding the transaction are *in writing*. The broker is responsible for maintaining copies of records pertaining to any transaction for at least *three years following consummation* of the transaction and is required to produce the records for examination by the commission upon written request. All parties to a contract must receive a copy of the executed agreement.

LICENSE RELATIONSHIPS

The Real Estate Licensing and Registration Act, amended November 1998, defines an *agency relationship* as: "a relationship whereby the broker or licensees in the employ of the broker act as fiduciaries for a consumer of real estate services by the express authority of the consumer of real estate services." The following definitions include for whom the licensee is working and the various roles that a licensee can enter into in a real estate transaction.

    a. *Consumer*—A person who is the recipient of any real estate service.

        Principal—A consumer of real estate services who has entered into an agency relationship with a broker.

    b. *Seller agent*—Any licensee who has entered into an agency relationship with a seller of real estate.

    c. *Subagent*—A broker, not in the employ of the listing broker, who is engaged to act for or cooperate with the listing broker in selling property as an agent of the seller. A subagent is deemed to have an agency relationship with the seller.

    d. *Listing broker*—A broker engaged as a seller's agent, dual agent or transaction licensee to market the property of a seller/landlord.

    e. *Dual agent*—A licensee who acts a an agent for the buyer and seller or lessee and landlord in the same transaction.

    f. *Designated agent*—One or more licensees designated by the employing broker with the consent of the principal to act exclusively as an or as agents on behalf of the principal to the exclusion of all other licensees within the broker's employ.

    g. *Transaction licensee*—a licensed broker or salesperson who provides communication or document preparation services or performs acts described under the definition of "broker" or "salesperson" for which a license is required, without being an agent or advocate of the consumer.

The broker of a real estate company will ultimately determine the role or roles that the licensees will assume.

GENERAL DUTIES OF THE LICENSEE

Regardless of whether a licensee is acting within the scope of an agency relationship with a consumer, a licensee owes the following to all consumers:

1. reasonable professional skill and care;

2. honest dealings in good faith;

3. presentation of all written offers, written notices and other written communications in a timely manner, except when otherwise waived;

4. compliance with those obligations imposed upon a licensee by the "Real Estate Seller Disclosure Act";

5. an accounting, in a timely manner, of all money and property received from or on behalf of any consumer to a transaction;

6. adequate information at the initial interview;

7. timely disclosure of any conflicts of interest;

8. guidance regarding the use of expert advice on matters relating to the transaction that are beyond the licensee's expertise;

9. providing all services in a reasonable, professional and competent manner;

10. ongoing advisement regarding the status of the transaction;

11. information regarding tasks that must be completed to satisfy an agreement or condition for settlement, regarding document preparation or regarding compliance with laws pertaining to real estate transactions;

12. timely presentation of all offers and counteroffers, unless otherwise directed in writing; and

13. disclosure of any financial interest, including a referral fee or commission. (For additional specific information regarding disclosure, refer to Section 606.1 of the Act.)

Refer to Section 606.2, 606.3, 606.4, 606.5, and 606.6 of the Act itself for additional dutues that must be performed when assuming a specific agency role.

Preagreement Disclosures

Certain information must be disclosed to seller/landlord or buyer/tenant during the initial interview. The initial interview is the first contact between a licensee and a consumer of real state-related services where a substantial discussion about real estate needs takes place. Such disclosure must be provided on a form and must include

- a disclosure of the relationship in which the broker may engage with the consumer; the disclosure must describe the duties that the broker owes in each relationship.

- a statement informing sellers and buyers of their option to have an agency relationship with a broker, and that an agency relationship is not presumed and will exist only as set forth in a written agreement between the parties;

- a statement that a real estate consumer can negotiate the fee and the specific activities or practices that the broker will provide;

- a statement identifying any possibility that the broker may provide services to another consumer who may be a party to the transaction, along with an explanation of those duties if applicable;

- a statement that the broker may designate one or more licensees affiliated with the broker to represent the separate interests of the parties to the transaction;

- a statement of the broker's policies regarding cooperation with other brokers, including the sharing of fees;

- a statement that a buyer's broker may be paid a fee that is a percentage of the purchase price, and that the buyer's broker, even if compensated by the listing broker, will represent the interests of the buyer; and

- a statement that the broker's fees and the duration of the broker's employment are negotiable.

Agreements with Broker

Section 608.1 of the Act requires the following information to appear in *written* agreements with a broker:

- a statement that the broker's fee and the duration of the contract have been determined as a result of negotiations between the broker and the consumer;

- a statement describing the nature and extent of the broker's services to be provided;

- a statement identifying any possibility that the broker or any licensee employed by the broker may provide services to more than one consumer in a single transaction, along with an explanation of the duties owed to each party;

- a statement of the broker's policies and compensation regarding cooperation with subagents and buyer agents;

- a statement identifying and disclosing how compensation from the seller will be received and distributed among the types of brokers;

- a statement describing the purpose of the Real Estate Recovery Fund and the telephone number where a seller may receive further information; and

- a statement disclosing any possible conflicts of interest in a timely manner.

Exclusive Listing Agreements (Section 35.332 of the Regulations) must contain the following information, in addition to that listed above:

- Sale or lease price

- Commission expected on the sale or lease price

- Duration of the agreement

If the listing is an exclusive-right-to-sell or exclusive-right-to-lease, there must be a statement in boldface type that the *broker earns a commission on the sale or lease during the listing period by whomever the sale is made, including the owner.*

An exclusive listing *may not* contain

- a listing period exceeding one year;

- an automatic renewal clause;

- a cancellation notice to terminate the agreement at the end of the listing;

- authority of the broker to execute a signed agreement of sale or lease for the owner;

- an option by the broker to purchase the listed property; or

- authority of the broker to confess judgment against the owner for the commission.

Agreements of Sale

Section 608.2 of the Act requires that an agreement of sale contain

- a statement identifying the capacity in which the broker is engaged in the transaction, and whether the broker or any licensee affiliated with the broker has provided services relating to the subject transaction to any other party in the transaction;

- a statement describing the purpose of the Real Estate Recovery Fund and the telephone number at the commission where a consumer can receive further information;

- a statement of the zoning classification of the property, except in cases where the property or each parcel of the property, if subdividable, is zoned solely or primarily to permit single-family dwellings; failure to comply with this requirement shall render the sales agreement or sales contract voidable at the option of the buyer and, if voided, any deposits tendered by the buyer shall be returned to the buyer without requirement for court action;

- a statement that access to a public road may require issuance of a highway occupancy permit from the Department of Transportation; and

- in any sales agreement or sales contract, a cemetery broker must be subject to the requirements of Section 608.2 as it relates to the Real Estate Recovery Fund and the disclosure of information.

Mortgage contingencies (Section 35.333 of the Regulations). An agreement of sale conditioned on the ability of the buyer to obtain a mortgage loan shall contain the

- type of mortgage;

- mortgage principal;

- maximum interest rate of the mortgage;

- minimum term of the mortgage;

- deadline for the buyer to obtain the mortgage; and

- nature and extent of assistance that the broker will render to the buyer in obtaining the mortgage.

Statements of estimated cost and return (Section 35.334 of the Regulations).
Before an agreement of sale is executed, the brokers involved in the transaction shall provide each party with a written estimate of the reasonably foreseeable expenses associated with the sale that the parties may be expected to pay. The estimates of costs shall be as accurate as may be reasonably expected of a person having knowledge of and experience in real estate sales. These include such items as the

- broker's commission;

- mortgage payments and financing costs;

- taxes and assessments; and

- settlement expenses.

Time-Share and Campground Membership Contracts

A purchaser shall have the right to cancel the purchase of a time-share or a campground membership until *midnight of the fifth day following the date on which the purchaser executed the contract*. The right-to-cancel notice shall be printed conspicuously in boldface type immediately above the signature of the purchaser and must be separately initialed. The right of cancellation shall not be waivable by any purchaser nor can the purchaser be held liable for any damages resulting from exercising this right. The statement required by Section 609 of the Act is as follows:

"You, the purchaser, may cancel this purchase at any time prior to midnight of the fifth day following the date of this transaction. If you desire to cancel, you are required to notify the seller, in writing, at [address]. Such notice shall be given by certified return receipt mail or by any other bona fide means of delivery which provides you with a receipt. Such notice shall be effective upon being postmarked by the U.S. Postal Service or upon deposit of notice with any bona fide means of delivery which provides you with a receipt."

Within ten days after receipt of a notice of cancellation, all payments made under the contract shall be refunded to the purchaser and an acknowledgment that the contract is void shall be sent to the purchaser. Any promotional prizes, gifts and premiums issued to the purchaser by the seller shall remain the property of the purchaser.

All of these provisions apply to time-share and campground memberships located in Pennsylvania as well as outside the state if the purchase contract *was executed by the purchaser in Pennsylvania.*

ESCROW REQUIREMENTS

Section 604(5) of the Act and Sections 35.321-35.328 of the Regulations set forth detailed requirements for handling escrow funds. Brokers are responsible for depositing funds they receive that belong to others (for example, hand money and security deposits) into an escrow account in a federally or state-insured bank or depository *pending consummation or termination of the transaction.*

The escrow account must be used exclusively for escrow purposes. The broker may not *commingle* these monies with the broker's business or personal funds nor may the broker misappropriate money that should be held in escrow with the broker's business or personal funds. However, the broker is permitted to deposit personal money into the escrow account to cover service charges assessed by the banking institution on the account.

If escrow money is expected to be held for more than six months, the broker is encouraged to deposit the funds into an interest-bearing account. The interest follows the principal amount of the escrow funds, unless the parties state otherwise in the agreement.

The broker's duty to escrow *cannot be waived or altered* by agreement between the parties to the transaction.

The account is established in the name of the broker as it appears on the license, with the broker being designated as trustee of the account. The broker may give written authority to an employee to make deposits and authority to a licensed employee to make withdrawals. However, the broker remains responsible for seeing that the requirements of the Regulations are met. Records must be maintained, including the name of the party from whom the money is received; the name of the party to whom the money belongs; and the dates the money is received, deposited and withdrawn. These records are subject to inspection by the commission.

Responsibility for Deposits

If a sales deposit is tendered by a buyer to the *listing broker* rather than the selling broker, the listing broker shall assume the escrow duty. If the sales deposit is tendered by a buyer to the *selling broker,* the selling broker assumes responsibility.

In cobrokerage transactions, however, it may be the intention of the listing broker to escrow the sales deposit, but the money is tendered to the selling broker. In this case, there must be written notice to the buyer that the selling broker intends to deliver the deposit to the listing broker. The listing broker then assumes the responsibility for the funds. The buyer must acknowledge in writing, prior to signing an agreement of sale, the name of the listing broker; that the selling broker is receiving these funds on behalf of the listing broker; and that the listing broker is to be designated as payee if the buyer's deposit is in the form of a check.

Deadlines for Deposits

A broker is responsible for depositing the funds in escrow *by the end of the next business day following receipt.* In the case of multiple office firms, the deadline applies to receipt by the office out of which the account is administered. If the money has been tendered in the form of a check when an offer to purchase or lease is made, the broker may, with *written permission* of both the buyer and the seller, refrain from depositing the money pending *acceptance* of the offer. In this case, the broker must deposit the funds within *one business day following acceptance of the offer.*

Withdrawal of Funds

A broker must retain all escrow funds received in the escrow account until the transaction is consummated or terminated. Consummation is simple to identify if, in the case of an agreement of sale, the sale proceeds through to settlement and the seller delivers title. However, there are situations in which, following the signing of an agreement of sale, a dispute arises between the parties and the sale does not proceed to closing. The broker may not appropriate any part of the earnest money as compensation as the broker's commission. The broker must retain the escrow money until the dispute is resolved and the parties agree as to whom the deposit money belongs. If resolution of the dispute appears remote without legal Action, the broker may, following 30 days' notice to the parties, petition the county court to interplead the rival claimants.

Rental Management Account

Rents that a broker receives as a property manager for a lessor shall be deposited into a rental management account. This account is separate from the broker's escrow account (in which security deposits are held) and the general business accounts.

GENERAL ETHICAL RESPONSIBILITIES

Subchapter D in the Regulations, "Standards of Conduct and Practice," lists a number of responsibilities. Preagreement disclosures to buyers and sellers, retention of records, supervising appraisal and property management activities or salespersons, reporting crimes and disciplinary actions and posting suspension notices have already been discussed. Many of the practices discussed in this chapter of the Regulations correspond to Section 604 of the Act, "Prohibited Practices."

Misleading Advice, Assurances and Representations

According to Section 35.282 of the Regulations, licensees may not give assurances or advice concerning any aspect of a real estate transaction that they know are *incorrect, inaccurate or improbable*. This includes information it is reasonable to believe that a licensee *should* know. Licensees may not knowingly be a party to a *material false or inaccurate representation* in a written document regarding a real estate transaction when acting in a representative capacity.

Conflict of Interest

Section 35.283 of the Regulations states that licensees must *disclose any ownership interest* they have in a property involved in a real estate transaction in which they are participating. It also says that a broker who manages rental property *may not accept commission, rebate or profit on expenditures made for the lessor* without the owner's *written consent*. The Regulations intend to ensure that licensees protect the interests of the people they are supposed to be serving and not use their position for personal profit.

The Regulations also require that if a licensee *represents more than one party* in a transaction (dual agency), there must be *written consent* from all parties to the multiple representation. This consent intends to ensure that the parties are aware that conflicts can arise when the licensee is attempting to represent two opposite parties in the same transaction.

Disclosure of Real Estate Affiliations

Because the franchise, network or other parent real estate company with which a broker is affiliated is not part of the license name, Section 35.285 of the Regulations requires that the commission be notified of this affiliation.

Duties When Selling or Leasing Own Real Estate

Once licensed, brokers or salespersons are bound to comply with all requirements of the Act and Section 35.288 of the Regulations when selling or leasing their own property. They must disclose their license status to a prospective buyer or tenant before the purchaser or tenant enters into an agreement with the licensee. Brokers who sell or lease their own real estate must disclose that they are licensed when advertising their properties.

ADVERTISING AND SOLICITATION

A licensee may not advertise, solicit prospective buyers or tenants, or place a "for sale" or "for rent" sign on a property without the *written consent of the owner*. A rental listing referral agent may not publish information about a rental property if the lessor or property manager expressly states that the property is not to be included in the lists prepared by the rental listing referral agent.

Business Name

When advertising a property for sale or rent, the broker's business name as it appears on the broker's license must appear in the ad; "blind ads" (advertisements by a broker without including the broker's business name) are prohibited. Advertising by employee licensees of a broker must include the business name of the employing broker. The business name of the broker and the broker's phone number must be given greater prominence than that of the employee if that employee's name and phone number appear.

Advertisement of Lotteries, Contests, Prizes, Certificates, Lots and Gifts

According to Section 604 of the Act and 35.306 of the Regulations, advertisement for the solicitation or sale of real estate that employ lotteries or contests or that offer prizes, certificates, gifts or free lots shall contain

- a description of each prize, certificate, gift or lot offered;
- the prerequisites for receiving the awards;
- the limitation on the number of awards;
- the *fair market value* (not suggested retail value) of each award; and
- the odds of winning or receiving the award.

If the awards are offered through the mail, the licensee shall maintain records that contain the number of awards that were made and the names and addresses of both the individuals who receive and the individuals who do not receive them. The commission requires that disclosures be made if there is a possibility that a particular award is not available and prohibits advertising an award that is not available for distribution. The description of an award cannot be misleading, and a statement of value and odds shall be printed in a clear and conspicuous manner. If the prizewinner must pay any fees, such as dealer preparation, shipping, handling or insurance, they must be disclosed.

Advertising Sales Volume, Market Position and Number of Offices

According to Section 35.307 of the Regulations, advertising by a broker about "sales volume" or "production" shall refer only to closed transactions. These are listings or sales that have gone to settlement or in which a fully executed deed has been delivered. An advertisement by a broker about production or position in the "market" shall identify the municipality that the market comprises. An advertisement about the number of offices that the broker operates shall refer only to offices that have been issued branch office licenses.

Harassment

According to Section 35.302 of the Regulations, a licensee, whether acting on behalf of a prospective buyer or not, must not solicit the sale or other disposition of real estate with such frequency as to amount to clear harassment of the owner of the property. This includes the use of telephone, mail, advertising or personal contact.

Panic Selling

In Section 35.303 of the Regulations, panic selling is defined as frequent efforts to sell residential real estate in a particular neighborhood because of fear of declining real estate values when that fear is not based on facts relating to the intrinsic value of the real estate. The commission regards an attempt by a licensee to bring about panic selling in order to profit from it to be *bad faith* under Section 604 of the Act. Proof of systematic solicitation of sales listings may be considered sufficient, but not conclusive, evidence of an attempt to bring about panic selling.

PROHIBITED ACTS   Section 604 of the Act lists 28 specific prohibited Acts. Licensees who engage in the performance of any of these practices are subject to suspension or revocation of their licenses, in addition to fines. Many of these practices have been discussed elsewhere in this chapter. For easy reference, a summary of the prohibited Acts follows.

1. Making any substantial misrepresentation

2. Making any false promise to influence, persuade or induce a person into a contract when the licensee could not or did not intend to keep the promise

3. Pursuing a continued and flagrant course of misrepresentation or making false promises through any licensee or any medium of advertising

4. Using misleading or untruthful advertising; using any other trade name or insignia of a real estate association of which the licensee is not a member

5. Failing to comply with all of the escrow requirements

6. Failing to preserve records relating to any real estate transaction for three years following consummation of the transaction

7. Acting for more than one party in a transaction without the knowledge of and consent in writing from all parties

8. Placing a "for sale" or "for rent" sign on or advertising any property without the written consent of the owner

9. Failing to voluntarily furnish a copy of any contract to all signatories at the time of execution

10. Failing to specify a definite termination date that is not subject to prior notice in any listing agreement

11. Inducing any party to a contract to break the contract for the purpose of substituting a new contract, when the substitution is motivated by personal gain of the licensee

12. Accepting a commission or other valuable consideration from any person except the licensed broker who is the employer; paying of a commission by a broker to anyone other than the broker's licensed employee or another broker

13. Failing to disclose in writing to the owner the licensee's interest in purchasing or acquiring an interest in a property listed with the licensee's office

14. Being convicted in court of, or pleading guilty or nolo contendere to, forgery, embezzlement, obtaining money under false pretenses, bribery, larceny, extortion, conspiracy to defraud or any felony

15. Violating any rule or Regulation of the commission

16. In the case of a broker, failing to exercise adequate supervision over the activities of the employed licensees

17. Failing to provide information requested by the commission as the result of a formal or informal complaint

18. Soliciting or selling real estate by offering free lots, conducting lotteries or contests, or offering prizes for the purpose of influencing a purchase by deceptive conduct

19. Paying or accepting, giving or charging undisclosed commission, rebate or compensation on expenditures for a principal

20. Performing any Act that demonstrates bad faith, dishonesty, untrustworthiness or incompetency

21. Performing any Act for which an appropriate license is required if such license is not currently in effect

22. Violating any provision of the Pennsylvania Human Relations Act, such as accepting listing with the understanding that illegal discrimination is to be practiced, giving false information for the purpose of discriminating, making a distinction in location of housing or dates of availability for the purpose of discriminating

23. Violating the Pennsylvania statutes relating to burial grounds (if a cemetery company registrant)

24. Violating Sections 606 and 608 of the Act

25. Failing as a broker, campground membership salesperson or time share salesperson to comply with the requirements for handling deposits or other monies

26. Failing to provide a disclosure required by this Act, or any other federal or state law imposing a disclosure obligation on licensees in connection with real estate transactions

PROMOTIONAL LAND SALES

Section 605 of the Act requires that any person who proposes to engage in real estate transactions of a promotional nature in Pennsylvania, regardless of whether the property is located in or outside Pennsylvania, shall first register with the commission. The Act specifies the information that must be submitted for the commission to grant approval before the property can be promoted. "Promotional real estate" is an interest in property that is part of a promotional plan that offers real estate through advertising by mail, newspaper or periodical, or by radio, television, telephone or other electronic means. Promotional real estate does not involve fewer than 50 lots or shares or land areas of less than 25 acres. The registration is not required if the promotional property is already registered with the Department of Housing and Urban Development under the Interstate Land Sales Full Disclosure Act.

•   •   •   •   •   •   •

KEY TERMS

associate broker	cemetery salesperson
broker	Real Estate Licensing and Registration
broker of record	Act
builder-owner salesperson	Real Estate Recovery Fund
business name	rental listing referral agent
campground membership	Rules and Regulations
campground membership salesperson	salesperson
cemetery associate broker	State Real Estate Commission
cemetery broker	time-share salesperson

SUMMARY

Real estate licenses are granted to qualified individuals, corporations and part-nerships under the provisions of the Real Estate Licensing and Registration Act. The Act is administered by the State Real Estate Commission. The commission has the authority to promulgate Rules and Regulations, which elaborate on the license law and provide additional legal guidance for Pennsylvania licensees. The purpose of the Act and the Regulations is to protect the public interest.

A real estate licensee is required to perform for others, and for a fee, such activi-ties as brokerage, property management, leasing and exchanging. Licenses are issued to brokers, salespersons, builder-owner salespersons, cemetery brokers and cemetery salespersons, rental listing referral agents, time-share salesper-sons and campground membership salespersons.

Certain individuals are exempt from licensure requirements, such as owners, attorneys-in-fact, attorneys-at-law (within the scope of the attorney-client rela-tionship), officers and directors of banking institutions (when dealing with insti-tution-owned real estate), trustees, executors, auctioneers, and officers and employees of banking institutions when appraising real estate on behalf of the institution.

Licenses are issued by the Department of State to individuals who meet the requirements for the licenses. The licenses are renewed every two years, and such renewal includes the payment of appropriate fees. Brokers and sales-persons must also satisfy a 14-hour continuing education requirement for license renewal.

The Act regulates such matters as the general operation of a real estate business, real estate documents, earnest money deposits, advertising and ethical consid-erations. There are procedures for the commission to investigate the activities and take disciplinary actions against licensees. The law establishes the Real Estate Recovery Fund, from which aggrieved persons may collect unpaid judgments resulting from a civil court suit for damages due to fraud, mis-representation or deceit.

Questions

1. A broker may pay a commission to a/an
   a. developer.
   b. licensed salesperson who works for another broker.
   c. attorney.
   d. licensed salesperson employed by the broker.

2. If a licensed salesperson violates a provision of the license law without the consent or knowledge of the supervising broker
   a. the salesperson may lose his or her license.
   b. only the broker may lose his or her license.
   c. both the salesperson and the broker may lose their licenses.
   d. the broker will be fined for the salesperson's violation.

3. All of the following are true regarding the requirements for a broker's office *except*
   a. the broker's license must be prominently displayed.
   b. the office must be equipped with a telephone.
   c. the licenses of the salespersons must be prominently displayed.
   d. the business name must be prominently displayed on the outside of the place of business.

4. A broker must keep records of all real estate transactions
   a. for at least one year following the closing date.
   b. for at least three years following the listing date.
   c. for at least three years following the consummation date.
   d. indefinitely.

5. The Real Estate Commission may take disciplinary action against a licensee for all of the following *except* violating the
   a. Real Estate Licensing and Registration Act.
   b. Rules and Regulations.
   c. Pennsylvania Human Relations Act.
   d. Blue Sky Laws.

6. When advertising a property for sale, the broker must include which of the following in the ad?
   a. Listing price
   b. Legal description of the property
   c. Broker's address
   d. Broker's business name

7. Which of the following is true regarding the Real Estate Recovery Fund?
   a. The maximum amount that may be paid the aggrieved person is $30,000.
   b. The licensee's license is automatically revoked.
   c. The aggrieved person may sue the licensee for further damages if the amount paid is insufficient.
   d. The licensee's license is suspended until he or she repays the full amount recovered out of the fund, plus interest.

8. An agreement of sale must include all of the following *except*
   a. the rate of commission.
   b. the names of the parties.
   c. disclosure of whom the broker represents.
   d. a description of the real estate to be conveyed.

9. Which of the following is *not* cause for disciplinary action against a licensee?
   a. Accepting a listing with the
      understanding that illegal discrimination
      will be exercised in the sale of the
      property
   b. Failure to provide the client with a copy
      of the listing contract at the time it is
      signed
   c. Placing a "for sale" sign on a property
      without written permission of the owner
   d. Payment of a commission by a licensed
      broker to another licensed broker

10. A licensed salesperson may do which of the
    following?
    a. Leave the employment of one broker
       and become associated with another
       broker without reporting the change to
       the commission
    b. Place an advertisement using only the
       salesperson's name and phone number
    c. Sell the salesperson's own property
       without telling a buyer that she is
       licensed
    d. Sell condominiums

11. Licensure is required for which of the fol-
    lowing activities?
    a. Owners selling their own properties
    b. Trustees selling trust properties
    c. Bank employees appraising property for
       the banking institution
    d. Selling campground memberships

12. A broker of record
    a. is employed by another broker.
    b. is the licensee responsible for the
       activities in a real estate corporation.
    c. is a broker who is permitted to sell
       dwellings only for the builder-owner.
    d. oversees the activities of a cemetery
       broker.

13. Which of the following is true regarding the
    laws for escrow accounts?
    a. Rents the broker collects must be
       deposited in the broker's escrow account.
    b. The salesperson must deposit escrow
       funds as soon as they are received.
    c. Escrow funds must be deposited in an
       interest-bearing account.
    d. The buyer and seller can agree in writ-
       ing that the escrow money will not be
       deposited until the agreement of sale is
       accepted.

14. All of the following must satisfy an educa-
    tion requirement prior to licensure *except*
    a. cemetery salespersons.
    b. campground membership salespersons.
    c. time-share salespersons.
    d. rental listing referral agents.

15. All of the following must take a license ex-
    amination *except*
    a. brokers.
    b. salespersons.
    c. builder-owner salespersons.
    d. time-share salespersons.

Section Two

REAL ESTATE PRACTICE

• • • • • • •

Real estate transactions are complex business dealings, beginning with the introduction of a property in the marketplace and progressing to the settlement or closing of the transaction. Because of the complex nature of these transactions, consumers rely on the expertise of real estate licensees to assist them. Real estate licensees provide a variety of services to buyers, sellers, property owners and tenants. As licensees provide these services, certain procedures and ethical behavior are followed to protect the interests of consumers.

Real Estate Practice introduces the various facets of the real estate business and the techniques, procedures and ethics involved in a real estate transaction. The concepts covered in this section and the chapters in which they are discussed are

14

The Real Estate Business

THE REAL ESTATE BUSINESS IS "BIG" BUSINESS

Billions of dollars circulate in our economy each year because of real estate. Property is bought and sold, rents are paid and collected and millions of dollars of loans are made to support the purchase and development of real estate. The talent and expertise of a number of professional people is needed to help today's buyers and sellers, landlords and tenants, investors, developers and lenders make their real estate decisions. Not only do millions of people depend on real estate professionals to help orchestrate their transactions, but millions of people also depend on some aspect of the real estate business for their livelihood.

Although some people see the real estate industry as a business comprised of brokers and salespeople who sell houses, many other highly trained people play an important role as well, especially as the technical aspects of real estate grow more complex. People trained in areas of specialization such as appraisal, property management, financing, subdivision and development, counseling and education provide valuable expertise in the industry. Attorneys, banks, trust companies, abstract and title insurance companies, architects, surveyors, accountants and government agencies also depend on real estate specialists.

Real Estate Activities

The real estate business offers many opportunities for people to pursue their individual interests. Some people become generalists, that is, they develop expertise in several areas of real estate practice; others become specialists, becoming highly skilled in a selected area. To appreciate the variety of the options that are available, consider the following discussion as we explore various real estate activities.

Brokerage. Brokerage is the aspect of the business that brings people together in a real estate transaction. It involves people who are interested in purchasing and selling or leasing and renting real estate. They may be interested in housing, commercial or industrial properties or other types of real estate. Some real estate practitioners broker several types of property, and others specialize, for example, in selected kinds of housing or in selected kinds of commercial property.

The way real estate practitioners provide brokerage services will be discussed in Chapter 15. In Pennsylvania, the real estate license law requires that people who are brokering property that they do not personally own must have a real estate license. In accordance with the state's law, there is a hierarchy in the real estate firm. The licensed broker in the company determines how the firm provides its services and will be compensated; the broker can hire licensed salespeople to provide these services on behalf of the broker.

Appraisal. Appraisal is the process of estimating a property's value. Although all real estate licensees must have some understanding of valuation, appraisers are trained specifically in the intricacies of valuing properties and developing appraisal reports. Their professional opinions of value, known as appraisals, are commonly used by lending institutions when property is financed, when property is sold by court order or is condemned or partitioned, when tax assessments are appealed and to value property for an estate. Appraisers may be employed by the government, lending institutions or trust companies, or they may be independent business owners. There are also certain requirements for licensing or certification that they must meet. Appraising is discussed in Chapter 19.

Property management. A property manager operates a property for its owner. The property manager's basic responsibility is to protect the value of the owner's investment while maximizing the owner's return on that investment. In that role, the property manager might be responsible for soliciting tenants, collecting rents, altering or constructing new space for tenants, ordering repairs and overseeing the general maintenance of the property. The scope of a property manager's responsibilities varies according to the terms of the individual employment contract, known as a management agreement. Property management is discussed in Chapter 22.

Financing. Financing is the business of providing the funds necessary to complete real estate transactions. Most transactions are financed by means of a mortgage loan, in which the property is pledged as security for the eventual payment of the loan. Individuals involved in financing real estate work in a variety of settings, such as commercial banks, savings and loan associations, mortgage banking and mortgage brokerage companies. It is not uncommon today for real estate brokerage companies and mortgage lenders to be affiliated with one another to provide one-stop services to buyers.

Subdivision and development. Subdivision entails dividing a large parcel of real estate into smaller ones. The subdivider surveys the land and drafts a map of the newly created parcels in the subdivision, often referred to as a *plat map*. (Subdividing is discussed in Chapter 2.) Development relates to the construction of improvements on land. These improvements fall into two categories. Off-site improvements, such as water lines and storm sewers under city streets, are made on public lands. On-site improvements, such as a new house, office building or shopping center, are made on individual parcels. While subdivision and development are normally related, particularly in housing, they are independent processes that can occur separately. People may specialize in one or both activities.

Counseling. Counseling involves providing clients with skilled, independent and professional guidance on a variety of real estate problems. Real estate investment decisions are highly individual and can be very complex, with many financial and tax consequences. A real estate counselor's role is to increase the client's knowledge and provide direction as the client makes real estate investment decisions.

Education. Education is the provision of real estate information to both practitioners and consumers. Colleges, universities and proprietary real estate schools conduct courses that are required for licensure and continuing education, and they along with trade associations and professional designation groups provide a broad range of courses and seminars for professional development. Many of these institutions as well as real estate companies conduct programs that are designed specifically to help consumers understand today's real estate transactions.

Other areas. Many other people are also part of the real estate business. These include those who are associated with mortgage banking firms, persons who negotiate mortgage loans for banks and savings and loan associations, people in property management and real estate departments of corporations, and officials and employees of government agencies such as zoning boards and assessing offices.

Types of Real Property

Just as there are many areas of specialization within the real estate industry, there are different types of property in which to specialize. Real estate can generally be classified as follows:

- residential—all property used for housing, from acreage to small city lots, both single-family and multifamily, in urban, suburban and rural areas
- commercial—business property, including office space, shopping centers, storefronts, theaters, hotels, parking facilities
- industrial—warehouses, factories, land in industrial districts, power plants
- agricultural—farms, timberland, pastureland, ranches, orchards
- special-purpose—churches, schools, cemeteries, government-held lands
- recreational—vacation property such as time shares, campground membership

In theory, a real estate company can provide all of the services that have been mentioned for all of these types of property, unless restricted by licensing laws. As a practical matter, this is not likely to be feasible. Each type of property as well as professional activity requires considerable expertise. Most real estate firms specialize to some degree, especially in urban areas. Some companies are highly specialized by only offering appraisal services, managing office buildings or concentrating on specialized market niches such as vacation properties or condominiums.

IN PRACTICE...	*Before engaging in any real estate activity, consider the licenses or certifications that may be required. Use Chapter 13 and Appendix C to identify the education and experience that is required and the procedures that must be followed to obtain the various real estate licenses. In addition, the activities of appraisers and mortgage bankers are governed by separate laws, copies of which can be obtained from the Bureau of Professional and Occupational Affairs in Harrisburg.*

Professional Organizations

The real estate business has many trade associations, the largest being the National Association of REALTORS® (NAR). State and local associations are chartered under the national organization. Active members of these affiliated state associations and local boards subscribe to the associations' Code of Ethics and are known as REALTORS®. Not all real estate licensees are REALTORS®. REALTOR® is a registered trademark of the National Association of REALTORS®. Some local boards offer a separate category of membership, Realtor-Associate, to salespeople affiliated with a REALTOR® and actively engaged in the real estate business as employees or independent contractors. The mission of NAR is to promote programs and services to enhance the ability of its members to conduct business successfully and ethically and to promote the preservation of the right to own, transfer and use real property.

NAR sponsors many specialized institutes that offer professional designations. People seeking these designations must satisfy certain requirements, including course work and experience in specialized fields of practice. For example, there are designations for counselors in real estate; specialists in farm and land; specialists in commercial, industrial, office or international property; property managers; real estate securities; residential brokers and sales specialists.

Among the many other professional associations is the National Association of Real Estate Brokers (NAREB), whose members also subscribe to a code of ethics. Members of NAREB are known as Realtists. The National Association of Exclusive Buyer Agents and Real Estate Buyer Agent's Council comprise real estate practitioners whose practices are devoted solely to providing services to buyers as clients. The Appraisal Institute and the National Association of Independent Fee Appraisers are professional associations of appraisers. The Real Estate Educators Association is a professional association of individuals and organizations involved in real estate education. (See Figure 14.1.)

THE REAL ESTATE MARKET

In literal terms a **market** is a place where goods can be bought and sold, where value for those goods can be established and where it is advantageous for buyers and sellers to trade. The function of the market is to facilitate this exchange by providing a setting in which the forces of supply and demand can establish market value.

To understand the real estate business, it's important to understand the real estate market. The "goods" in the real estate market are the properties. How readily can buyers and sellers trade properties? What is the value of the properties they are trading? Commonly the terms "buyer's market" and "seller's market" are used to describe the prevailing conditions in the marketplace. What do these

Figure 14.1 Examples of Professional Organizations in Real Estate	Organization	Professional Designation
	Appraisal Institute	RM (Residential Member) SRA (Senior Residential Appraisal) MAI (Member of the Appraisal Institute)
	Building Owners and Managers Association (BOMA)	RPA (Real Property Administrator) FMA (Facilities Management Administrator) SMA (Systems Maintenance Administrator)
	Institute of Real Estate Management (IREM)	CPM (Certified Property Manager) ARM (Accredited Residential Manager)
	National Association of Exclusive Buyer Agents (NAREB)	CEBA (Certified Exclusive Buyer Agent)
	National Association of Independent Fee Appraisers	IFA (Independent Fee Appraiser) IFSA (Senior Independent Fee Appraiser)
	National Association of Industrial and Office Properties (NAIOP)	
	National Association of Real Estate Brokers	Realtists
	National Association of REALTORS®	REALTORS® GRI (Graduate REALTORS® Institute)
	Real Estate Buyer Agent's Council (REBAC)	ABR (Accredited Buyer Representative)
	Real Estate Educators Association (REEA)	DREI (Designated Real Estate Instructor)
	REALTORS® Land Institute (RLI)	
	REALTORS® National Marketing Institute Residential Sales Council Real Estate Brokerage Council Commercial Investment Real Estate	CRS (Certified Residential Specialist) CRB (Certified Real Estate Brokerage Manager) CCIM (Certified Commercial-Investment Member)
	Society of Industrial and Office REALTORS®	SIOR (Society of Industrial and Office REALTORS®)
	Women's Council of REALTORS® (WCR)	LTG (Leadership Training Graduate)

Note: These are some of the many professional associations, councils and societies that are organized for the benefit of members engaged in various specialties in real estate and related practices.

terms mean to the industry and the individual buyers and sellers? To answer these questions, look at the how the forces of supply and demand interact.

The economic forces of **supply** and **demand** continually interact in the market to establish and maintain price levels. Essentially, *when supply goes up and demand remains stable, prices will drop as more producers or sellers compete for buyers. When demand increases and supply remains stable, prices will rise as more buyers compete for the product.* Greater supply means producers need to attract more buyers, so they lower prices. Greater demand means producers can raise their prices because buyers compete with one another for the product.

Following this theory a "buyer's market" is characterized by a relatively large number of properties available for sale, while a "seller's market" is characterized by fewer properties. This theory also says that in a buyer's market the buyers would not be paying as high a price as the seller could command in a seller's market.

However, because of the physical characteristics of real estate, real estate markets are relatively slow to adjust to the forces of supply and demand. Real estate is not a standardized product. Despite the fact that several units in one development may be built to the same specifications, each parcel has its own geographic location. Therefore, no two parcels are ever exactly alike. The general supply of properties may be large, but because each property is unique, its unique differences must appeal to a purchaser.

Land is immobile so real estate cannot be relocated to satisfy demand where supply is low. Nor can buyers always relocate to an area with greater supply. It is relatively difficult to affect supply and demand in a short period of time. Withdrawing a property from the market or adding property by constructing or renovating buildings will have an effect but it may not be immediate. It is also important to remember that the local character of the properties and the preferences of buyers create conditions that tend to make real estate markets unique.

Even when supply and demand can be forecast with some accuracy, natural disasters such as hurricanes, tornadoes or floods, sudden changes in the financial markets, new legislation or local events such as plant closings, can dramatically disrupt market trends. In those cases, communities face formidable challenges to meet the unanticipated demand of dislocated families and businesses whose properties are damaged or destroyed.

Historically, the geographic area in which real estate firms do business has been very local. Each geographic market is a mix of different types of real estate and different price ranges. For example, prices of inexpensive homes could be rising, prices for expensive homes could be stable, while condominiums and commercial real estate are declining in value. Certainly considerable expertise is needed to market properties and a company's services even in a small locale. Today, however, with technology and the volume of information that can be exchanged electronically, real estate companies can conduct business professionally and competently in a much larger geographic area, which may mean covering many, and perhaps quite different, markets. In fact, this is what today's consumers expect real estate firms to do.

Factors Affecting Supply

Factors that tend to affect supply in the real estate market include the labor force, construction costs, government controls and fiscal policies.

Labor force and construction costs. Any shortage of skilled labor or building materials or increase in cost of materials or labor can decrease the amount of new construction. Higher construction costs will be passed along to buyers and tenants. There is a limit to how much more they are willing to pay for what they are buying. Technological advances that result in cheaper materials and more efficient means of construction tend to counteract some price increases.

Government controls and financial policies. Government monetary policy can have a substantial impact on the real estate market. The Federal Reserve Board and such government agencies as the Federal Housing Administration (FHA), the Government National Mortgage Association (GNMA) and the Federal Home Loan Mortgage Corporation (FHLMC) can affect the amount of money available for mortgage loans, which ultimately affects the ability of buyers to purchase and builders to develop properties.

The federal government's fiscal policies also influence how much money is available for real estate investment. For example, taxation takes money out of circulation. The government puts money into circulation through spending programs ranging from welfare to farm subsidies.

Real estate taxation is one of the primary sources of revenue for local government. Taxation policies can have either positive or negative effects. High taxes may deter investors or even discourage homebuyers from considering a certain community. On the other hand, tax incentives can attract new businesses and industries. And, of course, along with these enterprises come increased employment and expanded residential real estate markets.

Local governments can also influence supply with their land-use policies. Communities can use building codes and zoning ordinances to encourage or discourage building or development. Community amenities such as schools and parks also shape the market. By establishing redevelopment districts and favorable zoning ordinances, communities can encourage developers to invest in blighted or previously undesirable neighborhoods. This can increase supply as well as enhance the value of properties in surrounding neighborhoods and increase tax revenue for the community.

Factors Affecting Demand

Factors that tend to affect demand in the real estate market include population, demographics and employment and wage levels.

Population. Shelter is a basic human need, so the need for housing grows as the population grows. Although the total population of the country continues to increase, the demand for real estate increases faster in some areas than in others. The Sunbelt, for example, is still attracting mobile retirees, but community incentives have succeeded in drawing businesses and young families as well. Similar local controls have also made other areas attractive for newcomers.

In other locations growth has ceased altogether or population has plummeted. For example, a local airbase or manufacturing plant might close. The result can be a dwindling population or mass exodus, with an accompanying drop in demand for real estate.

Demographics. The makeup of the population—or demographics—affects demand as strongly as simple numbers. Family size and the ratio of adults to children, the number of people moving into retirement care facilities and retirement communities, the effect of "doubling up" (two or more families using one housing unit) and the changing number of single-parent households all contribute to the amount and type of housing needed. Another factor is the number of young people who would prefer to rent or own their own residences but share with roommates or remain in their parent's homes for economic reasons.

Employment and wage levels. The real estate market is closely tied to the job market. As employment opportunities increase and decline as businesses move into or out of an area or expand or downsize their operations, the demand for housing increases and declines depending on the number of potential buyers and sellers. When job opportunities are scarce, wage levels are low or workers are insecure about their continued employment, demand for real estate usually drops. On the other hand, favorable employment conditions generally increase the demand for housing. It's important to keep abreast of local employment conditions to anticipate demand for real estate.

The general economic climate in the area also affects demand. The level of confidence people have in the economy affects their decisions about whether to spend or save, buy or rent, invest in the community or go elsewhere. All of these decisions ultimately affect the demand for real estate.

THE HOUSING MARKET

Everyone needs a place to live; communities thrive because of their residents. When people have a vested interest in the community, they demand services such as education, transportation, health care and cultural and recreational opportunities, all of which use real estate. People are the "engine" that drives communities.

Many of the factors of supply and demand that were discussed have a direct affect on the housing market. In addition, the individual needs and preferences of buyers impact the market. Real estate ownership represents more than the shelter of "brick and mortar"; it is a psychological as well as a financial investment. People want a place to belong and the ability to control their quality of life. Ownership also gives them a sense of pride. Therefore, the motivation to own is great, but frequently people, particularly first-time homebuyers, are unaware that they can become stakeholders in the community. Many people can indeed become homeowners once they understand the housing market and the economic considerations involved in homeownership.

Types of Housing

The housing market consists of many types of housing, especially because of social changes, demographic shifts and economic considerations. As mentioned in the discussion about demographics, the profile of today's homebuyer is quite diverse. As the needs of buyers become more specialized, the residential market is evolving to meet those needs. Common types of housing that are currently available, in addition to single-family homes, are discussed in the following paragraphs. Some are not only innovative uses of real estate but also incorporate a variety of ownership concepts.

Apartment complexes, groups of apartment buildings with any number of units in each building continue to be popular. The buildings may be low-rise or high-rise, and the amenities may include parking as well as clubhouses, swimming pools and, even, golf courses.

The *condominium* is a popular form of ownership, particularly for people who want the security of owning property but do not want the responsibilities of caring for and maintaining a house. Management and maintenance of building exteriors and common facilities such as halls, elevators, swimming pools, club houses, tennis courts and surrounding grounds is provided by an agreement with the condominium association, which is made up of the unit owners, who pay periodic assessments for the expenses. Office buildings and shopping centers may also be established as condominiums, allowing businesses to build equity in the space they occupy while avoiding unpredictable rent increases. Condominiums are discussed in detail in Chapter 7.

A *cooperative* is similar to a condominium because it has units within a larger building with common walls and facilities. The owners, however, do not actually own the units. Instead they buy shares of stock in the corporation that holds title to the building. In return for stock in the corporation, they receive a *proprietary lease* entitling them to occupy a particular unit. Like condominium unit owners, cooperative unit owners pay their share of the building's expenses. Cooperatives are discussed in detail in Chapter 7.

Planned residential developments (PRDs) merge a variety of residential housing types under one development. *Planned unit developments (PUDs)* merge such diverse land uses as housing, recreation and commercial units in one self-contained development. PRDs and PUDs are zoned under special cluster zoning requirements that allow them to make high density use of the land and maximize the use of open space by reducing lot sizes and street areas. Owners do not have direct ownership interest in the common areas. A community association is formed to maintain these areas with fees collected from the owners.

Converted-use properties are factories, office buildings, hotels, schools and churches that have been converted to residential use. Usually the property was abandoned and bought by developers who found it both aesthetically and economically appealing to renovate for use as rental or condominium units. An abandoned warehouse may be transformed into luxury loft condominium units, a closed hotel may become an apartment building and an old factory may become a shopping complex.

Retirement communities, often structured as PUDs, may provide shopping, recreational opportunities and health-care facilities, in addition to residential units. Because of the recent amendments to the fair housing laws, retirement communities cannot exclude families with children unless they meet the legal requirements for "housing for older persons." This is defined as housing to be occupied solely by persons 62 years of age or older or housing in which at least 80 percent of the units are to be occupied by at least one person who is 55 years of age or older. The laws also require that there must be facilities and services to meet the physical, recreational and social needs of older persons.

High-rise developments often combine office space, stores, theaters and apartment units. These buildings usually are self-contained and include laundry facilities, restaurants, food stores, valet shops, beauty parlors, barbershops, swimming pools and other attractive and convenient features. The most successful developments also effectively use natural assets such as rivers, lakes and forest preserves.

Mobile homes were once considered useful only as temporary residences or for travel. But in times of high-priced housing, they are often used as principal residences or stationary vacation homes. Relatively low cost, coupled with the increased living space available in the newer, double-wide and triple-wide models, has made mobile homes more attractive. Increased sales have in turn resulted in growing numbers of mobile-home parks in some communities. These parks offer complete residential environments with permanent community facilities as well as semipermanent foundations and hookups for gas, water and electricity.

Modular homes are also gaining popularity as the price of newly constructed homes rises. Each room, preassembled at the factory, is lowered into place on the building site by a crane; workers later finish the structure and connect plumbing and wiring. Entire developments can be built at a fraction of the time and cost of conventional types of construction.

Through *time-shares* purchasers share ownership of one vacation home. Each owner is entitled to use the property for a certain period of time each year, usually one week. In addition to the purchase price, each owner pays an annual maintenance fee. Due to high initial marketing costs and the uncertain resale market, time-share resale prices can be significantly lower than their original purchase prices.

HOUSING AFFORDABILITY

Housing affordability has become a major issue in recent years. Periods of high inflation of the 1970s caused housing prices to rise rapidly, but individual incomes failed to keep pace. Although the recession of the early 1990s slowed the rapid price increases and appreciation of the 1980s, the general economic climate and employment conditions in some areas of the state inhibited the ability of many people to take advantage of more affordable housing prices that flattened, or even declined, in some markets.

Homeownership has declined most severely among young people and low-to-moderate income purchasers. First-time homebuyers, for example, often have difficulty saving the downpayment and closing costs needed for a conventional loan. Real estate and related industry groups, along with Congress, state legislatures and local government bodies, have been working to develop solutions that will increase the availability of suitable and affordable housing for all segments of the population.

Certainly not all people should own homes. Home ownership involves substantial commitment and responsibility, and the flexibility of renting suits some individuals' needs. People whose work requires frequent moves or whose financial position is uncertain will particularly benefit from renting. Investing in a home may not be suitable for people who rely on income-producing assets to live. Renting also provides more leisure time by freeing tenants from management and maintenance.

The decision to purchase rather than rent must be weighed carefully. Current mortgage loan terms, expenses of ownership, investment and tax should be considered in light of a person's individual financial circumstances.

Mortgage Loans

Because many people finance their purchases, the amount of cash needed for a down payment and the interest rate and other finance charges affect their ability to own a home.

Down payment requirements have been liberalized over the years. The *loan-to-value-ratio* (the amount of the loan in relation to the value of the property) has increased to 95 percent, depending on the specific type of loan. Under certain circumstances and typically with higher interest rates, the loan-to-value-ratio can be 97% to 100%. Although the down payment can be, for example, 20 percent of the purchase price, people who do not have this much cash to invest can purchase with smaller down payments. Low down payment loans are available under programs sponsored by the Federal Housing Administration (FHA), the Department of Veterans Affairs (commonly called the VA), the Pennsylvania Housing Finance Agency and local community reinvestment loans.

The trade-off, however, is that the amount of the down payment affects the amount of the loan. When the down payment is small, the borrower must be able to afford the monthly payments on a higher loan amount. The annual interest rate is also normally higher on these loans, which increases the monthly payment as well. But, as will be discussed later, income-tax deductions for mortgage interest may offset the added expense, depending on a person's individual tax situation. Buyers may also be able to qualify for loans with adjustable interest rates; many of these loans have lower initial interest rates.

The length of loan also affects housing affordability. For some borrowers, a 15-year loan-term is desirable. If they can afford the higher payment to pay off the loan faster, they can own their homes free-and-clear in a shorter period of time. For others, stretching out payments over a 30 year loan-term fits better into the monthly budget because the payments are lower.

Cash for closing costs, in addition to the down payment, can be problematic for buyers, but there are ways to cope with this situation as well. Specific loan programs offer lower closing costs, particularly those for first-time homebuyers. It is also possible to have the seller agree to assist with some of the costs as an incentive to get the house sold.

Buyer's Ability to Pay

Home ownership involves expenses for utilities (electricity, natural gas, water), trash removal, sewer charges and maintenance and repairs plus real estate taxes and property insurance, as well as the mortgage loan payment.

To determine whether a prospective buyer can afford a certain purchase, lenders traditionally have used a "rule of thumb" formula. The monthly cost of buyer and maintaining a home (mortgage payment plus tax and insurance) should not exceed 28 percent of gross (pretax) monthly income. This payment plus the payments on all recurring debts should not exceed 38 percent of monthly income. These formulas may vary, however, depending on the type of loan program and the borrower's earnings, number of debts, credit history, number of dependents and other factors.

Investment Considerations

Purchasing a home offers several financial advantages. As the total mortgage debt is reduced through monthly payments, the owner's interest in the property, called **equity,** increases. Some people view this as forced savings because as they repay the loan, they are gaining an asset.

Another advantage is the possibility of the property gaining in value, appreciating, during the time it is owned. This means a sale could bring more money than the owner paid for the property. There are many variables that affect whether this possibility becomes a reality. The specific kind of property, the neighborhood and value of surrounding properties, the general condition of the

Table 14.1 Homeowners' Tax Benefits	**Income Tax Deductions**	**Homeowner's Exclusions**
	Loan interest on first and second homes, subject to limitation Loan origination fees Some loan discount points Loan Prepayment penalties Real estate taxes	Single individuals can exclude $250,000 gain or profit from income. Married couples, filing jointly, can exclude $500,000 gain or profit from income
	Deferment of Tax on Profit	Additionally, first-time home buyers may make penalty-free withdrawals from their tax-deferred IRAs, to a maximum down payment of $10,000.
	Tax on some or all of profit on sale is postponed if another personal residence is purchased within 24 months before or after sale.	

local economy and the interaction of supply and demand when the property is sold all affect the amount of appreciation that can be realized. Real estate values have historically been less volatile than other investments, and the rate of appreciation has at least equaled, and in many cases exceeded, the rate of interest that could be earned if the cash were invested elsewhere.

Tax Benefits

To encourage home ownership the federal government allows homeowners certain income-tax advantages. Homeowners may deduct from their income some or all of the mortgage interest paid, as well as real estate taxes and certain other expenses. They may even defer or eliminate tax on the profit received from selling the home. Depending on a person's individual circumstances, tax considerations may be an important factor when deciding whether to purchase a home. (See Table 14.1.)

Tax deductions. Homeowners may deduct from their gross income

- mortgage interest payments on first and second homes that meet the definition of "qualified residence interest"

- real estate taxes (but *not* interest paid on overdue taxes)

- certain loan origination fees

- discount points, whether paid by buyer or seller and

- loan prepayment penalties.

"Qualified residence interest" is limited as follows: All debt secured by a principal and second residence and used to buy, construct or substantially improve those residences, called *acquisition indebtedness,* must equal no more than $1 million. Home equity loans—loans secured by the property and in amounts not exceeding the owner's equity in the property—may not be more than $100,000.

Capital gains. Capital gains Capital gains is the profit realized from the sale or exchange of an asset, including real property. To stimulate investment, Congress has allowed part of a taxpayer's capital gain to be free from income tax.

In August 1997, retroactively to May 1997, a law was passed allowing an unmarried individual an exclusion of $250,000 gain or profit from income on the sale or exchange of a residence and $500,000 exclusion if married, filing jointly.

The exemption may be used repeatedly, as long as the homeowners have occupied the property as their primary residence for at least two of the previous five years. For most homeowners, the net result of this law is that they will never pay capital gains tax on the sale of their homes.

IN PRACTICE... *The circumstances of all investors and taxpayers are not the same. A taxpayer who does not itemize deductions, for example, may not have the same tax advantages as a taxpayer who does itemize. Also the tax laws constantly change, which can alter the tax benefits and deductions for homeowners. A real estate licensee should not attempt to give tax advice to clients and customers. They should be referred to the Internal Revenue Service, a certified public accountant or other tax specialist for specific information about their personal situations.*

INSURANCE

Although real estate and insurance are separate businesses, there is a logical connection between the two. Once people invest in real estate, they want to protect their investment by insuring it. In fact, lenders, to lessen their own risk of loss when the debt is secured by real estate, usually require property owners to have insurance. Many years ago it was not uncommon for real estate brokers to also be insurance brokers, providing real estate purchasers with an additional service by brokering insurance policies.

To fully understand the role of insurance in a real estate transaction, it's important to look as the various events insurance covers. Although a homeowner can insure against the destruction of the property by fire or windstorm, injury to others on the premises and theft of personal property, most people choose to buy a packaged **homeowner's insurance policy** to cover all of these events.

Homeowners' Insurance

Although coverage provided may vary among policies, all homeowners' policies have three common characteristics.

First, they all have *fixed ratios of coverage*. That is each type of coverage, such as on household contents and other items, must be a fixed percentage of the amount of insurance on the building itself. While the amount of contents coverage may be increased, it cannot be reduced below the standard percentage.

Second, homeowners' policies have an *indivisible premium,* which means that the insured receives coverage for all perils included in the policy for a single rate and may not choose to exclude certain perils from coverage.

Finally, *first-party and third-party insurance* protects the owner whose acts or negligence cause injury to another. Not only actual damage or loss but also the homeowner's legal liability for losses, damages or injuries are included in this **liability coverage.**

The basic form of homeowners' insurance provides coverage against

- fire or lightning

- glass breakage

- windstorm or hail

- explosion

- riot or civil commotion

- damage by aircraft

- damage from vehicles

- damage from smoke

- vandalism and malicious mischief

- theft and

- loss of property removed from the premises when endangered by fire or other perils.

A broad form, in addition to the coverage listed above, also covers

- falling objects

- weight of ice, snow or sleet

- collapse of the building or any part of it

- bursting, cracking, burning or bulging of a steam or hot-water heating system, or of appliances used to heat water

- accidental discharge, leakage or overflow of water or steam from within a plumbing, heating or air-conditioning system

- freezing of plumbing, heating and air-conditioning systems and domestic appliances and

- injury to electrical appliances, devices, fixtures and wiring from short circuits or other accidentally generated currents.

Further coverage is available from policies that cover almost all possible perils. Other policies include a broad-form policy designed specifically for apartment renters and a broad-form policy for condominium owners. Apartment and condominium policies generally provide fire and windstorm, theft and public liability coverage for injuries or losses sustained within the unit but do not usually extend to cover losses or damages to the structure. The structure is insured by either the landlord or the condominium owners' association (except, in condominium ownership, for additions or alterations made by the unit owner, which are not covered by the association's master policy).

Most homeowners' insurance policies contain a **coinsurance clause** to cover partial losses. This provision usually requires the insured to maintain fire insurance on his or her property in an amount equal to at least 80 percent of the **replacement cost** of the dwelling (not including the land). If the owner carries such a policy, a claim may be made for the cost of the repair or replacement of the damaged property without deduction for depreciation. Homeowners should periodically review their policies to be certain that the coverage is equal to at least 80 percent of the current replacement cost of their homes.

Most insurance policies have a **subrogation** clause that applies when the insured collects for damage from the insurance company. It provides that any rights the insured may have to sue the person who caused the damage will be assigned to the insurance company. The insurer may pursue legal action to collect the amount paid out from the party at fault. The clause prevents the insured from collecting twice for the same damage.

Federal Flood Insurance Program

The National Flood Insurance Act of 1968 was enacted by Congress to help owners of property in flood-prone areas by subsidizing flood insurance and by taking land use and control measures to improve future management for flood-plain areas. The Department of Housing and Urban Development (HUD) administers the flood program. The Army Corps of Engineers has prepared maps that identify specific flood-prone areas throughout the country. Owners in flood-prone areas need to obtain flood insurance to finance property by federal or federally related mortgage loans, grants or guarantees or provide a survey showing that the lowest part of the building is located above the 100-year flood mark.

In designated areas, flood insurance coverage is required on all types of buildings—residential, commercial, industrial and agricultural—for either the value of the property or the amount of the mortgage loan, subject to the maximum limits available. Policies are written annually and can be purchased from any licensed property insurance broker, the National Flood Insurance Program or the designated servicing companies in each state.

Mine Subsidence Insurance

One of the limitations of homeowners' insurance is that damage or loss of an insured's property due to mine subsidence is not covered. Any property owner who is concerned about this type of damage or loss should seek additional insurance specifically for such an event. Policies are available through the Coal Mines Subsidence Insurance Fund under the Department of Mines and Minerals Industries in Pennsylvania. The recoverable loss under these policies is limited to damage to the structure; damage to the surrounding site is not covered. The Bureau of Mines is a good resource to consult regarding the location of mines and to help evaluate the likelihood of subsidence.

•   •   •   •   •   •   •

KEY TERMS

capital gain
coinsurance clause
demand
equity
homeowner's insurance policy

liability coverage
market
replacement cost
subrogation
supply

SUMMARY

Although brokerage is the most widely recognized activity of the real estate business, many other services are also provided by the industry, such as appraisal, property management, property development, counseling, property financing and education. Most real estate firms specialize in only one or two of these areas.

Real property can be classified according to its general use as residential, commercial, industrial, agricultural, special-purpose or recreational. Although many brokers deal with more than one type of real property, they tend to specialize to some degree.

A market is a place where goods and services can be bought and sold and price levels established. The ideal market allows for a continual balancing of the forces of supply and demand. Because of its unique characteristics, real estate is relatively slow to adjust to the forces of supply and demand.

The supply of and demand for real estate are affected by many factors, including changes in population numbers and demographics, wage and employment levels, construction costs and availability of labor, and government monetary policy and controls.

The housing market includes apartment complexes, condominiums, cooperatives, planned unit developments, retirement communities, high-rise developments, converted-use properties, modular homes, mobile homes and time shares in addition to single family homes.

Prospective buyers should be aware of both the advantages and disadvantages of home ownership. Although a homeowner gains financial security and pride of ownership, the costs of ownership—both the initial price and the continuing expenses—must be considered.

One of the income-tax benefits available to homeowners is the ability to deduct mortgage-interest payments (within certain limitations) and property taxes from their federal income-tax returns. An individual can exclude $250,000 in gain from income and $500,000 if married. The exclusion can be used on a continuing basis, but not more than once every two years.

To protect their investment in real estate, most homeowners purchase insurance. A standard homeowner's insurance policy covers fire, theft and liability and can be extended to cover many types of less common risks. Another type of insurance, which covers personal property only, is available to people who live in apartments and condominiums.

Many homeowners' policies contain a coinsurance clause to cover partial losses that requires the policyholder to maintain fire insurance in an amount equal to 80 percent of the replacement cost of the home. If this percentage is not met, the policyholder may not be reimbursed for the full repair costs if a loss occurs. A subrogation clause enables an insurer to sue the party responsible for damage to the insured's property.

In addition to homeowners' insurance, the federal government makes flood insurance available for people living in flood-prone areas. The Coal Mines Subsidence Insurance Fund in Pennsylvania provides insurance to cover loss resulting from mine subsidence.

Questions

1. Commercial real estate includes all of the following *except*

    a. an office building for sale.
    b. apartments for rent.
    c. a retail space for lease.
    d. fast-food restaurants.

2. In general, when the supply of a certain commodity increases

    a. prices tend to rise.
    b. prices tend to drop.
    c. demand tends to rise.
    d. demand tends to drop.

3. All of the following factors tend to affect supply *except*

    a. the labor force.
    b. construction costs.
    c. government controls.
    d. employment and wage level.

4. Which of the following is an example of special-purpose real estate?

    a. An apartment building
    b. A public library
    c. A shopping center
    d. An industrial park

5. The real cost of owning a home includes certain costs or expenses that many people tend to overlook. Which of the following is *not* a cost or expense of owning a home?

    a. Interest paid on borrowed capital
    b. Homeowner's insurance
    c. Maintenance and repairs
    d. Taxes on personal property

6. When a person buys a house using a mortgage loan, the difference between the amount owed on the property and what it is worth represents the homeowner's

    a. tax basis.
    b. equity.
    c. replacement cost.
    d. capital gain.

7. A building that is remodeled into residential units and is no longer used for the purpose for which it was originally built is

    a. converted-use property.
    b. an example of urban homesteading.
    c. a planned unit development.
    d. a modular home.

8. In a homeowner's insurance policy, *coinsurance* refers to

    a. the specific form of policy purchased by the owner.
    b. the stipulation that the homeowner must purchase insurance coverage equal to at least 80 percent of the replacement cost of the structure to collect the full insured amount in the event of a loss.
    c. the stipulation that the homeowner must purchase fire insurance coverage equal to at least 70 percent of the replacement cost of the structure to be able to collect the full insured amount in the event of a loss.
    d. combined coverage for fire and flood damage.

9. Federal income-tax laws do *not* allow a homeowner to deduct which of the following expenses from gross income?

    a. Mortgage origination fees
    b. Real estate taxes
    c. Routine home maintenance
    d. Mortgage prepayment penalties

10. A townhouse is most closely associated
    with which of the following types of
    housing?
    a. High-rise development
    b. Condominium
    c. Mobile home
    d. Urban homestead

11. What is the capital gains tax exclusion avail-
    able to homeowners who file their income
    singly?
    a. $125,000   c. $225,000
    b. $250,000   d. $500,000

12. One result of the 1997 tax law is that *most*
    homeowners
    a. will pay capital gains tax at an 8 percent
       lower rate on their home sales.
    b. may use a one-time $500,000 exclusion
       if they file their taxes jointly.
    c. will never pay capital gains tax on the
       sale of their homes.
    d. will be taxed at a lower rate as they get
       older.

15

Real Estate Brokerage and Agency

The nature of real estate brokerage services, particularly those provided in residential sales transactions, has changed significantly in recent years. Through the 1950s real estate brokerage companies were primarily one-office, minimally staffed, family-run operations. The broker listed an owner's property for sale and found a buyer without assistance from other companies. Then the sale was negotiated and closed. It was relatively clear that the broker represented the seller's interests.

In the 1960s, however, the way buyers and sellers were brought together in a transaction began to change. Brokers started to share information about houses they had listed, resulting in two brokers cooperating with one another to sell a property. The brokers formalized this exchange of information by creating multiple-listing services (MLSs). The MLS expedited sales by increasing exposure to potential buyers and thus became a widely used industry service.

Confusion arose about who the broker represented in these cooperative transactions. With two different brokers involved in a sale, people naturally assumed was that there was a clear division of responsibility: the broker who had the property listed for sale represented the seller; and the broker who found the buyer represented the buyer. However, this was *not* the case. In those shared transactions, both brokers represented the seller.

Such misunderstandings ultimately led buyers to question exactly how their interests were being protected. This is one of many examples of a growing trend in which all consumers are demanding protections. In fact, lawmakers in many states have departed from the common law doctrine of *caveat emptor*—let the buyer beware—toward greater consumer protection. Buyers want not only accurate, factual information so that they can make informed decisions, but they also want advice. Buyers want someone to guide them and look out for their interests, particularly as real estate transactions become more complex. Why shouldn't they be able to have real estate licensees represent them, to provide the same level of service for buyers that they have been providing to sellers?

The real estate industry has responded. Homebuyers who had to either represent themselves or hire lawyers to represent them are now being represented by real estate licensees. This transformation in the industry is not as easy or simple as it may sound. Brokers have major decisions to make—whether to represent buyers (new for many brokers), to represent sellers (the "traditional" practice) or whether to do both. There's also the possibility of servicing buyers and sellers *without* representing either through **transactional brokerage.**

Although this historical perspective tracks developments in residential practices, buyers and sellers of nonresidential properties or landlords and tenants have similar concerns. The broker's decisions are essentially the same—whether to represent the prospective tenant for a storefront or to represent the owner of a shopping center, for example. The distinctive characteristic of representation is rooted in the law of agency. By understanding how the law of agency works, it is easier to understand the dilemmas brokers face when making their decisions.

LAW OF AGENCY

The *law of agency* is the basic framework of the law that governs the legal responsibilities of the broker to the people whom he or she represents. This is common law, that is, law based on usage, general acceptance and custom, and it is manifested in court decrees and judgments. Common law originated in England and was then incorporated into the U.S. legal system. The law of agency evolved from the master-servant relationship under English common law. The servant owed absolute loyalty to the master. This loyalty superseded the servant's personal interest as well as loyalty the servant might owe to others.

Under the **law of agency,** a relationship is created in which one person, the **principal,** delegates to another person, the **agent,** the right to act on his or her behalf in business transactions. This relationship must be *consensual:* the principal *delegates* authority; the agent *consents* to act. The agent has the right to reject an agency that he or she is incapable of performing. The parties must mutually agree to form the relationship. A fiduciary relationship then exists, meaning that the agent has certain duties and obligations when representing the principal. The agent is obligated to high standards of loyalty similar to the loyalty the servant owes to the master. As masters used the services of servants to accomplish what they could not or did not want to do for themselves, the principal uses the services of the agent. The agent is regarded as an expert on whom the principal can rely for specialized professional advice.

The following terms have specific legal definitions under the law of agency. (See Figure 15.1.)

- **Agent**—the individual who is authorized to and consents to act on behalf of and represent the interest of another person. In the real estate business the broker of the firm is the agent.

- **Principal**—the individual who hires and delegates to the agent the responsibility of representing his or her interests. In the real estate business this is the buyer or seller. The landlord or tenant may also be the principal.

- **Agency**—the fiduciary relationship between the principal and the agent

- **Fiduciary**—the relationship in which the agent is placed in the position of trust and confidence to the principal

- **Client**—the principal

- **Customer**—the third party for whom some service is provided

**Figure 15.1
Definitions in
Agency Law**

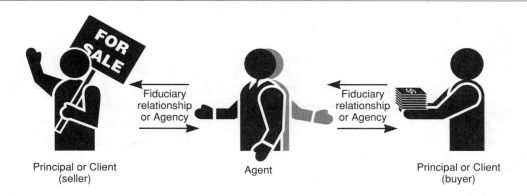

Principal or Client   Agent   Principal or Client
(seller)   (buyer)

Fiduciary relationship or Agency

Fiduciary relationship or Agency

The authorized activity of an agent is as simple or as complex as the principal allows. An agent may be classified as a general agent or special agent, based on the scope of his or her authority.

A **general agent** is empowered to represent the principal in a *broad range of matters* and may bind the principal to any contracts within the scope of the agent's authority. This type of agency can be created by a general power of attorney, which makes the agent an *attorney-in-fact*. The broker does *not* typically have this scope of authority as an agent in real estate transactions.

A **special agent** is authorized to represent the principal in *one specific act or business transaction, under detailed instructions*. A real estate broker is generally a special agent. If hired by a seller, for example, the broker's duty is to find a ready, willing and able buyer for the property. As a special agent, the broker is *not authorized* to bind the principal to any contract. The principals must bind themselves to the terms of contracts.

Real estate brokers and salespeople have commonly been referred to as "agents." Legally, however, this term refers to the strictly defined legal relationship. The salesperson and broker are not necessarily a person's agent. Sometimes the seller, for example, is the principal, which means that the broker is the seller's agent; and other times the buyer is the principal, which means that the broker is the buyer's agent. The salesperson is essentially the broker's representative, providing agency services to whomever the broker represents. The salesperson does not become the agent of a buyer or seller independently from the broker.

It is important to distinguish between *client-level* and *customer-level* services. The *client* is the principal to whom the agent has fiduciary obligations and provides *advice* and *counsel*. Advice is an opinion or recommendation offered as a guide for future action or conduct. It implies that the person who gives the advice has professional or technical knowledge, although the licensee does not provide legal advice unless separately licensed to do so. In contrast, the *customer* is provided factual *information* and, under the consumer laws, is entitled to fair and honest treatment. As a customer, the person does not receive advice and counsel. The agent works *for* the principal and *with* the customer. Essentially the agent is the principal's advocate.

**Figure 15.2
Agent's
Responsibilities**

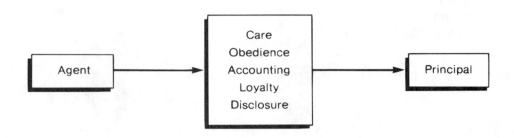

**Fiduciary
Responsibilities**

The cornerstone of the law of agency is the legal duties—the *fiduciary responsibilities*—an agent assumes on behalf of the principal. These duties are not simply moral or ethical, they are the law—the law of agency. To understand what client-level services are, it is important to understand the specific duties the agent owes the principal. These are the duties of *care, obedience, accounting, loyalty* and *disclosure,* easily remembered by the acronym COALD. (see Figure 15.2.)

Care. The agent must exercise a reasonable degree of care while transacting business entrusted to the agent by the principal. The principal expects the agent's skill and expertise in real estate matters to be superior to that of the average person. The most fundamental way in which the broker exercises care is to use that skill and knowledge in the principal's behalf. This means that the broker should know all facts that are pertinent to the principal's affairs. A broker who does not make a reasonable effort to properly represent the interest of the principal could possibly be found negligent. The broker is liable to the principal for any loss resulting from the broker's negligence or carelessness.

If the broker represents the seller, care and skill include helping the seller arrive at an appropriate and realistic listing price, discovering facts that affect the seller and disclosing them, and properly presenting the contracts that the seller signs. It also means making reasonable efforts to market the property, such as advertising and holding open houses, and helping the seller evaluate the terms and conditions of offers to purchase.

A broker who represents the buyer is expected to help the buyer locate suitable property and evaluate property values, neighborhood and property conditions, financing alternatives and offers and counteroffers with the buyer's interest in mind.

Obedience. The fiduciary relationship obligates the broker to act in good faith at all times, obeying the principal's instructions in accordance with the contract. That obedience is not absolute, however. The broker *may not* obey any instructions that are unlawful or unethical. For example, the broker may not follow instructions that violate the fair housing laws or to conceal a defect in the property. Because illegal acts do not serve the principal's best interests, obeying such instructions violates the broker's duty of loyalty. On the other hand, a broker who exceeds the authority granted by the principal will be liable for any injury the broker causes the principal.

Accounting. The broker must be able to report the status of all funds received from or on behalf of the principal. Brokers are required to deposit and account for escrow funds in the manner prescribed in Pennsylvania's license law. They are also not permitted to commingle these monies with personal or general business funds. Brokers are also required to give accurate copies of all documents to all parties affected by them and keep copies of these documents for at least three years.

Loyalty. The broker owes the principal the utmost loyalty. This means placing the principal's interest above those of all others, including the broker's self-interest. *Confidentiality about the personal affairs of the principal is a key element of loyalty* (similar to the relationship between a client and an attorney).

An agent may not, for example, disclose the principal's financial position. When the principal is the seller, the broker may not reveal that the principal will accept less than the listing price or is anxious to sell unless authorized by the seller to disclose this information. The broker, however, must disclose material facts about the *property*. If the principal is the buyer, the broker may not disclose that the buyer will pay more than the offered price or any similar facts that might harm the buyer's bargaining position.

Because an agent may not act out of self-interest, the broker must conduct the negotiation of sales agreements without regard to the amount of commission the broker will earn. According to Pennsylvania's license law, the broker must disclose any personal interest he or she has in purchasing a listed property and obtain the principal's consent. Licensees must also inform purchasers of personal interests licensees have in the properties being sold.

Disclosure. The agent has the duty to keep the principal informed of all facts or information that could affect the transaction. Duty of disclosure includes relevant information or *material facts* that the agent knows or *should have known* that could affect a principal's decision. The agent is obligated to discover facts that a reasonable person would feel are important in choosing a course of action, regardless of whether they are favorable or unfavorable to the principal's position. The broker may be held liable for damages for failure to disclose such information. For example, a broker representing a seller has the duty to disclose

- all offers;
- the identity of the prospective purchasers, including the agent's relationship, if any, to them (such as a relative or the broker's being a participating purchaser);
- the ability of the purchaser to complete the sale or offer a higher price;
- any interest the broker has in the buyer (such as the buyer's asking the broker to manage the property after it is purchased); or
- the buyer's intention to resell the property for a profit.

A broker representing a buyer must disclose deficiencies of a property, as well as sales contract provisions and financing that do not suit the buyer's interests. The broker would suggest the lowest price that the buyer should pay based on comparable values, regardless of the listing price. The broker would also disclose such information as how long the property has been listed or why the seller is selling, which would affect the buyer's ability to negotiate the lowest purchase price. This information, if the broker is representing the seller, violates the fiduciary to the seller.

Creation of Agency

Agents are employed for their expertise. However, providing services does not in itself create an agency relationship. As previously mentioned, no agency exists without mutual consent between the principal and the agent. The agent consents to undertake certain duties on behalf of the principal, subject to the principal's control. The principal authorizes the agent to perform these acts when dealing with others.

Express agency. Principal and agent may make an **express agreement** in which the parties state the contract's terms and express their intention either orally or in writing. An agency relationship between a seller and a broker is generally created by a written employment contract, commonly referred to as a **listing agreement,** which authorizes the broker to find a buyer or tenant for the owner's property. An agency relationship between a buyer and a broker is created by a **buyer-agency agreement.** Similar to a listing agreement, it stipulates the activities and responsibilities the buyer expects from the broker in finding suitable property for purchase or rent.

Pennsylvania Real Estate Commission's Rules and Regulations require that all exclusive listing agreements and other contracts of employment must be in writing. The regulations also prohibit a licensee from marketing or advertising the sale or lease of real estate or otherwise solicit prospective buyers without the authority of the seller or owner (or the owner's agent).

Implied agency. A written contract is not necessary to create an agency relationship. An agency may be created by **implied agreement.** This occurs when the *actions* of the parties indicate that they have mutually consented to an agency. A person acts on behalf of another as agent; the other person, as principal, delegates the authority to act.

The parties may not have consciously planned to create an agency relationship. Nonetheless, it can result *unintentionally, inadvertently* or *accidentally* by their actions. An implied agency with a buyer, for example, can result from the words and actions of a salesperson. If the salesperson legally represents the seller, then there is one agency in conflict with another. Dual representation, which will be discussed in detail later, may occur even though it was not intended.

Compensation

An exchange of consideration can be bargained for (a contractual relationship) or there may be no consideration (a gratuitous agency). As previously mentioned, the basis of an agency relationship is authorization and consent, not compensation. The fiduciary obligations are exactly the same regardless of whether or not there is an agreement to pay compensation.

The source of the compensation does not determine who is being represented. A buyer or a seller, for example, may compensate any agent, either their own or someone else's. Common practice in residential real estate has been for sellers to compensate the brokers as agreed to in the listing contracts. In this case the agent is being compensated by the principal. With the emergence of buyer agency, alternative compensation arrangements are becoming more common. For example, the broker who is representing the buyer may be compensated by the seller rather than the buyer-client. Or the compensation in the transaction may be shared by the buyer and seller. The listing contracts and buyer agency agreements normally indicate the specific compensation arrangements.

**Termination
of Agency**

An agency may be terminated at any time (except in the case of an agency coupled with an interest) for any of the following reasons:

- death or incapacity of either party (notice of death is not necessary);

- destruction or condemnation of the property;

- expiration of the terms of the agency;

- mutual agreement to terminate the agency;

- breach by one of the parties, such as abandonment by the agent or revocation by the principal (in which case breaching party may be liable for damages);

- by operation of law, as in a bankruptcy of the principal (bankruptcy terminates the agency contract and title to the property transfers to a court-appointed receiver); or

- completion, performance or fulfillment of the purpose for which the agency was created.

An **agency coupled with an interest** is an agency relationship in which the agent is given an interest in the subject of the agency, such as the property being sold. Such an agency *cannot be revoked by the principal, nor can it be terminated upon the principal's death.* For example, a broker might agree to supply the financing for a condominium development in exchange for the exclusive right to sell the completed condo units. Because this is an agency coupled with an interest, the developer would not be able to revoke the listing agreement after the broker provided the financing.

**TYPES OF AGENCY
RELATIONSHIPS**

The broker has to decide for whom the real estate company will provide client-level services and for whom it will provide customer-level services. Because fiduciary obligations cannot be taken lightly, the broker must be sure that the company's agency policies are consistent with the company's ability to perform the services.

The Pennsylvania Real Estate Licensing and Registration Act permits a broker to represent (provide client-level services to) buyers and tenants, sellers and landlords, or the broker may represent *two opposing parties* in the same transaction. This means that the broker may represent both the buyer and seller, for example, in the same sales transaction. The law also provides that the broker does not have to *represent* a person (an individual or an entity) in the transaction, which means that the broker can provide customer-level services for both the buyer and seller, for example, in the transaction.

To understand what Pennsylvania's license law means, look at the types of agency relationships that can be created.

Single Agency

Single agency is the practice of representing only one party to a transaction. The broker owes a fiduciary exclusively to one principal, who may be the buyer, seller, landlord or tenant. In single agency, the broker represents, for example, *either* the buyer *or* the seller, never both in the same transaction. The agent provides client-level services to one party and customer-level services to the other. (See Figure 15.3.)

**Figure 15.3
Single Agency
Relationship**

Buyer   Agent   Agent   Seller

• **Single Agency**

Seller as principal. If a seller contracts with a broker to market the seller's real estate, the broker becomes an *agent* of the seller; the seller is the *principal,* the broker's *client.* The traditional practice in residential sales has been that the broker represents the seller and, therefore, is the one with which most licensees are familiar. This agency relationship is normally created with a listing agreement, which is a contract between the seller and the broker. All licensed salespeople affiliated with the broker also represent the seller.

A buyer who contacts the broker to review properties listed with the broker's firm is the customer. Though obligated to deal fairly with all parties to a transaction and to comply with all aspects of the license law, the broker is strictly accountable *only to the principal*—in this case, the seller. The customer (in this case the buyer) represents himself or herself.

Owner as principal. An owner may employ a broker to market, lease, maintain and manage the owner's property. This is known as *property management.* The broker becomes the agent of the property owner through a property management agreement. The broker has a fiduciary responsibility to the client-owner to provide services within the scope of the property management agreement. The owner may employ a broker only to market the property to prospective tenants. In this case, the broker's responsibility is to find suitable tenants for the owner's property.

Buyer as principal. If a buyer contracts with a broker to locate property that is suitable for the buyer's specific purposes, the broker becomes an *agent* of the buyer; the buyer is the *principal,* the broker's *client.* The broker has fiduciary obligations to the buyer, and the seller is the broker's customer. A buyer agency contract between the buyer and the broker also obligates all licensed salespeople affiliated with the broker to represent the buyer. Contrary to popular belief, buyer agency is not a new phenomenon; brokers have been representing buyers in commercial transactions for years. As previously mentioned, a growing number of homebuyers want to be represented in sales transactions.

As the broker decides the policies for the company, he or she must decide whether to represent buyers exclusively or sellers exclusively. In a company

**Figure 15.4
Subagency**

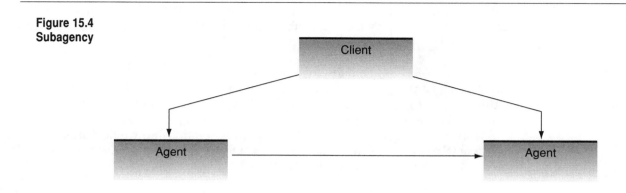

that represents buyers exclusively, for example, this means that the sellers of all properties the buyer is shown are customers of that broker. Conversely, in a company that represents sellers exclusively, all buyers that are shown properties are customers. A broker can decide to represent both buyers and sellers *in separate transactions.* This must be done carefully, however, to avoid the problems that can arise in dual agency, which will be discussed later in this chapter.

Tenant as principal. If a tenant contracts with a broker to locate property that is suitable for the tenant's specific purposes, the broker becomes an *agent* of the tenant; the tenant is the *principal,* the broker's *client.* This relationship is similar to the one a broker has with a buyer-client, except that the broker has fiduciary obligations to the tenant and the landlord/property owner is the broker's customer. It is not uncommon in commercial transactions for brokers to represent tenants in their quest for suitable office or retail space.

Subagency. Subagency is the theory under common law that an agent of a principal can authorize other agents to act on the principal's behalf. Subagency is created when the principal's agent delegates authority to another licensee, as a **subagent,** who assumes the same fiduciary obligations to the principal that the agent has. Subagency should be authorized by the principal. (See Figure 15.4.)

In real estate subagency arises when the broker, as the agent, authorizes other brokers to act on the principal's behalf as subagents. This subagency arose primarily as a result of multiple-listing services. The broker/agent who listed a property for sale would use the services of other brokers in the MLS, as long as this was authorized by the seller, to produce a ready, willing and able buyer for the property. The relationship of a salesperson or an associate broker to an employing broker is also an agency. These licenses are thus agents of the broker, in addition to being subagents of the broker's principal.

Because of the potential liability associated with subagency, the use of subagency in MLSs has become controversial in recent years, and in some areas, it is no longer practiced. Principals are liable for misrepresentations and other misconduct of their agents, which means that their liability increases when they authorize the use of subagents. Once principals understand these risks, they may refuse to authorize subagency. Agents are liable for the actions of subagents, which means that the agents' risk that the principals' interests are being properly served increases with subagency. A listing broker, for example, is liable for the actions of the subagents/brokers as well as all of the licensees affiliated with them. By avoiding subagency, the broker can minimize his or her liability and protect the seller's interests.

As mentioned earlier, the participation of more than one broker in a sales transaction can lead the buyer to assume erroneously that a *selling broker* (who has not listed the property) is representing the buyer as the client. To receive client-level services, however, the buyer would have to *engage the services* of this broker as his or her representative. The resulting relationship would not be subagency but *single agency*: the selling broker would represent the buyer and the listing broker would represent the seller.

It is important to distinguish between the terms *subagent* and *cooperating broker*. They are not necessarily synonymous. The cooperating broker, normally referred to as the selling broker, may be either a subagent acting on behalf of the seller or a buyer's agent who cooperates with the listing broker to bring the buyer and seller together to effect a sale. The spirit of cooperation among brokers who are also competitors is a unique relationship and one that benefits both the industry and the consumer. Even when subagency is not authorized, the seller/client benefits from the larger pool of potential buyers that results from brokers cooperating with one another. In fact, a listing broker who refuses to cooperate with a buyer's agent may injure the seller.

Dual Agency

Dual agency is the practice of one agent representing two parties as principals in the same transaction. Under the law of agency, this means that the agent has fiduciary obligations to two separate principals at the same time. Dual agency arises, for example, when the broker is the agent of the buyer *and* either the agent or subagent of the seller. The salespeople, as agents of the broker, have fiduciary responsibilities to the same principals as well. (See Figure 15.5.)

The challenge in dual agency is to fulfill the fiduciary obligations to one principal without compromising the other principal, especially when their interests are not only separate but may also be opposite. The principals in dual agency are not necessarily adversaries; both principals ultimately have a common goal—a contract and the satisfactory conclusion of a transaction. Each must eventually find common ground for agreement. The agents are in the middle during the process, however, as they try to balance their roles with both parties.

The basic controversy in dual agency arises from concerns about how an agent can serve two masters. In the strictest terms of the law of agency the agent must provide utmost loyalty to two principals and protect the confidences of each. The confidential information of one, however, may be material to the bargaining position of the other. For example, a buyer who confides in the agent that he or she will pay $5,000 more than the offered price provides information that the agent should communicate to the seller because the agent also represents the seller. This puts the dual agent in a compromising position. To avoid conflicting agencies or even the appearance of conflict, many agents and principals avoid dual agency entirely.

Disclosed dual agency. Pennsylvania's licensing law prohibits acting for more than one party in a transaction without the knowledge and written consent of all parties being represented. The Real Estate Commission has determined that dual agency is legal under the license law as long as it is conducted in such a manner to

**Figure 15.5
Dual Agency
Relationship**

Buyer   Agent   Seller

• Dual Agency

ensure that all parties being represented are knowledgeable about the dual agency and give their written consent. This is known as *disclosed dual agency.*

The agent must fully disclose to both the buyer and seller, for example, all the elements of agency, the agent's responsibilities and the consequences of dual agency. The principals must understand the conflicts of interest that can arise and how their respective positions can be compromised when the agent represents both parties. Merely disclosing the fact that the agent is representing two opposing principals in the same transaction is not sufficient. The disclosure must provide sufficient information to enable the parties to make an intelligent determination as whether to agree to dual representation. This is known as *informed consent.*

Although the possibility of conflict of interest still exists, disclosure in dual agency is intended to minimize the risk for the broker and the principals and ensure that both principles are aware of its effect on their respective interests. The agent is not relieved of the duty of confidentiality and loyalty unless authorized by the clients. These duties may be preserved or eliminated to the extent desired by the principals, but clients should specify in a written agency contract the modifications that they authorize.

There is considerable debate about whether brokers can properly represent both buyers and sellers in the same transaction, even when the dual agency is disclosed, particularly when the buyer-principal wants to purchase a property listed by the same broker-agent (known as an in-house sale). Some brokers decide to avoid this situation by practicing exclusive single agency. By representing only buyers, for example, and not listing properties, the brokers are never dual agents.

Recently, a number of states, including Pennsylvania, have passed laws that attempt to avoid dual agency in in-house sales. These laws permit the broker to designate certain licensees with the firm who are the legal representatives of a principal, known as **designated agents.** The broker would, however, be considered a dual agent. This is one of many examples of the ways the state legislatures are attempting to cope with the challenges posed by recent agency developments in the real estate industry.

Undisclosed dual agency. A broker may not intend to create a dual agency. However, by a salesperson's words or actions it may occur unintentionally or inadvertently. Sometimes the cause is carelessness. Other times the salesperson does not fully understand his or her fiduciary responsibilities. Some salespeople lose sight of other responsibilties when they focus intensely on bringing buyers and seller together.

For example, a salesperson representing the seller might tell a buyer that the seller will accept less than the listing price. Or the salesperson might promise to persuade the seller to accept an offer that is in the buyer's interest. Giving the buyer any specific advice on how much to offer can lead the buyer to believe that the salesperson is an advocate for the buyer. These actions create an *implied agency* (to be discussed later) with the buyer and violate the duties of loyalty and confidentiality to the seller-client. Because neither party has been informed of that situation on been given the opportunity to seek separate representation, the interests of both are jeopardized. This undisclosed dual agency is a violation of licensing laws. Also it can result in the rescission of the agreement of sale, forfeiture of commission or a suit for damages.

Disclosure

Because of the variety of agency relationships that may be created and the confusion about agency practices or misunderstandings that can occur, it is important for licensees to discuss agency with prospective customers and clients. People need to know how their respective interests will be protected and the scope of service they can expect from the licensee. In fact, as discussed in Chapter 13, the license law requires disclosure of agency relationships at the initial interview and before parties sign listing contracts and agreements of sale.

Mandatory agency disclosure forms must be used by licensees in Pennsylvania. Mandatory agency disclosure that went into effect in November of 1999 requires the licensee to disclose and explain:

• the various types of agency relationships that are permitted in Pennsylvania;

• that an agency relationship is not to be presumed and that it exists only in a written agreement between the broker and consumer of real estate;

• the specific types of agency the licensee's firm provides;

• who the licensee represents in a specific transaction;

• that the broker may designate one or more licensees affiliated with the broker to represent the separate interest of the parties to the transaction (dual agency) and the specific consequences and potential conflicts of interest that can arise and how the duties of confidentiality and undivided loyalty are to be handled;

• the broker's policies regarding cooperation with other brokers, including the sharing of fees, especially in the case of a buyer's broker, even if compensated by the listing broker, who will still represent the interests of the buyers; and

• the duration of the broker's employment and that the broker's fees are negotiable.

These disclosures are intended to give a prospective buyer/tenant or seller/landlord an understanding of the services that are provided to a client versus a customer.

IN PRACTICE. . .	*As licensees become familiar with the various types of agency relationships and the activities that they perform for clients versus customers, they can not only properly explain their services to prospective buyers and sellers but also conduct themselves in ways that are consistent with the level of service that they are to provide.*

CUSTOMER-LEVEL SERVICE

Anytime a licensee is providing customer-level services, the licensee is responsible for adhering to the consumer protection laws and the ethical provisions of the licensing law. This includes times when the licensee is representing a client and working with a customer and when the licensee is not representing anyone in the transaction.

The Pennsylvania license law permits *transactional brokerage.* In this relationship, a broker or salesperson provides communications, document preparation services and otherwise assists both parties in a transaction without being an agent or advocate of either party. While permissible under the law, it is not very common. In practice, licensees usually represent at least one party in a transaction and provide customer-level service to the other party.

Duties of licensees when providing services to anyone including customers are

- reasonable care and skill;
- honest and fair dealing; and
- disclosure of all facts the licensee knows or should reasonably be expected to know that materially affect the value or desirability of the property.

As previously mentioned, the doctrine of caveat emptor has changed in favor of consumers to offer them greater protections. In order for consumers to make wise decisions, they need information. Under caveat emptor they had to make decisions based on the information they could gather themselves, which meant asking questions. Unless they asked, providers of goods and services were under no obligation to volunteer information about what they were selling. Today's laws have shifted the responsibility to the providers of goods and services, obligating them to provide information that is material to the consumers' decisions. This affects licensees as well as property owners by requiring them to make numerous disclosures.

What do consumers need to know? Chapter 3 discussed the importance of environmental issues in today's real estate transactions and ways that purchasers can be protected. Buyers are also concerned about the properties' structural and mechanical conditions.

Pennsylvania's Real Estate Sellers Disclosure Act requires sellers to complete disclosure forms to indicate what they know about the condition of their property. These disclosures must describe both the physical and environmental conditions of a property.

| IN PRACTICE... | *Regardless of whether the licensees are providing client or customer services, it's incumbent on them to safeguard the interests of all parties when they are preparing legal contracts and ensure that the parties get the advice of any experts they need in the transactions, including the counsel of attorneys.* |

Opinion versus Fact

Is a statement made by a licensee an opinion or a fact? People tend to assume that statements made by licensees, because they are thought to have specialized knowledge, are factual, even though the licensee may not have any knowledge of the truth or accuracy of the statement. A statement by a salesperson such as "I believe the zoning ordinance permits your proposed use" could be merely the salesperson's opinion. But the customer or client could hear this comment as a statement of fact. While licensees are permitted to offer opinions without any intention to deceive, they must be sure that the customers understand the statements are opinions.

Fraud and Misrepresentations

Fraud is the *intentional* misrepresentation of a material fact for the purpose of deceiving and gaining an advantage over another person. This includes not only making false statements about a property, but also intentionally concealing or failing to disclose important facts. A party must have suffered injury by relying on the statement or conduct. A fraudulent statement is intentionally false or made without regard to whether it is truthful. Statements of fact, however, must be accurate.

If licensees make statements that are not true, fail to verify information or are careless about what they say, even if there is no intention to deceive, they may be guilty of a negligent misrepresentation. Charges of negligence arise out of how a licensee *should* have acted to prevent a party from being injured. Negligence is established by comparing the conduct with a standard that is commensurate with the level of service that should be provided by a competent professional. Statements that exaggerate a property's benefits are called **puffing.** Although the general characterizations in puffing may be legal, a misrepresentation of a fact is not legal. Licensees must ensure that none of their statements can be misinterpreted.

The Pennsylvania Real Estate Commission's Rules and Regulations specifically state that a licensee must not make representations or give assurances or advice concerning any aspect of a real estate transaction that is known (or should be known) to be incorrect, inaccurate or improbable. It is not necessary to *intend* to misrepresent; an unintentional (negligent) misrepresentation of a material fact that induces a buyer to purchase creates liability as well.

If a contract to purchase real estate is obtained as a result of fraudulent misstatements, the contract may be disaffirmed or renounced by the purchaser. The licensee will not only lose a commission but also can be liable for damages if either party suffers loss because of a licensee's misrepresentations. To avoid misrepresentations that arise because of the owner's inaccurate statements about the property, the licensee should clearly state that the information is based on the seller's representations.

Latent Defects

The seller has a duty to discover and disclose any latent defects that threaten structural soundness or personal safety. *A latent defect is a hidden structural defect that is not discoverable by ordinary inspection.* Examples of a latent defect are cases such as a house built over a ditch that was covered with decaying timber, a buried drain tile causing water to accumulate or a driveway built partly on adjoining property. Buyers have been able either to cancel sales contracts or receive damages when such defects have not been revealed. The courts have also decided in favor of the buyer when the seller has neglected to reveal violations of zoning or building codes.

Stigmatized Properties

In recent years questions have been raised about stigmatized properties, properties that society has branded as undesirable because of events that occurred on them. Typically the stigma is a criminal event such as a homicide, a shooting, illegal drug manufacturing, a gang-related activity or some other tragedy such as a suicide. Because of the potential liability of a broker's inadequately researching the facts concerning a property's condition and the inherent responsibility of a broker to disclose material facts to a prospective buyer, brokers are cautioned to seek competent counsel when dealing with a stigmatized property. Though laws and court cases in Pennsylvania have not, as yet, specifically addressed socially stigmatized properties, there is a developing body of law from elsewhere in the country.

IN PRACTICE...

Because real estate licensees have enormous exposure to liability under the law, some brokers purchase what are known as errors and omissions insurance *policies for their firms. Similar to malpractice insurance in the medical field, such policies generally cover liability for errors, mistakes and negligence in the usual listing and selling activities of a real estate company. Individual salespeople should be sure they are also insured. However, no insurance will protect a licensee from litigation arising from criminal acts. Also, insurance companies normally exclude coverage for violation of civil rights laws.*

REAL ESTATE BROKERAGE

As defined in Chapter 14, **brokerage** is the business of bringing parties together for the purpose of purchasing, selling, leasing or exchanging property. The issues discussed so far in this chapter describe the various ways that real estate companies provide their services to sellers, lessors, buyers or tenants to bring these people together. Now we look more closely at the real estate brokerage companies.

Today's real estate company uses many tools to compete in the marketplace and to enhance the services it provides. Some companies are independently owned and may also be affiliated with national franchises or referral companies; other companies are nationally owned but operated by local brokers. Many companies are affiliated with multiple-listing services (MLSs) so that they can expand the range of properties they offer for sale or rent. By investigating a number of brokerage operations in an area, prospective licensees can learn about how the companies do business and the benefits they derive from their various affiliations.

The real estate industry is becoming an information and service business, more so than a land and building business. Today's consumers crave information, and as their lives become more hectic, they look for expedient ways to do business. Instant and convenient ways to communicate and access information, all of which are possible because of technology, are essential to their way of life. To provide the services consumers expect, real estate licensees are using technology to communicate more rapidly, provide more information and produce more comprehensive and professional documents than was previously possible.

The provincial way of providing services has given way to a more global approach. Technology has expanded the geographic area licensees serve with regional MLSs. National, and even global, exchange of property information is also possible. Because of computers, information about mortgage loans, demographics, neighborhoods and school districts, cost-of-living comparisons, job-growth and economic conditions, cultural opportunities—just about any information buyers and sellers need is readily available. Real estate licensees are a resource to not only provide but also interpret information. The latter will become increasingly important because of the volume of information consumers can access themselves on the information superhighway.

Today's brokerage company also hires a variety of personnel. In addition to licensed salespeople, more firms are hiring support staff. These people, who are not licensed, perform clerical and administrative tasks for the company and the salespeople. This frees the licensees to devote more time to sales activities and less time to the paperwork. Salespeople may also hire their own personal assistants, but these people are not permitted to perform activities for which licensure is required unless they are properly licensed.

Many of the procedures brokers must follow in running their companies are governed by the license laws. As discussed in Chapter 13, these include the brokers' authority and responsibility for the activities of the licensees, requirements for establishing offices and branch offices, advertising and escrow account procedures and preparing and handling documents. (See the act and regulations in Appendix C.)

Broker-Salesperson Relationship

A real estate salesperson is licensed to perform real estate activities on behalf of a licensed broker. The broker is responsible for the actions of all licensees affiliated with the broker. In turn, *all of a salesperson's activities must be performed in the name of the broker*. The salesperson is permitted to perform only those activities assigned by the broker and is entitled to receive compensation for the real estate activities *only* from the employing broker. As an agent of the broker, the salesperson has no authority to make contracts with or receive compensation from any other party, be it the principal, another broker, the buyer or the seller.

Independent contractor versus employee. The broker can hire the salesperson as an employee or an an independent contractor. An **employee** is a person who works under the supervision and control of another. On the other hand, an **independent contractor** is a person who is retained to perform a certain act but who is not subject to the control and direction of another. The critical distinction, which is established by the income tax laws, is the degree of *control* an employer can exercise over a person's activities. The employer cannot control *how* an independent contractor performs the activities for which he or she is hired. (See Figure 15.6.)

**Figure 15.6
Independent
Contractor
versus
Employee**

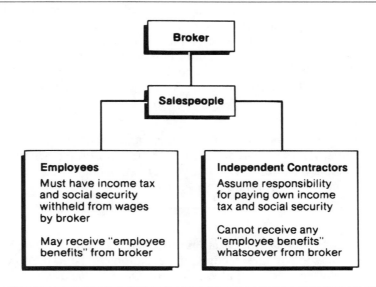

The state's license law treats the salesperson as the employee of the broker because of the broker's legal accountability and responsibility for the salesperson's actions, regardless of whether the salesperson is considered an employee or an independent contractor for tax purposes.

A broker can *require* an employee to follow rules governing such matters as working hours, office routine, attendance at office meetings and dress codes. As an employer, a broker is required by the federal government to withhold income, social security and Medicare taxes from wages paid to employees. In Pennsylvania, the broker is also required to withhold state income tax and pay unemployment and workers' compensation. In addition, employees might receive benefits such as health insurance and profit-sharing.

A broker's relationship with an independent contractor is very different. As an independent contractor, a salesperson operates more independently than an employee. The broker may control *what* the independent contractor will do but not *how* it will be done. The broker cannot *require* the independent contractor to keep specific office hours or attend sales meetings. Independent contractors are responsible for paying their own income, social security and Medicare taxes. They cannot receive anything from the broker that could be construed as an employee benefit such as health insurance.

To ensure that a salesperson is indeed an independent contractor, the federal tax laws require that

- a person must be properly licensed,

- gross income must be based on production rather than on the number of hours worked and

- work must be done pursuant to a written agreement in which the independent contractor status is clearly stated.

Because the IRS scrutinizes claims of independent contractor status, it is essential to meet at least these three requirements, otherwise known as the safe harbor test. In addition, the employer must also appropriately supervise the person as an independent contractor and not as an employee. The agreement between a broker and a salesperson should also define their respective obligations and responsibilities. (See Figure 15.7 for a sample independent contractor agreement.)

IN PRACTICE...	*Specific questions about the legal and tax implications for independent contractors should be referred to an attorney. Independent contractors should also get advice about keeping income and expense records and filing the appropriate tax returns.*

Broker's Compensation

The broker's compensation is normally specified in the listing, buyer agency or management agreement. Compensation can be in the form of a **commission** or brokerage fee computed as a *percentage of the amount of consideration in a transaction* (for example, sales price), as a *flat fee* or at an *hourly rate*. According to the state's license law, commissions must be determined as a result of negotiations. Attempting, however subtly, to impose uniform commission rates is also a clear violation of state and federal antitrust laws (discussed later in this chapter). A broker may, however, set the amount of compensation that is acceptable for that broker's firm. The important point is that the broker and the client or customer must agree on the compensation arrangements before any services are rendered.

Commission is usually considered to be earned when the work for which the broker was hired has been accomplished. Most sales commissions are *payable* when the sale is consummated by *delivery of the seller's deed*. The commission is generally considered to be *earned* when the broker has produced a ready, willing and able buyer who signs an agreement of sale, which is then accepted and executed by the seller, and when copies of the contract have been delivered to all parties.

To be entitled to a sales commission, one must be a licensed broker, be the procuring cause of a sale, and have been employed to perform the service under a valid contract. That broker should then compensate the salesperson who may have represented him or her in the transaction. To be considered the **procuring cause** of a sale, the broker must have taken action to start or to cause a chain of events that resulted in the sale. The specific actions that cause the chain of events is unique in each transaction. The important point is that merely being involved in a transaction is different from being the procuring cause.

Once a seller accepts an offer from a ready, willing and able buyer, the seller is technically liable for the broker's commission. A **ready, willing and able buyer** is one who is *prepared to buy on the seller's terms and ready to take positive steps toward consummation of the transaction*. Courts may prevent the broker from receiving a commission if the broker knew the buyer was unable to perform. If the transaction is *not* consummated, the broker may still be entitled to a commission if the seller

• has a change of mind and refuses to sell,

**Figure 15.7
Independent
Contractor
Agreement**

BROKER / SALESPERSON   Form 150-2
INDEPENDENT CONTRACTOR AGREEMENT
COPYRIGHT PENNSYLVANIA ASSOCIATION OF REALTORS® 1994
This form recommended and approved for, but not restricted to, use by the members of the Pennsylvania Association of REALTORS®

This Agreement is entered into this _____day of _____, 19_____ between _____
hereinafter referred to as "Broker," and _____, hereinafter referred to as "Salesperson".

Whereas, Broker is engaged in business as a Real Estate Broker and is duly licensed to engage in the activities of a "Broker" as defined by the Pennsylvania Licensing and Registration Act, Act of February 19, 1980, P.L. 15, No. 9, as amended, and

Whereas, Broker maintains one or more offices properly equipped with furnishings, listing books and other equipment necessary and incidental to the proper operation of said business, and staffed with clerical employees, and is thereby suitable to serving the public as a real estate broker; and

Whereas, Salesperson is duly licensed by the Commonwealth of Pennsylvania as a real estate "salesperson" or "associate broker" as defined by the Pennsylvania Licensing and Registration Act, and whereas it is deemed to be to the mutual advantage of Broker and Salesperson to enter this contract upon the terms and conditions hereinafter set forth.

NOW THEREFORE, for and in consideration of the mutual covenants and promises herein contained, the undersigned hereby enter into the following articles of agreement:

1. *Independent Contractor.*
The relationship of Salesperson to Broker is that of an independent contractor. In performing the activities of a real estate "salesperson" as defined by the Real Estate Licensing and Registration Act (hereinafter referred to as "Act"), salesperson shall be free to devote such portion of his/her time, energy, efforts and skill, as he/she deems appropriate. In keeping with the independent contractor status, Salesperson shall be responsible for completing any training required by the Act or other laws of the Commonwealth of Pennsylvania; Salesperson shall work on a commission basis and receive no salary, fringe benefits, medical benefits, pension benefits, or profit sharing; no state, local, unemployment, Social Security or business privilege taxes (where applicable) shall be withheld from Salesperson. Salesperson shall pay all professional licensing fees, errors and omissions insurance premiums (except as otherwise provided herein), multi-listing fees and/or computer access fees. **Salesperson shall not be treated as an employee with respect to the services performed hereunder for federal or state tax purposes or for purposes under the Worker's Compensation Act.**

2. *Sales Effort.*
Salesperson agrees to act as an independent real estate salesperson and shall faithfully, loyally and legally engage his/her efforts to sell, trade, lease or rent any and all real estate listed with Broker, to solicit additional listings, customers and clients for Broker, and to otherwise promote the business of serving the public in real estate transactions to the end that each of the parties hereto may derive the greatest profit possible.

3. *Office Facilities.*
Broker shall from time to time designate the office with which the Salesperson shall be associated. That office shall be provided with such furnishings and equipment as deemed necessary at the discretion of Broker for the proper operation of a real estate office. Broker shall make available to the Salesperson all current listings of the office, and agrees, upon request, to assist the Salesperson in his/her work by advice, instruction, and cooperation, to the extent deemed appropriate by Broker. Salesperson shall pay for long distance telephone charges and for such other forms, equipment, supplies as shall be set forth in Broker's written office policies.

4. *Automobile.*
Salesperson shall furnish his/her own automobile and pay all related expenses and Broker shall have no responsibility relating to Salesperson's automobile or transportation. Salesperson agrees to carry liability insurance upon his/her automobile with minimum liability limits of $300,000 for each person and $500,000 for each accident and with property damage liability limits of $50,000. Salesperson agrees to furnish Broker with a certificate certifying compliance with this requirement to be deposited with Broker on or before the effective date and each renewal date of this Agreement, or at other times as Broker may reasonably request.

5. *Commissions.*
Salesperson shall be entitled to a share of the commissions earned and received by Broker in accordance with Broker's Salesperson Commission Schedule in effect on the date of the act entitling Salesperson to a commission (*e.g.,* obtaining listing, placing property under agreement of sale, etc.) or as otherwise agreed by the parties in writing as to a particular transaction. Broker may alter its Salesperson Commission Schedule from time to time without prior notification. Revisions to the schedule shall be immediately applicable to all future transactions. The division of commissions between Broker and Salesperson shall follow deduction of all expenses according to the Salesperson Commission Schedule. In no case shall Broker be liable to Salesperson for any commissions not collected. All commissions derived from a transaction shall be deposited with the Broker as required by the Act and/or Rules and Regulations of the Real Estate Commission and subsequently paid according to the Salesperson Commission Schedule. This distribution shall take place as soon as practicable after collection and receipt of such commissions. It is understood and agreed that the Salesperson's only renumeration for the services being rendered under this Agreement is the Salesperson's share of the commissions paid by the parties to real estate transactions.

6. *Client Fees.*
In no event shall Salesperson charge less than the commission or fee established by the Broker without the prior written consent of Broker. If Broker shall have entered into a special contract or agreement pertaining to any particular transaction, Broker shall advise Salesperson of such special arrangement. All commissions and fees from a particular transaction shall be payable to the Broker. Salesperson shall not be personally liable to Broker for any commissions not received by Broker from parties to a transaction unless such nonpayment is the result of collusion, intentional or reckless conduct. Broker shall have the exclusive right to determine whether to commence litigation to collect a commission or fee, or to settle any claim for the same.

7. *Ethic and Trade Associations.*
Salesperson and Broker shall conduct business and regulate working schedules so as to maintain and to increase the good will, business, profits, and reputation of Broker and Salesperson and each agrees to conform to and abide by all laws, rules and regulations, and code of ethics that are binding on, or applicable to, real estate brokers and salespersons. Salesperson and Broker shall be governed by the Code of Ethics of the National Association of REALTORS®, the Act, Rules and Regulations of the Real Estate Commission, as the same may be from time to time amended or supplemented, the constitution and by-laws of the local realty board (or such other board or association as may be agreed upon), and the rules and regulations of any multiple listing service with which Broker may now or in the future be affiliated. Broker and Salesperson shall retain membership in good standing with the National Association of REALTORS®, the Pennsylvania Association of REALTORS®, and the local realty board or association designated by Broker or as may be agreed upon by the parties. Whenever Broker is a member of any real estate organization which requires membership of Salesperson in said organization, then Salesperson agrees that he/she shall become a member and pay fees or dues required by such membership. Broker and Salesperson agree to be bound by the rules and regulations of such organizations pertaining to ethics and standards of conduct and procedure. Salesperson acknowledges possession of a current copy of the Pennsylvania Real Estate Licensing and Registration Act, the Rules and Regulations of the Pennsylvania Real Estate Commission, and the Code of Ethics of the National Association of REALTORS® and agrees to be apprised of the provisions thereof so that Salesperson will conduct all activities in a manner consistent with such laws and ethics.

8. *Real Estate License and Dues.*
Salesperson shall pay the cost of any real estate license required by the provisions of any law or regulation of the Commonwealth of Pennsylvania. Salesperson shall further ensure that the requirements for licensure as a real estate salesperson by the Commonwealth of Pennsylvania are satisfied in every respect, including the timely satisfaction of mandatory continuing educational requirements. Salesperson shall pay all dues for membership in the associations set forth in the preceeding paragraph of this Agreement in a timely fashion and shall pay all taxes as may be levied upon income or productivity by the federal government, the Internal Revenue Service, the Commonwealth of Pennsylvania, or any local municipality or school district or other such taxing authority including but not limited to income taxes, occupation and occupation privilege taxes, per capita taxes, mercantile or business privilege taxes.

9. *Authority to Contract.*
Salesperson shall have no authority to bind, obligate or commit Broker by any promise or representation, unless specifically authorized by Broker in writing; provided, however, that Salesperson is and shall be authorized to execute listing agreements, buyer agency contracts, lease management contracts, as well as all addenda and agreements appurtenant thereto for and on behalf of Broker where not in conflict with Broker's agency practices and provided that the commission involved in such transaction is not less than that determined for such transaction or service by Broker. Prior to entering into any such contract or agreement, Salesperson shall determine the agency and management practices of Broker.

10. *Errors and Ommissions Insurance.*
Salesperson shall cooperate fully with Broker in obtaining errors and ommissions coverage in an amount, and with deductible, as shall from time to time be determined by Broker. Said insurance shall protect Salesperson against liability which may arise in connection with the conduct of Salesperson as an active real estate licensee. Said policy or policies shall contain an endorsement naming Broker and any subsidiaries of Broker as an additional insured and shall not be subject to cancellation except on a minimum of ten (10) days prior written notice to Broker. A certificate of said insurance shall be deposited with Broker on or before the effective date and each renewal date of this Agreement. The cost of said insurance shall be paid pursuant to the written policy of Broker, or, in the absence thereof, such cost shall be borne by Broker and Salesperson in the same proportion as they would normally share in the commission resulting from a listing and sale of a property as is set forth in the Salesperson Commission Schedule.

**Figure 15.7
(continued)**

11. *Listings, Contracts, Correspondence, Records and Forms.*
Salesperson agrees that any and all listings of property, agency agreements, and all actions taken in connection with the real estate business, shall be in the name of Broker.   Listings and agency contracts shall be filed with Broker within twenty-four (24) hours after receipt by Salesperson.   All listings and agency contracts shall be and remain the exclusive property of Broker.   All correspondence received, copies of correspondence written, plats, listing information, memoranda, files, photographs, reports, legal opinions, accounting information, and any and all other instruments, documents or information of any nature whatsoever concerning transactions handled by Broker or Salesperson, or jointly, are and shall remain the property of Broker provided that Salesperson is entitled to a copy of such instruments and information upon reasonable request concerning any transaction in which he/she is personally involved.   The parties hereto shall mutually approve and agree upon all correspondence from the office of Broker pertaining to transactions handled by Salesperson, and shall further agree on the forms to be used and the contents of all contracts and other forms before they are presented to clients and customers for signature.

12. *Deposits.*
All deposits received by Salesperson in the course of a real estate transaction of any nature shall be immediately transferred to Broker for deposit pursuant to the Act, the Rules and Regulations of the Real Estate Commission and the agreement of the parties to the transaction; provided, however, that any deposit to be maintained by another broker of record pursuant to the Act, Rules and Regulations of the Real Estate Commission and agreement of the parties to a transaction shall be immediately transferred to such broker with the appropriate notice to the person making such deposit and to Broker.

13. *Indemnification.*
Salesperson shall indemnify and hold Broker harmless from any and all claims, costs, liabilities, and judgments, including attorney's fees, arising from the intentional or reckless acts of Salesperson, or acts outside the scope of Salesperson's authority.   When litigation or a dispute arises concerning a transaction in which Salesperson was involved, the parties hereto shall mutually cooperate with each other.   In disputes or litigation where there is a claim to the effect that Salesperson has acted intentionally or recklessly or outside the scope of Salesperson's authority, Salesperson shall bear the costs, expenses and liabilities including judgments and awards arising from the dispute or litigation.   In disputes or litigation where there is a claim to the effect that Salesperson has acted negligently, Salesperson shall share the costs, expenses and liabilities including judgments and awards arising from the dispute or litigation.   Such sharing shall be in the same proportion as the division of commission was, or would have been, from the subject transaction.   The sharing of costs, expenses, and liabilities shall be without prejudice to Broker's rights of indemnification unless there has been a resolution of the indemnification issue between the parties hereto.   Broker shall select counsel to represent Broker's and Salesperson's interests in litigation with costs borne by the parties in proportion as set forth above pertaining to the sharing of costs.

14. *Termination.*
This Agreement, and the relationship created hereby, may be terminated by either party hereto, with or without cause, at any time upon written notice.   Upon termination, all negotiations commenced by Salesperson during the term of this Agreement shall be handled through Broker and with such assistance and cooperation by Salesperson as is reasonable under the circumstances for the protection of the interests of the parties to the real estate transactions involved.   Salesperson, upon termination, shall furnish Broker with a bona fide list of all prospects, leads, and probable transactions developed by Salesperson as well as all correspondence and documents described in Paragraph 11 above, which are deemed to be the property of Broker.   Salesperson further agrees that upon termination, or in anticipation thereof, he/she will not furnish to any person, firm, company or corporation engaged in the real estate business any information as to Broker's clients, customers, properties, prices, terms of negotiations nor Broker's policies or relationships with clients and customers nor any other information concerning Broker and/or his/her business.   Salesperson shall not, after termination of this Agreement, or in contemplation thereof, remove from the files or from the office of Broker any materials, data, publications, correspondence, files or information that is property of Broker.   Salesperson shall be entitled to copies of certain instruments pertaining to transactions in which Salesperson has a bona fide interest or pertaining to earnings of Salesperson.

15. *Commissions upon Termination.*
Upon termination, Salesperson's share of commissions on any transactions where a sales contract exists but the transaction has not closed, shall, after the closing of such transaction, be paid to Salesperson in accord with the Salesperson Commission Schedule in effect at the time of termination.   There shall be deducted from such share, however, a servicing charge of $_____ or _____% of the amount of the listing and/or sales commission, whichever is higher.   No commission other than for those properties on which an agreement has been signed and accepted in writing by the buyer and seller on or before termination shall be deemed earned by Salesperson, unless otherwise agreed in writing.   Likewise, no commission resulting from the listing for rent, or the rental of property shall be paid to Salesperson following termination with the exception of commissions arising from leases fully executed prior to termination and to the extent that lease payments are received prior to termination.   Salesperson shall not, however, share in the commissions payable in the future and based upon the lease options or lease payments not yet due and payable.

16. *Termination Procedure.*
Upon termination by either party, Salesperson shall immediately:
a) submit a letter of termination with a complete accounting of commissions, listings and buyer clients;
b) return all supplies, client/customer prospect lists, keys and documents considered property of Broker pursuant to the provisions of this Agreement;
c) meet with Broker for purposes of attempting to mutually agree upon a final accounting of commissions due and payable;
d) cooperate in the notification of the Real Estate Commission regarding the termination of the relationship of Broker and Salesperson.

17. *Arbitration of Disputes.*
Disagreements or disputes between Salesperson and Broker, or between Salesperson and a real estate licensee associated with or contracted to Broker, and which arise out of, or in connection with, the real estate business, and which cannot be adjusted by and between the parties involved, shall be submitted for arbitration in accordance with Article XIV of the Code of Ethics of the National Association of REALTORS®.   By this Agreement said arbitration shall be mandatory and Broker and Salesperson agree to provide a written agreement to the local association of REALTORS® as may be required by said association as a condition precedent to arbitration.   Broker and Salesperson agree to be bound by the decision of the arbitration panel of the local association or the Pennsylvania Association of REALTORS® which has entertained the dispute or disagreement.   The conduct of the arbitration shall be governed by the *Code of Ethics and Arbitration Manual* most recently published by the National Association of REALTORS® prior to Arbitration, as amended by the local association hearing the dispute.

18. *Amendments.*
This Agreement may be amended only by the parties hereto, in writing.

19. *Governing Law.*
This Agreement shall be governed by and interpreted pursuant to the laws of the Commonwealth of Pennsylvania.

20. *Successors in Interest.*
This Agreement shall inure to the benefit and be binding upon the successors in interest of Broker.   This Agreement, however, is based on the personal services of Salesperson and Salesperson shall not delegate or assign any of Salesperson's rights or duties hereunder without the prior written consent of Broker.

21. *Policy Manual.*
Any office policy or rules and procedures manual now existing or hereafter adopted or amended shall be binding on the parties.

22. *Entire Agreement.*
This Agreement constitutes the entire agreement between the Broker and Salesperson, and there are no agreements or understandings not expressed herein.

IN WITNESS WHEREOF, this Agreement has been executed on the date first above written.

Witness (or attest):

_____   By _____
                                                                                    Broker

Witness:

_____   By _____
                                                                                    Salesperson

Broker should ensure that written office policies describing Salesperson's financial obligations with respect to office supplies, telephone, etc., and a Salesperson Commission Schedule are provided to Salesperson.

COPIES: WHITE, BROKER;   YELLOW, SALESPERSON

PENNSYLVANIA ASSOCIATION OF REALTORS® 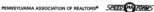   10/94

- has a spouse who refuses to sign the deed,

- has a title with uncorrected defects,

- commits fraud with respect to the transaction,

- is unable to deliver possession within a reasonable time,

- insists on terms not in the listing (for example, the right to restrict the use of the property) or

- has a mutual agreement with the buyer to cancel the transaction.

In other words, a *broker is generally due a commission if a sale is not consummated because of the principal's default.*

According to Pennsylvania license law, it is illegal for a broker to pay a commission to anyone *other than* the salesperson licensed with the broker or to another broker. Fees, commission or other compensation cannot be paid to unlicensed persons for services for which real estate licensure is required. These laws have been construed to include as compensation gifts of certain items of personal property (a new television, or other premiums, such as vacations and the like). This is not to be confused with referral fees paid between brokers for leads. Such fees are legal if the individuals are licensed.

Salesperson's Compensation

The compensation of a salesperson is set by a mutual agreement between the broker and the salesperson. A broker may agree to pay a salary or a share of the commissions from transactions originated by a salesperson. Many companies have graduated commission programs in which the salespeople earn higher shares of the gross commissions they generate for the company as their production increases. In some cases a salesperson may draw from an account against earned shares of commissions. Some brokers require salespeople to pay certain expenses such as all or part of the expense of advertising listed properties.

Some firms have adopted a *100-percent commission plan.* Salespeople in these companies pay a monthly service charge to their broker to cover the costs of office space, telephones and supervision in return for 100 percent of the commissions from the sales they negotiate.

However the salesperson's compensation is structured, only the employing broker can pay it. In cooperating transactions, the cooperating broker pays the commission to the employing broker who then pays the salesperson. (See Math Concept, Sharing Commissions, that follows.)

ANTITRUST LAWS

The real estate industry is subject to federal and state **antitrust laws**. Generally, these laws prohibit monopolies and conspiracies that unreasonably restrain trade. The most common antitrust violations are price fixing, group boycotting, allocating markets or territories and tying agreements.

Price fixing is the practice of setting prices for products or services rather than letting competition in the open market establish those prices. In real estate, price fixing occurs when brokers agree to set sales commissions, fees or management rates, and this is *illegal*. Brokers must independently determine commission rates or fees for their firms only. These decisions must be based on the

MATH CONCEPT
Sharing Commissions

A commission might be shared by many people: the listing broker, the listing salesperson, the selling broker and the selling salesperson. Drawing a diagram can help you determine which person is entitled to receive what amount of the total commission.

Salesperson *E,* while working for broker *H,* took a listing on a $73,000 house at a 6% commission rate. Salesperson *T,* while working for broker *M,* found the buyer for the property. If the property sold for the listed price, the listing broker and the seller broker shared the commission equally, and the selling broker kept 45% of what he received, how much did salesperson *T* receive? (If the broker retained 45% of the total commission that he received, his salesperson would receive the balance: 100% − 45% = 55%.)

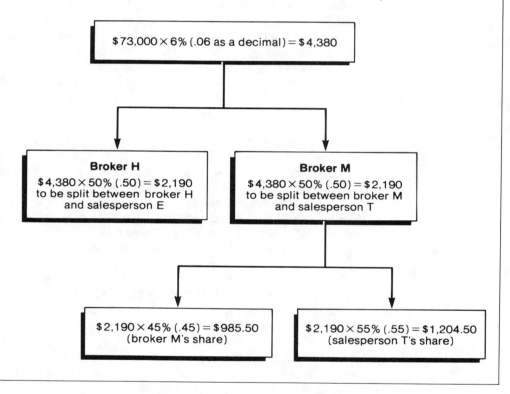

broker's business judgment and revenue requirements without input from other brokers.

Multiple-listing organizations, REALTOR® associations and other professional organizations may not set fees or commission splits; nor are they allowed to deny membership to brokers based on the fees the brokers charge. Either practice could lead the public to believe that the industry sanctions not only the unethical practice of withholding cooperation from certain brokers, but also the illegal practice of restricting open market competition.

The broker's challenge is to avoid *any* appearance of attempts at price fixing as well as the actual practice. Hinting in any way to prospective clients that there is a "going rate" of commission or fee simply implies that rates are in fact standardized. Likewise, discussions of rates among licensees from different firms could be construed as a price-fixing activity and should be avoided scrupulously.

Group boycotting occurs when two or more businesses conspire against other businesses or agree to withhold their patronage to reduce competition. This is also illegal under the antitrust laws. Examples include several brokers conspiring together to avoid cooperating with "discount" brokers or brokers who practice a different kind of agency representation than they do.

Allocating markets or territories involves an agreement between brokers to divide their markets and refrain from competing for each other's business. These agreements conspire to eliminate competition. Examples of allocations include geographic areas with brokers agreeing to specific territories within which they will operate exclusively, price range or type of property.

Tying agreements involve arrangements in which a party agrees to sell one product only on the condition that the buyer also purchases a different or *tied* product. Frequently the tied product is less unique than the other one. These agreements restrain competition because the buyer has to relinquish his or her choice of tied product to gain access to the tying product. An example is requiring a party to use the broker's services to purchase a property as a condition of a listing.

The penalties for antitrust violations are severe. Violations of the Sherman Antitrust Act are felony offenses punishable by a maximum $100,000 fine and/or imprisonment up to three years for individuals: fines for corporations are higher. In a civil suit a person who has suffered a loss because of the antitrust activities may recover triple the value of the actual damages plus attorney's fees and costs.

●   ●   ●   ●   ●   ●   ●   ●

KEY TERMS

agency	general agent
agency coupled with an interest	implied agreement
agent	independent contractor
antitrust laws	law of agency
brokerage	listing agreement
buyer-agency agreement	principal
commission	procuring cause
designated agent	puffing
dual agency	ready, willing and able buyer
employee	single agency
express agreement	special agent
fiduciary relationship	subagent
fraud	transactional brokerage

SUMMARY

Real estate brokerage is the bringing together, for a fee or commission, of people who wish to buy, sell, exchange or lease real estate. An important part of real estate brokerage is the law of agency. A real estate broker is the agent, hired by the seller or buyer to sell or find a particular parcel of real estate. The person who hires the broker is the principal. The principal and the agent have a fiduciary relationship under which the agent owes the principal the duties of care, obedience, accounting, loyalty and disclosure.

The law of agency governs the principal-agent relationship. Agency relationships may be expressed either by the words of the parties or written agreements or implied by their actions. In single-agency relationships the broker/agent represents one party in a transaction. The agent may seek the participation of subagents to assist the broker in serving the principal. Representing two opposite parties in the same transaction is dual agency. Disclosed dual agency requires that both principals be informed and consent to the broker's multiple representation. Licensees must be careful not to create a dual agency when none was intended. This unintentional or inadvertent dual agency is illegal and can result in the sales contract being rescinded and commission being forfeited or a suit in court.

The state's license law requires licensees to make certain disclosures about agency, including informing prospective purchasers and sellers about the agency alternatives and how client- versus customer-level services differ. The source of compensation for the services does not determine the party who is being represented.

Licensees have certain duties and obligations when providing customer-level services. Consumers are entitled to fair and honest dealings and information that is necessary for them to make informed decisions. This includes disclosing accurate information about the property.

The broker's compensation in a real estate sale may take the form of a commission, a flat fee or an hourly rate. The broker is considered to have earned a commission when he or she procures a ready, willing and able buyer for a seller.

A broker may hire salespeople to assist in this work. The salesperson works on the broker's behalf as either an employee or an independent contractor.

The state and federal antitrust laws prohibit brokers from conspiring to restrain competition with activities such as price fixing, group boycotting, allocating markets and tying agreements.

Questions

1. A person who has the authority to enter into contracts concerning all business affairs of another is called
   a. a general agent.   c. a special agent.
   b. a secret agent.   d. an attorney.

2. The term *fiduciary* refers to
   a. the sale of real property.
   b. principles by which a seller must conduct his or her business affairs.
   c. one who has legal power to act on behalf of another.
   d. the principal-agent relationship.

3. The legal relationship between broker and seller is generally
   a. a special agency.
   b. a general agency.
   c. a secret agency.
   d. a universal agency.

4. A real estate broker acting as the agent of the seller
   a. is obligated to render faithful service to the seller.
   b. can make a profit, if possible, in addition to the commission.
   c. can agree to a change in price without the seller's approval.
   d. can accept a commission from the buyer without the seller's approval.

5. The statement "to recover a commission for brokerage services, a broker must be employed" means
   a. the broker must work in a real estate office.
   b. the seller must have made an agreement to pay a commission to the broker for selling the property.
   c. the broker must have asked the seller the price of the property and then found a ready, willing and able buyer.
   d. the broker must have a salesperson employed in the office.

6. A broker is entitled to represent both the seller and the buyer when
   a. the broker holds a state license.
   b. the buyer and the seller are related.
   c. both parties give informed consent to such a transaction.
   d. both parties have attorneys.

7. In a fiduciary relationship, the agent is primarily responsible to the
   a. customer.
   b. client.
   c. lender.
   d. selling broker.

8. Under the law of agency, a real estate broker owes all of the following to the principal *except*
   a. care.   c. disclosure.
   b. obedience.   d. advertising.

9. A real estate broker will lose the right to a commission in a real estate transaction if he or she
    a. does not advertise the property.
    b. is not licensed when employed as an agent.
    c. does not personally market and sell the listing.
    d. accepts a commission from another licensee.

10. A real estate broker hired by an owner to sell a parcel of real estate must comply with
    a. any instructions of the owner.
    b. any instructions of the buyer.
    c. the concept of caveat emptor.
    d. the law of agency.

11. While in the employ of a real estate broker, a salesperson has the authority to
    a. act as an agent for the seller.
    b. assume responsibilities assigned by the broker.
    c. accept a commission from another broker.
    d. advertise the property on his or her own behalf.

12. M, a real estate broker, learns that her neighbor, V, wishes to sell his house. M knows the property well and is able to persuade E to make an offer for the property. M then asks V if she can present an offer to him, and V agrees. At this point,
    a. V is not obligated to pay M a commission.
    b. E is obligated to pay M for locating the property.
    c. V must pay M a commission.
    d. M has become a subagent of V.

13. A real estate broker who engages salespeople as independent contractors must
    a. withhold income tax from all commissions earned by them.
    b. require them to participate in office insurance plans offered to other salespeople hired as employees.
    c. withhold social security from all commissions earned by them.
    d. refrain from controlling how the salesperson conducts his or her business activities.

14. Salesperson T was listing seller J's house. J informed T that he would not sell to a member of a particular religious sect. T would be wise to do any of the following except
    a. accept the listing and ignore J's comment.
    b. attempt to convince J to change his mind.
    c. discuss the situation with his broker.
    d. refuse the listing.

15. Broker D lists K's residence for $87,000. K's employer has transferred her to another state, and she must sell her house quickly. To expedite the sale, D tells a prospective purchaser that K will accept at least $5,000 less than the listed price for the property. Based on these facts, all of the following statements are true except
    a. D has violated his agency responsibilities to K.
    b. D should not have disclosed this information, regardless of its accuracy.
    c. D should have disclosed only the lowest price that K would accept.
    d. D has a special agency relationship with K.

16. A broker has the right to dictate which of the following to an independent contractor who works for him?
    a. The number of hours that the person has to work
    b. The work schedule that the person has to follow
    c. The minimum acceptable dress code for the office
    d. The commission rate that the person receives

17. A buyer who is a client of the broker wants to purchase a house that the broker has listed for sale. Which of the following is true?
    a. If the listing salesperson and selling salesperson are two different people, there is no problem.
    b. The broker should refer the buyer to another broker to negotiate the sale.
    c. The seller and buyer must be informed and agree to the broker's representing both of them.
    d. The buyer should not have been shown a house listed by another broker.

16 Ethical Practices and Fair Housing

PROFESSIONAL ETHICS

Professional conduct involves more than just complying with laws of the industry. In real estate, the licensing laws set forth activities that are illegal and, therefore, prohibited. Licensees may be performing legally, yet not be performing ethically. **Ethics** is a system of *moral* principles, rules and standards of conduct. The ethical system of a profession establishes conduct that *exceeds* legal compliance. These moral principles establish standards for integrity and competence in dealing with the consumers of an industry's services, as well as a code of conduct between the professionals of that industry.

The basic rule of professional ethics is to *above all do no harm*. A course of action may appear to be justified because it is not illegal. However, if it causes harm to the client, the customer, the public or other licensees, it violates the rule of ethical behavior.

Code of Ethics

One way that many organizations address ethics among their members or in their respective businesses is by adopting codes of professional conduct. A **code of ethics** is a written system of standards for ethical conduct. These codes contain statements that are designed to advise, guide and regulate job behavior. They usually include references to topics such as conflict of interest, compliance with the law, commitment to protecting the public good and maintaining a high standard of business conduct. To be effective, a code of ethics must be specific by dictating rules that either prohibit or demand certain behavior rather than being purely aspirational. These codes must also provide for sanctions for violators so that the codes are enforced.

The real estate business is only as good as its reputation; reputations are built on fair dealings with the public. There are organizations within the real estate industry that have established codes of ethics for their members. These codes are expected to increase the level of professional conduct of their subscribers, thereby enhancing their reputation. A high standard of ethics is needed in the principal-agent relationship to ensure that the agent performs his or her fiduciary duties in the best interest of the principal.

The National Association of REALTORS® (NAR), the largest trade association in the country, adopted a Code of Ethics for its members in 1913. REALTORS® are expected to subscribe to this strict code of conduct. Not all licensees are REALTORS®, only those who are members of NAR. NAR has established procedures for Professional Standards committees at the local, state and national levels of the organization to administer compliance. Interpretations of the Code are known as Standards of Practice. The Code of Ethics has proved helpful because it contains practical applications of business ethics. The REALTORS® Code of Ethics and Standards of Practice are provided in Figure 16.1.

Code for Equal Opportunity

The NAR has adopted a *Code for Equal Opportunity* that sets forth standards of conduct for REALTORS® so that they may comply with the letter as well as the spirit of the fair housing laws, which will be discussed later in this chapter. The code provides these five basic guides to conduct:

1. In the sale, purchase, exchange, rental or lease of real property, REALTORS® have the responsibility to offer equal service to all clients and prospects without regard to race, color, religion, sex, handicap, familial status or national origin. This encompasses:

   a. entering broker-client relationships to sell or show property equally to members of all races, creeds or ethnic groups;

   b. receiving all formal written offers and communicating them to the owner;

   c. exerting their best efforts to conclude all transactions; and

   d. maintaining equal opportunity employment practices.

2. Members, individually and collectively, in performing their agency functions, have no right or responsibility to volunteer information regarding the racial, creed or ethnic composition of any neighborhood or any part thereof.

3. Members shall not engage in any activity that has the purpose of inducing panic selling.

4. Members shall not print, display or circulate any statement or advertisement with respect to the sale or rental of a dwelling that indicates any preference, limitations or discrimination based on race, color, religion, sex or ethnic background.

5. Members who violate the spirit or any provision of this Code of Equal Opportunity shall be subject to disciplinary action.

The NAR has also entered into a Fair Housing Partnership Agreement with HUD to jointly promote fair housing and address common fair housing concerns. The Fair Housing Partnership Agreement is based on several principles, including an understanding that all parts of the housing community share a responsibility for the achievement of fair housing.

The NAR supports voluntary compliance with fair housing laws and the principles of the Fair Housing Partnership. The organization encourages the development of local partnerships and encourages REALTORS® to publicly support and implement fair housing in their day-to-day business. The partnership envisions cooperation with all parts of the housing community.

Figure 16.1
Code of Ethics
and Standards
of Practice

Code of Ethics and Standards of Practice
of the NATIONAL ASSOCIATION OF REALTORS®
Effective January 1, 1999

Where the word REALTORS® is used in this Code and Preamble, it shall be deemed to include REALTOR-ASSOCIATE®s.

While the Code of Ethics establishes obligations that may be higher than those mandated by law, in any instance where the Code of Ethics and the law conflict, the obligations of the law must take precedence.

Preamble...

Under all is the land. Upon its wise utilization and widely allocated ownership depend the survival and growth of free institutions and of our civilization. REALTORS® should recognize that the interests of the nation and its citizens require the highest and best use of the land and the widest distribution of land ownership. They require the creation of adequate housing, the building of functioning cities, the development of productive industries and farms, and the preservation of a healthful environment.

Such interests impose obligations beyond those of ordinary commerce. They impose grave social responsibility and a patriotic duty to which REALTORS® should dedicate themselves, and for which they should be diligent in preparing themselves. REALTORS®, therefore, are zealous to maintain and improve the standards of their calling and share with their fellow REALTORS® a common responsibility for its integrity and honor.

In recognition and appreciation of their obligations to clients, customers, the public, and each other, REALTORS® continuously strive to become and remain informed on issues affecting real estate and, as knowledgeable professionals, they willingly share the fruit of their experience and study with others. They identify and take steps, through enforcement of this Code of Ethics and by assisting appropriate regulatory bodies, to eliminate practices which may damage the public or which might discredit or bring dishonor to the real estate profession.

Realizing that cooperation with other real estate professionals promotes the best interests of those who utilize their services, REALTORS® urge exclusive representation of clients; do not attempt to gain any unfair advantage over their competitors; and they refrain from making unsolicited comments about other practitioners. In instances where their opinion is sought, or where REALTORS® believe that comment is necessary, their opinion is offered in an objective, professional manner, uninfluenced by any personal motivation or potential advantage or gain.

The term REALTOR® has come to connote competency, fairness, and high integrity resulting from adherence to a lofty ideal of moral conduct in business relations. No inducement of profit and no instruction from clients ever can justify departure from this ideal.

In the interpretation of this obligation, REALTORS® can take no safer guide than that which has been handed down through the centuries, embodied in the Golden Rule, "Whatsoever ye would that others should do to you, do ye even so to them."

Accepting this standard as their own, REALTORS® pledge to observe its spirit in all of their activities and to conduct their business in accordance with the tenets set forth below.

Duties to Clients and Customers

Article 1

When representing a buyer, seller, landlord, tenant, or other client as an agent, REALTORS® pledge themselves to protect and promote the interests of their client. This obligation of absolute fidelity to the client's interests is primary, but it does not relieve REALTORS® of their obligation to treat all parties honestly. When serving a buyer, seller, landlord, tenant or other party in a non-agency capacity, REALTORS® remain obligated to treat all parties honestly. *(Amended 1/93)*

- **Standard of Practice 1-1**
  REALTORS®, when acting as principals in a real estate transaction, remain obligated by the duties imposed by the Code of Ethics. *(Amended 1/93)*

- **Standard of Practice 1-2**
  The duties the Code of Ethics imposes are applicable whether REALTORS® are acting as agents or in legally recognized non-agency capacities except that any duty imposed exclusively on agents by law or regulation shall not be imposed by this Code of Ethics on REALTORS® acting in non-agency capacities.

  As used in this Code of Ethics, "client" means the person(s) or entity(ies) with whom a REALTOR® or a REALTOR®'s firm has an agency or legally recognized non-agency relationship; "customer" means a party to a real estate transaction who receives information, services, or benefits but has no contractual relationship with the REALTOR® or the REALTOR®'s firm; "agent" means a real estate licensee (including brokers and sales associates) acting in an agency relationship as defined by state law or regulation; and "broker" means a real estate licensee (including brokers and sales associates) acting as an agent or in a legally recognized non-agency capacity. *(Adopted 1/95, Amended 1/99)*

- **Standard of Practice 1-3**
  REALTORS®, in attempting to secure a listing, shall not deliberately mislead the owner as to market value.

**Figure 16.1
(continued)**

- **Standard of Practice 1-4**
  REALTORS®, when seeking to become a buyer/tenant representative, shall not mislead buyers or tenants as to savings or other benefits that might be realized through use of the REALTOR®'s services. *(Amended 1/93)*

- **Standard of Practice 1-5**
  REALTORS® may represent the seller/landlord and buyer/tenant in the same transaction only after full disclosure to and with informed consent of both parties. *(Adopted 1/93)*

- **Standard of Practice 1-6**
  REALTORS® shall submit offers and counter-offers objectively and as quickly as possible. *(Adopted 1/93, Amended 1/95)*

- **Standard of Practice 1-7**
  When acting as listing brokers, REALTORS® shall continue to submit to the seller/landlord all offers and counter-offers until closing or execution of a lease unless the seller/landlord has waived this obligation in writing. REALTORS® shall not be obligated to continue to market the property after an offer has been accepted by the seller/landlord. REALTORS® shall recommend that sellers/landlords obtain the advice of legal counsel prior to acceptance of a subsequent offer except where the acceptance is contingent on the termination of the pre-existing purchase contract or lease. *(Amended 1/93)*

- **Standard of Practice 1-8**
  REALTORS® acting as agents or brokers of buyers/tenants shall submit to buyers/tenants all offers and counter-offers until acceptance but have no obligation to continue to show properties to their clients after an offer has been accepted unless otherwise agreed in writing. REALTORS® acting as agents or brokers of buyers/tenants shall recommend that buyers/tenants obtain the advice of legal counsel if there is a question as to whether a pre-existing contract has been terminated. *(Adopted 1/93, Amended 1/99)*

- **Standard of Practice 1-9**
  The obligation of REALTORS® to preserve confidential information (as defined by state law) provided by their clients in the course of any agency relationship or non-agency relationship recognized by law continues after termination of agency relationships or any non-agency relationships recognized by law. REALTORS® shall not knowingly, during or following the termination of professional relationships with their clients:
  1) reveal confidential information of clients; or
  2) use confidential information of clients to the disadvantage of clients; or
  3) use confidential information of clients for the REALTOR®'s advantage or the advantage of third parties unless:
     a) clients consent after full disclosure; or
     b) REALTORS® are required by court order; or

c) it is the intention of a client to commit a crime and the information is necessary to prevent the crime; or
d) it is necessary to defend a REALTOR® or the REALTOR®'s employees or associates against an accusation of wrongful conduct. *(Adopted 1/93, Amended 1/99)*

- **Standard of Practice 1-10**
  REALTORS® shall, consistent with the terms and conditions of their property management agreement, competently manage the property of clients with due regard for the rights, responsibilities, benefits, safety and health of tenants and others lawfully on the premises. *(Adopted 1/95)*

- **Standard of Practice 1-11**
  REALTORS® who are employed to maintain or manage a client's property shall exercise due diligence and make reasonable efforts to protect it against reasonably foreseeable contingencies and losses. *(Adopted 1/95)*

- **Standard of Practice 1-12**
  When entering into listing contracts, REALTORS® must advise sellers/landlords of:
  1) the REALTOR®'s general company policies regarding cooperation with and compensation to subagents, buyer/tenant agents and/or brokers acting in legally recognized non-agency capacities;
  2) the fact that buyer/tenant agents or brokers, even if compensated by listing brokers, or by sellers/landlords may represent the interests of buyers/tenants; and
  3) any potential for listing brokers to act as disclosed dual agents, e.g. buyer/tenant agents. *(Adopted 1/93, Renumbered 1/98, Amended 1/99)*

- **Standard of Practice 1-13**
  When entering into buyer/tenant agreements, REALTORS® must advise potential clients of:
  1) the REALTOR®'s general company policies regarding cooperation and compensation; and
  2) any potential for the buyer/tenant representative to act as a disclosed dual agent, e.g. listing broker, subagent, landlord's agent, etc. *(Adopted 1/93, Renumbered 1/98, Amended 1/99)*

Article 2

REALTORS® shall avoid exaggeration, misrepresentation, or concealment of pertinent facts relating to the property or the transaction. REALTORS® shall not, however, be obligated to discover latent defects in the property, to advise on matters outside the scope of their real estate license, or to disclose facts which are confidential under the scope of agency duties owed to their clients. *(Amended 1/93)*

- **Standard of Practice 2-1**
  REALTORS® shall only be obligated to discover and disclose adverse factors reasonably apparent to someone with expertise in those areas required by their real estate licensing authority. Article 2 does not impose upon the REALTOR® the obligation of expertise in other professional or technical disciplines. *(Amended 1/96)*

**Figure 16.1
(continued)**

- **Standard of Practice 2-2**
  (Renumbered as Standard of Practice 1-12 1/98)

- **Standard of Practice 2-3**
  (Renumbered as Standard of Practice 1-13 1/98)

- **Standard of Practice 2-4**
  REALTORS® shall not be parties to the naming of a false consideration in any document, unless it be the naming of an obviously nominal consideration.

- **Standard of Practice 2-5**
  Factors defined as "non-material" by law or regulation or which are expressly referenced in law or regulation as not being subject to disclosure are considered not "pertinent" for purposes of Article 2. *(Adopted 1/93)*

Article 3
REALTORS® shall cooperate with other brokers except when cooperation is not in the client's best interest. The obligation to cooperate does not include the obligation to share commissions, fees, or to otherwise compensate another broker. *(Amended 1/95)*

- **Standard of Practice 3-1**
  REALTORS®, acting as exclusive agents or brokers of sellers/landlords, establish the terms and conditions of offers to cooperate. Unless expressly indicated in offers to cooperate, cooperating brokers may not assume that the offer of cooperation includes an offer of compensation. Terms of compensation, if any, shall be ascertained by cooperating brokers before beginning efforts to accept the offer of cooperation. *(Amended 1/99)*

- **Standard of Practice 3-2**
  REALTORS® shall, with respect to offers of compensation to another REALTOR®, timely communicate any change of compensation for cooperative services to the other REALTOR® prior to the time such REALTOR® produces an offer to purchase/lease the property. *(Amended 1/94)*

- **Standard of Practice 3-3**
  Standard of Practice 3-2 does not preclude the listing broker and cooperating broker from entering into an agreement to change cooperative compensation. *(Adopted 1/94)*

- **Standard of Practice 3-4**
  REALTORS®, acting as listing brokers, have an affirmative obligation to disclose the existence of dual or variable rate commission arrangements (i.e., listings where one amount of commission is payable if the listing broker's firm is the procuring cause of sale/lease and a different amount of commission is payable if the sale/lease results through the efforts of the seller/landlord or a cooperating broker). The listing broker shall, as soon as practical, disclose the existence of such arrangements to potential cooperating brokers and shall, in response to inquiries from cooperating brokers, disclose the differential that would result in a cooperative transaction or in a sale/lease that results through the efforts of the seller/landlord. If the cooperating broker is a buyer/tenant representative, the buyer/tenant representative must disclose such information to their client. *(Amended 1/94)*

- **Standard of Practice 3-5**
  It is the obligation of subagents to promptly disclose all pertinent facts to the principal's agent prior to as well as after a purchase or lease agreement is executed. *(Amended 1/93)*

- **Standard of Practice 3-6**
  REALTORS® shall disclose the existence of an accepted offer to any broker seeking cooperation. *(Adopted 5/86)*

- **Standard of Practice 3-7**
  When seeking information from another REALTOR® concerning property under a management or listing agreement, REALTORS® shall disclose their REALTOR® status and whether their interest is personal or on behalf of a client and, if on behalf of a client, their representational status. *(Amended 1/95)*

- **Standard of Practice 3-8**
  REALTORS® shall not misrepresent the availability of access to show or inspect a listed property. *(Amended 11/87)*

Article 4
REALTORS® shall not acquire an interest in or buy or present offers from themselves, any member of their immediate families, their firms or any member thereof, or any entities in which they have any ownership interest, any real property without making their true position known to the owner or the owner's agent. In selling property they own, or in which they have any interest, REALTORS® shall reveal their ownership or interest in writing to the purchaser or the purchaser's representative. *(Amended 1/91)*

- **Standard of Practice 4-1**
  For the protection of all parties, the disclosures required by Article 4 shall be in writing and provided by REALTORS® prior to the signing of any contract. *(Adopted 2/86)*

Article 5
REALTORS® shall not undertake to provide professional services concerning a property or its value where they have a present or contemplated interest unless such interest is specifically disclosed to all affected parties.

Article 6
REALTORS® shall not accept any commission, rebate, or profit on expenditures made for their client, without the client's knowledge and consent.

When recommending real esatate products or services (e.g., homeowner's insurance, warranty programs, mortgage financing, title insurance, etc.), REALTORS® shall disclose to the client or customer to whom the recommendation is made any

**Figure 16.1
(continued)**

financial benefits or fees, other than real estate referral fees, the REALTOR® or REALTOR®'s firm may receive as a direct result of such recommendation. *(Amended 1/99)*

- **Standard of Practice 6-1**
  REALTORS® shall not recommend or suggest to a client or a customer the use of services of another organization or business entity in which they have a direct interest without disclosing such interest at the time of the recommendation or suggestion. *(Amended 5/88)*

Article 7
In a transaction, REALTORS® shall not accept compensation from more than one party, even if permitted by law, without disclosure to all parties and the informed consent of the REALTOR®'s client or clients. *(Amended 1/93)*

Article 8
REALTORS® shall keep in a special account in an appropriate financial institution, separated from their own funds, monies coming into their possession in trust for other persons, such as escrows, trust funds, clients' monies, and other like items.

Article 9
REALTORS®, for the protection of all parties, shall assure whenever possible that agreements shall be in writing, and shall be in clear and understandable language expressing the specific terms, conditions, obligations and commitments of the parties. A copy of each agreement shall be furnished to each party upon their signing or initialing. *(Amended 1/95)*

- **Standard of Practice 9-1**
  For the protection of all parties, REALTORS® shall use reasonable care to ensure that documents pertaining to the purchase, sale, or lease of real estate are kept current through the use of written extensions or amendments. *(Amended 1/93)*

Duties to the Public

Article 10
REALTORS® shall not deny equal professional services to any person for reasons of race, color, religion, sex, handicap, familial status, or national origin. REALTORS® shall not be parties to any plan or agreement to discriminate against a person or persons on the basis of race, color, religion, sex, handicap, familial status, or national origin. *(Amended 1/90)*

- **Standard of Practice 10-1**
  REALTORS® shall not volunteer information regarding the racial, religious or ethnic composition of any neighborhood and shall not engage in any activity which may result in panic selling. REALTORS® shall not print, display or circulate any statement or advertisement with respect to the selling or renting of a property that indicates any preference, limitations or discrimination based on race, color, religion, sex, handicap, familial status or national origin. *(Adopted 1/94)*

Article 11
The services which REALTORS® provide to their clients and customers shall conform to the standards of practice and competence which are reasonably expected in the specific real estate disciplines in which they engage; specifically, residential real estate brokerage, real property management, commercial and industrial real estate brokerage, real estate appraisal, real estate counseling, real estate syndication, real estate auction, and international real estate.

REALTORS® shall not undertake to provide specialized professional services concerning a type of property or service that is outside their field of competence unless they engage the assistance of one who is competent on such types of property or service, or unless the facts are fully disclosed to the client. Any persons engaged to provide such assistance shall be so identified to the client and their contribution to the assignment should be set forth. *(Amended 1/95)*

- **Standard of Practice 11-1**
  The obligations of the Code of Ethics shall be supplemented by and construed in a manner consistent with the Uniform Standards of Professional Appraisal Practice (USPAP) promulgated by the Appraisal Standards Board of the Appraisal Foundation.

  The obligations of the Code of Ethics shall not be supplemented by the USPAP where an opinion or recommendation of price or pricing is provided in pursuit of a listing, to assist a potential purchaser in formulating a purchase offer, or to provide a broker's price opinion, whether for a fee or not. *(Amended 1/96)*

- **Standard of Practice 11-2**
  The obligations of the Code of Ethics in respect of real estate disciplines other than appraisal shall be interpreted and applied in accordance with the standards of competence and practice which clients and the public reasonably require to protect their rights and interests considering the complexity of the transaction, the availability of expert assistance, and, where the REALTOR® is an agent or subagent, the obligations of a fiduciary. *(Adopted 1/95)*

- **Standard of Practice 11-3**
  When REALTORS® provide consultive services to clients which involve advice or counsel for a fee (not a commission), such advice shall be rendered in an objective manner and the fee shall not be contingent on the substance of the advice or counsel given. If brokerage or transaction services are to be provided in addition to consultive services, a separate compensation may be paid with prior agreement between the client and REALTOR®. *(Adopted 1/96)*

**Figure 16.1
(continued)**

Article 12

REALTORS® shall be careful at all times to present a true picture in their advertising and representations to the public. REALTORS® shall also ensure that their professional status (e.g., broker, appraiser, property manager, etc.) or status as REALTORS® is clearly identifiable in any such advertising. *(Amended 1/93)*

- **Standard of Practice 12-1**

  REALTORS® may use the term "free" and similar terms in their advertising and in other representations provided that all terms governing availability of the offered product or service are clearly disclosed at the same time. *(Amended 1/97)*

- **Standard of Practice 12-2**

  REALTORS® may represent their services as "free" or without cost even if they expect to receive compensation from a source other than their client provided that the potential for the REALTOR® to obtain a benefit from a third party is clearly disclosed at the same time. *(Amended 1/97)*

- **Standard of Practice 12-3**

  The offering of premiums, prizes, merchandise discounts or other inducements to list, sell, purchase, or lease is not, in itself, unethical even if receipt of the benefit is contingent on listing, selling, purchasing, or leasing through the REALTOR® making the offer. However, REALTORS® must exercise care and candor in any such advertising or other public or private representations so that any party interested in receiving or otherwise benefiting from the REALTOR®'s offer will have clear, thorough, advance understanding of all the terms and conditions of the offer. The offering of any inducements to do business is subject to the limitations and restrictions of state law and the ethical obligations established by any applicable Standard of Practice. *(Amended 1/95)*

- **Standard of Practice 12-4**

  REALTORS® shall not offer for sale/lease or advertise property without authority. When acting as listing brokers or as subagents, REALTORS® shall not quote a price different from that agreed upon with the seller/landlord. *(Amended 1/93)*

- **Standard of Practice 12-5**

  REALTORS® shall not advertise nor permit any person employed by or affiliated with them to advertise listed property without disclosing the name of the firm. *(Adopted 11/86)*

- **Standard of Practice 12-6**

  REALTORS®, when advertising unlisted real property for sale/lease in which they have an ownership interest, shall disclose their status as both owners/landlords and as REALTORS® or real estate licensees. *(Amended 1/93)*

- **Standard of Practice 12-7**

  Only REALTORS® who participated in the transaction as the listing broker or cooperating broker (selling broker) may claim to have "sold" the property. Prior to closing, a cooperating broker may post a "sold" sign only with the consent of the listing broker. *(Amended 1/96)*

Article 13

REALTORS® shall not engage in activities that constitute the unauthorized practice of law and shall recommend that legal counsel be obtained when the interest of any party to the transaction requires it.

Article 14

If charged with unethical practice or asked to present evidence or to cooperate in any other way, in any professional standards proceeding or investigation, REALTORS® shall place all pertinent facts before the proper tribunals of the Member Board or affiliated institute, society, or council in which membership is held and shall take no action to disrupt or obstruct such processes. *(Amended 1/99)*

- **Standard of Practice 14-1**

  REALTORS® shall not be subject to disciplinary proceedings in more than one Board of REALTORS® or affiliated institute, society or council in which they hold membership with respect to alleged violations of the Code of Ethics relating to the same transaction or event. *(Amended 1/95)*

- **Standard of Practice 14-2**

  REALTORS® shall not make any unauthorized disclosure or dissemination of the allegations, findings, or decision developed in connection with an ethics hearing or appeal or in connection with an arbitration hearing or procedural review. *(Amended 1/92)*

- **Standard of Practice 14-3**

  REALTORS® shall not obstruct the Board's investigative or professional standards proceedings by instituting or threatening to institute actions for libel, slander or defamation against any party to a professional standards proceeding or their witnesses based on the filing of an arbitration request, an ethics complaint, or testimony given before any tribunal. *(Adopted 11/87, Amended 1/99)*

- **Standard of Practice 14-4**

  REALTORS® shall not intentionally impede the Board's investigative or disciplinary proceedings by filing multiple ethics complaints based on the same event or transaction. *(Adopted 11/88)*

**Figure 16.1
(continued)**

Duties to REALTORS®

Article 15
REALTORS® shall not knowingly or recklessly make false or misleading statements about competitors, their businesses, or their business practices. *(Amended 1/92)*

Article 16
REALTORS® shall not engage in any practice or take any action inconsistent with the agency or other exclusive relationship recognized by law that other REALTORS® have with clients. *(Amended 1/98)*

- **Standard of Practice 16-1**

  Article 16 is not intended to prohibit aggressive or innovative business practices which are otherwise ethical and does not prohibit disagreements with other REALTORS® involving commission, fees, compensation or other forms of payment or expenses. *(Adopted 1/93, Amended 1/95)*

- **Standard of Practice 16-2**

  Article 16 does not preclude REALTORS® from making general announcements to prospective clients describing their services and the terms of their availability even though some recipients may have entered into agency agreements or other exclusive relationships with another REALTOR®. A general telephone canvass, general mailing or distribution addressed to all prospective clients in a given geographical area or in a given profession, business, club, or organization, or other classification or group is deemed "general" for purposes of this standard. *(Amended 1/98)*

  Article 16 is intended to recognize as unethical two basic types of solicitations:

  First, telephone or personal solicitations of property owners who have been identified by a real estate sign, multiple listing compilation, or other information service as having exclusively listed their property with another REALTOR®; and

  Second, mail or other forms of written solicitations of prospective clients whose properties are exclusively listed with another REALTOR® when such solicitations are not part of a general mailing but are directed specifically to property owners identified through compilations of current listings, "for sale" or "for rent" signs, or other sources of information required by Article 3 and Multiple Listing Service rules to be made available to other REALTORS® under offers of subagency or cooperation. *(Amended 1/93)*

- **Standard of Practice 16-3**

  Article 16 does not preclude REALTORS® from contacting the client of another broker for the purpose of offering to provide, or entering into a contract to provide, a different type of real estate service unrelated to the type of service

currently being provided (e.g., property management as opposed to brokerage). However, information received through a Multiple Listing Service or any other offer of cooperation may not be used to target clients of other REALTORS® to whom such offers to provide services may be made. *(Amended 1/93)*

- **Standard of Practice 16-4**

  REALTORS® shall not solicit a listing which is currently listed exclusively with another broker. However, if the listing broker, when asked by the REALTOR®, refuses to disclose the expiration date and nature of such listing; i.e., an exclusive right to sell, an exclusive agency, open listing, or other form of contractual agreement between the listing broker and the client, the REALTOR® may contact the owner to secure such information and may discuss the terms upon which the REALTOR® might take a future listing or, alternatively, may take a listing to become effective upon expiration of any existing exclusive listing. *(Amended 1/94)*

- **Standard of Practice 16-5**

  REALTORS® shall not solicit buyer/tenant agreements from buyers/tenants who are subject to exclusive buyer/tenant agreements. However, if asked by a REALTOR®, the broker refuses to disclose the expiration date of the exclusive buyer/tenant agreement, the REALTOR® may contact the buyer/tenant to secure such information and may discuss the terms upon which the REALTOR® might enter into a future buyer/tenant agreement or, alternatively, may enter into a buyer/tenant agreement to become effective upon the expiration of any existing exclusive buyer/tenant agreement.
  (Adopted 1/94, Amended 1/98)

- **Standard of Practice 16-6**

  When REALTORS® are contacted by the client of another REALTOR® regarding the creation of an exclusive relationship to provide the same type of service, and REALTORS® have not directly or indirectly initiated such discussions, they may discuss the terms upon which they might enter into a future agreement or, alternatively, may enter into an agreement which becomes effective upon expiration of any existing exclusive agreement. *(Amended 1/98)*

- **Standard of Practice 16-7**

  The fact that a client has retained a REALTOR® as an agent or in another exclusive relationship in one or more past transactions does not preclude other REALTORS® from seeking such former client's future business. *(Amended 1/98)*

- **Standard of Practice 16-8**

  The fact that an exclusive agreement has been entered into with a REALTOR® shall not preclude or inhibit any other REALTOR® from entering into a similar agreement after the expiration of the prior agreement. *(Amended 1/98)*

- **Standard of Practice 16-9**

  REALTORS®, prior to entering into an agency agreement or other exclusive relationship, have an affirmative obligation

**Figure 16.1
(continued)**

to make reasonable efforts to determine whether the client is subject to a current, valid exclusive agreement to provide the same type of real estate service. *(Amended 1/98)*

- **Standard of Practice 16-10**
  REALTORS®, acting as agents of, or in another relationship with, buyers or tenants, shall disclose that relationship to the seller/landlord's agent or broker at first contact and shall provide written confirmation of that disclosure to the seller/landlord's agent or broker not later than execution of a purchase agreement or lease. *(Amended 1/98)*

- **Standard of Practice 16-11**
  On unlisted property, REALTORS® acting as buyer/tenant agents or brokers shall disclose that relationship to the seller/landlord at first contact for that client and shall provide written confirmation of such disclosure to the seller/landlord not later than execution of any purchase or lease agreement.

  REALTORS® shall make any request for anticipated compensation from the seller/landlord at first contact. *(Amended 1/98)*

- **Standard of Practice 16-12**
  REALTORS®, acting as agents or brokers of sellers/landlords or as subagents of listing brokers, shall disclose that relationship to buyers/tenants as soon as practicable and shall provide written confirmation of such disclosure to buyers/tenants not later than execution of any purchase or lease agreement. *(Amended 1/98)*

- **Standard of Practice 16-13**
  All dealings concerning property exclusively listed, or with buyer/tenants who are subject to an exclusive agreement shall be carried on with the client's agent or broker, and not with the client, except with the consent of the client's agent or broker or except where such dealings are initiated by the client. *(Adopted 1/93, Amended 1/98)*

- **Standard of Practice 16-14**
  REALTORS® are free to enter into contractual relationships or to negotiate with sellers/landlords, buyers/tenants or others who are not subject to an exclusive agreement but shall not knowingly obligate them to pay more than one commission except with their informed consent. *(Amended 1/98)*

- **Standard of Practice 16-15**
  In cooperative transactions REALTORS® shall compensate cooperating REALTORS® (principal brokers) and shall not compensate nor offer to compensate, directly or indirectly, any of the sales licensees employed by or affiliated with other REALTORS® without the prior express knowledge and consent of the cooperating broker.

- **Standard of Practice 16-16**
  REALTORS®, acting as subagents or buyer/tenant agents or brokers, shall not use the terms of an offer to purchase/lease to attempt to modify the listing broker's offer of compensation to subagents or buyer's agents or brokers nor make the submission of an executed offer to purchase/lease contingent on the listing broker's agreement to modify the offer of compensation. *(Amended 1/98)*

- **Standard of Practice 16-17**
  REALTORS® acting as subagents or as buyer/tenant agents or brokers, shall not attempt to extend a listing broker's offer of cooperation and/or compensation to other brokers without the consent of the listing broker. *(Amended 1/98)*

- **Standard of Practice 16-18**
  REALTORS® shall not use information obtained by them from the listing broker, through offers to cooperate received through Multiple Listing Services or other sources authorized by the listing broker, for the purpose of creating a referral prospect to a third broker, or for creating a buyer/tenant prospect unless such use is authorized by the listing broker. *(Amended 1/93)*

- **Standard of Practice 16-19**
  Signs giving notice of property for sale, rent, lease, or exchange shall not be placed on property without consent of the seller/landlord. *(Amended 1/93)*

- **Standard of Practice 16-20**
  REALTORS®, prior to or after terminating their relationship with their current firm, shall not induce clients of their current firm to cancel exclusive contractual agreements between the client and that firm. This does not preclude REALTORS® (principals) from establishing agreements with their associated licensees governing assignability of exclusive agreements. *(Adopted 1/98)*

Article 17

In the event of contractual disputes or specific non-contractual disputes as defined in Standard of Practice 17-4 between REALTORS® associated with different firms, arising out of their relationship as REALTORS®, the REALTORS® shall submit the dispute to arbitration in accordance with the regulations of their Board or Boards rather than litigate the matter.

In the event clients of REALTORS® wish to arbitrate contractual disputes arising out of real estate transactions, REALTORS® shall arbitrate those disputes in accordance with the regulations of their Board, provided the clients agree to be bound by the decision. *(Amended 1/97)*

- **Standard of Practice 17-1**
  The filing of litigation and refusal to withdraw from it by REALTORS® in an arbitrable matter constitutes a refusal to arbitrate. *(Adopted 2/86)*

- **Standard of Practice 17-2**
  Article 17 does not require REALTORS® to arbitrate in those circumstances when all parties to the dispute advise the Board in writing that they choose not to arbitrate before the Board. *(Amended 1/93)*

Figure 16.1
(continued)

- **Standard of Practice 17-3**
  REALTORS®, when acting solely as principals in a real estate transaction, are not obligated to arbitrate disputes with other REALTORS® absent a specific written agreement to the contrary. *(Adopted 1/96)*

- **Standard of Practice 17-4**
  Specific non-contractual disputes that are subject to arbitration pursuant to Article 17 are:

  1) Where a listing broker has compensated a cooperating broker and another cooperating broker subsequently claims to be the procuring cause of the sale or lease. In such cases the complainant may name the first cooperating broker as respondent and arbitration may proceed without the listing broker being named as a respondent. Alternatively, if the complaint is brought against the listing broker, the listing broker may name the first cooperating broker as a third-party respondent. In either instance the decision of the hearing panel as to procuring cause shall be conclusive with respect to all current or subsequent claims of the parties for compensation arising out of the underlying cooperative transaction. *(Adopted 1/97)*

  2) Where a buyer or tenant representative is compensated by the seller or landlord, and not by the listing broker, and the listing broker, as a result, reduces the commission owed by the seller or landlord and, subsequent to such actions, another cooperating broker claims to be the procuring cause of sale or lease. In such cases the complainant may name the first cooperating broker as respondent and arbitration may proceed without the listing broker being named as a respondent. Alternatively, if the complaint is brought against the listing broker, the listing broker may name the first cooperating broker as a third-party respondent. In either instance the decision of the hearing panel as to procuring cause shall be conclusive with respect to all current or subsequent claims of the parties for compensation arising out of the underlying cooperative transaction. *(Adopted 1/97)*

  3) Where a buyer or tenant representative is compensated by the buyer or tenant and, as a result, the listing broker reduces the commission owed by the seller or landlord and, subsequent to such actions, another cooperating broker claims to be the procuring cause of sale or lease.

In such cases the complainant may name the first cooperating broker as respondent and arbitration may proceed without the listing broker being named as a respondent. Alternatively, if the complaint is brought against the listing broker, the listing broker may name the first cooperating broker as a third-party respondent. In either instance the decision of the hearing panel as to procuring cause shall be conclusive with respect to all current or subsequent claims of the parties for compensation arising out of the underlying cooperative transaction. *(Adopted 1/97)*

  4) Where two or more listing brokers claim entitlement to compensation pursuant to open listings with a seller or landlord who agrees to participate in arbitration (or who requests arbitration) and who agrees to be bound by the decision. In cases where one of the listing brokers has been compensated by the seller or landlord, the other listing broker, as complainant, may name the first listing broker as respondent and arbitration may proceed between the brokers. *(Adopted 1/97)*

The Code of Ethics was adopted in 1913. Amended at the Annual Convention in 1924, 1928, 1950, 1951, 1952, 1955, 1956, 1961, 1962, 1974, 1982, 1986, 1987, 1989, 1990, 1991, 1992, 1993, 1994, 1995, 1996, 1997 and 1998.

Explanatory Notes

The reader should be aware of the following policies which have been approved by the Board of Directors of the National Association:

In filing a charge of an alleged violation of the Code of Ethics by a REALTOR®, the charge must read as an alleged violation of one or more Articles of the Code. Standards of Practice may be cited in support of the charge.

The Standards of Practice serve to clarify the ethical obligations imposed by the various Articles and supplement, and do not substitute for, the Case Interpretations in *Interpretations of the Code of Ethics.*

Modifications to existing Standards of Practice and additional new Standards of Practice are approved from time to time. Readers are cautioned to ensure that the most recent publications are utilized.

NATIONAL ASSOCIATION
OF REALTORS®
430 North Michigan Avenue
Chicago, Illinois 60611

EQUAL OPPORTUNITY

Civil rights laws that affect real estate have been enacted to create a marketplace in which all persons of similar financial means have a similar range of choices in the purchase, rental or financing of real property. The goal is to create an open, unbiased housing market in which every person has the opportunity to live where he or she chooses. Owners, real estate licensees, apartment management companies, real estate organizations, lending agencies, builders and developers must all take part in creating this single housing market. Federal, state and local fair housing or equal opportunity laws affect every phase of a real estate transaction, from listing to closing.

The U.S. Congress and the Supreme Court have labored to create a legal framework that preserves the rights granted to all citizens under the Constitution. Discrimination in this nation has a long history, dating back to the beginning of slavery. Although the passage of laws establishes a code for public conduct, centuries of discriminatory practices result in attitudes and stereotypes that are not easily affected by law. Real estate licensees cannot allow their own prejudices or those of property owners or prospective property seekers to affect compliance with the fair housing laws.

Potential licensees must have a thorough knowledge of the fair housing laws to avoid illegal practices. Illegal activity is not limited to racial discrimination; amendments to the fair housing laws have expanded the number of protected classes. *Failure to comply with fair housing laws is not only a criminal act but also grounds for disciplinary action against the licensee.*

FEDERAL LAWS

The efforts of the federal government to guarantee equal housing opportunities to all U.S. citizens began more than 100 years ago with the passage of the **Civil Rights Act of 1866.** This law prohibits any type of discrimination based on race: "All citizens of the United States shall have the same right in every state and territory as is enjoyed by white citizens thereof to inherit, purchase, lease, sell, hold, and convey real and personal property."

In 1896, the U.S. Supreme Court established the "separate but equal" doctrine, which provided that separate but equal accommodations for the races were not in conflict with the Constitution. However, this segregated the races, creating classes among citizens. Although accommodations were separate, they rarely were equal. Patterns of segregation were perpetuated by zoning ordinances and restrictive covenants. The FHA, in administering its mortgage insurance programs, encouraged practices that maintained segregated housing patterns. Not until 1948 did the U.S. Supreme Court decide that racially restrictive covenants violated rights granted under the Constitution and were, therefore, unenforceable. In 1950, the federal government prohibited insuring mortgages on property encumbered by racially restrictive covenants.

It was not until the civil rights efforts of the 1960s that discriminatory conduct in housing was singled out for specific legislation. In 1962, President John F. Kennedy issued an executive order that guaranteed nondiscrimination in all housing financed by FHA and VA loans. The Civil Rights Act of 1964 prohibited discrimination in any housing program that receives whole or partial federal funding. However, both of these efforts had limited impact on discriminatory housing practices, particularly because a relatively small percentage of housing was affected by these programs. Finally, in 1968, Title VIII of the Civil Rights Act addressed specific practices in housing that are prohibited.

Fair Housing Act   Title VIII of the Civil Rights Act of 1968 prohibits discrimination in housing because of race, color, religion and national origin. In 1974, the Housing and Community Development Act added sex; in 1988, the Fair Housing Amendments Act added handicap and familial status as protected classes. Today the **Fair Housing Act,** as it is known, prohibits discrimination on the basis of *race, color, religion, sex, handicap, familial status and national origin.* The act also prohibits discrimination against individuals because of their *association* with persons in the protected classes. This law is administered by the Department of Housing and Urban Development (HUD), which has promulgated Rules and Regulations that further interpret the practices defined by the law.

The Regulations define housing as a "dwelling," being any building, or portion thereof (including a single-family house, condominium, cooperative or mobile home), designed for occupancy as a residence by one or more families. This also includes vacant land for sale or lease for the location or construction of these structures. Relating to persons in the protected classes, it shall be unlawful to

- refuse to sell, rent or refuse to negotiate with any person or otherwise make a dwelling unavailable;

- differentiate in terms, conditions or services for the purpose of discriminating;

- practice discrimination through any statement or advertisement that indicates any preference, limitation or discrimination;

- represent that a property is not available when in fact it is available for sale or rent;

- make a profit by inducing owners to sell or rent because of the prospective entry into the neighborhood of persons in the protected classes;

- alter the terms or conditions for a loan for the purchase, construction, improvement or repair of a dwelling as a means of discrimination; or

- deny membership or limit the participation in any real estate organization as a means of discriminating.

In addition to these general provisions of the law, HUD has issued rules and regulations that define specific procedures that affect practices in the real estate industry, mortgage lending and advertising.

Familial status. The most recent amendment to the Fair Housing Act included familial status as a protected class. Congress intended that this would assist families with children to find suitable housing that previously was unavailable, particularly in rentals. *Familial status* is defined as one or more individuals who have not reached the age of 18 being domiciled with a parent or another person who has legal custody. It also includes a person who is pregnant. Unless a property meets the standards for exemption as "housing for older persons," all properties must be made available under the same terms and conditions as are available to all other persons. Including families with children as a protected class requires property owners and licensees to change their standards for occupancy and their advertising and marketing practices. It is no longer legal to advertise "adults only" or other similar references. The number of persons who are permitted to reside in a property cannot be restrictive with the intent or effect of eliminating families with children.

Handicap. *Handicap* is defined as a physical or mental impairment or having a history of such impairment that substantially limits one or more of a person's major life activities. It does *not* include the current illegal use of or addiction to a controlled substance. However, an individual in an addiction recovery program may qualify under the handicap definition. Individuals with the AIDS virus, with or without evidence of disease, *are* protected by the fair housing laws under the handicap classification.

It is unlawful to discriminate against any prospective buyer or tenant because of a handicap. People are entitled to terms and conditions, privileges and access to service or facilities that are not discriminatory because of their disabilities. People with disabilities must be permitted, at their own expense, to make reasonable modifications to the existing premises that may be necessary for full enjoyment of the premises. In the case of a rental, the landlord can require, if it is reasonable to do so, that the person restore the interior of the premises to its previous condition if these modifications would make the property undesirable to the general population.

The law does not prohibit restricting occupancy exclusively to persons with a handicap in dwellings that are designed specifically for their accommodation.

For new construction of certain multifamily properties constructed with federally related funds, a number of accessibility and usability requirements must be met. Access is specified for public and common-use portions of the buildings and adaptive and accessible design features within the interior of the dwelling units.

Exemptions to the Fair Housing Act

The federal Fair Housing Act provides for certain exemptions. It is, however, important to know in what situations they apply. There are *no* exemptions involving race *or* in transactions involving a real estate licensee. Most of the exemptions in the federal law also do not apply under Pennsylvania law (which will be discussed later in this chapter).

- The sale or rental of a single-family home is exempted when the home is owned by an individual who does not own more than three such homes at one time, when a real estate licensee is not used and discriminatory advertising is not used. Only one such sale by an owner not living in the dwelling at the time of the transaction or not the most recent occupant is exempt from the law within any 24-month period. *This exemption does not apply under Pennsylvania law.*

- The rental of rooms or units is exempted in an owner-occupied one-family to four-family dwelling. *Pennsylvania law only recognizes an exemption in the rental of an owner-occupied rooming house with a common entrance or, in the case of sex, the rental or leasing of housing accommodations in a single-sex dormitory.*

- Dwelling units owned by religious organizations and not operated for commercial purposes may be limited or give preference to people of the same religion if membership in the organization is not restricted on the basis of race, color or national origin.

• A private club that is not in fact open to the public may restrict the rental or occupancy of lodgings that it owns to its members, as long as the lodgings are not operated commercially. The private club may not discriminate in its requirements for membership.

Housing for older persons. Although the Fair Housing Act protects families with children, certain properties can be restricted for occupancy by the elderly. Housing occupied (or intended to be occupied) solely by persons age 62 or older or housing occupied (or intended to be occupied) by at least one person 55 years of age or older per unit in 80 percent of the units is exempt from the familial status protection. There also must be published policies and procedures that demonstrate the intent to provide housing for these individuals.

Other provisions. The Fair Housing Act does not require that housing be made available to individuals whose tenancy would constitute a direct threat to the health or safety of other individuals or that would result in substantial physical damage to the property of others. Nor are individuals who have been *convicted* of the illegal manufacture or distribution of a controlled substance protected under this law.

Jones v. Mayer. In 1968, the Supreme Court heard the case of *Jones v. Alfred H. Mayer Company,* 392 U.S. 409 (1968). In its decision, the Court upheld the Civil Rights Act of 1866, which "prohibits all racial discrimination, private or public, in the sale and rental of property." This decision is important because, although the federal law exempts individual homeowners and certain groups, the 1866 law *prohibits all racial discrimination without exception.* An aggrieved person may seek remedy for racial discrimination under the 1866 law. *Where race is involved, no exceptions apply.*

Supreme Court interpretation. In 1987, the U.S. Supreme Court clarified the definition of *race* beyond the way the court viewed the term as was understood in the 19th century when the Civil Rights Act of 1866 was passed. In the decision of two cases the court used the criteria of ancestry or ethnic characteristics, meaning that one possesses certain physical, cultural or linguistic characteristics commonly shared by a "national origin group" to define "race." Discrimination on the basis of race, as it is now defined to refer to more than nonwhite persons, affords due process of complaints under the provisions of the Civil Rights Act of 1866.

Equal Housing Opportunity Poster

The Fair Housing Act instituted the use of an equal housing opportunity poster. This poster, obtainable from HUD and illustrated in Figure 16.2, features the equal housing opportunity slogan, an equal housing statement pledging adherence to the Fair Housing Act and support of affirmative marketing and advertising programs, and the equal housing opportunity logo (shown in Figure 16.3). The use of the equal housing logo and slogan in advertising is discussed in HUD's regulations.

When HUD investigates a broker for discriminatory practices, it may consider failure to prominently display the poster in the broker's place of business prima facie evidence of discrimination.

Figure 16.2
Equal Housing
Opportunity Poster

U.S. Department of Housing and Urban Development

EQUAL HOUSING
OPPORTUNITY

We Do Business in Accordance With the Federal Fair Housing Law
(The Fair Housing Amendments Act of 1988)

It is Illegal to Discriminate Against Any Person Because of Race, Color, Religion, Sex, Handicap, Familial Status, or National Origin

- In the sale or rental of housing or residential lots
- In advertising the sale or rental of housing
- In the financing of housing

- In the provision of real estate brokerage services
- In the appraisal of housing
- Blockbusting is also illegal

Anyone who feels he or she has been discriminated against may file a complaint of housing discrimination with the:
1-800-424-8590 (Toll Free)
1-800-424-8529 (TDD)

U.S. Department of Housing and Urban Development
Assistant Secretary for Fair Housing and Equal Opportunity
Washington, D.C. 20410

Previous editions are obsolete

form **HUD-928.1** (3-89)

**Figure 16.3
Equal Housing
Opportunity
Symbol**

**EQUAL HOUSING
OPPORTUNITY**

**Equal Credit
Opportunity Act**

The federal **Equal Credit Opportunity Act (ECOA)** prohibits discrimination based on race, color, religion, national origin, sex, marital status or age (if the applicant has reached the age of contractual capacity) in the granting of credit. Note the dissimilarity in the protected classes between the Fair Housing Act and the ECOA in which marital status and age are included. As in the Fair Housing Act, ECOA requires that credit applications be considered only on the basis of income, net worth, job stability and credit rating.

**Americans with
Disabilities Act**

The Americans with Disabilities Act (ADA), which was signed into law in 1990, intends to enable people with disabilities to become part of the economic and social mainstream of society by "opening doors" both literally and physically. The law mandated equal access to employment, public services (such as transportation provided by state and local governments as well as by national services such as Amtrak), goods and services offered by both public and private entities and telecommunications. Title I prohibits discrimination against qualified job applicants who have a disability. Title III provides that no person with a disability shall be discriminated against in the full and equal enjoyment of goods, facilities, privileges or accommodations.

The passage of ADA has focused considerable attention on employment practices. Title I of ADA requires employers with 15 or more employees to adopt nondiscriminatory employment procedures. (The Pennsylvania Human Relations Act is broader by requiring employers in Pennsylvania with *4 or more employees* to adopt nondiscriminatory practices.) The law does not expect preferential treatment or preference for people with disabilities, but rather prevents employers from basing hiring and employment decisions on assumptions about the effects of a disability. Recruitment, job application procedures, hiring, firing, advancement, compensation, training and other privileges of employment cannot be discriminatory, and employers must provide any reasonable accommodations that a person with a disability needs to perform the essential functions of a job.

According to ADA, anyone who provides goods and services to the public must do so in ways that enable people with disabilities to access them. Public accommodations include establishments such as lodging facilities, eating establishments, entertainment and amusement facilities, museums and libraries, and retail and consumer services. The Pennsylvania Human Relations Act includes commercial property (any building or vacant land used for the purpose of operating a business, an office or a manufacturing facility). These properties must be free of architectural and communication barriers or other accommodations must be provided if this is not feasible. The Americans with Disabilities Act Accessibility Guidelines for buildings and facilities (ADAAG) include specifications for parking, passenger loading zones, curb ramps, stairs, elevators, doors, drinking fountains and water coolers, alarms and detectable warnings, toilet facilities, signage and telephones.

Because of the large number of existing commercial buildings, eliminating all architectural barriers is a massive undertaking. Many of these buildings are difficult to retrofit not only because of their existing design but also because of the enormous expense that could be involved. The ADA provides reasonable approaches for bringing existing buildings into compliance. Barriers must be removed in existing buildings to maximize accessibility if it is *readily achievable* to do so; that is, with little difficulty or expense as defined in the law. If a barrier cannot be removed, *reasonable accommodations* must be provided such as installing a call button at a door that cannot be made accessible.

New construction of commercial properties must be designed to be readily accessible and usable as defined in ADAAG to the extent that it is not structurally impractical. It is estimated that incorporating accessibility features in new construction is normally less than 1 percent of the overall construction cost. ADAAG contains general design standards for both the building and the site.

What does ADA mean in the real estate business? The broker's office space and functions for the public such as seminars, meetings, conferences or classes must be accessible to people with disabilities or the broker must provide reasonable accommodations that will enable a person to access the broker's services. Because communications as well as architectural barriers impede accessibility, auxiliary aids such as interpreters, signers or large print materials may be provided in accordance with the laws to help people during a real estate transaction. Brokers also should consider how a person with hearing loss will communicate with their offices or how a person with a physical disability can be accommodated at an open house if the property or model home is not accessible.

ADA may affect the broker's hiring practices depending on the number of employees. Managers of commercial property, as the agents of the real estate owners, are affected by ADA. Noncompliance creates liability for the owner as well as for the property manager. Appraisers must be aware of ADA; conspicuous property features that are barriers to people with disabilities may affect the value of a property.

PENNSYLVANIA HUMAN RELATIONS ACT

The **Pennsylvania Human Relations Act (PHRA)** is the state law that prohibits certain practices of discrimination in housing and employment. The protected classes and prohibited acts are *essentially equivalent to those cited in the federal law.* The PHRA protects familial status and defines protected classes relating to handicap more specifically: *handicap or disability, use of guide animal because of blindness or deafness, use of support animal because of a physical handicap, a handler or trainer of a support or guide animal, or* *because of the handicap or disability of a person with whom an individual has a relationship or association.* Despite the differences in the language, the protections are basically the same. When the Pennsylvania law was most recently amended to make it "substantially equivalent" to the federal law, an additional protection was added to include *age* (being a person 40 years of age or older).

Housing accommodations and commercial property. A major difference between Pennsylvania and federal law is that the state law applies to housing accommodations and *commercial property.* The discussions earlier in this chapter regarding unlawful practices do not apply only to dwellings. Prospective purchasers or tenants of commercial property in Pennsylvania are afforded the same protections as those seeking housing.

Exemptions

Exemptions, as defined in the federal Fair Housing Act, have limited application in Pennsylvania. In Pennsylvania, the federal exemptions apply only to privately owned or government housing located in the state that is *federally assisted.* In the previous discussion relating to exemptions, pay particular attention to the explanations regarding Pennsylvania law.

Pennsylvania Real Estate Licensing and Registration Act

Violating any provision of the Pennsylvania Human Relations Act is a violation of the licensing law. Section 604 of the Pennsylvania Real Estate Licensing and Registration Act specifically prohibits accepting listings that illegally discriminate against certain persons or groups in the sale or rental of property; giving false information for the purpose of discrimination; and making distinctions, for discriminatory purposes, in the location of housing or dates of availability. The State Real Estate Commission can take disciplinary action against a licensee, in addition to any action by the Human Relations Commission.

Official Notice and Poster

The Pennsylvania Human Relations Commission prepares and distributes fair housing and fair lending posters that any individual subject to the Pennsylvania Human Relations Act *must* display prominently in the place of business. The Commission also requires that all licensees furnish an individual seeking to list a property with an "Official Notice" (Figure 16.4). It lists the types of practices considered to be discriminatory under the Pennsylvania Human Relations Act and summarizes the Civil Rights Act of 1866, applicable federal laws and the parts of the Pennsylvania Real Estate Licensing and Registration Act that relate to discriminatory practices. This notice is intended to inform the property owner of the obligations of both the licensee and the owner to comply with the fair housing laws.

FAIR HOUSING PRACTICES

It is important for licensees to know the classes of people whose rights are protected under the laws described in this chapter and the practices that are prohibited. For the civil rights laws to accomplish their goals of eliminating discrimination, they must be applied in daily practice. In the following section the topics are selected for discussion because they are either clearly illegal or provide insight into the specific situations that confront real estate licensees.

Figure 16.4
Official Notice

The Commonwealth of Pennsylvania
HUMAN RELATIONS COMMISSION

OFFICIAL NOTICE

Responsibilities of Owners of Real Property
under
the PENNSYLVANIA HUMAN RELATIONS ACT of
October 27, 1955, P.L. 744, as amended

The Pennsylvania Legislature has made it illegal: To refuse to sell, lease, finance, or otherwise deny or withhold residential or commercial property located in the Commonwealth of Pennsylvania because of any person's ...

Race, Color, Sex, Religious Creed, Ancestry, National Origin, Disability, Age or Familial Status

or

To refuse to lease, or discriminate in the terms of selling or leasing, or in furnishing facilities, services or privileges in connection with the ownership, occupancy or use of any residential or commercial property because of any person's ...

Race, Color, Sex, Religious Creed, Ancestry, National Origin, Disability, Age, Familial Status, Use of a Guide or Support Animal Because of the Blindness, Deafness or Physical Disability of the User or Because the User is a Handler or Trainer of Support or Guide Animals

or

Figure 16.4
(continued)

Construct, operate, offer for sale, lease or rent or otherwise make available housing or commercial property which is not accessible. The term **"accessible"** means being in compliance with the applicable standards as provided under the **Fair Housing Act, the Americans with Disabilities Act of 1990 and the Universal Accessibility Act.**

IT IS ALSO UNLAWFUL FOR:

Any person to retaliate against an individual because the individual has filed a complaint with the Commission, or has otherwise participated in any Commission proceeding, or for any person to aid or abet any unlawful discriminatory practice under the Human Relations Act.

OR, BECAUSE OF:

The disability of an individual with whom the person is known to have a relationship or association.

OTHER APPLICABLE LAWS EXPLAINED:

1. The **CIVIL RIGHTS ACT OF 1866** provides that all citizens of the United States shall have the same right in every state and territory thereof to inherit, purchase, lease, sell, hold and convey real and personal property, and prohibits all racial and ethnic discrimination without exception in the sale or rental of property.

2. **TITLE VIII** of the **FEDERAL CIVIL RIGHTS ACT OF 1968** prohibits discrimination in housing based on **race, color, sex, religion, national origin, familial status, disability or intimidation.**

3. **COURT AWARDS:** Under either of the above laws, federal courts may award successful plaintiffs actual and punitive damages, attorney's fees, and injunctive relief.

4. **TITLE IX** of the **CIVIL RIGHTS ACT OF 1968** provides criminal penalties for the willful or attempted injury, intimidation or interference with any person because of his/her **race, color, sex, religion, national origin, familial status or disability** who is selling, purchasing, renting, financing or occupying any dwelling or contracting or negotiating for the sale, purchase, rental, financing or occupation of any dwelling or applying for or participating in any service, organization or facility relating to the business of selling or renting dwellings.

5. **REAL ESTATE BROKERS LICENSE ACT OF MAY 1, 1929, P.L. 1216,** as amended, makes it unlawful for a real estate broker or salesperson to accept a listing with an understanding that illegal discrimination in the sale or rental of property is to be practiced.

6. **LOCAL ORDINANCES** prohibiting discrimination in housing may exist in your locality, and should be consulted for any additional protection these ordinances may provide.

**Figure 16.4
(continued)**

7. **AMERICANS WITH DISABILITIES ACT OF 1990** prohibits discrimination because of a disability in employment, public service and public accommodation (which includes commercial property).

8. **UNIVERSAL ACCESSIBILITY ACT (PA ACT 166)** requires accessibility for person with disabilities in certain new and rehabilitated residential and commercial property.

TO OWNERS OF REAL PROPERTY WITHIN THE COMMONWEALTH:

■ **YOU ARE LEGALLY RESPONSIBLE** for your own actions and the actions of any agent acting on your behalf. Under the Pennsylvania Human Relations Act and other state and federal legislation which prohibit discrimination in housing, you bear the responsibility for seeing that discriminatory acts do not occur.

■ **PROTECT YOURSELF** by providing your agent with verbal and written instructions that in all transactions relating to your property — including all services provided in connection with the transactions — you wish to comply with all civil rights ordinances including, but not limited to: **The Pennsylvania Human Relations Act, The Civil Rights Act of 1866, Title VIII of the Civil Rights Act of 1968, the Americans with Disabilities Act of 1990 and the Universal Accessibility Act (PA Act 166).**

■ **UNDER THE PENNSYLVANIA HUMAN RELATIONS ACT, NEITHER YOU NOR YOUR BROKER/SALESPERSON OR AGENT MAY ...**

1. Steer or otherwise direct a property seeker's attention to a particular neighborhood based on the race, color, religion, national origin, ancestry, sex, disability, age, familial status, or use of a guide or support animal because of the blindness, deafness or physical disability of the user, or because the user is a handler or trainer of support or guide animals, of either the property seekers or persons already residing in that neighborhood.

2. Volunteer information to or invite questions from property seekers concerning the race, color, religion, national origin, ancestry, sex, disability, age, familial status, or use of a guide or support animal because of the blindness, deafness or physical disability of the user or because the user is a handler or trainer of support or guide animals of persons already residing in a neighborhood.

3. Answer questions from or initiate a discussion with persons who are selling, renting or otherwise making housing or commercial property available concerning the race, color, religion, national origin, ancestry, sex, disability, age, familial status, or use of a guide or support animal

Figure 16.4
(continued)

because of the blindness, deafness or physical disability of the user or because the user is a handler or trainer of support or guide animals of prospective buyers, applicants or others seeking housing.

4. Engage in certain practices which attempt to induce the sale, or discourage the purchase or lease of housing accommodations or commercial property by making direct or indirect reference to the present or future composition of the neighborhood in which the facility is located with respect to race, color, religion, sex, ancestry, national origin, disability, age, familial status or guide or support animal dependency.

5. Engage in any course of action which could be construed as reluctant or delayed service having the effect of withholding or making unavailable housing accommodations or commercial property to persons because of their race, color, religion, nation origin, ancestry, sex, disability, age, familial status or use of a guide or support animal.

■ **RULES AND REGULATIONS OF THE PENNSYLVANIA HUMAN RELATIONS COMMISSION** (16 Pennsylvania Code 43.14) require that all licensed brokers or salespersons with whom you list your property for sale or rent **shall provide you with a copy of this notice** in order that you may be made aware of the laws you are required to obey.

The Commission provides equal opportunity in employment and service to the public.

For further information, write, phone or visit:

Pennsylvania Human Relations Commission
Headquarters Office
101 South Second Street
Executive House, Suite 300
Harrisburg, PA 17101

Telephone: (717) 783-8274 (VOICE)
(717) 787-4087 (TT)

To file a compaint contact the regional office nearest you:

Pittsburgh	Riverfront Office Center	**Philadelphia**
11th Floor State Office Building	1101 South Front Street	711 State Office Building
300 Liberty Avenue	5th Floor	Broad & Spring Garden Sts.
Pittsburgh, PA 15222-1210	Harrisburg, PA 17104	Philadelphia, PA 19130-4088
(412) 565-5395 (VOICE	(717) 787-9784 (VOICE)	(215) 560-2496 (VOICE)
(412) 565-5711 (TT)	(717) 787-7279 (TT)	(215) 560-3599 (TT)

Blockbusting

Blockbusting is the unlawful activity of inducing or attempting to induce a person to sell or rent a dwelling by making representations regarding the entry or prospective entry into the neighborhood of a person in one of the protected classes. Any action, including uninvited solicitations, that conveys the message that the neighborhood is undergoing changes and encourages the property owner to sell or rent is considered blockbusting. Asserting that the entry of certain persons will result in undesirable consequences such as a lowering of property values, an increase in criminal or antisocial behavior or a decline in the quality of schools to encourage a sale or rental is also illegal. A critical element in blockbusting, according to HUD's regulations, is that profit is a motive for engaging in this activity. A property owner may be intimidated into selling the property at a depressed price to the blockbuster who, in turn, resells the property to another person at a higher price. Another term for this activity is *panic selling*. To avoid accusations of blockbusting, real estate licensees should use good judgment when choosing locations and methods for soliciting listings.

Steering

Steering is the channeling of homeseekers to or away from particular neighborhoods, thereby limiting their choices. This practice makes certain homes unavailable, which is contrary to the fair housing laws. Steering may be done to either preserve the homogeneity of a neighborhood or purposely change its character. Many cases of steering are subtle, motivated by *assumptions or perceptions* about a homeseeker's desires or preferences for a neighborhood or assumptions about financial ability. Assumptions are dangerous—they could be wrong.

The salesperson's role is to qualify the prospective homeseeker *objectively* to identify housing requirements and determine financial ability. The salesperson then makes recommendations based on the individual's needs and finances. The prospective homeseeker selects the neighborhoods or specific properties to be viewed. The licensee cannot *assume* that a prospective homeseeker expects to be directed to certain neighborhoods or properties. Steering anyone is illegal.

Intent and Effect

If the owner or real estate licensee *purposely* sets different sales or rental prices or different down payment or security deposit requirements to "chill the interest" of certain individuals or establishes policies to segregate families with children in certain parts of a housing complex, for example, the *intention* to discriminate is obvious. However, owners and licensees must scrutinize their policies and procedures to determine if, even without intent, they have the *effect* of discriminating. Whenever such practices *result* in unequal treatment of individuals in the protected classes, they are regarded as being discriminatory. This is known as the *effects test,* which is used by compliance agencies to determine if an individual has been discriminated against. Certain policies and procedures may have been adopted to serve other business purposes unrelated to discriminating against persons in the protected classes. But if they affect those individuals differently from others, the policies and procedures are discriminatory. This effect is known as *disparate impact.*

Advertising

Any printed or published advertisement of property for sale or rent cannot include language that indicates a preference or limitation, regardless of how subtle the choice of words. HUD's regulations cite examples that are considered discriminatory: "adult building, Jewish home, restricted, private, integrated, traditional." References to a property's location can also imply discriminatory preference or limitation, such as in its relation to landmarks that are associated with a nationality or religion. References to a parish or a synagogue or to a club or school used exclusively by one sex are also examples. Pictorial representations using human models as residents or customers that depict one segment of the population while not including others are discriminatory. The media used for promoting property or real estate services cannot target one population to the exclusion of others. The selective use of media, whether by language or geography, for example, may have discriminatory impact.

The Pennsylvania Human Relations Act provides the Human Relations Commission with sensible real estate advertising guidelines. Words that *would appear* discriminatory must not appear in advertising. The accepted rule is: "Always describe property: never describe people." Consult HUD's regulations for a full list of words that are acceptable and not acceptable for advertising purposes.

Appraising

People who prepare appraisals or any statements of valuation, whether they are formal or informal, oral or written (including a comparative market analysis), may consider any factors that affect value. However, race, color, religion, national origin, sex, handicap or familial status are *not* factors that may be taken into consideration.

Redlining

The practice of refusing to make mortgage loans or issue insurance policies in specific areas for reasons other than the economic qualifications of the applicants is known as **redlining.** This practice, which often contributes to the deterioration of older, transitional neighborhoods, was frequently based on racial grounds rather than on any real objections to the applicant. The federal Fair Housing Act prohibits discrimination in mortgage lending and covers not only the actions of primary lenders but also activities in the secondary mortgage market. However, a lending institution can refuse a loan solely on *sound* economic grounds.

In an effort to counteract redlining, the federal government passed the *Home Mortgage Disclosure Act* in 1975. This act requires all institutional mortgage lenders with assets in excess of $10 million and one or more offices in a given geographic area to make annual reports by census tracts of all mortgage loans the institution makes or purchases. This law enables the government to detect lending or insuring patterns that might constitute redlining.

ENFORCEMENT OF THE FAIR HOUSING ACT

The federal Fair Housing Act is administered by the Office of Fair Housing and Equal Opportunity (OFHEO) under the direction of the Secretary of HUD. Any aggrieved person who believes illegal discrimination has occurred may file a complaint with HUD within one year of the alleged act. HUD may also initiate its own complaint. Complaints may be reported to the Office of Fair Housing and Equal Opportunity, Dept. of Housing and Urban Development, Washington, DC 20410, or to the Office of Fair Housing and Equal Opportunity, care of the nearest HUD regional office.

Upon receipt of a complaint, HUD will initiate an investigation and, within 100 days of the filing of the complaint, either determine that reasonable cause exists to bring a charge that illegal discrimination has occurred or dismiss the complaint. During this investigation period HUD can attempt to resolve the dispute informally through conciliation. *Conciliation* is a process initiated to resolve the complaint by obtaining assurance that the respondent (the person against whom the complaint was filed) will remedy any violation of the rights of the aggrieved party and take such action as will ensure the elimination or prevention of discriminatory practices in the future. These agreements can be enforced through civil action, if necessary.

The aggrieved person has the right to seek relief through administrative proceedings before an administrative law judge (ALJ) at any time during the investigation period or after a charge has been decided. The ALJ has the authority to award actual damages to the aggrieved person or persons and, if it is believed the public interest will be served, also to impose penalties. The penalties range from up to $10,000 for the first offense to $25,000 for a second violation within five years and $50,000 for further violations within seven years. The ALJ also has the authority to issue an injunction to order the offender to either do something—rent to the complaining party, for example—or refrain from doing something.

The parties may elect civil (judicial) action in federal court at any time within two years of the discriminatory act. For cases heard in federal court, punitive damages can be awarded in addition to actual damages. There is no limit on the amount of punitive damages that can be awarded. The court can also issue injunctions. As noted in a previous chapter, errors and omissions insurance carried by licensees normally does not pay on violations of the fair housing laws.

Whenever the Attorney General has reasonable cause to believe that any person or group is engaged in a pattern or practice of resistance to the full enjoyment of any of the rights granted by the federal fair housing laws, the Attorney General may commence a civil action in any federal district court. Civil penalties may result in an amount not to exceed $50,000 for a first violation and an amount not to exceed $100,000 for second and subsequent violations.

Complaints brought under the Civil Rights Act of 1866 are taken directly to a federal court. The only time limit for action would be the state's statute of limitation for *torts,* that is, injuries done by one individual to another.

Pennsylvania Law

Whenever a state or municipality has a fair housing law that has been ruled *substantially equivalent* to the federal law, all complaints in the state that are filed with HUD are referred to and handled by the local enforcement agency responsible for those laws. In Pennsylvania, that would be the Pennsylvania Human Relations Commission. To be considered substantially equivalent, the local law and its related regulations must contain prohibitions comparable to those in the federal law. In addition, the state or locality must show that its local enforcement agency is taking sufficient affirmative action in processing and investigating complaints and in finding remedies for discriminatory practices. The procedures for handling complaints under the Pennsylvania Human Relations Act are essentially the same as under the federal law.

Some municipalities have ordinances that deal with discriminatory housing practices. The real estate licensee should be familiar with any local laws.

Threats or Acts of Violence

The federal Fair Housing Act of 1968 contains criminal provisions protecting the rights of those who seek the benefits of the open housing law as well as owners, brokers or salespeople who aid or encourage the enjoyment of open housing rights. Unlawful actions involving threats, coercion and intimidation are punishable by civil action. In such cases, the victim should report the incident immediately to the local police and to the nearest office of the Federal Bureau of Investigation.

In Pennsylvania, a victim of such harassment is further protected by the Ethnic Intimidation and Vandalism Act, which prohibits coercion, intimidation or threats. It prohibits retaliation against those who seek protection of their rights by filing a complaint or against those who are fair housing activists. Licensees who conduct their business in compliance with the fair housing laws are also protected against any intimidation or retaliation. In Pennsylvania, the Interagency Task Force on Civil Tension has been established to investigate incidents of this kind.

IMPLICATIONS FOR BROKERS AND SALESPEOPLE

An enormous responsibility for effecting and maintaining an open housing market falls on the real estate industry. Brokers and salespeople promote themselves as the real estate experts in the community. With this visibility comes the *social,* as well as the *legal,* responsibility for ensuring that the civil rights of all persons are protected. The community has the right to expect the real estate industry to do its part in overcoming discrimination. The reputation of the industry cannot afford *any* appearance that its licensees are not committed to the principles of fair housing. Licensees and the industry must be publicly conspicuous in their equal opportunity efforts. Establishing relationships with community and fair housing groups to discuss common concerns and develop programs to address problems is constructive activity.

Fair housing *is* the law. (See Figure 16.5). The consequences for anyone who violates the law are serious and potentially very expensive. That the offense was unintentional is no defense. Although there are overt acts of discrimination, many are very subtle. Licensees must scrutinize their practices and be careful not to fall victim to clients or customers who expect to discriminate.

Complaints may be filed by anyone who even *suspects* that illegal discrimination has occurred. The enforcement agency is responsible for uncovering the facts during an investigation to determine if there are grounds for the complaint. *The complainant does not have to prove guilty knowledge or specific intent.* Licensees should be scrupulous in their conduct to avoid a complaint being filed. An investigation can be time consuming and expensive, even if the complaint is unfounded.

It is essential that the broker establish office policies and procedures that ensure compliance with the laws. The Pennsylvania Human Relations Commission and the Pennsylvania Association of REALTORS® have jointly authored the Fair Housing Guidelines, a useful resource. A *standardized inventory* of properties

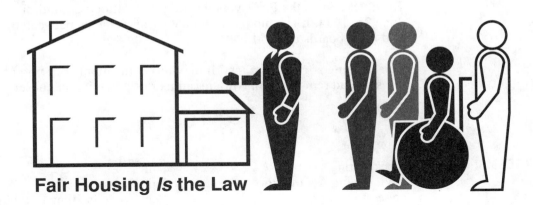

Fair Housing _Is_ the Law

available for sale or rent will ensure that all persons who inquire about availability will be offered a uniform listing of properties. _Consistent practices_ for qualifying prospective purchasers and tenants, showing properties, following the progress of a transaction and presenting offers ensure equal treatment for everyone. Establishing _verifiable and measurable criteria_ that can be justified for prudent business decisions is essential for qualifying all tenant applicants equally. _Written documentation_ of applications, conversations, showings and follow-up contacts are essential evidence to defend against a complaint. A major pitfall for licensees is failing to communicate with all parties. The complexities of a real estate transaction are commonplace to a licensee, but they can be a confusing maze for a client or customer. Actions can be misinterpreted if they are not completely explained.

All parties deserve the same standard of service, that is, "equal treatment," within an individual's property requirements, financial ability and experience in the marketplace. A good test is to answer the question, "Are we doing this for everyone?" If an act is not consistently performed or if an act affects some individuals differently than it does others, it could be construed as discriminatory.

The prejudices and stereotypes individuals have can surface in a real estate transaction and can result in discriminatory behavior. Even innocent actions may be viewed later as prejudicial. For instance, a seller asks the nationality of a prospective purchaser. The licensee must consider the _effect_ his or her response will have on the transaction. If the seller refuses to negotiate or decides to pursue a different course of negotiations based on the response, the question of discrimination could arise. A licensee cannot control effect and must be aware of how actions could be construed.

HUD and the Pennsylvania Human Relations Commission require that fair housing posters be displayed in any place of business where real estate is offered for sale or rent. Following HUD's advertising procedures and using the fair housing slogan and logo help the public know of the broker's commitment to equal opportunity. The public must know that it is the broker's policy, for example, not to offer any information on the racial, ethnic or religious composition of a neighborhood or place restrictions on listing, showing or providing information on the availability of homes.

A Memorandum of Understanding between the Pennsylvania Association of REALTORS® and the Pennsylvania Human Relations Commission was signed on June 25, 1974. It is a model for voluntary agreements between the Commission and local boards of REALTORS®.

Fair housing is *good business*. It maximizes the number of properties available for sale and rent to the maximum number of potential purchasers and tenants.

●   ●   ●   ●   ●   ●   ●

KEY TERMS

blockbusting
Civil Rights Act of 1866
code of ethics
Equal Credit Opportunity Act
    (ECOA)

ethics
Fair Housing Act
Pennsylvania Human Relations Act (PHRA)
redlining
steering

SUMMARY

A real estate business is only as good as its reputation. Real estate licensees can maintain good reputations by demonstrating good business ability and adhering to an ethical standard of business practices. Many licensees subscribe to a code of ethics as members of professional real estate organizations. The Code of Ethics of the National Association of REALTORS® is reprinted in this chapter. The provisions of this and the Code for Equal Opportunity suggest an excellent set of standards for all licensees to follow.

The federal regulations regarding equal opportunity in housing are principally contained in two laws. The Civil Rights Act of 1866 prohibits all racial discrimination, and the Fair Housing Act (Title VIII of the Civil Rights Act of 1968), as amended, prohibits discrimination on the basis of race, color, religion, sex, handicap, familial status or national origin in the sale, rental or financing of residential property. Discriminatory actions include refusing to deal with an individual or a specific group, changing any terms of a real estate or loan transaction, changing the services offered for any individual or group, making statements or advertisements that indicate discriminatory restrictions, or otherwise attempting to make a dwelling unavailable to any person or group because of race, color, religion, sex, handicap, familial status or national origin.

Complaints under the Fair Housing Act may be reported to and investigated by the Department of Housing and Urban Development (HUD). Such complaints may also be taken directly to a U.S. district court. In states and localities that have enacted fair housing legislation that is "substantially equivalent to the federal law," complaints are handled by state and local agencies and state courts. Complaints under the Civil Rights Act of 1866 must be taken to a federal court.

The Pennsylvania Human Relations Act has been ruled "substantially equivalent" to the federal Fair Housing Act. For this reason, complaints filed under the federal law are handled by the state agency.

Questions

1. Which of the following acts is permitted under the federal Fair Housing Act?
   a. Advertising property for sale only to a special group
   b. Altering the terms of a loan for a member of a minority group
   c. Refusing to sell a home to an individual because he or she has a poor credit history
   d. Telling an individual that an apartment has been rented when in fact it has not

2. Complaints relating to the Civil Rights Act of 1866
   a. are taken directly to a federal court.
   b. are no longer reviewed in the courts.
   c. are handled by HUD.
   d. are handled by state enforcement agencies.

3. The Civil Rights Act of 1866 is unique because it
   a. has been broadened to protect age.
   b. adds welfare recipients as a protected class.
   c. contains "choose your neighbor" provisions.
   d. provides no exceptions to racial discrimination.

4. "I hear they're moving in; there goes the neighborhood. Better sell to me today!" is an example of
   a. steering.   c. redlining.
   b. blockbusting.   d. testing.

5. The act of channeling homeseekers to a particular area either to maintain or to change the character of a neighborhood is
   a. blockbusting.
   b. redlining.
   c. steering.
   d. permitted under the Fair Housing Act of 1968.

6. A lender's refusal to lend money to potential homeowners attempting to purchase property located in predominantly minority neighborhoods is known as
   a. redlining.   c. steering.
   b. blockbusting.   d. qualifying.

7. Which of the following would *not* be permitted under the federal Fair Housing Act?
   a. The Harvard Club in New York will rent rooms only to graduates of Harvard who belong to the club.
   b. The owner of a 20-unit apartment building rents to women only.
   c. A Catholic convent refuses to furnish housing for a Jewish man.
   d. An owner refuses to rent the duplex home in which she lives to families with children.

8. Under federal law, families with children may be refused rental or purchase in a building where occupancy is reserved exclusively for those aged at least
   a. 40.   c. 62.
   b. 60.   d. 65.

9. Guiding prospective buyers to a particular area because the agent feels they belong there may be regarded as
   a. blockbusting.   c. steering.
   b. redlining.   d. bird-dogging.

10. A minority real estate broker's practice of offering a special discount to minority clients is

   a. satisfactory.
   b. illegal.
   c. legal but ill advised.
   d. not important.

11. Under the Supreme Court decision in the case of *Jones v. Alfred H. Mayer Company*

   a. racial discrimination is prohibited by any party in the sale or rental of real estate.
   b. sales by individual residential homeowners are exempted, provided the owner does not employ a broker.
   c. laws against discrimination apply only to federally related transactions.
   d. persons with handicaps are a protected class.

12. After broker *G* takes a sale listing of a residence, the owner specifies that he will not sell his home to a minority. The broker should *not*

   a. show the property to anyone who is interested.
   b. explain to the owner that this violates federal law and he cannot do it.
   c. abide by the principal's directions.
   d. put the listing in the multilist.

13. The fine for a first violation of the Fair Housing Act could be as much as

   a. $500.   c. $5,000.
   b. $1,000.   d. $10,000.

14. The REALTORS® Code of Ethics suggests a set of standards for all brokers and salespeople to follow who are members of its association. Which of the following provisions is *not* contained in the Code?

   a. A REALTOR® should not engage in the practice of law.
   b. A REALTOR® must protect the public against fraud and unethical practices in the real estate field.
   c. A REALTOR® should not accept compensation from more than one party without the full knowledge of all parties to the transaction.
   d. In the event of a REALTOR®'s controversy with another REALTOR®, the matter should be settled through litigation.

17 Agency Contracts

The majority of agency relationships in the real estate brokerage business are created by written agreement. An agency contract may hire the broker to represent the buyer, the seller, the landlord or the tenant, depending on the broker's agency policies. These are *employment contracts* rather than real estate contracts, that is, they contract for the personal professional services of the broker, not the transfer of real estate or real estate interest.

Although it is possible to create an agency relationship orally or by the parties' actions, creating agency relationships purposely by written agreement serves both a legal and practical purpose. The state's license law requires most of these contracts to be in writing, and written contracts provide proof of what the parties are expected to do. This is also important if a broker has to institute a court action to collect a commission.

Under agency and license laws, only a broker can act as the agent. A salesperson who lists, leases or sells property or provides other services to the principal does so in the name and under the supervision of the broker. Listing agreements and buyer agency agreements are discussed in this chapter. Throughout this chapter, unless otherwise stated, the terms *broker, agent* and *firm* are intended to include both broker and salesperson.

LISTING AGREEMENTS

Just as a supermarket needs inventory or products to sell, real estate brokers need properties to sell. Brokers obtain listings to acquire their inventory. A listing agreement creates a special agency relationship between a broker (agent) and a seller (principal), whereby the agent is authorized to represent the principal's property for sale, solicit offers and submit the offers to the principal.

There are several different types of listing agreements. The type of contract determines the specific rights and obligations of the parties.

Exclusive-Right-to-Sell Listing

In an **exclusive-right-to-sell listing,** one broker is appointed as the sole agent of the seller and is given the exclusive right, or *authorization,* to market the seller's property. If the property is sold while the listing is in effect, the seller must pay the broker a commission *regardless of who sells the property.* In other words, if the seller finds a buyer without the broker's assistance, the seller must *still* pay the broker a commission. Brokers strongly favor this form of listing agreement because if offers the broker the greatest opportunity to receive a commission. In turn, the seller can benefit because the broker feels freer to spend money for marketing, advertising, brochures, fliers, open houses and other selling expenses.

The Pennsylvania Real Estate Commission's Rules and Regulations require that all exclusive-right-to-sell or exclusive-right-to-lease agreements must contain statements in boldface type that the broker earns a commission on the sale or lease of the property, regardless of who, including the owner, makes the sale or lease during the listing period. (An example of this form of listing agreement is reproduced in Figure 17.1.)

The Rules and Regulations also require that certain terms be included in every exclusive-agency and exclusive-right-to-sell listing:

• the seller's asking price;

• the broker's expected commission on the sale price;

• that the commission and time period of the listing have been determined as a result of negotiations between the broker and the seller;

• notice of the Real Estate Recovery Fund; and

• that payments of money received by the broker shall be held by the broker in an escrow account.

The listing period *cannot* exceed 12 months. There cannot be an automatic renewal clause or a cancellation notice to terminate the agreement at the end of the listing period set forth in the contract. The broker cannot have authority to execute a signed agreement of sale for the owner or have an option to purchase the listed property. The broker cannot have authority to confess judgment for the commission in the event of a sale.

Exclusive-Agency Listing

In an **exclusive-agency listing,** *one broker* is authorized to act as the exclusive agent of the principal. However, the seller *retains the right to sell the property himself or herself* without obligation to the broker. The seller is obligated to pay a commission to the broker only if the broker or a subagent of the broker has been the procuring cause of the sale.

Open Listing

In an **open listing** (also known in some areas as a nonexclusive listing or a simple listing), the seller retains the right to employ any number of brokers as agents. These brokers can act simultaneously, and the seller is obligated to pay a commission only to that broker who successfully produces a ready, willing and able buyer. If the seller personally sells the property *without the aid of any of the brokers,* the seller is not obligated to pay any of them a commission. If a broker was in any way a procuring cause in the transaction, however, he or she may be entitled to a commission. The Commission's Rules and Regulations

**Figure 17.1
Exclusive-
Right-to-Sell
Agreement**

LISTING CONTRACT
EXCLUSIVE RIGHT TO SELL REAL PROPERTY

*Residential
XLS-3*

This form recommended and approved for, but not restricted to use by, the members of the Pennsylvania Association of REALTORS®

1. **SELLER** (list all Owners)
   Name_____ SS#_____
   Mailing Address _____
   Phone Number _____
   Name_____ SS#_____
   Mailing Address _____
   Phone Number _____
   If there are other owners, give names, addresses, phone numbers, and social security numbers on an additional sheet.
2. **BROKER**
   Broker is_____
   Address _____
   Phone Number _____
   Salesperson is _____, who works for the Broker.
3. **PROPERTY**
   Address _____
   _____
   Municipality (city, borough, township) _____
   County _____ School District _____
   Zoning and Present Use _____
   Salesperson: Complete
   Identification Number (For example, tax identification number, parcel number, deed book, page, recording date) _____
4. **LISTED PRICE $** _____
5. **STARTING AND ENDING DATES OF LISTING CONTRACT** (also called "Term")
   A. No Association of REALTORS® has set or recommended the term of this contract. By law, the length or term of a listing contract may not exceed one year. Seller and Broker have discussed and agreed upon the length or term of this contract.
   B. **Starting Date:** This Contract starts when signed by the Seller and Salesperson or Broker.
   C. **Ending Date:** This Contract ends on _____ unless Seller is negotiating a sale. In that case, the Broker will continue to represent the Seller until negotiations end.
6. **BROKER'S DUTY** Seller is hiring Broker to find a buyer for the Property. During the length or term of this Contract, Seller will not hire any other broker to sell the Property.
7. **BROKER'S FEE**
   A. No Association of REALTORS® has set or recommended the Broker's Fee. Seller and Broker have negotiated the fee that Seller will pay Broker.
   B. The Broker's Fee is _____ of/from the sale price and paid by Seller. Salesperson has explained Broker's company policies about cooperating with other brokers. Seller and Broker agree that Broker will pay from Broker's Fee:
      (1) **A fee to another broker (SUBAGENT), who represents the Seller.**
          ☐ No ☐ Yes   If Yes, amount: _____ of/from the sale price.
      (2) **A fee to another broker (BUYER'S AGENT), who represents a buyer.**
          ☐ No ☐ Yes   If Yes, amount: _____ of/from the sale price.
8. **PAYMENT OF BROKER'S FEE**
   A. **Seller must pay Broker's Fee if Property is sold or exchanged during the length or term of this Contract by Broker, Broker's agents, Seller, or by any other person or broker, at the listed price or any price acceptable to Seller.**
   B. Broker will earn Broker's Fee after the Ending Date of this Contract IF:
      (1) A sale occurs within _____ days of the Ending Date, AND
      (2) The buyer was shown or negotiated to buy the Property during the term of this contract.
      Seller will not owe Broker's Fee if the Property is listed under an "exclusive right to sell contract" with another broker at the time of the sale.
9. **BROKER'S FEE IF SALE DOES NOT OCCUR**
   A. **Seller must pay Broker's Fee if a ready, willing, and able buyer is found by Broker or by anyone, including Seller. A** *willing buyer* **is one who will pay the listed price or more for the Property.**
   B. If the Property or any part of it is taken by any government for public use (Eminent Domain) Seller must pay Broker _____ of/from any money paid by the government.
   C. If a buyer signs an agreement of sale then refuses to buy the Property, or if a buyer is unable to buy because of failing to do all the things required of the buyer in the agreement of sale, Seller must pay Broker:
      (1) _____ of/from buyer's deposit monies,
      OR
      (2) the **Broker's Fee** in Paragraph 7B, whichever is less.
10. **SETTLEMENT AND POSSESSION**
    A. Preferred Settlement Date: _____
    B. Seller will give possession of the Property to Buyer at settlement or on _____ , ___.
    C. (1) If the Property, or any part of it, is rented, Seller will give any leases to Broker before signing this Contract.
       (2) If any leases are oral, Seller will provide a written summary of the terms, including amount of rent, ending date, and tenant's responsibilities.
       (3) Seller will not enter into or renew any lease during the term of this Contract except as follows: _____

Seller's Initials _____   Page 1 of 3   Broker's/Salesperson's Initials _____

R Pennsylvania Association of
REALTORS®
The Voice for Real Estate® in Pennsylvania

COPYRIGHT PENNSYLVANIA ASSOCIATION OF REALTORS® 1996
COPIES: WHITE–SELLER: BLUE–   : YELLOW–SALESPERSON
2/98

Reprinted with the permission of the Pennsylvania Association of REALTORS®.

11. TAXES AND ASSOCIATION FEES
    A. At settlement, Seller will pay one-half of the total Real Estate Transfer Taxes.
    B. Real Estate Property Tax Assessment $ _____
        Yearly Taxes $ _____
        Trash $ _____
        Water $ _____
        Wage/Income Tax_____
        Per Capita Tax $_____
    C. Association Fees $_____
        Association Fees Include: _____
    D. Other _____

12. TITLE
    A. At settlement, Seller will give full rights of ownership (fee simple) to a buyer except as follows:
        (1) Mineral Rights Agreements _____
        (2) Other_____
    B. Seller has:
        ☐ Yes   ☐ No   Mortgage with _____
                                 Amount of balance $_____
        ☐ Yes   ☐ No   Equity loan with _____
                                   Amount of balance $_____
        ☐ Yes   ☐ No   Seller authorizes Broker to receive mortgage payoff and/or equity loan payoff information from the lender.
        ☐ Yes   ☐ No   Past Due Taxes   Amount owed $ _____
        ☐ Yes   ☐ No   Judgments   Amount $ _____
                            Type_____
        ☐ Yes   ☐ No   Municipal Assessments   Amount $ _____
        ☐ Yes   ☐ No   Other _____
                            Amount $_____

13. BUYER FINANCING   Seller will accept the following arrangements for buyer to pay for the Property
    ☐ Cash
    ☐ Buyer will apply for a mortgage. Type(s) of mortgages acceptable to Seller are:
        ☐ Yes ☐ No Conventional   ☐ Yes ☐ No FHA
        ☐ Yes ☐ No VA   ☐ Yes ☐ No _____
    ☐ Seller's help to buyer (if any):_____

14. MULTIPLE LISTING SERVICE (MLS) (Complete if Broker is a member of an MLS)
        ☐ Broker will use a Multiple Listing Service to advertise the Property to other real estate salespersons, who can tell their clients and customers about it. Seller agrees that the MLS, the Broker, and the Salesperson are not responsible for mistakes in the MLS description of the Property.
        ☐ Broker will not use a Multiple Listing Service to advertise the Property to other real estate salespersons.

15. PUBLICATION OF SALE PRICE
    A. Seller is aware that newspapers may publish the final sale price after settlement.
    B. Seller will allow publishing of the sale price after Seller accepts an Agreement of Sale.
        ☐ Yes   ☐ No

16. SIGNS & KEYS Seller allows (where permitted):
    ☐ Yes ☐ No Sale Sign   ☐ Yes ☐ No Sold Sign
    ☐ Yes ☐ No Key in Office   ☐ Yes ☐ No Lock Box
    ☐ Yes ☐ No

17. ITEMS INCLUDED IN THE PRICE OF THE PROPERTY
The following items are included in the purchase and price of the Property:
    (1) _____
    (2) ☐ See attached sheet for additional items included in the sale.

18. ITEMS NOT INCLUDED IN THE PRICE OF THE PROPERTY
The following items are not included in the purchase and price of the Property
    (1) _____
    (2) Items rented by the Seller.
    (3) ☐ See attached sheet for additional items not included in the sale.

19. SELLER MUST REVEAL DEFECTS AND ENVIRONMENTAL HAZARDS
Seller must tell Salesperson, Broker, and any interested buyers about any known material defects or environmental hazards in or on the Property. A material defect is a problem or condition that
    (1) is a possible danger to those living in the Property or
    (2) might affect a reasonable buyer's decision to buy it.
    A. If Seller fails to tell of known material defects and environmental hazards,
        (1) Seller will not hold Broker or Salesperson responsible in any way;
        (2) Seller will protect Salesperson and Broker from any claims, lawsuits, and actions that result;
        (3) Seller will pay all of Broker's and Salesperson's costs that result. This includes attorney fees and court-ordered payments or settlements (money Broker or Salesperson pays to end a lawsuit or claim).
    B. ☐ Seller has noted all known material defects and environmental hazards on a separate disclosure statement.
        ☐ Seller has noted known material defects and environmental hazards on a separate disclosure statement and also notes the following defects: _____
        _____
        ☐ Seller knows of no material defects and conditions.
        ☐ Seller knows of no environmental hazards.

Seller's Initials _____   Page 2 of 3   Broker's/Salesperson's Initials _____

Figure 17.1 (continued)

20. **IF PROPERTY WAS BUILT BEFORE 1978**
The Residential Lead-Based Paint Hazard Reduction Act says that any Seller of property built before 1978 must give the Buyer an EPA pamphlet titled *Protect Your Family from Lead in Your Home*. The Seller also must tell the Buyer and the Broker what the Seller knows about lead-based paint and lead-based paint hazards that are in or on the property being sold. Seller must tell the Buyer how the Seller knows that lead-based paint and lead-based paint hazards are on the property, where the lead-based paint and lead-based paint hazards are, the condition of the painted surfaces, and any other information Seller knows about lead-based paint and lead-based paint hazards on the property. Any Seller of a pre-1978 structure must also give the Buyer any records and reports that the Seller has or can get about lead-based paint or lead-based paint hazards in or around the property being sold, the common areas, or other dwellings in multi-family housing. According to the Act, a Seller must give a Buyer 10 days (unless Seller and Buyer agree to a different period of time) from the time an Agreement of Sale is signed to have a "risk assessment" or inspection for possible lead-based paint hazards done on the property. Buyers may choose not to have the risk assessment or inspection for lead paint hazards done. If Buyer chooses not to have the assessment or inspection, Buyer must inform the Seller in writing of the choice. The Act does not require the Seller to inspect for lead paint hazards or to correct lead paint hazards on the property. The Act does not apply to housing built in 1978 or later.

21. **DEPOSIT MONEY**
    A. Broker, or any person Seller and the buyer name in the Agreement of Sale, will keep all deposit monies paid by or for the buyer in an escrow account. This escrow account will be held as required by real estate licensing laws and regulations until the sale or exchange of the Property is final. Seller agrees that the person keeping the deposit monies may wait to deposit any uncashed check that is received as deposit money until Seller has accepted an offer.
    B. If Seller joins Salesperson or Broker in a lawsuit for the return of deposit monies, Seller will pay Salesperson's and Broker's attorney's fees and costs.

22. **RECOVERY FUND**
Pennsylvania has a Real Estate Recovery Fund (the Fund) to repay any person who has received a final court ruling (civil judgment) against a Pennsylvania real estate licensee because of fraud, misrepresentation, or deceit in a real estate transaction. The Fund repays persons who have not been able to collect the judgment after trying all lawful ways to do so. For complete details about the Fund, call (717) 783-3658.

23. **TRANSFER OF THIS CONTRACT**
    A. Seller agrees that Broker may transfer this Contract to another real estate broker when:
       (1) Broker stops doing business,
       (2) Broker forms a new real estate business,
       (3) Broker joins his business with another, or
       (4) Other_____
       Broker will notify Seller immediately in writing when a transfer occurs or Broker will lose the right to transfer this Contract. Seller will follow all requirements of this Contract with the new broker.
    B. Should Seller give or transfer the Property, or an ownership interest in it, to anyone during the term of this Contract, all owners must follow the requirements of this Contract.

24. **NOTICE TO PERSONS OFFERING TO SELL OR RENT HOUSING IN PENNSYLVANIA**
Federal and state laws make it illegal for Seller, Broker, or anyone to use RACE, COLOR, RELIGION or RELIGIOUS CREED, SEX, DISABILITY (physical or mental), FAMILIAL STATUS (children under 18 years of age), AGE (40 or older), NATIONAL ORIGIN or USE OR HANDLING/TRAINING OF SUPPORT OR GUIDE ANIMALS, or the FACT OF RELATIONSHIP OR ASSOCIATION TO AN INDIVIDUAL KNOWN TO HAVE A DISABILITY as reasons for refusing to sell, show, or rent properties, loan money, or set deposit amounts, or as reasons for any decision relating to the sale of property.

25. **NO OTHER CONTRACTS**
Seller will not enter into another listing agreement with another broker that begins before the Ending Date of this Contract.

26. **ADDITIONAL OFFERS**
ONCE SELLER ENTERS INTO AN AGREEMENT OF SALE, BROKER IS NOT REQUIRED TO PRESENT OTHER OFFERS.

27. **CONFIDENTIALITY**
Salesperson and Broker will not tell any private (confidential) information given to them by Seller during the term of this Contract. *Private information* means information that Seller gives to Salesperson or Broker which Seller does not want any buyers to know. Salesperson and Broker will continue to keep the information confidential after this Contract ends.
NOTE: Seller must always tell of material defects or conditions.

28. **ENTIRE CONTRACT**
This Contract is the entire agreement between Broker and Seller. Any verbal or written agreements that were made before are not a part of this Contract.

29. **CHANGES TO THIS CONTRACT**   Requirements for any change to this Listing Contract:
       (1) All changes must be in writing
       AND
       (2) Signed by all the parties: Seller and Salesperson or Broker.

30. **NOTICE BEFORE SIGNING**
THIS LISTING AGREEMENT IS A LEGAL CONTRACT. IF SELLER HAS LEGAL QUESTIONS ABOUT THIS CONTRACT, SELLER IS ADVISED TO TALK TO A LAWYER.

SELLER _____ DATE _____
SELLER _____ DATE _____
SELLER _____ DATE _____
All Sellers must sign this Contract.

BROKER (Company Name)_____
ACCEPTED BY _____ DATE _____
              (signature of Broker or Salesperson)

Page 3 of 3

stipulate that any broker taking an *oral* open listing must give the parties involved a written memorandum stating all the terms of the listing agreement.

Special Listing Provisions

Multiple listing. A multiple listing clause may be included in an exclusive-agency or exclusive-right-to-sell contract. It may be used by brokers who are members of **multiple-listing services (MLSs).** These are marketing organizations whose members share their listings with one another. MLSs offer advantages to both the brokers and the sellers. Brokers develop a sizable inventory of properties to sell and are assured a portion of the commission if they list a property or participate in the sale of another broker's listing. Sellers gain because their properties are exposed to a larger market.

The contractual obligations among the member brokers of a multiple listing service vary widely. Most MLSs require the broker to turn new listings over to the MLS within a specific, normally a fairly short period of time. There are also procedures for the way members cooperate with one another depending on whether they are subagents (as long as the principals authorize subagency) or buyers' agents and procedures for sharing commissions. The brokers must also determine procedures to protect their fiduciary obligations to their principals. If a broker represents a buyer for a property in the multiple-listing service, that broker should notify the listing broker before any other communication takes place.

IN PRACTICE. . .

Technology enhances the benefits of MLS membership. Not only do MLSs provide instant access to information about listings from a broad geographic area as well as properties that are sold and are off the market, often they also provide a wide range of other useful information about mortgage loans, real estate taxes and assessments, and municipalities and school districts.

Net listing. A **net listing** provision specifies that the seller will receive a net amount of money from any sale with the excess being given to the listing broker as a commission. The broker is free to offer the property at any price higher than that net amount. However, net listings can create a conflict of interest between the broker's fiduciary responsibility to the seller and the broker's profit motive. For this reason, the use of net listings is discouraged, although prohibition of net listings by the real estate industry has been viewed by the courts as a restraint of trade.

TERMINATION OF LISTINGS

A listing agreement may be terminated for any of the following reasons:

* fulfillment of the purpose of the listing;

* expiration of the time period stated in the agreement;

* breach or cancellation by one of the parties, although that party may be liable to the other for damages;

- transfer of title to the property by operation of law, as in a bankruptcy;

- mutual consent;

- death or incapacity of either party; and

- destruction of the property or a change in property use by outside forces (such as a change in zoning or condemnation by eminent domain).

A listing agreement is a *personal service contract*. Its success depends on the personal efforts of the broker who is a party to the agreement. The broker cannot turn the listing over to another broker without the principal's written consent. Failing to perform any work toward its fulfillment or revoking the agreement constitutes abandonment of the listing. The property owner cannot force the broker to comply in that event but can sue the broker for damages. The property owner also can fail to fulfill the terms of the agreement. A property owner who refuses to cooperate with reasonable requests of the broker, such as allowing tours of the property by prospective buyers or refusing to proceed with a sales contract, could be liable for damages to the other party.

Expiration of Listing Period

All listings should specify a definite period of time, not to exceed one year by law in Pennsylvania, during which the broker is to be employed. As previously mentioned, the use of an automatic renewal clause and cancellation notice to terminate in exclusive listings is *prohibited*. An example of an **automatic renewal** is a listing that provides for a base period of 90 days and "continues thereafter until terminated by either party hereto by 30 days' notice in writing."

Some listing contracts contain a "broker protection clause." This clause provides that the property owner will pay the listing broker a commission if, within a specified number of days after the listing expires, the owner sells the property to someone with whom the broker negotiated during the original term of the contract. This clause protects a broker who introduces the parties and is the procuring cause, only to have the parties enter into a contract and complete the transaction after the listing agreement expires. The times for such clauses usually parallel the terms of the listing agreement: for example, a six-month listing may carry a broker protection clause of six months after the listing's expiration. To protect the owner and prevent any liability of the owner for two separate commissions, most of these clauses stipulate that they cannot be enforced if the property is relisted under a new contract, either with the original listing broker or with another broker.

THE LISTING PROCESS

Prior to signing a contract, the broker and seller must discuss a variety of issues. The seller's most critical concerns typically will be the selling price of the property and the net amount that the seller will receive from its sale. The licensee has several professional tools to provide information about a property's value and calculate the proceeds from a sale. Most sellers will ask other question such as: How quickly will the property sell? What services will the broker provide during the listing period? This is the licensee's opportunity to explain the various types of listing agreements, the ramifications of agency relationships and the marketing services the broker provides. At the end of this process, the seller should feel comfortable with the decision to list with this brokerage firm.

Similarly, before the listing agreement is finalized, the broker should feel well equipped to fulfill the fiduciary obligations that the agreement will impose. The seller should have provided comprehensive information about the property and the personal concerns of the seller so that the broker can accept the listing with confidence that its purpose can be served.

Pricing the Property

Although it is the responsibility of the broker or salesperson to advise and assist, it is ultimately the *seller* who must determine a listing price for the property. Because the average seller usually does not have the background to make an informed decision about a fair market price, real estate agents must be prepared to offer their knowledge, information and expertise.

A salesperson can help the seller determine a listing price for the property by developing a **comparative market analysis** (CMA). This is a study of the market including a comparison of the prices of recently sold homes that are similar in location, size, age, style and amenities to the seller's property. To assist in evaluating the competition, properties that are currently listed for sale are also included. If no adequate comparisons can be made or if the property is unique in some way, the seller may prefer that a formal *appraisal*—a detailed estimate of a property's value—be prepared by a professional appraiser.

Whether a CMA or a formal appraisal is used, the figure sought is the property's market value. Market value, as discussed in the appraising chapter, is *the most probable price a property would bring in an arm's-length transaction under normal conditions on the open market.* A salesperson performing a CMA will estimate market value as likely to fall within a range of figures. A salesperson should be familiar with methods of valuing properties to prepare a CMA, but a CMA should not be confused with an appraisal. (It is illegal for a licensee to accept compensation for developing a CMA.)

Although it is the property owner's privilege to set whatever listing price he or she chooses, the seller should be cautioned against setting a price that is substantially exaggerated or severely out of line with the CMA or appraisal. These tools are the best indications of what a buyer will likely pay for the property. A licensee does the seller an injustice by taking a listing that is priced too high. It gives the seller false hopes and also wastes the broker's time and money to market the property that is unlikely to sell. Licensees are advised to reject such a listing.

Seller's Return

Through simple calculations the broker can show the seller roughly how much the seller will net from a given sales price or what sales price will produce a certain net. The mathematical examples show the net the seller would receive after the sales commission. In addition there are other expenses that the seller incurs. (See Chapter 21.)

MATH CONCEPT
Calculating Sales Prices, Commissions and Nets to Seller

When a property sells, the sales price is equal to 100% of the money being transferred. Therefore, if a broker is to receive a 6% commission, 94% will be left for the seller's other expenses and equity.

To calculate a commission using a sales price of $80,000 and a commission rate of 6% (.06 as a decimal), multiply the sales price by the commission rate:

$$\$80,000 \times .06 = \$4,800 \text{ commission}$$

To calculate a sales price using a commission of $4,550 and a commission rate of 7% (.07 as a decimal), divide the commission by the commission rate:

$$\$4,550 \div .07 = \$65,000 \text{ sales price}$$

To calculate a commission rate using a commission of $3,200 and a sales price of $64,000, divide the commission by the sales price:

$$\$3,200 \div \$64,000 = .05 \text{ as a decimal} = 5\% \text{ commission rate}$$

To calculate the net to the seller using a sales price of $85,000 and a commission rate of 8% (.08 as a decimal), multiply the sales price by *100% minus the commission rate:*

$$\$85,000 \times (100\% - 8\%) = \$85,000 \times .92 = \$78,200$$

The same result could be achieved by calculating the commission ($85,000 × .08 = $6,800) and deducting it from the sales price ($85,000 − $6,800 = $78,200). However, this involves unnecessary extra calculations.

Sales price × commission rate = commission
Commission ÷ commission rate = sales price
Commission ÷ sales price = commission rate
Sales price × (100% − commission rate) = net to seller

IN PRACTICE...

Licensees must comply with certain requirements that are detailed in the Real Estate Licensing and Registration Act and Rules and Regulations when they are listing real estate. See Sections 604, 606 and 608 in the act and Sections 35.301–.307, 35.284 and 35.331–.332 in the rules and regulations. (Refer to Chapter 13 and Appendix C.)

Information Needed for Listing Agreements

Once the real estate licensee and the owner have agreed on a listing price consistent with the owner's wishes and what the market will bear, the licensee obtains specific detailed information about the property. Obtaining as much factual information as possible ensures that most contingencies can be anticipated and provided for. This is particularly important when the listing will be shared with other brokers through a multiple-listing service and any other licensee who must rely on the information taken by the lister.

Information generally includes (where appropriate):

- names and relationships, if any, of the owners;

- street address of the property;

- asking price;

- size of lot and number and sizes of rooms and other improvements;

- age of the improvements and the type of construction;

- information about the neighborhood (schools, parks and recreational areas, public transportation, etc.);

- current (or most recent) taxes and any pending special assessments;

- financing (interest, payments, other costs and whether or not the loan is assumable) and possibility of seller financing;

- utilities and average payments;

- any real property to be removed by the seller or personal property to be included in the sale;

- date of occupancy or possession;

- any disclosures about property conditions; and

- zoning classification (especially important for vacant land).

Real Estate Seller Disclosure Act

Under Act 84, the **Real Estate Seller Disclosure Act,** which became effective in September of 1996, any seller of residential real property (an individual, partnership, corporation, trustee or combination thereof) who intends to transfer an interest in such property must disclose to the buyer any and all material defects. This must be done through the use of a Seller's Property Disclosure Statement. (See Figure 17.2.)

The broker, associate broker or salesperson representing the seller must advise the seller of this responsibility and must provide the seller with a blank copy of the disclosure form. The signed and dated disclosure statement must be presented to a prospective buyer prior to the signing of a written agreement. It must be completed accurately and honestly by the seller (not the licensee) to avoid litigation arising from fraudulent or careless misrepresentations.

The term *material defect* is defined under the law to mean "a problem with the property or any portion of it that would have a significant adverse impact on the value of the residential real property or that involves an unreasonable risk to people on the land."

Figure 17.2
Seller's Property
Disclosure Statement

SELLER'S PROPERTY DISCLOSURE STATEMENT   Form 128–2

1 **Property Address:**_____

2 _____

3 **Seller:**_____

4   A seller must disclose to a buyer all known material defects about property being sold that are not readily observable. This disclosure

5 statement is designed to assist Seller in complying with disclosure requirements and to assist Buyer in evaluating the property being

6 considered.

7   This Statement discloses Seller's knowledge of the condition of the property as of the date signed by Seller and **is not a substitute for**

8 **any inspections or warranties that Buyer may wish to obtain.** This Statement is not a warranty of any kind by Seller or a warranty or

9 representation by any listing real estate broker (Agent for Seller), any real estate broker, or their agents. Buyer is encouraged to address

10 concerns about the conditions of the property that may not be included in this Statement. This Statement does not relieve Seller of the

11 obligation to disclose a material defect that may not be addressed on this form.

12   A material defect is a problem with the property or any portion of it that would have a significant adverse impact on the value of the

13 residential real property or that involves an unreasonable risk to people on the land.

15 **1. SELLER'S EXPERTISE** Seller does not possess expertise in contracting, engineering, architecture, or other areas related to the

16   construction and conditions of the property and its improvements, except as follows:_____

18 **2. OCCUPANCY** Do you, Seller, currently occupy this property? ☐ Yes ☐ No

19   If "no," when did you last occupy the property?

21 **3. ROOF**

22   (a) Date roof installed:_____ Documented? ☐ Yes ☐ No ☐ Unknown

23   (b) Has the roof been replaced or repaired during your ownership? ☐ Yes ☐ No

24   If yes, were the existing shingles removed? ☐ Yes ☐ No ☐ Unknown

25   (c) Has the roof ever leaked during your ownership? ☐ Yes ☐ No

26   (d) Do you know of any problems with the roof, gutters or down spouts? ☐ Yes ☐ No

27   Explain any "yes" answers that you give in this section: _____

30 **4. BASEMENTS AND CRAWL SPACES (Complete only if applicable)**

31   (a) Does the property have a sump pump? ☐ Yes ☐ No ☐ Unknown

32   (b) Are you aware of any water leakage, accumulation, or dampness within the basement or crawl space? ☐ Yes ☐ No

33   If "yes," describe in detail:_____

35   (c) Do you know of any repairs or other attempts to control any water or dampness problem in the basement or crawl space?

36   ☐ Yes ☐ No

37   If "yes," describe the location, extent, date, and name of the person who did the repair or control effort: _____

40 **5. TERMITES/WOOD DESTROYING INSECTS, DRYROT, PESTS**

41   (a) Are you aware of any termites/wood destroying insects, dryrot, or pests affecting the property? ☐ Yes ☐ No

42   (b) Are you aware of any damage to the property caused by termites/wood destroying insects, dryrot, or pests? ☐ Yes ☐ No

43   (c) Is your property currently under contract by a licensed pest control company? ☐ Yes ☐ No

44   (d) Are you aware of any termite/pest control reports or treatments for the property in the last five years? ☐ Yes ☐ No

45   Explain any "yes" answers that you give in this section: _____

48 **6. STRUCTURAL ITEMS**

49   (a) Are you aware of any past or present water leakage in the house or other structures? ☐ Yes ☐ No

50   (b) Are you aware of any past or present movement, shifting, deterioration, or other problems with walls, foundations, or other struc-

51   tural components? ☐ Yes ☐ No

52   (c) Are you aware of any past or present problems with driveways, walkways, patios, or retaining walls on the property?

53   ☐ Yes ☐ No

54   Explain any "yes" answers that you give in this section. When explaining efforts to control or repair, please describe the loca-

55   tion and extent of the problem, and the date and person by whom the work was done, if known: _____

Page 1 of 4   **Seller's Initials:** _____

Figure 17.2
(continued)

59 7. **ADDITIONS/REMODELS**   Have you made any additions, structural changes, or other alterations to the property?   59
60   ☐ Yes   ☐ No   60
61   If yes, describe: _____   61
62   _____   62
63   63
64 8. **WATER AND SEWAGE**   64
65   (a) What is the source of your drinking water?   65
66   ☐ Public   ☐ Community System   ☐ Well on Property   Other (explain) _____   66
67   (b) If your drinking water source is not public   67
68   When was your water last tested? _____ What was the result of the test?_____   68
69   Is the pumping system in working order? ☐ Yes   ☐ No   69
70   If "no," explain: _____   70
71   (c) Do you have a softener, filter, or other purification system?   ☐ Yes   ☐ No   71
72   If yes, is the system   ☐ Leased   ☐ Owned   72
73   (d) What is the type of sewage system?   ☐ Public Sewer   ☐ Community Sewer   73
74   ☐ On-Site (or Individual) sewage system   74
75   If On-Site, what type?   ☐ Cesspool   ☐ Drainfield   ☐ Unknown   ☐ Other (specify): _____   75
76   Is there a septic tank on the Property?   ☐ Yes   ☐ No   ☐ Unknown   76
77   If yes, what is the type of tank?   ☐ Metal/steel   ☐ Cement/concrete   ☐ Fiberglass   ☐ Unknown   77
78   ☐ Other (specify):_____   78
79   Other type of sewage system (explain):_____   79
80   _____   80
81   (e) When was the on-site sewage disposal system last serviced?_____   81
82   (f) Is there a sewage pump?   ☐ Yes   ☐ No   82
83   If yes, is it in working order?   ☐ Yes   ☐ No   83
84   (g) Is either the water or sewage system shared?   ☐ Yes   ☐ No   84
85   If "yes," explain: _____   85
86   (h) Are you aware of any leaks, backups, or other problems relating to any of the plumbing, water, and sewage-related items?   86
87   ☐ Yes   ☐ No   87
88   If "yes," explain: _____   88
89   89
90 9. **PLUMBING SYSTEM**   90
91   (a) Type of plumbing: ☐ Copper   ☐ Galvanized   ☐ Lead   ☐ PVC   ☐ Unknown   91
92   Other (explain): _____   92
93   (b) Are you aware of any problems with any of your plumbing fixtures (e.g., including but not limited to: kitchen, laundry, or bath-   93
94   room fixtures; wet bars; hot water heater; etc.)?   ☐ Yes   ☐ No   94
95   If "yes," explain: _____   95
96   96
97 10. **HEATING AND AIR CONDITIONING**   97
98   (a) Type of air conditioning: ☐ Central Electric   ☐ Central Gas   ☐ Wall   ☐ None   98
99   Number of window units included in sale _____ Location _____   99
100   (b) List any areas of the house that are not air conditioned:_____   100
101   _____   101
102   (c) Type of heating: ☐ Electric   ☐ Fuel Oil   ☐ Natural Gas   ☐ Propane (On-site)   102
103   Are there wood or coal burning stoves? ☐ Yes   ☐ No   If yes, how many? ____   Are they working? ☐ Yes   ☐ No   103
104   Are there any fireplaces?   ☐ Yes   ☐ No   If yes, how many? ____   Are they working?   ☐ Yes   ☐ No   104
105   Other types of heating systems (explain): _____   105
106   _____   106
107   (d) Are there any chimneys?   ☐ Yes   ☐ No   If yes, how many? ____   Are they working? ☐ Yes   ☐ No   107
108   When were they last cleaned? _____   108
109   (e) List any areas of the house that are not heated:_____   109
110   _____   110
111   (f) Type of water heating: ☐ Electric   ☐ Gas   ☐ Solar   111
112   Other: _____   112
113   (g) Are you aware of any underground fuel tanks on the property?   ☐ Yes   ☐ No   113
114   If yes, describe: _____   114
115   Are you aware of any problems with any item in this section?   ☐ Yes   ☐ No   115
116   If "yes," explain: _____   116
117   117
118 11. **ELECTRICAL SYSTEM**   Are you aware of any problems or repairs needed in the electrical system?   ☐ Yes   ☐ No   118
119   If "yes," explain: _____   119
120   **Page 2 of 4**   **Seller's Initials:** _____   120

**Figure 17.2
(continued)**

121 **12. OTHER EQUIPMENT AND APPLIANCES INCLUDED IN SALE (Complete only if applicable)** 121
122 Equipment and appliances ultimately included in the sale will be determined by negotiation and according to the terms of the 122
123 Agreement of Sale. 123
124 (a) ☐ Electric Garage Door Opener   No. of Transmitters _____ 124
125 (b) ☐ Smoke Detectors   How many? _____   Location _____ 125
126 (c) ☐ Security Alarm System   ☐ Owned   ☐ Leased   Lease Information_____ 126
127 (d) ☐ Lawn Sprinkler   No. _____   ☐ Automatic Timer 127
128 (e) ☐ Swimming Pool   ☐ Pool Heater   ☐ Spa/Hot Tub 128
129 Pool/Spa Equipment (list): _____ 129
130 (f) ☐ Refrigerator   ☐ Range   ☐ Microwave Oven   ☐ Dishwasher   ☐ Trash Compactor   ☐ Garbage Disposal 130
131 (g) ☐ Washer   ☐ Dryer 131
132 (h) ☐ Intercom 132
133 (i) ☐ Ceiling fans   No. _____   Location _____ 133
134 (j) Other: _____ 134
135 Are any items in this section in need of repair or replacement?   ☐ Yes   ☐ No   ☐ Unknown 135
136 If "yes," explain: _____ 136
137 137

138 **13. LAND (SOILS, DRAINAGE, AND BOUNDARIES)** 138
139 (a) Are you aware of any fill or expansive soil on the property?   ☐ Yes   ☐ No 139
140 (b) Are you aware of any sliding, settling, earth movement, upheaval, subsidence, or earth stability problems that have occurred on 140
141 or affect the property?   ☐ Yes   ☐ No 141
142 *Note to Buyer: The property may be subject to mine subsidence damage. Maps of the counties and mines where mine subsi-* 142
143 *dence damage may occur and mine subsidence insurance are available through:* Department of Environmental Protection, Mine 143
144 Subsidence Insurance Fund, 3913 Washington Road, McMurray, PA 15317 (412) 941-7100. 144
145 (c) Are you aware of any existing or proposed mining, strip-mining, or any other excavations that might affect this property? 145
146 ☐ Yes   ☐ No 146
147 (d) To your knowledge, is this property, or part of it, located in a flood zone or wetlands area?   ☐ Yes   ☐ No 147
148 (e) Do you know of any past or present drainage or flooding problems affecting the property?   ☐ Yes   ☐ No 148
149 (f) Do you know of any encroachments, boundary line disputes, or easements?   ☐ Yes   ☐ No 149
150 *Note to Buyer: Most properties have easements running across them for utility services and other reasons. In many cases, the* 150
151 *easements do not restrict the ordinary use of the property, and Seller may not be readily aware of them. Buyers may wish to* 151
152 *determine the existence of easement and restrictions by examining the property and ordering an Abstract of Title or searching* 152
153 *the records in the Office of the Recorder of Deeds for the county before entering into an Agreement of Sale.* 153
154 (g) Are you aware of any shared or common areas (e.g., driveways, bridges, docks, walls, etc.) or maintenance agreements? 154
155 ☐ Yes   ☐ No 155
156 Explain any "yes" answers that you give in this section: _____ 156
157 _____ 157
158 158

159 **14. HAZARDOUS SUBSTANCES** 159
160 (a) Are you aware of any underground tanks or hazardous substances present on the property (structure or soil) such as, but not 160
161 limited to, asbestos, Polychlorinated biphenyls (PCBs), Urea Formaldehyde Foam Insulation (UFFI), etc.?   ☐ Yes   ☐ No 161
162 (b) To your knowledge, has the property been tested for any hazardous substances?   ☐ Yes   ☐ No 162
163 (c) Do you know of any other environmental concerns that might impact upon the property?   ☐ Yes   ☐ No 163
164 Explain any "yes" answers that you give in this section: _____ 164
165 _____ 165
166 (d) Do you know of any tests for radon gas that have been performed in any buildings on the Property?   ☐ Yes   ☐ No 166
167 If yes, list date, type, and results of all tests below: 167
168 DATE   TYPE OF TEST   RESULTS (picoCuries/liter or working levels) 168
169 _____   _____   _____ 169
170 _____   _____   _____ 170
171 _____   _____   _____ 171
172 (e) Are you aware of any radon removal system on the Property?   ☐ Yes   ☐ No 172
173 If yes, list date installed and type of system, and whether it is in working order below: 173
174 DATE INSTALLED   TYPE OF SYSTEM   WORKING ORDER 174
175 _____   _____   ☐ Yes   ☐ No 175
176 _____   _____   ☐ Yes   ☐ No 176
177 _____   _____   ☐ Yes   ☐ No 177
178 (f) If Property was constructed, or if construction began, before 1978, you must disclose any knowledge of lead-based paint on the 178
179 Property. Are you aware of any lead-based paint or lead-based paint hazards on the Property?   ☐ Yes   ☐ No 179
180 If yes, explain how you know of it, where it is, and the condition of those lead-based paint surfaces:_____ 180
181 _____ 181

182 **Page 3 of 4**   Seller's Initials: _____ 182

**Figure 17.2
(continued)**

183 (g) If Property was constructed, or if construction began, before 1978, you must disclose any reports or records of lead-based paint 183
184 on the Property. Are you aware of any reports or records regarding lead-based paint or lead-based paint hazards on the Property? 184
185 ☐ Yes ☐ No 185
186 If yes, list all available reports and records: _____ 186
187 _____ 187
188 188
189 **15. CONDOMINIUMS AND OTHER HOMEOWNERS ASSOCIATIONS (Complete only if applicable)** 189
190 Type: ☐ Condominium ☐ Cooperative ☐ Homeowners Association or Planned Community 190
191 Other _____ 191
192 *Notice regarding Condominiums, Cooperatives, and Planned Communities: According to Section 3407 of the Uniform Condo-* 192
193 *minium Act [68 Pa. C.S. §3407 (relating to resale of units) and 68 Pa. C.S. §4409 (relating to resale of cooperative interests)] and* 193
194 *section 5407 of the Uniform Planned Community Act [68 Pa. C.S. §5407 (relating to resale of units)], a buyer of a resale unit in a* 194
195 *condominium, cooperative, or planned community must receive a copy of the declaration (other than the plats and plans), the by-* 195
196 *laws, the rules or regulations, and a certificate of resale issued by the association in the condominium, cooperative, or planned com-* 196
197 *munity. The buyer will have the option of canceling the agreement with the return of all deposit monies until the certificate has been* 197
198 *provided to the buyer and for five days thereafter or until conveyance, whichever occurs first.* 198
199 199
200 **16. MISCELLANEOUS** 200
201 (a) Are you aware of any existing or threatened legal action affecting the property? ☐ Yes ☐ No 201
202 (b) Do you know of any violations of federal, state, or local laws or regulations relating to this property? ☐ Yes ☐ No 202
203 (c) Are you aware of any public improvement, condominium or homeowner association assessments against the property that remain 203
204 unpaid or of any violations of zoning, housing, building, safety or fire ordinances that remain uncorrected? ☐ Yes ☐ No 204
205 (d) Are you aware of any judgment, encumbrance, lien (for example co-maker or equity loan) or other debt against this property that 205
206 cannot be satisfied by the proceeds of this sale? ☐ Yes ☐ No 206
207 (e) Are you aware of any reason, including a defect in title, that would prevent you from giving a warranty deed or conveying title to the 207
208 property? ☐ Yes ☐ No 208
209 (f) Are you aware of any material defects to the property, dwelling, or fixtures which are not disclosed elsewhere on this form? 209
210 ☐ Yes ☐ No 210
211 A material defect is a problem with the property or any portion of it that would have a significant adverse impact on the value of 211
212 the residential real property or that involves an unreasonable risk to people on the land. 212
213 Explain any "yes" answers that you give in this section: _____ 213
214 _____ 214
215 215
216 216
217 **The undersigned Seller represents that the information set forth in this disclosure statement is accurate and complete to the best** 217
218 **of Seller's knowledge. Seller hereby authorizes the Agent for Seller to provide this information to prospective buyers of the prop-** 218
219 **erty and to other real estate agents. SELLER ALONE IS RESPONSIBLE FOR THE ACCURACY OF THE INFORMATION** 219
220 **CONTAINED IN THIS STATEMENT. Seller shall cause Buyer to be notified in writing of any information supplied on this form** 220
221 **which is rendered inaccurate by a change in the condition of the property following completion of this form.** 221
222 222
223 223
224 224
225 225
226 SELLER _____ DATE _____ 226
227 SELLER _____ DATE _____ 227
228 SELLER _____ DATE _____ 228
229 229
230 **EXECUTOR, ADMINISTRATOR, TRUSTEE SIGNATURE BLOCK** 230
231 231
232 According to the provisions of the "Real Estate Seller Disclosure Act," the undersigned executor, administrator or trustee is not required to fill out a Seller's Property 232
233 Disclosure Statement. The executor, administrator or trustee, should, however, disclose any known material defect(s) of the property. 233
234 _____ **DATE** _____ 234
235 235
236 **RECEIPT AND ACKNOWLEDGEMENT BY BUYER** 236
237 The undersigned Buyer acknowledges receipt of this Disclosure Statement. Buyer acknowledges that this Statement is not a warranty and that, unless 237
238 stated otherwise in the sales contract, Buyer is purchasing this property in its present condition. It is Buyer's responsibility to satisfy himself or herself as 238
239 to the condition of the property. Buyer may request that the property be inspected, at Buyer's expense and by qualified professionals, to determine the con- 239
240 dition of the structure or its components. 240
241 **BUYER** _____ **DATE** _____ 241
242 **BUYER** _____ **DATE** _____ 242
243 **BUYER** _____ **DATE** _____ 243
244 **Page 4 of 4** 244

THE LISTING CONTRACT FORM

A variety of listing contract forms are available. The individual specifics may vary. However, most listing contracts require similar information because the same considerations arise in almost all real estate transactions. Figure 17.1 is a typical listing agreement. Important provisions of the sample listing agreement are:

- *Exclusive Right to Sell*. The title specifies that this document is an "exclusive right to sell" real property.

- *Date*. The date of the listing contract is the date it is executed; however, this may not necessarily be the date that the contract becomes effective.

- *Names and signatures*. The names of all persons having an interest in the property should be specified and all should enter into the agreement. All legal owners of the listed property or their authorized agents (such as a holder of a power of attorney) must sign the contract.

- *Broker or Firm*. The name of the broker or firm entering into the listing must be clearly stated in the agreement. The listing salesperson and/or broker should sign the listing agreement. The listing salesperson can sign the contract in the broker's name if authorized by the broker.

- *Owner's Granting of the Listing*. This section establishes the document as a legal contract and states the promises by both parties that create and bind the agreement.

- *Commission*. This paragraph establishes the broker's commission (or a minimum amount of commission) and must be so stated in the contract.

- *Protection Clause*. This section protects the broker if the owner or another person sells the property after the listing expires to a person with whom the original broker negotiated. In other words, the broker is guaranteed a commission for a set period of time after the agreement expires (generally three to six months) if he or she was the procuring cause of the sale, even if the broker did not actually consummate the transaction. This protection clause does not apply, however, if the owner signs a new listing agreement with another broker after the original agreement expires.

- *Broker's Responsibilities*. This paragraph defines the rights and duties of the broker.

- *Broker's Authority*. Here the broker is given the authority to place a sign on the property and show it to buyers, as well as the permission to supply the buyers with any and all information that may appear on the listing form. Without such permission, this information would be confidential and could not be revealed to anyone without breaching the agency doctrine of confidence.

- *Listing Price*. The listing price is a gross sales price, and the owner should understand that any obligations such as taxes, mortgages and assessments remain the owner's responsibility and must be paid out of the proceeds of the sale.

- *Encumbrances*. This paragraph points out responsibilities of encumbrances, especially important to the broker because they determine whether or not the property is, in fact, salable.

- *Evidence of Ownership and Deed.* The type of deed to be executed and proof of ownership in the form of a title are stated here.

- *Liabilities.* The owner protects both buyer and broker with this statement.

- *Civil Rights Legislation.* This clause serves to alert the owner that both federal and state legislation exist to protect against discrimination. This is the Official Notice required by the Pennsylvania Human Relations Act.

- *Termination of Agreement.* Both the exact time and the date serve to remove any ambiguity in regard to termination of the contract. A particular termination date does not necessarily include that day itself, unless the phrase "up to and including" is used.

- *Disclosures Required by the Pennsylvania Real Estate Licensing and Registration Act, Sec. 606.*

- *Revealing Defects and Environmental Hazards.* These sections define the responsibility of the seller to disclose all material defects and environmental hazards the seller is aware of to the broker and potential purchasers. It also defines *material defect* and details the broker's protection from lawsuits and action if this is not done.

- *Lead-Based Paint Disclosure.* Reviews the requirements under The Residential Lead-Based Paint Hazard Reduction Act regarding lead-based paint hazards for property built before 1978.

- *Recovery Fund.* This paragraph informs the seller that a state fund exists to repay any person legally determined to have been a victim of fraud or misrepresentation.

The sample exclusive-right-to-sell agreement (see Figure 17.1) is published by the Pennsylvania Association of REALTORS® for use by any licensee throughout the state. A local MLS may publish similar form for use by its members.

BUYER AGENCY AGREEMENT

A **buyer agency agreement** is also an employment contract. However, in this case the broker is being employed as the agent of the buyer to find a suitable property. The buyer becomes the principal, rather than the seller. As discussed in a previous chapter, the buyer may choose to have a degree of representation in a real estate purchase that is only possible through a fiduciary relationship with the broker. This is effected through a buyer agency agreement.

Types of Buyer Agency Agreements

There are several types of buyer agency agreements. (See Figure 17.3 for an example of a buyer agency agreement.)

- Exclusive buyer agency agreement is a 100 percent exclusive agency agreement. The buyer is bound to compensate the agent whenever he or she purchases a property of the type described in the contract, regardless of whether the property was located by the agent, the buyer or another licensee.

- Exclusive agency buyer agreement is an exclusive contract with the agent, but it gives the buyer the flexibility to locate a property himself or herself without being obligated to compensate the agent.

- Open buyer agency agreement permits do not have any exclusive provision. The buyer can sign agency contracts with a number of brokers an be obligated to compensate only the broker who locates the property the buyer purchases.

Contracting with Buyers

Just as when listing a property, there are a number of issues the broker and prospective client must discuss before signing a buyer agency agreement. The licensee is required to make the same kind of agency disclosures that were previously discussed. This is also an opportunity to explain exactly how the agent will represent the buyer and the specific services that are provided to a buyer-client. Because the agency contract employs the agent to represent the buyer and locate a suitable property, the licensee needs certain information in order to properly represent the buyer's interests. This includes financial information and the specific property requirements.

A buyer-agency agreement is similar to a listing contract in that it specifies the rights and obligations of the parties, including the compensation arrangements. As mentioned in Chapter 15, the source of compensation does not determine which party is being represented. Compensation may be a flat fee, an hourly rate or a percentage of the purchase price of a property. The agent may collect a retainer fee at the time the agency contract is signed and apply it as a credit toward fees that are due at the settlement of the purchase agreement. It is also possible that the seller may agree to compensate the buyer's agent. Of course, all compensation arrangements are negotiable.

● ● ● ● ● ● ● ●

KEY TERMS

automatic renewal
buyer agency agreement
comparative market analysis
exclusive-agency listing
exclusive right-to-sell listing

multiple listing service (MLS)
net listing
open listing
Real Estate Seller Disclosure Act

SUMMARY

To acquire an inventory of property to sell, brokers must obtain listings. Types of listing agreements include open listings, exclusive-agency listings and exclusive-right-to-sell listings.

With an exclusive-right-to-sell listing, the seller employs only one broker and must pay that broker a commission, regardless of whether it is the broker or the seller who finds a buyer, so long as the buyer is found within the listing period.

Under an exclusive-agency listing, the broker is given the exclusive right to represent the seller, but the seller can avoid paying the broker a commission if the owner sells the property without the broker's help.

In an open listing, the seller is permitted to contract with any number of brokers and is obligated to compensate only the broker who procures the buyer.

A multiple-listing provision in a listing contract gives the broker the authority to distribute the listing to other brokers in the multiple-listing service. A net

**Figure 17.3
Buyer Agency
Contract**

REAL ESTATE BROKER EMPLOYMENT CONTRACT
COPYRIGHT PENNSYLVANIA ASSOCIATION OF REALTORS®
This form recommended and approved for, but not restricted to, use by the members of the Pennsylvania Association of REALTORS®

**BAC 1991
(5-95)**

1. BUYER (list all Buyers)

Name _____ SS#_____

Mailing Address _____

Phone Number _____

Name _____ SS#_____

Mailing Address _____

Phone Number _____

If there are other buyers, give names, addresses, phone numbers, and social security numbers on an additional sheet.

2. BROKER

Broker is _____

Address _____

Phone Number _____

Salesperson is _____, who works for the Broker.

3. PURPOSE OF THIS CONTRACT

A. (1) Buyer is hiring broker to find a property for Buyer and to act in Buyer's best interest in its purchase.

(2) During the term of this Contract, Buyer will not hire or work with any other Broker to help Buyer find a property.

(3) Buyer will give Broker any information Broker needs to help Buyer.

B. (1) Broker will act only in Buyer's best interest, including negotiating terms and price.

(2) Broker will use Broker's knowledge and skill to help Buyer.

(3) Broker will give Buyer any information Broker has to help Buyer make a decision.

(4) Broker will not reveal any confidential information that Buyer gives to Broker during the term of this Contract. Broker will continue to keep the information confidential after the Ending Date of this Contract.

(5) Broker will tell all sellers and listing brokers at first contact that Broker is representing Buyer.

4. DESCRIPTION OF PROPERTY

This Contract applies to any property Buyer chooses to buy. The following information is a general description of the property Buyer would like to buy.

A. Price Range _____

B. Location (counties of) _____

C. _____

5. STARTING AND ENDING DATES OF THIS CONTRACT (also called "Term")

A. The term of this Contract is a result of negotiations between Buyer and Broker and has not been set or recommended by any Association of REALTORS®. The term of this contract cannot be more than one year.

B. **Starting Date:** The Starting Date of this Contract is: _____

C. **Ending Date:** This Contract ends on _____ unless Buyer has signed an agreement of sale or unless a purchase is being negotiated. In either case, the Broker will continue to represent the Buyer until negotiations end.

6. BROKER'S FEE

A. The Broker's Fee is a result of negotiations between Buyer and Broker. The Broker's fee has not been set or recommended by any Association of REALTORS®.

B. The Broker's Fee is to be paid in one or more of the following ways:
(Instruction: Fill in "N/A" in the sections that do Not Apply)

(1) **Flat Fee:** $ _____ to be paid at settlement.

(2) **Percentage Fee:** _____ % of the purchase price, to be paid at settlement.

(3) **Time Fee:** $ _____ ☐ hourly ☐ daily to be paid by Buyer when bill is received.

(4) **Advanced Fee (NON-REFUNDABLE):** $ _____
This amount ☐ will ☐ will not be applied to Flat, Percentage, or Time Fees.

(5) An **additional** fee of _____ will be paid if property to be bought is not listed with a broker.

(6) Other Fee: _____

C. Buyer must pay Broker's Fee directly to Broker. Broker may receive the fee (or part of it) from a seller, from a listing broker, from a mortgage lender, or from any other source.
Special Instructions: _____

D. Broker will tell Buyer of any other fees that Broker receives in connection with Buyer's purchase of a property. Buyer allows Broker to accept additional fees.

E. If Buyer buys a property within _____ days after the Ending Date of this Contract, **Buyer will pay Broker's Fee if Buyer learned of the property during the term of this Contract.**

F. If Buyer signs an agreement of sale then refuses to buy the property, or if Buyer is unable to buy it because of failing to do all the things required of Buyer in the agreement of sale, then Buyer must immediately pay any Broker's Fee that would have been due at settlement.

7. DEPOSIT MONEY

A. Broker will keep (or will give to the listing broker, who will keep) all deposit monies that Salesperson or Broker receives in an escrow account as required by real estate licensing laws and regulations until the sale or exchange of the property is final. Buyer agrees that Broker may wait to deposit any uncashed check that is received as deposit money until Buyer's offer has been accepted.

B. If Buyer joins Salesperson or Broker in a lawsuit for the return of deposit monies, Buyer will pay Salesperson's and Broker's attorney's fees and costs.

**Figure 17.3
(continued)**

8. **OTHER BUYERS.**
   Buyer agrees that Broker may show or present the same properties to other buyers.
9. **CONFLICT OF INTERESTS**
   A. Broker represents Buyer's interests. If the Broker, or any of Broker's salespeople, has a *conflict of interest*, Broker will immediately tell Buyer and **this Contract will be ended in regard to that conflict only.**
   B. A *conflict of interest* could be:
      1. If the property is listed with Broker.
      2. If Broker has financial or personal interest in the property.
      3. Any other case where Broker would not be able to put Buyer's interests before any other.
   C. If this Contract ends because of a conflict of interest
      1. Broker will not reveal any confidential information that Buyer has given Broker during the term of this Contract.
      2. Buyer may continue to buy the property knowing that Broker has a conflict of interest and that Broker may represent the other party. Buyer may also wish to hire another broker or lawyer to represent Buyer's interest.
      3. No Broker's Fee will be due except money owed under the Time Fee. Any money that Broker has already received will be kept by Broker.
10. **TRANSFER OF THIS CONTRACT**
    Buyer agrees that Broker may transfer this Contract to another real estate broker if
       1. Broker stops doing business,
       2. Broker forms a new real estate business,
       3. Broker joins Broker's business with another, or
       4. for any other reason.
    If a transfer occurs, Buyer will follow all requirements of this Contract with new broker.
11. **CIVIL RIGHTS ACTS**
    Federal and state laws make it illegal for a seller, Broker, or anyone to use RACE, COLOR, RELIGION or RELIGIOUS CREED, SEX, DISABILITY (physical or mental), FAMILIAL STATUS (children under 18 years of age), AGE (40 or older), NATIONAL ORIGIN or USE OR HANDLING/TRAINING OF SUPPORT OR GUIDE ANIMALS, or the FACT OF RELATIONSHIP OR ASSOCIATION TO AN INDIVIDUAL KNOWN TO HAVE A DISABILITY as reasons for refusing to sell, show, or rent properties, loan money, or set deposit amounts, or as reasons for any decision relating to the sale of property.
12. **RECOVERY FUND.**
    Pennsylvania has a Real Estate Recovery Fund to repay any person who has received a final civil judgment against a Pennsylvania real estate licensee because of fraud, misrepresentation, or deceit in a real estate transaction, and who has not been unable to collect the judgment after trying all legal and equitable remedies. For complete details about the Fund, call (717) 783-3658.
13. **CHANGES TO THIS CONTRACT.**
    Any changes to this Contract must be in writing and signed by Buyer and Salesperson or Broker.
14. **CONFIDENTIALITY**
    Salesperson and Broker will not reveal any confidential information given to them by Buyer during the term of this Contract. Salesperson and Broker will continue to keep the information confidential after the Ending Date of this Contract.
15. **ENTIRE CONTRACT**
    This Contract is the entire Contract between Broker and Buyer. Any verbal or written agreements that were made before are not a part of this Contract.
16. **NOTICE BEFORE SIGNING**
    WHEN SIGNED, THIS CONTRACT IS BINDING. IF BUYER HAS LEGAL QUESTIONS ABOUT THIS CONTRACT, BUYER IS ADVISED TO TALK TO A LAWYER.

BUYER _____ DATE _____
BUYER _____ DATE _____
BUYER _____ DATE _____
All Buyers must sign this Contract.
BROKER (Company Name): _____

ACCEPTED BY: _____
                  (signature of Broker or Salesperson)

Buyer gives permission to Broker to do the following

A. Order Title Insurance from any reputable company   ☐ No   ☐ Yes _____
                                                                           Buyer's initials
B. Order insurance in the amount of the purchase price
      ☐ Homeowners   ☐ Fire & Extended Coverage   ☐ Flood (if necessary)   _____
                                                                           Buyer's initials
C. _____ _____
                                                                           Buyer's initials

PENNSYLVANIA ASSOCIATION OF REALTORS®   SPEED PAR FORMS   5/95 listing is based on the net price the seller will receive if the property is sold. The broker under a net listing is free to offer the property for sale at the highest available price and retain as his or her commission any amount over and above the seller's net. The use of a net listing is discouraged because of the potential conflict of interest between the broker's fiduciary responsibility and the broker's profit motive.

A listing agreement may be terminated for the same reasons as any other agency relationship.

When listing a property for sale, the seller is concerned about the selling price and the net amount that will be received from the sale. A competitive market analysis is a comparison of the prices of recently sold properties that are similar to the seller's property. The CMA or a formal appraisal report can be used to help the seller determine a reasonable listing price. The amount the seller will net from the sale is calculated by subtracting the broker's commission and any other expenses that the seller incurs from the selling price.

Listing contracts are typically preprinted forms that include such information as the type of listing, the broker's authority and responsibilities, listing price, duration of the listing, information about the property, terms for the payment of commission and the buyer's possession and nondiscrimination laws.

A buyer agency agreement is the contract in which a buyer employs the broker to represent the buyer in the purchase of a property. Types of buyer agency agreements include an exclusive buyer agency agreement, an exclusive agency buyer agreement and an open buyer agency agreement.

Before any agency agreement is signed, disclosures of agency must be made in accordance with state laws.

Questions

1. A listing taken by a real estate salesperson belongs to the
   a. broker.
   b. seller.
   c. salesperson.
   d. salesperson and the broker equally.

2. Which of the following is a similarity between an exclusive-agency and an exclusive-right-to-sell listing?
   a. Under both types of listings, the seller retains the right to sell the real estate without the broker's help without paying the broker a commission.
   b. Under both, the seller authorizes only one particular salesperson to show the property.
   c. Both give the responsibility of representing the seller to one broker only.
   d. Both are open listings.

3. All of the following may terminate a listing *except*
   a. expiration of the contract.
   b. death or incapacity of the broker.
   c. nonpayment of the commission by the seller.
   d. destruction of the improvements on the property.

4. Seller *M* has listed his property under an exclusive-agency listing with broker *K*. If *M* sells his property himself during the term of the listing without using *K*'s services, he will owe *K*
   a. no commission.
   b. the full commission.
   c. a partial commission.
   d. only reimbursement for broker *K*'s costs.

5. A broker sold a residence for $88,000 and received $6,160 as her commission in accordance with the terms of the listing. What percentage of the sales price was the broker's commission?
   a. 6 percent
   b. 6.5 percent
   c. 7 percent
   d. 7.5 percent

6. A seller's residence is listed with a broker, and the seller stipulates that she wants to receive $85,000 from the sale but the broker can sell the property for as much as possible and keep the difference as the commission. The broker agrees. Which of the following *best* describes this type of listing arrangement?
   a. Exclusive-right-to-sell listing
   b. Exclusive-agency listing
   c. Open listing
   d. Net listing

7. All of the following provisions are usually found in a listing agreement *except*
   a. rate of commission.
   b. monthly utility bills.
   c. price the seller wants.
   d. contract expiration date.

8. The listed price for a property should be based on
   a. the net to the seller.
   b. the appraised value.
   c. what the seller chooses.
   d. the maximum of a range of values.

9. Which of the following is true about a listing contract?

   a. It is an employment contract for the personal and professional services of the broker.
   b. It obligates the seller to convey the property if the broker procures a ready, willing and able buyer.
   c. It obligates the broker to work diligently for both the buyer and the seller.
   d. It automatically requires the payment of a commission while the broker protection clause is in effect.

10. Seller W hired broker N under the terms of an exclusive-right-to-sell listing. While the listing was in effect, W—without informing N— sold the property to his neighbor. Seller W must pay

    a. no commission to broker N.
    b. broker N's marketing expenses.
    c. full commission to broker N.
    d. half commission to broker N.

11. Seller G listed her residence with broker D. Broker D brought an offer at full price and terms of the listing from buyers who were willing and able to pay cash for the property. Then seller G rejected the buyers' offer. In this situation seller G

    a. must sell her property.
    b. owes a commission to broker D.
    c. is liable to the buyers for specific performance.
    d. is liable to the buyers for compensatory damages.

12. Which is a similarity between an open listing and exclusive-agency listing?

    a. Under both the seller avoids paying the broker a commission if the seller sells the property himself or herself.
    b. Under both the seller is guaranteed to net a certain amount.
    c. Under both the broker earns a commission regardless of who sells the property, as long as it is sold within the listing period.
    d. Both grant an exclusive right to sell to whichever broker procures a buyer for the seller's property.

13. The parties to the listing contract are

    a. the seller and the buyer.
    b. the seller and the broker.
    c. the seller and the salesperson.
    d. the broker and the salesperson.

14. A competitive market analysis

    a. is the same as an appraisal.
    b. can help the seller price the property.
    c. by law must be completed for each listing taken.
    d. should not be retained in the property's listing file.

15. A property was listed with a broker who belonged to a multiple-listing service and was sold by another member broker for $53,500. The total commission was 6 percent of the sale price. The selling broker received 60 percent of the commission, and the listing broker received the balance. What was the listing broker's commission?

    a. $1,284   c. $1,926
    b. $1,464   d. $2,142

16. All of the following provisions must, by state regulation, be included in exclusive-listing agreements *except*

    a. amount of commission.
    b. seller's asking price.
    c. date the agreement terminates.
    d. zoning classification.

17. After a buyer signs an agency agreement with a broker, the buyer also signs other agency agreements with other brokers. Despite all of these agency relationships, the buyer finds a house on his own. Under the terms of these agency agreements, the buyer does not owe any broker a commission. What kind of an agency agreements were these?

    a. Exclusive agency agreements
    b. Exclusive agency buyer agency agreements
    c. Exclusive buyer agency agreements
    d. Open buyer agency agreements

18 Sales Contracts

The culmination of the agent's efforts to market a seller's property or help a buyer find a suitable home is when a buyer and seller negotiate an agreement of sale. The process begins with an offer that, if it is accepted, "ripens into" a contract and binds the parties to certain obligations.

Because licensees work with a number of contracts in their business, they must understand both the legal and practical implications of the contracts that are used. The most common kind of sales contract is an agreement of sale, though option agreements and installment contracts are also used. *The agreement of sale is an important document*—it sets out in detail the agreement between the buyer and seller and establishes their legal rights and obligations. In effect, it dictates the contents of the deed.

PREPARING CONTRACTS

The use of preprinted forms is common because of the similarities among transactions. These forms are a useful tool; however, the licensee must exercise care in completing them. Certain printed language may not be applicable to a particular transaction; the blanks must be filled in properly, and certain clauses or agreements may need to be added to the "standard form." Licensees who are careless in completing these documents risk injuring the buyer or seller and create liability for themselves.

Real estate licensees are not authorized to practice law. Situations that are beyond the expertise of a licensee should be referred to a lawyer. All parties to a transaction should have the opportunity to seek independent counsel to be sure they understand their rights and the obligations to which they are being legally bound.

Essential Requirements of a Contract

Any agreement between two or more parties must meet certain basic requirements for it to be a legally valid contract. These were more fully discussed in a previous chapter. The fundamental essentials include:

- *Offer and acceptance.* There must be an offer by one party that is communicated to another party for acceptance. The acceptance must be communicated to the offering party. This process satisfies the requirement of *mutual assent* or "meeting of the minds."

- *Consideration.* Something of value must be given in exchange for a promise. A promise to another is not enforceable without consideration in exchange. Consideration that is "good and valuable" between the parties satisfies the legal requirement for consideration.

- *Legally competent parties.* All parties must be of legal age and have sufficient mental capacity to understand the nature and consequences of their actions. If these conditions are absent, a contract may be void or voidable.

- *Legality of object.* The parties must agree to acts that are consistent with the law and public policy. All or part of a contract may be unenforceable if it contemplates acts that violate criminal or civil laws.

Validity of Contracts

A *valid* contract is one that contains all of the essential requirements of a contract that make it legally sufficient to be enforceable. A *void* contract is one that has no legal force or effect. A *voidable* contract is one that may be disaffirmed or rescinded. The laws protect people from their actions in certain circumstances when enforcing the contract would subject them to injury.

Reality of Consent

A contract may be void or voidable because of circumstances in which there is no "reality of consent" between the parties, even though the contract meets all the essential requirements. People must be able to act prudently, knowledgeably and without undue influence when they enter into contracts. When a person has been injured by an action that prevents this from happening, the contract is either void or voidable such as in circumstances of *fraud* or *misrepresentation* (described in Chapter 11).

Undue influence means persuading a person in such as way as to completely overpower the person's free will to prevent him or her from acting intelligently and voluntarily. *Duress* forces a party into contract under the threat of physical harm or by exciting fear of violence. A party who is unable to exercise his or her free will and judgment in this situation may void the contract within a reasonable time after the threat is removed. All of these situations are complex and require legal interpretation. A real estate licensee needs to be aware of these conditions, however, so as to protect the enforceability of a contract.

AGREEMENT OF SALE

The **agreement of sale** sets forth all details of the agreement between a buyer and a seller for the purchase and sale of a parcel of real estate. When it has been prepared and signed by the purchaser, it is an offer to purchase the subject real estate. If the document is accepted and signed by the seller, it then becomes, or "ripens into," an agreement of sale. A real estate sales contract is shown in Figure 18.1.

Details to be included in a real estate sales contract are the price, terms, accurate description of the real estate, kind and condition of the title, form of deed the seller will deliver, kind of title evidence required, who will provide title evidence and how defects in the title, if any, are to be eliminated. The contract

**Figure 18.1
Real Estate
Agreement
of Sale**

STANDARD AGREEMENT FOR THE SALE OF REAL ESTATE   A/S Residential
This form recommended and approved for, but not restricted to use by, the members of the Pennsylvania Association of REALTORS® (PAR)

PA LICENSED BROKER

AGENT FOR SELLER _____ PH _____
  ADDRESS _____ FAX _____
SUBAGENT FOR SELLER _____ PH _____
  ADDRESS _____ FAX _____
AGENT FOR BUYER _____ PH _____
  ADDRESS _____ FAX _____

1. **This Agreement,** dated _____, is between
SELLER(S): _____

Address _____
_____ Zip Code _____ hereafter "Seller," and
BUYER(S): _____

Address _____
_____ Zip Code _____ hereafter "Buyer."

2. **PROPERTY (1-98)** Seller hereby agrees to sell and convey to Buyer, who hereby agrees to purchase:
ALL THAT CERTAIN lot or piece of ground with buildings and improvements thereon erected, if any, known as:
_____
_____ in the _____ of _____,
County of _____ in the Commonwealth of Pennsylvania, Zip Code _____
Identification (e.g., Tax ID#; Parcel #; Lot, Block; Deed Book, Page, Recording Date) _____
_____

3. **TERMS (1-98) (A)** Purchase Price _____
_____ **Dollars**
which shall be paid to Seller by Buyer as follows:
  (B) Cash or check at signing this Agreement: _____ $ _____
  (C) Cash or check on or before: _____ $ _____
  (D) _____ $ _____
  (E) Cash, cashier's or certified check at time of settlement: _____ $ _____
                                  TOTAL $ _____
  (F) Deposits to be held by Agent for Seller, unless otherwise stated here: _____
  (G) Written approval of Seller to be on or before: _____
  (H) Settlement to be made on or before: _____
  (I) Conveyance from Seller will be by fee simple deed of special warranty unless otherwise stated here: _____
_____ .
  (J) Payment of transfer taxes will be divided equally between Buyer and Seller unless otherwise stated here: _____
  (K) At time of settlement, the following shall be adjusted pro-rata on a daily basis between Buyer and Seller, reimbursing where applicable: taxes; rents; interest on mortgage assumptions; condominium fees and homeowner association fees, if any; water and/or sewer rents, if any, together with any other lienable municipal service. The charges are to be pro-rated for the period(s) covered: Seller will pay up to and including the date of settlement; Buyer will pay for all days following settlement, unless otherwise stated here: _____
_____ .

4. **FIXTURES AND PERSONAL PROPERTY (1-98)**
  (A) INCLUDED in this sale and purchase price are all existing items permanently installed in the Property, free of liens, including plumbing; heating; lighting fixtures (including chandeliers and ceiling fans); water treatment systems; pool and spa equipment; garage door openers and transmitters; television antennas; shrubbery, plantings and unpotted trees; any remaining heating and cooking fuels stored on the Property at the time of settlement; wall to wall carpeting; shades, blinds, window covering hardware; built-in air conditioners; built-in appliances; and the range/oven unless otherwise stated. Also included: _____
_____
  (B) EXCLUDED fixtures and items: _____
_____

5. **SPECIAL CLAUSES (1-98)**
  (A) ☐ Buyer and Seller acknowledge having received a statement of their respective estimated closing costs before signing this Agreement of Sale.
  (B) ☐ Buyer acknowledges receipt of Seller's Property Disclosure Statement before signing this Agreement, if required by law. (See Notice, Information Regarding the Seller's Property Disclosure Act.)
  (C) ☐ Buyer acknowledges receipt of the Deposit Money Notice (for cooperative sales when Agent for Seller is holding deposit money) before signing this Agreement.
  (D) The following are a part of this Agreement if checked:
    ☐ Limited Dual Agency Addendum (PAR Form 140)   ☐ Settlement of Other Property Contingency
    ☐ Sale & Settlement of Other Property   (PAR Form 133)
      Contingency Addendum (PAR Form 130)   ☐ Tenant-Occupied Property Addendum (PAR Form TOP)
    ☐ Sale & Settlement of Other Property Contingency ☐ _____
      with Right to Continue Marketing Addendum   ☐ _____
      (PAR Form 131)   ☐ _____

Buyer Initials: _____   A/S Residential Page 1 of 8   Seller Initials: _____

**Figure 18.1
(continued)**

68	**6. MORTGAGE CONTINGENCY (1-98)**	68

68 **6. MORTGAGE CONTINGENCY (1-98)**
69 ☐ WAIVED. This sale is NOT contingent on mortgage financing.
70 ☐ ELECTED
71 (A) This sale is contingent upon Buyer obtaining mortgage financing as follows:
72   1. Amount of mortgage loan $_____
73   2. Minimum Term _____ years
74   3. Type of mortgage _____
75   4. Interest rate _____ %; however, **Buyer agrees to accept the interest rate as may be committed by the mortgage lender,** not to
76   exceed a maximum interest rate of _____%.
77   5. Discount points, loan origination, loan placement and other fees charged by the lender as a percentage of the mortgage loan (excluding
78   any mortgage insurance premiums or VA funding fee) not to exceed _____% of the mortgage loan.
79   The interest rate and fees provisions required by Buyer are satisfied if a mortgage lender makes available to Buyer the right to guarantee an
80   interest rate at or below the Maximum Interest Rate specified herein with the percentage fees at or below the amount specified herein. Buyer
81   gives Seller the right, at Seller's sole option and as permitted by the lending institution and applicable laws, to contribute financially, without
82   promise of reimbursement, to the Buyer and/or lender to make the above terms available to Buyer.
83 (B) Within 10 days of the execution of this Agreement, Buyer shall make a completed, written mortgage application to a responsible mortgage lend-
84   ing institution through the office of Agent for Buyer, if any, otherwise through the office of Subagent for Seller, if any, or Agent for Seller, if
85   any. **This Agent is authorized to communicate with the lender for the purposes of assisting in the mortgage loan process.**
86 (C) 1. Upon receipt of a mortgage commitment, Buyer and/or Agent will promptly deliver a copy of the commitment to Agent for Seller, if any,
87   otherwise to Seller.
88   2. Mortgage commitment date _____ . If a written commitment is not received by
89   Agent for Seller, if any, otherwise by Seller, by the above date, **Buyer and Seller agree to extend the commitment date until Seller ter-
90   minates this Agreement in writing.**
91   3. Seller has the option to terminate this Agreement in writing, on or after the mortgage commitment date, if the mortgage commitment:
92   a. Is not valid until the date of settlement, OR
93   b. Is conditioned upon the **sale and settlement of any other property**, OR
94   c. Contains any other condition not specified in this Agreement.
95   4. In the event Seller does not terminate this Agreement as provided above, Buyer has the option to terminate this Agreement in writing if
96   the mortgage commitment:
97   a. Is not obtained by or valid until the date of settlement, OR
98   b. Is conditioned upon the **sale and settlement of any other property** which do not occur by the date of settlement, OR
99   c. Contains any other condition not specified in this Agreement which Buyer is unable to satisfy by the date of settlement.
100   5. If this Agreement is terminated as specified in paragraphs 6 (C) (2), (3) or (4), all deposit monies paid on account of purchase price shall
101   be returned to Buyer. Buyer will be responsible for any premiums for mechanics lien insurance and/or title search, or fee for cancellation
102   of same, if any; AND/OR any premiums for flood insurance and/or fire insurance with extended coverage, insurance binder charges or
103   cancellation fee, if any; AND/OR any appraisal fees and charges paid in advance to mortgage lender.
104 (D) If the mortgage lender requires repairs to the Property, Buyer will, upon receipt, deliver a copy of the mortgage lender's requirements to Agent
105   for Seller, if any, otherwise to Seller. Seller shall, within 5 days of receipt of the lender's requirements, notify Buyer whether Seller shall make
106   the required repairs at Seller's expense.
107   1. If Seller chooses to make repairs, Buyer shall accept the Property and agree to the RELEASE set forth in paragraph 26 of this Agreement.
108   2. If Seller chooses not to make the required repairs, Buyer will, within 5 days, notify Seller in writing of Buyer's choice to terminate the
109   Agreement of Sale OR make the required repairs at Buyer's expense and with Seller's permission, which shall not be unreasonably with-
110   held. If Seller denies Buyer permission to make the required repairs, Buyer may, within 5 days of Seller's denial, terminate this Agreement.
111   If Buyer terminates this Agreement, all deposit monies paid on account of purchase price shall be returned promptly to Buyer and this
112   Agreement of Sale will be NULL and VOID.
113 (E) **Seller Assist**
114   ☐ NOT APPLICABLE
115   ☐ APPLICABLE. Seller shall pay:
116   ☐ $ _____ , maximum, toward Buyer's costs as permitted by the mortgage lender.
117   ☐ _____
118   _____
119
120   **FHA/VA, IF APPLICABLE**
121 (F) It is expressly agreed that notwithstanding any other provisions of this contract, Buyer shall not be obligated to complete the purchase of the
122   Property described herein or to incur any penalty by forfeiture of earnest money deposits or otherwise unless Buyer has been given, in accor-
123   dance with HUD/FHA or VA requirements, a written statement by the Federal Housing Commissioner, Veterans Administration, or a Direct
124   Endorsement Lender setting forth the appraised value of the Property of not less than $ _____ (the dollar amount to be
125   inserted is the sales price as stated in the Agreement). Buyer shall have the privilege and option of proceeding with consummation of the con-
126   tract without regard to the amount of the appraised valuation. The appraised valuation is arrived at to determine the maximum mortgage the
127   Department of Housing and Urban Development will insure. HUD does not warrant the value nor the condition of the Property. Buyer should
128   satisfy himself/herself that the price and condition of the Property are acceptable.
129   **Warning:** Section 1010 of Title 18, I.S.C., Department of Housing and Urban Development provides, "Whoever for the purpose of . . . influ-
130   encing in any way the action of such department . . . makes, passes, utters or publishes any statement knowing the same to be false . . . shall be
131   fined not more than $5,000 or imprisoned not more than two years, or both."
132 (G) **U.S. Department of Housing and Urban Development (HUD) NOTICE TO PURCHASERS:**
133   **THE IMPORTANCE OF A HOME INSPECTION**
134   **HUD does not warrant the condition of a property.** (See Notices and Information on Property Condition Inspections.)
135 (H) **Certification** We the undersigned, Seller(s) and Buyer(s) party to this transaction each certify that the terms of this contract for purchase are
136   true to the best of our knowledge and belief, and that any other agreement entered into by any of these parties in connection with this transac-
137   tion is attached to this Agreement of Sale.
138 **7. INSPECTIONS (1-98)**
139 (A) Seller hereby agrees to permit inspections by authorized appraisers, reputable certifiers, insurer's representatives, surveyors, municipal officials
140   and/or Buyer as may be required by the lending institutions, if any, or insuring agencies. Seller further agrees to permit any other inspections
141   required by or provided for in the terms of this Agreement.
142 (B) Buyer reserves the right to make a pre-settlement walk-through inspection of the Property. Buyer's right to make this inspection is not waived
143   by any other provision of this Agreement.
144 (C) Seller will have heating and all utilities (including fuel(s)) on for the inspections.
145 **8. PROPERTY INSPECTION CONTINGENCY (1-98)**
146   ☐ WAIVED. Buyer understands that Buyer has the option to request inspections of the Property (see Property Inspection and Environmental
147   Notices). BUYER WAIVES THIS OPTION and agrees to the RELEASE set forth in paragraph 26 of this Agreement.
148 **Buyer Initials:** _____   **A/S Residential Page 2 of 8**   **Seller Initials:** _____

**Figure 18.1
(continued)**

149 ☐ ELECTED

150 (A) Within _____ days of the execution of this Agreement, Buyer, at Buyer's expense, may choose to have inspections and/or certifications completed by licensed or otherwise qualified professionals (see Property Inspection and Environmental Notices). Other provisions of this Agreement may provide for inspections and/or certifications that are not waived or altered by Buyer's election here. If Buyer is not satisfied with the condition of the Property as stated in any written report, Buyer will, **within the time given for completing inspections:**

154 ☐ **Option 1**

155   1. Accept the Property with the information stated in the report(s) and agree to the RELEASE set forth in paragraph 26 of this Agreement, OR

157   2. Terminate the Agreement of Sale in writing by notice to Agent for Seller, if any, otherwise to Seller, within the time given for inspection, in which case all deposit monies paid on account of purchase price shall be returned promptly to Buyer and this Agreement will be NULL and VOID.

160 ☐ **Option 2**

161   1. Accept the Property with the information stated in the report(s) and agree to the RELEASE set forth in paragraph 26 of this Agreement, UNLESS the total cost to correct the conditions contained in the report(s) is more than $ _____ .

163   2. If the total cost to correct the conditions contained in the report(s) EXCEEDS the amount specified in paragraph 8(A) (Option 2) 1, **Buyer will deliver the report(s) to Agent for Seller, if any, otherwise to Seller, within the time given for inspection.**

165   a. Seller will, within _____ days of receiving the report(s), inform Buyer in writing of Seller's choice to:

166   1) Make repairs before settlement so that the remaining cost to repair conditions contained in the report(s) is less than or equal to the amount specified in paragraph 8 (A) (Option 2) 1.

168   2) Credit Buyer at settlement for the difference between the estimated cost of repairing the conditions contained in the report(s) and the amount specified in paragraph 8 (A) (Option 2) 1. This option must be acceptable to the mortgage lender, if any.

170   3) Not make repairs and not credit Buyer at settlement for any defects in conditions contained in the report(s).

171   b. If Seller chooses to make repairs or credit Buyer at settlement as specified in paragraph 8 (A) (Option 2) 2, Buyer shall accept the Property and agree to the RELEASE set forth in paragraph 26 of this Agreement.

173   c. If Seller chooses not to make repairs and not to credit Buyer at settlement, or **if Seller fails to choose any option within the time given,** Buyer will within _____ days:

175   1) Accept the Property with the information stated in the report(s) and agree to the RELEASE set forth in paragraph 26 of this Agreement, OR

177   2) Terminate the Agreement of Sale in writing by notice to Agent for Seller, if any, otherwise to Seller, in which case all deposit monies paid on account of purchase price shall be returned promptly to Buyer and this Agreement of Sale will be NULL and VOID.

180 (B) **Buyer's failure to exercise any of Buyer's options within the time limits specified in this paragraph shall constitute a WAIVER of this contingency and Buyer accepts the Property and agrees to the RELEASE set forth in paragraph 26 of this Agreement.**

182 **9. WOOD INFESTATION CONTINGENCY (1-98)**

183 ☐ WAIVED. Buyer understands that Buyer has the option to request that the Property be inspected for wood infestation by a certified Pest Control Operator. BUYER WAIVES THIS OPTION and agrees to the RELEASE set forth in paragraph 26 of this Agreement.

185 ☐ ELECTED

186 (A) Within _____ days of the execution of this Agreement,

187   ☐ Buyer, at Buyer's expense,

188   ☐ Buyer, at Seller's expense, not to exceed $ _____ ,

189 shall obtain a written "Wood-Destroying Insect Infestation Inspection Report" from a certified Pest Control Operator and will deliver it and all supporting documents and drawings provided by the Pest Control Operator to Agent for Seller, if any, otherwise to Seller. The report is to be made satisfactory to and in compliance with applicable laws, mortgage and lending institutions, and/or Federal Insuring and Guaranteeing Agency requirements, if any. The inspection will include all readily visible and accessible areas of all structures on the Property except the following structures, which will not be inspected: _____

195 (B) If the inspection reveals evidence of active infestation(s), Seller agrees, at Seller's expense and before settlement, to treat for active infestation(s), in accordance with applicable laws.

197 (C) If the inspection reveals damage from active infestation(s) or previous infestation(s), Buyer, at Buyer's expense, has the option to obtain a written report by a professional contractor, home inspection service, or structural engineer that is limited to structural damage to the Property caused by wood-destroying organisms and a proposal to repair the damage. Buyer will deliver the structural damage report and corrective proposal to Agent for Seller, if any, otherwise to Seller, within _____ days of delivering the original inspection report.

201 (D) Within 5 days of receiving the structural damage report and corrective proposal, Seller shall advise Buyer whether Seller will repair, at Seller's expense and before settlement, any structural damage from active or previous infestation(s).

203 (E) If Seller chooses to repair structural damage revealed by the report, Buyer agrees to accept the Property as repaired and agrees to the RELEASE set forth in paragraph 26 of this Agreement.

205 (F) If Seller chooses not to repair structural damage revealed by the report, Buyer, within 5 days of receiving Seller's notice, will notify Seller in writing of Buyer's choice to:

207   1. Accept the Property with the defects revealed by the inspection, without abatement of price and agree to the RELEASE set forth in paragraph 26 of this Agreement, OR

209   2. Make the repairs before settlement, if required by the mortgage lender, if any, at Buyer's expense and with Seller's permission, which shall not be unreasonably withheld, in which case Buyer accepts the Property and agrees to the RELEASE set forth in paragraph 26 of this Agreement. If Seller denies Buyer permission to make the repairs, Buyer may, within 5 days of Seller's denial, terminate this Agreement. If Buyer terminates this Agreement, all deposit monies paid on account of purchase price shall be returned promptly to Buyer and this Agreement of Sale will be NULL and VOID, OR

214   3. Terminate this Agreement, in which case all deposit monies paid on account of purchase price shall be returned promptly to Buyer and this Agreement of Sale will be NULL and VOID.

216 (G) **Buyer's failure to exercise any of Buyer's options within the time limits specified in this paragraph shall constitute a WAIVER of this contingency and Buyer accepts the Property and agrees to the RELEASE set forth in paragraph 26 of this Agreement.**

218 **10. CERTIFICATE OF OCCUPANCY (1-98)**

219 ☐ NOT APPLICABLE

220 ☐ APPLICABLE

221 (A) Buyer and Seller acknowledge that a certificate permitting occupancy of the Property may be required by the municipality and/or governmental authority.

223 (B) If a certificate is required, Seller shall, at Seller's expense and within _____ days of the execution of this Agreement, order the certificate for delivery to Buyer on or before settlement.

225 (C) In the event repairs/improvements are required for the issuance of the certificate, Seller shall, within 5 days of Seller's receipt of the requirements, notify Buyer of the requirements and whether Seller shall make the required repairs/improvements at Seller's expense.

227 (D) If Seller chooses not to make the required repairs/improvements, Buyer will, within 5 days, notify Seller in writing of Buyer's choice to terminate the Agreement of Sale OR make the repairs/improvements at Buyer's expense and with Seller's permission, which shall not be unreasonably withheld. If Seller denies Buyer permission to make the required repairs, Buyer may, within 5 days of Seller's denial, terminate this Agreement. If Buyer terminates this Agreement, all deposit monies paid on account of purchase price shall be returned promptly to Buyer and this Agreement of Sale will be NULL and VOID.

232 **11. RESIDENTIAL LEAD-BASED PAINT HAZARD REDUCTION ACT NOTICE REQUIRED FOR PROPERTIES BUILT BEFORE 1978 (1-98)**

234 ☐ NOT APPLICABLE

235 ☐ APPLICABLE

236 (A) **Seller represents that:** (check 1 OR 2)

237   ☐ 1. Seller has no knowledge concerning the presence of lead-based paint and/or lead-based paint hazards in or about the Property.

238   ☐ 2. Seller has knowledge of the presence of lead-based paint and/or lead-based paint hazards in or about the Property. (Provide the basis for determining that lead-based paint and/or hazards exist, the location(s), the condition of the painted surfaces, and other available information concerning Seller's knowledge of the presence of lead-based paint and/or lead based paint hazards.)_____

245 **Buyer Initials:** _____ A/S Residential Page 3 of 8 **Seller Initials:** _____

**Figure 18.1
(continued)**

246　　(B) **Records/Reports** (check 1 OR 2)

247　　　　☐ 1. Seller has no reports or records pertaining to lead-based paint and/or lead-based paint hazards in or about the Property.

248　　　　☐ 2. Seller has provided Buyer with all available records and reports pertaining to lead-based paint and/or lead-based paint hazards in or about

249　　　　　　the Property. (List documents) _____

250　　　　　　_____

251　　(C) **Buyer's Acknowledgment**

252　　　　☐ 1. Buyer has received the pamphlet *Protect Your Family from Lead in Your Home* and has read the Lead Warning Statement contained in this

253　　　　　　Agreement (See Environmental Notices).

254　　　　　　**Buyer's Initials** _____ **Date** _____

255　　　　☐ 2. Buyer has reviewed Seller's disclosure of known lead-based paint and/or lead-based paint hazards, as identified in paragraph 11(A) and

256　　　　　　has received the records and reports pertaining to lead-based paint and/or lead-based paint hazards identified in paragraph 11(B).

257　　　　　　**Buyer's Initials** _____ **Date** _____

258　　(D) **RISK ASSESSMENT/INSPECTION.** Buyer acknowledges that before Buyer is obligated to buy a residential dwelling built before 1978,

259　　　　Buyer has a 10 day period (unless Buyer and Seller agree in writing to a different period of time) to conduct a risk assessment or inspection of

260　　　　the Property for the presence of lead-based paint and/or lead-based paint hazards.

261　　☐　　WAIVED. Buyer understands that Buyer has the right to conduct a risk assessment or inspection of the Property to determine the presence of

262　　　　lead-based paint and/or lead-based paint hazards. BUYER WAIVES THIS RIGHT and agrees to the RELEASE set forth in paragraph 26 of

263　　　　this Agreement.

264　　☐　　ELECTED

265　　　　1.　Buyer, at Buyer's expense, chooses to obtain a risk assessment and/or inspection of the Property for lead-based paint and/or lead-based

266　　　　　　paint hazards. The risk assessment and/or inspection shall be completed within _____ days of the execution of this Agreement of Sale

267　　　　　　(insert "10" unless Buyer and Seller agree to a different period of time).

268　　　　**2.　Within the time set forth above for obtaining the risk assessment and/or inspection of the Property for lead-based paint and/or**

269　　　　　　**lead-based paint hazards, Buyer may deliver to Agent for Seller, if any, otherwise to Seller,** a written list of the specific hazardous

270　　　　　　conditions cited in the report and those corrections requested by Buyer, along with a copy of the risk assessment and/or inspection report.

271　　　　3.　Seller may, within _____ days of receiving the list and report(s), submit a written corrective proposal to Buyer. The corrective proposal

272　　　　　　will include, but not be limited to, the name of the remediation company and a completion date for corrective measures. Seller will pro-

273　　　　　　vide certification from a risk assessor or inspector that corrective measures have been made satisfactorily on or before the completion date.

274　　　　4.　Upon receiving the corrective proposal, Buyer, within 5 days, will:

275　　　　　　a.　Accept the corrective proposal and the Property in writing, and agree to the RELEASE set forth in paragraph 26 of this Agreement,

276　　　　　　　　OR

277　　　　　　b.　Terminate this Agreement in writing, in which case all deposit monies paid on account of purchase price shall be returned promptly

278　　　　　　　　to Buyer and this Agreement of Sale will be NULL and VOID.

279　　　　5.　Should Seller fail to submit a written corrective proposal within the time set forth in paragraph 11(D)3 of this Agreement, then Buyer,

280　　　　　　within 5 days, will:

281　　　　　　a.　Accept the Property in writing, and agree to the RELEASE set forth in paragraph 26 of this Agreement, OR

282　　　　　　b.　Terminate this Agreement of Sale in writing, in which case all deposit monies paid on account of purchase price shall be returned

283　　　　　　　　promptly to Buyer and this Agreement of Sale will be NULL and VOID.

284　　　　**6.　Buyer's failure to exercise any of Buyer's options within the time limits specified in this paragraph shall constitute a WAIVER of**

285　　　　　　**this contingency and Buyer accepts the Property and agrees to the RELEASE set forth in paragraph 26 of this Agreement.**

286　　(E) **Certification** By signing this Agreement, Buyer and Seller certify the accuracy of their respective statements, to the best of their knowledge.

287　**12.　RADON CONTINGENCY (1-98)**

288　　(A) Seller represents that: (check appropriate response(s))

289　　　　☐ 1. Seller has no knowledge concerning the presence or absence of radon.

290　　　　☐ 2. Seller has knowledge that the Property was tested on the dates, by the methods (e.g., charcoal canister, alpha track, etc.), and with the

291　　　　　　results of all tests indicated below:

292　　　　　　DATE　　　　METHOD　　　　　　RESULTS (picoCuries/liter or working levels)

293　　　　　　_____　_____　_____

294　　　　　　_____　_____　_____

295　　　　　　_____　_____　_____

296　　　　　　COPIES OF ALL AVAILABLE TEST REPORTS will be delivered to Buyer with this Agreement. SELLER DOES NOT WARRANT

297　　　　　　EITHER THE METHODS OR RESULTS OF THE TESTS.

298　　　　☐ 3. Seller has knowledge that the Property underwent radon reduction measures on the date(s) and by the method(s) indicated below:

299　　　　　　DATE　　　　RADON REDUCTION METHOD

300　　　　　　_____　_____

301　　　　　　_____　_____

302　　　　　　_____　_____

303　　☐　　WAIVED. Buyer understands that Buyer has the option to request that the Property be inspected for radon by a certified inspector (see Radon

304　　　　Notice). BUYER WAIVES THIS OPTION and agrees to the RELEASE set forth in paragraph 26 of this Agreement.

305　　☐　　ELECTED

306　　(B) Buyer, at Buyer's expense, has the option to obtain, from a certified inspector, a radon test of the Property and will deliver a copy of the test

307　　　　report to Agent for Seller, if any, otherwise to Seller, within _____ days of the execution of this Agreement. (See Radon Notice.)

308　　　　1.　If the test report reveals the presence of radon below 0.02 working levels (4 picoCuries/liter), Buyer accepts the Property and agrees to the

309　　　　　　RELEASE set forth in paragraph 26 of this Agreement.

310　　　　2.　If the test report reveals the presence of radon at or exceeding 0.02 working levels (4 picoCuries/liter), Buyer will, within _____ days

311　　　　　　of receipt of the test results:

312　　☐　　**Option 1**

313　　　　　　a.　Accept the Property in writing and agree to the RELEASE set forth in paragraph 26 of this Agreement, OR

314　　　　　　b.　Terminate this Agreement in writing, in which case all deposit monies paid on account of purchase price shall be returned promptly

315　　　　　　　　to Buyer and this Agreement of Sale will be NULL and VOID, OR

316　　　　　　c.　Submit a written, corrective proposal to Agent for Seller, if any, otherwise to Seller. The corrective proposal will include, but not be

317　　　　　　　　limited to, the name of the certified mitigation company; provisions for payment, including retests; and completion date for correc-

318　　　　　　　　tive measures.

319　　　　　　　　1)　Within 5 days of receiving the corrective proposal, Seller will:

320　　　　　　　　　　a)　Agree to the terms of the corrective proposal in writing, in which case Buyer accepts the Property and agrees to the

321　　　　　　　　　　　　RELEASE set forth in paragraph 26 of this Agreement, OR

322　　　　　　　　　　b)　Not agree to the terms of the corrective proposal.

326　**Buyer Initials:** _____　　　　　A/S Residential Page 4 of 8　　　　　**Seller Initials:** _____

**Figure 18.1
(continued)**

2) Should Seller not agree to the terms of the corrective proposal or fail to respond within the given time, Buyer will, within 5 days, elect to:
   a) Accept the Property in writing and agree to the RELEASE set forth in paragraph 26 of this Agreement, OR
   b) Terminate this Agreement in writing, in which case all deposit monies paid on account of purchase price shall be returned promptly to Buyer and this Agreement of Sale will be NULL and VOID.

☐ **Option 2**
   a. Accept the Property in writing and agree to the RELEASE set forth in paragraph 26 of this Agreement, OR
   b. Submit a written, corrective proposal to Agent for Seller, if any, otherwise to Seller. The corrective proposal will include, but not be limited to, the name of the certified mitigation company; provisions for payment, including retests; and completion date for corrective measures. Seller shall pay a maximum of $ _____ toward the total cost of remediation and retests, which shall be completed by settlement.
      1) If the total cost of remediation and retests EXCEEDS the amount specified in paragraph 12(B) (Option 2) b, Seller will, within 5 days of receipt of the cost of remediation, notify Buyer of Seller's choice to pay for the total cost of remediation and retests OR not pay for the total cost of remediation and retests.
      2) If the Seller chooses not to pay for the total cost of remediation and retests, Buyer will, within 5 days of receipt of Seller's notification, notify Seller, in writing, of Buyer's choice to:
         a) Pay the difference between Seller's contribution to remediation and retests and the actual cost thereof, in which case Buyer accepts the Property and agrees to the RELEASE set forth in paragraph 26 of this Agreement, OR
         b) Terminate this Agreement, in which case all deposit monies paid on account of purchase price shall be returned promptly to Buyer and this Agreement of Sale will be NULL and VOID.

(C) **Buyer's failure to exercise any of Buyer's options within the time limits specified in this paragraph shall constitute a WAIVER of this contingency and Buyer accepts the Property and agrees to the RELEASE set forth in paragraph 26 of this Agreement.**

13. **STATUS OF WATER (1-98)**
(A) Seller represents that this property is served by:
   ☐ Public Water
   ☐ On-site Water
   ☐ Community Water
   ☐ None
   ☐ _____

(B) **WATER SERVICE INSPECTION CONTINGENCY**
   ☐ WAIVED. Buyer acknowledges that Buyer has the option to request an inspection of the water service for the Property. BUYER WAIVES THIS OPTION and agrees to the RELEASE set forth in paragraph 26 of this Agreement.
   ☐ ELECTED
      1. Buyer has the option, within _____ days of the execution of this Agreement and at Buyer's expense, to deliver to Agent for Seller, if any, otherwise to Seller, a written inspection report by a qualified, professional water testing company of the quality and/or quantity of the water service.
      2. Seller agrees to locate and provide access to the on-site (or individual) water system, if applicable, at Seller's expense, if required by the inspection company. Seller also agrees to restore the Property prior to settlement.
      3. If the report reveals that the water service does not meet the minimum standards of any applicable governmental authorities and/or fails to satisfy the requirements for quality and/or quantity set by the mortgage lender, if any, then Seller shall, within _____ days of receipt of the report, notify Buyer in writing of Seller's choice to:
         a. Upgrade the water service to the minimum acceptable levels, before settlement, in which case Buyer accepts the Property and agrees to the RELEASE set forth in paragraph 26 of this Agreement, OR
         b. Not upgrade the water service.
      4. **If Seller chooses not to upgrade the water service to minimum acceptable levels, Buyer will**, within _____ days of Seller's notice not to correct, either:
         a. Accept the Property and the water service and, if required by the mortgage lender, if any, and/or any governmental authority, upgrade the water service before settlement or within the time required by the mortgage lender, if any, and/or any governmental authority, at Buyer's expense and with Seller's permission, which shall not be unreasonably withheld, and agree to the RELEASE set forth in paragraph 26 of this Agreement. If Seller denies Buyer permission to upgrade the water service, Buyer may, within 5 days of Seller's denial, terminate this Agreement. If Buyer terminates this Agreement, all deposit monies paid on account of purchase price shall be returned promptly to Buyer and this Agreement of Sale will be NULL and VOID, OR
         b. Terminate this Agreement, in which case all deposit monies paid on account of purchase price shall be returned promptly to Buyer and this Agreement of Sale will be NULL and VOID.
      5. **Buyer's failure to exercise any of Buyer's options within the time limits specified in this paragraph shall constitute a WAIVER of this contingency and Buyer accepts the Property and agrees to the RELEASE set forth in paragraph 26 of this Agreement.**

14. **STATUS OF SEWER (1-98)**
(A) Seller represents that Property is served by:
   ☐ Public Sewer
   ☐ Individual On-lot Sewage Disposal System (See Sewage Notice 1)
   ☐ Individual On-lot Sewage Disposal System in Proximity to Well (See Sewage Notice 1; see Sewage Notice 4, if applicable)
   ☐ Community Sewage Disposal System
   ☐ Ten-acre Permit Exemption (See Sewage Notice 2)
   ☐ Holding Tank (See Sewage Notice 3)
   ☐ None (See Sewage Notice 1)
   ☐ None Available/Permit Limitations in Effect (See Sewage Notice 5)
   ☐

(B) **INDIVIDUAL ON-LOT SEWAGE DISPOSAL INSPECTION CONTINGENCY**
   ☐ WAIVED. Buyer acknowledges that Buyer has the option to request an individual on-lot sewage disposal inspection of the Property. BUYER WAIVES THIS OPTION and agrees to the RELEASE set forth in paragraph 26 of this Agreement.
   ☐ ELECTED
      1. Buyer has the option, within _____ days of the execution of this Agreement and at Buyer's expense, to deliver to Agent for Seller, if any, otherwise to Seller, a written inspection report by a qualified, professional inspector of the individual on-lot sewage disposal system.
      2. Seller agrees to locate and provide access to the individual on-lot sewage disposal system, and, if required by the inspection company, empty the septic tank, at Seller's expense. Seller also agrees to restore the Property prior to settlement.
      3. If the report reveals defects that do not require expansion or replacement of the existing sewage disposal system, Seller shall, within _____ days of receipt of the report, notify Buyer in writing of Seller's choice to:
         a. Correct the defects before settlement, including retests, at Seller's expense, in which case Buyer accepts the Property and agrees to the RELEASE set forth in paragraph 26 of this Agreement, OR
         b. Not correct the defects, in which case **Buyer will**, within _____ days of Seller's notice not to correct the defects, either:
            1) Accept the Property and the system and, if required by the mortgage lender, if any, and/or any governmental authority, correct the defects before settlement or within the time required by the mortgage lender, if any, and/or any governmental authority, at Buyer's sole expense and with Seller's permission, which shall not be unreasonably withheld, and agree to the RELEASE set forth in paragraph 26 of this Agreement. If Seller denies Buyer permission to correct the defects, Buyer may, within 5 days of Seller's denial, terminate this Agreement. If Buyer terminates this Agreement, all deposit monies paid on account of purchase price shall be returned promptly to Buyer and this Agreement of Sale will be NULL and VOID, OR
            2) Terminate this Agreement in writing, in which case all deposit monies paid on account of purchase price shall be returned promptly to Buyer and this Agreement of Sale will be NULL and VOID.
      4. If the report reveals the need to expand or replace the existing individual on-lot sewage disposal system, Seller may, within _____ days of receipt of the report, submit a corrective proposal to Agent for Buyer, if any, otherwise to Buyer. The corrective proposal will include, but not be limited to, the name of the remediation company; provisions for payment, including retests; and completion date for corrective measures. Within 5 days of receiving Seller's corrective proposal, or if no corrective proposal is received within the given time, **Buyer will:**
         a. Agree to the terms of the corrective proposal, if any, in writing, in which case Buyer accepts the Property and agrees to the RELEASE set forth in paragraph 26 of this Agreement, OR

Buyer Initials: _____   A/S Residential Page 5 of 8   Seller Initials: _____

Figure 18.1 (continued)

424   b.   Accept the Property and the system and, if required by the mortgage lender, if any, and/or any governmental authority, correct the
425   defects before settlement or within the time required by the mortgage lender, if any, and/or any governmental authority, at Buyer's
426   sole expense and with Seller's permission, which shall not be unreasonably withheld, and agree to the RELEASE set forth in para-
427   graph 26 of this Agreement. If Seller denies Buyer permission to correct the defects, all deposit monies paid on account of purchase
428   price shall be returned promptly to Buyer and this Agreement of Sale will be NULL and VOID, OR
429   c.   Terminate this Agreement in writing, in which case all deposit monies paid on account of purchase price shall be returned promptly
430   to Buyer and this Agreement of Sale will be NULL and VOID.
431   5.   **Buyer's failure to exercise any of Buyer's options within the time limits specified in this paragraph shall constitute a WAIVER of**
432   **this contingency and Buyer accepts the Property and agrees to the RELEASE set forth in paragraph 26 of this Agreement.**

15. NOTICES & ASSESSMENTS (1-98)

434   (A)   Seller represents as of Seller's execution of this Agreement, that no public improvement, condominium or homeowner association assessments
435   have been made against the Property which remain unpaid and that no notice by any government or public authority has been served upon Seller
436   or anyone on Seller's behalf, including notices relating to violations of zoning, housing, building, safety or fire ordinances which remain
437   uncorrected, and that Seller knows of no condition that would constitute violation of any such ordinances which remains uncorrected, unless
438   otherwise specified here: _____ .
439   (B)   Seller knows of no other potential notices and assessments except as follows: _____
440   _____ .
441   (C)   In the event notices and assessments are received after execution of this Agreement and before settlement, Seller will notify Buyer in writing,
442   within 5 days of receiving the notice or assessment, that Seller shall:
443   1.   Comply with notices and assessments at Seller's expense, in which case Buyer accepts the Property and agrees to the RELEASE set forth
444   in paragraph 26 of this Agreement, OR
445   2.   NOT comply with notices and assessments at Seller's expense, in which case Buyer will notify Seller within 5 days in writing that
446   Buyer shall:
447   a.   Comply with the notices and assessments at Buyer's expense and agree to the RELEASE set forth in paragraph 26 of this Agreement,
448   OR
449   b.   Terminate this Agreement, in which case all deposit monies paid on account of purchase price shall be returned promptly to Buyer
450   and this Agreement of Sale will be NULL and VOID.
451   **If Buyer fails to notify Seller within the given time, Buyer accepts the Property and agrees to the RELEASE set forth in paragraph**
452   **26 of this Agreement.**
453   (D)   Buyer is advised that access to a public road may require issuance of a highway occupancy permit from the Department of Transportation.
454   (E)   If required by law, Seller shall deliver to Agent for Buyer, if any, otherwise to Buyer, on or before settlement, a certification from the appropri-
455   ate municipal department or departments disclosing notice of any uncorrected violation of zoning, housing, building, safety or fire ordinances.

16. TITLE, SURVEYS, AND COSTS (1-98)

457   (A)   The Property is to be conveyed free and clear of all liens, encumbrances, and easements, EXCEPTING HOWEVER the following: existing
458   deed restrictions, building restrictions, ordinances, easements of roads, easements visible upon the ground, easements of record, privileges or
459   rights of public service companies, if any; otherwise the title to the above described real estate shall be good and marketable and such as will
460   be insured by a reputable Title Insurance Company at the regular rates.
461   (B)   In the event Seller is unable to give a good and marketable title and such as will be insured by a reputable Title Company at the regular rates,
462   as specified in paragraph 16(A), Buyer shall have the option of taking such title as Seller can give without changing the price or of being repaid
463   all monies paid by Buyer to Seller on account of purchase price and Seller shall reimburse Buyer for any costs incurred by Buyer for those items
464   specified in paragraph 16(C) and in paragraph 16(D) items (1), (2), (3); and in the latter event there shall be no further liability or obligation on
465   either of the parties hereto and this Agreement shall become NULL and VOID.
466   (C)   Any survey or surveys which may be required by the Title Insurance Company or the abstracting attorney, for the preparation of an adequate
467   legal description of the Property (or the correction thereof), shall be secured and paid for by Seller. However, any survey or surveys desired by
468   Buyer or required by the mortgage lender shall be secured and paid for by Buyer.
469   (D)   Buyer shall pay for the following: (1) The premium for mechanics lien insurance and/or title search, or fee for cancellation of same, if any;
470   (2) The premiums for flood insurance and/or fire insurance with extended coverage, insurance binder charges or cancellation fee, if any;
471   (3) Appraisal fees and charges paid in advance to mortgage lender, if any; (4) Buyer's customary settlement costs and accruals.

17. ZONING CLASSIFICATION (1-98)

473   Failure of this Agreement to contain the zoning classification (except in cases where the property {and each parcel thereof, if subdividable} is
474   zoned solely or primarily to permit single-family dwellings) shall render this Agreement voidable at the option of the Buyer, and, if voided, any
475   deposits tendered by the Buyer shall be returned to the Buyer without any requirement for court action.
476   **Zoning Classification:** _____
477   ☐   ELECTED. Within _____ days of the execution of this Agreement, Buyer will verify that the existing use of the Property as
478   _____ is permitted. In the event the use is not permitted, **Buyer will, within the time given for**
479   **verification**, notify Agent for Seller, if any, otherwise Seller, in writing that the existing use of the Property is not permitted and this Agreement
480   will be NULL and VOID, in which case all deposit monies paid on account of purchase price shall be returned promptly to Buyer. **Buyer's fail-**
481   **ure to respond within the given time shall constitute a WAIVER of this contingency and all other terms of this Agreement of Sale remain**
482   **in full force and effect.**

18. COAL NOTICE

484   ☐   NOT APPLICABLE
485   ☐   APPLICABLE
486   THIS DOCUMENT MAY NOT SELL, CONVEY, TRANSFER, INCLUDE OR INSURE THE TITLE TO THE COAL AND RIGHTS OF SUPPORT UNDERNEATH THE SURFACE LAND
487   DESCRIBED OR REFERRED TO HEREIN, AND THE OWNER OR OWNERS OF SUCH COAL MAY HAVE THE COMPLETE LEGAL RIGHT TO REMOVE ALL SUCH COAL AND
488   IN THAT CONNECTION, DAMAGE MAY RESULT TO THE SURFACE OF THE LAND AND ANY HOUSE, BUILDING OR OTHER STRUCTURE ON OR IN SUCH LAND. (This
489   notice is set forth in the manner provided in Section 1 of the Act of July 17, 1957, P.L. 984.) "Buyer acknowledges that he may not be obtaining the
490   right of protection against subsidence resulting from coal mining operations, and that the property described herein may be protected from damage
491   due to mine subsidence by a private contract with the owners of the economic interests in the coal. This acknowledgment is made for the purpose of
492   complying with the provisions of Section 14 of the Bituminous Mine Subsidence and the Land Conservation Act of April 27, 1966." Buyer agrees
493   to sign the deed from Seller which deed will contain the aforesaid provision.

19. POSSESSION (1-98)

495   (A)   Possession is to be delivered by deed, keys and:
496   1.   Physical possession to a vacant building (if any) broom clean, free of debris at day and time of settlement, AND/OR
497   2.   Assignment of existing lease(s), together with any security deposits and interest, at time of settlement, if Property is tenant occupied at the
498   execution of this Agreement or unless otherwise specified herein. Buyer will acknowledge existing lease(s) by initialing said lease(s) at
499   time of signing of this Agreement of Sale, if Property is tenant occupied.
500   (B)   Seller shall not enter into any new leases, written extension of existing leases, if any, or additional leases for the Property without expressed
501   written consent of Buyer.

20. RECORDING (3-85) This Agreement shall not be recorded in the Office for the Recording of Deeds or in any other office or place of public record
503   and if Buyer causes or permits this Agreement to be recorded, Seller may elect to treat such act as a breach of this Agreement.

21. ASSIGNMENT (3-85) This Agreement shall be binding upon the parties, their respective heirs, personal representatives, guardians and successors,
505   and to the extent assignable, on the assigns of the parties hereto, it being expressly understood, however, that Buyer shall not transfer or assign this
506   Agreement without the written consent of Seller.

22. DEPOSIT AND RECOVERY FUND (1-98)

508   (A)   Deposits paid by Buyer within 30 days of settlement shall be by cashier's or certified check. Deposits, regardless of the form of payment and
509   the person designated as payee, shall be paid to Agent identified in paragraph 3(F), who shall retain them in an escrow account until consum-
510   mation or termination of this Agreement in conformity with all applicable laws and regulations. Agent may hold any uncashed check tendered
511   as deposit pending the acceptance of this offer.
512   (B)   In the event of a dispute over entitlement to deposit monies, the Agent holding the deposit is required by the Rules and Regulations of the State
513   Real Estate Commission (49 Pa. Code §35.327) to retain the monies in escrow until the dispute is resolved. In the event of litigation for the
514   return of deposit monies, Agent shall distribute the monies as directed by a final order of court or the written Agreement of the parties. Buyer
515   and Seller agree that, in the event any Agent herein is joined in litigation for the return of deposit monies, the attorneys' fees and costs of the
516   Agent(s) will be paid by the party joining the Agent.

520   **Buyer Initials:** _____   A/S Residential Page 6 of 8   **Seller Initials:** _____

**Figure 18.1
(continued)**

521   (C) A Real Estate Recovery Fund exists to reimburse any persons who have obtained a final civil judgment against a Pennsylvania real estate
522   licensee owing to fraud, misrepresentation, or deceit in a real estate transaction and who have been unable to collect the judgment after exhaust-
523   ing all legal and equitable remedies. For complete details about the Fund, call (717) 783-3658, or (800) 882-2113 (within Pennsylvania) and
524   (717) 783-4854 (outside Pennsylvania).

525 **23. CONDOMINIUM RESALE ACT NOTICE (8-95)**
526   ☐ NOT APPLICABLE
527   ☐ APPLICABLE
528   (A) Buyer acknowledges that the Property is a unit of a condominium that is primarily run by a unit owners' association.
529   (B) §3407 of the Uniform Condominium Act of Pennsylvania requires Seller to furnish Buyer with a Certificate of Resale and copies of the condo-
530   minium declaration (other than plats and plans), the bylaws, and the rules and regulations of the association.
531   (C) Within _____ days of the execution of this Agreement, Seller shall submit a request to the association for a Certificate of Resale and the doc-
532   uments necessary to enable Seller to comply with the Act. The Act provides that the association is required to provide these documents within
533   10 days of Seller's request.
534   (D) Under the Act, Seller is not liable to Buyer for the failure or delay of the association to provide the Certificate in a timely manner, nor is Seller
535   liable to Buyer for any erroneous information provided by the association and included in the Certificate.
536   (E) Buyer may declare the Agreement of Sale VOID at any time before Buyer's receipt of the Certificate of Resale and for 5 days thereafter, OR
537   until settlement, whichever occurs first. Buyer's notice declaring the Agreement void must be in writing; thereafter all deposit monies shall be
538   returned to Buyer.

539 **24. PLANNED COMMUNITY (HOMEOWNER ASSOCIATION) NOTICE FOR PURPOSES OF RESALE ONLY (1-97)**
540   ☐ NOT APPLICABLE
541   ☐ APPLICABLE
542   (A) Buyer acknowledges that the Property is part of a planned community as defined by the Uniform Planned Community Act. (See Definition of
543   Planned Community Notice for the definition contained in the Act).
544   (B) §5407(a) of the Act requires Seller to furnish Buyer with a copy of the Declaration (other than plats and plans), the bylaws, the rules and regu-
545   lations of the association, and a Certificate containing the provisions set forth in §5407(a) of the Act.
546   (C) Within _____ days of the execution of this agreement, Seller shall submit a request to the association for a Certificate and the documents nec-
547   essary to enable Seller to comply with the Act. The Act provides that the association is required to provide these documents within 10 days of
548   Seller's request.
549   (D) Under the Act, Seller is not liable to Buyer for the failure or delay of the association to provide the Certificate in a timely manner, nor is Seller
550   liable to Buyer for any erroneous information provided by the Association and included in the Certificate.
551   (E) Buyer may declare the Agreement of Sale VOID at any time before Buyer's receipt of the association documents and for 5 days thereafter, OR
552   until settlement, whichever occurs first. Buyer's notice declaring the Agreement void must be in writing; thereafter all deposit monies shall be
553   returned to Buyer.

554 **25. MAINTENANCE AND RISK OF LOSS (1-98)**
555   (A) Seller shall maintain the Property, grounds, fixtures, and any personal property specifically scheduled herein in its present condition, normal
556   wear and tear excepted.
557   (B) In the event any system or appliance included in the sale of the Property fails and Seller does not repair or replace the item, Seller will promptly
558   notify Buyer in writing of Seller's choice to: .
559   1. Repair or replace the failed system or appliance before settlement or credit Buyer at settlement for the fair market value of the failed sys-
560   tem or appliance (this option must be acceptable to the mortgage lender, if any). In each case, Buyer accepts the Property and agrees to
561   the RELEASE set forth in paragraph 26 of this Agreement.
562   2. Make no repairs or replacements, and not credit Buyer at settlement for the fair market value of the failed system or appliance, in which
563   case Buyer will notify Seller in writing within 5 days or before settlement, whichever is sooner, that Buyer shall:
564   a. Accept the Property and agree to the RELEASE set forth in paragraph 26 of this Agreement, OR
565   b. Terminate this Agreement, in which case all deposit monies paid on account of purchase price shall be returned promptly to Buyer
566   and this Agreement of Sale will be NULL and VOID.
567   (C) Seller shall bear risk of loss from fire or other casualties until time of settlement. In the event of damage by fire or other casualties to any prop-
568   erty included in this sale that is not repaired or replaced prior to settlement, Buyer shall have the option of rescinding this Agreement and
569   promptly receiving all monies paid on account of purchase price or of accepting the Property in its then condition together with the proceeds
570   of any insurance recovery obtainable by Seller. Buyer is hereby notified that Buyer may insure Buyer's equitable interest in this Property as of
571   the time of execution of this Agreement.
572   **Buyer's failure to exercise any of Buyer's options within the time limits specified in this paragraph shall constitute a WAIVER of this con-**
573   **tingency and Buyer accepts the Property and agrees to the RELEASE set forth in paragraph 26 of this Agreement.**

574 **26. RELEASE (7-96) — Buyer hereby releases, quit claims and forever discharges SELLER, ALL AGENTS, their SUBAGENTS, EMPLOY-**
575   **EES, and any OFFICER or PARTNER of any one of them and any other PERSON, FIRM, or CORPORATION who may be liable by or**
576   **through them, from any and all claims, losses or demands, including, but not limited to, personal injuries and property damage and all of**
577   **the consequences thereof, whether now known or not, which may arise from the presence of termites or other wood-boring insects, radon,**
578   **lead-based paint hazards, environmental hazards, any defects in the individual on-lot sewage disposal system or deficiencies in the on-site**
579   **water service system, or any defects or conditions on the Property. This release shall survive settlement.**

580 **27. REPRESENTATIONS (1-98)**
581   (A) Buyer understands that any representations, claims, advertising, promotional activities, brochures or plans of any kind made by Seller, Agents
582   or their employees are not a part of this Agreement, unless expressly incorporated or stated in this Agreement.
583   (B) **It is understood that Buyer has inspected the Property before signing this Agreement of Sale (including fixtures and any personal prop-**
584   **erty specifically scheduled herein), or has waived the right to do so, and has agreed to purchase it in its present condition unless**
585   **otherwise stated in this Agreement. Buyer acknowledges that the Agents have not made an independent examination or determination**
586   **of the structural soundness of the Property, the age or condition of the components, environmental conditions, the permitted uses, or**
587   **of conditions existing in the locale where the Property is situated; nor have they made a mechanical inspection of any of the systems**
588   **contained therein.**
589   (C) It is further understood that this Agreement contains the whole agreement between Seller and Buyer and there are no other terms, obligations,
590   covenants, representations, statements or conditions, oral or otherwise of any kind whatsoever concerning this sale. Furthermore, this
591   Agreement shall not be altered, amended, changed, or modified except in writing executed by the parties.
592   (D) The headings, captions, and line numbers in this Agreement are meant only to make it easier to find the paragraphs.

593 **28. DEFAULT-TIME OF THE ESSENCE (1-98)**
594   The said time for settlement and all other times referred to for the performance of any of the obligations of this Agreement are hereby agreed to be
595   of the essence of this Agreement. For the purposes of this Agreement, number of days shall be counted from the date of execution, by excluding the
596   day this Agreement was executed and including the last day of the time period. Should Buyer:
597   (A) Fail to make any additional payments as specified in paragraph 3; OR
598   (B) Furnish false or incomplete information to Seller, Agent for Seller, Agent for Buyer, or the mortgage lender, if any, concerning Buyer's legal or
599   financial status, or fail to cooperate in the processing of the mortgage loan application, which acts would result in the failure to obtain the
600   approval of a mortgage loan commitment; OR
601   (C) Violate or fail to fulfill and perform any other terms or conditions of this Agreement;
602   then in such case, Seller shall have the option of retaining all deposit monies and other sums paid by Buyer on account of purchase price,
603   whether required by this Agreement or not, only as elected below: (Check only one)
604   ☐ As liquidated damages. In this event Buyer and Seller shall be released from further liability or obligation and this Agreement shall be
605   NULL and VOID.
606   ☐ On account of purchase price, or as monies to be applied to Seller's damages, or as liquidated damages for such breach, as Seller may
607   elect. In the event of liquidated damages, Buyer and Seller shall be released from further liability or obligation and this Agreement shall
608   be NULL and VOID.

609 **29. AGENT(S) (1-98)** It is expressly understood and agreed between the parties that the named Agent for Seller, any Subagents, their salespeople,
610   employees, officers and/or partners, are Agent(s) for Seller, and that the named Agent for the Buyer, their salespeople, employees, officers and/or
611   partners, are Agent(s) for Buyer. If there is no Agent for Buyer, Agent for Seller or Subagent for Seller may perform services for Buyer in connec-
612   tion with financing, insurance and document preparation, with written disclosure to Buyer and Seller.

617   **Buyer Initials:** _____   A/S Residential Page 7 of 8   **Seller Initials:** _____

**Figure 18.1
(continued)**

618 **30. MEDIATION (7-96)**
619   ☐   NOT AVAILABLE
620   ☐   WAIVED. Buyer and Seller understand that they may choose to mediate at a later date, should a dispute arise, but that there will be no oblig-
621   ation on the part of any party to do so.
622   ☐   ELECTED
623   (A) Buyer and Seller will try to resolve any dispute or claim that may arise from this Agreement of Sale through mediation, in accordance with the
624   Rules and Procedures of the Home Sellers/Home Buyers Dispute Resolution System. Any agreement reached through a mediation conference
625   and signed by the parties will be binding.
626   (B) Buyer and Seller acknowledge that they have received, read, and understand the Rules and Procedures of the Home Sellers/Home Buyers
627   Dispute Resolution System. (See Mediation Notice.)
628   (C) This agreement to mediate disputes arising from this Agreement shall survive settlement.
629
630 **Buyer and Seller acknowledge that they have read and understand the notices and explanatory information regarding property condition inspec-**
631 **tions set forth on the back of this form.**
632
633   **NOTICE TO PARTIES: WHEN SIGNED, THIS AGREEMENT IS A BINDING CONTRACT. Return by facsimile transmission (FAX) of this**
634 **Agreement of Sale, and all addenda, bearing the signatures of all parties, constitutes acceptance of this Agreement. Parties to this transaction**
635 **are advised to consult an attorney before signing if they desire legal advice.**
636
637 **WITNESS** _____ **BUYER** _____ **DATE** _____
638 **WITNESS** _____ **BUYER** _____ **DATE** _____
639 **WITNESS** _____ **BUYER** _____ **DATE** _____
640
641
642 Seller hereby approves the above contract this _____ day of _____ A.D. _____
643 and in consideration of the services rendered in procuring the Buyer, Seller agrees to pay the named Agent for Seller a fee of _____
644 off/from the herein specified sale price. In the event Buyer defaults hereunder, any monies paid on account shall be divided _____ ,
645 Seller, _____ , Agent for Seller, but in no event will the sum paid to the Agent for Seller be in excess of the above specified
646 Agent's fee.
647
648 **WITNESS** _____ **SELLER** _____ **DATE** _____
649 **WITNESS** _____ **SELLER** _____ **DATE** _____
650 **WITNESS** _____ **SELLER** _____ **DATE** _____
651
652 **Services to Buyer**
653 In conjunction with this Agreement of Sale, by initialing below, Buyer authorizes Subagent for Seller, if any, or Agent for Seller to perform the following
654 services on Buyer's behalf:
655
656 _____ Order Title Insurance from any reputable Title Insurance Company.
657 Buyer's Initials
658
659 _____ Order Homeowner's Insurance with coverage in the amount of $ _____ .
660 Buyer's Initials
661
662 _____ Order Fire & Extended Coverage Insurance with coverage in the amount of $ _____ .
663 Buyer's Initials
664
665 _____ Order Flood Insurance with coverage in the amount of $ _____ .
666 Buyer's Initials
667
668 _____ Buyer's Services_____ Fee: $ _____ .
669 Buyer's Initials
670
671 _____ _____ .
672 Buyer's Initials
673
674 **Seller's Acknowledgment**
675 _____ Seller acknowledges receipt of a separate Buyer's services agreement with Agent for Seller or Subagent for Seller.
676 Seller's Initials
677
678
679 **Broker's/Agent's Certifications (check all that are applicable):**
680   ☐   **Regarding Lead-Based Paint Hazards Disclosure: Required if Property was built before 1978:** The undersigned Agents involved in this
681   transaction, on behalf of themselves and their brokers, certify that their statements are true to the best of their knowledge and belief.
682   **Agents' Acknowledgment:** The Agents involved in this transaction have informed Seller of Seller's obligations under The Residential Lead
683   Paint Hazard Reduction Act, 42 U.S.C. 4852(d), and are aware of their responsibility to ensure compliance.
684
685   ☐   **Regarding FHA Mortgages:** The undersigned Agents involved in this transaction, on behalf of themselves and their brokers, certify that the
686   terms of this contract for purchase are true to the best of their knowledge and belief, and that any other agreement entered into by any of these
687   parties in connection with this transaction is attached to this Agreement of Sale.
688
689   ☐   **Regarding Mediation:** The undersigned
690   ☐ Agent for Seller ☐ Agent for Buyer ☐ Subagent for Seller
691   on behalf of themselves and their brokers, agree to submit to mediation in accordance with paragraph 30 of this Agreement.
692
693
694 AGENT FOR SELLER (Company Name) _____
695   ACCEPTED BY _____ DATE _____
696   (Signature of Broker or Salesperson)
697
698
699 SUBAGENT FOR SELLER (Company Name) _____
700   ACCEPTED BY _____ DATE _____
701   (Signature of Broker or Salesperson)
702
703
704 AGENT FOR BUYER (Company Name) _____
705   ACCEPTED BY _____ DATE _____
706   (Signature of Broker or Salesperson)
707
708
709
710
711 **Buyer Initials:** _____   **A/S Residential Page 8 of 8**   **Seller Initials:** _____

SELLER'S COPY

must be specific about the rights and privileges of the parties. When a contract is vague and one party sues the other based on one of the terms of the agreement, the court may refuse to uphold the contract. Real estate licensees who are at fault because of the vagueness or inadequacy of a contract they have prepared can be liable for the injury a party to the contract suffers.

Offer

A broker lists an owner's real estate for sale at the price and conditions set by the owner. This is considered to be an invitation for prospective buyers to make offers to purchase. A buyer who wants to purchase the property prepares a proposal—an offer—and signs it. Then the agent presents the offer to the seller.

Earnest money. It is customary for a purchaser to provide a deposit, usually in the form of a check, when making an offer. This is known as an **earnest money** or *hand money* deposit. *It gives evidence of the purchaser's intention to carry out the terms of the contract.* The earnest money is given to the broker, who is then required to deposit it in the escrow account by the end of the next business day after it is received. If agreed to in writing by all principals, the earnest money can be held by either the listing broker or the selling broker, depending upon who is indicated in the sales agreement. With the written permission of both the buyer and seller, the broker may refrain from depositing the money until the offer is accepted. If the offer is not accepted, the earnest money is returned to the would-be buyer.

The amount of the deposit is a matter to be agreed upon by the parties. The agent of the seller is obliged to accept a reasonable amount as earnest money. The deposit should be sufficient to discourage the buyer from defaulting, to compensate the seller for taking the property off the market and to cover any expenses the seller might incur if the buyer defaults. The escrow money deposit (less any previously agreed-upon amount of commission that may be owed the broker) becomes the seller's property as liquidated damages if the buyer defaults.

The agent must accurately represent to the seller the form of the earnest money—for example, cash, check or note. The seller must be aware of the potential difficulty in collecting the funds if a note is given. Although the note is made payable to the broker (as is a check), it should be a negotiable instrument containing a confession of judgment. The defaulted note may be endorsed to the seller to pursue collection. The broker is also at considerable risk when misrepresenting that earnest money exists when, if in fact, it does not. In the event the buyer defaults and there are no funds being held on behalf of the seller, the broker may be liable to the seller for damages.

Under state law a broker shall deposit money received that belongs to another into an **escrow account** in a federally or state-insured bank or depository. This money cannot be *commingled,* or mixed, with a broker's business or personal funds. However, the law does permit a broker to deposit personal monies into the escrow account to cover service charges assessed by the banking institution. A broker may not use escrow funds for his or her own personal use; this illegal act is known as *conversion.* A broker does not need to open a special escrow account for each earnest money deposit received; all funds can be deposited into one account. A broker should maintain full, complete and accurate records of all earnest money deposits.

The escrow account is not normally an interest-bearing account. However, if the money is expected to be held for more than six months, the broker is encouraged to deposit it in an interest-bearing escrow account. Interest should be held and disbursed in the same manner as the principal amount, unless the parties to the transaction direct otherwise in the agreement. Refer to the Pennsylvania licensing law and Real Estate Commission's Rules and Regulations for specific requirements governing escrow accounts.

There is some uncertainty as to exactly who owns the earnest money once it is put on deposit. Until the offer is officially accepted, the money is, in a sense, the buyer's. Once the seller accepts the offer, however, the buyer may not secure the return of the money, even though the seller is not entitled to it until the transaction has been completed. Under no circumstances does the money belong to the broker. It is absolutely necessary to be sure that these funds are properly protected pending a final decision on their disbursement.

Binder. A shorter document, known as a *binder,* may be prepared for the purchaser to sign. This document states the essential terms of the purchaser's offer and acknowledges receipt of the deposit. It also provides that the parties agree to have a more formal and complete contract of sale drawn up by an attorney when the seller accepts and signs the binder. A binder receipt may be customary in some parts of the country or in situations in which the details of the transaction are too complex for the standard sales contract form.

The Statute of Frauds provides that in order to bring an action for performance, the contract for the sale of real estate must be in writing and signed by the seller. A written agreement establishes the interest of the purchaser and the purchaser's rights to enforce that interest by court action. It prevents the seller from selling the property to another person who might offer a higher price. The signed contract agreement also obligates the buyer to complete the transaction according to the terms agreed upon in the contract.

Counteroffer

Any attempt by the seller to change the terms proposed by the buyer creates a *counteroffer.* The original offer ceases because the seller has rejected it, which also relieves the buyer from the offer. The buyer can accept the seller's counteroffer or can reject it and, if desired, make another counteroffer. Any change in the last offer made results in a counteroffer, until one party finally agrees to the other party's last offer and both parties sign the final contract.

An offer or counteroffer *may be withdrawn at any time before it has been accepted,* even if the person making the offer or counteroffer has agreed to keep the offer open for a set period of time.

Acceptance

If the seller agrees to the offer *exactly as it was made* and signs the contract, the offer has been *accepted* and the contract is *valid*. The broker must then communicate the seller's acceptance, preferably by delivering a signed copy of the contract, to the buyer.

An offer is not considered accepted until the person making the offer has been *notified of the other party's acceptance.* When the parties are communicating through agents or at a distance, questions may arise regarding whether an acceptance, a rejection or a counteroffer has effectively occurred. Currently, the use of telephones and electronic communication devices is popular. However, the lender will most likely request an original at closing. A signed agreement that is faxed would constitute adequate communication. The real estate broker or salesperson must transmit all offers, acceptances or other responses as soon as possible to avoid questions of proper communication.

Negotiation of an agreement of sale creates certain responsibilities for the salesperson, who has the duty to present *all* offers and counteroffers and to communicate acceptances *as soon as possible.* As simple as this sounds, the process can be complicated when multiple offers are generated at the same time, during negotiations involving a counteroffer or after the seller has accepted an offer. A great deal of care is required to ensure that the seller-client's interests are protected. The salesperson has no authority, on behalf of the seller, to decide the merits of an offer; thus, all offers must be presented. Because the seller can perform only on one agreement, the seller must be cautioned about the liability of signing multiple agreements. Good communications between the salesperson and the buyer, seller and cooperating broker (if one is involved) during the negotiations can avoid any question about whether an acceptance, a rejection or a counteroffer has occurred.

Equitable title. When buyers sign a contract to purchase real estate, they do not receive title to the land; title transfers only by delivery and acceptance of a deed. However, after both buyer and seller have executed a sales contract, the buyer acquires an interest in the land known as **equitable title.** Equitable title is the right to obtain absolute ownership to a property when the legal title is held in another person's name. Acquisition of equitable title gives the buyer an insurable interest in the property, which the buyer can protect with an insurance binder until legal title transfers. If the parties decide not to go through with the purchase and sale, the buyer may be required to release the equitable interest in the real estate.

Destruction of premises. In Pennsylvania, once the sales contract is signed by both parties but before the deed is delivered (and unless the contract provides otherwise), the buyer must bear the loss of any damage to or *destruction* of the property by fire or other casualty. Through laws and court decisions, however, a growing number of states have placed the risk of any such loss on the seller. The seller may be held liable for a loss if the seller was negligent, is unable to deliver good title or has delayed the closing of the transaction. In practice, the agreement of sale usually explains risk of loss to avoid confusion. In any case, the seller should maintain adequate insurance through the date of closing, and the buyer commonly insures the equitable interest.

IN PRACTICE...	*Most residential licensees use preprinted forms for agreements of sale. Because there are several forms that are commonly used, it is important that licensees have a thorough understanding of the form they are using. Salespeople should be able to explain the form to buyers and sellers before they sign a contract. However, licensees should not practice law by interpreting how specific provisions affect a person's individual position. A buyer and seller should be given the opportunity to have their attorneys review a contract before they sign it.*
	Nonresidential saleas transactions are rarely as similar to one another as residential ones are, so most contracts are individually drafted to provide for the specific conditions of these sales. Preprinted forms normally are not satisfactory, and forms that are designed for residential transactions should not be used for the sale of nonresidential properties.

Parts of an Agreement of Sale

All real estate sales contracts can be divided into a number of general parts. Although each form of contract will contain these divisions, their location in the contract may vary. Study the sample contract in Figure 18.1 to determine the exact terms of agreement. This contract is divided into the following main sections:

- identification of the seller and buyer;

- legal or adequate description of the real estate involved;

- statement of the type of deed the seller agrees to give, including the conditions and provisions (interests of others) to which the deed will be made subject, sometimes known as the "subject to" section of the contract;

- consideration statement of the purchase price and how the purchaser intends to pay for the property, including provision for an earnest money deposit and the conditions of any mortgage financing the purchaser intends to obtain;

- provisions for the closing and the purchaser's possession of the property, including dates;

- provisions for title evidence;

- provisions for prorations, which are adjustments for taxes, insurance, fuel and the like;

- provisions in the event of destruction or damage to premises;

- provisions for default;

- provisions for contingencies;

- miscellaneous provisions; and

- dates and signatures.

Although it is not an essential requirement under basic contract law, the Statute of Frauds requires real estate agreements of sale to include the signatures of the seller and an adequate legal description of the property being conveyed. When sellers are co-owners, all must sign if the entire ownership is being transferred. Corporate seals are required, accompanied by the signature of the authorized corporate representative, when a corporation is a party to a contract. An individual holding a properly executed power of attorney may execute his or her signature on behalf of an owner. A power of attorney to convey real estate must be notarized to be recorded; it must be recorded to be effective. Section 35.332 of the Commission's Regulations prohibit a listing agreement from giving the broker authority to execute a signed agreement of sale for the owner.

Addenda

An agreement of sale may include an **addenda**, which are additional agreements attached to and made part of the agreement of sale. *Addendum* is the singular term. Because of a buyer's concerns about the property's physical and environmental conditions, common addenda include provisions for inspections. Experts in these fields can be hired to provide inspection reports so that the purchaser is adequately informed about these conditions. Inspections may include those for wood-boring insects, structural and mechanical systems, sewage facilities and radon or other hazardous substances.

Contingencies create additional conditions that must be satisfied before an agreement is fully enforceable. They specify actions that are necessary to satisfy the contingency, the time frame in which these actions must be performed and who is responsible for paying any cost that might be involved. The most common is a mortgage contingency, which protects the buyer's earnest money until a lender has committed to the mortgage loan. A common practice in some areas is to make the agreement of sale contingent on the inspections referred to above.

A purchaser who has another house to sell may make the contract contingent on the sale of the buyer's current home. A "kick out" or "back out" clause, as this is known, protects the buyer from being legally bound to the purchase before being assured that the existing home is sold. The seller may insist on an escape clause that would allow the seller to continue to solicit additional buyers. If an offer that is more favorable to the seller comes forth, the original buyer retains the right to either eliminate the contingency or to void the contract.

Disclosures Required by License Law

According to Section 608.2 of the state's license law, the agreement of sale must contain a statement disclosing that the broker is an agent of the seller or an agent of the buyer. It must also contain a statement describing the purpose of the Real Estate Recovery Fund established by the Act and the telephone number of the Real Estate Commission at which the purchaser can receive further information about the fund. (This disclosure was already made to the seller in the listing contract.)

There must be a statement of the zoning classification of the property, except in cases where the property is zoned solely or primarily to permit single-family dwellings. Failure to comply with this requirement shall render the sales agreement voidable at the option of the buyer. If voided, any deposits tendered by the buyer shall be returned without any requirement for court action.

There must be a statement that access to a public road may require issuance of a highway occupancy permit from the Department of Transportation.

The buyer must read and acknowledge receipt of the Seller's Property Disclosure Statement prior to signing the agreement of sale.

A lead-based paint disclosure is included for property built prior to 1978, and a sewage facilities disclosure is included informing the buyer if the property is not serviced by a community sewage system or indicating to the buyer the type of septic system that is currently on the property.

Finally, if the agreement involves the sale of a time-share, condominium or planned community (with a homeowner's association), the law requires additional disclosures regarding the buyer's right to rescind the purchase.

Estimated Statements of Closing Costs

Before an agreement of sale is signed, real estate licensees are required to provide each party with written *estimated statements of closing costs.* These estimates are to include any reasonably foreseeable expenses that are associated with the sale of the property. They include broker's commission, mortgage payments and financing costs, taxes and assessments, and settlement expenses. The estimated cost forms should be as accurate as can be expected of persons having knowledge of and experience in the field.

IN PRACTICE...

Licensees must comply with certain requirements that are detailed in the Real Estate Licensing and Registration Act and Rules and Regulations when they are selling real estate. See Sections 604 and 607 in the Act and Sections 35.281, 35.321–.324, 35.327, 35.281, 35.333–.334 in the Rules and Regulations. (Refer to Chapter 13 and Appendix C.)

OPTION AGREEMENTS

An **option** is a *unilateral contract by which an optionor (generally an owner) gives an optionee (a prospective purchaser or lessee) the right to buy or lease the owner's property at a fixed price within a stated period of time.* The optionee pays a fee (the agreed-upon consideration) for this option right and assumes no obligation until he or she decides, within the specified time, to exercise the option right (to buy or lease the property) or to allow the option right to expire. The owner may be bound to sell; the optionee is not bound to buy. An option is enforceable by only one party—the optionee.

For example, for a consideration of a specified amount of money, a present owner (optionor) agrees to give an optionee an irrevocable right to buy real estate at a certain price for a limited period of time. At the time the option is signed by the parties, the owner does not sell nor does the optionee buy. They merely agree that the optionee will have the right to buy and the owner will be obligated to sell *if* the optionee decides to exercise his or her right of option. Options must contain all the terms and provisions required for a valid contract.

The option agreement, which is a unilateral contract, requires the optionor to act only after the optionee gives notice that he or she elects to execute the option and buy. If the option is not exercised within the time specified, then the optionor's obligation and the optionee's right expire, unless the contract provides for a renewal. The optionee cannot recover the consideration paid for the option right. The contract may state whether the money paid for the option is to be applied to the purchase price of the real estate if the option is exercised.

A common application of an option is a lease that includes an option for the tenant to purchase the property. Options on commercial real estate are frequently made dependent on the fulfillment of specific conditions, such as obtaining a zoning change or a building permit. The optionee is usually obligated to exercise the option if the conditions are met. Similar terms could also be included in a sales contract.

INSTALLMENT CONTRACTS

A real estate sale can be made under an **installment contract,** sometimes called a *contract for deed, land contract of sale* or *articles of agreement.* Under a typical installment contract the seller, also known as the *vendor,* retains fee ownership, while the buyer, known as the *vendee,* takes possession and gets an equitable interest in the property. The buyer agrees to give the seller a down payment and pay regular monthly installments of principal and interest over a number of years. The buyer also agrees to pay real estate taxes, insurance premiums and repairs and upkeep on the property. Although the buyer obtains possession when the contract is signed by both parties, *the seller is not obligated to execute and deliver a deed to the buyer until the terms of the contract have been satisfied.* Under most installment contracts, the buyer is entitled to a deed as soon as he or she is able to complete the terms of the contract.

Real estate is occasionally sold with the new buyer assuming an existing installment contract from the original buyer/vendee. Generally, the seller/vendor must approve the new purchaser.

Default of Contract

Installment contracts usually include a provision that a *default* by the buyer permits the seller to forfeit the contract, retain all payments already made and evict the buyer. In some states, however, laws have been enacted that require the seller to refund to the buyer any payments received in excess of a reasonable rental or use value of the property. A defaulted installment contract may have to be foreclosed in the same manner as a mortgage.

IN PRACTICE...

Legislatures and courts have not looked favorably on the harsh provisions of some real estate installment contracts. A seller and buyer contemplating such a sale should first consult an attorney to make sure that the agreement meets all legal requirements and addresses the individual concerns of the parties.

KEY TERMS

agreement of sale
addenda
contingencies
earnest money

escrow account
equitable title
installment contract
option

SUMMARY

Contracts frequently used in the sale of real estate include agreements of sale, options and installment contracts. To be enforceable, these contracts must be in writing and contain the essential elements for a valid contract.

An agreement of sale binds a buyer and a seller to a definite transaction, as described in detail in the contract. The buyer is bound to purchase the property for the amount stated in the agreement. The seller is bound to deliver a good and marketable title, free from liens and encumbrances (except those allowed by the "subject to" clause of the contract). These contracts frequently include additional provisions and contingencies that must be satisfied.

In Pennsylvania, an agreement of sale must include disclosures of whom the broker represents, the existence of the Real Estate Recovery Fund, zoning classification (unless the property is zoned for single-family dwellings), a statement regarding highway access, the Seller's Property Disclosure Statement, the lead-based paint statement, and the sewage facilities statement.

Under an option agreement, the optionee purchases from the optionor for a limited time period the exclusive right to purchase or lease the optionor's property. For a potential purchaser or lessee, an option is a means of buying time to consider or complete arrangements for a transaction.

An installment contract, or contract for deed, is a sales/financing arrangement under which a buyer purchases a seller's real estate "on time." The buyer may take possession of and responsibility for the property but does not receive the deed until the terms of the contract are complete.

Questions

1. A real estate purchaser is said to have *equitable title* when
   a. the sales contract is signed by both buyer and seller.
   b. the transaction is closed.
   c. escrow is opened.
   d. a contract for deed is paid off.

2. The sales contract says *J* will purchase only if his wife flies up and approves the sale by the following Saturday. Her approval is a
   a. contingency.   c. warranty.
   b. reservation.   d. consideration.

3. When the buyer promises to purchase the seller's property only if he can sell his present home, the buyer can be protected from owning two homes by
   a. an escrow.
   b. an option.
   c. an equitable title.
   d. a contingency.

4. An option to purchase binds
   a. the buyer only.
   b. the seller only.
   c. neither buyer nor seller.
   d. both buyer and seller.

5. Which of the following best describes a land contract or installment contract?
   a. A contract to buy land only
   b. A mortgage on land
   c. A means of conveying title immediately whereby the purchaser pays for the property in installments
   d. A method of selling real estate whereby the purchaser pays in regular installments while the seller retains title

6. The purchaser of real estate under an installment contract
   a. generally pays no interest charge.
   b. receives title immediately.
   c. is not required to pay property taxes for the duration of the contract.
   d. is called a vendee.

7. The *F*s offer in writing to purchase a house for $120,000, including its draperies, with the offer to expire on Saturday at noon. The *W*s reply in writing on Thursday, accepting the $120,000 offer but excluding the draperies. On Friday, while the *F*s are considering this counteroffer, the *W*s decide to accept the original offer, draperies included, and state that in writing. At this point, the *F*'s
   a. must buy the house and have the right to insist on the draperies.
   b. are not bound to buy.
   c. must buy the house but are not entitled to the draperies.
   d. must buy the house and can deduct the value of the draperies from the $120,000.

8. *Q* makes an offer to purchase certain property listed with broker *M* and leaves a deposit with broker *M* to show good faith. *M* should
   a. immediately apply the deposit to the listing expenses.
   b. put the deposit in an account as provided by state law.
   c. give the deposit to the seller when the offer is presented.
   d. put the deposit in her checking account.

9. A buyer wants to make an offer to purchase a house that she suspects has a wet basement. The buyer is afraid that the house may be sold to someone else before she has a chance to get information about the structure. How should she proceed?

   a. Ask the real estate salesperson to guarantee that the basement is dry
   b. Ask the seller to repair the basement before she makes an offer
   c. Make an offer to purchase that is contingent on a structural inspection
   d. Hire a contractor to give an estimate for repair before making an offer

10. An agreement of sale in Pennsylvania must contain all of the following *except* a

   a. disclosure of whom the broker represents.
   b. disclosure that the rate of commission has been negotiated.
   c. statement about the recovery fund.
   d. statement about the zoning classification, except for single-family zoning.

11. Estimated statements of closing costs must be provided to buyers and sellers

   a. prior to settlement.
   b. after acceptance of an offer.
   c. within 24 hours of communication of acceptance of an offer.
   d. prior to signature of the agreement of sale.

12. A buyer makes an offer to purchase. The broker cannot locate the seller to present the offer. In the meantime, the broker receives an offer for a higher price from another buyer. How should the broker proceed?

   a. Decide which offer is best to present to the seller
   b. Present the offer for the higher price
   c. Call the first buyer and tell the buyer the broker cannot present the offer because it is too low
   d. Present both offers to the seller

19 Appraising Real Estate

APPRAISING

Formal appraisal reports are relied on by mortgage lenders, investors, public utilities, governmental agencies, businesses and individuals. Home mortgage lenders, for instance, need to know a property's market value to be sure that the amount of the loan is based on an accurate valuation of the collateral.

An **appraisal** is a supportable estimate or opinion of **value.** The appraiser is an independent third party required to provide an *unbiased* estimate of value. Appraising is a professional service performed for a fee based on the amount of time and effort needed to accomplish the task.

Regulating Appraisal Activities

To ensure that appraisals are performed by competent individuals whose professional conduct is subject to effective supervision, appraisers must be either certified or licensed by the state. But a real estate license is not required for general or residential certified appraisers. (Also, the apprasier is *not* in an agency relationship.) Federal law requires that only state-certified appraisers perform appraisals for federally related transactions. A *federally related transaction* is any real estate-related financial transaction in which a federal financial institution, a regulatory agency or the Resolution Trust Corporation engages. This includes transactions involving the sale, lease, purchase, investment or exchange of real property and the financing, refinancing or the use of real property as security for a loan or investment, including mortgage-backed securities.

The Appraisers Certification Act in Pennsylvania specifies three classes of certification. Appraisals performed for federally related transactions involving all types of real property (residential and nonresidential) valued over $250,000 must be performed by a **certified general real estate appraiser**. One-unit to four-unit properties valued over $250,000 must be appraised by a **certified residential real estate appraiser** for federally related transactions. The third class of certification, involving properties valued under $250,000, is the **broker/appraiser.** This certification was offered to all brokers who responded on or before September 3, 1998.

The State Board of Certified Appraisers has promulgated rules and regulations that specify the education and experience requirements necessary to obtain the certifications. It is important to remember that not all appraisals are performed for federally related financing because valuations are used for a wide variety of purposes in addition to mortgage lending.

Comparative Market Analysis

Not all estimates of value are prepared by professional appraisers, nor are the estimates as comprehensive or technical as an appraisal. Often salespeople help a seller arrive at a listing price or a buyer determine a price to offer for property. A *comparative market analysis* (CMA) is a report compiled from research of properties that have sold that are similar to the property the salesperson is trying to list or the buyer is considering purchasing. In order to compile the market data, salespeople need to be familiar with the methods appraisers use.

Although an appraisal identifies a specific value for a property, a CMA identifies what is expected to be a realistic range of prices within which a property should sell. A CMA is often used when preparing a marketing plan for selling an owner's property and, therefore, also includes properties that are currently for sale to identify the competition. Because a CMA may be biased by a salesperson's anticipated agency relationship, and because a salesperson is not authorized to prepare a formal appraisal, a comparative market analysis should *never* be represented as an appraisal.

VALUE

Value is an abstract word with many definitions. In a broad sense, **value** may be defined as the monetary worth arising from the ownership of a desired object. In the marketplace value is the power of a good or service to command other goods or services in exchange. The value of an object to an individual owner, based on its usefulness to that owner, may differ from the value of that object to other individuals in the marketplace. In terms of real estate appraisal, value may be described as the *present worth of future benefits arising from the ownership of real property.*

To have value in the real estate market, a property must have the following characteristics:

- *demand:* the need or desire for possession or ownership backed by the financial means to satisfy that need;

- *utility:* the capacity to satisfy human needs and desires;

- *scarcity:* a finite supply; and

- *transferability:* the relative ease with which ownership rights are transferred from one person to another.

Market Value

A given parcel of real estate may have many different kinds of value at the same time, such as market value (used to estimate selling price), assessed value (used for property taxes), insured value, book value, mortgage value, salvage value, condemnation value and depreciated value. Generally, the goal of an appraiser is to estimate market value. The **market value** of real estate is *the most probable price that a property should bring in a competitive and open market under all conditions requisite to a fair sale, given that the buyer and seller are each acting prudently and knowledgeably and assuming the price is not affected by undue stimulus.* The following conditions are essential to market value.

- The *most probable* price is not the average or highest price.

- The buyer and seller are unrelated and acting without *undue pressure*.

- Both buyer and seller must be *well informed* as to the property's use and potential, including its assets and defects.

- A *reasonable time* is allowed for exposure in the open market.

- Payment is made in cash or its equivalent.

- The price represents a normal consideration for the property sold, unaffected by special financing amounts and/or terms, services, fees, costs or credits incurred in the market transaction.

Market value versus market price. Market value is an opinion of value based on an analysis of data, which may include not only an analysis of comparable sales but also an analysis of potential income and expenses and replacement costs (less depreciation). *Market price,* on the other hand, is what a property *actually* sells for—its sales price. Theoretically, the market price should be the same as the market value. Market price can be taken as accurate evidence of current market value, however, *only* if the conditions essential to market value exist. There are circumstances under which a property may be sold below market value, such as when the seller is forced to sell quickly or when a sale is arranged between relatives.

Market value versus cost. There is an important distinction between market value and *cost.* One of the most common misconceptions about valuing property is that cost represents market value. Cost and market value *may* be equal and often are when the improvements on a property are new. But more often, cost does not equal market value. For example, two homes are identical in every respect, except that one is located on a street with heavy traffic and the other is on a quiet, residential street. The value of the former may be less than that of the latter, although the cost of each may be exactly the same. A homeowner may improve a house by adding an addition; however, the cost of the improvement may not significantly affect the value of the property. (See the principle of contribution later in the chapter.)

Basic Principles of Value

A number of economic principles can affect the value of real estate. The most important are defined in the text that follows.

Anticipation. The principle of **anticipation** says that value is created by the expectation that certain benefits will be realized in the future. Value can increase or decrease in anticipation of some future benefit or detriment affecting the property. For example, the value of a house may be affected if there are rumors that an adjacent property may be converted to commercial use in the near future.

Change. The cause and effect of social and economic forces constantly cause property values to be in transition. No physical or economic condition remains constant. Real estate is subject to natural phenomena, such as tornadoes, fires and routine wear and tear of the elements. The real estate business is also subject to the demands of its market, as is any business. It is an appraiser's job to be knowledgeable about the past and, perhaps, predictable effects of natural phenomena and the behavior of the marketplace.

Competition. **Competition** is the interaction of supply and demand. Excess profits tend to attract competition. For example, the success of a retail store may cause investors to open similar stores in the area. This tends to mean less profit for all stores concerned, unless the purchasing power in the area increases substantially.

Conformity. The principle of **conformity** says that value is created when the components of the property are in harmony with the surroundings. Maximum value is realized if the use of land conforms to existing neighborhood standards. In residential areas of single-family houses, for example, buildings should be similar in design, construction, size and age.

Contribution. The principle of **contribution** says that the value of any component of a property is measured by the amount it contributes to the value of the whole or the amount its absence detracts from the value of the whole. For example, the cost of installing an air-conditioning system and remodeling an older office building may be greater than is justified by any increase in market value (a function of expected net increase) that may result from the improvement to the property.

Highest and best use. The most profitable single use to which the property may be adapted or the use that is likely to be in demand in the reasonably near future is the property's **highest and best use.** The use must be legally permitted, financially feasible, physically possible and maximally productive. The highest and best use of a site can change with social, political and economic forces. Highest and best use is noted in every appraisal but may also be the object of a more extensive analysis. For example, a highest-and-best-use study may show that a parking lot in a busy downtown area does not maximize the productivity of the land to the degree that a building would.

Increasing and diminishing returns. The addition of more improvements to land and structures will increase value only to a certain point, that being the point of the asset's maximum value. After this point, additional improvements will no longer have an effect on the property's value. As long as money spent on improvements produces an increase in income or value, the *law of increasing returns* is applicable. At the point where additional improvements will not produce a proportionate increase in income or value, the *law of diminishing returns* applies.

Plottage. The principle of **plottage** holds that the merging or consolidation of adjacent lots held by separate landowners into one larger lot may produce a higher total land value than the sum of the values of the two sites valued separately. For example, if two adjacent lots are valued at $35,000 each, their total value if consolidated into one larger lot under a single use might be $90,000. The process of merging the two lots under one owner is known as **assemblage.**

Regression and progression. The principle that between dissimilar properties, the worth of the better property is adversely affected by the presence of the lesser-quality property is known as **regression.** Thus, in a neighborhood of modest homes, a structure that is larger, better maintained and/or more luxurious would tend to be valued in the same range as the others. Conversely, the principle of **progression** states that the worth of a lesser property tends to increase if it is located among better properties.

Substitution. The principle of **substitution** says that the maximum value of a property tends to be set by the cost of purchasing an equally desirable and valuable substitute property.

Supply and demand. The principle of **supply and demand** says that the value of a property depends on the number of properties available in the marketplace and their respective prices and the number of prospective market participants and the price they are willing to pay. For example, the last lot to be sold in a residential area where the demand for homes is high would probably be worth more than the first lot sold in that area.

THE THREE APPROACHES TO VALUE

To arrive at an accurate estimate of value, appraisers traditionally use three basic valuation techniques: the sales comparison approach, the cost approach and the income capitalization approach. Each method serves as a check against the others and narrows the range within which the final estimate of value will fall. Each method is generally considered most reliable for specific types of property.

The Sales Comparison Approach

In the **sales comparison approach** an estimate of value is obtained by comparing the subject property (the property under appraisal) with recently sold comparable properties (properties similar to the subject). This approach is the best example of the principle of substitution. Because no two parcels of real estate are exactly alike, each comparable property must be analyzed for differences and similarities between it and the subject property. The sales prices must be adjusted for any dissimilarities. The principal factors for which adjustments must be made include:

- *Property rights*: An adjustment must be made in cases when less than the full fee simple legal bundle of rights is involved, such as land leases, ground rents, life estates, easements, deed restrictions and encroachments.

- *Financing concessions*: The financing terms must be considered, including adjustments for differences such as mortgage loan terms and owner financing or any other type of typical financing.

- *Conditions of sale:* Adjustments must be made for motivational factors that would affect the sale, such as foreclosure, a sale between family members or some nonmonetary incentive.

- *Date of sale:* An adjustment must be made if economic changes occur between the date of sale of the comparable property and the date of the appraisal.

- *Location:* An adjustment may be necessary to compensate for locational differences. For example, similar properties might differ in price from neighborhood to neighborhood, or even between locations within the same neighborhood.

- *Physical features and amenities:* Physical features that may cause adjustments include age of building, size of lot, landscaping, construction, number of rooms, square feet of living space, interior and exterior condition, presence or absence of a garage, fireplace or air-conditioner, and so forth.

After a careful analysis of the differences between comparable properties and the subject property, the appraiser must adjust the comparables to reflect the market's reaction to the differences. Following the principle of contribution, the value of an amenity or the impact of date of sale, location or terms of a sale are assigned by the market. The appraiser *estimates either dollar or percentage adjustments* reflective of the value of these differences.

The value of a feature present in the subject but not in the comparable property is *added* to the sale price of the comparable. This presumes that, all other conditions being equal, a property having a feature not present in the comparable property (such as a fireplace or wet bar) would tend to have a higher market value solely because of this feature. (The feature need not be a physical amenity; it may be a locational or aesthetic feature.) Likewise, the value of a feature present in the comparable but not in the subject property is *subtracted*. The adjusted sales prices of the comparables represent the probable range of value of the subject property. From this range, a single market value estimate can be selected.

The sales comparison approach is essential in almost every appraisal of real estate. It is considered the most reliable of the three approaches in appraising residential property, where the intangible benefits may be difficult to measure otherwise. Most appraisals include a minimum of three comparable sales reflective of the subject property. Some appraisal forms require the inclusion of currently listed properties that are similar to the subject to indicate the current market competition. An example of the sales comparison approach is shown in Table 19.1.

The Cost Approach

The **cost approach** to value is also based on the principle of substitution. The cost approach consists of these steps:

1. Estimate the value of the land as if it were vacant and available to be put to its highest and best use.

2. Estimate the current cost of constructing buildings and site improvements.

3. Estimate the amount of accrued depreciation of the building resulting from physical deterioration, functional obsolescence and/or external depreciation.

4. Deduct accrued depreciation from the estimated construction cost of new building(s) and site improvements.

5. Add the estimated land value to the depreciated cost of the building(s) and site improvements to arrive at the total property value.

Land value (step 1) is usually estimated by using the sales comparison approach; that is, the location and site improvements (such as the presence of utilities and sewer lines) of the subject property are compared with those of similar nearby sites, and adjustments are made for significant differences.

There are two ways to look at the construction cost of a building for appraisal purposes (step 2): reproduction cost and replacement cost. **Reproduction cost** is the construction cost at current prices of an *exact duplicate* of the subject improvement, including both the benefits and the drawbacks of the property. **Replacement cost** is the construction cost at current prices of improvements with utility or function similar to the subject property, but not necessarily an

Table 19.1
Sales Comparison
Approach to Value

Comparables

	Subject Property	A	B	C	D	E
Sales price		$118,000	$112,000	$121,000	$116,500	$110,000
Financing Concessions	none	none	none	none	none	none
Date of Sale		current	current	current	current	current
Location	good	same	poorer +6,500	same	same	same
Age	6 years	same	same	same	same	same
Size of Lot	60′ × 135′	same	same	larger –5,000	same	larger –5,000
Landscaping	good	same	same	same	same	same
Construction	brick	same	same	same	same	same
Style	ranch	same	same	same	same	same
No. of Rooms	6	same	same	same	same	same
No. of Bedrooms	3	same	same	same	same	same
No. of Baths	1½	same	same	same	same	same
Sq. Ft. of Living Space	1,500	same	same	same	same	same
Other Space (basement)	full basement	same	same	same	same	same
Condition—Exterior	average	better –1,500	poorer +1,000	better –1,500	same	poorer +2,000
Condition—Interior	good	same	same	better –500	same	same
Garage	2-car attached	same	same	same	same	none +5,000
Other Improvements	none	none	none	none	none	none
Net Adjustments		–1,500	+7,500	–7,000	-0-	+2,000
Adjusted Value		$116,500	$119,500	$114,000	$116,500	$112,000

Note: Because the value range of the properties in the comparison chart (excluding comparable B) is close, and comparable D required no adjustment, an appraiser would conclude that the indicated market value of the subject is $116,500.

exact duplicate. Replacement cost is more frequently used in appraising older structures because it eliminates obsolete features and takes advantage of current construction materials and techniques.

An example of the cost approach to value is shown in Table 19.2.

Determining reproduction or replacement cost. An appraiser using the cost approach computes the reproduction or replacement cost of a building using one of the following four methods:

1. **Square-foot method:** The cost per square foot of a recently built comparable structure is multiplied by the number of square feet (using exterior dimensions) in the subject building. This is the most common and easiest method of cost estimation. The example in Table 19.2 uses the square-foot method, which is also referred to as the *comparison method*. For some properties the cost per *cubic*

foot of a recently built comparable structure is multiplied by the number of cubic feet in the subject structure.

2. **Unit-in-place method:** In the unit-in-place method the cost of a structure is estimated based on the construction cost per unit of measure of individual building components, including material, labor, overhead and builder's profit. Most components are measured in square feet, although items such as plumbing fixtures are estimated by cost. The sum of the components is the cost of the new structure.

3. **Quantity-survey method:** The quantity and quality of all materials (such as lumber, brick and plaster) and the labor are estimated on a unit cost basis. These factors are added to indirect costs (building permit, survey, payroll, taxes, builder's profit) to arrive at the total cost of the structure. Because it is so detailed and time-consuming, this method is usually used only in appraising historic properties.

4. **Index method:** A factor representing the percentage increase to the present time of construction costs is applied to the original cost of the subject property. Because this method fails to take into account individual property variables, it is useful only as a check of the estimate reached by one of the other methods.

Depreciation. In a real estate appraisal, **depreciation** refers to any condition that adversely affects the value of an improvement to real property. Land usually does not depreciate—it retains its value indefinitely, except in such rare cases as downzoned urban parcels, improperly developed land or misused farmland. Depreciation is considered to be curable or incurable, depending on the contribution of the expenditure to the value of the property. For appraisal purposes (as opposed to depreciation for tax purposes, which is discussed in Chapter 23), depreciation is divided into three classes according to its cause.

1. **Physical deterioration**—*curable:* an item in need of repair, such as painting (deferred maintenance), that is economically feasible and would result in an increase in appraised value equal to or exceeding the cost.

   Physical deterioration—incurable: a defect caused by physical wear and tear if its correction would not be economically feasible or contribute a comparable value to the building. A major repair, such as replacement of weatherworn siding, may not warrant the financial investment.

2. **Functional obsolescence**—*curable:* outmoded or unacceptable physical or design features that are no longer considered desirable by purchasers but could be replaced or redesigned at a cost that would be offset by the anticipated increase in ultimate value. Outmoded fixtures, such as plumbing, are usually easily replaced. Room function may be redefined at no cost if the basic room layout allows for it. A bedroom adjacent to a kitchen may be converted to a family room.

   Functional obsolescence—incurable: currently undesirable physical or design features that could not be easily remedied because the cost of effecting a cure would be greater than its contribution to the value. An office building that cannot be air-conditioned, for example, suffers from incurable functional obsolescence if the cost outweighs its contribution to the value.

3. **External depreciation**—*usually incurable*: caused by negative factors not on the subject property, such as environmental, social or economic forces. This type of depreciation usually cannot be considered curable because the loss in value cannot be affected by expenditures to the property. Proximity to a

Table 19.2 **Cost Approach** **to Value**	**Land Valuation:** Size 60′ × 135′ @$450 per front foot		= $27,000
	Plus site improvements: driveway, walks, landscaping, etc.		= 8,000
	Total Land Value		$35,000
	Building Valuation: Replacement Cost		
	1,500 sq. ft. @$65 per sq. ft. =	$97,500	
	Less Depreciation:		
	Physical depreciation		
	curable		
	(items of deferred maintenance)		
	exterior painting	$4,000	
	incurable (structural deterioration)	9,750	
	Functional obsolescence	2,000	
	External depreciation	-0-	
	Total Depreciation	−15,750	
	Depreciated Value of Building		$ 81,750
	Indicated Value by Cost Approach		$116,750

nuisance, such as a polluting factory or a deteriorating neighborhood, would be unchangeable factors that could not be cured by the owner of the subject property.

In determining a property's depreciation, most appraisers use the *breakdown method* in which depreciation is broken down into all three classes with separate estimates for curable and incurable factors in each class. Depreciation, however, is difficult to measure; and the older the building, the more difficult it is to estimate. The easiest but least precise way to determine depreciation is the **straight-line method,** also called the *economic age-life method.* Depreciation is assumed to occur at an even rate over a structure's **economic life,** the period during which it is expected to remain useful for its original intended purpose. The property's cost is divided by the number of years of its expected economic life to derive the amount of annual depreciation.

For example, a $120,000 property may have a land value of $30,000 and an improvement value of $90,000. If the improvements are expected to last 60 years, the annual straight-line depreciation would be $1,500 ($90,000 divided by 60 years). Such depreciation can be calculated as an annual dollar amount or as a percentage of the improvement's replacement cost.

Much of the functional obsolescence and all the external depreciation can be evaluated only by considering the actions of buyers in the marketplace.

The cost approach is most helpful in the appraisal of newer buildings or special-purpose buildings such as schools, churches and public buildings. Some properties are difficult to appraise using other methods because there are seldom many local sales to use as comparables and the properties do not ordinarily generate income.

The Income Approach

The **income approach** to value is based on the present value of the rights to future income. It assumes that the income derived from a property will, to a large extent, control the value of that property. The income approach is used for valuation of income-producing properties—apartment buildings, office buildings, shopping centers and the like. In estimating value using the income approach, an appraiser must take the following steps:

1. Estimate annual *potential gross rental income*. An estimate of economic rental income must be made based on market studies. Current rental income may not reflect the current market rental rates, especially in the cases of short-term leases or leases about to terminate. Potential income includes other income to the property from such sources as vending machines, parking fees and laundry machines.

2. Deduct an appropriate allowance for vacancy and rent loss, based on the appraiser's experience, and arrive at *effective gross income*.

3. Deduct the annual *operating expenses* from the effective gross income to arrive at the annual *net operating income*. See Table 19.3, Income Capitalization Approach to Value, for expenses. Management costs are always included even if the current owner manages the property. Mortgage payments (principal and interest) are *debt service* and are not considered operating expenses.

4. Estimate the price a typical investor would pay for the income produced by this particular type and class of property. This is done by estimating the rate of return (or yield) that an investor will demand for the investment of capital in this type of building. This rate of return is called the **capitalization** (or cap) **rate** and is determined by comparing the relationship of net operating income to the sales prices of similar properties that have sold in the current market. For example, a comparable property that is producing an annual net income of $15,000 is sold for $187,500. The capitalization rate is $15,000 divided by $187,500 or 8 percent. It may be concluded that 8 percent is the rate that the appraiser should apply to the subject property if other comparable properties sold at prices that yielded substantially the same rate.

5. Apply the capitalization rate to the property's annual net operating income to arrive at the estimate of the property's value.

With the appropriate capitalization rate and the projected annual net operating income, the appraiser can obtain an indication of value by the income approach in the following manner:

I = Income   R = Rate   V = Value

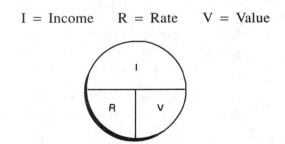

Net Operating Income ÷ Capitalization Rate = Value

Example: $18,000 income ÷ 9% cap rate = $200,000 value or

$18,000 income ÷ 8% cap rate = $225,000 value

Note the inverse relationship between the rate and value. As the rate goes down, the value increases.

This formula and its variations are important in dealing with income property.

$$\frac{\text{Income}}{\text{Rate}} = \text{Value} \qquad \frac{\text{Income}}{\text{Value}} = \text{Rate} \qquad \text{Value} \times \text{Rate} = \text{Income}$$

A very simplified version of the computations used in applying the income approach is illustrated in Table 19.3.

IN PRACTICE...	*The most difficult step in the income approach to value is determining the appropriate capitalization rate for the property. This rate must be selected to accurately reflect the recapture of the original investment over the building's economic life, give the owner an acceptable rate of return on investment and provide for the repayment of borrowed capital. Note that an income property that carries with it a great deal of risk as an investment generally requires a higher rate of return than a property considered a safe investment.*

**Table 19.3
Income
Capitalization
Approach to
Value**

Potential Gross Annual Income		
Market Rent		$60,000
Income from other sources		
(vending machines and pay phones)		+600
		$60,600
Less vacancy and collection losses (estimated) @ 4%		−2,424
Effective Gross Income		$58,176
Expenses:		
Real estate taxes	$9,000	
Insurance	1,000	
Heat	2,800	
Maintenance	6,400	
Utilities, electricity, water, gas	800	
Repairs	1,200	
Decorating	1,400	
Replacement of equipment	800	
Legal and accounting	600	
Management	3,000	
Total Expenses		$27,000
Annual Net Operating Income		$31,176

Capitalization Rate = 10%

Capitalization of annual net income: $\dfrac{\$31,176}{.10}$

Indicated Value by Income Approach = $311,760

Gross rent or gross income multipliers. Certain properties, such as single-family homes or two-unit buildings, are not purchased primarily for income. As a substitute for a more elaborate income capitalization analysis, the **gross rent multiplier** (GRM) and **gross income multiplier** (GIM) are often used in the appraisal process. Each relates the sales price of a property to its rental income.

Because both single-family and one-to-four-unit residences usually produce only a rental income, the gross rent multiplier is used. This relates the sales price to *monthly* rental income. However, commercial and industrial properties generate income from many other sources (rent, concessions, escalator clause income and so forth), and they are valued using their *annual* income from all sources.

The formulas are as follows:

$$\frac{\text{Sales Price}}{\text{Gross Income}} = \frac{\text{Gross Income Multiplier}}{\text{(GIM)}}$$

or

$$\frac{\text{Sales Price}}{\text{Gross Rent}} = \frac{\text{Gross Rent Multiplier}}{\text{(GRM)}}$$

For example, if a home recently sold for $82,000 and its monthly rental income was $650, the GRM for the property would be computed thus:

$$\frac{\$82,000}{\$650} = 126.2 \text{ GRM}$$

To establish an accurate GRM, an appraiser must have recent sales and rental data from at least four properties that are similar to the subject property. The resulting GRM can then be applied to the estimated fair market rental of the subject property to arrive at its market value. The formula would then be

Rental Income × GRM = Estimated Market Value

Table 19.4 shows some examples of GRM comparisons.

Table 19.4
Gross Rent
Multiplier

Comparable No.	Sales Price	Monthly Rent	GRM
1	$93,600	$650	144
2	78,500	450	174
3	95,500	675	141
4	82,000	565	145
Subject	?	625	?

Note: Based on an analysis of these comparisons, a GRM of 145 seems reasonable for homes in this area. In the opinion of an appraiser, then, the estimated value of the subject property would be $625 × 145, or $90,625.

IN PRACTICE...	*Much skill is required to use multipliers accurately because there is no fixed multiplier for all areas or all types of properties and the data for each comparable must be carefully scrutinized. Therefore, many appraisers view the technique simply as a quick, informal way to check the validity of a property value obtained by one of the other appraisal methods.*

Reconciliation

When the three approaches to value are applied to the same property, they will normally produce three separate indications of value. **Reconciliation** is the art of analyzing and effectively weighing the findings from the three approaches.

Although each approach may serve as an independent guide to value, all three approaches should be used whenever possible as a check on the final estimate of value. The process of reconciliation is more complicated than simply taking the average of the three derived value estimates. An average implies that the data and logic applied in each of the approaches are equally valid and reliable and should therefore be given equal weight. In fact, however, certain approaches are more valid and reliable with some kinds of properties than with others.

For example, in appraising a home the income approach is rarely valid, and the cost approach is of limited value unless the home is relatively new; therefore, the sales comparison approach is usually given greatest weight in valuing single-family residences. In the appraisal of income or investment property, the income approach would normally be given the greatest weight. In the appraisal of churches, libraries, museums, schools and other special-use properties where there is little or no income or sales revenue, the cost approach would usually be assigned the greatest weight. From this analysis, or reconciliation, a single estimate of market value is produced.

THE APPRAISAL PROCESS

Although appraising is not an exact or precise science, the key to an accurate appraisal lies in the methodical collection of data. The appraisal process is an orderly set of procedures used to collect and analyze data to arrive at an ultimate value conclusion. The data are divided into two basic classes:

1. *General data,* covering the nation, region, city and neighborhood. Of particular importance is the neighborhood where an appraiser finds the physical, economic, social and political influences that directly affect the value and potential of the subject property.

2. *Specific data,* covering details of the subject property as well as comparative data relating to costs, sales and income and expenses of properties similar to and competitive with the subject property.

The following list outlines the steps an appraiser takes in carrying out an appraisal assignment.

1. *State the problem.* The kind of value to be estimated must be specified and the valuation approach(es) most valid and reliable for the kind of property under appraisal must be selected.

2. *List the data needed and their sources.* Based on the approach(es) the appraiser will be using, the types of data needed and the sources to be consulted are listed.

3. *Gather, record and verify the general data.* Detailed information concerning the economic, political and social conditions of the region and/or city and comments on the effects of these data on the subject property must be obtained. Specific data about the subject site and improvements must be collected and verified.

    Depending on the approach(es) used, comparative information relating to sales, income and expenses, and construction costs of comparable properties must be collected. All data should be verified, usually by checking the same information against two different sources. In the case of sales data,one source should be a person directly involved in the transaction.

4. *Determine highest and best use.* The appraiser analyzes market forces such as competition and current versus potential uses to determine the reasonableness of the property's present use in terms of its profitability.

5. *Estimate land value.* The best method is to consider the features and sales prices of comparable sites as compared with the subject to determine the value of the land alone.

6. *Estimate value by each of the three approaches.* The sales comparison, cost and income approaches are used to estimate the value of the subject property.

7. *Reconcile estimated values for final value estimate.* The appraiser reconciles the findings of the three approaches and forms an opinion of the value estimate of the property.

8. *Report final value estimate.* After the three approaches have been reconciled and an opinion of value reached, the appraiser prepares an oral or formal written report for the client. Uniform Standards of Professional Appraisal Practice (USPAP), which were established by the Appraisal Standards Board of the Appraisal Foundation (a national body composed of representatives of the major appraisal and related organizations), identifies three levels of written reports. Each differs because of the amount of information required to support the appraiser's reasoning and conclusions. According to USPAP rules, any written report should

    a. identify the real estate being appraised;

    b. state the real property interest being appraised;

    c. state the purpose and intended use of the appraisal;

    d. define the value to be estimated;

    e. state the effective date of value and date of the appraisal;

    f. state the extent of process of collecting, confirming and reporting data;

    g. state all assumptions and limiting conditions that affect analysis, opinion and conclusion;

    h. describe information considered, the appraisal procedures followed and the reasoning that supports the analysis, opinion and conclusions;

    i. describe the appraiser's opinion of the highest and best use of the real estate, when such an opinion is necessary and appropriate;

j. explain and support the exclusion of any of the usual valuation approaches;

k. describe any additional information that may be appropriate to show compliance with or clearly identify and explain permitted departures, from the specific guidelines of standard #1; and

l. include two signed certifications in accordance with standards rules 2-3.

IN PRACTICE...

The role of an appraiser is not to determine value, but to develop a supportable and objective report about the value of the subject property. The appraiser relies on experience and expertise in valuation theories to evaluate market data. The appraiser does not create numbers or "pick them from the air." It is not what the appraiser thinks the property is worth, but what the market indicates the value is that the appraiser can verify. This is important to remember, particularly when dealing with a property owner who may, understandably, lack the necessary objectivity to see the property realistically. The possible lack of objectivity can complicate the salesperson's ability to list a property within the most probable range of market value, as well.

KEY TERMS

anticipation	income approach
appraisal	index method
assemblage	market value
broker/appraiser	physical deterioration
capitalization rate	plottage
certified general real estate appraiser	progression
certified residential real estate appraiser	quantity-survey method
change	reconciliation
competition	regression
conformity	replacement cost
contribution	reproduction cost
cost approach	sales comparison approach
depreciation	square-foot method
economic life	straight-line method
external depreciation	substitution
functional obsolescence	supply and demand
gross income multiplier	unit-in-place method
gross rent multiplier	value
highest and best use	

SUMMARY

To appraise real estate means to estimate its value. Although there are many types of value, the most common objective of an appraisal is to estimate market value—the most probable sale price of a property. Basic to appraising are certain underlying economic principles, such as highest and best use, substitution, supply and demand, conformity, anticipation, increasing and diminishing returns, regression, progression, plottage, contribution, competition and change.

Appraisals are concerned with values, prices and costs; it is vital to understand the distinctions among the terms. Value is an estimate of future benefits, cost represents a measure of past expenditures and price reflects the actual amount of money paid for a property.

A professional appraiser analyzes a property through three approaches to value. In the sales comparison approach, the value of the subject property is compared with the values of others like it that have sold recently. Because no two properties are exactly alike, adjustments must be made to account for any differences. With the cost approach, an appraiser calculates the cost of building a similar structure on a similar site. The appraiser then subtracts depreciation (losses in value), which reflects the differences between new properties of this type and the present condition of the subject property. The income approach is an analysis based on the relationship between the rate of return that an investor requires and the net income that a property produces.

An informal version of the income approach, called the gross rent multiplier (GRM), may be used to estimate the value of single-family residential properties that are not usually rented but could be. The GRM is computed by dividing the sales price of a property by its gross monthly rent. For commercial or industrial property, a gross income multiplier (GIM), based on annual income from all sources, may be used.

Normally, the application of the three approaches results in three different estimates of value. In the process of reconciliation, the validity and reliability of each approach are weighed objectively to arrive at the single best and most supportable estimate of value.

Questions

1. Which of the following approaches to value makes use of a rate of investment return?
   a. Sales comparison approach
   b. Cost approach
   c. Income approach
   d. Gross income multiplier

2. The elements of value include which of the following?
   a. Competition   c. Anticipation
   b. Scarcity   d. Balance

3. The principle of value that states that two adjacent parcels of land combined into one larger parcel would have a greater value than the two parcels valued separately is called
   a. substitution.   c. regression.
   b. plottage.   d. progression.

4. The amount of money a property commands in the marketplace is its
   a. market price.
   b. market value.
   c. capitalization rate.
   d. index.

5. *H* has his "dream house" constructed for $100,000 in an area where most newly constructed homes are not as well equipped as his and typically sell for only $80,000. The value of *H*'s house is likely to be affected by the principle of
   a. progression.   c. change.
   b. assemblage.   d. regression.

6. In question 5, the owners of the lesser-valued homes in *H*'s immediate area may be affected by the principle of
   a. progression.
   b. increasing returns.
   c. competition.
   d. regression.

7. Accrued depreciation for appraisal purposes is *not* caused by which of the following?
   a. Functional obsolescence
   b. Physical deterioration
   c. External depreciation
   d. Acceleration depreciation

8. *Reconciliation* refers to which of the following?
   a. Loss of value due to any cause
   b. Separating the value of the land from the total value of the property to compute depreciation
   c. Analyzing the results obtained by the three approaches to value to determine a final estimate of value
   d. The process by which an appraiser determines the highest and best use for a parcel of land

9. One method an appraiser uses to determine a building's cost new involves an estimate of the raw materials needed to build the structure plus the cost of such materials, labor and other expenses. This is called the
   a. square-foot method.
   b. quantity-survey method.
   c. cubic-foot method.
   d. unit-in-place method.

10. If a property's annual net income is $24,000 and it is valued at $300,000, what is its capitalization rate?

    a. 12.5 percent   c. 15 percent
    b. 10.5 percent   d. 8 percent

11. Certain figures must be determined by an appraiser before value can be computed by the income approach. Which one of the following is *not* required for this process?

    a. Annual net operating income
    b. Capitalization rate
    c. Accrued depreciation
    d. Annual gross income

12. The income approach would be given the most weight in the valuation of a(n)

    a. single-family residence.
    b. industrial property.
    c. strip shopping center.
    d. school.

13. The market value of a parcel of real estate is

    a. the cost of the land and any improvements.
    b. the amount of money paid for the property.
    c. an estimate of the most probable price it should bring.
    d. its value without improvements.

14. Capitalization is the process by which annual net income is used as the basis to

    a. determine cost.
    b. estimate value.
    c. establish depreciation.
    d. determine potential tax value.

15. From the reproduction or replacement cost of the building, an appraiser deducts depreciation, which represents

    a. the remaining economic life of the building.
    b. remodeling costs to increase rentals.
    c. loss of value due to any cause.
    d. costs to modernize the building.

16. In the sales comparison approach to value, the probable sales price of a building may be estimated by

    a. capitalizing net operating income.
    b. considering sales of similar properties.
    c. deducting accrued depreciation.
    d. determining construction costs.

17. Which factor would be least important in comparing properties under the sales comparison approach to value?

    a. Difference in dates of sale
    b. Difference in financing terms
    c. Difference in appearance and condition
    d. Difference in type of heating system

18. In the income approach to value

    a. the reproduction or replacement cost of the building must be computed.
    b. the capitalization rate must be estimated.
    c. depreciation must be determined.
    d. sales of similar properties must be considered.

19. In the cost approach to value, it is necessary to

    a. determine a dollar value for depreciation.
    b. estimate future expenses and operating costs.
    c. check sales prices of recently sold homes in the area.
    d. reconcile differing value estimates.

20. The appraised value of a residence with four bedrooms and one bathroom would probably be reduced because of

    a. external obsolescence.
    b. functional obsolescence.
    c. physical deterioration—curable.
    d. physical deterioration—incurable.

20 Financing the Real Estate Transaction

COST OF CREDIT

When buyers must rely on other people's money to finance their purchases, the cost of credit is a necessary part of a business transaction. From a lender's point of view, a loan is an investment and the finance and interest charges for a loan represent income. Because the lender has something the borrower needs, that is money, the borrower in a sense must pay the price the lender charges to use that money. In addition to the interest paid during the term of the loan, the borrower pays a *loan origination fee* and may also have to pay a *service fee* or *points* to acquire the loan.

As discussed in Chapter 12, the loan origination fee is charged by most lenders as an expense for generating the loan. The origination fee is typically 1 percent of the amount of the loan, but it may be higher. A service fee or points may also be charged when the loan is originated. Points represent prepaid interest charged to produce additional income on the loan. One point is equal to 1 percent of the loan. Depending on the terms of the agreement of sale, the seller may assist the buyer by paying some or all of the points.

If a borrower's down payment is small in relation to the amount of the mortgage loan, the lender may also require private mortgage insurance on the loan. The *insurance premium* is collected at closing and may also be collected with the monthly payments during a partial term of the loan.

Discount Points

The lender may sell the loan to an investor in the secondary market instead of collecting the principal and interest over the life of the loan. By selling loans, lending institutions replenish their supply of funds for additional loans.

The stated rate of interest that a lender charges could be less than the yield (true rate of return) required by the investors who might purchase the loan. For this reason, the lender charges **discount points** to make up the difference between the stated interest rate and the yield the investor wants. The number of points varies, depending both on the difference between the interest rate and the required yield and on the average time the lender expects the loan to be outstanding. The average 30-year loan is in effect for 7 to 12 years.

One discount point equals 1 percent of the loan amount (*not* the purchase price) and is charged as prepaid interest at the closing. For example, a charge of three discount points on a $100,000 loan equals $3,000 ($100,000 × 3%).

Application for Credit

Prospective borrowers must file an application for credit to provide the lender with the basic information needed to evaluate the acceptability of the proposed loan. The application includes information about the purpose and amount of the loan, the interest rate and the proposed terms of repayment. This is considered a preliminary offer of a loan agreement; final terms may require lengthy negotiations. The FNMA/FHLMC Uniform Loan Application is a form widely used by borrowers in Pennsylvania.

A common practice today is for buyer prospects to be *prequalified* by a lender or lenders before beginning the search for a home.

IN PRACTICE...

The information provided in a loan application must be accurate and verifiable. There are serious legal consequences when people obtain loans as a result of false statements made in loan applications. No one, *licensees included, should participate in falsifying any information—these are criminal offenses.*

What should a person know about making applications for credit? Credit reporting agencies hold the key to a person being able to get credit and even employment. But consumer groups have complained that the agencies have been unreasonable and far too slow in fixing mistakes in credit files. To avoid this embarrassment and frustration, the potential borrower should order a credit report to review before applying for a mortgage loan.

If there are mistakes in a credit report, they can be remedied more easily because of the *Credit Reporting Reform Act* of 1994. This law makes it cheaper for consumers to look at their own credit files and forces reporting agencies to correct mistakes and remove disputed information from the files unless the creditor verifies it. Credit reporting agencies are also required to set up toll-free phone numbers so that consumers can check the accuracy of their reports and request corrections.

To evaluate the quality of the investment the lender will be making, the lender needs certain information about both the borrower and the property that will be pledged as security for the loan. A prospective borrower must provide personal information, including employment, earnings, assets and financial obligations. Information about the real estate includes the legal description, description of the improvements, title and tax information and a survey. For loans on income property or those made to corporations, additional information such as financial and operating statements, schedules of leases and tenants, and balance sheets will be required.

The lender investigates the information provided in the application and studies credit reports and an appraisal of the property before deciding whether to grant the loan. The lender's acceptance of the application is written in the form of a *loan commitment,* which creates a contract to make a loan and sets forth the details. In some cases the commitment may be conditional; that is, the lender commits to lending the money subject to the borrower meeting certain conditions. Common conditions include selling a current property or providing a title insurance policy at settlement.

IN PRACTICE...

Shopping for credit is relatively easy primarily because of technology. Although there are many mortgage lenders offering various types of loans, each with different down payment requirements, finance charges, interest rates and terms, borrowers do not have to visit each lender to compare loan possibilities. The latest information is readily available via computers networked in many brokers' offices, which is also where the salespeople can help buyers evaluate the loan products and identify the most suitable ones for their specific needs. Some brokers even offer computerized loan originations (CLOs) that enable a borrower to make a loan application electronically and receive a conditional commitment conveniently in the broker's office.

LOAN REPAYMENT

A variety of repayment plans are available for mortgage loans. Different payment plans tend alternately to gain and lose favor as the cost and availability of mortgage money fluctuate. Fully amortized loans seem to be the most frequently used. As discussed in Chapter 12, the payment on an amortized loan includes principal and interest during the term, as opposed to a *straight* loan, which is the payment of interest only. As each payment is made, it is applied first to the interest owed and the balance is applied to the principal. Regular payments are made usually over terms of 15 to 30 years.

In addition to fixed-interest/fixed-payment amortized loans, the following payment programs have evolved.

Adjustable-Rate Mortgage (ARM)

Adjustable-rate mortgages (ARMs) are generally originated at one rate of interest, with the rate fluctuating up or down during the loan term based on some economic indicator. Because the interest may change, so may the borrower's loan payments. Details of how and when the rate of interest on the loan will change are included in the provisions of the note. Common components of an ARM include the following.

- The interest rate is tied to the movement of an *index,* such as the cost-of-funds index for federally chartered lenders. Most indexes are tied to U.S. Treasury securities.

- Usually the interest rate is the index rate plus a premium, called the *margin,* which is the lender's cost of doing business, such as profits and costs. For example, the loan rate may be 2 percent over the U.S. Treasury bill rate.

- *Rate caps* limit the amount the interest rate may change. Most ARMs have both periodic rate caps, which limit the amount the rate may increase at any one time, and aggregate rate caps, which limit the amount the rate may increase over the entire life of the loan.

- The mortgagor is protected from unaffordable individual payments by the *payment cap,* which sets a maximum amount for payments. With a payment cap, however, a rate increase could result in negative amortization—an increase in the loan balance.

- The *adjustment period* establishes how often the rate may be changed. Common adjustment periods are monthly, quarterly and annually.

- Lenders may offer a *conversion option,* which enables the mortgagor to convert from an adjustable to a fixed-rate loan at certain intervals during the loan. The option will stipulate the terms and conditions for the conversion.

Balloon Payment Loan

When the periodic payments are not large enough to fully amortize the loan by the time the final payment is due, the final payment is larger than the others. This is called a **balloon payment.** It is a *partially amortized loan.* For example, a loan made for $80,000 at 11.5 percent interest may be computed on a 30-year amortization schedule but paid over a 20-year term, with a final balloon payment due at the end of the 20th year. In this case each monthly payment would be $792.24 (the amount taken from a 30-year amortization schedule), with a final balloon payment of $56,340 (the amount of principal still owing after 20 years). It is frequently assumed that, if the payments are made promptly the lender will extend the balloon payment for another limited term. The lender, however, is in no way legally obligated to grant this extension and can require payment in full when the note is due.

Growing Equity Mortgage (GEM)

The **growing equity mortgage (GEM),** or *rapid-payoff mortgage,* uses a fixed interest rate, but payments of principal are increased according to an index or a schedule. The total payment thus increases, but the borrower's income is expected to keep pace and the loan is paid off more quickly.

Reverse Annuity Mortgage (RAM)

A **reverse annuity mortgage (RAM)** is one in which regular monthly payments are made *to the borrower,* based on the equity the homeowner has in the property pledged as security for the loan. A reverse loan allows senior citizens on fixed incomes to benefit from the equity buildup in their homes without having to sell. The borrower is charged a fixed rate of interest and the loan is eventually paid from the sale of the property or from the borrower's estate upon his or her death.

LOAN PROGRAMS

Mortgage loans are generally classified based on their **loan-to-value ratio,** that is, the ratio of debt to value of the property. Value is the sale price or the appraised value, whichever is lower. The lower the ratio of debt to value means a higher down payment by the borrower. For the lender, the higher down payment means a more secure loan, minimizing the lender's risk.

Conventional Loans

Conventional loans are viewed as the most secure loans because the loan-to-value ratio is lowest. Usually the ratio is 80 percent of the value of the property or lower; the borrower makes a down payment of 20 percent or more. The security for the loan is provided solely by the mortgage. The payment of the debt rests upon the ability of the borrower to pay. In making these loans, the lender relies primarily on its appraisal of the security (the real estate) and information from credit reports that indicate the reliability of the prospective borrower. No additional insurance or guarantee is necessary to protect the lender's interest.

Lenders can set criteria by which the borrower and the collateral are evaluated to qualify for the loan. However, in recent years the secondary mortgage market has had a significant impact on the borrower qualifications, standards for the collateral and documentation procedures that lenders follow. For loans to be salable to the Federal National Mortgage Association (FNMA) and Federal Home Loan Mortgage Association (FHLMC), they must meet their requirements. Lenders can still be flexible in their lending decisions but would have to retain loans that are unsalable in the secondary market.

Private Mortgage Insurance

One way borrowers can obtain loans with a lower down payment is under **private mortgage insurance (PMI)** programs. Because the loan-to-value ratio is higher than for other conventional loans, up to 97 percent of the appraised value of the property (up to 100 percent under certain circumstances), the lender requires additional security to minimize its risk. The lender purchases insurance from a private mortgage insurance company as additional security to insure the lender against the borrower's default.

Private mortgage insurance insures the difference between the down payment and 20 percent of the purchase price. The borrower is normally charged a fee for this coverage at closing, plus additional monthly fees while the insurance is in force. Because only a portion of the loan is insured, once the loan is repaid to a certain level, the lender terminates the coverage. The borrower should keep track of when that 20 percent has been reached and then advise the lender to remove the PMI. However, the lender should have already removed the PMI, in accordance with the law.

FHA-Insured Loans

Another alternative for borrowers to finance real estate with a low down payment is with FHA-insured loans. The Federal Housing Administration (FHA), which operates under the Department of Housing and Urban Development, insures these high **loan-to-value ratio** loans in a effort to make more affordable loans available. Much like private mortgage insurance, the FHA insurance protects the lender against loss from a borrower's default. The common term **FHA loan** refers to a loan that is not made by the agency but is *insured* by it. These loans must be made by approved FHA lending institutions.

In addition to low down payments, FHA loans are attractive because the interest rates are competitive with other types of loans and the FHA offers a variety of incentives for borrowers to use its programs. Borrowers have the option of 15- or 30-year fixed-rate loans or 1-year adjustable-rate loans. The FHA qualifying ratios (debt to income) are higher than for other types of loans. Although FHA limits the maximum loan amounts, the limits are set regionally to reflect the housing prices in the area. Borrowers are charged a premium for the FHA insurance, but this amount may be paid at closing by the borrower or someone else, or it may be added to the loan amount. There may also be an annual premium, but this amount varies depending on the loan-to-value ratio and the term of the loan.

There are a number of FHA programs, each serving different purposes. Some insure loans for owner occupancy of a one- to four-family residence. There is a program to help residents or investors repair or rehabilitate single-family properties. Another program is designed for condominium purchases as long as the condominium complex meets the FHA ratio of owner occupants to renters. All properties to be acceptable collateral must meet FHA standards for the type and construction of the properties and the quality of the neighborhoods.

A borrower may prepay an FHA loan on a one- to four-family residence without penalty. However, the borrower must give the lender written notice of intention to exercise this privilege at least 30 days before the anticipated prepayment. Otherwise the lender has the option of charging up to 30 days' interest.

FHA loans are assumable. However, the assumption rules vary depending on the date that the loan was originated, the type of property and the specific FHA loan program under which the original loan was granted. In some cases, there are no restrictions on their assumption. In other cases, assumptions are permitted only when the assuming buyer has been qualified for the loan.

Contact your local FHA office or mortgage lender for loan amounts in your area and specific loan requirements. The programs change from time to time.

VA-Guaranteed Loans

Under the Servicemen's Readjustment Act of 1944 and subsequent federal legislation, the Department of Veterans Affairs is authorized to guarantee loans to purchase or construct homes for eligible veterans. VA loans assist veterans to finance the purchase of homes with little or no down payment at competitive interest rates.

As with the term FHA loan, **VA loan** is something of a misnomer. The term *VA loan* does not refer to a loan that is made by the agency but one that is guaranteed by it. This is normally a high loan-to-value ratio loan as well. A veteran obtains a loan from a VA-approved lending institution; the VA partially guarantees loans made by these institutions. The guarantee provides the lender with additional security in place of insurance. The lender would receive the amount of the guarantee from the VA if a foreclosure sale did not bring enough to cover the outstanding balance.

Maximum loan terms are 30 years for one- to four-family dwellings and 40 years for farm loans. The interest rates are negotiable between the lender and borrower, and the VA guarantees fixed-rate and adjustable-rate loans. Lenders are permitted to charge reasonable closing costs plus no more than a 1 percent loan origination fee. A VA funding fee to be paid either at closing or to be included in the loan amount is also charged. The amount of the fee varies depending on the amount of the down payment, the type of property and the eligibility status of the borrower. Residential property purchased with a VA loan must be owner occupied. The VA also requires that the real estate meet certain requirements.

To determine whether someone is eligible for a VA loan, the person should contact the Department of Veterans Affairs. Eligibility varies depending on the length of service and the years during which the veteran served on active duty. Certain people who serve in the National Guard or in the Reserves are eligible as well. The veteran should also obtain a *certificate of eligibility*. The certificate establishes the maximum loan guarantee to which the veteran is entitled. While there is no VA limit on the amount of the loan a veteran can obtain, the VA does limit the amount of loan it will guarantee. For individuals with full eligibility, no down payment would be required for loans up to a certain maximum.

The VA also issues a *certificate of reasonable value* (CRV) for the property being purchased, stating its current market value based on a VA-approved appraisal. The CRV places a ceiling on the amount of a VA loan allowed for the property. No down payment is required if the purchase price does not exceed the amount cited in the CRV; if the purchase price is greater, the veteran must pay the difference in cash.

Although VA loans are assumable, the procedures vary depending on the date the original loan was made. In some cases the assuming borrower must be approved. The original veteran-borrower, however, remains personally liable for repayment of the loan unless the VA approves a *release of liability*. The release is issued if the buyer assumes all the veteran's liabilities on the loan and the VA or the lender approves the buyer and the assumption agreement. A funding fee is also required. A release would also be possible if another veteran used his or her own entitlement in assuming the loan. Any release of liability issued by the VA does not release the veteran's liability to the lender. This must be obtained separately from the lender.

As with an FHA loan, the borrower under a VA loan can repay the debt at any time without penalty.

Contact your local VA office or mortgage lender for specific requirements for VA loans. The programs change from time to time.

Farmers Home Administration. The function of the Farmers Home Administration (FmHA) has been to guarantee loans for the purchase or improvement of single-family homes in rural areas or the operation of family farms. The loans are made and serviced by a private lender and are guaranteed for a specific percentage by the government agency. Loans are made to low- and moderate-income families, and the interest rate charged can be as low as 1 percent, depending on the borrower's income. The original functions of Farmers Home Administration have been moved under the umbrella of the Department of Agriculture. *Rural Economic and Community Development Services* (RECD) is responsible for the residential loans. *Farm Service Agency* (FSA) handles the agricultural or farm loans.

OTHER FINANCING TECHNIQUES

A variety of other financing techniques have been created to meet specific needs of borrowers and lenders. The following loans, which do not fit strictly into the categories previously described, are among the most common.

Purchase-Money Mortgages

A **purchase-money mortgage** is a note and mortgage created at the time of purchase to facilitate the sale. The term is used in two ways—to refer to *any* security instrument originating at the time of sale or, most often, to refer to the instrument *given by the purchaser to a seller who "takes back" a note for part or all of the purchase price*. As with a conventional mortgage, the buyer receives the deed at closing.

Package Loans

A **package loan** includes not only the real estate but also *all personal property and appliances installed on the premises.* In recent years this kind of loan has been used extensively in financing furnished condominium units in some parts of the country. Such loans usually include furniture, drapes, carpets, kitchen range, refrigerator, dishwasher, garbage disposal unit, washer and dryer, food freezer and other appliances as part of the real estate in the sales price of the home. However, package mortgages are not permitted in Pennsylvania. State law stipulates that only real estate and fixtures may be made subject to the lien of a mortgage on real estate.

Blanket Loans

A **blanket loan** covers *more than one parcel or lot.* It is usually used to finance subdivision developments, though it can be used to finance the purchase of improved properties or to consolidate loans as well. These loans usually include a provision known as a *partial release clause,* so that the borrower may obtain the release of any one lot or parcel from the lien by repaying a certain amount of the loan. The lender issues a partial release for each parcel released from the mortgage lien; this release form includes a provision that the lien will continue to cover all other unreleased lots.

Wraparound Loans

A **wraparound loan** enables a borrower who is paying off an existing mortgage loan to obtain additional financing from a second lender. *The new lender assumes payment of the existing loan and gives the borrower a new, increased loan at a higher interest rate.* The total amount of the new loan includes the existing loan as well as the additional funds needed by the borrower. The borrower makes payments to the new lender on the larger loan. The new lender makes the payments on the original loan out of the borrower's payments.

A wraparound mortgage is frequently used as a method of refinancing real property or financing the purchase of real property when an existing mortgage cannot be prepaid. It also is used to finance the sale of real estate when the buyer wishes to put up a minimum amount of initial cash for the sale. The buyer executes a wraparound mortgage to the seller, who will collect payments on the new loan and continue to make payments on the old loan. To protect themselves in the case of the seller's default on the old loan, buyers should require a protective clause in the document granting the right to make payments directly to the original lender.

IN PRACTICE. . .

A wraparound loan is possible only if the original loan permits such refinancing. An acceleration and alienation or due-on-sale clause in the original loan documents may prevent a sale under these terms. Real estate licensees could be subject to disciplinary action by licensing authorities if they encourage or assist in any financing that violates loan provisions.

Open-End Loans

An **open-end loan** secures a *note* executed by the borrower to the lender as well as any future *advances* of funds made by the lender to the borrower. The interest rate on the initial amount borrowed is fixed, but interest on future advances may be the market rate then in effect. Often a less costly alternative to a home improvement loan, this financing technique allows the borrower to "open" the mortgage to increase the debt to its original amount, or the amount stated in the note, after the debt has been reduced by payments over a period of time. The mortgage usually includes a statement about the maximum amount that can be secured and the terms and conditions under which the loan can be opened and provisions for repayment.

Construction Loans

A **construction loan** is made to *finance the construction of improvements* on real estate such as homes, apartments and office buildings. The lender commits to the full amount of the loan but disburses the funds in payments during construction. These payments, also known as draws, are made to the general contractor or the owner for that part of the construction work that has been completed since the previous payment. Before each payment, the lender inspects the work. The general contractor must provide the lender with adequate waivers of lien that release all mechanic's lien rights for the work covered by the payment.

This kind of loan generally bears a higher-than-market interest rate because of the risks assumed by the lender. These risks include the inadequate releasing of mechanic's liens, possible delays in completing the construction or the financial failure of the contractor or subcontractors. This type of financing is generally *short-term* or *interim financing.* The borrower pays interest only, periodically, on the monies that have been disbursed to that payment date. The borrower is expected to arrange for a permanent loan, also known as an *end loan* or *take-out loan,* that will repay or "take out" the construction financing lender when the work is completed.

Sale-and-Leaseback

Sale-and-leaseback arrangements are used as an alternative to financing large commercial or industrial properties. The land and building, usually used by the seller for business purposes, are sold to an investor, such as an insurance company. The real estate is then leased back by the buyer (the investor) to the seller, who continues to conduct business on the property as a tenant. The buyer becomes the lessor, and the original owner becomes the lessee. This enables a business firm with money invested in the real estate to free that money so it can be used as working capital.

Sale-and-leaseback arrangements are complex. They involve complicated legal procedures, and their success is usually related to the effects the transaction has on the firm's tax situation. Legal and tax experts should be involved in this type of transaction.

Installment Contracts/ Contracts for Deed

Real estate can be purchased under an *installment contract,* also known as a *contract for deed, land contract of sale, agreement of sale* or *articles of agreement for deed.* Real estate is often sold on contract if mortgage financing is unavailable or too expensive. If the purchaser does not have a sufficient down payment to cover the difference between a mortgage loan and the selling price to assume the seller's loan, an installment contract could be used, provided the terms of the original mortgage do not prevent an assumption. The purchaser under an installment contract makes installment payments according to the terms of the contract and receives title to the real estate only after the terms have been met.

Buydowns

A **buydown** is a way of temporarily lowering the initial interest rate on a mortgage loan. Perhaps a homebuilder wishes to stimulate sales by offering a lower-than-market rate. Or a particular buyer is having trouble qualifying for a loan at the prevailing rates, and some relatives or the sellers want to help the buyer qualify. By donating in advance or "prepaying" some of the interest to the lender on the borrower's behalf, one can "buy down" the original interest rate for a period of time. Typical buydown arrangements reduce the interest rate by 1 to 3 percent over the first one to three years of the loan term.

Home Equity Loans

Home equity loans are a source of funds for homeowners who wish to finance the purchase of expensive items, consolidate existing installment loans on credit card debt or pay for medical, education, home improvement or other expenses. Use of this type of financing has increased in recent years, partly because interest on consumer loans is no longer deductible under the income tax laws. Home equity loans are secured by the borrower's residence, and the interest charged is deductible up to a loan limit of $100,000.

A home equity loan can be taken out as a fixed loan amount or as an equity line of credit. With the home equity line of credit, the lender extends a line of credit that the borrowers can use whenever they want. The borrowers can receive their money by a check sent to them, deposits made in a checking or savings account, or a book of drafts the borrowers can use up to their credit limit.

Using the equity buildup in the home to finance purchases is an alternative to refinancing. The original mortgage loan remains in place; the home equity loan is junior to that lien. If the homeowner refinances, the original mortgage loan is paid off and replaced by a new loan. The homeowner must compare the costs for a new mortgage loan, interest rates, total monthly payments and income-tax consequences to decide which alternative is best.

FINANCING LEGISLATION

The federal government regulates the lending practices of mortgage lenders through the Truth-in-Lending Act, Equal Credit Opportunity Act and the Real Estate Settlement Procedures Act.

Truth-in-Lending Act and Regulation Z

Regulation Z, which was promulgated pursuant to the *Truth-in-Lending Act,* requires credit institutions to inform borrowers of the true cost of obtaining credit so that the borrower can compare the costs of various lenders and avoid the uninformed use of credit. Regulation Z applies when credit is extended to individuals for personal, family or household uses and the amount of credit is $25,000 or less. Regardless of the amount, Regulation Z always applies when a credit transaction is secured by a residence. The regulation does not apply to business or commercial loans or to agricultural loans of more than $25,000.

The regulation requires that the consumer be fully informed of all finance charges, as well as the true annual interest rate, before a transaction is consummated. The finance charges must include any loan fees, finders' fees, service charges and points, as well as interest. In the case of a mortgage loan made to finance the purchase of a dwelling, the lender must compute and disclose the *annual percentage rate (APR)* but does not have to indicate the total interest payable during the term of the loan. Also, the lender does not have to include as part of the finance charge such actual costs as title fees, legal fees, appraisal fees, credit reports, survey fees and closing expenses.

Creditor. A *creditor,* for purposes of Regulation Z, is a person who extends consumer credit more than 25 times a year—or more than five times a year, if the transaction involves a dwelling as security. The credit must be subject to a finance charge or payable in more than four installments by written agreement.

Advertising. Regulation Z provides strict regulation of real estate advertisements that include mortgage financing terms. General phrases like "liberal terms available" may be used, but if details are given, they must comply with this act. By the provisions of the act, the annual percentage rate—which includes all charges—rather than the interest rate alone *must be stated.*

Specific credit terms, such as the down payment, monthly payment, dollar amount of the finance charge or term of the loan, may not be advertised unless the following information is set forth as well: cash price; required down payment; number, amount and due dates of all payments; and annual percentage rate. The total of all payments to be made over the term of the mortgage must also be specified unless the advertised credit refers to a first mortgage to finance acquisition of a dwelling.

Three-day right of rescission. In the case of most consumer credit transactions covered by Regulation Z, the borrower has three days in which he or she may rescind the transaction by merely notifying the lender. This right of rescission does not apply to residential first mortgage loans, but it does apply to refinancing.

Penalties. Regulation Z provides penalties for noncompliance. The penalty for violation of an administrative order enforcing Regulation Z is $10,000 for each day the violation continues. A fine of up to $10,000 may be imposed for engaging in an unfair or deceptive practice. In addition, a creditor may be liable to a consumer for twice the amount of the finance charge, for a minimum of $100 and a maximum of $1,000, plus court costs, attorney's fees and any actual damages. Willful violation is a misdemeanor punishable by a fine of up to $5,000, one year's imprisonment or both.

Equal Credit Opportunity Act

The federal **Equal Credit Opportunity Act (ECOA),** in effect since 1975, prohibits lenders and others who grant or arrange credit to consumers from discriminating against credit applicants on the basis of race, color, religion, national origin, sex, marital status, age (provided the applicant is of legal age) or dependency upon public assistance. In addition, lenders and other creditors must inform all rejected credit applicants, in writing, of the principal reasons why credit was denied or terminated.

Real Estate Settlement Procedures Act

The federal Real Estate Settlement Procedures Act (RESPA) was created to encourage homeownership by protecting consumers from unreasonable expenses for settlement. This law will be discussed in detail in the next chapter.

•   •   •   •   •   •   •

KEY TERMS

adjustable-rate mortgage (ARM)   loan-to-value ratio
balloon payment   open-end loan
blanket loan   package loan
buydown   private mortgage insurance (PMI)
construction loan   purchase-money mortgage
conventional loan   Regulation Z
discount points   reverse annuity mortgage (RAM)
Equal Credit Opportunity Act (ECOA)   sale and leaseback
FHA loan   VA loan
growing equity mortgage (GEM)   wraparound loan
home equity loan

SUMMARY

The cost for credit when financing a real estate purchase includes finances charges such as loan origination fees, points and, in some cases, mortgage insurance premiums that are paid at closing, and the recurring cost of interest and any mortgage insurance premiums.

For the lender to sell a mortgage loan, its income must be competitive in the money market. Discount points may be charged to increase the yield of the loan. Points may be paid by the buyer, the seller or shared by both.

There are many types of loan repayment plans in addition to fully amortized, fixed interest and straight loans. Adjustable-rate mortgages, growing equity mortgages and reverse annuity mortgages have been developed.

The types of mortgage programs available include conventional loans and those insured by FHA or private mortgage insurance companies or guaranteed by the VA. FHA and VA loans must meet certain requirements for the borrower to obtain the benefits of government backing, which induces the lender to lend its funds.

Other types of real estate financing include purchase-money mortgages, blanket loans, package loans, open-end loans, wraparound loans, construction loans, sale-and-leaseback agreements, installment contracts and buydowns.

Regulation Z requires lenders to inform prospective borrowers who use their homes as security for credit of all finance charges involved in such a loan. Severe penalties are provided for noncompliance. The federal Equal Credit Opportunity Act prohibits creditors from discriminating against credit applicants on the basis of race, color, religion, national origin, sex, marital status, age or dependency on public assistance. The Real Estate Settlement Procedures Act protects the consumer from unreasonable expenses for settlement.

Questions

1. The *M*'s are purchasing a lakefront summer home in a new resort development. The house is completely equipped, and the *M*'s are seeking a loan that covers the purchase price of the residence, including furnishings and appliances. This kind of financing is
   a. a wraparound loan.
   b. a package loan.
   c. a blanket loan.
   d. an unconventional loan.

2. The *D*'s purchased a residence for $95,000. They made a down payment of $15,000 and agreed to assume the seller's existing mortgage, which had a current balance of $23,000. The *D*'s financed the remaining $57,000 of the purchase price by executing a mortgage and note to the seller. This type of loan, by which the seller becomes the mortgagee, is called a
   a. wraparound mortgage.
   b. package mortgage.
   c. balloon note.
   d. purchase-money mortgage.

3. *F* continues to live in the home she purchased 30 years ago, but she now receives monthly checks, thanks to her
   a. straight mortgage.
   b. adjustable-rate mortgage.
   c. reverse annuity mortgage.
   d. overriding deed of trust.

4. A purchaser obtains a fixed-rate loan to finance a home. Which of the following characteristics is true of this type of loan?
   a. The amount of interest to be paid is predetermined.
   b. The loan cannot be sold in the secondary market.
   c. The monthly payment amount will fluctuate each month.
   d. The interest rate change may be based on an index.

5. In a loan that requires periodic payments that do not fully amortize the loan balance by the final payment, what term best describes the final payment?
   a. Adjustment payment
   b. Acceleration payment
   c. Balloon payment
   d. Variable payment

6. A developer received a loan that covers five parcels of real estate and provides for the release of the mortgage lien on each parcel when certain payments are made on the loan. This type of loan arrangement is called a
   a. purchase-money mortgage.
   b. blanket loan.
   c. package loan.
   d. wraparound loan.

7. Funds for Federal Housing Administration (FHA) loans are usually provided by
   a. the Federal Housing Administration (FHA).
   b. the Federal Reserve.
   c. qualified lenders.
   d. the seller.

8. Under the provisions of the Truth-in-Lending Act (Regulation Z), the annual percentage rate (APR) of a finance charge includes all of the following components *except*

    a. discount points.
    b. the broker's commission.
    c. the loan origination fee.
    d. the loan interest rate.

9. A home is purchased using a fixed-rate, fully amortized mortgage loan. Which of the following is true regarding this mortgage?

    a. A balloon payment will be made at the end of the loan.
    b. Each payment amount is the same.
    c. Each payment reduces the principal by the same amount.
    d. The principal amount in each payment is greater than the interest amount.

10. A borrower obtains a mortgage loan to make repairs on her home. The loan is not insured or guaranteed by a government agency, and the mortgage document secures the amount of the loan as well as any future funds advanced to the borrower by the lender. This borrower has obtained a(n)

    a. wraparound mortgage.
    b. conventional loan.
    c. open-end loan.
    d. growing equity mortgage.

11. The federal Equal Credit Opportunity Act prohibits lenders from discriminating against potential borrowers on the basis of all of the following *except*

    a. race.
    b. sex.
    c. source of income.
    d. amount of income.

12. Which of the following is an example of a conventional loan?

    a. A mortgage loan insured by the Federal Housing Administration
    b. A second loan for home improvements secured through a credit union
    c. A loan obtained through a private lender with a VA guarantee
    d. An installment sale

21 Closing the Real Estate Transaction

CLOSING THE TRANSACTION

Closing or *settlement* is the consummation of the real estate transaction, which actually involves two events: The promises made in the sales contract are fulfilled, and the buyer's loan is closed, that is, the mortgage loan funds are dispersed by the lender. The preceding chapters discussed the various steps that lead to this point. An agreement of sale is the blueprint for completing the transaction. Before exchanging documents and funds the parties should assure themselves that the stipulations of the agreement of sale have been met.

The buyer wants to be sure that the seller is delivering good title and that the property is in the promised condition. This involves inspecting the title evidence, the deed the seller will give and any documents showing that liens have been removed, the survey, the termite report and leases if there are tenants on the premises. The seller wants to be sure that the buyer has obtained the appropriate funds to complete the sale. Both parties will want to inspect the closing statement to make sure that all monies involved in the transaction have been accounted for properly. The parties may wish to be accompanied by their attorneys at closing.

When the parties are satisfied that everything is in order, the exchange is made and all pertinent documents are then recorded. The documents must be recorded in the correct order to avoid creating a defect in the title. For example, if the seller is paying off an existing loan and the buyer is obtaining a new loan, the seller's satisfaction of mortgage must be recorded before the deed to the buyer is recorded. The buyer's new mortgage must then be recorded after the deed because the buyer cannot pledge the property as security for the loan until he or she owns it.

A real estate professional should assist in preclosing arrangements. This includes estimating the approximate amount of money the buyer will need and the seller will receive at the closing. The closing represents the culmination of the service the real estate firm provides. The sale that the licensee has negotiated is completed, and the broker's commission (and thus the salesperson's commission) is usually paid out of the proceeds at the closing.

Title Procedures

As mentioned in the preceding overview, the buyer and the buyer's lender want assurance that the seller's title complies with the requirements of the agreement of sale. In Pennsylvania, the buyer is responsible for determining that he or she is taking good title to the property. This is usually done by obtaining an *abstract of title* from an attorney or a title insurance company. The abstract sets forth the status of the seller's title, showing recorded liens, encumbrances, easements, conditions or restrictions that encumber the seller's title.

The abstract should be reviewed by the buyer and seller and their representatives (either agents or attorneys) *before* closing. This allows time to resolve problems that could delay the settlement. When a buyer is purchasing a title insurance policy, any matters that would prevent the title from being insurable are normally raised by the title company and resolved before a policy is issued. This must occur before closing so that the title policy can be issued for settlement.

Unless the buyer has agreed to take title subject to certain liens, the seller will have to satisfy any liens in order to convey clear title. When the purchaser pays cash or obtains a new loan to purchase the property, the seller's existing mortgage usually is paid in full and satisfied on the record. To know the exact amount required to satisfy the existing mortgage, the seller secures a *payoff statement* from the lender. The payoff statement indicates the figures as of the date of settlement, including the unpaid amount of principal, interest due through the date of payment, the fee for issuing the satisfaction piece and credits (if any) for tax and insurance reserves. The same procedure would be followed for any other liens that must be released before the buyer takes title.

For transactions in which the buyer assumes the seller's existing mortgage loan, the buyer needs to know the exact balance of the loan as of the closing date. In some areas, it is customary for the buyer to obtain a *mortgage reduction certificate* from the lender, certifying the amount owed on the mortgage loan, the interest rate and the last interest payment made.

Because the buyer's abstract is prepared several days or weeks before the closing, this may not necessarily be accurate as of the date of settlement. For this reason a second search is made after the closing and immediately before the new deed is recorded to identify any recordings since the previous search.

Checking the Property

The property should be checked before closing for several reasons. One is to determine if there are any encroachments. Commonly, a survey is used to spot the location of all buildings, driveways, fences and other improvements located primarily on the premises being purchased. A survey also indicates any improvements located on adjoining property that may encroach on the premises. Depending on the nature of the encroachments, they may pose title problems. As a practical matter, it is useful for the new owner to be able to identify the property boundaries and any easements that might be indicated on the survey. Many buyers have the surveyor place stakes to physically identify boundaries.

The buyer is also concerned about the physical condition of the property. Shortly before the closing the buyer usually makes a *final inspection* to be sure that the property will be delivered in the condition stated in the agreement of sale. The inspection reveals that any repairs that were agreed to have been made, that both the inside and outside of the property have been well maintained, that all fixtures are in place and that there has been no unauthorized removal or alteration of any part of the improvements. It is also important to determine that there are no unauthorized parties in possession of the property. As a practical matter, it is easier to resolve problems relating to these issues before closing rather than resorting to legal proceedings after settlement.

CONDUCTING CLOSINGS

Closings may be held at a number of locations, including the office of the title company, the lending institution, one of the parties' attorneys, the broker or the recorder of deeds. Those attending a closing may include

- the buyer;
- the seller;
- the real estate salesperson or broker (from the selling and/or listing office[s]);
- the attorney(s) for the seller and/or buyer;
- the representatives and/or attorneys for lending institutions involved with the buyer's new mortgage loan or the buyer's assumption of the seller's existing loan; and
- the representative of the title insurance company.

Closing agent or closing officer. One person usually conducts the proceedings at a closing and calculates the official settlement, or division of incomes and expenses, between the parties. In some areas of Pennsylvania, real estate brokers preside; in others the closing agent is the buyer's or seller's attorney, a representative of the lender or the representative of a title company. Some title companies and law firms employ paralegal assistants who conduct closings for their firms. Before closing, the title insurance or title certificate, surveys, property insurance policy and other items must be ordered and reviewed; arrangements must be made with the parties for the time and place of closing; and closing statements and other documents must be prepared.

IRS reporting requirements. Every real estate transaction must be reported to the Internal Revenue Service by the closing agent on a Form 1099. Information includes the sales price and the seller's social security number. If the person responsible for conducting the closing does not notify the IRS, the responsibility then falls on (in the following order) the mortgage lender, the seller's broker, the buyer's broker or other persons as designated in the IRS regulations.

Licensee's Role at Closing

Depending on the local custom, the licensee's role at a closing can vary from appearing to collect the commission or acting as the authorized representative of one of the parties to the broker conducting the closing. Although the licensee's job is essentially over when the sales contract is signed, generally the licensee continues to oversee a variety of details so that the transaction can proceed smoothly to closing.

The licensee or staff member of the brokerage firm follows the transaction to see that any contingencies in the agreement of sale are satisfied. This could include helping a buyer locate a mortgage lender or coordinating inspections or repairs for wood-boring insects, structural conditions, water supplies, sewage facilities or toxic substances. Licensees, however, must be careful not to *recommend* people to conduct these inspections because of the liability created in the event the buyer is injured by a provider's service.

Once contingencies are satisfied, the licensee or staff assistant coordinates arrangements for closing exhibits with whomever is conducting the closing. Exhibits at closing include a fire and hazard insurance policy, title insurance policy, survey, lien payoff statements, real estate tax receipts or other documents that might be required by the lender or title insurance company.

Lender's Interest in Closing

Whether a buyer is obtaining new financing or assuming the seller's existing loan, the lender wants to protect its security interest in the real estate. This is done by making sure that the buyer is getting marketable title so that there will be no liens with greater priority than the mortgage lien and by ensuring that the value of the collateral is protected in case the property is damaged or destroyed. The lender frequently requires a title insurance policy, a fire and hazard insurance policy, additional information such as a survey, a termite or other inspection report or a certificate of occupancy and a reserve or escrow account for tax and insurance payments. The lender may be represented by its own attorney at the closing.

RESPA REQUIREMENTS

The federal **Real Estate Settlement Procedures Act (RESPA)** intends to further the goal of encouraging homeownership by aiding consumers during the mortgage loan settlement process and protecting them from abusive lending practices. RESPA provides consumers with greater and more timely information about certain aspects of mortgage lending and the costs of settling or closing mortgage loans and eliminates *kickbacks,* certain types of referral fees and other costs associated with a loan that tend to unnecessarily increase the settlement costs.

RESPA requirements apply when the purchase is financed by a federally related mortgage loan. Federally related loans include those made by banks, savings and loan associations or other lenders whose deposits are insured by federal agencies; loans insured by the FHA or guaranteed by the VA; loans administered by the U.S. Department of Housing and Urban Development; or loans intended to be sold by the lender to Fannie Mae, Ginnie Mae or Freddie Mac. RESPA is administered by HUD.

RESPA regulations apply to first lien, residential mortgage loans made to finance the purchase, either for investment or occupancy, of one- to four-family homes, cooperatives and condominiums. They also apply to second or subordinate liens for home equity loans. A transaction financed solely by a purchase-money mortgage taken back by the seller, an installment contract (contract for deed) or the buyer's assumption of the seller's existing loan would not be covered by RESPA, unless the terms of the assumed loan were modified or the lender charged more than $50 for the assumption.

Computerized Loan Origination

Recent changes in RESPA rules help the real estate industry and affiliated businesses provide services that enhance the homebuying process and satisfy consumer demand for one-stop-shopping. Computerized loan originations (CLOs) are automated systems that enable a purchaser/borrower to locate a lender, submit a loan application and obtain a conditional loan commitment right in the real estate office. The consumer can comparison shop a variety of lenders and their various loan products. Although these systems must offer the products of multiple lenders, consumers must also be informed that other lenders' products are available to enhance their ability to comparison shop. CLOs also enable the consumer to make multiple loan applications if desired to see which program is most suitable and where they can obtain a commitment in the shortest time.

Controlled Business Arrangements

Another service that appeals to one-stop-shop consumers is controlled business arrangements (CBAs). These are networks of interrelated companies that offer real estate–related services. Real estate firms, title insurance companies, mortgage brokerage firms and even pest control or moving companies may be affiliated with one another. One of the concerns about these arrangements is that consumers could be hurt rather than helped if they are unaware of the relationship among the various firms or if they are coerced into using the services of an affiliated business. RESPA permits CBAs as long as the relationship between the firms is disclosed in writing to consumers, they are free to obtain the services elsewhere and fees are *not* exchanged among the affiliated companies *simply for the referral* of business.

Disclosure Requirements

Lenders and settlement agents have certain *disclosure* obligations at the time of a loan application and at the closing of a loan.

- *Special information booklet:* Lenders must provide a copy of the HUD booklet *Settlement Costs and You* to every person from whom they receive or for whom they prepare a loan application. The booklet provides the borrower with general information about settlement (closing) costs and explains the various provisions of RESPA, including a line-by-line discussion of the Uniform Settlement Statement. Loan applicants must be given the booklet at the time the application is made or within three days thereafter. Licensees should review a copy of the booklet to be familiar with its contents.

- *Good-faith estimate of settlement costs:* No later than three business days after the receipt of the loan application, the lender must provide the borrower with a good-faith estimate of the settlement costs the borrower is likely to incur. This estimate may be a specific figure or a range of costs based upon comparable past transactions in the area. In addition, if the lender requires use of a particular attorney or title company to conduct the closing, the lender must state whether it has any business relationship with that firm and must estimate the charges for this service.

- *Uniform Settlement Statement (HUD Form 1):* RESPA requires that a special HUD form be completed to itemize all charges to be paid by the borrower and seller in connection with settlement. The Uniform Settlement Statement includes all charges that will be collected at closing, whether required by the lender or a third party. Items paid by the borrower and seller outside closing that are not required by the lender are not included on HUD-1. Charges required by the lender that are paid for before closing are indicated as "paid outside of closing" (POC).

A completed settlement statement must be made available for inspection by the borrower *at or before* settlement. Borrowers have the right to inspect the completed HUD-1, to the extent that the figures are available *one business day before the closing.* (Under the act, sellers are not entitled to this privilege.)

Lenders must retain these statements for two years after the date of closing, unless the loan (and its servicing) is sold or otherwise disposed of. The Uniform Settlement Statement may be altered to allow for local custom, and certain lines may be deleted if they do not apply in the area.

IN PRACTICE. . .	*Real estate licensees in Pennsylvania are required to prepare statements of estimated closing costs for buyers and sellers on appropriate* forms *prior to their signing the agreement of sale. The buyers should already have a general idea of the cash requirements needed for settlement before making the loan application. Figures 21.1 and 21.2 are examples of these forms.*
	Although RESPA requires the lender to keep settlement statements for two years after closing, the State Real Estate Commission requires that the broker retain documents of all real estate transactions for three years following the consummation of the transaction.

Escrow Accounts

RESPA prohibits lenders from requiring borrowers to deposit excessive amounts of money in escrow accounts for taxes and insurance, thus preventing the lender from taking advantage of the borrower by overbilling. Escrow rules prevent lenders from accumulating a cushion of more than two months' payments for taxes and insurance rather than four or five months that some lenders use to collect. Because lenders can set up only one escrow account per home loan (instead of one for taxes and a separate one for insurance), the two-month calculation is based on the total disbursements for taxes and insurance. Lenders must pay the tax and insurance bills from the account on a timely basis.

Within 45 days of settlement lenders are required to conduct an escrow account analysis before establishing the account and to prepare a statement for the borrower detailing the amount of the mortgage loan payment and the portion that will go into the escrow account. These amounts can be provided in the HUD-1 settlement statement. RESPA regulations are quite detailed about procedures for analyzing, reporting and adjusting escrow accounts during the term of the loan.

The specifics for calculating the two-month reserve amount can be confusing but they can be explained by the lender. Consumer guides and computer programs are also available for homeowners to calculate escrow accounts on their existing loans.

Kickbacks and Referral Fees

RESPA explicitly *prohibits the payment of kickbacks, or unearned fees* incident to or as part of a real estate settlement service. It prohibits the *payment* or *receipt* of any fee, kickback or thing of value when *no* services are actually rendered. This includes referrals for settlement services such as making mortgage loans, title searches, title insurance, services rendered by attorneys, surveys, credit reports or appraisals. Fee splitting or referral fees between cooperating brokers or members of multiple listing services, brokerage referral arrangements or the division of a commission between a broker and the broker's salespeople are not prohibited under RESPA.

In CLO systems, brokers may charge a fair fee for providing the mortgage loan accessing service, but the *borrower must pay the fee,* not the mortgage broker or lender. RESPA regulations clarify that these services and fee arrangements are

**Figure 21.1
Buyer's Estimated
Closing Costs**

PENNSYLVANIA ASSOCIATION OF REALTORS'
This form recommended and approved for, but not restricted to, use by members of the Pennsylvania Association of REALTORS'

REALTOR'

**BUYER'S CLOSING COSTS
ESTIMATED**

RE PROPERTY: _____

SETTLEMENT DATE: _____ PURCHASE PRICE $ _____

1. Title   Charges
  (a) Title Search $
  (b) Settlement/Notary Fees $
  (c) Title Insurance $
  (d) End's #100, #300, #710 others $
  (e) Mechanics Lien Insurance $
  (f) Recording Fees: Mortgage and/or Deed $
  (g) Transfer Tax $
  (h) Survey $
2. Agent's Services $
3. Hazard Insurance $
4. Tax Adjustments: (+/−)
  (a) School $
  (b) County $
  (c) Municipality $
  (d) $
  (e) $
5. Lienable (+/−) e.g. water, sewer, condo/associations
  (a) $
  (b) $
6. $
7. $
8. Lender
  (a) Fees (Part payment may be required before settlement) $
  (b) Appraisal & Credit Report (s) (Paid with application) $
  (c) Mortgage Insurance Premium $
  (d) Preparation Mortgage Documents $
  (e) VA Funding Fee $
  (f) Interest from   to $
  (g) $
  (h) $
9. Reserves Deposited With Lender (Escrow Account)
  (a) Hazard Insurance $
  (b) Mortgage Insurance Premium $
  (c) Taxes:
    (1) School $
    (2) County $
    (3) Municipality $
  (d) $

        Estimated Costs $

I/We understand the estimated costs are based on the best information available at this date and may be higher or lower at settlement.
MORTGAGE TYPE: ☐ FIXED RATE ☐ ADJUSTABLE RATE ☐ _____

**Estimated Monthly Payments
INITIALLY**
Based on $ _____ . for _____ years, at _____ %
Prinicpal and Interest.......... $
Taxes......................... $
Hazard Insurance............. $
Mortgage Insurance Premium ... $
      $
    Estimated Total $

**Estimated Maximum Monthly Payments
INITIALLY**
Based on $ _____ . for _____ years, at _____ %
Prinicpal and Interest.......... $
Taxes......................... $
Hazard Insurance............. $
Mortgage Insurance Premium ... $
      $
    Estimated Total $

If the interest rate charged by the mortgage lender is higher or lower than the above rates, the total monthly payments will be higher or lower. Because mortgage types and terms vary greatly, Buyer should consult the mortgage lender in regards to mortgage costs and terms.

An agreement for the sale of real estate must contain the zoning classification of the property except for a single family dwelling. A real estate recovery fund exists to reimburse persons who have suffered monetary loss and have obtained an uncollectable judgment due to fraud, misrepresentation or deceit in a real estate transaction by a Pennsylvania licensee. For complete details, call 717-783-3658.

THE AGENT REPRESENTS THE SELLER, however, the Agent may perform services for the Buyer in connection with financing, insurance and document preparation.

We also understand and have received a copy of these estimated closing costs and estimated monthly payments before signing the agreement of sale.

AGENT: _____   BUYER: _____ (seal)
Prepared by: _____   BUYER: _____ (seal)
DATE: _____   BUYER: _____ (seal)
404   5/85

**Figure 21.2
Seller's Estimated
Closing Costs**

PENNSYLVANIA ASSOCIATION OF REALTORS®   Form 405-2
This form recommended and approved for, but not restricted to, use by
members of the Pennsylvania Association of REALTORS®

SELLER'S CLOSING COSTS
ESTIMATED

RE PROPERTY: _____
SETTLEMENT DATE: _____   SALE PRICE $ _____

                                                                    Charges

1. Agents Fee _____ $ _____

2. Preparation of Deed _____ $ _____

3. Transfer Tax_____ $ _____

4. Tax Adjustments (+/—)
   (a) School _____ $ _____
   (b) County _____ $ _____
   (c) Municipality_____ $ _____
   (d) _____ $ _____
   (e) _____ $ _____

5. Lienable Items (+/—) e.g. water, sewer, condo/associations
   (a) _____ $ _____
   (b) _____ $ _____

6. Mortgage Placement Fee _____ $ _____

7. Wood-Infestation Report _____ $ _____

8. Municipal Certification _____ $ _____

9. Settlement Fee_____ $ _____

10. Notary Fees _____ $ _____

11. Survey_____ $ _____

12. _____ $ _____

13. _____ $ _____

                        Estimated Costs $ _____

Sale Price _____ $ _____
Less Estimated Costs _____ $ _____
                    Estimated Proceeds $ _____

The estimated proceeds do not take into account any mortgages, liens, assessments or other obligations which may be
against the property.

The above figures are approximated closing costs and will be adjusted as of date of final settlement, if necessary.

I/We understand and have received a copy of these estimated closing costs.

AGENT: _____   SELLER: _____(seal)
BY:_____   SELLER: _____(seal)
                                            SELLER: _____(seal)
DATE: _____   SELLER: _____(seal)
COPIES: WHITE; SELLER, YELLOW; AGENT   8/83
PENNSYLVANIA ASSOCIATION OF REALTORS®   SPEED PAR FORMS

permissible as long as they are properly disclosed, fees are charged for services actually rendered and the mortgage broker or lender does not pay a referral fee for the loan. As previously mentioned, affiliated companies in CBAs cannot exchange fees simply for referring business.

IN PRACTICE...	*The RESPA rules are very detailed about CLOs, CBAs and kickbacks and referral fees, and interpretations and clarifications of the rules continue to emerge. The purpose of this introduction to RESPA is to alert licensees to the provisions of the law. Specific questions about activities governed by RESPA should be referred to HUD or legal counsel.*

PREPARATION OF SETTLEMENT STATEMENTS

Both the buyer and the seller incur expenses in a typical sales transaction. These include items prepaid by the seller for which he or she must be reimbursed, such as prepaid taxes, and items for which the seller has some responsibility but that the buyer will pay sometime after settlement, such as taxes that are due later in the year. The financial responsibility for these items must be *prorated,* or divided, between the buyer and the seller. All expenses and prorated items are accounted for on the settlement statement to determine the cash required by the buyer and the net proceeds to the seller.

How the Settlement Statement Works

The completion of a *settlement statement* involves an accounting of the parties' debits and credits. A **debit** is a charge, an amount that the party being debited owes and must pay at the closing. A **credit** is an amount entered in a person's favor—an amount that has already been paid, an amount being reimbursed or an amount the buyer promises to pay in the form of a loan.

To determine the amount the buyer needs at the closing, the buyer's debits are totaled—any expenses and prorated amounts for items prepaid by the seller are added to the purchase price. Then the buyer's credits are totaled. These include the earnest money (already paid), the amount of the loan the buyer is obtaining or assuming and the seller's share of any prorated items that the buyer will pay in the future. Finally, the total of the buyer's credits is subtracted from the total amount the buyer owes (debits) to arrive at the actual amount of cash the buyer must bring to the closing. Usually the buyer brings a bank cashier's check or a certified personal check.

A similar procedure is followed to determine how much money the seller will actually receive. The seller's debits and credits are each totaled. The credits include the purchase price plus the buyer's share of any prorated items that the seller has prepaid. The seller's debits include expenses, the seller's share of prorated items to be paid later by the buyer and the balance of any mortgage loan or other lien that the seller is paying off. Finally, the total of the seller's charges is subtracted from the total credits to arrive at the amount the seller will receive.

Expenses

In addition to the payment of the sales price and the proration of taxes, interest and the like, a number of other expenses and charges may be involved in a real estate transaction.

Broker's commission. The responsibility for paying the broker's commission will have been determined by previous agreement. The seller or the buyer may pay the commission or both may be responsible for a share of the commission, depending on the provisions of the agency agreements.

Attorney's fees. If either of the parties' attorneys will be paid from the closing proceeds, that party will be charged with the expense on the closing statement. This expense may include fees for the preparation or review of documents or for representing the parties at settlement.

Recording expenses. In Pennsylvania, the charge for recording a document varies according to the size of the document and the number of additional registrations involved.

The *seller* usually pays for recording charges (filing fees) that are necessary to clear all defects and furnish the purchaser with a clear title according to the terms of the contract. Items usually charged to the seller include recording the satisfaction of mortgages, quitclaim deeds, affidavits and satisfaction of mechanic's lien claims. The *purchaser* pays for recording charges relating to the actual transfer of the title. Usually such items include recording the deed that conveys title to the purchaser and the mortgage executed by the purchaser.

Transfer tax. Pennsylvania requires that transfer tax be paid on certain real estate transactions. Transfer taxes are charged at the rate of 1 percent of the consideration or 1 percent of value (if there is no consideration). In addition to the state tax, many cities and local municipalities in Pennsylvania charge transfer taxes. The buyer and the seller might share this expense equally, or they can agree to some other arrangement.

Title expenses. The responsibility for title expenses varies according to local custom. As discussed earlier, in Pennsylvania the buyer is normally responsible for charges associated with title evidence such as the title search and title insurance or certificate of title. The Pennsylvania Title Insurance Rating Bureau regulates the issuance of title insurance and has a set of combined, all-inclusive title insurance rates for buyers of real estate. The set rate covers the initial title search, the later search to "bring the title down" to the closing date and the title insurance policy. (See Figure 21.3.)

Municipal lien and sewage lien letters are required in some areas as further evidence that there are no pending liens. Any fees for these letters are, by custom, generally paid by the seller.

Tax certification letters, sometimes requiring a fee, may be necessary in cases in which the seller does not have any of the immediate past three years' tax receipts to deliver to the buyer. Because real estate tax liens in many areas are not immediately filed in the recorder's office, it may be necessary to provide the buyer with evidence that the taxes have been paid.

Deed preparation fee. This fee is charged by the preparer of the deed. It is customarily paid by the seller.

Loan fees. When the purchaser is securing a mortgage loan, the lender usually charges a loan origination fee of from 1 to 3 percent (or more) of the loan.

**Figure 21.3
Schedule of
All-Inclusive
Title Insurance
Rates**

ALL INCLUSIVE SCHEDULE OF RATES
Pennsylvania - Area I
$0-$350,000 Effective March 1, 1995

Unit of Insurance or Fraction Thereof		Area I	
		Basic	Reissue *
$0 - $30,000		380.00	330.00
$30,001 - $31,000		387.25	336.50
$31,001 - $32,000		394.50	343.00
$32,001 - $33,000		401.75	349.50
$33,001 - $34,000		409.00	356.00
$34,001 - $35,000		416.25	362.50
$35,001 - $36,000		423.50	369.00
$36,001 - $37,000		430.75	375.50
$37,001 - $38,000		438.00	382.00
$38,001 - $39,000		445.25	388.50
$39,001 - $40,000		452.50	395.00
$40,001 - $41,000		459.75	401.50
$41,001 - $42,000		467.00	408.00
$42,001 - $43,000		474.25	414.50
$43,001 - $44,000		481.50	421.00
$44,001 - $45,000		488.75	427.50
$45,001 - $46,000		494.75	433.00
$46,001 - $47,000		500.75	438.50
$47,001 - $48,000		506.75	444.00
$48,001 - $49,000		512.75	449.50
$49,001 - $50,000		518.75	455.00
$50,001 - $51,000		524.75	460.50
$51,001 - $52,000		530.75	466.00
$52,001 - $53,000		536.75	471.50
$53,001 - $54,000		542.75	477.00
$54,001 - $55,000		548.75	482.50
$55,001 - $56,000		554.75	488.00
$56,001 - $57,000		560.75	493.50
$57,001 - $58,000		566.75	499.00
$58,001 - $59,000		572.75	504.50
$59,001 - $60,000		578.75	510.00
$60,001 - $61,000		584.75	515.50
$61,001 - $62,000		590.75	521.00
$62,001 - $63,000		596.75	526.50
$63,001 - $64,000		602.75	532.00
$64,001 - $65,000		608.75	537
$65,001 - $66,000		614.75	
$66,001 - $67,000		620	
$67,001 - $68,000			
$68,001 - $69,0			
$69,0			

		1,690.50	
		1,953.75	1,694.75
$327,001 - $328,000		1,958.75	1,699.00
$328,001 - $329,000		1,963.75	1,703.25
$329,001 - $330,000		1,968.75	1,707.50
$330,001 - $331,000		1,973.75	1,711.75
$331,001 - $332,000		1,978.75	1,716.00
$332,001 - $333,000		1,983.75	1,720.25
$333,001 - $334,000		1,988.75	1,724.50
$334,001 - $335,000		1,993.75	1,728.75
$335,001 - $336,000		1,998.75	1,733.00
$336,001 - $337,000		2,003.75	1,737.25
$337,001 - $338,000		2,008.75	1,741.50
$338,001 - $339,000		2,013.75	1,745.75
$339,001 - $340,000		2,018.75	1,750.00
$340,001 - $341,000		2,023.75	1,754.25
$341,001 - $342,000		2,028.75	1,758.50
$342,001 - $343,000		2,033.75	1,762.75
$343,001 - $344,000		2,038.75	1,767.00
$344,001 - $345,000		2,043.75	1,771.25
$345,001 - $346,000		2,048.75	1,775.50
$346,001 - $347,000		2,053.75	1,779.75
$347,001 - $348,000		2,058.75	1,784.00
$348,001 - $349,000		2,063.75	1,788.25
$349,001 - $350,000		2,068.75	1,792.50

On the excess over $350,000		Basic Rate	Re-Issue Rate
$350,001 - $500,000	Add per $1,000	$5.00	$4.25
$500,001 - $1,000,000	Add per $1,000	$3.75	$3.50
$1,000,001 - $2,000,000	Add per $1,000	$2.75	$2.50

*NOTE: If the face amount of the current insurance exceeds the face amount of the insurance previously issued, the charge for the excess will be determined by the applicable basic fee. Buyer qualifies for reissue rate only

DISBURSEMENT CHARGE - Against the seller - $35.00

CANCELLATION CHARGES - If application is canceled after the orginal evidence of title is issued under Company or Agent Procedure, a minimum charge of $100.00 is to be made for such cancellation.

For Quotes over $2,000,000
Call your local Agent, Branch Office

Compilation Courtesy of T.A. Title Insurance Company.

Points also may be charged in addition to the origination fee. These charges are usually paid by the purchaser at settlement, unless there is an agreement that the seller will pay some portion. If the buyer is assuming the seller's existing financing, there may be an assumption fee.

The seller also may be charged fees by a lender. Under the terms of some mortgage loans, the seller may be required to pay a prepayment charge or penalty for paying off the mortgage loan in advance of its due date.

Tax and insurance reserves (escrow accounts). Many mortgage lenders require that borrowers provide a reserve fund or **escrow** account to pay future real estate taxes and insurance premiums. The borrower starts the account at closing by depositing funds to cover at least the amount of unpaid real estate taxes from the date of lien to the end of the current month. (The buyer receives a credit from the seller at closing for any unpaid taxes.) Thereafter, the borrower pays a portion of the taxes along with the loan payment. Because the borrower is responsible for maintaining adequate fire or hazard insurance as a condition of the mortgage loan, generally the first year's premium is paid in full at closing and a portion of the premium is paid thereafter in the loan payment. (See previous discussion about RESPA.)

Appraisal fees. Either the seller or the purchaser pays the appraisal fees, depending on who orders the appraisal. It is customary for the lender to require an appraisal when the buyer obtains a mortgage loan, for which the buyer will pay.

Survey fees. When obtaining a mortgage loan the purchaser customarily pays the survey fees. In some cases the agreement of sale may require the seller to furnish a survey.

Prorations

Most closings involve the division of financial responsibility between the buyer and the seller for such items as loan interest, taxes, rents, and fuel and utility bills. These allowances are called **prorations.** Prorations are necessary to ensure that expenses are fairly divided between the seller and the buyer. For example, the seller may owe current taxes that have not been billed; the buyer would want this settled at closing. Where taxes must be paid in advance, as in Pennsylvania, the seller is entitled to a rebate at the closing. If the buyer assumes the seller's existing mortgage, the seller usually owes the buyer an allowance for accrued interest through the date of closing.

Accrued items are items to be prorated that are owed by the seller but later will be paid by the buyer. The seller therefore pays for these items at closing by giving a credit to the buyer.

Prepaid items are items to be prorated that have been prepaid by the seller but not fully earned (not fully used up). They are therefore credits to the seller.

General rules for prorating. The rules or customs governing the computation of prorations for the closing of a real estate sale vary widely from state to state. In many states the real estate boards and the state bar associations have established closing rules and procedures. These rules may apply to closings for the entire state or they may merely affect closings within a given city, town or county.

Here are some general rules to guide you in studying the closing procedure and in preparing the closing statement.

- In Pennsylvania, the seller owns the property on the day of closing, and prorations are usually made *to and including the day of closing.*

- Mortgage interest, general real estate taxes, water bills, insurance premiums and similar expenses are usually computed by using *360 days in a year and 30 days in a month.* However, the rules in some areas provide for computing prorations on the basis of the actual number of days in the calendar month of closing. The agreement of sale may specify which method is to be used.

- Accrued or prepaid *general real estate taxes* are usually prorated at the closing. In Pennsylvania, taxes are generally prepaid and may be due in the early part of the year. The tax proration then could be for accrued or prorated taxes, depending on the time of year and the tax payment schedule.

- *Special assessments* for such municipal improvements as sewers, water mains or streets are usually paid in annual installments over several years. The municipality usually charges the property owner annual interest on the outstanding balance of future installments. In a sales transaction, the seller normally pays the current installment and the buyer assumes all future installments. *The special assessment installment generally is not prorated at the closing.* Some buyers, however, insist that the seller allow them a credit for the seller's share of the interest to the closing date. The agreement of sale may address the manner in which special assessments are to be handled at settlement.

- *Rents* are usually adjusted on the basis of the *actual* number of days in the month of closing. It is customary for the seller to receive the rents for the day of closing and to pay all expenses for that day. If any rents for the current month are uncollected when the sale is closed, the buyer will often agree by a separate letter to collect the rents if possible and remit the pro rata share to the seller.

- *Security deposits* made by tenants to cover the last month's rent of the lease or to cover the cost of repairing damage caused by the tenant are generally transferred by the seller to the buyer. Because of Pennsylvania's regulations regarding security deposits, it is wise to get the tenant's consent to such a transfer of the deposit.

- Depending on customary settlement procedures, evidence of *water and sewage charges,* whether billed monthly or quarterly, are presented at closing. The portion owed by the seller is debited through the date of closing; the prepaid portion is credited to the seller. Other utilities are not normally handled at closing; the utility company handles final billing.

You should verify these proration rules with the customs in your area.

Accounting for Credits and Charges

The items that must be accounted for in the closing statement fall into two general categories: prorations or other amounts due to either the buyer or seller (credit to) and paid for by the other party (debit to) *and* expenses or items paid by the seller or buyer (debit only).

The list on the top of page 376 shows which items are commonly credited to the buyer and which to the seller. Other items may be included in such a list, depending on the customs of your area.

The *buyer's earnest money,* although credited to the buyer, *is not debited to the seller.* The buyer receives a credit because that amount has already been paid toward the purchase price. As prescribed by state law, however, the money is held by the broker until settlement and will be included as part of the total amount due the seller. If the seller is paying off an existing loan and the buyer is obtaining a new one, these two items are accounted for with a debit *only to the seller for the amount of the payoff* and a credit *only to the buyer for the amount of the new loan.*

Accounting for expenses. Expenses paid out of the closing proceeds are debited only to the party making the payment. Occasionally, an expense item such as the state transfer tax is shared by the buyer and the seller, and each party will be debited for one-half the expense.

Items Credited to Buyer (debited to seller)	Items Credited to Seller (debited to buyer)
1. buyer's earnest money*	1. sales price*
2. unpaid principal balance of outstanding mortgage being assumed by buyer*	2. prorated premium for unearned (prepaid) portion of fire insurance
3. earned interest on existing assumed mortgage not yet payable (accrued)	3. coal or fuel oil on hand, usually figured at current market price (prepaid)
4. earned portion of general real estate tax not yet due (accrued)	4. insurance and tax reserve (if any) when outstanding mortgage is being assumed by buyer (prepaid)
5. unearned portion of current rent collected in advance	5. refund to seller of prepaid water charge and similar expenses
6. tenants' security deposits*	6. unearned portion of general real estate tax, if paid in advance
7. purchase-money mortgage	

*These items are not prorated; they are entered in full as listed.

THE ARITHMETIC OF PRORATING

Accurate prorating involves four questions:

1. What is the item being prorated?
2. Is it an accrued item that requires the determination of an earned amount?
3. Is it a prepaid item that requires that the unearned amount—a refund to the seller—be determined?
4. What arithmetic processes must be used?

The information contained in the previous sections will assist in answering the first three questions.

The computation of a proration involves identifying a yearly charge for the item to be prorated, then dividing by 12 to determine a monthly charge for the item. It is usually also necessary to establish a daily charge for the item by dividing the monthly charge by the number of days in the month. These smaller portions are then multiplied by the number of months and/or days in the prorated time period to determine the accrued or unearned amount that will be figured in the settlement.

Using this general principle, there are two methods of calculating prorations.

1. The yearly charge is divided by a *360-day year,* or 12 months of 30 days each.
2. The yearly charge is divided by 365 (366 in a leap year) to determine the daily charge. Then the actual number of days in the proration period is determined, and this number is multiplied by the daily charge.

In some cases, such as when a sale is closed on the 15th of the month, the one-half month's charge is computed by simply dividing the monthly charge by two.

The final proration figure will vary slightly, depending on which computation method is used. The final figure will also vary according to the number of decimal places to which the division is carried. *All of the computations in this text are computed by carrying the division to three decimal places.* The third decimal place is rounded off to cents only after the final proration figure is determined.

Accrued Items

When the taxes are levied for the calendar year but have not yet been paid, the accrued portion is for the period from January 1 to the date of closing. If the current tax bill has not yet been issued, the parties must agree on an estimated amount based on the previous year's bill and any known changes in assessment or tax levy for the current year.

For example, assume a sale is to be closed on April 17, and current real estate taxes of $1,200 are to be prorated accordingly. The accrued period, then, is 3 months, 17 days. First determine the prorated cost of the real estate tax per month and day:

$$\frac{\$100 \text{ per month}}{12)\$1,200} \qquad \frac{\$3.333 \text{ per day}}{30)\$100.000}$$

Next, multiply these figures by the accrued period and add the totals to determine the prorated real estate tax:

$100	$ 3.333	$300.000
× 3 months	× 17 days	+ 56.661
$300	$56.661	$356.661

Thus, the accrued real estate tax for 3 months, 17 days is $356.66 (rounded off to two decimal places after the final computation). This amount represents the seller's accrued earned tax; it will be *a credit to the buyer and a debit to the seller.*

Although these examples show proration as of the date of settlement, the agreement of sale may require otherwise. One possibility is the case in which the buyer's and seller's possession date does not coincide with the settlement date. The parties may elect to prorate according to the date of possession.

IN PRACTICE...

On Pennsylvania licensing examinations, tax prorations are usually based on a 30-day month (360-day year) unless specified otherwise in the problem. In practice, however, it is customary to base prorations on a 365-day year (366 days in leap years) in most areas. Title insurance companies provide proration charts that detail tax factors for each day in the year. To determine a tax proration using one of these charts, simply multiply the factor given for the closing date by the annual real estate tax.

Prepaid Items

A tax proration could be a prepaid item. As real estate tax may be paid in the early part of the year, tax prorations calculated for closings taking place later in the year must reflect the fact that the seller has already paid the tax. For example, in the above problem, suppose that the closing did not take place until

September 17 and that the taxes had been paid. The buyer, then, must reimburse the seller; the proration is *credited to the seller and debited to the buyer*.

In figuring the tax proration, it is necessary to ascertain the number of future days, months and years for which the taxes have been paid. The formula commonly used for this purpose is as follows:

	Years	Months	Days
Taxes paid to (Dec. 31, end of tax year)	1996	12	31
Date of closing (Sept. 17, 1996)	1996	9	17
Period for which tax must be paid		3	14

With this formula we can find the amount the buyer will reimburse the seller for the *unearned* portion of the real estate tax. The prepaid period, as determined using the formula for prepaid items, is 3 months, 14 days. Three months at $100 per month equals $300, and 14 days at $3.333 per day = $46.662. Add this up to determine that the proration is $346.662, or $346.66 *credited to the seller and debited to the buyer*.

Another example of a prepaid item is a water bill. Assume that the water is billed in advance by the city without using a meter. The six months' billing is $8 for the period ending October 31. The sale is to be closed on August 3. Because the water bill is paid to October 31, the prepaid time must be computed. Using a 30-day basis, the time period is the 27 days left in August plus two full months: $8 ÷ 6 = $1.333 per month. For one day, divide $1.333 by 30, which equals $0.044 per day. The prepaid period is 2 months, 27 days, so:

$$27 \text{ days} \quad \times \$0.044 = \$1.188$$
$$2 \text{ months} \times \$1.333 = \underline{\$2.666}$$
$$\$3.854 \text{ or } \$3.85$$

This is a prepaid item; it is *credited to the seller* and *debited to the buyer*.

To figure this on the basis of the actual days in the month of closing, the following process would be used:

$1.333 per month ÷ 31 days in August	=	$.043 per day
August 4 through August 31	=	28 days
28 days × $.043	=	$1.204
2 months × $1.333	=	$2.666
$1.204 + $2.666	=	$3.870 or *$3.87*

IN PRACTICE... | *Homeowner's insurance policies are not generally assumed. The typical policy is for one year. The seller will cancel the policy effective the date of closing and receive a refund of unused premium from the insurance company. The buyer purchases a new policy, effective the date of closing. Evidence of insurance coverage is required by the mortgage lender at closing.*

●   ●   ●   ●   ●   ●   ●

KEY TERMS   accrued item   prepaid item
                      credit   proration
                      debit   Real Estate Settlement Procedures
                      escrow   Act (RESPA)

SUMMARY   Closing a sale involves both title procedures and financial matters. The broker should be present at the closing to see that the sale is actually concluded and to account for the earnest money deposit.

Closings must be reported to the IRS on Form 1099.

The federal Real Estate Settlement Procedures Act (RESPA) requires disclosure of all settlement costs when a real estate purchase is financed by a federally related mortgage loan. RESPA requires lenders to use a Uniform Settlement Statement to detail the financial particulars of a transaction.

Usually the buyer orders and pays for the title evidence, such as title insurance, to ensure that the seller's title is acceptable.

The actual amount to be paid by the buyer at the closing is computed by preparation of a closing, or settlement, statement. This lists the sales price, earnest money deposit and all adjustments and prorations due between buyer and seller. The purpose of this statement is to determine the net amount due the seller at closing and the cash requirements of the buyer. The form is signed by both parties to evidence their approval.

Questions

•   •   •   •   •   •   •

1. Which of the following is true of real estate closings in Pennsylvania?
   a. Closings are generally conducted by real estate salespeople.
   b. The buyer usually receives the rents for the day of closing.
   c. The seller pays the commission.
   d. The buyer pays for title evidence.

2. All encumbrances and liens shown on the report of title, other than those waived or agreed to by the purchaser and listed in the contract, must be removed so that the title can be delivered free and clear. The removal of such encumbrances is the duty of the
   a. buyer.   c. broker.
   b. seller.   d. title company.

3. Legal title always passes from the seller to the buyer
   a. on the date of execution of the deed.
   b. when the closing statement has been signed.
   c. when the deed is placed in escrow.
   d. when the deed is delivered.

4. Which of the following would a lender generally require to be produced at the closing?
   a. Title insurance policy
   b. Market value appraisal
   c. Application
   d. Credit report

5. When an item to be prorated is owed but has not been paid by the seller,
   a. the amount owed is a credit to the buyer.
   b. the amount owed is a debit to the seller.
   c. the amount owed is a debit to the buyer.
   d. a and b

6. The RESPA Uniform Settlement Statement must be used to illustrate all settlement charges for
   a. every real estate transaction.
   b. transactions financed by VA and FHA loans only.
   c. residential transactions financed by federally related mortgage loans.
   d. all transactions involving commercial property.

7. A mortgage reduction certificate is executed by a(n)
   a. abstract company.
   b. attorney.
   c. lending institution.
   d. grantor.

8. The principal amount of the purchaser's new mortgage loan is a
   a. credit to the seller.
   b. credit to the buyer.
   c. debit to the seller.
   d. debit to the buyer.

9. The annual real estate taxes amount to $1,800 and have been paid in advance for the calendar year. If closing is set for June 15, which of the following is true?
   a. Credit seller $825; debit buyer $975
   b. Credit seller $1,800; debit buyer $825
   c. Credit buyer $975; debit seller $975
   d. Credit seller $975; debit buyer $975

10. The seller collected rent of $400, payable in advance, from the tenant on August 1. At the closing on August 15, the
    a. seller owes the buyer $400.
    b. buyer owes the seller $400.
    c. seller owes the buyer $200.
    d. buyer owes the seller $200.

11. Security deposits should be listed on a closing statement as a credit to the
    a. buyer.
    b. seller.
    c. lender.
    d. broker.

12. A building was bought for $50,000, with 10 percent down and a loan for the balance. If the lender charged the buyer two discount points, how much cash did the buyer need at closing?
    a. $6,900
    b. $5,900
    c. $5,200
    d. $900

13. A buyer of a $50,000 home has paid $2,000 as earnest money and has a loan commitment for 70 percent of the purchase price. How much more cash does the buyer need to complete the transaction?
    a. $10,000
    b. $13,000
    c. $15,000
    d. $35,000

14. At the closing, the seller's attorney gave credit to the buyer for certain accrued items. These items were
    a. bills relating to the property that have already been paid by the seller.
    b. bills relating to the property that will have to be paid by the buyer.
    c. all of the seller's real estate bills.
    d. all of the buyer's real estate bills.

15. The Real Estate Settlement Procedures Act (RESPA) applies to the activities of
    a. a broker selling commercial and office buildings.
    b. security salespersons selling limited partnerships.
    c. Ginnie Mae or Fannie Mae when purchasing loans.
    d. lenders financing the purchase of a borrower's residence.

16. The purpose of RESPA is to
    a. make sure buyers do not borrow more than they can repay.
    b. make real estate brokers more responsive to buyer's needs.
    c. help buyers know how much money is required.
    d. see that buyers and sellers know all settlement costs.

22 Property Management

The use of professional property managers for both residential and commercial properties has expanded in recent years. As the size of buildings increases, construction, maintenance and repairs become more complex and the number of buildings owned by large institutions, corporations and investors (all absentee owners) increases, the demand for the services of property managers increases as well. Today many brokerage firms maintain separate departments staffed by carefully selected, well-trained people. Corporate and institutional owners of real estate have also established property management departments. However, many real estate investors still manage their own property and thus must acquire the knowledge and skills of a property manager.

In Pennsylvania, property managers serving the public for a fee must be licensed real estate brokers. *Employees* of the owners of residential multi-family dwellings performing certain tasks need not be licensed. (See Real Estate Licensing and Registration Act, Section 304.)

THE PROPERTY MANAGER

The real estate specialty of property management involves the leasing, management, marketing and overall maintenance of real estate owned by others. The **property manager** is usually in a fiduciary relationship with the property owner and is responsible for the fiscal management (financial affairs), physical management (structure and grounds) and administrative management (files and records) for each property being managed. The property manager strives to maintain the investment and earn income for the owner. The objectives are to merchandise the property and control expenses to maximize income, and to maintain and modernize the physical property to preserve and enhance the owner's capital investment. Securing suitable tenants, collecting rents, caring for the physical premises, budgeting and controlling expenses, hiring and supervising employees, keeping proper accounts and making periodic reports to the owner are among the specific tasks of a property manager.

The property manager may be a licensee in a real estate firm or property management company that manages properties for a number of owners under management agreements (to be discussed later). The property manager has an agency relationship with the owner, which involves greater authority and discretion over the management decisions than an employee would have. A property manager or the owner may employ individual building managers to supervise the daily operations of a building. In some cases these individuals may be residents of the building.

Securing Management Business

Corporate owners, apartments and condominiums, homeowners' associations, investment syndicates, trusts and absentee owners are possible sources of management business. In securing business from any of these sources, word of mouth is often the best advertising. A manager who consistently demonstrates the ability to increase property income over previous levels should have no difficulty finding new business.

Before contracting to manage any property, however, the professional property manager should be certain that the building owner has realistic income expectations and is willing to spend money on necessary maintenance. Attempting to meet impossible owner demands by dubious methods can endanger the manager's reputation and be detrimental to obtaining future business.

The Management Agreement

The first step in taking over the management of any property is to enter into a **management agreement** with the owner. This agreement creates an agency relationship between the owner and the property manager. The property manager usually is considered to be a *general agent,* whereas a real estate broker in a listing agreement, for example, is usually considered to be a special agent. As agent, the property manager is charged with the fiduciary responsibilities of care, obedience, accounting, loyalty and disclosure. After entering into an agreement with a property owner, a manager handles the property as the owner would. In all activities the manager's first responsibility is to *realize the highest return that is consistent with the owner's instructions on the property.*

The management agreement should be in writing and should cover the following points:

- *Description* of the property
- *Time period* the agreement will cover
- *Definition of management's responsibilities:* All of the manager's duties should be stated in the contract; exceptions should be noted.
- *Statement of owner's purpose:* This statement should indicate what the owner desires the manager to accomplish with the property. One owner may wish to maximize net income and therefore instruct the manager to cut expenses and minimize reinvestment. Another owner may want to increase the capital value of the investment, in which case the manager should initiate a program for improving the property's physical condition.
- *Extent of manager's authority:* This provision should state what authority the manager is to have in such matters as hiring, firing and supervising employees; fixing rental rates for space; making expenditures and authorizing repairs within the limits established previously with the owner. Repairs that exceed a certain expense limit may require the owner's written approval.

MATH CONCEPT Rental Commissions

Residential commissions are usually based on the annualized rent from a property. For example, if an apartment unit rents for $475 per month and the commission payable is 8%, the commission will be calculated as follows:

$$\$475 \text{ per month} \times 12 \text{ months} = \$5,700; \$5,700 \times .08 \text{ (8\%)} = \$456$$

- *Reporting:* Agreement should be reached on the frequency and detail of the manager's periodic reports on operations and financial position. These reports serve as a means for the owner to monitor the manager's work and as a basis for both the owner and the manager to assess trends that can be used in shaping future management policy.

- *Management fee:* The fee can be based on a percentage of gross or net income, a fixed fee or a combination of both. If the property manager also leases, commissions are usually earned on the rentals as well. Management fees are subject to the same antitrust considerations as sales commissions. They cannot be standardized in the marketplace because that would be viewed as price fixing. The fee is the result of negotiation between the agent and the principal.

- *Allocation of costs:* The agreement should state which of the property manager's expenses, such as office rent, office help, telephone, advertising, association fees and social security, will be paid by the manager and which will be charged to the property's expenses and paid by the owner.

Property managers must also be aware of the provisions in the Section 604(19) of the Pennsylvania license law and Section 35.283 of the Regulations that prohibit their personally profiting from expenditures they make on behalf of the principal.

MANAGEMENT FUNCTIONS

A property manager must live up to both the letter and the spirit of the management agreement. The owner must be kept well informed on all matters of policy as well as on the financial condition of the property and its operation.

Budgeting Expenses

Before attempting to rent any property, a property manager should develop an operating budget based on anticipated revenues and expenses and reflecting the long-term goals of the owner. In preparing a budget, a manager should begin by allocating money for such continuous, fixed expenses as employees' salaries, real estate taxes, property taxes and insurance premiums. Although budgets should be as accurate as possible, adjustments may sometimes be necessary, especially in the case of new properties.

Next, the manager should budget for such variable expenses as repairs, decorating and supplies. The amount allocated can be computed from the previous yearly costs of the variable expenses.

Capital expenditures. If an owner and a property manager decide that modernization or renovation of the property will enhance its value, the manager should budget money to cover the costs of remodeling. The property manager should be thoroughly familiar with the *principle of contribution* (as discussed in the chapter on real estate appraisal) or seek expert advice when estimating any increase in value expected from an improvement. In the case of large-scale construction, the expenditures charged against the property's income should be depreciated over several years.

The cost of equipment to be installed in a modernization or renovation must be evaluated over its entire useful life. This is called **life cycle costing.** This term simply means that both the *initial* and the *operating* costs of equipment over its expected life must be measured to compare the total cost of one type of equipment with another.

Renting the Property

Effective rental of the property is essential to the success of a property manager. However, the role of the manager in managing a property should not be confused with that of a broker acting as a leasing agent who is solely concerned with renting space. The property manager may use the services of a leasing agent, but that agent does not undertake the full responsibility of maintenance and management of the property.

Setting rental rates. In establishing rental rates for a property, a basic concern must be that in the long term, the income from the rentable space covers the fixed charges and operating expenses and also provides a fair return on the investment. The property manager must also consider the prevailing rates in comparable buildings and the current level of vacancy in the property to be rented. In the short term, rental rates are primarily a result of supply and demand. Following a detailed survey of the competitive space available in the neighborhood, prices should be noted and adjusted for differences between neighboring properties and the property being managed. Annual rent adjustments are usually warranted.

Rental rates for residential space are usually stated in monthly amounts for a unit. Office, retail and industrial rentals, in contrast, are usually stated according to the annual rate per square foot.

If a high level of vacancy exists, the manager should immediately attempt to determine the reason. *A high level of vacancy does not necessarily indicate that rents are too high;* instead the problem may be inept management or defects in the property. The manager should attempt to identify and correct the problems first rather than immediately lower the rent. Conversely, *although a high percentage of occupancy may appear to indicate an effective rental program, it could also mean that rental rates are too low.* Whenever the occupancy level of an apartment house or office building exceeds 95 percent, serious consideration should be given to raising the rents.

Selecting tenants. Generally, the highest rents can be secured from satisfied tenants. Whereas a broker may sell a property and then have no further dealings with the purchaser, a building manager's success is greatly dependent on retaining sound, long-term relationships. The first and most important step is selection of tenants. The property manager should be sure that the premises are suitable for the tenant's needs. The manager should ascertain that the size of the space meets the tenant's requirements and that the tenant will be able to pay for the space. A commercial tenant's business should be compatible with the building and the other tenants. If the tenant is likely to expand in the future, ways to accommodate additional space requirements should also be considered.

The property manager must comply with all federal, state and local fair housing laws in the selection of both residential and commercial tenants.

Collecting rents. The best way to minimize rent collection problems is, again, to make a *careful selection* of tenants. The desire for a high level of occupancy should not override good judgment. A property manager should accept only those tenants who can be expected to meet their financial obligations to the property owner. The manager should investigate financial references given by the prospect, check with local credit bureaus and, when possible, interview the prospective tenant's former landlord.

The terms of rental payment should be spelled out in detail in the lease agreement, including the time and place of payment, provisions and penalties for late payment and provisions for cancellation and damages in case of nonpayment. The property manager should establish a *firm and consistent collection plan* with a sufficient system of notices and records. In cases of delinquency, every attempt must be made to make collections without resorting to legal action. For those cases in which legal action is required, a property manager must be prepared to initiate and follow through with the necessary steps in conjunction with the property owner's or management firm's legal counsel.

Maintaining Good Tenant Relations

The ultimate success of a property manager depends greatly on the his or her ability to maintain good relations with tenants. Dissatisfied tenants eventually vacate the property, and a high tenant turnover means greater expense for the owner in terms of advertising, redecorating and uncollected rents. The increased attention being given to landlord-tenant relationships by legal and judicial systems has added to the significance of this issue.

An effective property manager establishes good communication with tenants, uses intangible as well as tangible benefits to keep tenants satisfied, ensures that maintenance and service requests are attended to promptly and enforces all lease terms and building rules. A good manager is tactful and decisive and acts to the benefit of both owner and occupants. The property manager must be able to deal with residents who do not pay their rent on time or who break building regulations and breed dissatisfaction among other tenants. Careful record keeping will show whether rent is being remitted promptly and in the proper amount. Records of all lease renewal dates should be kept so that the manager can anticipate expiration and retain good tenants who might otherwise move when their leases end.

Maintaining the Property

One of the most important functions of a property manager is the supervision of property maintenance. A manager must learn to balance services provided with the costs they entail so as to satisfy the tenants' needs while minimizing operating expenses.

Efficient property maintenance demands accurate assessment of the needs of the building and the number and kinds of personnel necessary to meet these needs. Staffing and scheduling requirements vary with the type, size and regional location of the property; so owner and manager should agree in advance on maintenance objectives for the property. In some cases the most viable plan may be to operate with a low rental schedule and minimal expenditures for services and maintenance. Another property may be more lucrative if kept in top condition and operated with all possible tenant services, because it can then command premium rental rates.

A primary maintenance objective is to *protect the physical integrity of the property over the long term.* For example, preserving the property by repainting the exterior or replacing the heating system will keep the building functional and decrease routine maintenance costs. Keeping the property in good condition involves preventive maintenance, repair or corrective maintenance, routine maintenance and construction.

Preventive maintenance includes regularly scheduled activities, such as regular painting and periodic lubrication of gears and motors, that will preserve the long-range value and physical integrity of the building. Most authorities agree this is the most critical but most neglected maintenance responsibility. Failure to do preventive maintenance invariably leads to greater expense in other areas of maintenance.

Repair or corrective maintenance involves the actual repairs that keep the building's equipment, utilities and amenities functioning as contracted for by the tenants. Repairing a boiler, fixing a leaky faucet and repairing a broken air-conditioning unit are acts of repair maintenance.

A property manager must also *supervise the routine cleaning and repairs* of the building, including such day-to-day duties as cleaning common areas, doing minor carpentry and plumbing and providing regularly scheduled upkeep of heating, air-conditioning and landscaping.

Last is new or renovation *construction.* Especially when dealing with commercial or industrial space, a property manager will be called on to make **tenant improvements**—alterations to the interior of the building to meet the functional demands of a tenant. These alterations may range from repainting to completely gutting the interior and redesigning the space. Tenant improvements are especially important when renting new buildings because the interior is usually left incomplete so that it can be adapted to the needs of individual tenants. It must be clarified whether any improvements are to be considered as trade fixtures (personal property belonging to the tenant) or as belonging to the owner of the real estate.

Supervision of modernization or renovation of a building that has become functionally obsolete and thus unsuited to today's building needs is also important. The renovation of a building often increases its marketability and thus its possible income.

Hiring employees versus contracting for services. One of the major decisions a property manager faces is whether to contract for maintenance services from an outside firm or to hire on-site employees to perform such tasks. This decision should be based on a number of factors, including size of the building, complexity of tenants' requirements and availability of suitable labor.

Handling Environmental Concerns

With the proliferation of federal and state laws and increasing local regulation, environmental concerns have become a major responsibility of the property manager. Such concerns will require an increasing amount of management time and attention in the future. Although property managers are not expected to be experts in all the disciplines necessary to operate a modern building, they are expected to be knowledgeable in many diverse subjects, most of which are technical in nature. Environmental concerns are one such subject.

The property manager must be able to respond to a variety of environmental problems. He or she may manage structures containing asbestos or radon or may be called on to arrange an environmental audit of a property. The manager must see that any hazardous wastes produced by the manager's employer or tenants are properly disposed of. Even the normally nonhazardous waste of an office building must be controlled to avoid violation of laws requiring segregation of types of wastes. The property manager may have to provide recycling facilities and see that tenants sort their trash properly.

Complying with the ADA

The Americans with Disabilities Act (ADA) has a significant impact on the responsibilities of the property manager. Employment practices and the operation of accessible public facilities are the sections of the law that have the greatest affect on property managers.

Title I. Title I of the act prohibits discrimination against qualified job applicants and employees who have a disability. The property manager as an employer should be familiar with ADA to ensure that interview and selection procedures are not discriminatory. Employers are required also to make *reasonable accommodations* that enable an individual with a disability to perform essential job functions. Such accommodations include making the work site accessible, restructuring a job, perhaps by providing part-time or modified work schedules, and modifying equipment that is used on the job.

Employers with 15 or more employees must comply with ADA. However, the Pennsylvania Human Relations Act requires employers in Pennsylvania with 4 or more employees to adopt nondiscriminatory employment practices.

Title III. Property managers, as agents of the owners, must comply with Title III of ADA, which addresses the requirements for buildings in which business establishments are located and public services are provided. This section of the law prohibits discrimination against people with disabilities by ensuring access to the facilities and enjoyment of services in a full and equal manner. The property manager is typically responsible for procuring an audit of an existing building to determine if it meets the accessibility requirements of ADA and preparing and executing a plan for restructuring or retrofitting a building that is not in compliance. Experts who are versed in ADA and architectural design for individuals with disabilities should be consulted for audits and advice on achieving accessibility.

Existing barriers must be removed when it is *readily achievable* to do so, that is, easy to do at a low cost. Examples are ramping a small stoop or removing an obstacle from an otherwise accessible entrance, lowering telephones, adding raised letters and Braille markings on elevator buttons and installing auditory signals in elevators. Alternative methods can be used to provide accommodations if extensive restructuring or burdensome expense make retrofitting impractical. Examples are installing a cup dispenser at a water fountain that is too high for an individual in a wheelchair or providing assistance to retrieve merchandise from an inaccessible location. Newly constructed buildings and alterations must meet stricter accessibility requirements because it is less costly to incorporate accessible design into new construction than to retrofit an existing structure.

Fair Housing Laws

Property managers who are also leasing real estate must be sure to adopt leasing practices that comply with the fair housing laws. Discrimination in rentals is the basis of a majority of the complaints filed with the Pennsylvania Human Relations Commission and HUD. Commercial as well as residential property is covered under the Pennsylvania law. See the chapters on leasing and fair housing for a discussion of the fair housing laws.

RISK MANAGEMENT

Because enormous monetary losses can result from certain occurrences, one of the most critical areas of responsibility for a property manager is **risk management.** Risk management involves answering the question, "What will happen if something goes wrong?" The perils of any risk must be evaluated in terms of options. In considering the possibility of a loss, the property manager must decide whether it is better to

- *avoid it* by removing the source of risk, such as a swimming pool;

- *control it* by installing sprinklers, fire doors and other preventive measures;

- *transfer it* by taking out an insurance policy; or

- *retain it* to a certain extent, by insuring with a large *deductible* (loss not covered by the insurer).

Security of Tenants

The physical safety of tenants in the leased premises has become an important issue for property managers and owners. Recent court decisions in several parts of the country have held landlords and their agents responsible for physical harm that was inflicted on tenants by intruders. These decisions have prompted property managers and owners to evaluate measures to protect tenants from unauthorized entry to building complexes and to secure individual apartments from intruders.

Types of Insurance

Utilizing insurance is one of the major ways to protect against losses. Many types of insurance are available. A competent, reliable insurance agent familiar with the problems that typically arise with the type of property involved should be selected to survey the property and make recommendations. Additional insurance surveys should be obtained if any questions remain. Final decisions, however, must be made by the property owner.

Today, many insurance companies offer **multiperil policies** for apartment and business buildings. These policies offer the property manager an insurance package that includes standard types of commercial coverage as fire, hazard, public liability and casualty plus special coverage for natural events such as earthquakes or floods.

IN PRACTICE...	*The Real Estate Licensing and Registration Act prohibits an individual from receiving any undisclosed commission, rebate or compensation on expenditures made on behalf of the principal. A property manager's responsibilities often involve contracting for services and improvements on behalf of the owner. The licensee must be careful not to violate this provision of the license law in the course of those activities.*

●   ●   ●   ●   ●   ●   ●

KEY TERMS

life cycle costing
management agreement
multiperil policies

property manager
risk management
tenant improvements

SUMMARY

Property management is a specialized service to owners of income-producing properties through which the managerial function may be delegated to an individual or a firm with particular expertise in the field. The manager, as agent of the owner, becomes the administrator of the project and assumes the executive functions required for the care and operation of the property.

A management agreement establishing the agency relationship between owner and manager must be prepared carefully to define and authorize the manager's duties and responsibilities.

Projected expenses, combined with the manager's analysis of the condition of the building and the rent patterns in the neighborhood, form the basis on which rental rates for the property are determined. Once a rent schedule is established, the property manager is responsible for soliciting tenants whose needs are suited to the available space and who are financially capable of meeting the proposed rents. The manager is generally obligated to collect rents, maintain the building, hire necessary employees, pay taxes for the building and deal with tenant problems.

Maintenance includes safeguarding the physical integrity of the property and performing routine cleaning and repairs as well as making tenant improvements—adapting the interior space and overall design of the property to suit the tenants' needs and meet the demands of the market.

Questions

1. Apartment rents are usually expressed
   a. in monthly amounts.
   b. on a per-room basis.
   c. in square feet per month.
   d. in square feet per year.

2. From a management point of view, apartment building occupancy that reaches as high as 98 percent tends to indicate that
   a. the building is poorly managed.
   b. the building has reached its maximum potential.
   c. the building is a desirable place to live.
   d. rents should be raised.

3. Which of the following should *not* be a consideration in selecting a tenant?
   a. The size of the space versus the tenant's requirements
   b. The tenant's ability to pay
   c. The race and ethnicity of the tenant
   d. The compatibility of the tenant's business with other tenants' businesses

4. When a property manager chooses an insurance policy with a $250 deductible, the risk management technique being employed is
   a. avoiding risk.
   b. retaining risk.
   c. controlling risk.
   d. transferring risk.

5. Tenant improvements are
   a. fixtures.
   b. adaptations of space to suit tenants' needs.
   c. removable by the tenant.
   d. paid for by the landlord.

6. In preparing a budget, the property manager should set up for variable expenses a/an
   a. control account.
   b. floating allocation.
   c. cash reserve fund.
   d. asset account.

7. Rents should be determined on the basis of
   a. prevailing rental rates in the area.
   b. the local apartment owners' association.
   c. HUD.
   d. a tenants' union.

8. Which of the following might indicate rents are too low?
   a. A poorly maintained building
   b. Many For Lease signs in the area
   c. High building occupancy
   d. High vacancy level

9. Repairing a boiler is classified as which type of maintenance?
   a. Preventive
   b. Corrective
   c. Routine
   d. Construction

Pennsylvania Real Estate Licensing Examination

Modern Real Estate Practice in Pennsylvania is designed to introduce the reader to the basic knowledge necessary to engage in the real estate business. However, the license law in Pennsylvania, as detailed in Chapter 13, requires certain individuals seeking a license to pass an examination in addition to satisfying an education requirement. Testing is used not to keep people out of the business but to ensure that individuals who engage in real estate are competent to practice.

Experior is currently contracted by the Bureau of Professional and Occupational Affairs of the Department of State of Pennsylvania to develop and administer the real estate licensing examinations. Complete information about the testing procedures is provided in a Candidate Information Bulletin available from Experior at 261 Connecticut Drive, Burlington, NJ, 08016; phone 1-800-352-0637. The bulletin is also available from real estate education providers.

EXAMINATION ADMINISTRATION PROCEDURES

Brokers, cemetery brokers, associate brokers, real estate salespeople and rental listing referral agents must first prove that they are eligible to take the licensing examination. Candidates for an examination must submit documentation, including course transcripts and a Certificate of Examination Eligibility Registration Form to Experior. This may be mailed to Experior, 261 Connecticut Dr., Burlington, NJ, 08016, faxed to (609) 387-7971, or sent by e-mail to parealestate@worldnet.att.net. If you choose to fax or e-mail you must still mail the original registration form and documentation.

Upon receipt of the mail, fax or e-mail, Experior will check all candidates against the Disciplinary Action Data Bank, which is maintained by the Association of Real Estate License Law Officials, and review the supporting eligibility documentation. If approved, the candidate will receive by mail, e-mail, or fax, a confirmation letter outlining the examination scheduling process.

Test Reservations

After a candidate has the proper credentials to be admitted to the test site, the person needs to make a reservation to take the exam. Candidates will be instructed in their confirmation letter to contact the CSCC (Candidate Services

Call Center) to schedule the test date, time and site, and to authorize the $45 payment for the test. The CSCC is available Monday-Friday from 8:00 A.M. to 8:00 P.M. (EST) and on Saturday from 8:00 A.M. to 4:00 P.M. (EST).

Administration of the Exam

Examinations are offered daily (five to six days a week) in Sylvan Technology Centers. Operating hours vary between 8:00 A.M. and 7:00 P.M. (EST). The candidate bulletin provides a list of test sites.

Candidates should arrive 30 minutes prior to their scheduled exam and bring two forms of identification, one photobearing, both with signatures. Candidates may also bring a silent, simple (i.e., four-function) pocket calculator. All exams are closed-book.

The exam is given on a personal computer. Answers are recorded using a "mouse," a keyboard using the arrow keys or by typing a, b, c or d.

EXAMINATION CONTENT

The content of licensing examinations, as determined by the State Real Estate Commission, is to reflect information deemed to be necessary for licensees to practice in Pennsylvania.

The salesperson and brokers exams consist of two portions: the general theory portion, which consists of 95 multiple-choice questions including 5 pretest questions imbedded throughout the exam, and the state specific portion, which consists of 35 multiple-choice questions, including 5 pretest questions. Candidates will have three hours to complete the general portion and one hour to complete the State portion.

General Examination

The general theory portion of the examination covers the following information:

I. Business Practices and Ethics   15%
  A. Professional ethics
     1. Public and fiduciary responsibility
     2. Unlawful practice of law
  B. Federal requirements for real estate activities
     1. Fair Housing and anti-discrimination
     2. Violation of *Sherman Antitrust Act*
     3. Advertising
  C. Record keeping and document handling

II. Agency and Listing   15%
  A. Principles of agency
     1. Creating agency
     2. Liabilities
     3. Types and functions of agency
     4. Roles and responsibilities of licensees
     5. Terminating agency
  B. Types of listings
  C. Listing procedures
     1. Disclosing agency relationships
     2. Evaluating property

      3. Disclosure of property conditions
      4. Fraud and misrepresentations
   D. Listing agreement
      1. Legal requirements
      2. Fiduciary duties and representations
      3. Terminating listing

III. Property Characteristics, Descriptions, Ownership, Interests, and Restrictions*   15%
   A. Characteristics of property
      1. Legal description of property
      2. Interpreting physical and economic characteristics of property
      3. Real and personal property
   B. Ownership and estates in land
      1. Title
      2. Types of ownership
      3. Types of estates
   C. Government restrictions
      1. The four governmental powers (police power, eminent domain, escheat, taxation)
      2. Environmental regulations and disclosures
      3. Water rights
   D. Private restrictions
      1. Voluntary and involuntary liens
      2. Covenants, conditions, and restrictions
      3. Other encumbrances

IV. Property Valuation and the Appraisal Process*   10%
   A. Principles of valuation
      1. Value, price, and cost
      2. Characteristics of property that affect value
      3. Principles of value
   B. Determining value
      1. Direct sales comparison (market data) approach
      2. Cost approach
      3. Income approach
   C. Appraisal
      1. Purpose and use of appraisal
      2. Role of appraiser
      3. Role of licensee in property valuation

V. Real Estate Sales Contracts   15%
   A. Purpose, scope, and elements of real estate sales contracts
   B. Offers and counteroffers
      1. Purpose of offer and counteroffer
      2. Valid methods of communicating offers
   C. Earnest money
   D. Completion, termination, breach

VI. Financing Sources*   10%
   A. Essentials of financing
      1. Mortgages, deeds of trust, and their provisions
   B. Qualifying buyer for financing
      1. Pre-qualifying considerations
      2. Loan repayment

* Topic includes math items (8-12% of total items on exam)

C. Types of financing
   1. Loan programs, their benefits and requirements
   2. Financing methods
D. Foreclosure and alternatives
E. Pertinent laws and regulations
   1. *Truth-in-Lending Act* and *Regulation Z*
   2. *Equal Credit Opportunity Act*
   3. *Fair Credit Reporting Act*

VII. Closing/Settlement and Transferring Title*   15%
  A. Settlement statement and other critical documents
  B. Closing/settlement
    4. Purpose of closing/settlement
    5. Legal requirements (include RESPA)
  C. Transferring title
    6. Methods of transfer (includes deeds)
    7. Recording title
  D. Title insurance
    8. Purpose and scope of title insurance
    9. Essentials of title insurance

VIII. Property Management   5%
  A. Leases, estates, tenancies
  B. Property manager and owner relationships
  C. Laws affecting property management

State Specific Examination

The state-specific portion of the examination covers the following information:

I. Real Estate Commission
Salesperson 10%   Broker 10%
  A. Duties and powers
  B. Complaints, Investigations, and
  C. Real Estate Recovery Fund

II. Licensure
Salesperson 20%   Broker 20%
  A. Activities Requiring License
  B. Types of License
  C. Eligibility for License
  D. License Renewal
  E. Change of Employment
  F. Exclusions from Licensure
  G. Suspension and Revocation

III. Regulation of Conduct of Licensees
Salesperson 70%   Broker 70%
  A. Advertising
  B. Broker/Salesperson Relationship
  C. Compensation
  D. Prohibited Conduct
  E. Disclosures
  F. Documents and Forms
  G. Conflict of Interest
  H. Funds and Accounts

* Topic includes math items (8-12% of total items on exam)

    I.   Office Requirements and Inspections
    J.   Pennsylvania Human Relations Act
    K. Promotional Land Sales

Passing Scores

Upon completion of the exam, candidates will automatically receive their scores. Included in the score report will be diagnostic report outlining strengths and weaknesses. If the exam is passed, the salesperson or broker licensure application form will print at that time.

The examination candidate must achieve at least a score of 75 percent on *each portion* of the test to have passed the exam. The grading process is described in the candidate bulletin. In the event a candidate does not pass one portion of the test, there is no need to retake the entire exam; the candidate retakes only that portion. Both portions of the exam must be passed within three years of the date the person makes application for licensure.

EXAMINATION FORMAT

The questions are in the form of four-answer multiple-choice items.

Example: The purpose of requiring a prospective licensee to take an examination is to

  a. keep people out of the business.
  b. determine the competency of an individual to practice real estate.
  c. see if the licensee is good at taking a test.
  d. generate revenue from test fees.

The salesperson's exam is less difficult than the broker's. The broker's exam is designed to test the applicant in greater detail and includes information indicative of that licensee's practice.

Preparing for the Exam

The courses required by the State Real Estate Commission prior to licensure are not designed to "teach the test." The Commission has determined that their purpose is to develop a fundamental knowledge of real estate. That is the information presented in *Modern Real Estate Practice in Pennsylvania.* However, the information presented to the reader, enhanced by that presented by the instructor, is the basis of the material that should be studied to pass the license exam. The best way to prepare for the exam is to study rather than memorize. Be thoroughly familiar with the material, particularly *what the information means.* Being able to apply the knowledge to situations, combining facts and principles, is necessary to pass the exam.

Taking the Exam

For best results, go through the entire examination first and answer those questions about which you are certain, leaving the others for later. After all the questions you know are answered, return to the remaining questions. There is no penalty for guessing; guess if you are unable to arrive at an answer. Remain relaxed. If you are prepared and have an adequate knowledge of the subject, you should be able to complete the exam successfully.

Questions

The following sample questions deal with material for the state portion of the exam. (Review Appendix C.) They provide practice in thinking through multiple-choice test questions and are an aid in preparing for the exam.

1. The Real Estate Commission conducts its activities to
   a. safeguard all real estate licensees.
   b. protect the public interest.
   c. satisfy the legislature.
   d. assist the Commissioner of Professional and Occupational Affairs.

2. The Commission has the authority to
   a. issue licenses.
   b. conduct licensing examinations.
   c. appoint Commissioners.
   d. promulgate rules and regulations.

3. The Commission has authority to take disciplinary action against
   a. landlords.
   b. campground membership salespeople.
   c. attorneys-in-fact.
   d. licensed auctioneers.

4. The Commission can take which of the following actions if a salesperson advertises a property for sale without the owner's permission?
   a. Assess the salesperson a criminal penalty of $500
   b. Award the owner damages from the Recovery Fund
   c. Suspend the salesperson's license
   d. Tell the owner to file a complaint with a local real estate board

5. An individual has applied for a salesperson license. This person can do which of the following?
   a. Solicit listings
   b. Advertise a house for sale
   c. Negotiate an agreement of sale
   d. Attend the broker's sales training program

6. Applicants for licensure must satisfy an education requirement in all of the following cases *except*
   a. a builder-owner salesperson license.
   b. a campground membership salesperson license.
   c. a time-share salesperson license.
   d. a rental listing referral agent license.

7. A broker is responsible for which of the following activities?
   a. Conducting title searches
   b. Attending closings
   c. Training builder-owner salespersons
   d. Business that is conducted in branch offices

8. To be eligible for a broker license, an individual must do all of the following *except*
   a. obtain 240 hours of education.
   b. be at least 21 years of age.
   c. be a citizen of the United States.
   d. pass an examination.

9. When a salesperson owns the house that the salesperson is selling, which of the following is true?

   a. The salesperson must list the property with another broker.
   b. The salesperson must disclose to a prospective purchaser that the salesperson is licensed.
   c. The act does not apply to a licensee who is selling his or her own property.
   d. A salesperson cannot collect a commission on the sale of his or her own property.

10. If a salesperson is unable to collect from the employing broker a commission that the salesperson has earned, what recourse does the salesperson have to collect this money?

    a. File a complaint with the Commission
    b. Sue the broker
    c. Make application to the Recovery Fund
    d. Change employing brokers

11. A broker decides to open a branch office. Which of the following is true?

    a. The broker is not responsible for the branch office if an associate broker is the manager.
    b. A branch office license will be issued if the broker's license is suspended at the main office.
    c. The number of branch offices that a broker can open is limited by the Commission.
    d. The broker could open the branch office in his or her home if there is a separate entrance to the office.

12. A seller offers a $500 bonus to a salesperson who sells the house within 30 days. Which of the following is true?

    a. The seller may pay the bonus to the salesperson who produces a buyer.
    b. Bonuses of this nature are strictly prohibited.
    c. The salesperson who produces a buyer cannot accept this bonus directly from the seller.
    d. The bonus could be paid by the seller to a salesperson if it is a lesser amount.

13. Which of the following is true about a salesperson's license?

    a. The broker must display the license in the office where the salesperson works.
    b. The broker must display the license in the broker's main office.
    c. The license is issued to the salesperson and can be taken to any broker of the salesperson's choice.
    d. The salesperson cannot use the license until completion of the broker's training program.

14. Estimated statements of closing costs must meet which of the following requirements?

    a. They must be signed by the seller.
    b. They must be an exact representation of the costs incurred by a buyer and seller at settlement.
    c. They must be presented to a buyer and seller prior to their signing an agreement of sale.
    d. They must disclose whom the broker represents.

15. A broker can be subject to disciplinary action if a salesperson is found guilty of misconduct

    a. any time the salesperson's license is suspended.
    b. when the Commission files a complaint against the broker.
    c. if the broker directed the illegal course of action.
    d. only if the salesperson is licensed.

16. When a buyer gives the salesperson a check for escrow money, which of the following is true?

    a. The salesperson must deposit it immediately in the broker's escrow account.
    b. The salesperson must give the check to the seller.
    c. The check must be deposited in an interest-bearing account.
    d. The check must be deposited in the broker's escrow account by the end of the next business day after receipt.

17. When a property is advertised for sale by a salesperson, what information must be included in the ad?

    a. The address of the broker
    b. The business name of the broker
    c. The name of the salesperson
    d. The phone number of the salesperson

18. When a buyer and seller enter into an agreement of sale, the broker is responsible for all of the following *except*

    a. giving a copy of the agreement to the buyer and seller.
    b. keeping a copy for three years after the consummation of the sale.
    c. giving a copy to the mortgage lender.
    d. using a written contract.

19. A mortgage contingency must include all of the following information *except* the

    a. amount of the mortgage payment.
    b. amount of the loan.
    c. maximum interest rate for the loan.
    d. minimum number of years for the loan.

20. A salesperson is discussing the possibility of listing a seller's home. What information should the salesperson give to the seller before the listing agreement is signed?

    a. The common rate of commission charged in the area
    b. The approximate number of times the house will be advertised
    c. That a listing must last for at least one year
    d. Existence of the Real Estate Recovery Fund

21. A listing in which the seller owes a commission even if the seller finds the buyer is a(n)

    a. open listing.
    b. exclusive agency.
    c. multiple listing.
    d. exclusive-right-to-sell.

22. *K* signed an agreement of sale to purchase a time-share property. Three days later *K* decided that she didn't really want the property. Which of the following is true?

    a. *K* must return the cookware she received at the time of the purchase.
    b. *K* can recover her hand money from the Recovery Fund.
    c. *K* can cancel the contract.
    d. The broker is due a commission on the sale.

23. Under what circumstances can a broker deposit his or her own money in the escrow account?

    a. Never
    b. Only with the seller's permission
    c. To cover any fees for the account charged by the bank
    d. With permission from the Commission

24. The owner tells the salesperson not to rent an apartment to a family with children. What should the salesperson do?

    a. Follow the instructions because the owner is the client
    b. Tell the owner to rent the property himself
    c. Rent the apartment to anyone who is financially qualified
    d. Both the owner and the salesperson have the right to deny the apartment to a family with children

25. An agreement of sale must include certain information. Which of the following is *not* a requirement?

    a. Disclosure of whom the broker represents
    b. Disclosure that the amount of commission has been determined by negotiations
    c. Disclosure of the zoning classification unless the property is zoned for single family
    d. Disclosure of the existence of the Recovery Fund

26. The owner of a house does not want it to be rented to anyone who has a pet. The salesperson has a prospect with a visual disability who uses a guide dog. What should the salesperson do?

    a. Find the prospect a house to rent where pets are allowed
    b. Charge a higher security deposit and rent the house to the prospect
    c. Have the tenant sign a commitment to be responsible for any damage done by the guide dog
    d. Rent the house to the prospect without further concern for the pet restriction

27. A buyer was concerned about a clause in the agreement of sale. The salesperson, who represents the seller, told the buyer that it was not something for the buyer to worry about. In this situation

    a. the salesperson should have referred the buyer to a lawyer.
    b. the salesperson did the right thing.
    c. the salesperson should not have said anything because the salesperson doesn't represent the buyer.
    d. the license law does not apply.

28. A brokerage firm advertises that it is the best to do business with because it sells more property than any other firm in the area. This kind of advertising is

    a. good business.
    b. not addressed by the Commission.
    c. allowed if the claim is based on closed transactions.
    d. illegal under the act.

29. An exclusive-right-to-lease agreement must include certain information. Which of the following is *not* a requirement?

    a. An automatic renewal clause
    b. Lease price
    c. Duration of the agreement
    d. Commission expected on the lease

30. A buyer is concerned about how much a property will appreciate over the next five years. The salesperson assures the buyer that its value will double in eight years. Which of the following is true?

    a. This sounds like a good investment.
    b. The salesperson should not have made such a comment.
    c. The comment is good salesmanship.
    d. The buyer should rely on the comment because of the salesperson's knowledge and experience.

31. The *purpose* of the real estate license law is to

    a. keep criminals from practicing real estate.
    b. control the number of people who get a real estate license.
    c. ensure that the public interest is protected.
    d. create the State Real Estate Commission.

32. You have passed the salesperson's exam and selected a broker with whom you are going to work but your license hasn't been issued yet. Now your neighbor tells you he needs to list his home and get it sold quickly. How can you help him?

    a. Suggest your neighbor contact the broker you've selected to work for to list his property.
    b. Tell your neighbor to run an ad for an open house and that you will conduct the open house for him.
    c. Tell your neighbor that you can list the property but can't show it until your license comes.
    d. Do a competitive market analysis of the neighbor's property and negotiate a listing contract but don't date the contract yet.

33. A salesperson had an offer from a buyer-customer to purchase a property that was listed exclusively with another real estate company. The salesperson asked the seller to cancel the listing and sign a new listing with the salesperson's company before presenting the offer. This way the salesperson would earn more money by selling the company's own listing. Which of the following is true?

    a. The buyer should have made the offer through the company that listed the property rather than with this salesperson.
    b. The salesperson should not attempt to disrupt the exclusive relationship the seller has with the listing broker.
    c. The salesperson is permitted to do whatever is necessary to personally gain from a transaction and earn a living.
    d. The salesperson's broker rather than the salesperson should have approached the seller with the request to break the listing contract with the other company.

34. When a salesperson changes employing brokers, the salesperson should

    a. notify the local real estate association.
    b. notify a member of the Real Estate Commission.
    c. rely on the employing broker to notify the Commission.
    d. notify the Real Estate Commission in writing.

35. The broker's license will expire at the end of May. Which of the following is true as of June 1?

    a. The broker can renew the license as of June 1 and complete the continuing education courses within the following two years.
    b. The license will be inactive and the broker must cease practice on June 1 if the broker fails to renew it.
    c. The broker can continue to practice for 60 days after June 1 before renewing the license.
    d. If the broker has been in business for more than 25 years, he or she can renew the license as of June 1 without taking continuing education.

36. The broker wants to hire someone to handle the daily management of the sales office so that the broker can concentrate on other activities. A licensed salesperson, who currently works for the broker and is extremely competent, has been selling for 15 years. The broker wants to hire this person to manage the office. Which of the following is true?

    a. The broker can hire this licensed salesperson to manage the office as long as the person is not given the title of manager.
    b. Because the salesperson has 15 years experience, this salesperson can manage the office.
    c. The broker is the manager of the office unless someone else with a broker license is hired as the manager.
    d. This salesperson can become the manager as long as the person is in the process of qualifying for a broker license.

37. To obtain a salesperson license, as person must

    a. be at least 21 years of age.
    b. complete 30 hours of instruction.
    c. complete not less than 30 days of on-site training.
    d. pass an examination.

38. The purpose of the Recovery Fund is to

    a. enable people to get payment of uncollected judgments against licensees.
    b. enable sellers to recover money when buyers default on sales agreements.
    c. enable licensees to recover commissions that their brokers have failed to pay.
    d. enable sellers to recover escrow money that brokers have handled improperly.

39. On Thursday evening, a buyer makes an offer to purchase a property and gives the salesperson a check for $3,000 hand money. The offer is presented to the seller, then the seller makes a counteroffer. The buyer finally accepts the counteroffer and the acceptance is communicated to the seller on Monday evening. How is the check to be handled between Thursday and Monday evenings?

    a. The check should be held by the salesperson and given to the broker on Tuesday morning.
    b. The check should be given to the broker to hold until Tuesday.
    c. The broker is responsible for depositing the check by the end of business on Friday.
    d. The check should be given to the seller when the acceptance is communicated on Monday evening.

40. A buyer makes an offer on a house that is listed by another brokerage company. With the offer the buyer gives a hand money check that is made payable to the selling company. What should be done with the hand money check according to the Rules and Regulations?

    a. The salesperson should refuse to accept the check until the seller accepts the offer.
    b. The real estate company to whom the check is made payable is responsible for depositing it in its escrow account.
    c. The broker of the company to whom the check is made payable must endorse it over to the listing broker.
    d. The listing broker should ask the buyer for another hand money check.

Review Examination

The following exam questions can be used for review of the text material or for license examinations preparation. Note that the proration calculations are based on a 30-day month unless otherwise stated.

1. Which of the following is a lien on real estate?
   a. A recorded easement
   b. A recorded mortgage
   c. An encroachment
   d. A deed restriction

2. A contract agreed to under duress is
   a. voidable.   c. discharged.
   b. breached.   d. void.

3. A broker receives a check for earnest money from a buyer and deposits the money in an escrow or trust account to protect herself from the charge of
   a. commingling.
   b. novation.
   c. lost or stolen funds.
   d. embezzlement.

4. A mortgage loan that requires monthly payments of $875.70 for 20 years and a final payment of $24,095 is known as a(n)
   a. wraparound loan.
   b. accelerated loan.
   c. balloon loan.
   d. variable loan.

5. The borrower computed the interest she was charged for the previous month on her $60,000 loan balance as $412.50. What is her interest rate?
   a. 7.5 percent   c. 8.25 percent
   b. 7.75 percent   d. 8.5 percent

6. A loan originated by a bank may be sold in which of the following?
   a. Primary market
   b. Secondary market
   c. Mortgage market
   d. Investor market

7. The deed that contains five covenants is the
   a. warranty deed.   c. grant deed.
   b. quitclaim deed.   d. deed in trust.

8. Steering is
   a. leading prospective homeowners to or away from certain areas.
   b. refusing to make loans to persons residing in certain areas.
   c. a requirement to join a multiple-listing service.
   d. a practice of illegally setting commission rates.

9. *H* grants a life estate to her grandson and stipulates that upon the grandson's death the title to the property will pass to her son-in-law. This second estate is known as an
    a. estate in remainder.
    b. estate in reversion.
    c. estate at sufferance.
    d. estate for years.

10. Under joint tenancy
    a. a maximum of two people can own the real estate.
    b. the fractional interests can be different.
    c. additional owners can be added later.
    d. there is right of survivorship if properly designated.

11. The states in which the lender is the owner of mortgaged real estate are known as
    a. title theory states.
    b. lien theory states.
    c. statutory share states.
    d. strict forfeiture states.

12. What is a tenancy for years?
    a. A tenancy with the consent of the landlord
    b. A tenancy that expires on a specific date
    c. A tenancy created by the death of the owner
    d. A tenancy created by a testator

13. A residence with outmoded plumbing is suffering from
    a. functional obsolescence.
    b. curable physical deterioration.
    c. incurable physical deterioration.
    d. external obsolescence.

14. *K* built a structure that has six stories. Several years later an ordinance was passed in that area banning any building six stories or higher. This instance represents
    a. a nonconforming use.
    b. a situation in which the structure would have to be demolished.
    c. a conditional use.
    d. a violation of the zoning laws.

15. Assuming that the listing broker and the selling broker in a transaction split their commission equally, what was the sales price of the property if the commission rate was 6.5 percent and the listing broker received $2,593.50?
    a. $39,900   c. $79,800
    b. $56,200   d. $88,400

16. According to the Statute of Frauds in Pennsylvania, an oral lease for five years is
    a. a long-term lease.
    b. renewable.
    c. illegal.
    d. unenforceable.

17. The market value of a parcel of land
    a. is an estimate of the present worth of future benefits.
    b. represents a measure of past expenditures.
    c. is what the seller wants for the property.
    d. is the same as the market price.

18. Police powers include all of the following *except*
    a. zoning.
    b. deed restrictions.
    c. building codes.
    d. subdivision regulations.

19. The seller wants to net $65,000 from the sale of his house after paying the broker's fee of 6 percent. His gross sales price will be
    a. $69,149.   c. $61,321.
    b. $68,900.   d. $61,100.

20. An acre contains
    a. 360 degrees.   c. 160 square yards.
    b. 36 sections.   d. 43,560 square feet.

21. *W* is purchasing a condominium unit in a subdivision and obtaining financing from a local savings and loan association. In this situation, which of the following best describes *W?*
    a. Vendor   c. Grantor
    b. Mortgagor   d. Lessor

22. The current value of a property is $40,000. The property is assessed at 40 percent of its current value for real estate tax purposes, with an equalization factor of 1.5 applied to the assessed value. If the tax rate is $4 per $100 of assessed valuation, what is the amount of tax due on the property?
    a. $640
    b. $960
    c. $1,600
    d. $2,400

23. A building was sold for $60,000 with the purchaser putting 10 percent down and obtaining a loan for the balance. The lending institution charged a 1 percent loan origination fee. What was the total cash used for the purchase?
    a. $540
    b. $6,000
    c. $6,540
    d. $6,600

24. After a snowstorm a property owner offers to pay $10 to anyone who will shovel his driveway. This is an example of a(n)
    a. implied contract.
    b. executed contract.
    c. bilateral contract.
    d. unilateral contract.

25. Capitalization rates are
    a. determined by the gross rent multiplier.
    b. the rates of return a property will produce.
    c. a mathematical value determined by the sales price.
    d. determined by the amount of depreciation in the property.

26. An eligible veteran made an offer of $50,000 to purchase a home to be financed with a VA-guaranteed loan. Four weeks after the offer was accepted a certificate of reasonable value (CRV) for $47,800 was issued for the property. In this case the veteran may
    a. withdraw from the sale with a 1 percent penalty.
    b. purchase the property with a $2,200 down payment.
    c. not withdraw from the sale.
    d. withdraw from the sale upon payment of $2,200.

27. If a house was sold for $40,000 and the buyer obtained an FHA-insured mortgage loan for $38,500, how much money would be paid in discount points if the lender charged four points?
    a. $1,600
    b. $1,540
    c. $1,500
    d. $385

28. The commission rate is 7¾ percent on a sale of $50,000. What is the dollar amount of the commission?
    a. $3,500
    b. $3,875
    c. $4,085
    d. $4,585

29. All of the following will terminate an offer *except*
    a. revocation of the offer before its acceptance.
    b. the death of the offeror before acceptance.
    c. a counteroffer by the offeree.
    d. an offer from a third party.

30. G is purchasing a home under a land contract. Until the contract is paid in full, G has
    a. legal title to the premises.
    b. no interest in the property.
    c. a legal life estate in the premises.
    d. equitable title in the property.

31. F and K enter into an agreement wherein K will mow F's lawn every week during the summer. Shortly thereafter K decides to go into a different business. V would like to assume K's duties mowing F's lawn. F agrees and enters into a new contract with V. F and K tear up their original agreement. This is known as
    a. assignment.
    b. novation.
    c. substitution.
    d. rescission.

32. G borrowed $4,000 from a private lender using the services of a mortgage broker. After deducting the loan costs, G received $3,747. What is the face amount of the note?
    a. $3,747
    b. $4,000
    c. $4,253
    d. $7,747

33. An offer to purchase real estate becomes a contract when it is signed by which of the following?
    a. Buyer
    b. Buyer and seller
    c. Seller
    d. Seller and broker

34. A borrower has just made the final payment on his mortgage loan to his bank. Regardless of this fact, the lender will still hold a lien on the mortgaged property until which of the following is recorded?
    a. A satisfaction of the mortgage document
    b. A reconveyance of the mortgage document
    c. A novation of the mortgage document
    d. An estoppel of the mortgage document

35. If the annual net income from a commercial property is $22,000 and the capitalization rate is 8 percent, what is the value of the property using the income approach?
    a. $275,000
    b. $200,000
    c. $183,000
    d. $176,000

36. A broker enters into a listing agreement with a seller wherein the seller will receive $120,000 from the sale of a vacant lot and the broker will receive any sale proceeds over that amount. This type of agreement is called a(n)
    a. exclusive-agency listing.
    b. net listing.
    c. exclusive-right-to-sell listing.
    d. multiple listing.

37. Angela moved into a cooperative apartment after selling her house. Under the cooperative form of ownership she will
    a. become a stockholder in the corporation.
    b. not lose her apartment if she pays her share of the expenses.
    c. have to take out a new mortgage loan on her unit.
    d. receive a fixed-term lease for her unit.

38. A defect or a cloud on title to property may be cured by
    a. obtaining quitclaim deeds from all interested parties.
    b. bringing an action to register the title.
    c. paying cash for the property at the settlement.
    d. bringing an action to repudiate the title.

39. Discount points on a real estate loan are a potential cost to both the seller and the buyer. The points are
    a. set by FHA and VA for their loan programs.
    b. charged only on conventional loans.
    c. limited by government regulations.
    d. determined by the market for money.

40. Under the terms of a net lease the tenant would usually be responsible for paying all of the following except
    a. maintenance expenses.
    b. mortgage debt service.
    c. fire and extended-coverage insurance.
    d. real estate taxes.

41. The Civil Rights Act of 1866 prohibits in all cases discrimination based on a person's
    a. sex.
    b. religion.
    c. race.
    d. familial status.

42. What would it cost to put new carpeting in a den measuring 15′ × 20′ if the cost of the carpeting is $6.95 per square yard and laying it cost an additional $250?
    a. $232
    b. $482
    c. $610
    d. $2,335

43. What is the difference between a general lien and a specific lien?
    a. A general lien cannot be enforced in court while a specific lien can.
    b. A specific lien is held by only one person while a general lien must be held by two or more.
    c. A general lien is a lien against personal property while a specific lien is a lien against real estate.
    d. A specific lien is a lien against a certain parcel of real estate while a general lien covers all of the debtor's property.

44. In an option to purchase real estate the optionee
    a. must purchase the property but may do so at any time within the option period.
    b. is limited to a refund of the option consideration if the option is exercised.
    c. cannot obtain third-party financing on the property until after the option has expired.
    d. has no obligation to purchase the property during the option period.

45. An individual seeking to be excused from the requirements of a zoning ordinance should request a
    a. building permit.
    b. certificate of alternative usage.
    c. variance.
    d. certificate of nonconforming use.

46. *Acceleration* is a term associated with which of the following documents?
    a. Listings
    b. Mortgages
    c. Leases
    d. Purchase contracts

47. Under the terms in the mortgage the lender must be paid in full if the property is sold. This clause is known as the
    a. acceleration clause.
    b. due-on-sale clause.
    c. subordination clause.
    d. habendum clause.

48. The broker receives a deposit with a written offer that indicates that the offeror will leave the offer open for the seller's acceptance for ten days. On the fifth day, and prior to acceptance by the seller, the offeror notifies the broker that he is withdrawing his offer and demanding the return of his deposit. In this situation
    a. the offeror cannot withdraw the offer— it must be held open for the full ten-day period.
    b. the offeror has the right to withdraw the offer and secure the return of the deposit at any time before he is notified of the seller's acceptance.
    c. the offeror can withdraw the offer, and the seller and the broker will each retain one-half of the forfeited deposit.
    d. the offeror can withdraw the offer, and the broker will declare the deposit forfeited and retain all of it in lieu of a commission.

49. *C* and *L* are joint tenants in a parcel of property. *L* sells her interest to *F*. What is the relationship between *C* and *F* regarding the property?
    a. They are joint tenants.
    b. They are tenants in common.
    c. They are tenants by the entirety.
    d. There is no relationship, because *L* cannot sell her joint tenancy interest.

50. *S* and *W* orally enter into a six-month lease. If *W* defaults, then *S*
    a. may not bring a court action because of the parol evidence rule.
    b. may not bring a court action because of the statute of frauds.
    c. may bring a court action because six-month leases need not be in writing to be enforceable.
    d. may bring a court action because the statute of limitations does not apply to oral leases.

51. On Monday *T* offers to sell his vacant lot to *K* for $12,000. On Tuesday *K* counteroffers to buy the lot for $10,500. On Friday *K* withdraws his counteroffer and accepts *T*'s original price of $12,000. Under these circumstances
    a. there is a valid agreement because K accepted *T*'s offer exactly as it was made, even though it was not accepted immediately.
    b. there is a valid agreement because K accepted before *T* advised him that the offer was withdrawn.
    c. there is no valid agreement because *T*'s offer was not accepted within 72 hours of its having been made.
    d. there is no valid agreement because *K*'s counteroffer was a rejection of *T*'s offer, and once rejected, it cannot be accepted later.

52. The parcel of property over which an easement runs is known as the
    a. dominant tenement.
    b. servient tenement.
    c. prescriptive tenement.
    d. eminent tenement.

53. If the quarterly interest at 7.5 percent is $562.50, what is the principal amount of the loan?
    a. $7,500
    b. $15,000
    c. $30,000
    d. $75,000

54. Assume a house is sold for $84,500 and the commission rate is 7 percent. If the commission is split 60/40 between the selling broker and the listing broker, and each broker splits his or her share of the commission evenly with the salesperson, how much will the listing salesperson receive from this sale?
    a. $1,183
    b. $1,775
    c. $2,366
    d. $3,549

55. If the mortgage loan is 80 percent of the appraised value of a house and the interest rate of 8 percent amounts to $460 for the first month, what is the appraised value of the house?
    a. $92,875
    b. $86,250
    c. $71,875
    d. $69,000

56. Local zoning ordinances often regulate all of the following except
    a. the height of buildings in an area.
    b. the density of population.
    c. the appropriate use of the buildings.
    d. the market value of property.

57. A broker took a listing and later discovered that her client had previously been declared incompetent by the court. The listing is now
    a. unaffected because the broker was acting in good faith as the owner's agent.
    b. of no value to the broker because the contract is void.
    c. the basis for recovery of a commission if the broker produces a buyer.
    d. renegotiable between the broker and her client.

58. A borrower defaulted on his home mortgage loan payments, and the lender obtained a court order to foreclose on the property. At the foreclosure sale, however, the property sold for only $64,000; the unpaid balance of the loan at the time of the foreclosure was $78,000. What must the lender do in an attempt to recover the $14,000 that the borrower still owes?
    a. Sue for specific performance
    b. Sue for damages
    c. Seek a deficiency judgment
    d. Seek a judgment by default

59. All of the following are exemptions to the federal Fair Housing Act of 1968 *except*
    a. the sale of a single-family home where the listing broker does not advertise the property.
    b. the restriction of noncommercial lodgings by a private club to members of the club.
    c. the rental of a unit in an owner-occupied three-family dwelling where an advertisement is placed in the paper.
    d. the restriction of noncommercial housing in a convent where a certified statement has not been filed with the government.

60. *G* purchases a $37,000 property, depositing $3,000 as earnest money. If he can obtain a 75 percent loan-to-value loan on the property and no additional items are prorated, how much more cash will he need at the settlement?
    a. $3,250
    b. $3,500
    c. $5,250
    d. $6,250

61. In the appraisal of a building constructed in the 1920s, the cost approach would be the least accurate method because of difficulties in
    a. estimating changes in material costs.
    b. obtaining building codes from the 1920s.
    c. estimating changes in labor rates.
    d. estimating depreciation.

62. *G* sold his property to *W*. In the deed of conveyance *G*'s only guarantee was that the property was not encumbered during the time he owned it except as noted in the deed. The type of deed used in this transaction was a
    a. general warranty deed.
    b. special warranty deed.
    c. bargain and sale deed.
    d. quitclaim deed.

63. *S* and *T*, who are not married, own a parcel of real estate. Each owns an undivided interest, with *S* owning one-third and *T* owning two-thirds. The form of ownership under which *S* and *T* own their property is

a. severalty.
b. joint tenancy.
c. tenancy at will.
d. tenancy in common.

64. The buyers agree to purchase a house for $84,500. The buyers pay $2,000 as earnest money and obtain a new mortgage loan for $67,600. The purchase contract provides for a March 15 settlement. The buyers and sellers prorate the previous year's real estate taxes of $1,880.96, which have been prepaid. The buyers have additional closing costs of $1,250, and the sellers have other closing costs of $850. How much cash must the buyers bring to the settlement?

a. $19,638
b. $17,638
c. $17,238
d. $16,388

65. A broker was advertising a house he had listed for sale at the price of $47,900. *J*, a Mexican, saw the house and was interested in it. When *J* asked the broker the price of the house, the broker told *J* $53,000. Under the federal Fair Housing Act of 1968 such a statement is

a. legal because all that is important is that *J* be given the opportunity to buy the house.
b. legal because the representation was made by the broker and not directly by the owner.
c. illegal because the difference in the offering price and the quoted price was greater than 10 percent.
d. illegal because the terms of the potential sale were changed for *J*.

66. A deed must be signed by which of the following?

a. The grantor
b. The grantee
c. The grantor and the grantee
d. The grantee and at least two witnesses

67. An appraiser has been hired to prepare an appraisal report of a property for loan purposes. The property is an elegant old mansion that is now used as an insurance company office. To which approach to value should the appraiser give the greatest weight when making this appraisal?

a. Income approach
b. Sales comparison approach
c. Replacement cost approach
d. Gross rent multiplier

68. Which of the following is true about a term mortgage loan?

a. All of the interest is paid at the end of the term.
b. The debt is partially amortized over the life of the loan.
c. The length of the term is limited by state statutes.
d. The entire principal amount is due at the end of the term.

69. *J* recently moved into a condominium. She has the use of many facilities there, including a swimming pool, putting green and tennis courts. Under the typical condominium arrangement these facilities would be owned by

a. the association of homeowners in the condominium.
b. the corporation in which *J* and the other owners hold stock.
c. *J* and the other owners in the condominium in the form of divided interests.
d. all the condominium owners in the form of percentage undivided interests.

70. Which of the following is *not* usually prorated between the seller and the buyer at the settlement?

a. Recording charges
b. Real estate taxes
c. Prepaid rents
d. Utility bills

71. *T* believes that he has been the victim of an unfair discriminatory practice committed by a local real estate broker. In accordance with federal regulations, how long does *T* have to file his complaint against the broker?

    a. 90 days after the alleged discrimination
    b. 180 days after the alleged discrimination
    c. 9 months after the alleged discrimination
    d. 1 year after the alleged discrimination

72. A real estate loan that uses both real estate and personal property as collateral is known as a

    a. blanket loan.
    b. package loan.
    c. growing-equity loan.
    d. graduated-payment loan.

73. All of the following are true regarding the concept of adverse possession except

    a. the person taking possession of the property must do so without the consent of the owner of the property.
    b. occupancy of the property by the person taking possession must be continuous over a specified period of time.
    c. the person taking possession of the property must compensate the owner at the end of the adverse possession period.
    d. the person taking possession of the property could ultimately end up owning it.

74. What is the cost of constructing a fence 6′, 6″ high around a lot measuring 90′ × 175′, if the cost of erecting the fence is $1.25 per linear foot and the cost of materials is $.825 per square foot of fence?

    a. $1,752   c. $2,084
    b. $2,054   d. $3,505

75. *K,* who desires to sell his house, enters into a listing agreement with broker *E.* Broker *N* obtains a buyer for the house, and *E* does not receive a commission. The listing agreement between *K* and *E* was probably a(n)

    a. exclusive-right-to-sell listing.
    b. open listing.
    c. exclusive-agency listing.
    d. multiple listing.

76. Antitrust laws prohibit all *except*

    a. real estate companies agreeing on fees charged to sellers.
    b. real estate brokers allocating markets based on the value of homes.
    c. real estate companies allocating markets based on the location of commercial buildings.
    d. real estate salespersons allocating markets based on the location of homes.

77. Under the concept of riparian rights, the owners of property adjacent to navigable rivers or streams have the right to use the water and

    a. may erect a dam across the waterway if the owners on each side agree.
    b. are considered to own the submerged land to the center point of the waterway.
    c. are considered owners of the water adjacent to the land.
    d. are considered to own the land to the edge of the water.

78. The landlord of tenant *D* has sold his building to the state so that a freeway can be built. *D*'s lease has expired, but the landlord is letting him remain until the building is torn down. *D* continues to pay the same rent as prescribed in his lease. What kind of tenancy does *D* have?

    a. Holdover tenancy
    b. Month-to-month tenancy
    c. Tenancy at sufferance
    d. Tenancy at will

79. When a form of real estate sales contract has been agreed to and signed by the purchaser and spouse and then given to the seller's broker with an earnest money check,

    a. this transaction constitutes a valid contract.
    b. the purchasers can sue the seller for specific performance.
    c. this transaction is considered to be an offer.
    d. the earnest money will be forfeited if the purchasers default.

80. A seller gives an open listing to several brokers, specifically promising that if one of the brokers finds a buyer for the seller's property, the seller will then be obligated to pay a commission to that broker. Which of the following agreement best describes this offer by the seller?

    a. Executed   c. Unilateral
    b. Discharged   d. Bilateral

81. By paying his debt after a foreclosure sale, the borrower has the right to regain his property under which of the following?

    a. Acceleration   c. Reversion
    b. Redemption   d. Recovery

82. Which of the following is true of a sale-and-leaseback arrangement?

    a. The seller/vendor retains title to the real estate.
    b. The buyer/vendee gets possession of the property.
    c. The buyer/vendee is the lessor.
    d. This arrangement is disallowed in most states.

83. Fannie Mae and Ginnie Mae

    a. work together as primary market lenders.
    b. are both federal agencies.
    c. are both privately owned entities.
    d. are involved in the secondary market.

84. *Q* decided he could make more money from his tree farm by dividing it into small parcels and selling them to numerous buyers. Subsequently, *Q* entered into a series of purchase agreements in which he agreed to operate the property and distribute proceeds from its income to the buyers of the parcels. Under these circumstances *Q* has sold

    a. real estate because the object of the sale was the land.
    b. securities because the object of the purchase was the trees and the underlying land was merely incidental to the sale.
    c. real estate because the property was subdivided before the sales ever took place.
    d. securities because the buyers were investors relying on *Q*'s activities to generate a profit from the premises purchased.

85. All of the following situations are in violation of the federal Fair Housing Act of 1968 *except*

    a. the refusal of a property manager to rent an apartment to a Catholic couple who are otherwise qualified.
    b. the general policy of a loan company to avoid granting home improvement loans to individuals living in transitional neighborhoods.
    c. the intentional neglect of a broker to show an Asian family any property listings of homes in all-white neighborhoods.
    d. the insistence of a widowed woman on renting her spare bedroom only to another widowed woman.

86. If a storage tank that measures $12' \times 9' \times 8'$ was designed to store natural gas and the cost of the gas is $1.82 per cubic foot, what does it cost to fill the tank to one-half its capacity?

    a. $685   c. $864
    b. $786   d. $1,572

87. When a buyer signs a purchase contract and the seller accepts, the buyer acquires an immediate interest in the property known as

    a. legal title.   c. statutory title.
    b. equitable title.   d. defeasible title.

88. Which of the following requires that finance charges be stated as an annual percentage rate?

    a. Truth-in-Lending Act (Regulation Z)
    b. Real Estate Settlement Procedures Act
    c. Equal Credit Opportunity Act
    d. Federal Fair Housing Act

89. *J* owns an apartment building in a large city. After discussing the matter with his advisers, *J* decided to alter the type of occupancy in the building from rental to condominium status. This procedure is known as

    a. amendment.   c. deportment.
    b. partition.   d. conversion.

90. In the preceding question, after checking the applicable laws, *J* discovered that in connection with the change to condominium status he must initially offer to sell each unit to the tenant who currently occupies the unit. If the tenant rejects the offer, *J* may then offer the unit for sale to the general public. The requirement that *J* offer the property to the tenant in this situation is known as a

    a. contingent restriction.
    b. conditional sales option.
    c. right of first refusal.
    d. covenant of prior acceptance.

91. Which of the following real estate documents is least likely to be recorded?

    a. A standard form deed
    b. A long-term lease
    c. An option agreement
    d. A purchase agreement

92. Broker *U* represented the seller in a transaction. Her client told her that he did not want to recite the actual consideration that was paid for the house. In this situation Broker *U*

    a. must inform her client that only the actual price of the real estate may appear on the deed.
    b. may show the nominal consideration of only $10 on the deed.
    c. should inform the seller that either the full price should be stated in the deed or all references to consideration should be removed from it.
    d. may show a price on the deed other than the actual price, provided that the variance is not greater than 10 percent of the purchase price.

93. A broker obtained a listing agreement to act as the agent in the sale of a seller's house. A buyer has been found for the property, and all of the agreements have been signed. As an agent for the seller, the broker is responsible for the buyer's

    a. completing the loan application.
    b. receiving copies of all documents.
    c. qualification for the new mortgage loan.
    d. inspecting the property.

94. *G* and *M*, co-owners of a corner parcel of vacant commercial property, have executed three open listing agreements with three brokers around town. All three brokers would like to place For Sale signs on the sellers' property. Under these circumstances

    a. a broker does not have to obtain the sellers' permission before placing a sign on the property.
    b. only one For Sale sign may be placed on the property at one time.
    c. upon obtaining the sellers' written consent, all brokers can place their For Sale signs on the property.
    d. the broker who obtained the first open listing must consent to all signs being placed on the property.

95. In estimating the value of real estate using the cost approach, the appraiser should

    a. estimate the replacement cost of the improvements.
    b. deduct for the depreciation of the land and buildings.
    c. determine the original cost and adjust for inflation.
    d. review the sales prices of comparable properties.

Real Estate
Licensing and
Registration Act

COMMONWEALTH OF PENNSYLVANIA

STATE REAL ESTATE COMMISSION

REAL ESTATE LICENSING AND REGISTRATION ACT

PRINTING DATE: JANUARY 1992

"REAL ESTATE LICENSING &
REGISTRATION ACT"
Act of February 19, 1980, P.L. 15, No. 9
as amended through July 1990

TABLE OF CONTENTS

CHAPTER 1
GENERAL PROVISIONS

Section 101. Short title.

This act shall be known and may be cited as the "Real Estate Licensing and Registration Act."

CHAPTER 2
DEFINITIONS

Section 201. Definitions.

The following words and phrases when used in this act shall have, unless the context clearly indicates otherwise, the meanings given to them in this section:

"Associate broker." A broker employed by another broker.

"Broker." Any person who, for another and for a fee, commission or other valuable consideration:

(1) negotiates with or aids any person in locating or obtaining for purchase, lease or acquisition of interest in any real estate;

(2) negotiates the listing, sale, purchase, exchange, lease, time share and similarly designated interests, financing or option for any real estate;

(3) manages or appraises any real estate;

(4) represents himself as a real estate consultant, counselor, house finder;

(5) undertakes to promote the sale, exchange, purchase or rental of real estate: Provided, however, That this provision shall not include any person whose main business is that of advertising, promotion or public relations; or

(6) attempts to perform any of the above acts.

"Builder-owner salesperson." Any person who is a full-time employee of a builder-owner of single and multifamily dwellings located within the Commonwealth and as such employee shall be authorized and empowered to list for sale, sell or offer for sale, or to negotiate the sale or exchange of real estate, or to lease or rent, or offer to lease, rent or place for rent, any real estate owned by his builder-owner employer, or collect or offer, or attempt to collect, rent for the use of real estate owned by his builder-owner employer, for and on behalf of such builder-owner employer.

"Campground membership." An interest, other than in fee simple or by lease, which gives the purchaser the right to use a unit of real property for the purpose of locating a recreational vehicle, trailer, tent, tent trailer, pickup camper or other similar device on a periodic basis pursuant to a membership contract allocating use and occupancy rights between other similar users.

"Campground membership salesperson." A person who either as an employee or an independent contractor sells or offers to sell campground memberships. Such person shall sell campground memberships under the active supervision of a broker. A person licensed as a broker, as a salesperson or as a time-share salesperson shall not be required to be licensed as a campground membership salesperson as a condition for selling or offering to sell campground memberships.

"Cemetery." A place for the disposal or burial of deceased human beings, by cremation or in a grave, mausoleum, vault, columbarium or other receptacle, but the term does not include a private family cemetery.

"Cemetery broker." Any person engaging in or carrying on the business or acting in the capacity of a broker within this Commonwealth exclusively within the limited field or branch of business which applies to cemetery lots, plots and mausoleum spaces or openings.

"Cemetery company." Any person who offers or sells to the public the ownership, or the right to use, any cemetery lot.

"Cemetery salesperson." Any person employed by a broker or cemetery broker to perform duties as defined herein under "cemetery broker."

"Commission." The State Real Estate Commission.

"Commissioner." Commissioner of Professional and Occupational Affairs.

"Department." The Department of State acting through the Commissioner of Professional and Occupational Affairs.

"Employ, employed, employee, employment." The use of the words employ, employed, employee, or employment in this act shall apply to the relationship of independent contractor as well as to the relationship of employment, except as applied to builder-owner salespersons.

"Person." Any individual, corporation, corporate fiduciary, partnership, association or other entity, foreign or domestic.

"Real Estate." Any interest or estate in land, whether corporeal, incorporeal, freehold or nonfreehold, whether the land is situated in this Commonwealth or elsewhere including leasehold interests and time share and similarly designated interests. A sale of a mobile home shall be deemed to be a transfer of an interest in real estate if accompanied by the assignment of the lease or sale of the land on which the mobile home is situated.

"Rental listing referral agent." Any person who owns or manages a business which collects rental information for the purpose of referring prospective tenants to rental units or locations of such units. The term "rental listing referral agent" shall not include any employee or official of any public housing authority created pursuant to State or Federal law.

"Salesperson." Any person employed by a licensed real estate broker to list for sale, sell or offer for sale, to buy or offer to buy or to negotiate the purchase or sale or exchange of real estate or to negotiate a loan on real estate or to lease or rent or offer to lease, rent or place for rent any real estate or collect or offer or attempt to collect rent for the use of real estate for or in behalf of such real estate broker. No person employed by a broker to perform duties other than those activities as defined herein under "broker" shall be required to be licensed as a salesperson.

"School." Any person who conducts classes in real estate subjects but is not a college, university or institute of higher learning duly accredited by the Middle States Association of Colleges and Secondary Schools or equivalent accreditation.

"Time share." The right, however evidenced or documented, to use or occupy one or more units on a periodic basis according to an arrangement allocating use and occupancy rights of that unit or those units between other similar users. As used in this definition, the term "unit" is a building or portion thereof permanently affixed to real property and designed for separate occupancy or a campground or portion thereof designed for separate occupancy. The phrase "time share" does not include campground membership.

"Time-share salesperson." A person who either as an employee or independent contractor sells or offers to sell time shares. Such person shall sell time shares under the active supervision of a broker. A person licensed as a broker or as a salesperson shall not be required to be licensed as a time-share salesperson as a condition for selling or offering to sell time shares.

Section 202. State Real Estate Commission.

(a) The State Real Estate Commission is hereby created and shall consist of the Commissioner of Professional and Occupational Affairs; the Director of the Bureau of Consumer Protection, or his designee; three members who shall be persons representing the public at large; five other persons, each of whom shall at the time of his appointment be a licensed and qualified real estate broker under the existing law of this Commonwealth, and shall have been engaged in the real estate business in this Commonwealth for a period of not less than ten years immediately prior to his appointment; and one other person who shall have been licensed as a real estate broker, or cemetery broker, for a period of at least five years and shall have been engaged in selling cemetery lots for at least ten years immediately prior to his appointment. Each of said members of the commission shall be appointed by the Governor.

(b) The term of office of each of said members shall be five years from his appointment, or until his successor has been appointed and qualified but not longer than six months beyond the five-year period. In the event that any of said members shall die or resign during his term of office, his successor shall be appointed in the same way and with the same qualifications as above set forth and shall hold office for the unexpired term.

(c) A majority of the members currently serving on the commission shall constitute a quorum. The commission shall elect a chairman, vice-chairman and secretary from among its members. A commission member who fails to attend three consecutive meetings shall forfeit his seat unless the Commissioner of Professional and Occupational Affairs, upon written request from the member, finds that the member should be excused from a meeting because of illness or the death of a family member.

(d) Each member of the commission other than the Commissioner of Professional and Occupational Affairs shall receive reimbursement for reasonable expenses in accordance with Commonwealth regulations and per diem compensation at the rate of $60 per day for the time actually devoted to the business of the commission.

(e) In addition to regularly scheduled meetings of the commission, there shall be at least one public meeting each year in Pittsburgh, one public meeting each year in Philadelphia and one public meeting each year in Harrisburg. At least 15 days prior to the holding of any public meeting pursuant to this subsection, the commission shall give public notice of the meeting in a newspaper of general circulation in each of the areas where the public meeting is to be held. The purpose of these special meetings shall be to solicit from members of the public, suggestions, comments and objections about real estate practice in this Commonwealth.

CHAPTER 3
APPLICATION OF THE ACT AND PENALTIES

Section 301. Unlawful to conduct business without license or registration certificate.

It shall be unlawful for any person, directly or indirectly, to engage in or conduct, or to advertise or hold himself out as engaging in or conducting the business, or acting in the capacity of a broker or salesperson, cemetery broker, cemetery salesperson, campground membership salesperson, time-share salesperson, builder-owner salesperson, rental listing referral agent or cemetery company within this Commonwealth without first being licensed or registered as provided in this act, unless he is exempted from obtaining a license or registration certificate under the provisions of section 304.

Section 302. Civil suits.

No action or suit shall be instituted, nor recovery be had, in any court of this Commonwealth by any person for compensation for any act done or service rendered, the doing or rendering of which is prohibited under the provisions of this act by a person other than a licensed broker, salesperson, cemetery broker, cemetery salesperson, campground membership salesperson, time-share salesperson, builder-owner salesperson or rental listing referral agent, unless such person was duly licensed and registered hereunder as broker or salesperson at the time of offering to perform any such act or service or procuring any promise or contract for the payment of compensation for any such contemplated act or service.

Section 303. Criminal penalties.

Any person who shall engage in or carry on the business, or act in the capacity of a broker, salesperson, cemetery broker, cemetery salesperson, campground membership salesperson, time-share salesperson, builder-owner salesperson, rental listing referral agent or cemetery company, within this Commonwealth, without a license or registration certificate, or shall carry on or continue business after the suspension or revocation of any such license or registration certificate issued to him, or shall employ any person as a salesperson or cemetery salesperson to whom a license has not been issued, or whose license or registration certificate as such shall have been revoked or suspended, shall be guilty of a summary offense and upon conviction thereof for a first offense shall be sentenced to pay a fine not exceeding $500 or suffer imprisonment, not exceeding three months, or both and for a second or subsequent offense shall be guilty of a felony of the third degree and upon conviction thereof, shall be sentenced to pay a fine of not less than $2,000 but not more than $5,000 or to imprisonment for not less than one year but not more than two years, or both.

Section 304. Exclusions.

Except as otherwise provided in this act, the provisions of this act shall not apply to the following:

(1) An owner of real estate with respect to property owned or leased by such owner. In the case of a partnership or corporation, this exclusion shall not extend to more than five of its partners or officers, respectively, nor to other partnership or corporation personnel or employees.

(2) The employees of a public utility acting in the ordinary course of utility-related business under the provisions of Title 66 of the Pennsylvania Consolidated Statutes (relating to public utilities), with respect to negotiating the purchase, sale or lease of property.

(3) The officers or employees of a partnership or corporation whose principal business is the discovery, extraction, distribution or transmission of energy or mineral resources, provided that the purchase, sale or lease of real estate is a common and necessary transaction in the conduct of such principal business.

(4) The services rendered by an attorney-in-fact under an executed and recorded power of attorney from the owner or lessor (provided such power of attorney is not utilized to circumvent the intent of this act) or by an attorney at law.

(5) A person acting as trustee in bankruptcy, administrator, executor, trustee or guardian while acting under a court order or under the authority of a will or of a trust instrument.

(6) The elected officer or director of any banking institution, savings institution, savings bank, credit union or trust company operating under applicable Federal or State laws where only the real estate of the banking institution, savings institution, savings bank, credit union or trust company is involved.

(7) Any officer or employee of a cemetery company who, as incidental to his principal duties and without remuneration therefor, shows lots in such company's cemetery to persons for their use as a family burial lot and who accepts deposits on such lots for the representatives of the cemetery company legally authorized to sell the same.

(8) Cemetery companies and cemeteries owned or controlled by a bona fide church or religious congregation or fraternal organization or by any association created by a bona fide church or religious organization or by a fraternal organization.

(9) An auctioneer licensed under the act of September 29, 1961 (P.L. 1745, No. 708), known as "The Auctioneers' License Act," while performing authorized duties at any bona fide auction.

(10) Any person employed by an owner of real estate for the purpose of managing or maintaining multifamily residential property: Provided, however, That such person is not authorized or empowered by such owner to enter into leases on behalf of the owner, to negotiate terms or conditions of occupancy with current or prospective tenants or to hold money belonging to tenants other than on behalf of the owner. So long as the owner retains the authority to make all such decisions, the employees may show apartments and provide information on rental

amounts, building rules and regulations and leasing determinations.

(11) The elected officer, director or employee of any banking institution, savings institution, savings bank, credit union or trust company operating under applicable Federal or State laws when acting on behalf of the institution in performing appraisals or other evaluations of real estate in connection with a loan transaction.

Section 305. Civil penalty.

In addition to any other civil remedy or criminal penalty provided for in this act, the commission, by a vote of the majority of the maximum number of the authorized membership of the commission as provided by law, or by a vote of the majority of the duly qualified and confirmed membership or a minimum of five members, whichever is greater, may levy a civil penalty of up to $1,000 on any current licensee who violates any provision of this act or on any person who practices real estate without being properly licensed to do so under this act. The commission shall levy this penalty only after affording the accused party the opportunity for a hearing, as provided in Title 2 of the Pennsylvania Consolidated Statutes (relating to administrative law and procedure).

CHAPTER 4
POWERS AND DUTIES OF THE STATE REAL ESTATE COMMISSION - GENERAL

Section 401.   Duty to issue licenses and registration certificates.

It shall be the duty of the department to issue licenses and registration certificates to any person who shall comply with the provisions of this act.

Section 402. Approval of schools.

Any school which shall offer or conduct any course or courses of study in real estate shall first obtain approval from, and thereafter abide by the rules and regulations of the commission covering such schools.

Section 403. Authority to examine applicants.

The commission is empowered to prescribe the subjects to be tested. The department shall arrange for the services of professional testing services to write and administer examinations on behalf of the commission in accordance with commission guidance and approval.

Section 404. Power to promulgate regulations.

The commission shall have the power to promulgate rules or regulations in order to administer and effectuate the purposes of this act. All existing rules or regulations shall remain in full force and effect until modified by the commission.

Section 404a. Continuing education.

(a)   The commission shall adopt, promulgate and enforce rules and regulations consistent with the provisions of this act establishing requirements of continuing education to be met by individuals licensed as real estate brokers and real estate salespersons under this act as a condition for renewal of their licenses. The commission may waive all or part of the continuing education requirement for a salesperson or broker who shows evidence, to the commission's satisfaction, that he was unable to complete the requirement due to illness, emergency or hardship. Such regulations shall include any fees necessary for the commission to carry out its responsibilities under this section.

(b)   Beginning with the license period designed by regulation, each person licensed pursuant to this act shall be required to obtain 14 hours of mandatory continuing education during each two-year license period. A licensed broker or salesperson who wishes to activate a license which has been placed on inactive status shall be required to document 14 hours of continuing education.

(c)   All courses, materials, locations and instructors shall be approved by the commission. No credit shall be given for any course in office management.

(d)   The commission shall initiate the promulgation of regulations to carry out the provisions of this section within six months of the effective date of this section.

(e)   The commission shall inform licensees of the continuing education requirement prior to the renewal period when continuing education is required. Each renewal notice thereafter shall include the following additional information:

(1)   That licenses may be placed on inactive status for no more than five years.

(2)   That individuals must show evidence of 14 hours of continuing education in order to reactivate a license which has been placed on inactive status.

(3)   The procedure and fee required for activating an inactive license.

(4)   That a licensee who fails to activate his license after five years must retake the appropriate examination.

Section 405. Duty to keep records confidential.

Repealed. 1984, March 29, P.L. 162, No. 32, § 7.

Section 406. Administration and enforcement.

The commission shall have the power and its duty shall be to administer and enforce the laws of the Commonwealth relating to:

(1) Those activities involving real estate for which licensing is required under this act and to instruct and require its agents to bring prosecutions for unauthorized and unlawful practice.

(2) Those activities involving cemeteries and cemetery companies for which registration is required under this act and to instruct and require its agents to bring prosecutions for unauthorized or unlawful activities.

(3) Those activities involving campground memberships for which licensing is required under this act and to instruct and require its agents to bring prosecutions for unauthorized or unlawful activities.

Section 407. Fees.

(a) All fees required under this act shall be fixed by the commission, by regulation and shall be subject to review in accordance with the act of June 25, 1982 (P.L. 633, No. 181), known as the "Regulatory Review Act." If the projected revenues to be generated by fees, fines and civil penalties imposed in accordance with the provisions of this act are not sufficient to match expenditures over a two-year period, the commission shall increase those fees by regulation, subject to review in accordance with the "Regulatory Review Act," such that the projected revenue will meet or exceed projected expenditures.

(b) If the Bureau of Professional and Occupational Affairs determines that the fees established by the commission are inadequate to meet the minimum enforcement efforts required, then the bureau, after consultation with the commission, shall increase the fees by regulation, subject to review in accordance with the "Regulatory Review Act," so that adequate revenue is raised to meet the required enforcement effort.

Section 408. Reports to legislative committees.

(a) The commission shall submit annually a report to the Professional Licensure Committee of the House of Representatives and to the Consumer Protection and Professional Licensure Committee of the Senate a description of the types of complaints received, status of cases, board action which has been taken and the length of time from the initial complaint to final board resolution.

(b) The commission shall also submit annually to the House of Representatives and the Senate Appropriations Committees, 15 days after the Governor has submitted his budget to the General Assembly, a copy of the budget request for the upcoming fiscal year which the commission previously submitted to the department.

CHAPTER 5

QUALIFICATIONS AND APPLICATIONS FOR LICENSES AND REGISTRATION CERTIFICATES

SUBCHAPTER A
GENERAL

Section 501. Reputation; inactive licensee; revoked license.

(a) Licenses shall be granted only to and renewed only for persons who bear a good reputation for honesty, trustworthiness, integrity and competence to transact the business of broker, salesperson, cemetery broker, cemetery salesperson, campground membership salesperson, time-share salesperson, builder-owner salesperson or rental listing referral agent, in such manner as to safeguard the interest of the public, and only after satisfactory proof of such qualifications has been presented to the commission as it shall by regulation require.

(b) Any person who remains inactive for a period of five years without renewing his license shall, prior to having a license reissued to him, submit to and pass the examination pertinent to the license for which the person is reapplying.

(c) Unless ordered to do so by Commonwealth Court, the commission shall not reinstate the license, within five years of date of revocation, of any person whose license has been revoked under this act. Any person whose license has been revoked may reapply for a license at the end of the five-year period but must meet all of the licensing qualifications of this act for the license applied for, to include the examination requirement.

SUBCHAPTER B
BROKER'S LICENSE

Section 511. Qualifications for license.

The applicant for a broker's license, shall as a condition precedent to obtaining a license, take the broker's license examination and score a passing grade. Prior to taking the examination:

(1) The applicant shall be at least 21 years of age.

(2) The applicant shall be a high school graduate or shall produce proof satisfactory to the commission of an education equivalent thereto.

(3) The applicant shall have completed 240 hours in real estate instruction in areas of study prescribed by the rules of the commission, which rules shall require instruction in the areas of fair housing and professional ethics.

(4) The applicant shall have been engaged as a licensed real estate salesperson for at least three

years or possess educational or experience qualifications which the commission deems to be the equivalent thereof.

Section 512. Application for license.

(a)   An application for a license as real estate broker shall be made in writing to the department, upon a form provided for the purpose by the department and shall contain such information as to the applicant as the commission shall require.

(b)   The application shall state the place of business for which such license is desired.

(c)   The application shall be received by the commission within three years of the date upon which the applicant passed the examination.

Section 513.   Corporations, partnerships and associations.

If the applicant for a broker's license is a corporation, partnership or association, then the provisions of sections 511 and 512 shall apply to the individual designated as broker of record.   The employees of said corporation, partnership or association actually engaging in or intending to engage in the real estate business shall meet the provisions of section 521 and 522.

SUBCHAPTER C
SALESPERSON'S LICENSE

Section 521. Qualifications for license.

Each applicant shall as a condition precedent to obtaining a license, take the salesperson license examination and score a passing grade.   Prior to taking examination:

(1)   The applicant shall be at least 18 years of age.

(2)   The applicant shall have completed 60 hours in real estate instruction in areas of study prescribed by the rules of the commission, which rules shall require instruction in the areas of fair housing and professional ethics.

Section 522. Application for license.

(a)   An application for a license as salesperson shall be made, in writing to the department, upon a form provided for the purpose by the department, and shall contain such information as to the applicant, as the commission shall require.

(b)   The applicant shall submit a sworn statement by the broker with whom he desires to be affiliated certifying that the broker will actively supervise and train the applicant.

(c)   The application shall be received by the commission within three years of the date upon which the

applicant passed the examination.

SUBCHAPTER D
CEMETERY BROKER'S LICENSE

Section 531. Qualifications for license.

Each applicant for a cemetery broker's license shall as a condition to obtaining a license take the cemetery broker's license examination and score a passing grade. Prior to taking the examination:

(1)   The applicant shall be at least 21 years of age.

(2)   The applicant shall have been engaged full time as a salesperson or cemetery salesperson for at least three years or possess educational or experience qualifications which the commission deems to be the equivalent thereof.

Section 532. Application for license.

(a)   An application for a license as a cemetery broker shall be made, in writing, to the department, upon a form provided for the purpose by the department and shall contain such information as to the applicant, as the commission shall require.

(b)   The applicant shall have completed 60 hours in real estate instruction in areas of study prescribed by the rules of the commission, which rules shall require instruction in the areas of professional ethics.

(c)   The application shall be received by the commission within three years of the date upon which the applicant passed the examination.

Section 533.   Corporations, partnerships, associations or other entities.

If the applicant for a cemetery broker's license is a corporation, partnership, association, or other entity, foreign or domestic, then the provisions of sections 531 and 532 shall apply to the individual designated as Broker of Record, as well as those members actually engaging in or intending to engage in the real estate business.

SUBCHAPTER E
CEMETERY SALESPERSON'S LICENSE

Section 541. Qualifications for license.

The applicant for a cemetery salesperson's license shall be at least 18 years of age.

Section 542. Application for license.

(a)   An application for a license as a cemetery salesperson shall be made, in writing, to the department, upon a form provided for the purpose by the department, and shall contain such information as to the applicant, as the commission shall require.

(b)   The applicant for a license shall submit a sworn affidavit by the broker or cemetery broker with whom he desires to be affiliated certifying that the broker will actively supervise and train the applicant and certifying the truth and accuracy of the certification of the applicant.

SUBCHAPTER F
BUILDER-OWNER SALESPERSON'S LICENSE

Section 551. Qualifications for license.

Each applicant for a builder-owner salesperson's license, shall be a condition precedent to obtaining a license, take the standards real estate salesperson's license examination and score a passing grade. Prior to taking the examination:

(1)   The applicant shall be 18 years of age.

(2)   The applicant shall be employed by a builder-owner possessing those qualifications as contained in section 501.

Section 552. Application for license.

(a)   An application for a license as a builder-owner salesperson shall be made, in writing to the department, upon a form provided for the purpose by the department, and shall contain such information as to the applicant as the commission shall require.

(b)   The applicant shall submit a sworn statement by the builder-owner by whom he is employed certifying to such employment.

(c)   The application shall be received by the commission within three years of the date upon which the applicant passed the examination.

SUBCHAPTER G
RENTAL LISTING REFERRAL AGENT'S LICENSE

Section 561. Qualifications for license.

The qualification for licensure as a rental listing referral agent shall be the same as those set forth in section 521 and 522 except that the applicant need not be affiliated with a broker.

SUBCHAPTER H
CEMETERY COMPANY REGISTRATION CERTIFICATE

Section 571.   Application and fee for registration certificate.

An application for a registration certificate for a cemetery company to operate a cemetery shall be made, in writing to the department, upon a form provided for the purpose by the department, and shall contain such

information as to the applicant as the commission shall require.

SUBCHAPTER I.
CAMPGROUND MEMBERSHIP SALESPERSON'S LICENSE

Section 581.   Qualifications for license.

(a)   The applicant for a campground salesperson's license shall be at least 18 years of age.

(b)   The applicant shall have successfully completed 15 hours in the following areas of study:

(1)   Basic contract law.

(2)   Sales practices and procedures.

(3)   Sales ethics.

(4)   Basic theory of campground memberships.

(c)   The applicant shall undergo not less than 30 days of onsite training at a campground membership facility.

Section 582.   Application for license.

(a)   An application for a license as a campground membership salesperson shall be made in writing to the department upon a form provided for the purpose by the department and shall contain such information as to the applicant as the commission shall require.

(b)   The applicant for a license shall submit a sworn affidavit by a broker certifying that the broker will actively supervise and train the applicant and certifying the truth and accuracy of the certification of the applicant.

(c)   A license shall be renewed biennially.

(d)   The commission shall establish an application fee and a biennial renewal fee by regulation.

SUBCHAPTER J.
TIME-SHARE SALESPERSON'S LICENSE

Section 591.   Qualifications for license.

(a)   The applicant for a time-share salesperson's license shall be at least 18 years of age.

(b)   The applicant shall have successfully completed 30 hours of instruction in the following areas of study:

(1)   Basic contract law.

(2)   Sales practices and procedures.

(3)   Sales ethics.

(4)   Basic theory of resort time sharing.

(c)   The applicant shall undergo not less than 30 days of onsite training at a time-share facility.

Section 592.   Application for license.

(a)   An application for a license as a time-share salesperson shall be made in writing to the department upon a form provided for the purpose by the department and shall contain such information as to the applicant as the commission shall require.

(b)   The applicant shall submit a sworn statement by a broker certifying that the broker will actively supervise and train the applicant and certifying the truth and accuracy of the certification of the applicant.

(c)   A license shall be renewed biennially.

(d)   The commission shall establish an application fee and a biennial renewal fee by regulation.

CHAPTER 6
DUTIES OF LICENSEES

Section 601.   Duty of brokers, cemetery brokers and rental listing referral agents to maintain office.

(a)   Each resident licensed broker (which term in this section shall include cemetery broker) and rental listing referral agent shall maintain a fixed office within this Commonwealth. The current license of a rental listing referral agent or broker and of each licensee employed by such broker shall be prominently displayed in an office of the broker or rental listing referral agent. The address of the office shall be designated on the current license. In case of removal of a broker's office from the designated location, all licensees registered at that location shall make application to the commission before such removal or within ten days thereafter, designating the new location of the office, and shall pay the required fees, whereupon the commission shall issue a current license at the new location for the unexpired period, if the new location complies with the terms of this act. Each licensed broker shall maintain a sign on the outside of his office indicating the proper licensed brokerage name.

(b)   If the applicant for a broker's license intends to maintain more than one place of business within the Commonwealth, he shall apply for and obtain an additional license in his name at each office. Every such application shall state the location of such office. Each office shall be under the direction and supervision of a manager who is either the broker or an associate broker: Provided, however, That such broker or an associate broker may direct and supervise more than one office.

Section 602. Nonresident licensees.

Any nonresident of this Commonwealth who meets the equivalent experience requirements and other standards and qualifications, as the commission shall by rule provide, shall qualify for a license under this act.

Section 603.   Employment of associate brokers, salesperson.

(a)   No associate broker or salesperson (which term is this section shall include cemetery salesperson) shall be employed by any other broker than is designated upon the current license issued to said associate broker or said salesperson. Whenever a licensed salesperson or associate broker desires to change his employment from one licensed broker to another, he shall notify the commission in writing no later than ten days after the intended date of change, pay the required fee, and return his current license. The commission, shall upon receipt of acknowledgement from the new broker of the change of employment issue a new license. In the interim at such time as the change in affiliation of the salesperson or associate broker occurs, he shall maintain a copy of the notification sent to the commission as his temporary license pending receipt of his new current license. It shall be the duty of the applicant to notify the commission if a new license or other pertinent communication is not received from the commission within 30 days.

(b)   No campground membership salesperson or time-share salesperson shall be supervised by any other broker than is designated upon the current license issued to such salesperson. Whenever a campground membership salesperson or a time-share salesperson desires to be supervised by a different broker, such licensee and the commission shall follow the procedure specified in subsection (a) for real estate salespersons.

Section 604. Prohibited acts.

(a)   The commission may upon its own motion, and shall promptly upon the verified complaint in writing of any person setting forth a complaint under this section, ascertain the facts and, if warranted, hold a hearing for the suspension or revocation of a license or registration certificate or for the imposition of fines not exceeding $1,000, or both. The commission shall have power to refuse a license or registration certificate for cause or to suspend or revoke a license or registration certificate or to levy fines up to $1,000, or both, where the said license has been obtained by false representation, or by fraudulent act or conduct, or where a licensee or registrant, in performing or attempting to perform any of the acts mentioned herein, is found guilty of:

(1)   Making any substantial misrepresentation.

(2)   Making any false promise of a character likely to influence, persuade or induce any person to enter into any contract or agreement when he could not or did not intend to keep such promise.

(3)   Pursuing a continued and flagrant course of misrepresentation or making of false promises through salesperson, associate broker, other

persons, or any medium of advertising, or otherwise.

(4) Any misleading or untruthful advertising, or using any other trade name or insignia or membership in any real estate association or organization, of which the licensee is not a member.

(5) Failure to comply with the following requirements:

(i) all deposits or other moneys accepted by every person, holding a real estate broker license under the provisions of this act, shall be retained by such real estate broker pending consummation or termination of the transaction involved, and shall be accounted for in the full amount thereof at the time of the consummation or termination;

(ii) every salesperson and associate broker promptly on receipt by him of a deposit or other moneys on any transaction in which he is engaged on behalf of his broker-employer, shall pay over the deposit to the broker;

(iii) a broker shall not commingle the money or other property of his principal with his own;

(iv) every broker shall immediately deposit such moneys, of whatever kind of nature, belonging to others, in a separate custodial or trust fund account maintained by the broker with some bank or recognized depository until the transaction involved is consummated or terminated, at which time the broker shall account for the full amount received. Under no circumstances shall a broker permit any advance payment of funds belonging to others to be deposited in the broker's business or personal account, or to be commingled with any funds he may have on deposit;

(v) every broker shall keep records of all funds deposited therein, which records shall indicate clearly the date and from whom he received money, the date deposited, the dates of withdrawals, and other pertinent information concerning the transaction, and shall show clearly for whose account the money is deposited and to whom the money belongs. All such records and funds shall be subject to inspection by the commission. Such separate custodial or trust fund account shall designate the broker, as trustee, and such account must provide for withdrawal of funds without previous notice. All such records shall be available to the commission, or its

representatives, immediately after proper demand or after written notice given, or upon written notice given to the depository;

(vi) a broker is not required to hold in escrow rents that he receives for property management for a lessor. A broker shall deposit rents received into a rental management account that is separate from the broker's escrow account and general business accounts; or

(vii) a broker shall be permitted to deposit moneys into his escrow account to cover service charges to this account assessed by the banking institution.

(6) Failing to preserve for three years following its consummation records relating to any real estate transaction.

(7) Acting for more that one party in a transaction without the knowledge and consent in writing of all parties for whom he acts.

(8) Placing a "for sale" or "for rent" sign on or advertising any property without the written consent of the owner, or his authorized agent.

(9) Failing to voluntarily furnish a copy of any listing, sale, lease, or other contract relevant to a real estate transaction to all signatories thereof at the time of execution.

(10) Failing to specify a definite termination date that is not subject to prior notice, in any listing contract.

(11) Inducing any party to a contract, sale, or lease to break such contract for the purpose of substitution in lieu thereof of a new contract, where such substitution is motivated by the personal gain of the licensee.

(12) Accepting a commission or any valuable consideration by a salesperson or associate broker for the performance of any acts specified in this act, from any person, except the licensed real estate broker with whom he is affiliated.

(12.1) Paying of a commission or any valuable consideration by a broker to anyone other than his licensed employees or another real estate broker for the performance of any acts specified in this act.

(13) Failing to disclose to an owner in writing his intention or true position if he directly or indirectly through a third party, purchased for himself or acquires or intends to acquire any interest in or any option to purchase property which has been listed with his office to sell or lease.

(14) Being convicted in a court of competent jurisdiction in this or any other state, or Federal court, of forgery, embezzlement, obtaining money under false pretenses, bribery, larceny, extortion, conspiracy to defraud, or any similar offense or offenses, or any felony or pleading guilty or nolo contendere to any such offense or offenses.

(15) Violating any rule or regulation promulgated by the commission in the interest of the public and consistent with the provisions of this act.

(16) In the case of a broker licensee, failing to exercise adequate supervision over the activities of his licensed salespersons or associate brokers within the scope of this act.

(17) Failing, within a reasonable time as defined by the commission, to provide information requested by the commission as the result of a formal or informal complaint to the commission, which would indicate a violation of this act.

(18) Soliciting, selling or offering for sale real property by offering free lots, or conducting lotteries or contests or offering prizes for the purpose of influencing by deceptive conduct any purchaser or prospective purchaser of real property. The commission shall promulgate necessary rules and regulations to provide standards for the nondeception conduct under this paragraph.

    (i) Any offering by mail or by telephone of any prize, gift, award or bonus in relation to the offering of sale of real property, including time sharing, shall be accompanied by a statement of the fair market value, not suggested retail price, of all prizes offered, plus a statement of the odds of receiving any such prize. If the offering is by mail the statement of value and odds shall be printed in a clear and conspicuous manner.

    (ii) If a prize is to be awarded as a rebate, coupon or discount certificate, a statement of that fact shall be included. An offering by mail shall include a statement of any fees and the maximum amount of each which the prizewinner must pay in order to receive the prize. Such fees shall include, but not be limited to, dealer preparation, shipping, handling, redemption and shipping insurance. Each fee associated with a prize and the odds of receiving the prize shall appear in a clear and conspicuous manner on any offering by mail.

    (iii) An offering by mail shall be written in a clear and coherent manner, using common usages of words and terms. A concise description of the real property or interest being promoted shall appear in any offering and shall include a statement that the interest is a time share, where applicable. If the prospective prizewinner must personally visit and inspect the real property or interest being promoted and listen to a sales presentation in order to win a prize, the offering shall include a statement of that fact. An offering may include instructions for a recipient to contact a certain telephone number within a specified time period or by a specified date, if the offeror identifies the business entity and its relationship to the offeror and complies with this paragraph.

    (iv) Substitutions of prizes having equal or greater fair market value may be made if the offeror complies with this paragraph.

    (v) As used in this paragraph, the term "prize" includes, but is not limited to, money, personal property, vacations, travel certificates, motor vehicles and appliances.

(19) Paying or accepting, giving or charging any undisclosed commission, rebate, compensation or profit or expenditures for a principal, or in violation of this act.

(20) Any conduct in a real estate transaction which demonstrates bad faith, dishonesty, untrustworthiness, or incompetency.

(21) Performing any act for which an appropriate real estate license is required and is not currently in effect.

(22) Violating any provision of the act of October 27, 1955 (P.L. 744, No. 222), known as the "Pennsylvania Human Relations Act," or any order or consent decree of the Pennsylvania Human Relations Commission issued pursuant to such act if such order or consent decree resulted from a complaint of discrimination in the area of activities authorized by virtue of this act.

    (i) Such activities include but are not limited to:

        (A) Accepting listings on the understanding that illegal discrimination in the sale or rental of housing is to be practiced due to race, color, religious creed, sex, ancestry, national origin, physical handicap, disability or use of a guide dog because of blindness of user of a prospective lessee or purchaser.

(B) Giving false information for purposes of discrimination in the rental or sale of housing due to race, color, religious creed, sex, ancestry, national origin, physical handicap, disability or use of a guide dog because of blindness of user of a prospective lessee or purchaser.

(C) Making distinctions in locations of housing or dates of availability of housing for purposes of discrimination in the rental or sale of such housing due to race, color, religious creed, sex, ancestry, national origin, physical handicap, disability or use of a guide dog because of blindness of user of the prospective lessee or purchaser.

(ii) Nothing contained in this paragraph is intended to preclude the State Real Estate Commission from conducting its own investigation and maintaining its own file on any complaint of discrimination. The intent hereunder is to allow the Pennsylvania Human Relations Commission a reasonable period of time to conduct its own investigations, hold hearings, render its decisions and inform the State Real Estate Commission of its findings prior to the State Real Estate Commission taking action against any broker, salesperson or sales associate charged with a violation of this paragraph.

(iii) If in the event the Pennsylvania Human Relations Commission does not act on a discrimination complaint within 90 days after it is filed with the Pennsylvania Human Relations Commission then the State Real Estate Commission may proceed with action against such licensee.

(iv) The 90-day waiting period delaying State Real Estate Commission action against licensee accused of discrimination applies only in initial complaints against such licensee, second or subsequent complaints may be brought by individuals or the Pennsylvania Human Relations Commission directly to the State Real Estate Commission.

(v) The Pennsylvania Human Relations Commission shall notify the State Real Estate Commission of findings of violations by the Human Relations Commission against licensees under this act concerning the sale, purchase or lease of real estate in violation of the "Pennsylvania Human Relations Act."

(23) In the case of a cemetery company registrant, violating any provisions of Title 9 of the Pennsylvania Consolidated Statutes (relating to burial grounds).

(24) In the case of a cemetery company registrant, violating any provisions of the act of August 14, 1963 (P.L. 1059, No. 459), entitled "An act prohibiting future need sales of cemetery merchandise and services, funeral merchandise and services, except under certain conditions; requiring the establishment of and deposit into a merchandise trust fund of certain amount of the proceeds of any such sale; providing for the administration of such trust funds and the payment of money therefrom; conferring powers and imposing duties on orphans' courts, and prescribing penalties."

(25) Violating section 606 or 607.

(26) Violating section 609.

(27) In the case of a broker licensee, failing to exercise adequate supervision over the activities of a campground membership salesperson or a time-share salesperson within the scope of this act.

(28) Failure of a broker, campground membership salesperson or time-share salesperson to comply with the requirements of paragraph (5), or such alternative requirements established by the rules of the commission, in connection with deposits or other moneys received by the broker, campground membership salesperson or time-share salesperson in conjunction with the sale of a campground membership or a time share.

(b) All fines and civil penalties imposed in accordance with section 305 and this section shall be paid into the Professional Licensure Augmentation Account.

Section 605. Promotional land sales; approval

(a) Any person who proposes to engage in real estate transactions of a promotional nature in this Commonwealth for a property located inside or outside of this Commonwealth, shall first register with the commission for its approval before so doing, and shall comply with such restrictions and conditions pertaining thereto as the commission may impose by rule or regulation. Registration shall not be required for property located within or outside of this Commonwealth which is subject to a statutory exemption under the Federal Interstate Land Sales Full Disclosure Act (Public Law 90-448, 82 Stat. 590, 15 U.S.C. §1702).

(b) As used in this section the term "promotional real estate" means an interest in property as defined in this act which is a part of a common promotional plan undertaken by a single developer or group of developers acting together to offer interests in real estate for sale or lease through advertising by mail, newspaper or periodical, by radio, television, telephone or other electronic means which is contiguous, known, designated or advertised as a common unit or by a common name: Provided, however, That the term shall not mean real estate interest involving less than 50 lots or shares, cemetery lots and land involving less than 25 acres.

(c)   A person may apply to the commission for registration of promotional land sales by filing a statement of record and meeting the requirements of this section. Each registration shall be renewed annually. In lieu of registration or renewal, the commission shall accept registrations, property reports or similar disclosure documents filed in other states or with the Federal Government: Provided, That the commission may suspend or revoke the registration when the Federal Government or a registering state suspends or revokes a regulation. The commission shall, by rule and regulation, cooperate with similar jurisdictions in other states to establish uniform filing procedures and forms, public offering statements and similar forms. The commission shall charge an application fee as determined by regulation to cover costs associated with processing applications for registrations and renewals.

(d)   Unless prior approval has been granted by the commission or the promotional plan is currently registered with the Department of Housing and Urban Development pursuant to the Federal Interstate Land Sales Full Disclosure Act or pursuant to State law, the statement of record shall contain the information and be accompanied by documents specified as follows:

(1)   The name and address of each person having an interest in the property to be covered by the statement of record and the extent of such interest, except that in the case of a corporation the statement shall list all officers and all holders of 10% or more of the subscribed or issued stock of the corporations.

(2)   A legal description of, and a statement of the total area included in the property and a statement of the topography thereof, together with a map showing the division proposed and the dimensions of the property to be covered by the statement of record and their relation to existing streets and roads.

(3)   A statement of the condition of the title to the land comprising the property including all encumbrances, mortgages, judgments, liens or unpaid taxes and deed restrictions and covenants applicable thereto.

(4)   A statement of the general terms and conditions, including the range of selling prices or rents at which it is proposed to dispense of the property.

(5)   A statement of the present condition of access to the property, the existence of any unusual conditions relating to safety which are known to the developer, completed improvements including, but not limited to, streets, sidewalks, sewage disposal facilities and other public utilities, the proximity in miles of the subdivision to nearby municipalities and the nature of any improvements to be installed by the developer and his estimated schedule for completion.

(6)   A statement of any encumbrance, a statement of the consequences for the purchaser of a failure by the person or persons bound to fulfill obligations under any instrument or instruments creating such encumbrance and the steps, if any, taken to protect the purchaser in such eventuality.

(7)   A copy of the articles of incorporation with all amendments thereto, if the developer is a corporation, copies of all instruments by which a deed of trust is created or declared, if the developer is a trust, copies of articles of partnership or association and all other papers pertaining to its organization if the developer is a partnership, unincorporated association, joint stock company or other form of organization and if the purported holder of legal title is a person other than the developer, copies of the above documents for such person.

(8)   Copies of the deed or other instrument establishing title to the property in the developer or other person and copies of any instrument creating a lien or encumbrance upon the title of the developer or other person or copies of the opinion or opinions of counsel in respect to the title to the subdivision in the developer or other person or copies of the title insurance policy guaranteeing such title.

(9)   Copies of all forms of conveyance to be used in selling or leasing lots to purchasers.

(10) Copies of instruments creating easements or other restrictions.

(11) Certified financial statements of the developer or an uncertified financial statement if a certified statement is not available as may be required by the commission.

(12) Such other information and such other documents and certifications as the commission may require as being reasonably necessary or appropriate to assure that prospective purchasers have access to truthful and accurate information concerning the offering.

(13) Consent to submit to the jurisdiction of the Commonwealth Court with respect to any action arising under this section.

(e)   If at any time subsequent to the date of filing of a

statement of record with the commission, a change shall occur affecting any material facts required to be contained in the statement, the developer shall promptly file an amendment thereto.

(f)   If it appears to the commission that the statement of record or any amendment thereto, is on its face incomplete or inaccurate in any material respect, the commission shall so advise the developer within a reasonable time after the filing of the statement or amendment. Failure of the developer to provide the information requested by the commission within 90 days shall result in an automatic denial of an application or a suspension of registration.

(g)   If it appears to the commission that a statement of record includes any untrue statement of material facts or omits to state any material fact required to be stated therein or necessary to make the statements therein not misleading, the commission may reject such application. The commission shall make an investigation of all consumer complaints concerning real estate promotions in the absence of a reciprocal agreement to handle on-site inspections. Under no circumstances shall a member or an employee of the commission perform an on-site inspection. If the commission determines that a violation of this section has occurred, the commission may:

(1)   suspend or revoke any registration;

(2)   refer the complaint to the Consumer Protection Bureau of the Office of Attorney General; or

(3)   seek an injunction or temporary restraining order to prohibit the complained of activity in the Commonwealth Court.

(h)   Upon rejection of an application or amendment, the applicant may within 20 days after such notice request a hearing before the commission. Prior to, and in conjunction with such hearing, the commission, or its designee, shall have access to and may demand the production of any books and papers of, and may examine, the developer, any agents or any other person in respect of any matter relevant to the application. If the developer or any agents fail to cooperate or obstruct or refuse to permit the making of an investigation, such conduct shall be grounds for the denial of the application.

Section 606. Broker's disclosure to seller.

In any listing agreement or contract of agency, the broker shall make the following disclosures to any seller of real property:

(1)   A statement that the broker's commission and the time period of the listing have been determined as a result of negotiations between the broker and the seller.

(2)   A statement describing the purpose of the Real Estate Recovery Fund established under section

801 and the telephone number of the commission at which the seller can receive further information about the fund.

Section 607. Broker's disclosure to buyer.

In any sales agreement or sales contract, a broker shall make the following disclosures to any prospective buyer of real property:

(1)   A statement that the broker is the agent of the seller or that the broker is the agent of the buyer.

(2)   A statement describing the purpose of the Real Estate Recovery Fund established under section 801 and the telephone number of the commission at which the purchaser can receive further information about the fund.

(3)   A statement of the zoning classification of the property except in cases where the property (or each parcel thereof, if subdividable) is zoned solely or primarily to permit single-family dwellings. Failure to comply with this requirement shall render the sales agreement or sales contract voidable at the option of the buyer, and, if voided, any deposits tendered by the buyer shall be returned to the buyer without any requirement for any court action.

(4)   A statement that access to a public road may require issuance of a highway occupancy permit from the Department of Transportation.

Section 608. Information to be given at initial interview.

The commission shall establish rules or regulations which shall set forth the manner and method of disclosure of information to the prospective buyer or seller during the initial interview. Such disclosure shall include, but shall not be limited to:

(1)   A statement that the broker is the agent of the seller or that the broker is the agent of the buyer.

(2)   The purpose of the Real Estate Recovery Fund and the telephone number of the commission at which further information about the fund may be obtained.

(3)   A statement that the duration of the listing agreement or contract and the broker's commission are negotiable.

(4)   A statement that any sales agreement must contain the zoning classification of a property except in cases where the property (or each parcel thereof, if subdividable) is zoned solely or primarily to permit single-family dwellings.

Section 608a. Cemetery broker's disclosure.

In any sales agreement or sales contract, a cemetery broker shall be subject to the requirements of section 607(2) as it relates to the Real Estate Recovery Fund and the disclosure of information.

Section 609. Right to cancel purchase of time share and campground membership.

(a) A purchaser shall have the right to cancel the purchase of a time share or a campground membership until midnight of the fifth day following the date on which the purchaser executed the purchase contract.

(b) The right of cancellation shall be set forth conspicuously in boldface type of at least ten point in size immediately above the signature of the purchaser on the purchase contract in substantially the following form:

> "You, the purchaser, may cancel this purchase at any time prior to midnight of the fifth day following the date of this transaction. If you desire to cancel, you are required to notify the seller, in writing, at (address). Such notice shall be given by certified return receipt mail or by any other bona fide means of delivery which provides you with a receipt. Such notice shall be effective upon being postmarked by the United States Postal Service or upon deposit of the notice with any bona fide means of delivery which provides you with a receipt."

This clause is to be separately initialed by the purchaser. Copies of all documents which place an obligation upon a purchaser shall be given to the purchaser upon execution by the purchaser.

(c) Notice of cancellation shall be given by certified return receipt mail or by any other bona fide means of delivery, provided that the purchaser obtains a receipt. A notice of cancellation given by a bona fide means of delivery shall be effective on the date postmarked or on the date of deposit of the notice with any bona fide means of delivery.

(d) Within ten business days after the receipt of a notice of cancellation, all payments made under the purchase contract shall be refunded to the purchaser and an acknowledgement that the contract is void shall be sent to the purchaser. In the event of a cancellation pursuant to this section, any promotional prizes, gifts and premiums issued to the purchaser by the seller shall remain the property of the purchaser.

(e) The right of cancellation shall not be waivable by any purchaser.

(f) A purchaser who exercises the right of cancellation shall not be liable for any damages as a result of the exercise of that right.

(g) In addition to constituting a violation of this act, a violation of this section by any individual, corporation,

partnership, association or other entity shall also be deemed a violation of the act of December 17, 1968 (P.L. 1224, No. 387), known as the "Unfair Trade Practices and Consumer Protection Law." The Attorney General is authorized to enforce this section. Any actions brought by the Attorney General to enforce this section shall be in addition to any actions which the commission may bring under this act.

(h) The right of the purchaser to bring an action to enforce this section shall be independent of any rights of action which this section confers on the Attorney General and the commission.

(i) Nothing in this act shall affect any rights conferred upon the purchaser by 68 Pa. C.S. Pt. II Subpt. B (relating to condominiums).

(j) This act shall be applicable to time shares and campground memberships which are located within this Commonwealth and to time shares and campground memberships, which are located outside this Commonwealth but for which the purchase contract was executed by the purchaser within this Commonwealth.

CHAPTER 7
PROCEEDINGS BEFORE THE COMMISSION

Section 701. Hearings held by commission.

(a) The said hearings may be held by the commission or any members thereof, or by any of its duly authorized representatives, or by any other person duly authorized by the commission for such purpose in any particular case.

(b) The commission may adopt the findings in the report or may, with or without additional testimony, either return the matter to the representative for such further consideration as the commission deems necessary or make additional or other findings of fact on the basis of all the legally probative evidence of the record and enter its conclusions of law and order in accordance with the requirements for the issuance of an adjudication under Title 2 of the Pennsylvania Consolidated Statutes (relating to administrative law and procedure).

(c) Proceedings before the commission shall be conducted in accordance with Title 1, Part 2 of the Pennsylvania Code.

Section 702. Imputed knowledge, limitations.

(a) No violation of any of the provisions of this act on the part of any salesperson, associate broker, or other employee of any licensed broker, shall be grounds for the revocation or suspension of the license of the employer of such salesperson, associate broker, or employee, unless it shall appear upon the hearings held, that such employer had actual knowledge of such violation.

(b) No violation of any of the provisions of this act on the part of any cemetery broker or cemetery salesperson or other employee of any registered cemetery company, shall be grounds for the revocation or suspension of the registration certificate of the cemetery company, unless it shall appear that such cemetery company had actual knowledge of such violation.

(c)   A course of dealing shown to have been followed by such employee shall constitute prima facie evidence of such knowledge upon the part of his employer.

(d)   No violation of any of the provisions of this act on the part of any campground membership salesperson or time-share salesperson shall be grounds for the revocation or suspension of the license of the broker responsible for supervising such salesperson unless it shall appear upon the hearings held that such broker had actual knowledge of such violation. A course of dealing shown to have been followed by such salesperson shall constitute prima facie evidence of such knowledge upon the part of such broker.

CHAPTER 8
REAL ESTATE RECOVERY FUND

Section 801. Establishment of the fund.

(a)   There is hereby established the Real Estate Recovery Fund for the purposes hereinafter set forth in this act.

(b)   The Real Estate Recovery Fund shall not apply to the sale of, or the offer to sell, a campground membership or to a campground membership salesperson.

Section 802. Funding of the fund.

Each licensee entitled to renew his license on or after February 28, 1980, shall, when so renewing his license pay in addition to the applicable license fee a further fee of $10, which shall be paid and credited to the Real Estate Recovery Fund, thereafter any person upon receiving his initial real estate license or cemetery company registration certificate, shall, in addition to all fees, pay into the Real Estate Recovery Fund a sum of $10. If at the commencement of any biennial renewal period beginning in 1982 and thereafter, the balance of the fund is less than $300,000, the commission may assess an additional fee, in addition to the renewal fee, against each licensee and registrant in an amount not to exceed $10 which will yield revenues sufficient to bring the balance of the fund to $500,000. All said fees shall be paid into the State Treasury and credited to the Real Estate Recovery Fund, and said deposits shall be allocated solely for the purposes of the fund as provided in this act. The fund shall be invested and interest/dividends shall accrue to the fund.

Section 803. Application for recovery from fund.

(a)   When any aggrieved person obtains a final judgment in any court of competent jurisdiction against any person licensed under this act, upon grounds of fraud, misrepresentation or deceit with reference to any transaction for which a license or registration certificate is required under this act (including with respect to cemetery companies any violation of 9 Pa. C.S. §308(b) (relating to accounts of qualified trustee)) and which cause of action occurred on or after the effective date of this act, the aggrieved person may, upon termination of all proceedings, including reviews and appeals, file an application in the court in which the judgment was entered for an order directing payment out of the Real Estate Recovery Fund of the amount unpaid upon the judgment.

(b)   The aggrieved person shall be required to show:

(1)   That he is not a spouse of the debtor, or the personal representative of said spouse.

(2)   That he has obtained a final judgment as set out in this section.

(3)   That all reasonable personal acts, rights of discovery and such other remedies at law and in equity as exist have been exhausted in the collection thereof.

(4)   That he is making said application no more than one year after the termination of the proceedings, including reviews and appeals in connections with the judgment.

(c)   The commission shall have the right to answer actions provided for under this section, and subject to court approval, it may compromise a claim based upon the application of the aggrieved party.

(d)   When there is an order of the court to make payment or a claim is otherwise to be levied against the fund, such amount shall be paid to the claimant in accordance with the limitations contained in this section. Notwithstanding any other provisions of this section, the liability of that portion of the fund allocated for the purpose of this act shall not exceed $20,000 for any one claim and shall not exceed $100,000 per licensee. If the $100,000 liability of the Real Estate Recovery Fund as provided herein is insufficient to pay in full claims adjudicated valid of all aggrieved persons against any one licensee or registrant, such $100,000 shall be distributed among them in such ratio that the respective claims of the aggrieved applicants bear to the aggregate of such claims held valid. If, at any time, the money deposited in the Real Estate Recovery Fund is insufficient to satisfy any duly authorized claim or portion thereof, the commission shall, when sufficient money has been deposited in the fund, satisfy such unpaid claims or portions thereof, in the order that such claims or portions thereof were originally filed, plus accumulated interest at the rate of 6% a year.

(e)   Upon petition of the commission the court may require all claimants and prospective claimants against one licensee or registrant to be joined in one action, to the end that the respective rights of all such claimants to the Real Estate Recovery Fund may be equitably adjudicated and settled.

(f)   Should the commission pay from the Real Estate Recovery Fund any amount in settlement of a claim as provided for in this act against a licensee, the license of that person shall automatically suspend upon the effective date of the payment thereof by the commission. No such licensee shall be granted reinstatement until he has repaid in full plus interest at the rate of 10% a year, the amount paid from the Real Estate Recovery Fund.

(g)   Should the commission pay from the Real Estate Recovery Fund any amount in settlement of a claim as provided for in this act against a registrant the registrant shall automatically be denied the right to sell cemetery lots upon the effective date of the payment thereof by the commission. No such registrant shall be granted the right to sell cemetery lots until he has repaid in full plus interest at the rate of 10% a year, the amount paid from the Real Estate Recovery Fund.

CHAPTER 9
REPEALER AND EFFECTIVE DATE

Section 901. Repealer.

The act of May 1, 1929 (P.L. 1216, No. 427), known as the "Real Estate Brokers License Act of one thousand nine hundred and twenty-nine," is repealed to the following conditions:

(1)   All valid licenses issued prior to the effective date of this act under the provisions of said 1929 act shall continue with full force and validity during the period for which issued. For the subsequent license period, and each license period thereafter, the commission shall renew such licenses without requiring any license examination to be taken: Provided, however, That applicants for renewal or holders of such licenses shall be subject to all other provisions of this act.

(2)   All proceedings in progress on the effective date shall continue to proceed under the terms of the act under which they were brought.

(3)   All offenses alleged to have occurred prior to the effective date of this act shall be processed under the act of May 1, 1929 (P.L. 1216, No. 427).

Section 902. Effective date.

Section 561 shall take effect September 1, 1980 and the remaining provisions of this act shall take effect immediately.

Ch. 35 STATE REAL ESTATE COMMISSION 49 § 35.1

CHAPTER 35. STATE REAL ESTATE COMMISSION

Subchapter B. GENERAL PROVISIONS

§ 35.201. Definitions.

The following words and terms, when used in this chapter, have the following meanings, unless the context clearly indicates otherwise:

Act—The Real Estate Licensing and Registration Act (63 P. S. §§ 455.101—455.902).

Associate broker—An individual broker who is employed by another broker.

Broker—An individual or entity that, for another and for a fee, commission or other valuable consideration, does one or more of the following:

(i) Negotiates with or aids a person in locating or obtaining for purchase, lease or acquisition of interest in real estate.

(ii) Negotiates the listing, sale, purchase, exchange, lease, time share and similarly designated interests, financing or option for real estate.

(iii) Manages or appraises real estate.

35-16

COMMONWEALTH OF PENNSYLVANIA

STATE REAL ESTATE COMMISSION

RULES AND REGULATIONS

PRINTING DATE: JANUARY 1992

(iv) Represents himself or itself as a real estate consultant, counsellor or house finder.

(v) Undertakes to promote the sale, exchange, purchase or rental of real estate. This subparagraph does not apply to an individual or entity whose main business is that of advertising, promotion or public relations.

(vi) Attempts to perform one of the actions listed in subparagraphs (i)—(v).

Broker of record—The individual broker responsible for the real estate transactions of a partnership, association or corporation that holds a broker's license, or the individual broker or limited broker responsible for the real estate transactions of a partnership, association or corporation that holds a limited broker's license.

Builder-owner salesperson—An individual who is a full-time employe of a builder-owner of single- and multi-family dwellings located in this Commonwealth and who is authorized, on behalf of the builder-owner, to do one or more of the following:

(i) List for sale, sell or offer for sale real estate of the builder-owner.

(ii) Negotiate the sale or exchange of real estate of the builder-owner.

(iii) Lease or rent, or offer to lease, rent or place for rent, real estate of the builder-owner.

(iv) Collect or offer, or attempt to collect, rent for real estate of the builder-owner.

Bureau—The Bureau of Professional and Occupational Affairs of the Department.

Campground membership—An interest, other than in fee simple or by lease, which gives the purchaser the right to use a unit of real property for the purpose of locating a recreational vehicle, trailer, tent, tent trailer, pickup camper or other similar device on a periodic basis under a membership contract allocating use and occupancy rights between other similar users.

Campground membership salesperson—An individual who, either as an employe or an independent contractor, sells or offers to sell campground memberships. The individual shall sell campground memberships under the active supervision of a broker. A licensed broker, salesperson or time-share salesperson does not need to possess a campground membership salesperson's license to sell campground memberships.

Cemetery—A place for the disposal or burial of deceased human beings, by cremation or in a grave, mausoleum, vault, columbarium or other receptacle. The term does not include a private family cemetery.

Cemetery associate broker—An individual cemetery broker employed by another cemetery broker or by a broker.

Cemetery broker—An individual or entity that is engaged as, or carrying on the business or acting in the capacity of, a broker exclusively within the limited field or branch of business that applies to cemetery lots, plots and mausoleum spaces or openings.

Cemetery company—An individual or entity that offers or sells to the public the ownership, or the right to use, a cemetery lot.

Cemetery salesperson—An individual employed by a broker or cemetery broker exclusively to perform the duties of a cemetery broker.

Commission—The State Real Estate Commission.

Credit—A period of 15 hours of instruction.

Department—The Department of State of the Commonwealth.

Hour of instruction—A period of at least 50 minutes.

Manager of record—The individual rental listing referral agent responsible for the rental listing transactions of a partnership, association or corporation that holds a rental listing referral agent's license.

Real estate—An interest or estate in land—whether corporeal or incorporeal, whether freehold or nonfreehold, whether the land is situated in this Commonwealth or elsewhere—including leasehold interests and time share and similarly designated interests.

Real estate school—An individual or entity that conducts classes in real estate subjects. The term does not include a college, university or institute of higher learning accredited by the Middle States Association of Colleges and Secondary Schools or equivalent accreditation.

Rental listing referral agent—An individual or entity that owns or manages a business which collects rental information for the purpose of referring prospective tenants to rental units or locations of rental units. The term does not include an official or employe of a public housing authority that is created under State or Federal law.

Salesperson—An individual who is employed by a broker to do one or more of the following:

(i) Sell or offer to sell real estate, or list real estate for sale.

(ii) Buy or offer to buy real estate.

(iii) Negotiate the purchase, sale or exchange of real estate.

(iv) Negotiate a loan on real estate.

(v) Lease or rent real estate, or offer to lease or rent real estate or to place real estate for rent.

(vi) Collect rent for the use of real estate, or offer or attempt to collect rent for the use of real estate.

(vii) Assist a broker in managing or appraising property.

Time share—The right, however evidenced or documented, to use or occupy one or more units on a periodic basis according to an

Appendix C: Real Estate Licensing and Registration Act   433

arrangement allocating use and occupancy rights of that unit or those units between other similar users. As used in this definition, the term "unit" is a building or portion thereof permanently affixed to real property and designed for separate occupancy or a campground membership or portion thereof designed for separate occupancy. The term does not include a campground membership.

Time-share salesperson—An individual who, either as an employe or an independent contractor, sells or offers to sell time shares.

Authority

The provisions of this § 35.201 issued under act of February 19, 1980 (P. L. 15, No. 9) (63 P. S. §§ 455.101—455.902).

Source

The provisions of this § 35.201 adopted February 24, 1989, effective February 25, 1989, 19 Pa.B. 781; amended June 10, 1994, effective June 11, 1994, 24 Pa.B. 2904. Immediately preceding text appears at serial pages (135730) to (135732) and (185623).

§ 35.202. Exclusions from the act.

The following categories of individuals and entities are excluded from the act and this chapter:

(1) An owner of real estate with respect to property owned or leased by the owner. In the case of a corporation or partnership, this exclusion does not extend to more than five of the partnership's partners or the corporation's officers, nor to the other employes of the partnership or corporation.

(2) An employe of a public utility acting in the ordinary course of utility-related business under 66 Pa.C.S. §§ 101—3315 (relating to the Public Utility Code), with respect to negotiating the purchase, sale or lease of real estate.

(3) An officer or employe of a partnership or corporation whose principal business is the discovery, extraction, distribution or transmission of energy or mineral resources, if the purchase, sale or lease of real estate is a common and necessary transaction in the conduct of the principal business.

(4) An attorney in fact who renders services under an executed and recorded power of attorney from an owner or lessor of real estate, if the power of attorney is not used to circumvent the intent of the act. The Commission will consider it a circumvention of the intent of the act for an owner or lessor of real estate to grant a power of attorney to a property manager for the sole purpose of avoiding the necessity of having the property managed by a real estate broker licensed under the act.

(5) An attorney-at-law who receives a fee from his client for rendering services within the scope of the attorney-client relationship and does not hold himself out as a real estate broker.

(6) A trustee in bankruptcy, administrator, executor, trustee or guardian who is acting under authority of a court order, will or trust instrument.

(7) An elected officer or director of a banking institution, savings institution, savings bank, credit union or trust company operating under applicable Federal or State statutes when only the real estate of the banking institution, savings institution, savings bank, credit union or trust company is involved.

(8) An officer or employe of a cemetery company who, as an incidental part of his principal duties and without remuneration therefore, shows lots in the company's cemetery to persons for use as family burial lots and who accepts deposits on the lots for a representative of the cemetery company legally authorized to sell them.

(9) A cemetery company or cemetery owned or controlled by a bona fide church or religious congregation or fraternal organization or by an association created by a bona fide church or religious organization or fraternal organization.

(10) An auctioneer licensed under The Auctioneers' License Act (63 P. S. §§ 701—732) (Repealed) or The Auctioneer and Auction Licensing Act (63 P. S. §§ 734.1—734.34) while performing authorized duties at a bona fide auction.

(11) An individual who is employed by the owner of multifamily residential dwellings to manage or maintain the dwellings and who is not authorized by the owner to enter into leases on the owner's behalf, to negotiate terms and conditions of occupancy with current or prospective tenants, or to hold money belonging to the tenants other than on the owner's behalf. So long as the owner retains authority to make decisions, the individual may show apartments and provide information on rental amounts, building rules and regulations and leasing determinations.

(12) An elected officer, director or employe of a banking institution, savings institution, savings bank, credit union or trust company operating under applicable Federal or State statutes when acting on behalf of the banking institution, savings institution, savings bank, credit union or trust company in performing appraisals or other evaluations of real estate in connection with a loan transaction.

Authority

The provisions of this § 35.202 issued under act of February 19, 1980 (P. L. 15, No. 9) (63 P. S. §§ 455.101—455.902).

Ch. 35   STATE REAL ESTATE COMMISSION   49 § 35.203

Source

The provisions of this § 35.202 adopted February 24, 1989, effective February 25, 1989, 19 Pa.B. 781; amended June 10, 1994, effective June 11, 1994, 24 Pa.B. 2904. Immediately preceding text appears at serial pages (185623) to (185624).

§ 35.203. Fees.

The following fees are charged by the Commission:

Licensing examination for broker, cemetery broker, salesperson, builder-owner salesperson or rental listing referral agent $49.50

Review of qualifications of candidate for broker or cemetery broker licensing examination $25

Application for licensure of:

(i) Broker, cemetery broker or rental listing referral agent ... $55

(ii) Branch office $50

(iii) Associate broker, salesperson, cemetery associate broker, builder-owner salesperson, time-share salesperson, campground membership salesperson, or broker of record, partner or officer for a partnership, association or corporation $20

(iv) Cemetery salesperson $15

Application for registration of cemetery company $20

Initial licensure for broker, cemetery broker, branch office, rental listing referral agent, or broker of record, partner or officer for a partnership, association or corporation:

(i) If issued in first half of biennial period $60

(ii) If issued in second half of biennial period $30

Initial registration for cemetery company or initial licensure for associate broker, salesperson, cemetery associate broker, cemetery salesperson, builder-owner salesperson, time-share salesperson or campground membership salesperson:

(i) If issued in first half of biennial period $40

(ii) If issued in second half of biennial period $20

Biennial renewal of license of broker, cemetery broker, branch office, rental listing referral agent, or broker of record, partner or officer for a partnership, association or corporation $84

Biennial renewal of cemetery company registration or license of associate broker, salesperson, cemetery associate broker, cemetery salesperson, builder-owner salesperson, time-share salesperson or campground membership salesperson $64

Registration of promotional real estate $250

Annual renewal of registration of promotional real estate $75

Approval of real estate school $325

49 § 35.203   DEPARTMENT OF STATE   Pt. I

Annual renewal of approval of real estate school .. $250 plus $10 for each satellite location, course and instructor $55

Change of name or office location of broker, cemetery broker or rental listing referral agent $55

Change of name or address for cemetery company or change of employer, change of employer's name or change of employer's address for associate broker, cemetery associate broker, salesperson, cemetery salesperson, builder-owner salesperson, time-share salesperson, campground membership salesperson, or broker of record, partner or officer for a partnership, association or corporation $20

Change of ownership or directorship of real estate school $40

Change of name or location of real estate school $90

Addition of satellite location, course or instructor for real estate school $20

Certification of current status of licensure, registration or approval $15

Certification of history of licensure, registration or approval $30

Duplicate license $5

Late renewal of license .... In addition to the prescribed renewal fee, $5 for each month or part of the month beyond the renewal date.

Authority

The provisions of this § 35.203 issued under act of February 19, 1980 (P. L. 15, No. 9) (63 P. S. §§ 455.101—455.902).

Source

The provisions of this § 35.203 adopted February 24, 1989, effective February 25, 1989, 19 Pa.B. 781; amended July 31, 1992, effective August 1, 1992, except for the amendment relating to the biennial renewal fees for real estate licensees, which takes effect on, and be retroactive to, May 1, 1992, 22 Pa.B. 3984; amended November 5, 1993, effective upon publication and apply retroactively for July 1, 1993, 23 Pa.B. 5304; amended May 20, 1994, effective June 1, 1994, 24 Pa.B. 2613. Immediately preceding text appears at serial pages (185624) to (185626).

Cross References

This section cited in 49 Pa. Code § 35.221 (relating to general requirements); 49 Pa. Code § 35.243 (relating to licensure of branch office); 49 Pa. Code § 35.271 (relating to examination for broker's license); 49 Pa. Code § 35.272 (relating to examination for salesperson's license); 49 Pa. Code § 35.273 (relating to examination for limited broker's license); 49 Pa. Code § 35.274 (relating to examination for builder-owner salesperson's license); 49 Pa. Code § 35.275 (relating to examination for rental listing referral agent's license); 49 Pa. Code § 35.341 (relating to approval of real estate school); and 49 Pa. Code § 35.343 (relating to renewal of school approval).

Ch. 35   STATE REAL ESTATE COMMISSION   49 § 35.204

§ 35.204. Accuracy and veracity of papers filed with the Commission.

(a) An application, statement, character reference or other paper that is required to be filed by, or on behalf of, an applicant for examination, licensure, registration or approval under the act or this chapter will be subject to investigation by the Commission to confirm its accuracy and truthfulness.

(b) An applicant's knowing failure to provide accurate and truthful information in the application, or in the statements and papers that accompany the application, will be grounds for the Commission's denial of the application.

(c) A licensee's knowing failure to provide accurate and truthful information in connection with an application for examination, licensure, registration or approval under the act or this chapter will be grounds for disciplinary action against the licensee.

Authority

The provisions of this § 35.204 issued under act of February 19, 1980 (P. L. 15, No. 9) (63 P. S. §§ 455.101—455.902).

Source

The provisions of this § 35.204 adopted February 24, 1989, effective February 25, 1989, 19 Pa.B. 781.

Subchapter C. LICENSURE

LICENSURE REQUIREMENTS

---

49 § 35.221   DEPARTMENT OF STATE   Pt. I

OFFICES

STATUS OF LICENSURE

LICENSURE REQUIREMENTS

§ 35.221. General requirements.

In addition to meeting the other requirements of this subchapter pertaining to the specific license sought, an applicant for a Pennsylvania real estate license shall submit the following to the Commission with the license application:

(1) The license fee prescribed in § 35.203 (relating to fees).

(2) Complete details of a conviction of, or plea of guilty or nolo contendere to, a felony or misdemeanor and the sentence imposed. In the case of an applicant that is a corporation, partnership or association, this requirement applies to each member of the partnership or association and to each officer of the corporation.

(3) Written consent that valid and binding service of process may be made on the applicant by serving the Chairperson of the Commission and the Secretary of the Commonwealth if the service of process cannot be made on the applicant under 231 Pa. Code (relating to rules of civil procedure) for actions at law or in equity arising out of the applicant's real estate activities in this Commonwealth.

Authority

The provisions of this § 35.221 issued under act of February 19, 1980 (P. L. 15, No. 9) (63 P. S. §§ 455.101—455.902).

Source

The provisions of this § 35.221 adopted February 24, 1989, effective February 25, 1989, 19 Pa.B. 781.

§ 35.222. Licensure as broker.

(a) Except as provided in subsection (b), an individual who wants to obtain a Pennsylvania broker's license shall:

Ch. 35   STATE REAL ESTATE COMMISSION   49 § 35.222

(1) Have scored a passing grade on each part of the broker's examination within 3 years prior to the submission of a properly completed license application. See § 35.271 (relating to examination for broker's license).

(2) Comply with §§ 35.241 and 35.242 (relating to general office requirement; and office of broker or limited broker).

(3) Submit a completed license application to the Commission with recommendations attesting to the applicant's good reputation for honesty, trustworthiness, integrity and competence from:

(i) One real estate broker licensed by the Commission.

(ii) Two persons unrelated to the applicant who own property in the county where the applicant resides or has a place of business.

(iii) Two persons unrelated to the applicant who own property in the county where the applicant previously resided, if the applicant changed his county of residence within 1 year prior to the submission of the application.

(b) An individual holding a broker's license issued by another jurisdiction who wants to obtain a Pennsylvania broker's license either shall comply with subsection (a) or shall:

(1) Possess a broker's license issued by another jurisdiction that has been active within 5 years prior to the submission of a properly completed license application.

(2) Have scored a passing grade on the Pennsylvania portion of the broker's examination within 3 years prior to the submission of a properly completed license application. See § 35.271.

(3) Comply with §§ 35.241 and 35.242.

(4) Submit a completed license application to the Commission with a certification from the real estate licensing authority of the other jurisdiction containing the following information:

(i) The applicant's license number, the date of issuance of the license and confirmation that the applicant obtained initial licensure by written examination.

(ii) Whether the license has been active within the past 5 years.

(iii) A description of past disciplinary action taken by the licensing authority against the applicant.

(iv) The applicant's office address and the name of the applicant's employer.

(c) A partnership, association or corporation that wants to obtain a Pennsylvania broker's license shall:

(1) Ensure that each member of the partnership or association, or each officer of the corporation, who intends to engage in the real estate business is licensed by the Commission as a salesperson or broker.

49 § 35.223   DEPARTMENT OF STATE   Pt. I

(2) Designate an individual who is licensed by the Commission as a broker to serve as broker of record.

(3) Comply with §§ 35.241 and 35.242.

(4) Submit a completed license application to the Commission.

Authority

The provisions of this § 35.222 issued under act of February 19, 1980 (P. L. 15, No. 9) (63 P. S. §§ 455.101—455.902).

Source

The provisions of this § 35.222 adopted February 24, 1989, effective February 25, 1989, 19 Pa.B. 781; amended June 10, 1994, effective June 11, 1994, 24 Pa.B. 2904. Immediately preceding text appears at serial pages (135737) to (135738).

§ 35.223. Licensure as salesperson.

(a) Except as provided in subsection (b), an individual who wants to obtain a Pennsylvania salespersons's license shall:

(1) Have scored a passing grade on each part of the salesperson's examination within 3 years prior to the submission of a properly completed license application. See § 35.272 (relating to examination for salesperson's license).

(2) Submit a completed license application to the Commission with:

(i) A sworn statement from the broker with whom the applicant desires to be affiliated:

(A) Attesting to the applicant's good reputation for honesty, trustworthiness, integrity and competence.

(B) Certifying that he will actively supervise and train the applicant.

(ii) Official transcripts evidencing the acquisition of degrees or course credits required by § 35.272(a)(2).

(b) An individual holding a broker's or salesperson's license issued by another jurisdiction who wants to obtain a Pennsylvania salesperson's license shall comply with subsection (a) or shall:

(1) Possess a broker's or salesperson's license issued by another jurisdiction that has been active within 5 years prior to the submission of a properly completed license application.

(2) Have scored a passing grade on the Pennsylvania portion of the salesperson's examination within 3 years prior to the submission of a properly completed license application. See § 35.272.

(3) Submit a completed license application to the Commission with a certification from the real estate licensing authority of the other jurisdiction containing the following information:

Ch. 35   STATE REAL ESTATE COMMISSION   49 § 35.224

(i) The applicant's license number, the date of issuance of the license and confirmation that the applicant obtained initial licensure by written examination.

(ii) An indication of whether the license has been active within the past 5 years.

(iii) A description of past disciplinary action taken by the licensing authority against the applicant.

(iv) The applicant's office address and name of the applicant's employer.

Authority

The provisions of this § 35.223 issued under act of February 19, 1980 (P. L. 15, No. 9) (63 P. S. §§ 455.101—455.902).

Source

The provisions of this § 35.223 adopted February 24, 1989, effective February 25, 1989, 19 Pa.B. 781; amended June 10, 1994, effective June 11, 1994, 24 Pa.B. 2904. Immediately preceding text appears at serial pages (135739) to (135740).

§ 35.224. Licensure as cemetery broker.

(a) An individual who wants to obtain a Pennsylvania cemetery broker's license shall:

(1) Have scored a passing grade on each part of the salesperson's examination within 3 years prior to the submission of a properly completed license application. See § 35.273 (relating to examination for cemetery broker's license).

(2) Comply with §§ 35.241 and 35.242 (relating to general office requirement; and office of broker or cemetery broker).

(3) Submit a completed license application to the Commission with recommendations attesting to the applicant's good reputation for honesty, trustworthiness, integrity and competence from:

(i) One real estate broker licensed by the Commission.

(ii) Two persons unrelated to the applicant who own property in the county where the applicant resides or has a place of business.

(iii) Two persons unrelated to the applicant who own property in the county where the applicant previously resided, if the applicant changed his county of residence within 1 year prior to the submission of the application.

(b) A partnership, association or corporation that wants to obtain a Pennsylvania cemetery broker's license shall:

(1) Ensure that each member of the partnership, association, or each officer of the corporation, who intends to engage in the real estate business is licensed by the Commission as a broker or cemetery broker.

49 § 35.225   DEPARTMENT OF STATE   Pt. I

(2) Designate an individual who is licensed by the Commission as a broker or cemetery broker to serve as broker of record.

(3) Comply with §§ 35.241 and 35.242.

(4) Submit a complete license application to the Commission.

Authority

The provisions of this § 35.224 issued under act of February 19, 1980 (P. L. 15, No. 9) (63 P. S. §§ 455.101—455.902).

Source

The provisions of this § 35.224 adopted February 24, 1989, effective February 25, 1989, 19 Pa.B. 781; amended June 10, 1994, effective June 11, 1994, 24 Pa.B. 2904. Immediately preceding text appears at serial page (135740).

§ 35.225. Licensure as cemetery salesperson.

An individual who wants to obtain a Pennsylvania cemetery salesperson's license shall:

(1) Be 18 years of age or older.

(2) Submit a completed license application to the Commission with a sworn affidavit from the broker or cemetery broker with whom the applicant will be affiliated:

(i) Attesting to the applicant's good reputation for honesty, integrity, trustworthiness and competence.

(ii) Certifying that he will actively supervise and train the applicant.

Authority

The provisions of this § 35.225 issued under act of February 19, 1980 (P. L. 15, No. 9) (63 P. S. §§ 455.101—455.902).

Source

The provisions of this § 35.225 adopted February 24, 1989, effective February 25, 1989, 19 Pa.B. 781; amended June 10, 1994, effective June 11, 1994, 24 Pa.B. 2904. Immediately preceding text appears at serial pages (135740) to (135741).

§ 35.226. Licensure as builder-owner salesperson.

An individual who wants to obtain a Pennsylvania builder-owner salesperson's license shall:

(1) Have scored a passing grade on each part of the salesperson's examination within 3 years prior to the submission of a properly completed license application. See § 35.274 (relating to examination for builder-owner salesperson's license).

(2) Submit a completed license application to the Commission with a sworn statement from a builder-owner:

(i) Attesting to the applicant's good reputation for honesty, trustworthiness, integrity and competence.

(ii) Certifying that he:

(A) Is a builder-owner of single or multifamily dwellings.

(B) Employs the applicant.

Authority

The provisions of this § 35.226 issued under act of February 19, 1980 (P. L. 15, No. 9) (63 P. S. §§ 455.101—455.902).

Source

The provisions of this § 35.226 adopted February 24, 1989, effective February 25, 1989, 19 Pa.B. 781; amended June 10, 1994, effective June 11, 1994, 24 Pa.B. 2904. Immediately preceding text appears at serial page (135741).

§ 35.227. Licensure as rental listing referral agent.

(a) An individual who wants to obtain a Pennsylvania rental listing referral agent's license shall:

(1) Have scored a passing grade on each part of the salesperson's examination within 3 years prior to the submission of a properly completed license application. See § 35.275 (relating to examination for rental listing referral agent's license).

(2) Comply with § 35.241 (relating to general office requirement).

(3) Submit a completed license application to the Commission.

(b) A partnership, association or corporation that wants to obtain a Pennsylvania rental listing referral agent's license shall:

(1) Designate an individual who is licensed by the Commission as a rental listing referral agent to serve as manager of record.

(2) Comply with § 35.241.

(3) Submit a completed license application to the Commission.

Authority

The provisions of this § 35.227 issued under act of February 19, 1980 (P. L. 15, No. 9) (63 P. S. §§ 455.101—455.902).

Source

The provisions of this § 35.227 adopted February 24, 1989, effective February 25, 1989, 19 Pa.B. 781; amended June 10, 1994, effective June 11, 1994, 24 Pa.B. 2904. Immediately preceding text appears at serial pages (135741) to (135742).

§ 35.228. Licensure as campground membership salesperson.

(a) An individual who wants to obtain a Pennsylvania campground membership salesperson's license shall:

(1) Be 18 years of age or older.

35-29

(2) Have successfully completed the one-credit (15 hours), Commission-developed course titled Campground Membership Sales, provided the following conditions are met:

(i) The course was taken prior to onsite training.

(ii) The course was taught at an accredited college, university or institute of higher learning in this Commonwealth or a real estate school in this Commonwealth approved by the Commission.

(3) Have successfully completed 30 days of onsite training at a campground membership facility subject to the following conditions:

(i) The 30 days of onsite training shall be completed during a 90-day period within 3 years prior to the submission of a license application.

(ii) The trainee shall be actively supervised and trained by a broker.

(4) Submit a completed license application to the Commission with:

(i) An official transcript evidencing acquisition of the qualifying coursework or degree.

(ii) A sworn statement from the broker under whom the applicant received his onsite training certifying that he actively trained and supervised the applicant and providing other information regarding the onsite training as the Commission may require.

(b) An individual who sells campground memberships without a license may be subject to disciplinary action by the Commission for unlicensed practice as a campground membership salesperson under section 301 of the act (63 P. S. § 455.301).

Authority

The provisions of this § 35.228 issued under act of February 19, 1980 (P. L. 15, No. 9) (63 P. S. §§ 455.101—455.902).

Source

The provisions of this § 35.228 adopted June 10, 1994, effective June 11, 1994, 24 Pa.B. 2904.

§ 35.229. Licensure as time-share salesperson.

(a) An individual who wants to obtain a Pennsylvania time-share salesperson's license shall:

(1) Be at least 18 years of age.

(2) Have successfully completed the two-credit (30 hours), Commission-developed course titled Time Share Sales, provided the following conditions are met:

(i) The course was taken prior to onsite training.

35-30

(ii) The course was taught at an accredited college, university or institute of higher learning in this Commonwealth or a real estate school in this Commonwealth approved by the Commission.

(3) Have successfully completed 30 days of onsite training at a time share facility subject to the following conditions:

(i) The 30 days of onsite training shall be completed during a 90-day period within 3 years prior to the submission of a license application.

(ii) The trainee shall be actively supervised and trained by a broker.

(4) Submit a completed license application to the Commission with:

(i) An official transcript evidencing acquisition of the qualifying coursework or degree.

(ii) A sworn statement from the broker under whom the applicant received his onsite training certifying that he actively trained and supervised the applicant and providing other information regarding the onsite training the Commission may require.

(b) An individual who sells time shares without a license may be subject to disciplinary action by the Commission for unlicensed practice as a time-share salesperson under section 301 of the act (63 P. S. § 455.301).

Authority

The provisions of this § 35.229 issued under act of February 19, 1980 (P. L. 15, No. 9) (63 P. S. §§ 455.101—455.902).

Source

The provisions of this § 35.229 adopted June 10, 1994, effective June 11, 1994, 24 Pa.B. 2904.

OFFICES

§ 35.241. General office requirement.

(a) A broker, cemetery broker, or rental listing referral agent shall maintain a fixed office in this Commonwealth unless he maintains a fixed office in another jurisdiction where he is licensed.

(b) A broker, cemetery broker or rental listing referral agent may maintain more than one office in this Commonwealth. A branch office license is required for each additional office maintained by a broker or cemetery broker. See § 35.243 (relating to licensure of branch office).

Authority

The provisions of this § 35.241 issued under act of February 19, 1980 (P. L. 15, No. 9) (63 P. S. §§ 455.101—455.902).

Source

The provisions of this § 35.241 adopted February 24, 1989, effective February 25, 1989, 19 Pa.B. 781; amended June 10, 1994, effective June 11, 1994, 24 Pa.B. 2904. Immediately preceding text appears at serial page (135742).

Cross References

This section cited in 49 Pa. Code § 35.222 (relating to licensure as broker); 49 Pa. Code § 35.224 (relating to licensure as cemetery broker); and 49 Pa. Code § 35.227 (relating to licensure as rental listing referral agent).

§ 35.242. Office of broker or cemetery broker.

(a) The office of a broker or cemetery broker shall be devoted to the transaction of real estate business and be arranged to permit business to be conducted in privacy.

(b) If the office of a broker or cemetery broker is located in a private residence, the entrance to the office shall be separate from the entrance to the residence.

(c) The business name of the broker or cemetery broker, as designated on the license, shall be displayed prominently and in permanent fashion outside the office.

(d) A branch office operated by a broker or cemetery broker shall be in compliance with this section.

Authority

The provisions of this § 35.242 issued under act of February 19, 1980 (P. L. 15, No. 9) (63 P. S. §§ 455.101—455.902).

Source

The provisions of this § 35.242 adopted February 24, 1989, effective February 25, 1989, 19 Pa.B. 781; amended June 10, 1994, effective June 11, 1994, 24 Pa.B. 2904. Immediately preceding text appears at serial page (135743).

Cross References

This section cited in 49 Pa. Code § 35.222 (relating to licensure as broker); and 49 Pa. Code § 35.224 (relating to licensure as cemetery broker).

§ 35.243. Licensure of branch office.

(a) A broker or cemetery broker may not open a branch office in this Commonwealth without first obtaining a branch office license for that location from the Commission. A broker or cemetery broker who wants to obtain a Pennsylvania branch office license shall submit a completed license application to the Commission with the license fee prescribed in § 35.203 (relating to fees).

(b) A branch office license will be issued in the name under which the broker or cemetery broker is licensed to conduct business at the main office.

(c) A branch office license terminates automatically with the suspension, revocation or discontinuance, for whatever reason, of the license of the broker or cemetery broker to whom the branch office license was issued.

Authority

The provisions of this § 35.243 issued under act of February 19, 1980 (P. L. 15, No. 9) (63 P. S. §§ 455.101—455.902).

Source

The provisions of this § 35.243 adopted February 24, 1989, effective February 25, 1989, 19 Pa.B. 781; amended June 10, 1994, effective June 11, 1994, 24 Pa.B. 2904. Immediately preceding text appears at serial pages (135743) to (135744).

Cross References

This section cited in 49 Pa. Code § 35.241 (relating to general office requirement).

§ 35.244. Supervision and operation of office.

(a) The main or branch office of a broker shall be under the direction and supervision of a broker or associate broker.

(b) The main or branch office of a cemetery broker shall be under the direction and supervision of a broker, cemetery broker, associate broker or cemetery broker.

(c) A branch office may not be operated in a manner that permits, or is intended to permit, an employe to carry on the business of the office for the employe's sole benefit.

(d) The office of a rental listing referral agent shall be under the direction and supervision of a rental listing referral agent. A rental listing referral agent may not supervise more than one office.

Authority

The provisions of this § 35.244 issued under act of February 19, 1980 (P. L. 15, No. 9) (63 P. S. §§ 455.101—455.902).

Source

The provisions of this § 35.244 adopted February 24, 1989, effective February 25, 1989, 19 Pa.B. 781; amended June 10, 1994, effective June 11, 1994, 24 Pa.B. 2904. Immediately preceding text appears at serial page (135744).

§ 35.245. Display of licenses in office.

(a) The current license of a broker, cemetery broker or rental listing referral agent shall be displayed in a conspicuous place at the main office.

(b) The current license of an associate broker, salesperson, associate cemetery broker or cemetery salesperson shall be displayed in a conspicuous place at the office out of which the licensee works.

35-33

(c) The current license of a branch office shall be displayed in a conspicuous place at the branch office.

(d) A broker or cemetery broker shall maintain at the main office a list of licensed employes and the branch office out of which each licensed employe works.

Authority

The provisions of this § 35.245 issued under act of February 19, 1980 (P. L. 15, No. 9) (63 P. S. §§ 455.101—455.902).

Source

The provisions of this § 35.245 adopted February 24, 1989, effective February 25, 1989, 19 Pa.B. 781; amended June 10, 1994, effective June 11, 1994, 24 Pa.B. 2904. Immediately preceding text appears at serial pages (135744) to (135745).

§ 35.246. Inspection of office.

(a) *Routine inspections.* No more than four times a year during regular business hours, the Commission or its authorized representatives may conduct a routine inspection of the main office or branch office of a broker, cemetery broker or rental listing referral agent for the purpose of determining whether the office is being operated in compliance with the act and this chapter.

(b) *Special inspections.* In addition to the routine inspections authorized by subsection (a), the Commission or its authorized representatives may conduct a special inspection of a main or branch office:

(1) Upon a complaint or reasonable belief that the broker, cemetery broker or rental listing referral agent, or a licensed employe of a broker, cemetery broker or rental listing referral agent, has violated the act or this chapter.

(2) As a follow-up to a previous inspection that revealed the office's noncompliance with the act or this chapter.

(c) *Commission notice.* Prior to the start of a routine or special inspection, the Commission or its authorized representatives will advise the broker, cemetery broker, rental listing referral agent or other licensee who may be in charge of the office at the time of the inspection that the inspection is being made under this section and is limited in scope by this section.

(d) *Permissible Commission actions.* During the course of a routine or special inspection, the Commission or its authorized representatives will be permitted to:

(1) Examine the records of the office pertaining to:

(i) Real estate transactions or rental listing referrals.

(ii) The corporation, partnership or association that holds a broker's or cemetery broker's license.

35-34

Ch. 35

STATE REAL ESTATE COMMISSION 49 § 35.251

(2) Inspect all areas of the office.

(3) Interview the broker, cemetery broker, rental listing referral agent and other licensed or unlicensed employs who work in the office.

(4) Obtain the broker's or cemetery broker's written authorization to the bank or depository where the broker or cemetery broker maintains his escrow account that it may release copies of the records of the account to the Commission or its authorized representatives.

Authority

The provisions of this § 35.246 issued under act of February 19, 1980 (P. L. 15, No. 9) (63 P. S. §§ 455.101—455.902).

Source

The provisions of this § 35.246 adopted February 24, 1989, effective February 25, 1989, 19 Pa.B. 781; amended June 11, 1994, effective June 10, 1994, 24 Pa.B. 2904. Immediately preceding text appears at serial pages (135745) to (135746).

Cross References

This section cited in 49 Pa. Code § 35.286 (relating to retention and production of records); 49 Pa. Code § 35.325 (relating to escrow account); and 49 Pa. Code § 35.328 (relating to escrow records).

STATUS OF LICENSURE

§ 35.251. Relicensure following revocation.

The Commission will not authorize relicensure of an individual whose license has been revoked for at least 5 years following the date revocation begins. After the 5-year period, the individual may petition the Commission for relicensure. The decision to permit relicensure is within the Commission's discretion. If relicensure is permitted, the individual shall comply with current requirements for licensure before the license is issued.

Authority

The provisions of this § 35.251 issued under act of February 19, 1980 (P. L. 15, No. 9) (63 P. S. §§ 455.101—455.902).

Source

The provisions of this § 35.251 adopted February 24, 1989, effective February 25, 1989, 19 Pa.B. 781.

35-35

---

49 § 35.252 DEPARTMENT OF STATE Pt. I

§ 35.252. Termination of business of deceased broker with sole proprietorship.

(a) Within 15 days following the death of a broker with a sole proprietorship, the deceased broker's estate may notify the Commission that it has appointed another licensed broker to supervise the termination of the deceased broker's business for 90 days following the appointment. The appointment is subject to verification that the appointed broker has a current license.

(b) The appointed broker shall observe the following rules during the 90-day termination period:

(1) New listing agreements may not be entered into.

(2) Unexpired listing agreements may be promoted unless the seller or lessor elects to cancel the agreement. Unexpired listings will expire automatically at the conclusion of the 90-day termination period and may not be renewed.

(3) Pending agreements of sale or lease may proceed to consummation.

(4) New licensees may not be hired.

Authority

The provisions of this § 35.252 issued under act of February 19, 1980 (P. L. 15, No. 9) (63 P. S. §§ 455.101—455.902).

Source

The provisions of this § 35.252 adopted February 24, 1989, effective February 25, 1989, 19 Pa.B. 781.

Subchapter D. LICENSING EXAMINATIONS

Sec.
35.271. Examination for broker's license.
35.272. Examination for salesperson's license.
35.273. Examination for cemetery broker's license.
35.274. Examination for builder-owner salesperson's license.
35.275. Examination for rental listing referral agent's license.

§ 35.271. Examination for broker's license.

(a) An individual who wants to take the broker's examination for a Pennsylvania broker's license shall:

(1) Be 21 years of age or older.

(2) Be a high school graduate or have passed a high school general education equivalency examination.

35-36

(3) Have worked at least 3 years as a licensed salesperson, with experience qualifications that the Commission considers adequate for practice as a broker, or possess at least 3 years of other experience, education, or both, that the Commission considers the equivalent of 3 years' experience as a licensed salesperson.

(4) Have acquired 16 credits, or 240 hours of instruction, in professional real estate education as determined by the Commission under subsection (b).

(5) Submit a completed examination application to the Commission or its designee with:

(i) Official transcripts evidencing the acquisition of course credits.

(ii) A detailed resume of real estate activities performed by the candidate while working as a salesperson and a sworn statement from the candidate's employing broker confirming that these activities were performed if the candidate is a licensed salesperson.

(iii) A complete description of work experience and education that the candidate considers relevant to the requirements of paragraph (3) if the candidate is not a licensed salesperson.

(iv) A certification from the real estate licensing authority of the jurisdiction in which the candidate is licensed stating that the candidate had an active license for each year that credits are claimed if the candidate is applying brokerage experience to satisfy the professional education requirement.

(v) The fees for review of the candidate's qualifications to take the examination and for administration of the examination prescribed in § 35.203 (relating to fees).

(b) The Commission will apply the following standards in determining whether an examination candidate has met the education requirement of subsection (a)(4):

(1) A candidate who has obtained one of the following degrees will be deemed to have met the education requirement and will not be required to show completion of coursework in specific areas of study:

(i) A bachelor's degree with a major in real estate from an accredited college, university or institute of higher learning.

(ii) A bachelor's degree from an accredited college, university or institute of higher learning, having completed coursework equivalent to a major in real estate.

(iii) A juris doctor degree from an accredited law school.

(2) Except as provided in paragraph (6), at least eight of the required 16 credits shall be in real estate courses in four or more of the

Commission-developed courses listed in this paragraph. The remaining eight credits shall be in real estate courses but not necessarily those listed in paragraph. A candidate may not apply credits used to qualify for the salesperson's examination toward fulfillment of the broker education requirement.

(i) Real Estate Law.

(ii) Real Estate Finance.

(iii) Real Estate Investment.

(iv) Residential Property Management.

(v) Nonresidential Property Management.

(vi) Real Estate Sales.

(vii) Real Estate Brokerage and Office Management.

(viii) Residential Construction.

(ix) Appraisal of Residential Property.

(x) Appraisal of Income-Producing Property.

(3) To be counted toward the education requirement, a real estate course shall have been offered by:

(i) An accredited college, university or institute of higher learning, whether in this Commonwealth or outside this Commonwealth.

(ii) A real estate school in this Commonwealth approved by the Commission.

(iii) A real estate school outside this Commonwealth that has been approved by the real estate licensing authority of the jurisdiction where the school is located.

(iv) A real estate industry organization outside this Commonwealth, if the course is also offered by a real estate school in this Commonwealth approved by the Commission.

(4) A maximum of four credits will be allowed for each real estate course. A maximum of four credits will be allowed for each area of real estate study listed in paragraph (2), except that a maximum of six credits will be allowed for courses in Real Estate Appraisal.

(5) Courses shall have been completed within 10 years prior to the date of successful completion of the licensing examination.

(6) Two credits will be allowed for each year of active practice the candidate has had a licensed broker in another jurisdiction during the 10-year period immediately preceding the submission of the examination application.

Authority

The provisions of this § 35.271 issued under act of February 19, 1980 (P. L. 15, No. 9) (63 P. S. §§ 455.101—455.902).

Ch. 35   STATE REAL ESTATE COMMISSION   49 § 35.272

Source

The provisions of this § 35.271 adopted February 24, 1989, effective February 25, 1989, 19 Pa.B. 781; corrected July 14, 1989, effective February 25, 1989, 19 Pa.B. 3036; amended June 10, 1994, effective June 11, 1994, 24 Pa.B. 2904. Immediately preceding text appears at serial pages (135747) to (135748) and (138653).

Cross References

This section cited in 49 Pa. Code § 35.222 (relating to licensure as broker).

§ 35.272. Examination for salesperson's license.

(a) An individual who wants to take the salesperson's examination for the purpose of obtaining a Pennsylvania salesperson's license shall:

(1) Be 18 years of age or older.

(2) Have successfully completed four credits, or 60 hours of instruction, in basic real estate courses as determined by the Commission under subsection (b).

(3) Submit a completed examination application to the Commission or its designee with the examination fee prescribed in § 35.203 (relating to fees).

(b) The Commission will apply the following standards in determining whether an examination candidate has met the education requirement of subsection (a)(2):

(1) A candidate who has obtained one of the following degrees will be deemed to have met the education requirement and will not be required to show completion of coursework in specific areas of study:

(i) A bachelor's degree with a major in real estate from an accredited college, university or institute of higher learning.

(ii) A bachelor's degree from an accredited college, university or institute of higher learning, having completed coursework equivalent to a major in real estate.

(iii) A juris doctor degree from an accredited law school.

(2) Credits will be allowed for each of the Commission-developed real estate courses—Real Estate Fundamentals and Real Estate Practice—when offered by:

(i) An accredited college, university or institute of higher learning in this Commonwealth.

(ii) A real estate school in this Commonwealth approved by the Commission.

(3) Credits will be allowed for acceptable basic real estate courses when offered by:

(i) An accredited college, university or institute of higher learning located outside this Commonwealth.

35-39

49 § 35.273   DEPARTMENT OF STATE   Pt. I

(ii) A real estate school outside this Commonwealth that has been approved by the real estate licensing authority of the jurisdiction where the school is located.

(4) Courses shall have been completed within 10 years prior to the date of successful completion of the licensing examination.

Authority

The provisions of this § 35.272 issued under act of February 19, 1980 (P. L. 15, No. 9) (63 P. S. §§ 455.101—455.902).

Source

The provisions of this § 35.272 adopted February 24, 1989, effective February 25, 1989, 19 Pa.B. 781.

Cross References

This section cited in 49 Pa. Code § 35.223 (relating to licensure as salesperson).

§ 35.273. Examination for cemetery broker's license.

(a) An individual who wants to take the salesperson's examination for the purpose of obtaining a Pennsylvania cemetery broker's license shall:

(1) Be 21 years of age or older.

(2) Have worked at least 3 years as a licensed salesperson or cemetery salesperson, with experience qualifications that the Commission considers adequate for practice as a cemetery broker, or possess at least 3 years of other experience, education, or both, that the Commission considers the equivalent of 3 years' experience as a licensed salesperson or cemetery salesperson.

(3) Have successfully completed four credits, or 60 hours of instruction, in basic real estate courses as determined by the Commission under subsection (b).

(4) Submit a completed examination application to the Commission or its designee with:

(i) Official transcripts evidencing the acquisition of degrees or course credits.

(ii) A detailed resume of real estate activities performed by the candidate while working as a salesperson or cemetery salesperson, and a sworn statement from the candidate's employing broker confirming that these activities were performed if the candidate is a licensed salesperson or cemetery salesperson.

(iii) A complete description of work experience and education that the candidate considers relevant to the requirements of paragraph (2) if the candidate is not a licensed salesperson or cemetery salesperson.

35-40

(iv) The fees for review of the candidate's qualifications to take the examination and for administration of the examination prescribed in § 35.203 (relating to fees).

(b) The Commission will apply the following standards in determining whether an examination candidate has met the education requirement of subsection (a)(3):

(1) A candidate who has obtained one of the following degrees will be deemed to have met the education requirement and will not be required to show completion of course work in specific areas of study:

(i) A bachelor's degree with a major in real estate from an accredited college, university or institute of higher learning.

(ii) A bachelor's degree from an accredited college, university or institute of higher learning, having completed course work equivalent to a major in real estate.

(iii) A juris doctor degree from an accredited law school.

(2) Credits will be allowed for each of the Commission-developed real estate courses—Real Estate Fundamentals and Real Estate Practice—when offered by:

(i) An accredited college, university or institute of higher learning in this Commonwealth.

(ii) A real estate school approved by the Commission in this Commonwealth.

(3) Credits will be allowed for cemetery courses when offered by:

(i) An accredited college, university or institute of higher learning in this Commonwealth.

(ii) A real estate school in this Commonwealth approved by the Commission.

(4) Credits will be allowed for acceptable basic real estate courses when offered by:

(i) An accredited college, university or institute of higher learning located outside this Commonwealth.

(ii) A real estate school outside this Commonwealth that has been approved by the real estate licensing authority of the jurisdiction where the school is located.

(iii) A cemetery association outside this Commonwealth, if the course taught by the cemetery association is equivalent to a course taught by a real estate school in this Commonwealth approved by the Commission.

(5) Courses shall have been completed within 10 years prior to the date of successful completion of the licensing examination.

35-41

Authority

The provisions of this § 35.273 issued under act of February 19, 1980 (P. L. 15, No. 9) (63 P. S. §§ 455.101—455.902).

Source

The provisions of this § 35.273 adopted February 24, 1989, effective February 25, 1989, 19 Pa.B. 781; amended June 10, 1994, effective June 11, 1994, 24 Pa.B. 2904. Immediately preceding text appears at serial pages (138654) to (138655) and (135751) to (135752).

Cross References

This section cited in 49 Pa. Code § 35.224 (relating to licensure as cemetery broker).

§ 35.274. Examination for builder-owner salesperson's license.

An individual who wants to take the salesperson's examination for the purpose of obtaining a Pennsylvania builder-owner salesperson's license shall:

(1) Be 18 years of age or older.

(2) Be employed by a builder-owner who has a good reputation for honesty, trustworthiness, integrity and competence.

(3) Submit a completed examination application to the Commission or its designee with the examination fee prescribed in § 35.203 (relating to fees).

Authority

The provisions of this § 35.274 issued under act of February 19, 1980 (P. L. 15, No. 9) (63 P. S. §§ 455.101—455.902).

Source

The provisions of this § 35.274 adopted February 24, 1989, effective February 25, 1989, 19 Pa.B. 781.

Cross References

This section cited in 49 Pa. Code § 35.226 (relating to licensure as builder-owner salesperson).

§ 35.275. Examination for rental listing referral agent's license.

(a) An individual who wants to take the salesperson's examination for the purpose of obtaining a Pennsylvania rental listing referral agent's license shall:

(1) Be 18 years of age or older.

(2) Have successfully completed four credits, or 60 hours of instruction, in basic real estate courses as determined by the Commission under subsection (b).

(3) Submit a completed examination application to the Commission or its designee with the examination fee prescribed in § 35.203 (relating to fees).

35-42

Ch. 35   STATE REAL ESTATE COMMISSION   49 § 35.275

(b) The Commission will apply the following standards in determining whether an examination candidate has met the requirements of subsection (a)(2):

(1) A candidate who has obtained one of the following degrees will be deemed to have met the education requirement and will not be required to show completion of coursework in specific areas of study:

(i) A bachelor's degree with a major in real estate from an accredited college, university or institute of higher learning.

(ii) A bachelor's degree from an accredited college, university or institute of higher learning, having completed coursework equivalent to a major in real estate.

(iii) A juris doctor degree from an accredited law school.

(2) Credits will be allowed for each of the Commission developed real estate courses—Real Estate Fundamentals and Real Estate Practice—when offered by:

(i) An accredited college, university or institute of higher learning in this Commonwealth.

(ii) A real estate school in this Commonwealth approved by the Commission.

(3) Credits will be allowed for acceptable basic real estate courses when offered by:

(i) An accredited college, university or institute of higher learning located outside this Commonwealth.

(ii) A real estate school outside this Commonwealth that has been approved by the real estate licensing authority of the jurisdiction where the school is located.

(4) Courses shall have been completed within 10 years prior to the date of successful completion of the licensing examination.

Authority

The provisions of this § 35.275 issued under act of February 19, 1980 (P. L. 15, No. 9) (63 P. S. §§ 455.101—455.902).

Source

The provisions of this § 35.275 adopted February 24, 1989, effective February 25, 1989, 19 Pa.B. 781.

Cross References

This section cited in 49 Pa. Code § 35.227 (relating to licensure as rental listing referral agent).

DEPARTMENT OF STATE   Pt. I

Subchapter E. STANDARDS OF CONDUCT AND PRACTICE

GENERAL ETHICAL RESPONSIBILITIES

Sec.
35.281. Putting contracts, commitments and agreements in writing.
35.282. Misleading advice, assurances and representations.
35.283. Conflict of interest.
35.284. Preagreement disclosures to buyer and seller.
35.285. Disclosure of real estate affiliations.
35.286. Retention and production of records.
35.287. Supervised appraisal and property management assistance by salespersons.
35.288. Duties when selling or leasing own real estate.
35.289. Valid list of rentals.
35.290. Reporting of crimes and disciplinary actions.
35.291. Posting of suspension notice.

ADVERTISING AND SOLICITATION

35.301. Unauthorized advertising and solicitation.
35.302. Harassment.
35.303. Panic selling.
35.304. Disclosure of licensure when advertising own real estate.
35.305. Business name on advertisements.
35.306. Advertisements of lotteries, contests, prizes, certificates, gifts and lots.
35.307. Advertisements of sales volume, market position and numbers of offices.
35.308. Relationship with educational institution.

ESCROW REQUIREMENTS

35.321. Duty to deposit money belonging to another into escrow account.
35.322. Nonwaiver of escrow duty.
35.323. Responsibility for escrow in cobrokerage transactions.
35.324. Deadline for depositing money into escrow account.
35.325. Escrow account.
35.326. Prohibition against commingling or misappropriation.
35.327. Procedure when entitlement to money held in escrow is disputed.
35.328. Escrow records.

REAL ESTATE DOCUMENTS

35.331. Listing agreements generally.
35.332. Exclusive listing agreements.
35.333. Agreements of sale.
35.334. Statements of estimated cost and return.
35.335. Rental listing referral agreements.

GENERAL ETHICAL RESPONSIBILITIES

§ 35.281. Putting contracts, commitments and agreements in writing.

(a) A licensee who acts in a representative capacity in connection with a real estate transaction shall ensure that sale or lease contracts, commitments and agreements regarding the transaction that he has knowledge of, or that he reasonably should be expected to have knowledge of, are in writing.

(b) A licensee who enters into an oral open listing agreement shall provide the seller or lessor with a written memorandum stating the terms of the agreement.

(c) A rental listing referral agent shall ensure that the agreement between himself and a prospective tenant is in writing.

Authority

The provisions of this § 35.281 issued under act of February 19, 1980 (P. L. 15, No. 9) (63 P. S. §§ 455.101—455.902).

Source

The provisions of this § 35.281 adopted February 24, 1989, effective February 25, 1989, 19 Pa.B. 781.

§ 35.282. Misleading advice, assurances and representations.

(a) A licensee may not give assurances or advice concerning an aspect of a real estate transaction that he knows, or reasonably should be expected to know, is incorrect, inaccurate or improbable.

(b) A licensee may not knowingly be a party to a material false or inaccurate representation in a writing regarding a real estate transaction in which he is acting in a representative capacity.

Authority

The provisions of this § 35.282 issued under act of February 19, 1980 (P. L. 15, No. 9) (63 P. S. §§ 455.101—455.902).

Source

The provisions of this § 35.282 adopted February 24, 1989, effective February 25, 1989, 19 Pa.B. 781.

35-45

§ 35.283. Conflict of interest.

(a) A licensee may not participate in a real estate transaction involving property in which he has an ownership interest unless he first discloses his interest in writing to all parties concerned.

(b) A licensee may not represent, or purport to represent, more than one party to a real estate transaction without the written consent of all parties concerned.

(c) A broker who manages rental property may not accept a commission, rebate or profit on expenditures made for the lessor without the lessor's written consent.

(d) A broker who is engaged in the business of financing the purchase of real or personal property, or of lending money on the security of real or personal property, may not require, as a condition precedent to the activities, the negotiation by the buyer through a particular insurance company of a policy of insurance or the renewal of the insurance covering the property or the person involved, with the exception of a group creditor policy.

Authority

The provisions of this § 35.283 issued under act of February 19, 1980 (P. L. 15, No. 9) (63 P. S. §§ 455.101—455.902).

Source

The provisions of this § 35.283 adopted February 24, 1989, effective February 25, 1989, 19 Pa.B. 781.

§ 35.284. Preagreement disclosures to buyer and seller.

(a) A licensee shall disclose the following information to a prospective client-seller at the initial interview before the seller enters into a listing agreement:

(1) Whether the broker is the agent of the seller or the agent of the buyer.

(2) The broker's commission and the duration of the listing period are negotiable.

(3) The existence of a Real Estate Recovery Fund to reimburse a person who has obtained a final civil judgment against a Pennsylvania real estate licensee owing to fraud, misrepresentation or deceit in a real estate transaction and who has been unable to collect the judgment after exhausting legal and equitable remedies. Details about the Fund may be obtained by calling the Commission at (717) 783-3658.

(4) The requirement that an agreement of sale executed by the seller shall contain the zoning classification of the property, unless the property (or each parcel thereof, if subdividable) is zoned solely or primarily to permit single-family dwellings.

35-46

Ch. 35   STATE REAL ESTATE COMMISSION   49 § 35.285

(b) A licensee shall disclose the following information to a prospective buyer at the initial interview before the buyer enters into an agreement of sale:

(1) Whether the broker is the agent of the seller or the agent of the buyer.

(2) The existence of a Real Estate Recovery Fund to reimburse a person who has obtained a final civil judgment against a Pennsylvania real estate licensee owing to fraud, misrepresentation or deceit in a real estate transaction and who has been unable to collect the judgment after exhausting legal and equitable remedies. Details about the Fund may be obtained by calling the Commission at (717) 783-3658.

Authority

The provisions of this § 35.284 issued under act of February 19, 1980 (P. L. 15, No. 9) (63 P. S. §§ 455.101—455.902).

Source

The provisions of this § 35.284 adopted February 24, 1989, effective February 25, 1989, 19 Pa.B. 781; amended June 10, 1994, effective June 11, 1994, 24 Pa.B. 2904. Immediately preceding text appears at serial pages (135756) to (135757).

§ 35.285. Disclosure of real estate affiliations.

A licensee shall provide to the Commission or its representatives upon proper demand information regarding a franchisor, network or other parent real estate company with which the licensee is, or may become, affiliated.

Authority

The provisions of this § 35.285 issued under act of February 19, 1980 (P. L. 15, No. 9) (63 P. S. §§ 455.101—455.902).

Source

The provisions of this § 35.285 adopted February 24, 1989, effective February 25, 1989, 19 Pa.B. 781.

§ 35.286. Retention and production of records.

(a) A broker or cemetery broker shall retain copies of records pertaining to a real estate transaction for at least 3 years following consummation of the transaction and shall produce the records for examination by the Commission or its authorized representatives upon written request or pursuant to an office inspection under § 35.246 (relating to inspection of office).

49 § 35.287   DEPARTMENT OF STATE   Pt. I

(b) A corporation, partnership or association that holds a broker's or cemetery broker's license shall produce its corporate, partnership or association records for examination by the Commission or its authorized representatives upon written request or pursuant to an office inspection under § 35.246.

Authority

The provisions of this § 35.286 issued under act of February 19, 1980 (P. L. 15, No. 9) (63 P. S. §§ 455.101—455.902).

Source

The provisions of this § 35.286 adopted February 24, 1989, effective February 25, 1989, 19 Pa.B. 781; amended June 10, 1994, effective June 11, 1994, 24 Pa.B. 2904. Immediately preceding text appears at serial pages (135757) to (135758).

§ 35.287. Supervised appraisal and property management assistance by salespersons.

(a) A salesperson may assist in the preparation of an appraisal by the employing broker or an associate broker, if the employing broker or associate broker:

(1) Directly supervises and controls the salesperson's work, assuming total responsibility for the contents of the appraisal documents and value conclusions. The salesperson may not arrive at an independent determination of value.

(2) Personally makes a physical inspection of the interior and exterior of the subject property.

(3) Signs the appraisal document as "appraiser" and has the salesperson sign as "assistant to the appraiser."

(b) A salesperson may assist in the management of real estate if the salesperson's work is directly supervised and controlled by the employing broker. The salesperson may not independently negotiate the terms of a lease nor execute a lease on behalf of the lessor.

Authority

The provisions of this § 35.287 issued under act of February 19, 1980 (P. L. 15, No. 9) (63 P. S. §§ 455.101—455.902).

Source

The provisions of this § 35.287 adopted February 24, 1989, effective February 25, 1989, 19 Pa.B. 781.

§ 35.288. Duties when selling or leasing own real estate.

(a) A broker or salesperson who sells or leases his own real estate shall comply with the requirements of the act and this chapter.

(b) A broker or salesperson who is selling or leasing his own real estate shall disclose his licensed status to a prospective buyer or lessee before the buyer or lessee enters into an agreement of sale or lease. See § 35.304 (relating to disclosure of licensure when advertising own real estate).

Authority

The provisions of this § 35.288 issued under act of February 19, 1980 (P. L. 15, No. 9) (63 P. S. §§ 455.101—455.902).

Source

The provisions of this § 35.288 adopted February 24, 1989, effective February 25, 1989, 19 Pa.B. 781.

§ 35.289. Valid list of rentals.

The list of rental units that a rental listing referral agent gives to a prospective tenant shall meet the desired specifications sought by the prospective tenant as set forth in the rental listing agreement. The rental listing referral agent shall verify the availability of the rental units no more than 4 days prior to the date the agent collects a fee from the prospective tenant.

Authority

The provisions of this § 35.289 issued under act of February 19, 1980 (P. L. 15, No. 9) (63 P. S. §§ 455.101—455.902).

Source

The provisions of this § 35.289 adopted February 24, 1989, effective February 25, 1989, 19 Pa.B. 781.

§ 35.290. Reporting of crimes and disciplinary actions.

(a) A licensee shall notify the Commission of being convicted of, or pleading guilty or nolo contendere to, a felony or misdemeanor, within 30 days of the verdict or plea.

(b) A licensee shall notify the Commission of disciplinary action taken against him by the real estate licensing authority of another jurisdiction within 30 days of receiving notice of the disciplinary action.

Authority

The provisions of this § 35.290 issued under act of February 19, 1980 (P. L. 15, No. 9) (63 P. S. §§ 455.101—455.902).

Source

The provisions of this § 35.290 adopted February 24, 1989, effective February 25, 1989, 19 Pa.B. 781.

§ 35.291. Posting of suspension notice.

A broker or cemetery broker whose license is suspended by the Commission shall return his license to the Commission and shall post a notice of the Commission's action at the main office and at branch offices. The notice, which will be provided by the Commission, shall be posted prominently on or near the public entrance to each office. Failure to post the notice constitutes grounds for further disciplinary action by the Commission.

Authority

The provisions of this § 35.291 issued under act of February 19, 1980 (P. L. 15, No. 9) (63 P. S. §§ 455.101—455.902).

Source

The provisions of this § 35.291 adopted February 24, 1989, effective February 25, 1989, 19 Pa.B. 781; amended June 11, 1994, effective June 11, 1994, 24 Pa.B. 2904. Immediately preceding text appears at serial pages (135759) to (135760).

ADVERTISING AND SOLICITATION

§ 35.301. Unauthorized advertising and solicitation.

(a) A licensee may not advertise the sale or lease of real estate, or otherwise solicit prospective buyers or tenants for the real estate, without the authority of the seller or lessor or of the agent of the seller or lessor.

(b) A rental listing referral agent may not publish information about a rental property if the lessor or property manager expressly states that the property is not to be included in lists prepared by rental listing referral agents.

Authority

The provisions of this § 35.301 issued under act of February 19, 1980 (P. L. 15, No. 9) (63 P. S. §§ 455.101—455.902).

Source

The provisions of this § 35.301 adopted February 24, 1989, effective February 25, 1989, 19 Pa.B. 781.

§ 35.302. Harassment.

A licensee, whether acting on behalf of a prospective buyer or not, may not solicit—by personal contact, telephone, mail or advertising—the sale or other disposition of real estate with such frequency as to amount to clear harassment of the owner or other person who controls the sale or disposition of the real estate.

Authority

The provisions of this § 35.302 issued under act of February 19, 1980 (P. L. 15, No. 9) (63 P. S. §§ 455.101—455.902).

Source

The provisions of this § 35.302 adopted February 24, 1989, effective February 25, 1989, 19 Pa.B. 781.

§ 35.303. Panic selling.

(a) The Commission will regard an attempt by a licensee to bring about panic selling in order to profit from it as bad faith under section 604(a)(20) of the act (63 P. S. § 455.604(a)(20)). For purposes of this section, "panic selling," is frequent efforts to sell residential real estate in a particular neighborhood because of fear of declining real estate values when the fear is not based on facts relating to the intrinsic value of the real estate itself.

(b) Proof of systematic solicitation of sales listings may be considered sufficient, but not conclusive, evidence of an attempt to bring about panic selling.

Authority

The provisions of this § 35.303 issued under act of February 19, 1980 (P. L. 15, No. 9) (63 P. S. §§ 455.101—455.902).

Source

The provisions of this § 35.303 adopted February 24, 1989, effective February 25, 1989, 19 Pa.B. 781.

§ 35.304. Disclosure of licensure when advertising own real estate.

A broker who sells or leases his own real estate shall disclose that he is a real estate broker in advertisements for the property.

Authority

The provisions of this § 35.304 issued under act of February 19, 1980 (P. L. 15, No. 9) (63 P. S. §§ 455.101—455.902).

Source

The provisions of this § 35.304 adopted February 24, 1989, effective February 25, 1989, 19 Pa.B. 781.

Cross References

This section cited in 49 Pa. Code § 35.288 (relating to duties when selling or leasing own real estate).

§ 35.305. Business name on advertisements.

(a) A broker, cemetery broker or rental listing referral agent shall advertise or otherwise hold himself out to the public under the business name designated on the license.

(b) An advertisement by an associate broker, salesperson, cemetery associate broker or cemetery salesperson shall contain the business name and telephone number of the employing broker. The name and telephone number of the employing broker shall be given greater prominence in the advertisement than the name and telephone number of the employe.

Authority

The provisions of this § 35.305 issued under act of February 19, 1980 (P. L. 15, No. 9) (63 P. S. §§ 455.101—455.902).

Source

The provisions of this § 35.305 adopted February 24, 1989, effective February 25, 1989, 19 Pa.B. 781; amended June 11, 1994, 24 Pa.B. 2904. Immediately preceding text appears at serial pages (135761) to (135762).

§ 35.306. Advertisements of lotteries, contests, prizes, certificates, gifts and lots.

(a) An advertisement by a licensee for the solicitation, sale or offering for sale of real estate that employs lotteries or contests or that offers prizes, certificates, gifts or free lots shall contain:

(1) A description of each prize, certificate, gift or lot offered.

(2) The prerequisites for receiving each prize, certificate, gift or lot offered.

(3) Limitation on the number of prizes, certificates, gifts or lots offered.

(4) The fair market value of each prize, certificate, gift or lot offered. If the advertisement is in a print medium, the statement of fair market value shall be in the same size type as the description of the prize, certificate, gift or lot offered. For purposes of this paragraph, "fair market value" is the price or value that a prospective buyer would expect to pay, or be charged for, if he were to acquire a similar item of like quality and quantity in a retail outlet that offers the item for sale to the general public.

(5) The odds of winning or receiving each prize, certificate, gift or lot offered. If the advertisement is in a print medium, the statement of odds shall be the same size type as the description of the prize, certificate, gift or lot, and shall appear immediately adjacent to the description.

(b) A licensee who solicits, sells or offers for sale real estate by using the mails or by offering prizes, certificates, gifts or lots shall maintain records that contain:

(1) The number and description of each prize, certificate, gift or lot distributed or awarded.

(2) The name and address of each person who received a prize, certificate, gift or lot.

(3) The name and address of each person who responded to the advertisement or solicitation but did not receive a prize, certificate, gift or lot.

(c) The Commission will regard the following as deceptive conduct within the meaning of section 604(a)(18) of the act (63 P. S. § 455.604(a)(18)):

(1) Failure to comply with subsection (a) or (b).

(2) Failure to disclose the possibility that a particular prize, certificate, gift or lot may not be distributed or awarded.

(3) Advertising the availability of a prize, certificate, gift or lot when it is not available for distribution or awarding.

(4) Giving a misleading description of a prize, certificate, gift or lot.

Authority
The provisions of this § 35.306 issued under act of February 19, 1980 (P. L. 15, No. 9) (63 P. S. §§ 455.101—455.902).

Source
The provisions of this § 35.306 adopted February 24, 1989, effective February 25, 1989, 19 Pa.B. 781.

§ 35.307. **Advertisements of sales volume, market position and numbers of offices.**

(a) An advertisement by a broker about "sales volume" or "production" shall refer only to closed transactions. For purpose of this subsection, a "closed transaction" is either a listing sold or a sale made after a fully executed deed is delivered.

(b) An advertisement by a broker about his production or position in the "market" shall identify the municipality that the market comprises.

(c) An advertisement by a broker about the number of offices that he operates shall refer only to those offices that have been issued branch office licenses by the Commission.

Authority
The provisions of this § 35.307 issued under act of February 19, 1980 (P. L. 15, No. 9) (63 P. S. §§ 455.101—455.902).

35-53

Source
The provisions of this § 35.307 adopted February 24, 1989, effective February 25, 1989, 19 Pa.B. 781.

§ 35.308. **Relationship with educational institution.**

A real estate company, franchise or network may not promote, endorse or advertise its association, affiliation or connection with a real estate school or with a college, university or institute of higher learning regarding its offering of real estate instruction. This prohibition does not apply to individual licensees.

Authority
The provisions of this § 35.308 issued under act of February 19, 1980 (P. L. 15, No. 9) (63 P. S. §§ 455.101—455.902).

Source
The provisions of this § 35.308 adopted June 10, 1994, effective June 11, 1994, 24 Pa.B. 2904.

ESCROW REQUIREMENTS

§ 35.321. **Duty to deposit money belonging to another into escrow account.**

(a) Except as provided in subsection (b), a broker shall deposit money that he receives belonging to another into an escrow account in a Federally or State-insured bank or depository to be held pending consummation of the transaction, or a prior termination thereof that does not involve a dispute between the parties to the transaction, at which time the broker shall pay over the full amount to the party entitled to receive it. If a broker is a partnership, association or corporation, its broker of record shall be responsible for ensuring that the escrow duty is performed.

(b) A broker is not required to hold in escrow rents that he receives as a property manager for a lessor. A broker shall deposit rents received into a rental management account that is separate from the broker's escrow and general business accounts.

(c) If a broker receives money belonging to another under an installment land purchase agreement, the transaction shall be considered consummated, for purposes of subsection (a), when the buyer has been afforded the opportunity, by means of the seller's written acknowledgement on or affixed to the agreement, to record the agreement, unless the agreement specifies otherwise.

35-54

Ch. 35   STATE REAL ESTATE COMMISSION   49 § 35.322

(d) If a broker receives money belonging to another under an agreement of sale involving cemetery property, the transaction shall be considered consummated, for purposes of subsection (a), when the buyer receives a copy of the agreement of sale.

(e) If a broker receives a security deposit belonging to another under a lease agreement, the broker's duty to pay over the deposit, for purposes of subsection (a), shall arise when the tenancy ends.

Authority

The provisions of this § 35.321 issued under act of February 19, 1980 (P. L. 15, No. 9) (63 P. S. §§ 455.101—455.902).

Source

The provisions of this § 35.321 adopted February 24, 1989, effective February 25, 1989, 19 Pa.B. 781.

§ 35.322. Nonwaiver of escrow duty.

A broker's escrow duty may not be waived or altered by an agreement between the parties to the transaction, between the broker and the parties, or between the broker and other brokers who may be involved in the transaction.

Authority

The provisions of this § 35.322 issued under act of February 19, 1980 (P. L. 15, No. 9) (63 P. S. §§ 455.101—455.902).

Source

The provisions of this § 35.322 adopted February 24, 1989, effective February 25, 1989, 19 Pa.B. 781.

§ 35.323. Responsibility for escrow in cobrokerage transactions.

(a) If a sales deposit is tendered by a buyer to the listing broker rather than to the selling broker, the listing broker shall assume the escrow duty.

(b) If a sales deposit is tendered by a buyer to the selling broker with the buyer having prior notice that the selling broker intends to deliver the deposit to the listing broker, the listing broker shall assume the escrow duty. The selling broker shall require the buyer to acknowledge in writing, prior to his signing the agreement of sale, that the prior notice contained the following information:

(1) The name of the listing broker.

(2) That the selling broker's acceptance of the buyer's deposit is on behalf of the listing broker as subagent for the listing broker.

(3) That the listing broker is a licensed real estate broker who is required to hold the deposit in escrow.

49 § 35.324   DEPARTMENT OF STATE   Pt. I

(4) That the listing broker be designated as payee, if the buyer's deposit is in the form of a check.

(c) If a sales deposit is tendered by a buyer to the selling broker without the buyer having the prior notice in subsection (b), the selling broker shall assume the escrow duty.

Authority

The provisions of this § 35.323 issued under act of February 19, 1980 (P. L. 15, No. 9) (63 P. S. §§ 455.101—455.902).

Source

The provisions of this § 35.323 adopted February 24, 1989, effective February 25, 1989, 19 Pa.B. 781.

§ 35.324. Deadline for depositing money into escrow account.

(a) Except as provided in subsection (b), a broker shall deposit money belonging to another into an escrow account by the end of the next business day following its receipt in the real estate office where the escrow records are maintained.

(b) If the money of another has been tendered to the broker in the form of a check under an offer to purchase or lease real estate, the broker may, with the written permission of both the buyer and the seller or the lessee and the lessor, refrain from depositing the money into an escrow account by the deadline in subsection (a) pending the seller's or lessor's acceptance of the offer. The broker shall deposit the check into an escrow account within 1 business day of the seller's or lessor's acceptance of the offer.

Authority

The provisions of this § 35.324 issued under act of February 19, 1980 (P. L. 15, No. 9) (63 P. S. §§ 455.101—455.902).

Source

The provisions of this § 35.324 adopted February 24, 1989, effective February 25, 1989, 19 Pa.B. 781.

§ 35.325. Escrow account.

(a) An escrow account shall:

(1) Be maintained in a Federally- or State-insured bank or recognized depository.

(2) Designate the broker as trustee.

(3) Provide for the withdrawal of funds without prior notice.

(4) Be used exclusively for escrow purposes.

Ch. 35   STATE REAL ESTATE COMMISSION   49 § 35.326

(b) The employing broker or broker of record of a partnership, association or corporation may give an employe written authority to deposit money into an escrow account and may give a licensed employe written authority to withdraw funds from the escrow account for payments that are properly chargeable to the account.

(c) If money is expected to be held in escrow for more than 6 months, the broker is encouraged to deposit the money into an interest-bearing escrow account. Interest earned on an escrow account shall be held and disbursed, pro rata, in the same manner as the principal amount, unless the parties to the transaction direct otherwise by agreement. A broker may not claim the interest earned on an escrow account, unless the broker is a lessor as provided in section 511.2 of the Landlord and Tenant Act (68 P. S. § 250.511b).

(d) A broker shall provide the Commission or its authorized representatives, upon written request or under an office inspection under § 35.246 (relating to inspection of office), a letter addressed to the bank or depository where the escrow account is maintained authorizing the release of records pertaining to the account.

Authority

The provisions of this § 35.325 issued under act of February 19, 1980 (P. L. 15, No. 9) (63 P. S. §§ 455.101—455.902).

Source

The provisions of this § 35.325 adopted February 24, 1989, effective February 25, 1989, 19 Pa.B. 781.

§ 35.326. **Prohibition against commingling or misappropriation.**

(a) Except as provided in subsection (b), a broker may not commingle money that is required to be held in escrow—or interest earned on an escrow account—with business, personal or other funds.

(b) A broker may deposit business or personal funds into an escrow account to cover service charges assessed to the account by the bank or depository where the account is located or to maintain a minimum balance in the account as required by the regulations of the bank or depository.

(c) A broker may not misappropriate money that is required to be held in escrow—or interest earned on an escrow account—for business, personal or other purposes.

Authority

The provisions of this § 35.326 issued under act of February 19, 1980 (P. L. 15, No. 9) (63 P. S. §§ 455.101—455.902).

49 § 35.327   DEPARTMENT OF STATE   Pt. I

Source

The provisions of this § 35.326 adopted February 24, 1989, effective February 25, 1989, 19 Pa.B. 781; amended June 10, 1994, effective June 11, 1994, 24 Pa.B. 2904. Immediately preceding text appears at serial page (135767).

§ 35.327. **Procedure when entitlement to money held in escrow is disputed.**

If a dispute arises between the parties to a real estate transaction over entitlement to money that is being held in escrow by a broker, the broker shall retain the money in escrow until the dispute is resolved. If resolution of the dispute appears remote without legal action, the broker may, following 30 days' notice to the parties, petition the county court having jurisdiction in the matter to interplead the rival claimants.

Authority

The provisions of this § 35.327 issued under act of February 19, 1980 (P. L. 15, No. 9) (63 P. S. §§ 455.101—455.902).

Source

The provisions of this § 35.327 adopted February 24, 1989, effective February 25, 1989, 19 Pa.B. 781.

§ 35.328. **Escrow records.**

A broker shall keep records of monies received by him that are required to be held in escrow and shall produce the records for examination by the Commission or its authorized representatives upon written request or pursuant to an office inspection under § 35.246 (relating to inspection of office). The records shall contain:

(1) The name of the party from whom the broker received the money.

(2) The name of the party to whom the money belongs.

(3) The name of the party for whose account the money is deposited.

(4) The date the broker received the money.

(5) The date the broker deposited the money into the escrow account.

(6) The date the broker withdrew the money from the escrow account.

Authority

The provisions of this § 35.328 issued under act of February 19, 1980 (P. L. 15, No. 9) (63 P. S. §§ 455.101—455.902).

Ch. 35   STATE REAL ESTATE COMMISSION   49 § 35.331

Source

The provisions of this § 35.328 adopted February 24, 1989, effective February 25, 1989, 19 Pa.B. 781.

REAL ESTATE DOCUMENTS

§ 35.331. Listing agreements generally.

A listing agreement, of whatever type, shall state that:

(1) A Real Estate Recovery Fund exists to reimburse a person who has obtained a final civil judgment against a Commonwealth real estate licensee owing to fraud, misrepresentation or deceit in a real estate transaction and who has been unable to collect the judgment after exhausting legal and equitable remedies.

(2) Details about the Fund may be obtained by calling the Commission at (717) 783-3658.

(3) Payments of money received by the broker on account of a sale—regardless of the form of payment and the person designated as payee (if payment is made by an instrument)—shall be held by the broker in an escrow account pending consummation of the sale or a prior termination thereof.

Authority

The provisions of this § 35.331 issued under act of February 19, 1980 (P. L. 15, No. 9) (63 P. S. §§ 455.101—455.902).

Source

The provisions of this § 35.331 adopted February 24, 1989, effective February 25, 1989, 19 Pa.B. 781; amended June 10, 1994, effective June 11, 1994, 24 Pa.B. 2904. Immediately preceding text appears at serial page (135768).

§ 35.332. Exclusive listing agreements.

(a) An exclusive listing agreement may comprise one of the following:

(1) The exclusive agency of the broker.

(2) The exclusive right-to-sell or exclusive right-to-lease.

(b) An exclusive listing agreement shall contain:

(1) The sale or lease price.

(2) The commission expected on the sale or lease price.

(3) The duration of the agreement.

(4) In the case of an exclusive right-to-sell agreement, a statement in bold face type that the broker earns a commission on the sale of the property during the listing period by whomever made, including the owner.

49 § 35.332   DEPARTMENT OF STATE   Pt. I

(5) In the case of an exclusive right-to-lease agreement, a statement in bold print that the broker earns a commission on the lease of the property during the listing period by whomever made, including the lessor.

(c) An exclusive listing agreement may not contain:

(1) A listing period exceeding 1 year.

(2) An automatic renewal clause.

(3) A cancellation notice to terminate the agreement at the end of the listing period set forth in the agreement.

(4) Authority of the broker to execute a signed agreement of sale or lease for the owner or lessor.

(5) An option by the broker to purchase the listed property.

(6) Authority of the broker to confess judgment against the owner or lessor for the Commission in the event of a sale or lease.

(d) The following exclusive right-to-sell listing agreement is exemplary of the requirements of this section:

EXCLUSIVE RIGHT-TO-SELL LISTING AGREEMENT

_____ (hereinafter the "Seller") hereby grants _____ (hereinafter the "Agent") the exclusive right to sell property located at _____ for the sale price of $ _____ .

The Seller and the Agent agree that this agreement shall be in force for _____ months from the date of this agreement and shall then terminate unless extended in writing by the Seller and the Agent.

If the property is sold or exchanged during the term of this agreement by the Agent, or by the Seller, or by any other person, the Seller agrees to pay the Agent a commission of _____ of the gross sale price.

The Seller represents that he has the legal right to sell the property and has received an exact copy of this agreement.

The Seller authorizes the Agent to place a "For Sale" sign upon the property, which shall be the only such sign permitted to be displayed on the property during the term of this agreement.

The Seller understands that all payments received by the Agent on account of a sales agreement entered into between the Seller and a buyer shall be held in escrow by the Agent pending consummation of the sale, or a prior termination thereof, in accordance with the Real Estate Licensing and Registration Act and Regulations promulgated thereunder.

IN WITNESS WHEREOF, the Seller has hereunto set his hand and seal this _____ day of _____ 19 _____ .

(10) A statement that access to a public road may require issuance of a highway occupancy permit from the Department of Transportation.

(11) In the case of an agreement of sale for the purchase of a time share or campground membership, a statement regarding the purchaser's right of cancellation that is set forth conspicuously in bold face type of at least 10 point size immediately above the signature line for the purchaser and that is in substantially the following form:

"You, the purchaser, may cancel this purchase at any time prior to midnight of the fifth day following the date of this transaction. If you desire to cancel, you are required to notify the seller, in writing, at (insert address). Such notice shall be given by certified return receipt mail or by any other bona fide means of delivery which provides you with a receipt. Such notice shall be effective upon being postmarked by the United States Postal Service or upon deposit of the notice with any bona fide means of delivery which provides you with a receipt."

(b) An agreement of sale that is conditioned upon the ability of the buyer to obtain a mortgage shall contain:

(1) The type of mortgage.
(2) The mortgage principal.
(3) The maximum interest rate of the mortgage.
(4) The minimum term of the mortgage.
(5) The deadline for the buyer to obtain the mortgage.
(6) The nature and extent of assistance that the broker will render to the buyer in obtaining the mortgage.

(c) The following terms shall be printed in bold face if made part of an agreement of sale:

(1) A provision relieving the seller from responsibility for defects involving the sale property, or a provision requiring the buyer to execute a release to that effect at the time of settlement, or a provision of similar import.

(2) A provision reserving to the builder-seller the right to change, or depart from, the building specifications for the sale property.

(d) The requirements in subsection (a)(1)—(5) and (9) are applicable to an agreement of sale for a cemetery lot or plot or a mausoleum space or opening.

Authority

The provisions of this § 35.333 issued under act of February 19, 1980 (P. L. 15, No. 9) (63 P. S. §§ 455.101—455.902).

(189886) No. 240 Nov. 94

35-62

Accepted:

Agent _____ Seller
(SEAL)
Address _____ Seller
(SEAL)

Authority

The provisions of this § 35.332 issued under act of February 19, 1980 (P. L. 15, No. 9) (63 P. S. §§ 455.101—455.902).

Source

The provisions of this § 35.332 adopted February 24, 1989, effective February 25, 1989, 19 Pa.B. 781.

§ 35.333. Agreements of sale.

(a) An agreement of sale shall contain:

(1) The date of the agreement.
(2) The names of the buyer and seller.
(3) A description of the property and the interest to be conveyed.
(4) The sale price.
(5) The dates for payment and conveyance.
(6) The zoning classification of the property, except if the property (or each parcel thereof, if subdividable) is zoned solely or primarily to permit single-family dwellings, together with a statement that the failure of the agreement of sale to contain the zoning classification of the property shall render the agreement voidable at the option of the buyer and, if voided, deposits tendered by the buyer shall be returned to the buyer without a requirement of court action.
(7) A statement as to whether the broker is the agent of the seller or the agent of the buyer.
(8) A provision that payments of money received by the broker on account of the sale—regardless of the form of payment and the person designated as payee (if payment is made by an instrument)—shall be held by the broker in an escrow account pending consummation of the sale or a prior termination thereof.
(9) The following statement:

"A Real Estate Recovery Fund exists to reimburse any person who has obtained a final civil judgment against a Pennsylvania real estate licensee owing to fraud, misrepresentation, or deceit in a real estate transaction and who has been unable to collect the judgment after exhausting all legal and equitable remedies. For complete details about the Fund, call (717) 783-3658."

Ch. 35   STATE REAL ESTATE COMMISSION   49 § 35.334

Source

The provisions of this § 35.333 adopted February 24, 1989, effective February 25, 1989, 19 Pa.B. 781; amended June 10, 1994, effective June 11, 1994, 24 Pa.B. 2904. Immediately preceding text appears at serial pages (135770) to (135771).

§ 35.334. Statements of estimated cost and return.

(a) Before an agreement of sale is executed, the brokers involved in the transaction shall provide each party with a written estimate of reasonably foreseeable expenses associated with the sale that the party may be expected to pay, including, but not limited to:

(1) The broker's commission.

(2) The mortgage payments and financing costs.

(3) Taxes and assessments.

(4) Settlement expenses.

(b) The estimates of costs required under subsection (a) shall be as accurate as may be reasonably expected of a person having knowledge of, and experience in, real estate sales.

(c) The following statement of estimated costs to the buyer at settlement is exemplary of the requirements of subsection (a):

STATEMENT OF ESTIMATED COSTS TO BUYER AT SETTLEMENT

Estimated Settlement Date _____
Property _____
Broker _____
Purchase Price _____
Payment on Account _____
Balance at Settlement _____
Estimated Closing Expenses _____
Title Search and Insurance _____
Conveyancing or Preparation of Papers Charge _____
Recording Fees _____
Deed _____
Mortgage _____
Mortgagee's Charges _____
Appraisal Fee _____
Credit Report _____
Origination and Placement Fees _____
Mortgage Service Charge _____
Fire Insurance ($ _____ for _____ years) _____

35-63

(189887) No. 240 Nov. 94

---

49 § 35.334   DEPARTMENT OF STATE   Pt. I

Miscellaneous Charges _____
Local Realty Transfer Tax (_____ %)
Pennsylvania Realty Transfer Tax (_____ %)
Notary Fees _____
Other Charges _____
Total Closing Expenses _____
Costs for Rebates and Advances _____
Rebates to Seller _____
Insurance _____
Annual Taxes and Water-Sewer Rents _____
Advances by Buyer _____
Insurance _____
Taxes (Escrow) _____
Total Costs for Rebates and Advances _____
Total Estimated Costs at Settlement _____
Estimated Monthly Payments
First Lien $ _____ years at _____ %.
Interest and Principal _____
Monthly FHA Mortgage Insurance Premium _____
Real Estate Taxes $ _____
Fire Insurance $ _____
Water-Sewer Rents $ _____
Total Estimated Monthly Payments $ _____

I/we have read and received a copy of the estimated settlement costs and estimated monthly carrying charges prior to the signing of an agreement of sale to purchase the property noted above.

I/we understand that the above costs are estimated and based on the best information available at this date and that they are subject to change, particularly in the case of the escrow charges such as taxes, water and sewage, rent and insurance.

WITNESS:

_____   _____ (SEAL)
          Buyer

_____ (SEAL)
Buyer

(d) The following statement of estimated costs to the seller at settlement is exemplary of the requirements of subsection (a):

35-64

(189888) No. 240 Nov. 94

Ch. 35   STATE REAL ESTATE COMMISSION   49 § 35.335

STATEMENT OF ESTIMATED COSTS TO SELLER AT SETTLEMENT

Estimated Settlement Date _____

Property _____

Broker _____

Purchase Price _____
Payment on Account _____
Balance _____
Estimated Closing Expenses
Penna. Realty Transfer Tax
(_____%) _____
Local Realty Transfer Tax
(_____%) _____
Federal Documentary
Stamps _____
Notary Fee _____
Mortgage Discount _____
Unpaid Annual Taxes _____
Broker's Commission _____
Total Expenses _____
Estimated Closing Credits Tax
Refund _____
Estimated Net Charges _____
Estimated Net Proceeds _____

WITNESS:

_____ Seller

_____ Seller

Authority

The provisions of this § 35.334 issued under act of February 19, 1980 (P. L. 15, No. 9) (63 P. S. §§ 455.101—455.902).

Source

The provisions of this § 35.334 adopted February 24, 1989, effective February 25, 1989, 19 Pa.B. 781.

§ 35.335. **Rental listing referral agreements.**

The agreement between a rental listing referral agent and a prospective tenant shall contain:

(1) The rental specifications desired by the prospective tenant, such as location and rent.

(2) The following statement in bold print:

49 § 35.335   DEPARTMENT OF STATE   Pt. I

"We are a referral service only. We are not acting as real estate salespersons or brokers. We do not guarantee that the purchaser will find a satisfactory rental unit through our service. Our only purpose is to furnish the purchaser with lists of available rental units."

Authority

The provisions of this § 35.335 issued under act of February 19, 1980 (P. L. 15, No. 9) (63 P. S. §§ 455.101—455.902).

Source

The provisions of this § 35.335 adopted February 24, 1989, effective February 25, 1989, 19 Pa.B. 781.

Subchapter F. REAL ESTATE SCHOOLS

The provisions of this subchapter—Sections 35.341 through 35.363—discuss the approval of real estate schools, real estate school directors and the administration of real estate schools. Readers interested in this subchapter within the state's rules and regulations are encouraged to obtain it from the Department of State, Bureau of Professional and Occupational Affairs, State Real Estate Commission in Harrisburg.

Subchapter G. PROMOTIONAL LAND SALES

Sec.
35.371. General requirements.
35.372. Nonresident requirements.
35.373. Offering statements.
35.374. Review and approval of documents.
35.375. Affidavit of consent to service of jurisdiction.

§ 35.371. General requirements.

(a) A broker, developer or subdivider referred to in this subchapter as "applicant", who proposes to engage in sales of a promotional nature in this Commonwealth of property located outside of this Commonwealth shall submit to the Commission, for its approval before doing so, full particulars regarding the property and proposed terms of sale, and they and their salesmen shall comply with rules and regulations, restrictions and conditions pertaining thereto as the Commission may impose. Expenses reasonably incurred by the Commission in investigating and inspecting the property and proposed sale thereof in this Commonwealth shall be borne by the applicant. No broker, developer or salesman may refer to the Commission or to an official or employe of the Commission in selling, offering for sale or advertising, or otherwise promoting the sale, mortgage or lease of the property, nor make representation that the property has been inspected or approved or otherwise passed upon by the Commission, or by a State official, department or employe.

(b) An applicant approved to engage in sales set forth in this chapter shall notify the Commission at least 10 days in advance of the date, time and place of efforts to sell or advertise through parties or reception or other group media.

Authority

The provisions of this § 35.371 issued under act of February 19, 1980 (P. L. 15, No. 9) (63 P. S. §§ 455.101—455.902).

Source

The provisions of this § 35.371 adopted February 24, 1989, effective February 25, 1989, 19 Pa.B. 781.

Notes of Decisions

The possession of a salesperson's license for 3 or more years does not automatically qualify a person to sit for a broker's examination. *Bhala v. State Real Estate Commission*, 617 A.2d 841, 842 (Pa. Commw. 1992).

§ 35.372. Nonresident requirements.

(a) A nonresident applicant shall also file an irrevocable consent that suits and actions may be commenced against the applicant in the proper court of a county of this Commonwealth in which a cause of action may arise, or in which plaintiff may reside, by the service of a process or pleadings authorized by the laws of the Commonwealth on the Commission in Harrisburg, Pennsylvania. The consent shall stipulate and agree that the service of process or pleadings on the Commission shall be taken and held in all courts to be as valid and binding as if service had been made upon the applicant personally within this Commonwealth.

(b) If process or pleadings are served upon the Commission, they shall be by duplicate copy, one of which shall be filed in the office of the Commission and the other immediately forwarded by certified mail to the main office of the applicant against which the process or pleadings are directed.

Authority

The provisions of this § 35.372 issued under act of February 19, 1980 (P. L. 15, No. 9) (63 P. S. §§ 455.101—455.902).

Source

The provisions of this § 35.372 adopted February 24, 1989, effective February 25, 1989, 19 Pa.B. 781.

Cross References

This section cited in 49 Pa. Code § 35.375 (relating to affidavit of consent to service of jurisdiction).

§ 35.373. Offering statements.

(a) The Commission also requires the applicant to prepare and deliver at its own expense, to each prospective purchaser in this Commonwealth an offering statement which shall be revised annually. The offering statement shall be approved by the Commission and shall contain a detailed description, price and terms of the offer as well as financial information disclosing assets and liabilities of the applicant. The offering statement shall also inform prospective purchasers of the following:

(1) Tax liabilities.
(2) Basis for guarantees.
(3) Public transportation facilities.
(4) Terrain details.
(5) Climate.
(6) Proposed and existing improvements.
(7) Roads.
(8) Water supply.
(9) Public utilities.
(10) An objectionable condition of air, sight or terrain.
(11) Sewage disposal facilities.
(12) Recreational and community facilities.
(13) The distances to a nearby populated area.

(b) The offering statement shall also set forth on the front page in large bold face type or italics, the following statement:

49 § 35.374   DEPARTMENT OF STATE   Pt. I

"The State Real Estate Commission's requirements of this broker, developer or subdivider does not constitute approval of the land being offered for sale or lease. The State Real Estate Commission has not in any way passed upon the merits of such offer."

Authority

The provisions of this § 35.373 issued under act of February 19, 1980 (P. L. 15, No. 9) (63 P. S. §§ 455.101—455.902).

Source

The provisions of this § 35.373 adopted February 24, 1989, effective February 25, 1989, 19 Pa.B. 781.

§ 35.374. Review and approval of documents.

The following information and documents shall be furnished annually to the Commission in report form for its review and approval:

(1) Name of owner, including the following:
  (i) Names and addresses of the owners or partners.
  (ii) Lists of the officers and holders of 10% or more of total subscribed or issued stock of the corporation.
  (iii) Copy of most recent certified audit of records including financial statements.
(2) Names of subsidiary organizations or companies.
(3) Name of development.
(4) Address of development.
(5) Addresses of administrative offices.
(6) Representative of the Commonwealth, including a list of the sales offices and personnel in this Commonwealth.
(7) Status of property, including the following:
  (i) Owner of the land.
  (ii) Whether land is free and clear.
  (iii) If land is mortgaged, whether the mortgage is assignable, including the following:
    (A) Whether individual lots can be released.
    (B) Cost per lot.
  (iv) Whether there are judgments against or unpaid taxes due on the land.
  (v) Whether abstracts or title policies will be furnished.
  (vi) Copy of type of deed used.
  (vii) Whether deeds are issued in fee simple.
  (viii) Whether there is additional charge for issuing a deed.
(8) Improvements completed, including the following:
  (i) Paved streets.
  (ii) Sidewalks.

35-86

(189910) No. 240 Nov. 94

Ch. 35   STATE REAL ESTATE COMMISSION   49 § 35.374

  (iii) Street lights.
  (iv) Public utilities.
  (v) Whether improvements are paid for.
  (vi) Tax rates.
  (vii) If no improvements, plans for completion.
  (viii) If FHA approved, copy of approval.
(9) Whether bond has been posted with a governmental authority to guarantee completion of promised improvements, including the following:
  (i) Specification for what purpose.
  (ii) Amount.
  (iii) Name of bonding company.
  (iv) How this bond will protect the purchasers from the Commonwealth.
  (v) Certified copy of the bonds used.
(10) Sewage, including the following:
  (i) Sanitary sewers.
  (ii) Storm sewers.
  (iii) Whether water mains or individual wells are necessary.
  (iv) Whether septic tanks are necessary.
  (v) If septic tanks are necessary, whether they are authorized by appropriate government authorities.
  (vi) Whether level of land and type of soil is suitable for septic tanks.
(11) Drainage, including the following:
  (i) Whether land is dry.
  (ii) Copy of the drainage plan of the engineer.
  (iii) Depth of water table.
  (iv) Depth of average well.
(12) Zoning restrictions, including the following:
  (i) Copy of topographical map.
  (ii) Copy of State Board of Health Percolation Test one hole per 5 acres where septic tanks are used.
(13) Advertising, including the following:
  (i) Size of lots offered.
  (ii) Price and terms of sale.
  (iii) Whether these lots are large enough for building purposes that would comply with zoning requirements.
  (iv) If and where plot is recorded.
(14) Location, including the following:
  (i) Aerial photo showing exact area with at least 1 mile of bordering properties.
  (ii) How far property is presently from the following:

35-87

(189911) No. 240 Nov. 94

49 § 35.375   DEPARTMENT OF STATE   Pt. I

(A) Highway.
(B) Incorporated town.
(C) Major shopping center.
(D) Industrial area including type and size.
(E) Transportation including bus and train.
(F) Schools—public, trade, parochial or private.
(G) Lighted streets.
(H) Type of pavement and curbs.
(I) Fire protection.
(J) Garbage and trash removal.
(K) Police protection.
(L) Airport and airlines operated therefrom.
(15) Current selling price of lots in adjoining area and owners of these lots.
(16) Financial arrangements, including the following:
 (i) Whether the down payment will be placed in escrow and terms of release of the down payment.
 (ii) Type of financing obtainable and percent of interest charged.
 (iii) Closing costs, specifying for what.
 (iv) Specific listing of carrying charges.
 (v) Types of contracts used.

Authority

The provisions of this § 35.374 issued under act of February 19, 1980 (P. L. 15, No. 9) (63 P. S. §§ 455.101—455.902).

Source

The provisions of this § 35.374 adopted February 24, 1989, effective February 25, 1989, 19 Pa.B. 781.

§ 35.375. Affidavit of consent to service of jurisdiction.

The following affidavit of consent to service of jurisdiction is exemplary of the requirements of § 35.372 (relating to nonresident requirements):

AFFIDAVIT OF CONSENT TO SERVICE OF JURISDICTION

That the undersigned _____ (give legal designation of applicant, individual, partnership, corporation) does hereby irrevocably consent that any action brought against the above named applicant in the proper court of any county of the State of Pennsylvania or in which the plaintiff in such action may reside and that in the event proper service of process cannot be had upon such applicant in any such proceeding in such county, service of any process may be made therein by the sheriff of such county by the service of any process or pleadings authorized by the Laws of Pennsylvania on the Real Estate Commission, hereby stipulating and

35-88

Ch. 35   STATE REAL ESTATE COMMISSION   49 § 35.375

agreeing that such service of such process or pleadings on said Chairman shall be taken and held in all courts to be valid and binding as if due process had been made upon said applicant in the State of Pennsylvania.

President _____

Secretary _____

Corporate Seal

Witness _____

Personally appeared _____ before me the undersigned notary public in and for the above named county and state, the day and date above named, and acknowledged the execution of the foregoing instrument to be the voluntary act and deed of such applicant for the purpose therein set forth (if applicant is an individual, strike out the following) and that they are the President and Secretary, respectively, of such corporation and are duly authorized to execute the foregoing instrument.
(Seal)

State of _____ SS

COUNTY OF _____

Authority

The provisions of this § 35.375 issued under act of February 19, 1980 (P. L. 15, No. 9) (63 P. S. §§ 455.101—455.902).

Source

The provisions of this § 35.375 adopted February 24, 1989, effective February 25, 1989, 19 Pa.B. 781.

Subchapter H. CONTINUING EDUCATION

Sec.
35.381. Purposes and goals.
35.382. Requirement.
35.383. Waiver of continuing education requirement.
35.384. Qualifying courses; required and elective topics.
35.385. Approved continuing education providers.
35.386. Course content outlines and course titles.
35.387. Administration of curriculum.
35.388. Facilities.
35.389. Instructors.
35.390. Advertising, solicitation and promotion.

35-89

49 § 35.381   DEPARTMENT OF STATE   Pt. I

35.391. Course transcripts and certificates of instruction.
35.392. Investigations and inspections.

§ 35.381. Purposes and goals.

The purposes and goals of continuing education are to provide an education program through which a licensee may obtain the knowledge and skills to:

(1) Maintain and increase competency to engage in licensed real estate activities.

(2) Keep a licensee abreast of changes in laws, regulations, practices and procedures that affect the real estate business.

(3) Better ensure that the public is protected from incompetent practice by licensees.

Authority

The provisions of this § 35.381 issued under section 404.1 of the act of February 19, 1980 (P. L. 15, No. 9) (63 P. S. § 455.404a).

Source

The provisions of this § 35.381 adopted July 31, 1992, effective August 1, 1992, 22 Pa.B. 3980.

§ 35.382. Requirement.

(a) *Condition precedent to renewal of current license.* Beginning with the 1994-1996 biennial license period and continuing with each biennial license period thereafter, a broker or salesperson who desires to renew a current license shall, as a condition precedent to renewal, complete 14 hours of Commission-approved continuing education during the preceding license period.

(b) *Condition precedent to reactivation and renewal of noncurrent license.* Effective March 1, 1994, a broker or salesperson who desires to reactivate and renew a noncurrent license shall, as a condition precedent to reactivation and renewal, complete 14 hours of Commission-approved continuing education during the 2-year period preceding the date of submission of the reactivation application. A broker or salesperson may not use the same continuing education coursework to satisfy the requirements of this subsection and subsection (a).

(c) *Exception.* The continuing education requirement does not apply to cemetery brokers, cemetery salespersons, builder-owner salespersons, timeshare salespersons, campground membership salespersons and rental listing referral agents.

(189914) No. 240 Nov. 94

35-90

Ch. 35   STATE REAL ESTATE COMMISSION   49 § 35.383

Authority

The provisions of this § 35.382 issued under section 404.1 of the act of February 19, 1980 (P. L. 15, No. 9) (63 P. S. § 455.404a).

Source

The provisions of this § 35.382 adopted July 31, 1992, effective August 1, 1992, 22 Pa.B. 3980.

Cross References

This section cited in 49 Pa. Code § 35.383 (relating to waiver of continuing education requirement).

§ 35.383. Waiver of continuing education requirement.

(a) The Commission may waive all or part of the continuing education requirement of § 35.382 (relating to requirement) upon proof that the licensee seeking the waiver is unable to fulfill the requirement because of illness, emergency or hardship. Subsections (b)—(d) are examples of situations in which hardship waivers will be granted. Hardship waivers will be granted in other situations for good cause shown.

(b) A licensee who seeks to renew a current license that was initially issued within 6 months of the biennial license period for which renewal is sought will be deemed eligible, on the basis of hardship, for a full waiver of the continuing education requirement.

(c) A licensee who seeks to renew a current license that was reactivated from noncurrent status within 6 months of the biennial license period for which renewal is sought will be deemed eligible, on the basis of hardship, for a full waiver of the continuing education requirement.

(d) A licensee who is a qualified continuing education instructor will be deemed eligible, on the basis of hardship, for the waiver of 1 hour of continuing education for each hour of actual classroom instruction in an approved continuing education topic that the instructor is qualified to teach. Duplicate hours of instruction in the same topic during the same biennial license period will not be considered for waiver purposes.

Authority

The provisions of this § 35.383 issued under section 404.1 of the act of February 19, 1980 (P. L. 15, No. 9) (63 P. S. § 455.404a).

Source

The provisions of this § 35.383 adopted July 31, 1992, effective August 1, 1992, 22 Pa.B. 3980.

§ 35.384. Qualifying courses; required and elective topics.

(a) *Qualifying courses.* A licensee may satisfy the continuing education requirement by doing one of the following:

(189915) No. 240 Nov. 94

35-91

49 § 35.384   DEPARTMENT OF STATE   Pt. I

(1) Completing a 14-hour continuing education course comprising 5-to-8 hours in required topics and 6-to-9 hours in elective topics.

(2) Completing a 5-to-8-hour continuing education course in required topics and one of the following courses:

(i) A 6-to-9 hour continuing education course in elective topics.

(ii) A course approved by the Commission for broker licensure if 6-to-9 hours are in elective topics.

(b) *Required topics.* A minimum of 5 and a maximum of 8 hours shall be in required topics. A minimum of 2 hours shall be in the act and this chapter and a minimum of 3 hours shall be in fair housing laws and practices. The Commission may, for a given biennial license period and with adequate notice to licensees, require up to 3 hours in a topic that addresses a critical issue of current relevance to licensees.

(c) *Elective topics.* The balance of the 14 hours shall be in elective topics that have significant intellectual and practical content to increase the competency of licensees. A minimum of 2 hours shall be in each elective topic. The elective topics may address either real estate specialties or matters of general interest to licensees.

(1) Acceptable elective topics include:

(i) Real estate ethics.

(ii) New laws affecting real estate.

(iii) Real estate financing.

(iv) Real estate valuation and evaluation.

(v) Property management.

(vi) Land use and zoning.

(vii) Income taxation as applied to real property.

(viii) Ad valorem tax assessment and special assessments.

(ix) Consumer protection and disclosures.

(x) Agency relationships.

(xi) Landlord-tenant laws.

(xii) Environmental issues in real estate.

(xiii) Anti-trust issues in real estate.

(xiv) Current litigation related to real estate.

(xv) Legal instruments related to real estate transactions.

(xvi) Legalities of real estate advertising.

(xvii) Developments in building construction techniques, materials and mechanical systems.

(2) Unacceptable elective topics include:

(i) Mechanical office and business skills; for example, typing, speed writing, preparation of advertising copy, development of sales promotional devices, word processing, calculator and computer operation.

Ch. 35   STATE REAL ESTATE COMMISSION   49 § 35.385

(ii) Office management and related internal operations procedures that do not have a bearing on the public interest.

(iii) Real estate mathematics.

Authority

The provisions of this § 35.384 issued under section 404.1 of the act of February 19, 1980 (P. L. 15, No. 9) (63 P. S. § 455.404a).

Source

The provisions of this § 35.384 adopted July 31, 1992, effective August 1, 1992, 22 Pa.B. 3980.

Cross References

This section cited in 49 Pa. Code § 35.386 (relating to course content outlines and course titles).

§ **35.385. Approved continuing education providers.**

The following providers are approved to offer instruction for continuing education:

(1) An accredited college, university or institute of higher learning, whether in this Commonwealth or outside this Commonwealth.

(2) A real estate school in this Commonwealth approved by the Commission.

(3) A real estate school outside this Commonwealth that has been approved by the real estate licensing authority of the jurisdiction where the school is located.

(4) A real estate industry organization outside this Commonwealth, if the Commission has given its prior approval to the industry organization's continuing education curriculum.

Authority

The provisions of this § 35.385 issued under section 404.1 of the act of February 19, 1980 (P. L. 15, No. 9) (63 P. S. § 455.404a).

Source

The provisions of this § 35.385 adopted July 31, 1992, effective August 1, 1992, 22 Pa.B. 3980.

§ **35.386. Course content outlines and course titles.**

(a) *Course outlines.* The Commission will develop content outlines for the required continuing education topics and make them available to continuing education providers within a reasonable time prior to the biennial license period during which the required topics are taught. Each continuing education provider is responsible for developing content outlines for the elective continuing education topics.

(b) *Course titles.* The Commission will specify the titles for continuing education courses authorized under § 35.384(a)(1) and (2)(i) (relating to qualifying courses; required and elective topics).

Authority

The provisions of this § 35.386 issued under section 404.1 of the act of February 19, 1980 (P. L. 15, No. 9) (63 P. S. § 455.404a).

Source

The provisions of this § 35.386 adopted July 31, 1992, effective August 1, 1992, 22 Pa.B. 3980.

§ 35.387. Administration of curriculum.

A continuing education provider shall comply with the requirements of § 35.358 (relating to administration of curriculum) except for paragraphs (3), (5) and (6).

Authority

The provisions of this § 35.387 issued under section 404.1 of the act of February 19, 1980 (P. L. 15, No. 9) (63 P. S. § 455.404a).

Source

The provisions of this § 35.387 adopted July 31, 1992, effective August 1, 1992, 22 Pa.B. 3980.

§ 35.388. Facilities.

A continuing education course shall be taught at a facility that conforms to § 35.352(b) (relating to location and facilities).

Authority

The provisions of this § 35.388 issued under section 404.1 of the act of February 19, 1980 (P. L. 15, No. 9) (63 P. S. § 455.404a).

Source

The provisions of this § 35.388 adopted July 31, 1992, effective August 1, 1992, 22 Pa.B. 3980.

§ 35.389. Instructors.

A continuing education course shall be taught by an instructor who meets the requirements of § 35.353 (relating to selection of instructors).

Authority

The provisions of this § 35.389 issued under section 404.1 of the act of February 19, 1980 (P. L. 15, No. 9) (63 P. S. § 455.404a).

Source

The provisions of this § 35.389 adopted July 31, 1992, effective August 1, 1992, 22 Pa.B. 3980.

§ 35.390. Advertising, solicitation and promotion.

A continuing education provider shall comply with the requirements in §§ 35.354 and 35.355 (relating to prohibited forms of advertising and solicitation; and prospectus materials).

Authority

The provisions of this § 35.390 issued under section 404.1 of the act of February 19, 1980 (P. L. 15, No. 9) (63 P. S. § 455.404a).

Source

The provisions of this § 35.390 adopted July 31, 1992, effective August 1, 1992, 22 Pa.B. 3980.

§ 35.391. Course transcripts and certificates of instruction.

(a) Within 30 days after a continuing education course has ended, the continuing education provider shall issue a course transcript to each licensee who satisfactorily completed the course and a certificate of instruction to the course instructor if the instructor is also a licensee. The course transcript and certificate of instruction shall contain, to the extent applicable, the information in § 35.360(a)(5) (relating to records), as well as the licensee's license numbers.

(b) A continuing education provider shall retain attendance rosters, course transcripts and certificates of instruction for 4 years and shall issue a duplicate transcript or certificate to the licensee or the Commission upon request.

(c) A licensee shall provide the Commission with information necessary to establish the licensee's compliance with this subchapter.

Authority

The provisions of this § 35.391 issued under section 404.1 of the act of February 19, 1980 (P. L. 15, No. 9) (63 P. S. § 455.404a).

Source

The provisions of this § 35.391 adopted July 31, 1992, effective August 1, 1992, 22 Pa.B. 3980.

§ 35.392. Investigations and inspections.

(a) *Investigations.* Continuing education providers and licensees shall cooperate with investigations conducted by the Commission or its authorized representatives to ensure compliance with this subchapter.

49 § 35.392   DEPARTMENT OF STATE   Pt. I

(b) *Routine and special inspections.* No more than 4 times a year while classes are in session, the Commission or its authorized representatives may conduct a routine inspection of the facilities of a continuing education provider for the purpose of determining whether the provider or a licensee is in compliance with this subchapter. In addition to the routine inspections, the Commission or its authorized representatives may conduct a special inspection of the facilities of a provider upon a complaint or reasonable belief that the provider is not in compliance with this subchapter or as a follow-up to a previous inspection that revealed the provider's noncompliance with this subchapter.

(c) *Scope of inspection.* Prior to the start of a routine or special inspection, the Commission or its authorized representatives will advise the person in charge at the time of the inspection that the inspection is being made under this section and is limited in scope by this section. During the course of a routine or special inspection, the Commission or its authorized representatives will be permitted to:

(1) Examine continuing education records.

(2) Inspect all areas of the facility where continuing education courses are taught.

(3) Monitor the performance of continuing education instructors in classrooms.

(4) Interview the director of the continuing education program, the instructors and the students.

(d) *Combined inspections.* The Commission or its authorized representatives may combine an inspection under this section with an inspection under § 35.362 (relating to inspection of school).

Authority

The provisions of this § 35.392 issued under section 404.1 of the act of February 19, 1980 (P. L. 15, No. 9) (63 P. S. § 455.404a).

Source

The provisions of this § 35.392 adopted July 31, 1992, effective August 1, 1992, 22 Pa.B. 3980.

[Next page is 36-1.]

35-96

Math FAQs

ANSWERS TO YOUR MOST
FREQUENTLY ASKED
REAL ESTATE MATH QUESTIONS

CONTENTS

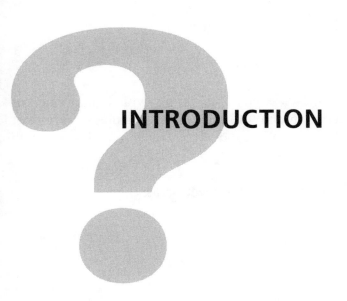

INTRODUCTION

Math is a part of the real estate profession, as it is of most careers. The amount of math and the complexity of the math will vary, depending on the area of real estate chosen. Today, we have calculators and computers that are great time-savers, but we still need to have a good basic knowledge of math. It is a matter of taking the math concepts we were taught in school and adapting them to the real estate profession.

People react differently to the word *math*. Some people like math. Some people are comfortable with math. Some people, though, are uncomfortable with math and become very anxious and stressed when they encounter numbers. If you're that kind of person, you will find the approach taken here very comfortable and helpful. Even if you're someone who's comfortable working with numbers, this clear and simple review will reinforce what you know—and maybe teach you a few tricks and shortcuts, too.

This book covers the basics of real estate math to prepare you for those real-world situations you will encounter as well as the math problems you will be most likely to find on your real estate licensing examination.

Study, review and practice will help you overcome stress and anxiety so you can become comfortable with math. Each time you review and practice your real estate math, you will find that your confidence and ability will increase.

Using This Book

This brief review book is designed to provide you with a quick checkpoint for your math knowledge and to help you reinforce what you already know. It's organized in a way that makes it easy for you to look up just the information you need, and the subject matter is presented in as straightforward a manner as we could think of, with a minimum of wordy explanation and a maximum of quick tips, examples, formulas, memory aids and shortcuts to help you overcome any remaining "math phobia."

The book is organized into five general subject areas:

1. Calculators
2. Fractions
3. Percentages
4. Measurement
5. Prorations

Within each general subject heading are a series of **frequently asked questions (FAQs)** and brief, clear explanations. If you read this book through from start to finish, you'll get a good, general review of real estate math principles. You also can use this book for last-minute review of difficult issues or even as a memory-jogger in your daily real estate practice. Simply check the Table of Contents to see if your question is listed: if it is, go directly to that page. If your question is more complicated or fact-specific, you may have to look at several different items to find your answer. Either way, you'll probably find it here.

Special Features

Throughout the text you will find **Math Tips** that offer insight into the trickier aspects of real estate math in general and the real estate exam's math content in particular. The **For Example . . .** feature applies formulas and concepts to practical situations to show how the concept works in the real world. A generous collection of **practice problems** at the end of the book gives you the opportunity to apply your understanding in an exam-style context, and the simple **T-Bar method** is offered as a shortcut that's both easy to understand and easy to apply.

We hope this Math Review helps you master real estate math. Good luck!

CHAPTER 1

Introduction to Calculators

Calculators are permitted when taking most state licensing examinations. The rules usually state that the calculator must be silent, hand-held, battery-operated and nonprinting.

What kind of calculator do I need?

A calculator that will add (+), subtract (−), multiply (×) and divide (÷) is all that is needed for licensing examinations. These calculators are available in many sizes, shapes and colors. The keys and display may be small or large. Some are battery-powered, some are solar-powered and others are solar-powered with a battery backup. A calculator with a battery only or solar power with a battery backup is recommended over solar-powered only. Choose a calculator that is most comfortable for you, and allow yourself time to learn to use it correctly and become comfortable with it before you take the licensing examination.

What are the specific real estate functions I should look for?

There are many business or financial calculators available that have additional functions and are very beneficial to the real estate professional. Some of the keys you would want are "N" (number of interest compounding periods/number of payments), "i" (interest rate per period), "PV" (present value of money/loan), "PMT" (amount of payment) and "FV" (future value of money). Business or financial calculators vary according to brand and/or model; therefore, the user's manual always should be followed to use the calculator properly. For example, some have "TERM" instead of "N"; therefore, you enter the number of years of the term instead of the number of payments or compounding periods. Some have "LOAN" instead of "PV". Some instruct you to enter the

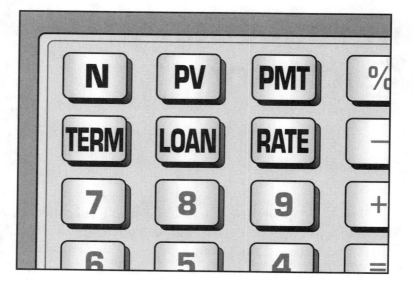

Figure 1   Calculator Functions To Look For

interest rate as an annual rate instead of a monthly rate. You may wish to purchase a business or financial calculator that contains these extra functions. Check with your state real estate commission to see if you will be permitted to use them.

MATH TIP: Be careful! Business or financial calculators are often set to round to two decimals at the factory. Follow the user's manual and set the decimal to float or to a minimum of five decimals. This will enable you to arrive at an answer with enough decimals to match multiple choice answers on exams. No matter which calculator you choose, *read the user's manual.*

Do all calculators work the same?

Your calculator may use chain logic or algebraic logic. In chain logic, the calculator computes the data entered in the order in which they are keyed.

For Example: 15 + 5 × 7 = **140**

Using *chain logic,* the calculator added 15 plus 5 to equal 20. Then the 20 was multiplied by 7 to equal 140.

In *algebraic logic,* the calculator computes the data in the order of multiplication, then division, then addition, then subtraction.

Using the same example as above: 15 + 5 × 7 = **50**

The calculator multiplied 5 by 7 to equal 35. Then the 35 was added to 15 to equal 50.

Some chain logic calculators use *Reverse Polish Notation* so-called because it was invented by the nineteenth-century Polish mathemetician Jan Lukasiewicz to simplify arithmetic expressions). These calculators have no "=" key. Using the above example of 15 + 5 × 7, the answer will still be 140, but you would enter the problem this way.

15 enter 5 + 7 × would give **140** as the answer.

MATH TIP: If you use the "%" key on calculators to solve percentage problems, read the user's manual for proper use of it. Some calculators require the use of the "%" key or the "=" key *but never both in the same calculation.* Other calculators require the use of *both* the "%" key *and* the "=" key to get a correct answer. No matter which calculator you choose, *read the user's manual.*

CHAPTER 2

Fractions, Decimals, and Percentages

What are the parts of a fraction?

The **denominator** shows the number of equal parts in the whole or total. The **numerator** shows the number of those parts with which you are working. In the example below, the whole or total has been divided into eight equal parts, and you have seven of those equal parts.

$$\frac{7}{8}$$ Numerator
Denominator

What is meant by a "proper fraction"?

⅞ is an example of a **proper fraction**. A proper fraction is less than the whole or less than 1.

What is an "improper fraction"?

$$\frac{11}{8}$$ Numerator
Denominator

This is an example of an **improper fraction**. An improper fraction is greater than the whole or greater than 1.

What is a mixed number?

11½ is a **mixed number**. You have a whole number plus a fraction. A mixed number is greater than the whole or greater than 1.

How do I convert fractions to decimals?

Fractions will sometimes be used in real estate math problems. Since calculators may be used on most licensing examinations, it is best to convert fractions to decimals.

> **MATH TIP:** To convert a fraction to a decimal, the numerator is divided by the denominator.

Using the previous three fractions, we can find the decimal equivalent.

$$
\begin{aligned}
\tfrac{7}{8} &= \quad 7 \div 8 = \mathbf{0.875} \\
\tfrac{11}{8} &= \quad 11 \div 8 = \mathbf{1.375} \\
11\tfrac{1}{2} &= \quad 1 \div 2 = 0.5 + 11 = \mathbf{11.5}
\end{aligned}
$$

Once fractions have been converted to decimals, other calculations can be easily completed using the calculator. Note that many calculators automatically add the zero before the decimal point.

How do I add or subtract decimals?

Line up the decimals, add or subtract and bring the decimal down in the answer.

$$
\begin{array}{r}
0.5 \\
+\ 3.25 \\
\hline
= \mathbf{3.75}
\end{array}
\qquad
\begin{array}{r}
8.2 \\
-\ 0.75 \\
\hline
= \mathbf{7.45}
\end{array}
$$

> **MATH TIP:** When you use a calculator, the decimal will be in the correct place in the answer.
>
> (0.5 + 3.25 = 3.75 and 8.2 − 0.75 = 7.45)

How do I multiply decimals?

Multiply the numbers, count the number of decimal places in each number and move the decimal the total number of decimal places to the left in the answer.

$$0.2$$
$$+\ 0.75$$
$$=\ \mathbf{.15}$$

$(2 \times 75 = 150.$, move the decimal **three places** to the **left** and the answer is **.150** or **.15**)

Note: When you use a calculator, the decimal will be in the correct place in the answer. $(0.2 \times 0.75 = \mathbf{0.15})$

How do I divide decimals?

Divide the **dividend** (the number being divided) by the **divisor** (the number you are dividing by) and bring the decimal in the dividend straight up in the **quotient** (answer). If the divisor has a decimal, move the decimal to the right of the divisor and move the decimal the same number of places to the right in the dividend. Now divide as stated above.

$$
\begin{array}{r}
= \mathbf{0.75} \\
2)\overline{1.5} \\
\underline{1.4} \\
10 \\
\underline{10} \\
0
\end{array}
\qquad
0.5)\overline{15.5} =
\begin{array}{r}
= \mathbf{31.} \\
5)\overline{155} \\
\underline{15} \\
5 \\
\underline{5} \\
0
\end{array}
$$

> **MATH TIP:** When you use a calculator, you can have a decimal in the divisor and the decimal will be in the correct place in the answer.
>
> $(1.5 \div 2 = 0.75$ and $15.5 \div 0.5 = 31)$

What is a percentage?

Percent (%) means *per hundred* or *per hundred parts*. The whole or total always represents 100 percent.

$5\% = 5$ parts of 100 parts, 0.05 or ¹⁄₂₀
$75\% = 75$ parts of 100 parts, 0.75 or ¾
$120\% = 120$ parts of 100 parts, 1.2 or 1⅕

Figure 2.1   *Converting Percentage to Decimal*

Percentage to Decimal

.20 ⬅ **20.%**

2 places left

Decimal to Percentage

.20 ➡ **20.%**

2 places right

How can I convert a percentage to a decimal?

Move the decimal *two places* to the *left* and *drop* the % sign.

$$20\%\% = 0.20 \text{ or } \mathbf{0.2}$$
$$1\% = \mathbf{0.01}$$
$$12\tfrac{1}{4}\% = 12.25\% = \mathbf{0.1225}$$

How can I convert a decimal to a percentage?

Move the decimal *two places* to the *right* and *add* the % sign.

$$0.25 = \mathbf{25\%}$$
$$0.9 = \mathbf{90\%}$$
$$0.875 = \mathbf{8.75\%} \text{ or } \mathbf{8\tfrac{3}{4}\%}$$

How do I multiply by percentages?

$$500 \times 25\% = 500 \times 25/100 = 12{,}500/100 = \mathbf{125}$$

or

$$500 \times 25\% = 500 \times 0.25 = \mathbf{125}$$

How do I divide by percentages?

$$100 \div 5\% = 100 \div 5/100 = 100 \times 100/5 = 10{,}000/5 = 2{,}000$$
$$\textbf{or}$$
$$100 \div 5\% = 100 \div 0.05 = \mathbf{2{,}000}$$

Is there any easy way to remember how to solve percentage problems?

These three formulas are important for solving all percentage problems.

$$
\begin{aligned}
\text{TOTAL} \times \text{RATE} &= \text{PART} \\
\text{PART} \div \text{RATE} &= \text{TOTAL} \\
\text{PART} \div \text{TOTAL} &= \text{RATE}
\end{aligned}
$$

There is a simple way to remember these formulas:

- *MULTIPLY* when PART is the UNKNOWN.
- *DIVIDE* when PART is the KNOWN.
- When you divide, always enter PART into the calculator first.

What is the "T-Bar" method?

The T-Bar is another tool to use to solve percentage problems. For some people, the "three-formula method" is more difficult to remember than the visual image of a *T*.

$$
\frac{\text{PART}}{\text{TOTAL} \mid \text{RATE}}
$$

How do I use the T-Bar?

The procedure for using the T-Bar is as follows:

1. Enter the two *known* items in the correct places.
2. If the line between the two items is *vertical*, you *multiply* to equal the missing item.
3. If the line between the two items is *horizontal*, you *divide* to equal the missing item. When you divide, the top (numerator/**Part**) always goes into the calculator first and is divided by the bottom (denominator/**Total** or **Rate**).

Figure 2.2   Using the T-Bar

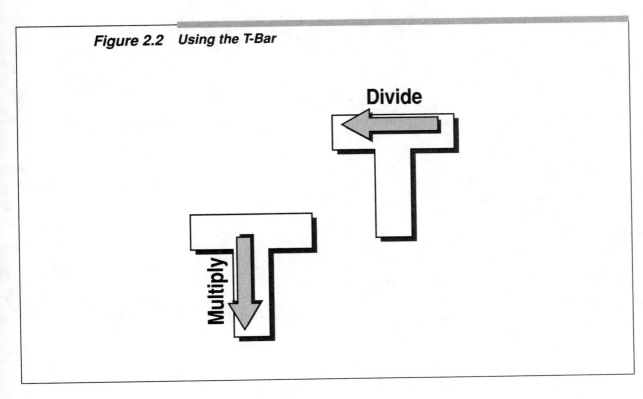

The following examples show how the T-Bar can be used to solve percentage problems. These examples deal with discounts because everyone
can relate to buying an item that is on sale. Later we will see how the
T-Bar can be used for many types of real estate problems.

For Example: John purchased a new suit that was marked $500.
How much did John save if it was on sale for 20 percent off?

$$\frac{= ?\ (\$100)}{\begin{array}{c|c} \$500 & 20\% \\ \text{Total Price} \times & 0.2 \end{array}} \quad \textbf{\$100 Saved}$$

How much did John pay for the suit?

$500 Total Price – $100 Discount **$400 Paid**

or

100% Total Price – 20% Discount = 80% Paid

$$\frac{= ?\ (\$400)}{\begin{array}{c|c} \$500 & 80\% \\ \text{Total Price} \times & 0.8 \end{array}} \quad \textbf{\$400 Saved}$$

For Example: Susie paid $112.50 for a dress that was reduced 25 percent. How much was it originally marked?

100% Original Price − 25% Discount = 75% Paid

$$= ? \ (\$150) \quad \frac{\$112.50 \text{ Paid}}{\begin{array}{c} 75\% \\ 0.75 \end{array}} \ \div \quad \textbf{\$150 Original Price}$$

For Example: Chris paid $127.50 for a coat that was marked down from the original price of $150. What percent of discount did Chris receive?

$150 Original Price − $127.50 Discount Price = $22.50 Discount

$$\div \quad \frac{\$22.50 \text{ Discount}}{\begin{array}{c} \$150 \\ \text{Original Price} \end{array}} \quad = ? \ (0.15 = 15\%) \quad \textbf{15\% Discount}$$

or

$$\div \quad \frac{\$127.50 \text{ Paid}}{\$150} \quad = ? \ (0.85 = 85\%)$$

85% was the percent paid; therefore,

100% Original Price − 85% Paid = **15% Discount**

Word problems can be tricky. How should I deal with them?

There are five important steps that must be taken to solve word problems.

1. **Read** the problem carefully and completely. Never touch the calculator until you have read the entire problem.
2. **Analyze** the problem to determine what is being asked, what facts are given that *will* be needed to solve for the answer and what facts are given that *will not* be needed to solve for the answer. Eliminate any information and/or numbers given that are not needed to solve the problem. Take the remaining information and/or numbers and determine which will be needed first, second, etc., depending on the number of steps it will take to solve the problem.
3. **Choose** the proper formula(s) and steps it will take to solve the problem.
4. **Insert** the known elements and calculate the answer.
5. **Check** your answer to be sure you keyed in the numbers and functions properly on your calculator. Be sure you finished the problem. For example, when the problem asks for the salesperson's share of the commission, do not stop at the broker's share of the commission and mark that answer just because it is one of the choices.

CHAPTER 3

Percentage Problems

How do I work commission problems?

The full **commission** is a percentage of the sales price unless stated differently in the problem. Remember that full commission rates, commission splits between brokers and commission splits between the broker and salespersons are always negotiable. Always read a problem carefully to determine the correct rate(s).

Full Commission	
Sales Price	Full Commission Rate

Sales Price × Full Commission Rate = **Full Commission**

Full Commission ÷ Full Commission Rate = **Sales Price**

Full Commission ÷ Sales Price = **Full Commission Rate**

Broker's Share of the Commission	
Full Commission	% of Full Commission to the Broker

Full Commission × % of Full Commission to the Broker = **Broker's Share of the Commission**

Broker's Share of the Commission ÷ % of Full Commission to the Broker = **Full Commission**

Broker's Share of the Commission ÷ Full Commission = **% of Full Commission to the Broker**

Salesperson's Share of the Commission	
Broker's Share of the Commission	Salesperson's % of the Broker's Share

Broker's Share of the Commission × Salesperson's % of the Broker's Share = **Salesperson's Share of the Commission**

Salesperson's Share of the Commission ÷ Salesperson's % of the Broker's Share = **Broker's Share of the Commission**

Salesperson's Share of the Commission ÷ Broker's Share of the Commission = **Salesperson's % of the Broker's Share**

For Example: A seller listed a home for $200,000 and agreed to pay a full commission rate of 5 percent. The home sold 4 weeks later for 90 percent of the list price. The listing broker agreed to give the selling broker 50 percent of the commission. The listing broker paid the listing salesperson 50 percent of her share of the commission and the selling broker paid the selling salesperson 60 percent of his share of the commission. How much commission did the selling salesperson receive?

= $180,000 Sales Price		
$200,000 List Price	×	90% or 0.9

= $9,000 Full Commission		
$180,000 Sales Price	×	5% or 0.05

$4,500 Broker's Share of the Commission		
$9,000 Full Commission	×	50% or 0.5

= $2,700 Selling Salesperson's Commission		
$4,500 Broker's Share of the Comm.	×	60% or 0.6

$2,700 Selling Salesperson's Commission is the answer.

What is meant by "net after commission"?

The amount of money left after the real estate commission is deducted from the sales price is called the **net after commission**. This net after commission will be used to pay the seller's other expenses and hopefully will leave some money for the seller.

Net after Commission	
Sales Price	Percent after Commission

Percent after Commission = 100% Sales Price − % Commission

Sales Price × Percent after Commission = **Net after Commission**

Net after Commission ÷ Percent after Commission = **Sales Price**

Net after Commission ÷ Sales Price = **Percent after Commission**

For Example: After deducting $5,850 in closing costs and a 5 percent broker's commission, the sellers received their original cost of $175,000 plus a $4,400 profit.. What was the sales price of the property?

$5,850 Closing Costs + $175,000 Original Cost + $4,400 Profit = $185,250 Net after Commission

100% Sales Price − 5% Commission = 95% Percent after Commission

$$\frac{\$185{,}250 \text{ Net after Commission}}{95\% \text{ or } 0.95} = \$195{,}000 \text{ Sales Price}$$

$195,000 Sales Price is the answer.

How do I determine interest?

Interest is the cost of using money. The amount of interest paid is determined by the agreed-on annual interest rate, the amount of money borrowed (loan amount) or amount of money still owed (loan balance) and the period of time the money is held. When a lender grants a loan for real estate, the loan-to-value ratio is the percentage of the sales price or appraised value, whichever is less, that the lender is willing to lend.

$$\frac{\text{Loan Amount}}{\text{Sales Price or Appraised Value (whichever is less)}} = \text{Loan-to-Value Ratio (LTV)}$$

Sales Price or Appraised Value (whichever is less) × Loan-to-Value Ratio (LTV) = **Loan Amount**

Loan Amount ÷ Loan-To-Value Ratio = **Sales Price** or **Appraised Value** (whichever is less)

Loan Amount ÷ Sales Price or Appraised Value (whichever is less) = **Loan-to-Value Ratio** (LTV)

$$\frac{\text{Annual Interest}}{\text{Loan Amount (Principal)}} = \text{Annual Interest Rate}$$

Loan Amount × Annual Interest Rate = **Annual Interest**

Annual Interest ÷ Annual Interest Rate = **Loan Amount**

Annual Interest ÷ Loan Amount = **Annual Interest Rate**

For Example: A parcel of real estate sold for $335,200. The lender granted a 90 percent loan at 7.5 percent for 30 years. The appraised value on this parcel was $335,500. How much interest is paid to the lender in the first monthly payment?

$$\begin{array}{c|c} \multicolumn{2}{c}{= \$301,680 \text{ Loan Amount}} \\ \hline \$335,200 & 90\% \\ \text{Sales Price} \qquad \times & \text{or } 0.9 \end{array}$$

$$\begin{array}{c|c} \multicolumn{2}{c}{= \$22,626 \text{ Annual Interest}} \\ \hline \$301,680 & 7.5\% \\ \text{Loan Amount} \qquad \times & \text{or } .075 \end{array}$$

$22,626 Annual Interest ÷ 12 Months = $1,885.50 Monthly Interest

$1,885.50 Interest in the First Monthly Payment is the answer.

How do I determine monthly principal and interest payments?

A **loan payment factor** can be used to calculate the monthly principal and interest (PI) payment on a loan. The factor represents the monthly principal and interest payment to amortize a $1,000 loan and is based on the annual interest rate and the term of the loan.

Loan Amount ÷ $1,000 × Loan Payment Factor = **Monthly PI Payment**

Monthly PI Payment ÷ Loan Payment Factor = **Loan Amount**

For Example: If the lender in the above example uses a loan payment factor of $6.99 per $1,000 of loan amount, what will be the monthly PI (principal and interest) payment?

$301,680 Loan Amount ÷ $1,000 × $6.99 = $2,108.74 Monthly PI Payment

$2,108.74 Monthly PI Payment is the answer.

How do I work problems about points?

One **point** equals 1 percent of the loan amount.

$$\frac{\text{Amount for Points}}{\text{Loan Amount} \quad | \quad \text{Points Converted to a Percent}}$$

Loan Amount × Points Converted to a Percent = **Amount for Points**

Amount of Points ÷ Points Converted to a Percent = **Loan Amount**

Amount of Points ÷ Loan Amount = **Points Converted to a Percent**

For Example: The lender will charge 3 ½ loan discount points on an $80,000 loan? What will be the total amount due?

$$\frac{= \$2,800 \text{ for Points}}{\substack{\$80,000 \\ \text{Loan Amount}} \quad \times \quad \substack{3.5\% \\ \text{or } 0.035}}$$

$2,800 for Points is the answer.

How do I determine profit?

A **profit** is made when we sell something for more than we paid for it. If we sell something for less than we paid, we have suffered a **loss**.

Sales Price − Cost = Profit

$$\frac{\text{Profit}}{\text{Cost} \quad | \quad \text{Percent of Profit}}$$

Cost × Percent of Profit = **Profit**

Profit ÷ Percent of Profit = **Cost**

Profit ÷ Cost = **Percent of Profit**

Cost + Profit = Sales Price

$$\frac{\text{Sales Price}}{\text{Cost} \quad | \quad \text{Percent Sold of Cost}}$$
(100% Cost + % Profit = % Sales Price)

Cost × Percent Sold of Cost = **Sales Price**

Sales Price ÷ Percent Sold of Cost = **Cost**

Sales Price ÷ Cost = **Percent Sold of Cost**

For Example: Your home listed for $125,000 and sold for $123,200, which gave you a 10 percent profit over the original cost. What was the original cost?

100% Original Cost + 10% Profit = 110% Sales Price

$$\frac{\$123,200 \text{ Sales Price}}{\begin{array}{c}= \$112,000 \\ \text{Original Cost}\end{array} \Big| \begin{array}{c}110\% \\ \text{or } 1.1\end{array}}$$

$112,000 Original Cost is the answer.

What is the difference between appreciation and depreciation?

Appreciation is increase in value. **Depreciation** is decrease in value. Both are based on the original cost. We only will cover the **straight-line method,** which is what should be used in math problems unless you are told differently. The straight-line method means that the value is increasing (appreciating) or decreasing (depreciating) the same amount each year. The amount of appreciation or depreciation is based on the original cost.

How do I solve appreciation problems?

$$\frac{\text{Annual Appreciation}}{\text{Cost} \Big| \text{Annual Appreciation Rate}}$$

Cost × Annual Appreciation Rate = **Annual Appreciation**

Annual Appreciation ÷ Annual Appreciation Rate = **Cost**

Annual Appreciation ÷ Cost = **Annual Appreciation Rate**

Annual Appreciation Rate × Number of Years = Total Appreciation Rate

100% Cost + Total Appreciation Rate = Today's Value as a Percent

$$\frac{\text{Today's Value (Appreciated Value)}}{\text{Cost} \Big| \text{Today's Value as a Percent}}$$

Cost × Today's Value as a Percent = **Today's Value**

Today's Value ÷ Today's Value as a Percent = **Cost**

Today's Value ÷ Cost = **Today's Value as a Percent**

How do I solve depreciation problems?

$$\frac{\text{Annual Depreciation}}{\text{Cost} \quad | \quad \text{Annual Depreciation Rate}}$$

Cost × Annual Depreciation Rate = **Annual Depreciation**

Annual Depreciation ÷ Annual Depreciation Rate = **Cost**

Annual Depreciation ÷ Cost = **Annual Depreciation Rate**

Annual Depreciation Rate × Number of Years = Total Depreciation Rate

100% Cost − Total Depreciation Rate = Today's Value as a Percent

$$\frac{\text{Today's Value (Depreciated Value)}}{\text{Cost} \quad | \quad \text{Today's Value as a Percent}}$$

Cost × Today's Value as a Percent = **Today's Value**

Today's Value ÷ Today's Value as a Percent = **Cost**

Today's Value ÷ Cost = **Today's Value as a Percent**

For Example: Seven years ago you purchased a piece of real estate for $93,700, including the original cost of the land, which was $6,700. What is the total value of the land today using an appreciation rate of 8 percent per year?

8% Appreciation per Year × 7 Years = 56% Total Appreciation Rate

100% cost + 56% Appreciation = 156% Today's Value

= $10,452 Today's Value

$80,000		156%
Original Cost	×	or 1.56

$10,452 Today's Value is the answer.

For Example: The value of a house without the lot at the end of four years is $132,300. What was the original cost of the house if the yearly rate of depreciation was 2.5 percent?

2.5% depreciation per year x 4 years = 10% total depreciation rate

100% cost − 10% depreciation = 90% today's value

$$\frac{\$132{,}300 \text{ Today's Value}}{= \$147{,}000 \quad | \quad 90\%}$$
$$\text{Original Cost} \qquad \times \qquad \text{or } 0.9$$

$147,000 Original Cost is the answer.

How do I determine value for income-producing properties?

When appraising income-producing property, the value is determined by using the annual net operating income (NOI) and the current market rate of return or capitalization rate. Annual scheduled gross income is adjusted for vacancies and credit losses to arrive at the annual effective gross income. The annual operating expenses are deducted from the annual effective gross income to arrive at the annual NOI.

Annual Scheduled Gross Income – Vacancies and Credit Losses = Annual Effective Gross Income

Annual Effective Gross Income – Annual Operating Expenses = Annual NOI

$$\frac{\text{Annual NOI}}{\text{Value} \quad | \quad \begin{array}{c}\text{Annual Rate of Return}\\ \text{or Annual Capitalization Rate}\end{array}}$$

Annual NOI ÷ Annual Rate of Return = **Value**

Value × Annual Rate of Return = **Annual NOI**

Annual NOI ÷ Value = **Annual Rate of Return**

For Example: An office building produces $132,600 annual gross income. If the annual expenses are $30,600 and the appraiser estimates the value using an 8.5 percent rate of return, what is the estimated value?

$132,600 Annual Gross Income – $30,600 Annual Expenses =

$102,000 Annual NOI

$$\frac{\$102{,}000 \text{ Annual NOI}}{= \$1{,}200{,}000 \text{ Value} \quad | \quad 8.5\%}$$
$$\text{or } .085$$

$1,200,000 Value is the answer.

The above formulas also can be used for investment problems. The total becomes *original cost* or *investment* instead of value.

For Example: You invest $335,000 in a property that should produce a 9 percent rate of return. What monthly NOI will you receive?

$$\frac{= \$30,150 \text{ Annual NOI}}{\underset{\text{Investment}}{\$335,000} \quad \times \quad \underset{\text{or } 0.09}{9\%}}$$

$30,150 Annual NOI ÷ 12 Months = $2,512.50

$2,512.50 Monthly NOI is the answer.

How do I solve problems involving percentage leases?

When establishing the rent to be charged in a lease for retail space, the lease may be a **percentage lease** instead of a lease based on dollars per square foot. In the percentage lease, there is normally a base or minimum monthly rent plus a percentage of the gross sales in excess of an amount set in the lease. The percentage lease also can be set up as a percentage of the total gross sales or of the base/minimum rent, whichever is larger. We shall look at the minimum plus percentage lease only.

Gross Sales – Gross Sales Not Subject to the Percentage = Gross Sales Subject to the Percentage

$$\frac{\text{Percentage Rent}}{\underset{\text{to the Percentage}}{\text{Gross Sales Subject}} \quad \text{\% in the Lease}}$$

Gross Sales Subject to the Percentage × % in the Lease = **Percentage Rent**

Percentage Rent ÷ % in the Lease = **Gross Sales Subject to the Percentage**

Percentage Rent ÷ Gross Sales Subject to the Percentage = **% in the Lease**

Percentage Rent + Base/Minimum Rent = Total Rent

For Example: A lease calls for monthly minimum rent of $900 plus 3 percent of annual gross sales in excess of $270,000. What was the annual rent in a year when the annual gross sales were $350,600?

$900 Monthly Minimum Rent × 12 Months = $10,800 Annual Minimum Rent

$350,600 Annual Gross Sales − $270,000 Annual Gross Sales Not Subject to the Percentage = $80,600 Annual Gross Sales Subject to the Percentage

=$2,418 Annual Percentage Rent

| $80,600 Annual Gross Sales | | 3% |
| Subject to the Percentage × | | or 0.03 |

$10,800 Annual Minimum Rent + $2,418 Annual Percentage Rent = $13,218

CHAPTER 4

Measurement Problems

What are linear measurements?

Linear measurement is line measurement. When the terms

- *per foot,*
- *per linear foot,*
- *per running foot* or
- *per front foot*

are used, you are being asked to determine the *total length* of the object whether measured in a straight line, crooked line or curved line.

What does the phrase "front foot" refer to?

When the term *per front foot* is used, you are dealing with the number of units on the **frontage** of a lot. The frontage is normally the street frontage, but it could be the water frontage if the lot is on a river, lake or ocean. If two dimensions are given for a tract of land, the first dimension given is the frontage if the dimensions are not labeled.

How do I convert one kind of linear measurement to another?

$$12 \text{ inches} = 1 \text{ foot}$$
$$\text{Inches} \div 12 = \text{Feet}$$
$$\text{Feet} \times 12 = \text{Inches}$$

$$36 \text{ inches} = 1 \text{ yard}$$
$$\text{Inches} \div 36 = \text{Yards}$$
$$\text{Yards} \times 36 = \text{Feet}$$

$$3 \text{ feet} = 1 \text{ yard}$$
$$\text{Feet} \div 3 = \text{Yards}$$
$$\text{Yards} \times 3 = \text{Feet}$$

$$5,280 \text{ feet} = 1 \text{ mile}$$
$$\text{Feet} \div 5,280 = \text{Miles}$$
$$\text{Miles} \times 5,280 = \text{Feet}$$

$$16\frac{1}{2} \text{ feet} = 1 \text{ rod}$$
$$\text{Feet} \div 16.5 = \text{Rods}$$
$$\text{Rods} \times 16.5 = \text{Feet}$$

$$320 \text{ rods} = 1 \text{ mile}$$
$$\text{Rods} \div 320 = \text{Miles}$$
$$\text{Miles} \times 320 = \text{Rods}$$

For Example: A rectangular lot is 50 feet × 150 feet. The cost to fence this lot is priced per linear/running foot. How many linear/running feet will be used to calculate the price of the fence?

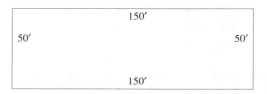

50 Feet + 150 Feet + 50 Feet + 150 Feet = 400 Linear/Running Feet

400 Linear/Running Feet is the answer.

For Example: A parcel of land that fronts on Interstate 45 in Houston, Texas, is for sale at $5,000 per front foot. What will it cost to purchase this parcel of land if the dimensions are 150′ by 100′?

150′ is the frontage because it is the first dimension given.

150 Front Feet × $5,000 = $750,000 Cost

$750,000 Cost is the answer.

How do I solve for area measurement?

Area is the two-dimensional surface of an object. Area is quoted in *square units* or in *acres*. We will look at calculating the area of squares, rectangles and triangles. Squares and rectangles are four-sided objects. All four sides of a square are the same. Opposite sides of a rectangle are the same. A triangle is a three-sided object. The three sides of a triangle can be the same dimension or three different dimensions.

> **MATH TIP:** When two dimensions are given, we assume it to be a rectangle unless told otherwise.

How do I convert one kind of area measurement to another?

144 square inches = 1 square foot
Square Inches ÷ 144 = Square Feet
Square Feet × 144 = Square Inches

1,296 square inches = 1 square yard
Square Inches ÷ 1,296 = Square Yards
Square Yards × 1,296 = Square Inches

9 square feet = 1 square yard
Square Feet ÷ 9 = Square Yards
Square Yards × 9 = Square Feet

43,560 square feet = 1 acre
Square Feet ÷ 43,560 = Acres
Acres × 43,560 = Square Feet

640 acres = 1 section = 1 square mile
Acres ÷ 640 = Sections (Square Miles)
Sections (Square Miles) × 640 = Acres

How do I determine the area of a square or rectangle?

FORMULA: LENGTH × WIDTH = AREA OF A SQUARE OR RECTANGLE

For Example: How many square feet are in a room 15′6″× 30′9″?

$$6'' \div 12 = 0.5' + 15' = 15.5' \text{ wide}$$

$$9'' \div 12 = 0.75' + 30' = 30.75' \text{ long}$$

$$30.75' \times 15.5' = 476.625 \text{ Square Feet}$$

476.625 Square Feet is the answer.

For Example: If carpet costs $63 per square yard to install, what would it cost to carpet the room in the previous example?

476.625 Square Feet ÷ 9 = 52.958333 Square Yards × $63 per Square Yard = $3,336.375 or $3,336.38 rounded

3,336.38 Carpet Cost is the answer.

For Example: How many acres are there in a parcel of land that measures 450′ × 484′?

484′ × 450′ = 217,800 Square Feet ÷ 43,560 = 5 Acres

5 Acres of Land is the answer.

How do I determine the area of a triangle?

FORMULA: **½ Base × Height = Area of a Triangle**

or

Base × Height ÷ 2 = Area of a Triangle

For Example: How many square feet are contained in a triangular parcel of land that is 400 feet on the base and 200 feet high?

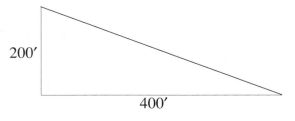

400′ × 200′ ÷ 2 = 40,000 Square Feet

40,000 Square Feet is the answer.

For Example: How many acres are in a three-sided tract of land that is 300′ on the base and 400′ high?

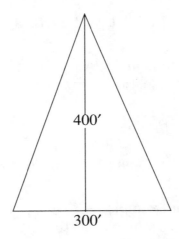

300′ × 400′ ÷ 2 = 60,000 Square Feet ÷ 43,560 = 1.377 Acres

1.377 Acres is the answer.

How do I solve for volume?

Volume is the space inside a three-dimensional object. Volume is quoted in *cubic units*. We will look at calculating the volume of boxes and triangular prisms.

How do I convert from one kind of volume measurement to another?

1,728 cubic inches = 1 cubic foot
   Cubic Inches ÷ 1,728 = Cubic Feet
   Cubic Feet × 1,728 = Cubic Inches

46,656 cubic inches = 1 cubic yard
   Cubic Inches ÷ 46,656 = Cubic Yards
   Cubic Yards × 46,656 = Cubic Inches

27 cubic feet = 1 cubic yard
   Cubic Feet ÷ 27 = Cubic Yards
   Cubic Yards × 27 = Cubic Feet

How do I determine the volume of a room?

For purposes of determining volume, think of a room as if it were a box.

FORMULA: Length × Width × Height = Volume of a Box

For Example: A building is 500 feet long, 400 feet wide and 25 feet high. How many cubic feet of space are in this building?

500′ × 400′ × 25′ = 5,000,000 Cubic Feet

5,000,000 Cubic Feet is the answer.

For Example: How many cubic yards of concrete would it take to build a sidewalk measuring 120 feet long; 2 feet, 6 inches wide; and 3 inches thick?

6″ ÷ 12 = .5′ + 2′ = 2.5′ Wide

3″ ÷ 12 = .25′ Thick

120′ 2.5′ × .25′ = 75 Cubic Feet ÷ 27 = 2.778 Cubic Yards (rounded)

2.778 Cubic Yards is the answer.

How do I determine the volume of a triangular prism?

The terms *A-frame*, *A-shaped* or *gable roof* on an exam describe a triangular prism.

FORMULA: ½ Base × Height × Width = Volume of a Triangular Prism

or

Base × Height × Width ÷ 2 = Volume of a Triangular Prism

For Example: An A-frame cabin in the mountains is 50 feet long and 30 feet wide. The cabin is 25 feet high from the base to the highest point. How many cubic feet of space does this A-frame cabin contain?

50 ′ × 30′ × 25′ ÷ 2 = 18,750 Cubic Feet

18,750 Cubic Feet is the answer.

497
MATH FAQs

For Example: A building is 40 feet by 25 feet with a 10-foot-high ceiling. The building has a gable roof that is 8 feet high at the tallest point. How many cubic feet are in this structure, including the roof?

40′ × 25′ × 10′ = 10,000 Cubic Feet in the Building

40′ × 25′ × 8′ ÷ 2 = 4,000 Cubic Feet in the Gable Roof

10,000 Cubic Feet + 4,000 Cubic Feet = 14,000 Total Cubic Feet

14,000 Cubic Feet is the answer.

CHAPTER 5

Proration Problems

Prorate means to divide proportionately. Some expenses and income may be prorated for the closing of a real estate transaction. We will look at prorating interest on a loan, ad valorem taxes on a property, homeowner's insurance on a property and rent on income-producing property.

What are the different calendars used for prorating?

When we prorate, we calculate the number of days owed for the expense or the rental income. The days may be calculated using a *banker's year, statutory year* or *calendar year*. The **banker's year** and **statutory year** are the same because they both contain 12 months with 30 days in each month. The total number of days in both a banker's year and a statutory year is 360 days. The **calendar year** contains 12 months with 28 to 31 days in each month. The total number of days in a calendar year is 365 days. The total number of days in a calendar *leap* year is 366 days. The following shows the days in each month.

	Banker's or Statutory Year	Calendar Year	Calendar Leap Year
January	30	31	31
February	30	28	29
March	30	31	31
April	30	30	30
May	30	31	31
June	30	30	30
July	30	31	31
August	30	31	31
September	30	30	30
October	30	31	31
November	30	30	30
December	30	31	31
Total days in year	360	365	366

What is the difference between prorating "through" and prorating "to" the day of closing?

In a proration problem, we will be told whether to prorate *through* the day of closing or *to* the day of closing. **This is very important when calculating the days owed.** When we prorate *through* the day of closing, the *seller* is responsible for the day of closing. When we prorate *to* the day of closing, the *buyer* is responsible for the day of closing.

How do I calculate proration problems?

Once we know the number of days owed, we then need to know the amount of the expense or income per day. We take either the annual amount divided by the total days in the year to get the daily amount or the monthly amount divided by the total days in the month to get the daily amount.

> **MATH TIP:** Be sure you are using the correct type of year (banker's or statutory year, calendar year, calendar leap year) when computing the daily amount.

The final step is to multiply the amount per day by the number of days owed to get the prorated amount.

What is the difference between "debit" and "credit" in a proration problem?

To calculate a proration problem, you need to know how expenses and income are posted on the closing statement. **Debit** takes money from a person. **Credit** gives money to a person. (See Figure 4.) When the prorated amount involves both the buyer and the seller, there always will be a double entry. If the seller owes the buyer, the prorated amount will be debited to the seller and credited to the buyer. If the buyer owes the seller, the prorated amount will be debited to the buyer and credited to the seller. When the prorated amount involves the buyer and someone other than the seller, there will be only a single entry. When the prorated amount involves the seller and someone other than the buyer, there will be only a single entry. We will discuss debits and credits as we learn to prorate each expense.

MATH FAQs

Figure 4.1   *The Debit/Credit Flow*

How do I calculate interest in a proration problem?

When a loan is assumed or paid off, the interest for the month of closing must be prorated. Interest is paid in arrears; therefore, the monthly payment made on the first day of the month pays interest for the entire previous month. The payment includes interest *up to but not including* the day of the payment unless specified otherwise. Not all payments are due on the first day of the month; therefore, pay attention when you are told what day the interest has been paid through. The sellers owe unpaid interest for the period of time they occupy the home. If the prorations are to be calculated *through* the day of closing, the seller will owe payments *including* the day of closing. If the prorations are to be calculated *to* the day of closing, the seller will owe *up to but not including* the day of closing. Remember to use the correct type of year. A banker's or statutory year has 360 days. A calendar year has 365 days. A calendar leap year has 366 days. On an assumption of the loan, the interest proration is a **debit** to the *seller* and a **credit** to the *buyer*. When a loan is paid off, unpaid interest is calculated and added to the outstanding loan balance and is a **debit** *to the seller only.*

For Example: A home was purchased on April 4, 1999, for $110,000, and the closing was set for May 8, 1999. The buyer assumed the balance of the seller's $93,600 loan with 11.5 percent interest and monthly payments of $990.29 due on the first day of each month. How much will the interest proration be, using a banker's year and prorating through the day of closing? Who will be debited and who will be credited?

Banker's Year/Statutory Year

Step 1. Find the exact number of days of earned or accrued interest.

Seller owes 8 days (May 1 *through* May 8).

Note: It would be 7 days (8 days minus 1 day) if the problem had said prorate *to* the day of closing.

Step 2. Find the daily interest charge. Outstanding Loan Balance × Annual Interest Rate = Annual Interest ÷ 360 Days per Year = Daily Interest.

$93,600 x 11.5% = $10,764 Annual Interest ÷ 360 Days = $29.90 Daily Interest

Step 3. Compute the total amount of accrued interest. Daily Interest × Days Owed = Interest Proration.

$29.90 Daily Interest × 8 Days = $239.20s

$239.20 Debit Seller, Credit Buyer is the answer.

Calendar Year (if the problem had said to use a calendar year)

Step 1. Find the exact number of days of earned or accrued interest.

Seller owes 8 days (May 1 *through* May 8).

Note: It would be 7 days (8 days minus 1 day) if the problem had said prorate *to* the day of closing.

Step 2. Find the daily interest charge. Outstanding Loan Balance × Annual Interest Rate = Annual Interest ÷ 365 Days per Year = Daily Interest.

$93,600 × 11.5% = $10,764 Annual Interest ÷ 365 Days = $29.49041096 Daily Interest

Step 3. Compute the total amount of accrued interest. Daily Interest × Days Owed = Interest Proration.

$29.49041096 Daily Interest × 8 Days = $235.92 Rounded

$235.92 Debit Seller, Credit Buyer is the answer.

How do I prorate taxes?

Real estate taxes are normally assessed from January 1 through December 31. The tax rate is *always* applied *to the assessed value of the property* instead of the market value. Taxes are usually paid in arrears; therefore, the seller will owe the buyer for accrued taxes from January 1 *through* the day of closing or *to* the day of closing. The most recent tax bill is used to compute the proration, and this is usually the past year's tax bill. Remember to use the correct type of year. A banker's or statutory year has 360 days. A calendar year has 365 days. A calendar leap year has 366 days. The tax proration will be a **debit** to the *seller* and a **credit** to the *buyer*.

> **For Example:** The market value of a home is $115,000. For tax purposes, the home is assessed at 90 percent of the market value. The annual tax rate is $2.50 per $100 of assessed value. If the closing is on March 13, 1999, what is the prorated amount? Prorations are calculated through the day of closing and using a statutory year.

Bankers Year/Statutory Year

Step 1. Find the exact number of days of accrued taxes from the beginning of the tax period (January 1, 1999) up to and including the day of closing (March 13, 1999).

2 Months (January and February) × 30 Days per Month = 60 Days + 13 Days in March = 73 Days

Note: It would be 72 days (73 days minus 1 day) if the problem had said prorate *to* the day of closing.

Step 2. Calculate the annual taxes. Market Value × Assessment Ratio = Assessed Value ÷ $100 × Tax Rate per Hundred = Annual Taxes.

$115,000 × 90% = $103,500 ÷ $100 × $2.50 = $2,587.50 Annual Taxes

Step 3. Find the tax amount per day. Annual Taxes ÷ 360 days per Year = Daily Taxes.

$2,587.50 ÷ 360 Days = $7.1875 Daily Taxes

Step 4. Compute the prorated tax amount. Daily Taxes × Days Owed = Daily Proration.

$7.1875 per Day   73 Days = $524.69 rounded

$524.69 Debit Seller, Credit Buyer is the answer.

Calendar Year (if the problem had said to use a calendar year)

Step 1. Find the exact number of days of accrued taxes from the beginning of the tax period (January 1, 1999) up to and including the day of closing (March 13, 1999).

31 Days in January + 28 Days in February + 13 Days in March = 72 Days

Note: It would be 71 days (72 days minus 1 day) if the problem had said prorate *to* the day of closing.

Step 2. Calculate the annual taxes. Market Value × Assessment Ratio = Assessed Value ÷ $100 × Tax Rate per Hundred = Annual Taxes.

$115,000 × 90% = $103,500 ÷ $100 × $2.50 = $2,587.50 Annual Taxes

Step 3. Find the tax amount per day. Annual Taxes ÷ 365 Days per Year = Daily Taxes.

$2,587.50 ÷ 365 Days = $7.089041096 Daily Taxes

Step 4. Compute the prorated tax amount. Daily Taxes × Days Owed = Tax Proration.

$7.089041096 per Day × 72 Days = $510.41 rounded

$510.41 Debit Seller, Credit Buyer is the answer.

Is insurance always prorated?

When buying a home, insurance coverage must be provided by the owners if they have a loan. The buyers normally purchase their own insurance policy. There will *not* be a proration if the buyers purchase a new policy because the sellers will cancel their existing policy effective as of the day of closing and the buyer's new policy will become effective as of the day of closing.

If insurance is prorated, how do I do it?

If the insurance company will allow a policy to be assumed and the buyers choose to do so, there will be an insurance proration. Today insurance policies are written for one year. The premiums are payable in advance; therefore, the sellers have paid the entire yearly premium. If the policy is transferred to the buyers, the buyers owe the sellers for the unused portion of the policy. If you are to prorate *through* the day of closing, the buyers owe the sellers from the day after closing until the expiration of the policy. If you are to prorate *to* the day of closing, the buyers owe the sellers starting with the day of closing until the expiration of the policy. Insurance policies become effective at 12:01 AM and expire exactly one year later at 12:01 AM; therefore, no coverage is counted on the day of expiration of the insurance policy. Remember to use the correct type of year. A banker's or statutory year has 360 days. A calendar year has 365 days. A calendar leap year has 366 days. The insurance proration will be a **debit** to the *buyer* and a **credit** to the *seller*.

> *For Example:* A 1-year fire insurance policy expires on August 20, 1999. The total premium for this policy was $425 and was paid in full in 1998. The house was sold and the closing date set for January 25, 1999. The proration is to be calculated through the day of closing using a banker's year. What will be the total credit to the seller to transfer the insurance policy to the buyer?

Banker's Year/Statutory Year

Step 1. Compute the number of days of insurance coverage that the buyer assumed.

```
    30 days in January
 –  25 day of closing
     5 days left in January
+ 180 days (6 months × 30 days per month/February–July)
+   19 days coverage in August
   204 days left on the policy
```

Note: It would be 205 days (204 days plus 1 day) if the problem had said prorate *to* the day of closing.

Step 2. Compute the amount of the policy cost per day. Annual Insurance Premium ÷ 360 Days per Year = Daily Insurance.

$425 Insurance Premium ÷ 360 Days = $1.1805556 Daily Insurance

Step 3. Calculate what the buyer owes. Daily Insurance × Days Left on the Policy = Insurance Proration.

$1.1805556 Daily Insurance × 204 Days = $240.83 rounded

$240.83 Credit Seller, Debit Buyer is the answer.

Calendar Year (if the problem had said to use a calendar year)

Step 1. Compute the number of days of insurance coverage that the buyer assumed.

```
    31 days in January
 –  25 day of closing
     6 days left in January
+   28 days in February
+   31 days in March
+   30 days in April
+   31 days in May
+   30 days in June
+   31 days in July
+   19 days coverage in August
   206 days left on the policy
```

Note: It would be 207 days (206 days plus 1 day) if the problem had said prorate *to* the day of closing.

Step 2. Compute the amount of the policy cost per day. Annual Insurance Premium ÷ 365 Days per Year = Daily Insurance.

$425 Insurance Premium ÷ 365 Days = $1.1643836 Daily Insurance

Step 3. Calculate what the buyer owes. Daily Insurance × Days Left on the Policy = Insurance Proration.

$1.1643836 Daily Insurance × 206 Days = $239.86 rounded

$239.86 Credit Seller, Debit Buyer is the answer.

How do I prorate rent?

When prorating rents, the amount of rent collected for the month of closing is the only amount prorated. The seller owes the buyer for the unearned rent starting with the day after closing through the end of the month if you are prorating *through* the day of closing. The seller owes the buyer for the unearned rent starting with the day of closing through the end of the month if you are prorating *to* the day of closing. If security deposits are being held by the seller, they are not prorated; therefore, the entire amount of security deposits are transferred to the buyer. Always use the actual number of days in the month of closing for rent prorations unless you are told differently. Both the rent proration and the security deposit will be a **debit** to the *seller* and a **credit** to the *buyer*.

> **For Example:** Bob is purchasing an apartment complex that contains 15 units that rent for $450 per month. A $450 security deposit is being held on each unit. The sale is to be closed on March 14, and the March rent has been received for all 15 units. Compute the rent proration by prorating through the day of closing. Compute the security deposit.

Calendar Days (remember to use actual days in the month unless specified differently)

Step 1. Compute the unearned days of rent for the month of closing.

$$
\begin{array}{r}
31 \text{ days in March} \\
- \ 14 \text{ day of closing} \\
\hline
17 \text{ days of unearned rent}
\end{array}
$$

Note: It would be 18 days (17 days plus 1 day) if the problem had said prorate *to* the day of closing.

Step 2. Compute the daily rent. Monthly Rent × Number of Units Paid = Total Rent Collected ÷ Number of Actual Days in the Month of Closing = Daily Rent.

$450 × 15 Units = $6,750 Monthly Rent Collected ÷ 31 Days in March = $217.7419355 Daily Rent

Step 3. Compute the prorated rent amount. Daily Rent × Days of Unearned Rent.

$217.7419355 Daily Rent × 17 Days = $3,701.61 rounded

Step 4. Compute the security deposit.

$450 per Unit × 15 Units = $6,750

$3,701.61 Rent Proration and **$6,750 Security Deposit** are the answers. They are both **Debit Seller and Credit Buyer.**

REAL ESTATE MATH PRACTICE PROBLEMS

1. The value of your house, not including the lot, is $91,000 today. What was the original cost if it has depreciated 5 percent per year for the past seven years?
   a. $67,407.41   c. $122,850.00
   b. $95,789.47   d. $140,000.00

2. What was the price per front foot for a 100′ × 125′ lot that sold for $125,000?
   a. $1,250   c. $556
   b. $1,000   d. $10

3. If the savings and loan gives you a 90 percent loan on a house valued at $88,500, how much additional cash must you produce as a down payment if you have already paid $4,500 in earnest money?
   a. $3,500   c. $4,350
   b. $4.000   d. $8,850

4. What did the owners originally pay for their home if they sold it for $98,672, which gave them a 12 percent profit over their original cost?
   a. $86.830   c. $89,700
   b. $88,100   d. $110,510

5. What would you pay for a building producing $11,250 annual net income and showing a minimum rate of return of 9 percent?
   a. $125,000   c. $101,250
   b. $123,626   d. $122,625

6. The sale of Mrs. Gates's home is to close on September 28. Included in the sale is a garage apartment that is rented to Sandy Dart for $350 per month. Sandy has paid the September rent. What is the rent proration, using actual days and prorating through the day of closing?
   a. $325.67   c. $350.00
   b. $23.33   d. $175.00

7. What is the total cost of a driveway 15′ wide, 40′ long and 4″ thick if the concrete costs $60.00 per cubic yard and the labor costs $1.25 per square foot?
   a. $527.25   c. $1,194.00
   b. $693.75   d. $1,581.75

8. An owner agrees to list his property on the condition that he will receive at least $47,300 after paying a 5 percent broker's commission and paying $1,150 in closing costs. At what price must it sell?
   a. $48,450   c. $50,875
   b. $50,815   d. $51,000

9. The Loving Gift Shop pays rent of $600 per month plus 2.5 percent of gross annual sales in excess of $50,000. What was the average monthly rent last year if gross annual sales were $75,000?
   a. $1,125.00   c. $600.00
   b. $756.25   d. $652.08

10. If your monthly rent is $525, what percent would this be of an annual income of $21,000?
    a. $25%   c. $33⅓%
    b. $30%   d. $40%

11. Two brokers split the 6 percent commission equally on a $73,000 home. The selling salesperson, Joe, was paid 70 percent of his broker's share. The listing salesperson, Janice, was paid 30 percent of her broker's share. How much did Janice receive?
    a. $657   c. $1,533
    b. $4,380   d. $1,314

12. Find the number of square feet in a lot with a frontage of 75 feet, 6 inches, and a depth of 140 feet, 9 inches.
    a. 10,626.63   c. 216.25
    b. 10,652.04   d. 25,510.81

13. You must attempt to appraise a 28-unit apartment house, employing the income approach. You discover that each unit rents for $775 a month, an amount that seems consistent with like rental units in the vicinity. For the past five years the annual expenses of operation have averaged $82,460. The complex has maintained a consistent occupancy rate of 95%. A potential investor is only interested if the return is 9.5 percent. What value would you arrive at using these variables?
a. $2,741,100   c. $1,736,000
b. $868,000   d. $1,873,100

14. How much interest will the seller owe the buyer for a closing date of August 10 if the outstanding loan balance is $43,580? The interest rate on this assumable loan is 10½ percent and the last payment was paid on August 1. Prorations are to be done through the day of closing and using a statutory year.
a. $127.11   c. $125.37
b. $254.22   d. $381.33

15. The buyer has agreed to pay $175,000 in sales price, 2.5 loan discount points and a 1 percent origination fee. If the buyer receives a 90 percent loan-to-value ratio, how much will the buyer owe at closing for points and the origination fee?
a. $1,575.00   c. $5,512.50
b. $3,937.50   d. $6,125.00

16. Calculate eight months' interest on a $5,000 interest-only loan at 9½ percent.
a. $475.00   c. $237.50
b. $316.67   d. $39.58

17. A 100-acre farm is divided into lots for homes. The streets require 1/8 of the whole farm, and there are 140 lots. How many square feet are in each lot?
a. 43,560   c. 31,114
b. 35,004   d. 27,225

18. The 1999 tax bill on the Burnses' home was $1,282 and was paid in December 1999. The Burnses' have sold their home and will close on April 23, 2000. How much will the tax proration be, using a calendar year and prorating to the day of closing?
a. 393.38   c. 396.89
b. 402.41   d. 427.33

19. What is the monthly net income on an investment of $115,000 if the rate of return is 12½ percent?
a. $1,150.00   c. $7,666.67
b. $1,197.92   d. $14,375.00

20. A salesperson sells a property for $58,500. The contract he has with his broker is 40% of the full commission earned. The com-mission due the broker is 6 percent. What is the salesperson's share of the commission?
a. $2,106   c. $3,510
b. $1,404   d. $2,340

21. Vicki buys 348,480 square feet of land at $0.75 per square foot. She divides the land into ½ acre lots. If she keeps three lots for herself and sells the others for $24,125 each, what percent of profit does she realize?
a. 47.4%   c. 20%
b. 32.2%   d. 16.7%

22. $437 was the insurance premium paid in full in 1999 for a one-year insurance policy that expires June 6, 2000. The house is sold and scheduled to close on February 16, 2000 The buyers are assuming the sellers' insurance policy. What is the amount of the insurance proration if a banker's year is used and all prorations are done through the day of closing?
a. $132.31   c. $302.26
b. $134.74   d. $304.69

23. What is the interest rate on a $10,000 loan with semiannual interest of $450?
    a. 7% c. 11%
    b. 9% d. 13.5%

24. A warehouse is 80′ wide and 120′ long with ceilings 14′ high. If 1,200 square feet of floor surface has been partitioned off, floor to ceiling, for an office, how many cubic feet of space will be left in the warehouse?
    a. 151,200 c. 133,200
    b. 134,400 d. 117,600

25. An office building produces $68,580 annual net operating income. What price would you pay for this property to show a minimum return of 12 percent on your investment?
    a. $489,857 c. $685,800
    b. $571,500 d. $768,096

26. A buyer is assuming the balance of a seller's loan. The interest rate is 8 percent and the last monthly payment of $578.16 was paid on April 1, leaving an outstanding balance of $18,450. Using a banker's year, compute the interest to be paid by the seller if the sale is to be closed on April 19. Prorate through the day of closing.
    a. $110.83 c. $77.90
    b. $82.00 d. $123.00

27. The lot you purchased five years ago for $15,000 has appreciated 3½ percent per year. What is it worth today?
    a. $12,375 c. $17,250
    b. $15,525 d. $17,625

28. A lot has a frontage of 100′ and a depth of 150′. If the building line regulations call for a setback of 25′ at the front and 6′ on the two sides, how many square feet of usable space are left for the building?
    a. 10,350 c. 11,750
    b. 11,000 d. 15,000

29. A lease calls for $1,000 per month minimum plus 2 percent of annual sales in excess of $100,000. What is the annual rent if the annual sales were $150,000?
    a. $12,000 c. $14,000
    b. $13,000 d. $15,000

30. The 1998 taxes on Don Mark's home were paid in full and amounted to $1,468. Don sold his home to Chuck Harris and closed the sale on August 29, 1999. What was the pro-rated tax amount using a calendar year if the proration was calculated to the day of closing?
    a. $965.26 c. $970.51
    b. $502.74 d. $497.49

31. There is a tract of land that is 1.25 acres. The lot is 150 feet deep. How much will the lot sell for at $65 per front foot?
    a. $9,750 c. $23,595
    b. $8,125 d. $8,125

32. If the broker received a 6.5 percent commission that was $5,200, what was the sales price of the house?
    a. $80,400 c. $77,200
    b. $80,000 d. $86,600

33. Sue earns $20,000 per year and can qualify for a monthly PITI payment equal to 25 percent of her monthly salary. If the annual tax and insurance is $678.24, what is the loan amount she will qualify for if the monthly PI payment factor is $10.29 per $1,000 of loan amount?
    a. $66,000 c. $40,500
    b. $43,000 d. $35,000

34. Find the cost of building a house 29′ × 34′ × 17′ with a gable roof 8′ high at the highest point. The cost of construction is $2.25 per cubic foot.
    a. $55,462.50 c. $37,714.50
    b. $46,588.50 d. $27,731.25

35. You invest $50,000 at a rate of return of 12 percent. What is the net operating income?
    a. $6,000
    b. $5,600
    c. $5,000
    d. $4,167

36. You pay $65.53 monthly interest on a loan bearing 9¼ percent annual interest. What is the loan amount rounded to the nearest hundred dollars?
    a. $1,400
    b. $2,800
    c. $6,300
    d. $8,500

37. What percentage of profit would you make if you paid $10,500 for a lot, built a home on the lot that cost $93,000 and then sold the lot and house together for $134,550?
    a. 13%
    b. 23%
    c. 30%
    d. 45%

38. You are purchasing a fourplex and going to close on November 4. Each apartment rents for $575 per month. On November 1, one apartment is vacant and the others paid the November rent. Compute the rent proration through the day of closing.
    a. $230.00
    b. $306.67
    c. $1,495.00
    d. $1,993.33

39. An income-producing property has $62,500 annual gross income and monthly expenses of $1,530. What is the appraised value if the appraiser uses a 10 percent capitalization rate?
    a. $441,400
    b. $625,000
    c. $183,600
    d. $609,700

40. A new house and lot cost Mr. Jones $65,000. Of this total price, it was estimated that the lot was worth $13,000. Mr. Jones held the prop-erty for eight years. Using the straight-line method, assuming an annual depreciation of 1 per-cent on the house and an annual increase of 8 percent on the lot, what would be the total value of the property at the end of eight years?
    a. $47,840
    b. $69,160
    c. $81,120
    d. $101,400

41. The seller received a $121,600 check at closing after paying a 7 percent commission, $31,000 in other closing costs and the $135,700 loan payoff. What was the total sales price?
    a. $288,300
    b. $306,300
    c. $308,500
    d. $310,000

42. A fence is being built to enclose a lot 125' by 350'. If there will be one 10' gate, how many running feet of fence will it take?
    a. 465
    b. 600
    c. 940
    d. $960

43. Alfred pays $2,500 each for four parcels of land. He subdivides them into six parcels and sells each of the six parcels for $1,950. What was Alfred's percentage of profit?
    a. 14.5%
    b. 17%
    c. 52%
    d. He lost money.

44. A property sells for $96,000. If it has appreciated 4 percent per year straight line for the past five years, what did the owner pay for the property five years ago?
    a. $76,800
    b. $80,000
    c. $92,300
    d. $115,200

45. Bill earns an annual income of $60,000, and Betty earns $2,400 per month. How much can Bill and Betty pay monthly for their mortgage payment if the lender uses a 28 percent qualifying ratio?
    a. $2,072
    b. $1,400
    c. $2,352
    d. $672

46. If Don borrows $4,400, agreeing to pay back principal and interest in 18 months, what annual interest rate is Don paying if the total payback is $5,588?
    a. 15%
    b. 18%
    c. 21.3%
    d. 27%

47. If you purchase a lot that is 125′ × 150′ for $6,468.75, what price did you pay per front foot?
    a. $23.52   c. $51.75
    b. $43.13   d. $64.69

48. Kelli has been granted a 90 percent loan for $340,500. How much will Kelli's monthly principal and interest payment be, using a loan payment factor of $7.16 per $1,000 of loan?
    a. $2,194.18   c. 2,437.98
    b. $4,755.59   d. $3,064.50

49. Calculate the amount of commission earned by a broker on a property selling for $61,000 if 6 percent is paid on the first $50,000 and 3 percent on the remaining balance.
    a. $3,330   c. $3,600
    b. $3,830   d. $3,930

50. A 50′ × 100′ lot has a 2,400-square-foot house on it that contains four bedrooms and three bathrooms. What percent of the lot is not taken up by the house?
    a. 21%   c. 50%
    b. 48%   d. 52%

ANSWER KEY FOR REAL ESTATE MATHEMATICS PRACTICE PROBLEMS

1. d $140,000.00 original cost
5% Depreciation per Year × 7 Years = 35% Total Depreciation
100% Original Cost − 35% Total Depreciation = 65% Today's Value

$$\frac{\$91,000 \text{ Today's Value}}{= \$140,000 \text{ Original Cost}} \quad \bigg| \quad \frac{65\%}{\text{or } 0.65}$$

2. a $1,250 per front foot
$125,000 Sales Price ÷ 100 Front Feet = **$1,250 per front foot**

3. c $4,350 due at closing
100% Value − 90% LTV = 10% Down Payment

$$\frac{= \$8,850 \text{ Down Payment}}{\$88,500 \text{ Value} \quad \times} \quad \bigg| \quad \frac{10\%}{\text{or } 0.1}$$

$8,850 Down Payment − $4,500 Earnest Money = **$4,350 Due at Closing**

4. b $88,100 original cost
100% Original Cost + 12% Profit = 112% Sales Price

$$\frac{\$98,672 \text{ Sales Price}}{= \$88,100 \text{ Original Cost}} \quad \bigg| \quad \frac{112\%}{\text{or } 1.12}$$

5. a $125,000 price

$$\frac{\$11,250 \text{ Annual Net Income}}{= \$125,000 \text{ Price}} \quad \bigg| \quad \frac{9\%}{\text{or } 0.09}$$

6. b $23.33 rent proration
30 Days in September − 28 Day of Closing = 2 Days Due
$350 Monthly Rent ÷ 30 Days = $11.666667 per Day × 2 Days = **$23.33 Rent Proration**

7. c $1,194.00 total cost
4″ ÷ 12 = 0.333′
Concrete: 40′ × 15′ × 0.333′ = 199.8 Cubic Feet ÷ 27 = 7.4 Cubic Yards × $60 per Cubic Yard = $444
Labor: 40′ × 15′ = 600 Square Feet × $1.25 per Square Foot = $750
$444 Concrete + $750 Labor = **$1,194.00 Total Cost**

8. d $51,000 sales price
$47,300 Net to Seller + $1,150 Closing Costs = $48,450 Net after Commission
100% Sales Price − 5% Commission = 95% Net after Commission

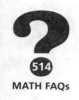

$$\frac{\$48,450 \text{ Net after Commission}}{= \$51,000 \quad | \quad 95\%}$$
Sales Price or 0.95

9. d $652.08 average monthly rent

$75,000 Gross Annual Sales − $50,000 = $25,000 Gross Annual Sales Subject to 2.5%

$$\frac{= \$625 \text{ Annual Percentage Rent}}{\$25,000 \quad | \quad 2.5\%}$$
Gross Annual Sales × or 0.25

$625 Annual Percentage Rent ÷ 12 Months = $52.08 Monthly Percentage Rent
$600 Monthly Minimum Rent + $52.08 Monthly Percentage Rent = **$652.08 Average Monthly Rent**

10. b 30%

$525 Monthly Rent × 12 Months = $6,300 Annual Rent

$$\frac{÷ \$6,300 \text{ Annual Rent}}{\$21,000 \text{ Annual Income} \quad | \quad = 0.3 \text{ or } 30\%}$$

11. a $657 commission to Janice

$$\frac{= \$4,380 \text{ Full Commission}}{\$73,000 \quad | \quad 6\%}$$
Sales Price × .06

$4,380 Full Commission ÷ 2 Brokers = $2,190 Broker's Share of the Commission

$$\frac{= \$657 \text{ Janice's Commission}}{\$2,190 \text{ Broker's Share} \quad | \quad 30\%}$$
of the Commission × .3

12. a 10,626.63 square feet

6″ ÷ 12 = 0.5′ + 75′ = 75.5′ Frontage
9″ ÷ 12 = 0.75′ + 140′ = 140.75′ Depth
140.75′ × 75.5′ = **10,626.63 Square Feet**

13. c $1,736,000 value

$775 Monthly Rent × 28 Units × 12 Months = $260,400 Annual Scheduled Gross Income

$$\frac{= \$247,380 \text{ Annual Effective Gross Income}}{\$260,400 \text{ Annual} \quad | \quad 95\%}$$
Scheduled Gross Income × .95

$247,380 Annual Effective Gross Income − $82,460 Annual Expenses = $164,920 Annual Net Operating Income

$$\dfrac{\$164{,}920 \text{ Annual Net Operating Income} \div}{= \$1{,}736{,}000 \text{ Value}} \quad \begin{array}{l} 9.5\% \\ \text{or } 0.095 \end{array}$$

14. a $127.11 interest due

Seller Owes Buyer 10 Days (August 1 *through* August 10)

$$\dfrac{= \$4{,}575.90 \text{ Annual Interest}}{\$43{,}850 \text{ Loan Balance} \quad \times} \quad \begin{array}{l} 10.5\% \\ 0.105 \end{array}$$

$4,575.90 Annual Interest ÷ 360 Days = $12.71083 per Day × 10 Days = **$127.11 Interest Due**

15. c $5,512.50 for points and the origination fee

2.5 Points Loan Discount + 1 Point Origination Fee = 3.5 Points

$$\dfrac{= \$157{,}500 \text{ Loan}}{\$175{,}000 \text{ Sales Price} \quad \times} \quad \begin{array}{l} 90\% \\ \text{or } 0.9 \end{array}$$

$$\dfrac{= \mathbf{\$5{,}512.50 \text{ for Points}}}{\$157{,}500 \text{ Loan} \quad \times} \quad \begin{array}{l} 3.5\% \\ \text{or } 0.035 \end{array}$$

16. b $316.67 Interest

$$\dfrac{= \$475 \text{ Annual Interest}}{\$5{,}000 \text{ Loan} \quad \times} \quad \begin{array}{l} 9.5\% \\ \text{or } 0.095 \end{array}$$

$475 Annual Interest ÷ 12 Months × 8 Months = **$316.67 Interest**

17. d 27,225 square feet

⅛ = 1 ÷ 8 = 0.125 for Streets
100 Acres × 0.125 = 12.5 Acres for Streets
100 Acres − 12.5 Acres for Streets = 87.5 Acres for Lots × 43,560 = 3,811,500 Square Feet ÷ 140 Lots = **27,225 Square Feet per Lot**

18. a $393.38 Tax Proration

Seller owes the Buyer January 1 *to* April 23

31 January
28 February
31 March
<u>22</u> April
112 Days Due

$1,282 Annual Tax ÷ 365 Days = $3.51233 per Day × 112 Days = **$393.38 Tax Proration**

19. b $1,197.92 monthly net operating income

$$\frac{= \$14,375 \text{ Annual Net Operating Income}}{\$115,000 \text{ Investment} \quad | \quad 12.5\%}$$
$$\times \qquad\qquad \text{or } 0.125$$

$14,375 Annual Net Operating Income ÷ 12 Months = $1,197.92 **Monthly Net Operating Income**

20. b $1,404 salesperson's commission

$$\frac{= \$3,510 \text{ Full Commission}}{\$58,500 \text{ Sales Price} \quad | \quad 6\%}$$
$$\times \qquad\qquad \text{or } 0.06$$

$$\frac{= \textbf{\$1,404 Salesperson's Commission}}{\$3,510 \text{ Full Commission} \quad | \quad 40\%}$$
$$\times \qquad\qquad \text{or } 0.4$$

21. c 20% Profit

348,480 Square Feet × $.75 per Square Foot = $261,360 Cost
348,480 Square Feet ÷ 43,560 = 8 Acres × 2 Lots per Acre = 16 Lots − 3 Lots = 13 Lots Sold × $24,125 Each = $313,625 Total Sales Price
$313,625 Sales Price − $261,360 Cost = $52,265 Profit

$$\frac{÷ \$52,265 \text{ Profit}}{\$261,360 \text{ Cost} \quad | \quad = \textbf{0.199973} \text{ or } \textbf{20\% Profit}}$$

22. a $132.31 insurance proration

```
    30 February
 − 16 Closing Date
    14 Days Left in February
    30 March
    30 April
    30 May
     5 June
   109 Days Due
```

$437 Annual Premium ÷ 360 Days = $1.21389 per Day × 109 Days Due = **$132.31 Insurance Proration**

23. b 9% annual interest rate
$450 × 2 = $900 Annual Interest

$$\frac{\div \ \$900 \ \text{Annual Interest}}{\$10,000 \ \text{Loan}} \quad \Big| \quad = \textbf{0.9 or 9\%}$$

24. d 117,600 cubic feet

120′ × 80′ = 9,600 Square Feet in Building − 1,200 Square Feet for Office = 8,400 Square Feet Left in Warehouse × 14′ Ceiling = **117,600 Cubic Feet** Left in Warehouse

25. b $571,500 price

$$\frac{\$68,580 \ \text{Annual Net Operating Income} \ \div}{= \ \textbf{\$571,500 Price}} \quad \Big| \quad \begin{array}{c} 12\% \\ \text{or } 0.12 \end{array}$$

26. c $77.90 interest proration

Seller owes Buyer 19 Days (April 1 *through* April 19)

$$\frac{= \ \$1,476 \ \text{Annual Interest}}{\$18,450 \ \text{Loan Balance} \qquad \times} \quad \Big| \quad \begin{array}{c} 8\% \\ \text{or } 0.08 \end{array}$$

$1,476 Annual Interest ÷ 360 Days = $4.10 per Day × 19 Days = **$77.90 Interest Proration**

27. d $17,625 today's value

3.5% Appreciation per Year × 5 Years = 17.5% Total Appreciation
100% Cost + 17.5% Total Appreciation = 117.5% Today's Value

$$\frac{= \ \textbf{\$17,625 Today's Value}}{\$15,000 \ \text{Original Cost} \qquad \times} \quad \Big| \quad \begin{array}{c} 117.5\% \\ \text{or } 1.175 \end{array}$$

28. b 11,000 square feet left

150′ Depth − 25′ Setback = 125′ Left
100′ Frontage − 6′ on One Side − 6′ on One Side = 88′ Left
125′ × 88′ = **11,000 Square Feet Left**

29. b $13,000 annual rent

$1,000 Monthly Minimum Rent × 12 Months = $12,000 Annual Minimum Rent
$150,000 Annual Sales − $100,000 = $50,000 Annual Sales Subject to 2%

$$\frac{= \ \$1,000 \ \text{Annual Percentage Rent}}{\begin{array}{c} \$50,000 \ \text{Annual Sales} \\ \text{Subject to 2\%} \qquad \times \end{array}} \quad \Big| \quad \begin{array}{c} 2\% \\ \text{or } 0.02 \end{array}$$

$12,000 Annual Minimum Rent + $1,000 Annual Percentage Rent = **$13,000 Annual Rent**

30. a $965.26 tax proration

Seller owes Buyer January 1 *to* August 29

```
 31 January
 28 February
 31 March
 30 April
 31 May
 30 June
 31 July
 28 August
240 Days Due
```

$1,468 Annual Tax ÷ 365 Days = $4.02192 per Day × 240 Days = **$965.26 Tax Proration**

31. c $23,595 sales price

1.25 Acres × 43,560 = 54,450 Square Feet ÷ 150′ Deep = 363′ Frontage × $65 per Front Foot = **$23,595 Sales Price**

32. b $80,000 sales price

$$\frac{\$5,200 \text{ Full Commission}}{6.5\% \text{ or } 0.065} = \textbf{\$80,000 Sales Price}$$

33. d $35,000 loan

$20,000 Annual Salary ÷12 Months = $1,666.67 Monthly Salary

$$\frac{\$1,666.67 \text{ Monthly Salary}}{25\% \text{ or } 0.25} = \$416.67 \text{ Monthly PITI Payment}$$

$678.24 Annual Tax and Insurance ÷ 12 Months = $56.52 Monthly Tax and Insurance
$416.67 Monthly PITI Payment − $56.52 Monthly TI = $360.15 Monthly PI Payment
$360.15 Monthly PI Payment ÷ $10.29 × $1,000 = **$35,000 Loan**

34. b $46,588.50 cost

29′ × 34′ × 17′ = 16,762 Cubic Feet in House
29′ × 34′ × 8′ ÷ 2 = 3,944 Cubic Feet in Roof
16,762 Cubic Feet + 3,944 Cubic Feet = 20,706 Cubic Feet Total × $2.25 per Cubic Foot = **$46,588.50 Cost**

35. a $6,000 annual net operating income

$$\frac{\$50,000 \text{ Investment}}{12\% \text{ or } 0.12} = \textbf{\$6,000 Annual Net Operating Income}$$

36. d $8,500 Loan

$65.53 Monthly Interest × 12 Months = $786.36 Annual Interest

$$\frac{\$786.36 \ \text{Annual Interest}}{9.25\% \ \text{or} \ 0.0925} = \$8,501.19$$
or **$8,500 Loan**

37. c 30%

$10,500 Cost of Lot + $93,000 Cost of Home = $103,500 Total Cost

$134,550 Sales Price − $103,500 Total Cost = $31,050 Profit

$$\frac{\div \ \$31,050 \ \text{Profit}}{\$103,500 \ \text{Total Cost}} = \textbf{0.3 or 30\%}$$

38. c $1,495.00 rent proration

   30 November
 − 4 Day of Closing
   26 Days Due

$575 Monthly Rent × 3 Units = $1,725 Monthly Rent ÷ 30 Days = $57.50 per Day × 26 Days = **$1,495 Rent Proration**

39. a $441,400 value

$1,530 Monthly Expenses × 12 Months = $18,360 Annual Expenses

$62,500 Annual Gross Income − $18,360 Annual Expenses = $44,140 Annual Net Operating Income

$$\frac{\$44,140 \ \text{Annual Net Operating Income} \div}{10\% \ \text{or} \ 0.1} = \textbf{\$441,400 Value}$$

40. b $69,160 property value

$65,000 Cost of House and Lot − $13,000 Cost of Lot = $52,000 Cost of House

Lot:
8% Annual Appreciation × 8 Years = 64% Total Appreciation
100% Cost + 64% Total Appreciation = 164% Today's Value

$$\frac{= \$21,320 \ \text{Today's Value of Lot}}{\$13,000 \ \text{Cost of Lot} \quad | \quad 164\% \ \text{or} \ 1.64}$$

House:
1% Annual Depreciation × 8 Years = 8% Total Depreciation
100% Cost − 8% Total Depreciation = 92% Today's Value

$$\frac{= \$47,840 \ \text{Today's Value of House}}{\$52,000 \ \text{Cost of House} \quad | \quad 92\% \ \text{or} \ 0.92}$$

$21,320 Lot + $47,840 House = **$69,160 Property Value**

41. d $310,000 sales price

$121,600 Seller's Net + $31,000 Closing Costs + $135,700 Loan Payoff = $288,300 Net after Commission

100% Sales Price − 7% Commission = 93% Net after Commission

$$\frac{\$288,300 \text{ Net after Commission} \div}{93\% \text{ or } 0.93} = \$310,000 \text{ Sales Price}$$

42. c 940 running feet

125′ + 350′ + 125′ + 350′ − 10′ Gate = **940 Running Feet**

43. b 17% profit

$2,500 Cost × 4 Parcels = $10,000 Total Cost
$1,950 Sales Price × 6 Parcels = $11,700 Sales Price
$11,700 Sales Price − $10,000 Cost = $1,700 Profit

$$\frac{\div \$1,700 \text{ Profit}}{\$10,000 \text{ Cost}} = \textbf{0.17 or 17\% Profit}$$

44. b $80,000 original cost

4% Annual Appreciation × 5 Years = 20% Total Appreciation
100% Cost + 20% Total Appreciation = 120% Today's Value

$$\frac{\$96,000 \text{ Today's Value} \div}{120\% \quad 1.2} = \$80,000 \text{ Original Cost}$$

45. a $2,072 monthly payment

$60,000 Annual Salary ÷ 12 Months = $5,000 Bill's Monthly Salary + $2,400 Betty's Monthly Salary = $7,400 Total Monthly Salary

$$\frac{= \$2,072 \text{ Monthly Payment}}{\$7,400 \text{ Total Monthly Salary} \times 28\% \text{ or } 0.28}$$

46. b 18% annual interest rate

$5,588 Payback (Principal + Interest) − $4,400 Loan (Principal) = $1,188 Interest for 18 Months ÷ 18 Months = $66 Monthly Interest × 12 Months = $792 Annual Interest

$$\frac{\div \$792 \text{ Annual Interest}}{\$4,400 \text{ Loan}} = \textbf{0.18 or 18\% Annual Interest Rate}$$

47. c $51.75 per front foot

$6,468.75 Price ÷ 125 Front Feet = **$51.75 per Front Foot**

48. c $2,437.98 monthly principal and interest payment

$340,500 Loan ÷ $1,000 × $7.16 = **$2,437.98 Monthly Principal and Interest Payment**

49. a $3,330 total commission

$$\frac{= \$3,000 \text{ Commission}}{\$50,000 \text{ Sales Price} \quad \underset{\times}{\big|} \quad \begin{matrix} 6\% \\ \text{or } 0.06 \end{matrix}}$$

$61,000 Total Sales Price − $50,000 Sales Price at 6% = $11,000 Sales Price at 3%

$$\frac{= \$330 \text{ Commission}}{\$11,000 \text{ Sales Price} \quad \underset{\times}{\big|} \quad \begin{matrix} 3\% \\ \text{or } 0.03 \end{matrix}}$$

$3,000 Commission + $330 Commission = **$3,330 Total Commission**

50. d 52% not taken up by house

50′ × 100′ = 5,000 Square Feet of Lot − 2,400 Square Feet of House = 2,600 Square Feet Not Taken up by House

$$\frac{\div 2,600 \text{ Square Feet}}{5,000 \text{ Square Feet Total} \quad \underset{\times}{\big|} \quad \begin{matrix} = 0.52 \text{ or } \textbf{52\% Not Taken} \\ \textbf{up by House} \end{matrix}}$$

Glossary of Real Estate Terms

abstract of title The condensed history of a title to a particular parcel of real estate, consisting of a summary of the original grant and all subsequent conveyances and encumbrances affecting the property and a certification by the abstractor that the history is complete and accurate.

acceleration clause The clause in a mortgage or trust deed that can be enforced to make the entire debt due immediately if the mortgagor defaults on an installment payment or other covenant.

accession Acquiring title to additions or improvements to real property as a result of the annexation of fixtures or the accretion of alluvial deposits along the banks of streams.

accrued interest The amount of interest that is due for the period of time since interest was last paid.

accrued items On a closing statement, expense items that are incurred but not yet payable, such as interest on a mortgage loan or taxes on real property.

acknowledgment A formal declaration made before a duly authorized officer, usually a notary public, by a person who has signed a document.

acre A measure of land equal to 43,560 square feet, 4,840 square yards, 4,047 square meters, 160 square rods, or 0.4047 hectares.

actual eviction The result of legal action, originated by a lessor, whereby a defaulted tenant is physically ousted from the rented property pursuant to a court order. (*See also* eviction.)

actual notice Express information or fact; that which is known; direct knowledge.

adjustable-rate mortgage (ARM) A loan characterized by a fluctuating interest rate, usually one tied to a bank or savings and loan association cost-of-funds index.

adjusted basis *See* basis.

ad valorem tax A tax levied according to value; generally used to refer to real estate tax. Also called the *general tax*.

adverse possession The actual, visible, hostile, notorious, exclusive and continuous possession of another's land under a claim of title. Possession for a statutory period may be a means of acquiring title.

agency The relationship between a principal and an agent, wherein the agent is authorized to represent the principal in certain transactions.

agency coupled with an interest An agency relationship in which the agent is given an estate or interest in the subject of the agency (the property).

agent One who acts or has the power to act for another. A fiduciary relationship is created under the *law of agency* when a principal authorizes a licensed real estate broker to be his or her agent.

agreement of sale An offer to purchase that has been accepted by the seller and has become a binding contract.

air lot A designated airspace over a piece of land. An air lot, just as surface property, may be transferred.

air rights The right to use the open space above a property, generally allowing the surface to be used for another purpose.

alienation The act of transferring property to another. Alienation may be voluntary, such as by gift or sale, or involuntary, such as through eminent domain or adverse possession.

alienation clause The clause in a mortgage that states that the balance of the secured debt becomes immediately due and payable at the mortgagee's option if the property is sold by the mortgagor. In effect, this clause prevents the mortgagor from assigning the debt without the mortgagee's approval.

allodial system A system of land ownership in which land is held free and clear of any rent or service due to the government; commonly contrasted with the feudal system. Land is held under the allodial system in the United States.

amenities Features, tangible and intangible, that enhance the value or desirability of real estate.

amortized loan A loan in which the principal as well as the interest is payable in monthly or other periodic installments over the term of the loan.

annual percentage rate The relationship of the total finance charges associated with a loan. This must be disclosed to borrowers by lenders under the Truth-in-Lending Act.

anticipation The appraisal principle that holds that value can increase or decrease based on the expectation of some future benefit or detriment produced by the property.

antitrust laws Laws designed to preserve the free enterprise of the open marketplace by making illegal certain private conspiracies and combinations formed to minimize competition. Violations of antitrust laws in the real estate business generally involve either *price fixing* (brokers conspiring to set fixed compensation rates) or *allocation of customers or markets* (brokers agreeing to limit their areas of trade or dealing to certain areas or properties).

apportionment clause Clause in an insurance policy providing that if the insured is covered by more than one policy, any payments will be apportioned according to the amount of coverage.

appraisal An estimate of the quantity, quality, or value of something. The process through which conclusions of property value are obtained; also refers to the report that sets forth the process of estimation and conclusion of value.

appreciation An increase in the worth or value of a property due to economic or related causes, which may prove to be either temporary or permanent; opposite of depreciation.

appurtenance A right, privilege or improvement belonging to, and passing with, the land.

appurtenant easement An easement that is annexed to the ownership of one parcel and allows the owner the use of the neighbor's land.

assemblage The combining of two or more adjoining lots into one larger tract to increase their total value.

assessment The imposition of a tax, charge or levy, usually according to established rates.

assignment The transfer in writing of interest in a bond, mortgage, lease or other instrument.

associate broker A person licensed as a real estate broker who chooses to work under the supervision of another broker.

assumption of mortgage Acquiring title to property on which there is an existing mortgage and agreeing to be personally liable for the terms and conditions of the mortgage, including payments.

attachment The act of taking a person's property into legal custody by writ or other judicial order to hold it available for application to that person's debt to a creditor.

attorney's opinion of title An abstract of title that an attorney has examined and has certified to be, in his or her opinion, an accurate statement of the facts concerning the property ownership.

automatic renewal A clause in a listing agreement that states that the agreement will continue automatically for a certain period of time after its expiration date. In many states, use of this clause is discouraged; in Pennsylvania it is prohibited.

avulsion The sudden tearing away of land, as by earthquake, flood, volcanic action or the sudden change in the course of a stream.

balance The appraisal principle that states that the greatest value in a property will occur when the type and size of the improvements are proportional to each other as well as the land.

balloon payment A final payment of a mortgage loan that is considerably larger than the required periodic payments because the loan amount was not fully amortized.

bargain and sale deed A deed that carries with it no warranties against liens or other encumbrances but that does imply that the grantor has the right to convey title. The grantor may add warranties to the deed at his or her discretion.

base line The main imaginary line running east and west and crossing a principal meridian at a definite point, used by surveyors for reference in locating and describing land under the rectangular survey (or government survey) system of legal description.

basis The financial interest that the Internal Revenue Service attributes to an owner of an investment property for the purpose of determining annual depreciation and gain or loss on the sale of the asset. If a property was acquired by purchase, the owner's basis is the cost of the property plus the value of any capital expenditures for improvements to the property, minus any depreciation allowable or actually taken. This new basis is called the *adjusted basis*.

benchmark A permanent reference mark or point established for use by surveyors in measuring differences in elevation.

beneficiary (1) The person for whom a trust operates or in whose behalf the income from a trust estate is drawn. (2) A lender in a deed of trust loan transaction.

bilateral contract *See* contract.

binder An agreement that may accompany an earnest money deposit for the purchase of real property as evidence of the purchaser's good faith and intent to complete the transaction.

blanket loan (mortgage) A mortgage covering more than one parcel of real estate, providing for each parcel's partial release from the mortgage lien upon repayment of a definite portion of the debt.

blockbusting The illegal practice of inducing homeowners to sell their properties by making representations regarding the entry or prospective entry of minority persons into the neighborhood.

blue-sky laws Common name for those state and federal laws that regulate the registration and sale of investment securities.

boot Money or property given to make up any difference in value or equity between two properties in an *exchange*.

branch office A secondary place of business apart from the principal or main office from which real estate business is conducted. A branch office generally must be run by a licensed real estate broker working on behalf of the broker who operates the principal office.

breach of contract Violation of any terms or conditions in a contract without legal excuse; for example, failure to make a payment when it is due.

broker One who buys and sells for another for a commission. *See also* real estate broker.

broker-appraiser One who provides an estimate of value for properties of non-federally related transactions under $250,000.

broker of record The individual broker responsible for the real estate transactions and activities of licensees in a partnership or corporation.

brokerage The bringing together of parties interested in making a real estate transaction.

buffer zone A strip of land, usually used as a park or designated for a similar use, separating land dedicated to one use from land dedicated to another use (e.g., residential from commercial).

builder-owner salesperson An individual who is a full-time employee of the owner or builder of single-family or multifamily residences who is licensed to perform certain acts on behalf of the builder-owner.

building code An ordinance that specifies minimum standards of construction for buildings in order to protect public safety and health.

building permit Written governmental permission for the construction, alteration or demolition of an improvement, showing compliance with building codes and zoning ordinances.

bulk transfer *See* Uniform Commercial Code.

bundle of legal rights The concept of land ownership that includes *ownership of all legal rights to the land*—for example, possession, control within the law, and enjoyment.

business name The name in which the broker's license is issued. Any time the name of the business appears, it must be represented exactly as it appears on the broker's license.

buydown A financing technique used to reduce the monthly payments for the first few years of a loan. Funds in the form of discount points are given to the lender to buy down or lower the effective interest rate paid by the buyer, thus reducing the monthly payments for a set time.

buyer-agency agreement A principal/agent relationship in which the broker is the agent for the buyer, with fiduciary responsibilities to the buyer. The broker represents the buyer under the law of agency.

campground membership An interest, other than in fee simple or by lease, that gives the purchaser the right to use a unit of real property for the purpose of locating a recreational vehicle, trailer, tent, camper or other similar device on a periodic basis pursuant to a membership contract.

campground membership salesperson A licensee who, either as an employee or independent contractor, sells campground memberships under the supervision of a broker.

capital gain Profit earned from the sale of an asset.

capitalization A mathematical process for estimating the value of a property using a proper rate of return on the investment and the annual net income expected to be produced by the property. The formula is expressed as

$$\frac{\text{Income}}{\text{Rate}} = \text{Value}$$

capitalization rate The rate of return a property will produce on the owner's investment.

cash flow The net spendable income from an investment, determined by deducting all operating and fixed expenses from the gross income. If expenses exceed income, a *negative cash flow* is the result.

cash rent In an agricultural lease, the amount of money given as rent to the landowner at the outset of the lease, as opposed to sharecropping.

caveat emptor A Latin phrase meaning "Let the buyer beware."

cemetery associate broker A licensed cemetery broker who is employed by another cemetery broker or broker.

cemetery broker An individual or entity licensed to engage exclusively in the sale of cemetery lots, plots and mausoleum spaces or openings.

cemetery salesperson A licensee employed by a broker or cemetery broker to sell cemetery lots exclusively.

certificate of reasonable value (CRV) A form indicating the appraised value of a property being financed with a VA loan.

certificate of sale The document generally given to the purchaser at a tax foreclosure sale. A certificate of sale does not convey title; generally, it is an instrument certifying that the holder received title to the property after the redemption period had passed and that the holder paid the property taxes for that interim period.

certificate of title A statement of opinion on the status of the title to a parcel of real property based on an examination of specified public records.

certified general real estate appraiser An individual who is certified under the state Certified Appraisers Act to perform appraisals of any type or value of property for federally related real estate transactions.

certified residential real estate appraiser An individual who is certified under the state Certified Appraisers Act to perform residential (one-unit to four-unit dwellings) appraisals for federally related real estate transactions.

chain of title The succession of conveyances, from some accepted starting point, whereby the present holder of real property derives title.

change The appraisal principle that holds that no physical or economic condition remains constant.

chattel *See* personal property.

Civil Rights Act of 1866 An act that prohibits racial discrimination in the sale and rental of housing.

closing statement A detailed cash accounting of a real estate transaction showing all cash received, all charges and credits made and all cash paid out in the transaction.

cloud on title Any document, claim, unreleased lien or encumbrance that may impair the title to real property or make the title doubtful; usually revealed by a title search and removed by either a quitclaim deed or suit to quiet title.

clustering The grouping of homesites within a subdivision on smaller lots than normal, with the remaining land used as common areas.

code of ethics A written system of standards for ethical conduct.

codicil A supplement or addition to a will, executed with the same formalities as a will, that normally does not revoke the entire will.

coinsurance clause A clause in insurance policies covering real property that requires the policyholder to maintain fire insurance coverage generally equal to at least 80 percent of the property's actual replacement cost.

commingling The illegal act by a real estate broker of placing client or customer funds with personal funds. By law brokers are required to maintain a separate *escrow account* for other parties' funds held temporarily by the broker.

commission Payment to a broker for services rendered, such as in the sale or purchase of real property; usually a percentage of the selling price of the property.

common elements Parts of a property that are necessary or convenient to the existence, maintenance and safety of a condominium or are normally in common use by all of the condominium residents. Each condominium owner has an undivided ownership interest in the common elements.

common law The body of law based on custom, usage and court decisions.

community property A system of property ownership based on the theory that each spouse has an equal interest in the property acquired by the efforts of either spouse during marriage. A holdover of Spanish law, found predominantly in western states; the system was unknown under English common law.

comparables Properties used in an appraisal report that are substantially equivalent to the subject property.

competition The appraisal principle that states that excess profits generate competition.

competitive market analysis (CMA) A comparison of the prices of recently sold homes that are similar to a listing seller's home in terms of location, style and amenities.

comprehensive plan *See* master plan.

condemnation A judicial or administrative proceeding to exercise the power of eminent domain, through which a government agency takes private property for public use and compensates the owner.

conditional-use permit Written governmental permission allowing a use inconsistent with zoning but necessary for the common good, such as locating an emergency medical facility in a predominantly residential area.

condominium The absolute ownership of a unit in a multiunit building based on a legal description of the airspace the unit actually occupies, plus an undivided interest in the ownership of the common elements, which are owned jointly with the other condominium unit owners.

confession of judgment clause Permits judgment to be entered against a debtor without the necessity of a creditor instituting legal proceedings.

conformity The appraisal principle that holds that the greater the similarity among properties in an area, the better they will hold their value.

consideration (1) That received by the grantor in exchange for his or her deed. (2) Something of value that induces a person to enter into a contract.

construction loan *See* interim financing.

constructive eviction Actions of a landlord that so materially disturb or impair the tenant's enjoyment of the leased premises that the tenant is effectively forced to move out and terminate the lease without liability for any further rent.

constructive notice Notice given to the world by recorded documents. All people are charged with knowledge of such documents and their contents, whether or not they have actually examined them. Possession of property is also considered constructive notice that the person in possession has an interest in the property.

contingency A provision in a contract that requires a certain act to be done or a certain event to occur before the contract becomes binding.

contract A legally enforceable promise or set of promises that must be performed and for which, if a breach of the promise occurs, the law provides a remedy. A contract may be either *unilateral,* by which only one party is bound to act, or *bilateral,* by which all parties to the instrument are legally bound to act as prescribed.

contribution The appraisal principle that states that the value of any component of a property is what it gives to the value of the whole or what its absence detracts from that value.

conventional loan A loan that is not insured or guaranteed by a government or private source.

conveyance A term used to refer to any document that transfers title to real property. The term is also used in describing the act of transferring.

cooperating broker *See* listing broker.

cooperative A residential multiunit building whose title is held by a trust or corporation that is owned by and operated for the benefit of persons living within the building, who are the beneficial owners of the trust or stockholders of the corporation, each possessing a proprietary lease.

co-ownership Title ownership held by two or more persons.

corporation An entity or organization created by operation of law, whose rights of doing business are essentially the same as those of an individual. The entity has continuous existence until it is dissolved according to legal procedures.

correction lines Provisions in the rectangular survey (government survey) system made to compensate for the curvature of the earth's surface. Every fourth township line (at 24-mile intervals) is used as a correction line on which the intervals between the north and south range lines are remeasured and corrected to a full six miles.

cost approach The process of estimating the value of a property by adding to the estimated land value the appraiser's estimate of the reproduction or replacement cost of the building, less depreciation.

cost recovery An Internal Revenue Service term for *depreciation.*

counteroffer A new offer made as a reply to an offer received. It has the effect of rejecting the original offer, which cannot be accepted thereafter unless revived by the offeror.

covenant A written agreement between two or more parties in which a party or parties pledge to perform or not perform specified acts with regard to property; usually found in such real estate documents as deeds, mortgages, leases and contracts for deed.

covenant of quiet enjoyment The covenant implied by law by which a landlord guarantees that a tenant may take possession of leased premises and that the landlord will not interfere in the tenant's possession or use of the property.

credit On a closing statement, an amount entered in a person's favor—either an amount the party has paid or an amount for which the party must be reimbursed.

curtesy A life estate, usually a fractional interest, given by some states to the surviving husband in real estate owned by his deceased wife. Most states have abolished curtesy.

datum A horizontal plane from which heights and depths are measured.

debit On a closing statement, an amount charged, that is, an amount that the debited party must pay.

decedent A person who has died.

dedication The voluntary transfer of private property by its owner to the public for some public use, such as for streets or schools.

deed A written instrument that, when executed and delivered, conveys title to or an interest in real estate.

deed in lieu of foreclosure A deed given by the mortgagor to the mortgagee when the mortgagor is in default under the terms of the mortgage. This is a way for the mortgagor to avoid foreclosure.

deed in trust An instrument that grants a trustee full power to sell, mortgage and subdivide a parcel of real estate. The beneficiary controls the trustee's use of these powers under the provisions of the trust agreement.

deed restrictions Clauses in a deed limiting the future uses of the property. Deed restrictions may impose a vast variety of limitations and conditions—for example, they may limit the density of buildings, dictate the type of structures that can be erected or prevent buildings from being used for specific purposes or even from being used at all.

default The nonperformance of a duty, whether arising under a contract or otherwise; failure to meet an obligation when due.

defeasance clause A clause used in leases and mortgages that cancels a specified right upon the occurrence of a certain condition, such as cancellation of a mortgage upon repayment of the mortgage loan.

defeasible fee estate An estate in which the holder has a fee simple title that may be divested upon the occurrence or nonoccurrence of a specified event. There are two categories of defeasible fee estates: fee simple on condition precedent (fee simple determinable) and fee simple on condition subsequent.

deficiency judgment A personal judgment levied against the borrower when a foreclosure sale does not produce sufficient funds to pay the mortgage debt in full.

demand The amount of goods people are willing and able to buy at a given price; often coupled with supply.

density zoning Zoning ordinances that restrict the average maximum number of houses per acre that may be built within a particular area, generally a subdivision.

depreciation (1) In appraisal, a loss of value in property due to any cause, including *physical deterioration, functional obsolescence* and *external obsolescence*. (2) In real estate investment, an expense deduction for tax purposes taken over the period of ownership of income property.

descent Acquisition of an estate by inheritance in which an heir succeeds to the property by operation of law.

developer One who attempts to put land to its most profitable use through the construction of improvements.

devise A gift of real property by will. The donor is the devisor and the recipient is the devisee.

discount point A unit of measurement used for various loan charges; one point equals 1 percent of the amount of the loan.

doctrine of prior appropriation *See* prior appropriation.

dominant tenement A property that includes in its ownership the appurtenant right to use an easement over another person's property for a specific purpose.

dower The legal right or interest, recognized in some states, that a wife acquires in the property her husband held or acquired during their marriage. During the husband's lifetime the right is only a possibility of an interest; upon his death it can become an interest in land.

dual agency Representing both parties to a transaction. This is unethical unless both parties agree to it, and it is illegal in many states.

due-on-sale clause. A provision in the mortgage that states that the entire balance of the note is immediately due and payable if the mortgagor transfers (sells) the property.

duress Unlawful constraint or action exercised upon a person whereby the person is forced to perform an act against his or her will. A contract entered into under duress is voidable.

earnest money Money deposited by a buyer under the terms of a contract, to be forfeited if the buyer defaults but applied to the purchase price if the sale is closed.

easement A right to use the land of another for a specific purpose, such as for a right-of-way or utilities; an incorporeal interest in land.

easement by condemnation An easement created by the government or government agency that has exercised its right under eminent domain.

easement by necessity An easement allowed by law as necessary for the full enjoyment of a parcel of real estate; for example, a right of ingress and egress over a grantor's land.

easement by prescription An easement acquired by continuous, open and hostile use of the property for the period of time prescribed by state law.

easement in gross An easement that is not created for the benefit of any *land* owned by the owner of the easement but that attaches *personally to the easement owner.* For example, a right granted by Eleanor Franks to Joe Fish to use a portion of her property for the rest of his life would be an easement in gross.

economic life The number of years during which an improvement will add value to the land.

emblements Growing crops, such as grapes and corn, that are produced annually through labor and industry; also called *fructus industriales.*

eminent domain The right of a government or municipal quasi-public body to acquire property for public use through the legal process called *condemnation.*

employee Someone who works as a direct employee of an employer and has employee status. The employer is obligated to withhold income taxes and social security taxes from the compensation of employees. *See also* independent contractor.

employment contract A document evidencing formal employment between employer and employee or between principal and agent. In the real estate business, this generally takes the form of a listing agreement or management agreement.

enabling acts State legislation that confers zoning powers on municipal governments.

encroachment A building or some portion of it—a wall or fence, for instance—that extends beyond the land of the owner and illegally intrudes on some land of an adjoining owner or a street or alley.

encumbrance Anything—such as a mortgage, tax, or judgment lien, an easement, a restriction on the use of the land or an outstanding dower right—that may diminish the value of a property.

Equal Credit Opportunity Act (ECOA) The federal law that prohibits discrimination in the extension of credit because of race, color, religion, national origin, sex, age or marital status.

equalization The raising or lowering of assessed values for tax purposes in a particular county or taxing district to make them equal to assessments in other counties or districts.

equalization factor A factor (number) by which the assessed value of a property is multiplied to arrive at a value for the property that is in line with statewide tax assessments. The *ad valorem tax* would be based on this adjusted value.

equitable lien *See* statutory lien.

equitable right of redemption The right of a defaulted property owner to recover the property prior to its sale by paying the appropriate fees and charges.

equitable title The interest held by a vendee under an installment contract or agreement of sale; the equitable right to obtain absolute ownership to property when legal title is held in another's name.

equity The interest or value that an owner has in the property over and above any mortgage indebtedness.

erosion The gradual wearing away of land by water, wind and general weather conditions; the diminishing of property caused by the elements.

escheat The reversion of property to the state or county, as provided by state law, in cases where a decedent dies intestate without heirs capable of inheriting, or when the property is abandoned.

escrow The closing of a transaction through a third party called an *escrow agent,* or *escrowee,* who receives certain funds and documents to be delivered upon the performance of certain conditions outlined in the escrow instructions.

escrow account The trust account established by a broker under the provisions of the license law for the purpose of holding funds on behalf of the broker's principal or some other person until the consummation or termination of a transaction.

estate (tenancy) at sufferance The tenancy of a lessee who lawfully comes into possession of a landlord's real estate but who continues to occupy the premises improperly after his or her lease rights have expired.

estate (tenancy) at will An estate that gives the lessee the right to possession until the estate is terminated by either party; the term of this estate is indefinite.

estate (tenancy) for years An interest for a certain, exact period of time in property leased for a specified consideration.

estate (tenancy) from period to period An interest in leased property that continues from period to period—week to week, month to month or year to year.

estate in land The degree, quantity, nature and extent of interest that a person has in real property.

estate taxes Federal taxes on a decedent's real and personal property.

estoppel Method of creating an agency relationship in which someone states incorrectly that another person is her or his agent, and a third person relies on that representation.

estoppel certificate A document in which a borrower certifies the amount owed on a mortgage loan and the rate of interest.

ethics The system of moral principles and rules that become standards for professional conduct.

eviction A legal process to oust a person from possession of real estate.

evidence of title Proof of ownership of property; commonly a certificate of title or title insurance.

exchange A transaction in which all or part of the consideration is the transfer of *like-kind* property (such as real estate for real estate).

exclusive-agency listing A listing contract under which the owner appoints a real estate broker as his or her exclusive agent for a designated period of time to sell the property, on the owner's stated terms, for a commission. The owner reserves the right to sell without paying anyone a commission if he or she sells to a prospect who has not been introduced or claimed by the broker.

exclusive-right-to-sell listing A listing contract under which the owner appoints a real estate broker as his or her exclusive agent for a designated period of time, to sell the property on the owner's stated terms, and agrees to pay the broker a commission when the property is sold, whether by the broker, the owner or another broker.

executed contract A contract in which all parties have fulfilled their promises and thus performed the contract.

execution The signing and delivery of an instrument. Also, a legal order directing an official to enforce a judgment against the property of a debtor.

executory contract A contract under which something remains to be done by one or more of the parties.

express agreement An oral or written contract in which the parties state the contract's terms and express their intentions in words.

express contract *See* express agreement.

external depreciation Reduction in a property's value caused by outside factors (those that are off the property).

Fair Housing Act The federal law that prohibits discrimination in housing based on race, color, religion, sex, handicap, familial status and national origin.

Fannie Mae A quasi-government agency established to purchase any kind of mortgage loans in the secondary mortgage market from the primary lenders.

Farmers Home Administration An agency of the federal government that provides credit assistance to farmers and other individuals who live in rural areas.

Federal Deposit Insurance Corporation (FDIC) An independent federal agency that insures the deposits in commercial banks.

Federal Home Loan Mortgage Corporation (FHLMC) A corporation established to purchase primarily conventional mortgage loans in the secondary mortgage market.

Federal National Mortgage Association (FNMA) *See* Fannie Mae.

Federal Reserve System The country's central banking system, which is responsible for the nation's monetary policy by regulating the supply of money and interest rates.

fee simple absolute The maximum possible estate or right of ownership of real property, continuing forever. Also known as *fee simple*.

fee simple defeasible *See* defeasible fee estate.

feudal system A system of ownership usually associated with precolonial England, in which the king or other sovereign is the source of all rights. The right to possess real property was granted by the sovereign to an individual as a life estate only. Upon the death of the individual title passed back to the sovereign, not to the decedent's heirs.

FHA loan A loan insured by the Federal Housing Administration and made by an approved lender in accordance with the FHA's regulations.

fiduciary One in whom trust and confidence is placed; usually a reference to a broker employed under the terms of a listing contract.

fiduciary relationship A relationship of trust and confidence, as between trustee and beneficiary, attorney and client or principal and agent.

Financial Institutions Reform, Recovery and Enforcement Act (FIRREA) This act restructured the savings and loan association regulatory system; enacted in response to the savings and loan crisis of the 1980s.

financing statement *See* Uniform Commercial Code.

FIRREA *See* Financial Institutions Reform, Recovery and Enforcement Act (FIRREA).

first mortgage The mortgage lien that takes first lien position by being recorded first.

fiscal policy The government's policy in regard to taxation and spending programs. The balance between these two areas determines the amount of money the government will withdraw from or feed into the economy, which can counter economic peaks and slumps.

fixture An item of personal property that has been converted to real property by being permanently affixed to the realty.

foreclosure A legal procedure whereby property used as security for a debt is sold to satisfy the debt in the event of default in payment of the mortgage note or default of other terms in the mortgage document. The foreclosure procedure brings the rights of all parties to a conclusion and passes the title in the mortgaged property to either the holder of the mortgage or a third party who may purchase the realty at the foreclosure sale, free of all encumbrances affecting the property subsequent to the mortgage.

fraud Deception intended to cause a person to give up property or a lawful right.

Freddie Mac *See* Federal Home Loan Mortgage Corporation (FHLMC).

freehold estate An estate in land in which ownership is for an indeterminate length of time, in contrast to a *leasehold estate*.

front footage The measurement of a parcel of land by the number of feet of street or road frontage.

functional obsolescence A loss of value to an improvement to real estate arising from functional problems, often caused by age or poor design.

future interest A person's present right to an interest in real property that will not result in possession or enjoyment until some time in the future, such as a reversion or right of reentry.

gap A defect in the chain of title of a particular parcel of real estate; a missing document or conveyance that raises doubt as to the present ownership of the land.

general agent One who is authorized by a principal to represent the principal in a specific range of matters.

general contractor A construction specialist who enters into a formal construction contract with a landowner or master lessee to construct a real estate building or project. The general contractor often contracts with several *subcontractors* specializing in various aspects of the building process to perform individual jobs.

general lien The right of a creditor to have all of a debtor's property—both real and personal—sold to satisfy a debt.

general partnership *See* partnership.

general warranty deed A deed in which the grantor fully warrants good clear title to the premises. Used in most real estate transfers, a general warranty deed offers the greatest protection of any deed.

Ginnie Mae *See* Government National Mortgage Association (GNMA).

government lot Fractional sections in the rectangular survey (government survey) system that are less than one quarter-section in area.

Government National Mortgage Association (GNMA) A government agency that plays an important role in the secondary mortgage market. It sells mortgage-backed securities that are backed by pools of FHA and VA loans.

government survey system *See* rectangular (government) survey system.

graduated-payment mortgage (GPM) A loan in which the monthly principal and interest payments increase by a certain percentage each year for a certain number of years and then level off for the remaining loan term.

grantee A person who receives a conveyance of real property from a grantor.

granting clause Words in a deed of conveyance that state the grantor's intention to convey the property at the present time. This clause is generally worded as "convey and warrant," "grant," "grant, bargain and sell" or the like.

grantor The person transferring title to or an interest in real property to a grantee.

gross income multiplier A figure used as a multiplier of the gross annual income of a property to produce an estimate of the property's value.

gross lease A lease of property under which a landlord pays all property charges regularly incurred through ownership, such as repairs, taxes, insurance and operating expenses. Most residential leases are gross leases.

gross rent multiplier (GRM) A figure used as a multiplier of the gross monthly income of a property to produce an estimate of the property's value.

ground lease A lease of land only, on which the tenant usually owns a building or is required to build as specified in the lease. Such leases are usually long-term net leases; the tenant's rights and obligations continue until the lease expires or is terminated through default.

growing-equity mortgage (GEM) A loan in which the monthly payments increase annually, with the increased amount being used to reduce directly the principal balance outstanding and thus shorten the overall term of the loan.

habendum clause That part of a deed beginning with the words, "to have and to hold," following the granting clause and defining the extent of ownership the grantor is conveying.

heir One who might inherit or succeed to an interest in land under the state law of descent if the owner dies without leaving a valid will.

highest and best use That possible use of a property that would produce the greatest net income and thereby develop the highest value.

holdover tenancy A tenancy whereby a lessee retains possession of leased property after the lease has expired and the landlord, by continuing to accept rent, agrees to the tenant's continued occupancy as defined by state law.

holographic will A will that is written, dated and signed in the testator's handwriting.

home equity loan A loan (sometimes called a *line of credit*) under which a property owner uses the equity in his or her residence as collateral and can then draw funds up to a prearranged amount against the property.

homeowner's insurance policy A standardized package insurance policy that covers a residential real estate owner against financial loss from fire, theft, public liability and other common risks.

homestead Land that is owned and occupied as the family home. In many states, a portion of the area or value of this land is protected or exempt from judgments for debts.

hypothecation The pledge of property as security for a loan.

impact fees Charges assessed developers by a municipality that relate to expenses incurred by the municipality for additional improvements necessitated by increased development.

implied agreement A contract under which the agreement of the parties is demonstrated by their acts and conduct.

implied contract *See* implied agreement.

implied warranty of habitability A theory in landlord/tenant law in which the landlord renting residential property implies that the property is habitable and fit for its intended use.

improvement (1) Any structure, usually privately owned, erected on a site to enhance the value of the property—for example, building a fence or a driveway. (2) A publicly owned structure added to or benefiting land, such as a curb, sidewalk, street or sewer.

income approach The process of estimating the value of an income-producing property by capitalization of the annual net income expected to be produced by the property during its remaining useful life.

incorporeal right A nonpossessory right in real estate; for example, an easement or a right-of-way.

independent contractor Someone who is retained to perform a certain act but who is subject to the control and direction of another only as to the end result and not as to the way in which he or she performs the act. Unlike an employee, an independent contractor pays for all his or her expenses and social security and income taxes and receives no employee benefits. Many real estate salespeople are independent contractors.

index method The appraisal method of estimating building costs by multiplying the original cost of the property by a percentage factor to adjust for current construction costs.

inflation The gradual reduction of the purchasing power of the dollar, usually related directly to the increases in the money supply by the federal government.

inheritance taxes State-imposed taxes on a decedent's real and personal property.

installment contract A contract for the sale of real estate whereby the purchase price is paid in periodic installments by the purchaser, who is in possession of the property even though title is retained by the seller until a future date, which may be not until final payment. Also called a *contract for deed* or *articles of agreement.*

installment sale A transaction in which the sales price is paid in two or more installments over two or more years. If the sale meets certain requirements, a taxpayer can postpone reporting such income until future years by paying tax each year only on the proceeds received that year.

interest A charge made by a lender for the use of money.

interim financing A short-term loan usually made during the construction phase of a building project (in this case, often referred to as a *construction loan*).

Interstate Land Sales Full Disclosure Act A federal law that regulates the sale of certain real estate in interstate commerce.

intestate The condition of a property owner who dies without leaving a valid will. Title to the property will pass to the decedent's heirs as provided in the state law of descent.

intrinsic value An appraisal term referring to the value created by a person's personal preferences for a particular type of property.

investment Money directed toward the purchase, improvement and development of an asset in expectation of income or profits.

involuntary alienation *See* alienation.

involuntary lien A lien placed on property without the consent of the property owner.

joint tenancy Ownership of real estate between two or more parties who have been named in one conveyance as joint tenants. Upon the death of a joint tenant, the decedent's interest passes to the surviving joint tenant or tenants by the *right of survivorship.*

joint venture The joining of two or more people to conduct a specific business enterprise. A joint venture is similar to a partnership in that it must be created by agreement between the parties to share in the losses and profits of the venture. It is unlike a partnership in that the venture is for one specific project only, rather than for a continuing business relationship.

judgment The formal decision of a court upon the respective rights and claims of the parties to an action or suit. After a judgment has been entered and recorded with the county recorder, it usually becomes a general lien on the property of the defendant.

judicial deed A deed that is delivered pursuant to court order.

judicial precedent In law, the requirements established by prior court decisions.

junior lien An obligation, such as a second mortgage, that is subordinate in right or lien priority to an existing lien on the same realty.

laches An equitable doctrine used by courts to bar a legal claim or prevent the assertion of a right because of undue delay or failure to assert the claim or right.

land The earth's surface, extending downward to the center of the earth and upward infinitely into space, including things permanently attached by nature, such as trees and water.

land contract *See* installment contract.

law of agency *See* agency.

lease A written or oral contract between a landlord (the lessor) and a tenant (the lessee) that transfers the right to exclusive possession and use of the landlord's real property to the lessee for a specified period of time and for a stated consideration (rent). By state law, leases for longer than a certain period of time must be in writing to be enforceable.

leasehold estate A tenant's right to occupy real estate during the term of a lease; generally considered to be a personal property interest.

lease option A lease under which the tenant has the right to purchase the property either during the lease term or at its end.

lease purchase The purchase of real property, the consummation of which is preceded by a lease, usually long-term. Typically done for tax or financing purposes.

legacy A disposition of money or personal property by will.

legal description A description of a specific parcel of real estate complete enough for an independent surveyor to locate and identify it.

legally competent parties People who are recognized by law as being able to contract with others; those of legal age and sound mind.

lessee *See* lease.

lessor *See* lease.

leverage The use of borrowed money to finance the bulk of an investment.

levy To assess; to seize or collect. To levy a tax is to assess a property and set the rate of taxation. To levy an execution is to officially seize the property of a person in order to satisfy an obligation.

liability coverage Insurance that indemnifies a property owner who is found liable for damage in the event of an individual's being injured on the insured's property.

license (1) A privilege or right granted to a person by a state to operate as a real estate broker or salesperson. (2) The revocable permission for a temporary use of land—a personal right that cannot be sold.

lien A right given by law to certain creditors to have their debt paid out of the property of a defaulting debtor, usually by means of a court sale.

lien theory Some states interpret a mortgage as being purely a lien on real property. The mortgagee thus has no right of possession but must foreclose the lien and sell the property if the mortgagor defaults.

life cycle costing In property management, comparing one type of equipment to another based on both purchase cost and operating cost over its expected useful lifetime.

life estate An interest in real or personal property that is limited in duration to the lifetime of its owner or some other designated person or persons.

life tenant A person in possession of a life estate.

limited partnership *See* partnership.

liquidated damages An amount predetermined by the parties to a contract as the total compensation to an injured party should the other party breach the contract.

liquidity The ability to sell an asset and convert it into cash, at a price close to its true value, in a short period of time.

lis pendens A recorded legal document giving constructive notice that an action affecting a particular property has been filed in either a state or a federal court.

listing agreement A contract between an owner (as principal) and a real estate broker (as agent) by which the broker is employed as agent to find a buyer for the owner's real estate on the owner's terms, for which service the owner agrees to pay a commission.

listing broker The broker in a multiple-listing situation from whose office a listing agreement is initiated, as opposed to the *cooperating broker,* from whose office negotiations leading up to a sale are initiated. The listing broker and the cooperating broker may be the same person.

littoral rights (1) A landowner's claim to use water in large navigable lakes and oceans adjacent to his or her property. (2) The ownership rights to land bordering these bodies of water up to the high-water mark.

loan origination fee A fee charged to the borrower by the lender for making a mortgage loan. The fee is usually computed as a percentage of the loan amount.

loan-to-value ratio The relationship between the amount of the mortgage loan and the value of the real estate being pledged as collateral.

lot-and-block (recorded plat) system A method of describing real property that identifies a parcel of land by reference to lot and block numbers within a subdivision, as specified on a recorded subdivision plat.

management agreement A contract between the owner of income property and a management firm or individual property manager that outlines the scope of the manager's authority.

market A place where goods can be bought and sold and a price established.

marketable title Good or clear title reasonably free from the risk of litigation over possible defects.

market value The most probable price property would bring in an arm's-length transaction under normal conditions on the open market.

master plan A comprehensive plan to guide the long-term physical development of a particular community.

mechanic's lien A statutory lien created in favor of contractors, laborers and materialmen who have performed work or furnished materials in the erection or repair of a building.

metes-and-bounds description A legal description of a parcel of land that begins at a well-marked point and follows the boundaries, using directions and distances around the tract, back to the place of beginning.

mill One-tenth of one cent. Some states use a mill rate to compute real estate taxes; for example, a rate of 52 mills would be $0.052 tax for each dollar of assessed valuation of a property.

minor Someone who has not reached the age of majority and therefore does not have legal capacity to transfer title to real property.

monetary policy Governmental regulation of the amount of money in circulation through such institutions as the Federal Reserve Board.

money judgment A court judgment ordering payment of money rather than specific performance of a certain action. *See also* judgment.

month-to-month tenancy A periodic tenancy under which the tenant rents for one month at a time. In the absence of a rental agreement (oral or written), a tenancy is generally considered to be month to month.

monument A fixed natural or artificial object used to establish real estate boundaries for a metes-and-bounds description.

mortgage A conditional transfer or pledge of real estate as security for the payment of a debt. Also the document creating a mortgage lien.

mortgage banker Mortgage loan companies that originate, service and sell loans to investors.

mortgage broker An agent of a lender who brings the lender and borrower together. The broker receives a fee for this service.

mortgagee A lender in a mortgage loan transaction.

mortgage lien A lien or charge on the property of a mortgagor that secures the underlying debt obligations.

mortgagor A borrower in a mortgage loan transaction.

multiperil policies Insurance policies that offer protection from a range of potential perils, such as those of a fire, hazard, public liability and casualty.

multiple-listing clause A provision in an exclusive listing for the additional authority and obligation on the part of the listing broker to distribute the listing to other brokers in the multiple-listing organization.

multiple-listing service (MLS) A marketing organization composed of member brokers who agree to share their listing agreements with one another in the hope of procuring ready, willing and able buyers for their properties more quickly than they could on their own. Most multiple-listing services accept exclusive-right-to-sell listings or exclusive agency listings from their member brokers, although any broker can sell a property listed in an MLS.

negotiable instrument A written promise or order to pay a specific sum of money that may be transferred by endorsement or delivery. The transferee then has the original payee's right to payment.

net lease A lease requiring the tenant to pay not only rent but also costs incurred in maintaining the property, including taxes, insurance, utilities and repairs.

net listing A listing based on the net price the seller will receive if the property is sold. Under a net listing the broker can offer the property for sale at the highest price obtainable to increase the commission. This type of listing is illegal in many states.

net operating income (NOI) The income projected for an income-producing property after deducting losses for vacancy and collection and operating expenses.

nonconforming use A use of property that is permitted to continue after a zoning ordinance prohibiting it has been established for the area.

nonhomogeneity A lack of uniformity; dissimilarity. Because no two parcels of land are exactly alike, real estate is said to be nonhomogeneous.

note *See* promissory note.

novation Substituting a new obligation for an old one or substituting new parties to an existing obligation.

nuncupative will An oral will declared by the testator in his or her final illness, made before witnesses and afterward reduced to writing.

obsolescence The loss of value due to factors that are outmoded or less useful. Obsolescence may be functional or economic.

offer and acceptance Two essential components of a valid contract; a "meeting of the minds."

offeror/offeree The person who makes the offer is the offeror. The person to whom the offer is made is the offeree.

Office of Thrift Supervision (OTS) Monitors and regulates the savings and loan industry. OTS was created by FIRREA.

open-end loan A mortgage loan that is expandable by increments up to a maximum dollar amount, the full loan being secured by the same original mortgage.

open listing A listing contract under which the broker's commission is contingent on the broker's producing a ready, willing and able buyer before the property is sold by the seller or another broker.

option An agreement to keep open for a set period an offer to sell or purchase property.

option listing Listing with a provision that gives the listing broker the right to purchase the listed property.

ostensible agency A form of implied agency relationship created by the actions of the parties involved rather than by written agreement or document.

package loan A real estate loan used to finance the purchase of both real property and personal property, such as in the purchase of a new home that includes carpeting, window coverings and major appliances.

parol evidence rule A rule of evidence providing that a written agreement is the final expression of the agreement of the parties, not to be varied or contradicted by prior or contemporaneous oral or written negotiations.

participation mortgage A mortgage loan wherein the lender has a partial equity interest in the property or receives a portion of the income from the property.

partition The division of co-tenants' interests in real property when the parties do not all voluntarily agree to terminate the co-ownership; takes place through court procedures.

partnership An association of two or more individuals who carry on a continuing business for profit as co-owners. Under the law a partnership is regarded as a group of individuals rather than as a single entity. A *general partnership* is a typical form of joint venture, in which each general partner shares in the administration, profits and losses of the operation. A *limited partnership* is a business arrangement whereby the operation is administered by one or more general partners and funded, by and large, by limited or silent partners, who are by law responsible for losses only to the extent of their investments.

party wall A wall that is located on or at a boundary line between two adjoining parcels of land and is used or is intended to be used by the owners of both properties.

patent A grant or franchise of land from the U.S. government.

payment cap The limit on the amount the monthly payment can be increased on an adjustable-rate mortgage when the interest rate is adjusted.

payoff statement *See* reduction certificate.

Pennsylvania Human Relations Act (PHRA) The state law that prohibits discrimination in the sale or rental of real estate, both housing and commercial properties, on the basis of race, color, religion, ancestry, national origin, sex, familial status, handicap or disability, use of guide or support animal due to a handicap or disability.

Pennsylvania Municipalities Planning Code The state law that governs the procedures municipalities must follow when enacting comprehensive plans, zoning and subdivision ordinances.

Pennsylvania Uniform Condominium Act The state law adopted from the national model act that governs condominiums.

percentage lease A lease, commonly used for commercial property, whose rental is based on the tenant's gross sales at the premises; it usually stipulates a base monthly rental plus a percentage of any gross sales above a certain amount.

percolation test A test of the soil to determine if it will absorb and drain water adequately to use a septic system for sewage disposal.

periodic tenancy *See* estate from period to period.

personal property Items, called *chattels,* that do not fit into the definition of real property; movable objects.

physical deterioration A reduction in a property's value resulting from a decline in physical condition; can be caused by action of the elements or by ordinary wear and tear.

planned unit development (PUD) A planned combination of diverse land uses, such as housing, recreation and shopping, in one contained development or subdivision.

plat map A map of a town, section or subdivision indicating the location and boundaries of individual properties.

plottage The increase in value or utility resulting from the consolidation *(assemblage)* of two or more adjacent lots into one larger lot.

point of beginning (POB) In a metes-and-bounds legal description, the starting point of the survey, situated in one corner of the parcel; all metes-and-bounds descriptions must follow the boundaries of the parcel back to the point of beginning.

police power The government's right to impose laws, statutes, and ordinances, including zoning ordinances and building codes, to protect the public health, safety and welfare.

power of attorney A written instrument authorizing a person, the *attorney-in-fact,* to act as agent on behalf of another person to the extent indicated in the instrument.

prepaid items On a closing statement, items that have been paid in advance by the seller, such as insurance premiums and some real estate taxes, for which he or she must be reimbursed by the buyer.

prepayment penalty A charge imposed on a borrower who pays off the loan principal early. This penalty compensates the lender for interest and other charges that would otherwise be lost.

price fixing *See* antitrust laws.

primary mortgage market The mortgage market in which loans are originated and consisting of such lenders as commercial banks, savings and loan associations and mutual savings banks.

principal (1) A sum loaned or employed as a fund or investment, as distinguished from its income or profits. (2) The original amount (as in a loan) of the total due and payable at a certain date. (3) A main party to a transaction—the person for whom the agent works.

principal meridian The main imaginary line running north and south and crossing a base line at a definite point, used by surveyors for reference in locating and describing land under the rectangular (government) survey system of legal description.

prior appropriation A concept of water ownership in which the landowner's right to use available water is based on a government-administered permit system.

priority The order of position or time. The priority of liens is generally determined by the chronological order in which the lien documents are recorded; tax liens, however, have priority even over previously recorded liens.

private mortgage insurance (PMI) Insurance provided by any private carrier that protects a lender against a loss in the event of a foreclosure and deficiency.

probate A legal process by which a court determines who will inherit a decedent's property and what the estate's assets are.

procuring cause The effort that brings about the desired result. Under an open listing the broker who is the procuring cause of the sale receives the commission.

progression An appraisal principle that states that, between dissimilar properties, the value of the lesser-quality property is favorably affected by the presence of the better-quality property.

promissory note A financing instrument that states the terms of the underlying obligation, is signed by its maker and is negotiable (transferable to a third party).

property manager Someone who manages real estate for another person for compensation. Duties include collecting rents, maintaining the property, and keeping up all accounting.

property reports The mandatory federal and state documents compiled by subdividers and developers to provide potential purchasers with facts about a property prior to their purchase.

proprietary lease A lease given by the corporation that owns a cooperative apartment building to the shareholder for the shareholder's right as a tenant to an individual apartment.

prorations Expenses, either prepaid or paid in arrears, that are divided or distributed between the buyer and seller at the closing.

protected class Any group of people designated as such by the Department of Housing and Urban Development (HUD) in consideration of federal and state civil rights legislation. Currently includes ethnic minorities, women, religious groups, individuals with handicaps and others.

public offering statement A disclosure document given to a prospective purchaser under applicable federal and state laws. It contains the material facts about the property to allow the consumer to make an informed decision.

puffing Exaggerated or superlative comments or opinions.

pur autre vie "For the life of another." A life estate pur autre vie is measured by the life of a person other than the grantee.

purchase-money mortgage (PMM) A note secured by a mortgage or deed of trust given by a buyer, as borrower, to a seller, as lender, as part of the purchase price of the real estate.

pyramiding The process of acquiring additional properties by refinancing properties already owned and investing the loan proceeds in additional properties.

quantity survey method The appraisal method of estimating building costs by calculating the cost of all of the physical components in the improvements, adding the cost to assemble them and then including the indirect costs associated with such construction.

quiet title A court action to remove a cloud on the title.

quitclaim deed A conveyance by which the grantor transfers whatever interest he or she has in the real estate, without warranties or obligations.

range A strip of land six miles wide, extending north and south and numbered east and west according to its distance from the principal meridian in the rectangular (government) survey system of legal description.

rate cap The limit on the amount the interest rate can be increased at each adjustment period in an adjustable-rate loan. The cap may also set the maximum interest rate that can be charged during the life of the loan.

ratification Method of creating an agency relationship in which the principal accepts the conduct of someone who acted without prior authorization as the principal's agent.

ready, willing and able buyer One who is prepared to buy property on the seller's terms and is ready to take positive steps to consummate the transaction.

real estate Land; a portion of the earth's surface extending downward to the center of the earth and upward infinitely into space, including all things permanently attached to it, whether naturally or artificially.

real estate investment syndicate *See* syndicate.

real estate investment trust (REIT) Trust ownership of real estate by a group of individuals who purchase certificates of ownership in the trust, which in turn invests the money in real property and distributes the profits back to the investors free of corporate income tax.

real estate license law State laws enacted to protect the public from fraud, dishonesty and incompetence in the purchase and sale of real estate.

Real Estate Licensing and Registration Act The Pennsylvania law that protects the public interest by governing real estate practices and the activities of licensees.

real estate mortgage investment conduit (REMIC) A tax entity that issues multiple classes of investor interests (securities) backed by a pool of mortgages.

Real Estate Recovery Fund A fund established for aggrieved parties who have obtained uncollectible judgments against real estate licensees for fraud, deceit or misrepresentation.

Real Estate Settlement Procedures Act (RESPA) The federal law that requires certain disclosures to consumers about mortgage loan settlements. The law also prohibits the payment or receipt of kickbacks and certain kinds of referral fees.

real property The interests, benefits and rights inherent in real estate ownership.

REALTORS® A registered trademark term reserved for the sole use of active members of local REALTOR® boards affiliated with the National Association of REALTORS®.

reconciliation The final step in the appraisal process, in which the appraiser reconciles the estimates of value received from the sales comparison, cost and income approaches to arrive at a final estimate of market value for the subject property.

recorder of deeds The county office in which matters relating to the real estate located within that county are filed.

recording The act of entering or recording documents affecting or conveying interests in real estate in the recorder's office established in each county. Until it is recorded, a deed or mortgage ordinarily is not effective against subsequent purchasers or mortgagees.

rectangular (government) survey system A system established in 1785 by the federal government, providing for surveying and describing land by reference to principal meridians and base lines.

redemption The right of a defaulted property owner to recover his or her property by curing the default.

redemption period A period of time established by state law during which a property owner has the right to redeem his or her real estate from a foreclosure or tax sale by paying the sales price, interest and costs. Many states do not have mortgage redemption laws.

redlining The illegal practice of a lending institution denying loans or restricting their number for certain areas of a community.

reduction certificate (payoff statement) The document signed by a lender indicating the amount required to pay a loan balance in full and satisfy the debt; used in the settlement process to protect both the seller's and the buyer's interests.

regression An appraisal principle that states that, between dissimilar properties, the value of the better-quality property is adversely affected by the presence of the lesser-quality property.

Regulation Z Implements the Truth-in-Lending Act requiring credit institutions to inform borrowers of the true cost of obtaining credit.

remainder interest The remnant of an estate that has been conveyed to take effect and be enjoyed after the termination of a prior estate, such as when an owner conveys a life estate to one party and the remainder to another.

rent A fixed, periodic payment made by a tenant of a property to the owner for possession and use, usually by prior agreement of the parties.

rent schedule A statement of proposed rental rates, determined by the owner or the property manager or both, based on a building's estimated expenses, market supply and demand, and the owner's long-range goals for the property.

rental listing referral agent A licensee who owns or manages a business that collects rental information for the purpose of referring prospective tenants to rental units or locations.

replacement cost The construction cost at current prices of a property that is not necessarily an exact duplicate of the subject property but serves the same purpose or function as the original.

reproduction cost The construction cost at current prices of an exact duplicate of the subject property.

restrictive covenants A clause in a deed that limits the way the real estate ownership may be used.

Resolution Trust Corporation The organization created by FIRREA to liquidate the assets of failed savings and loan associations.

reverse annuity mortgage (RAM) A loan under which the homeowner receives monthly payments based on his or her accumulated equity rather than a lump sum. The loan must be repaid at a prearranged date or upon the death of the owner or the sale of the property.

reversionary interest The remnant of an estate that the grantor holds after granting a life estate to another person.

reversionary right The return of the rights of possession and quiet enjoyment to the owner at the expiration of a lease or life estate.

right of survivorship *See* joint tenancy.

right-of-way The right given by one landowner to another to pass over the land, construct a roadway or use as a pathway, without actually transferring ownership.

riparian rights An owner's rights in land that borders on or includes a stream, river or lake. These rights include access to and use of the water.

risk management Evaluation and selection of appropriate property and other insurance.

Rules and Regulations Real estate licensing authority orders that govern licensees' activities; they usually have the same force and effect as statutory law.

sale-and-leaseback A transaction in which an owner sells his or her improved property and, as part of the same transaction, signs a long-term lease to remain in possession of the premises.

sales comparison approach The process of estimating the value of a property by examining and comparing actual sales of comparable properties.

salesperson A person who performs real estate activities while employed by or associated with a licensed real estate broker.

satisfaction of mortgage A document acknowledging the payment of a mortgage debt.

secondary mortgage market A market for the purchase and sale of existing mortgages, designed to provide greater liquidity for mortgages; also called the *secondary money market*. Mortgages are first originated in the *primary mortgage market*.

section A portion of a township under the rectangular (government) survey system. A township is divided into 36 sections, numbered 1 through 36. A section is a square with mile-long sides and an area of one square mile, or 640 acres.

security agreement *See* Uniform Commercial Code

security deposit A payment by a tenant, held by the landlord during the lease term and kept (wholly or partially) on default or destruction of the premises by the tenant.

separate property Under community property law, property owned solely by either spouse before the marriage, acquired by gift or inheritance after the marriage or purchased with separate funds after the marriage.

servient tenement Land on which an easement exists in favor of an adjacent property (called a *dominant estate*); also called *servient estate*.

setback The amount of space local zoning regulations require between a lot line and a building line.

severalty Ownership of real property by one person only, also called *sole ownership*.

severance Changing an item of real estate to personal property by detaching it from the land; for example, cutting down a tree.

sharecropping In an agricultural lease, the agreement between the landowner and the tenant farmer to split the crop or the profit from its sale, actually sharing the crop.

shared-appreciation mortgage (SAM) A mortgage loan in which the lender, in exchange for a loan with a favorable interest rate, participates in the profits (if any) the borrower receives when the property is eventually sold.

situs The personal preference of people for one area over another, not necessarily based on objective facts and knowledge.

special agent One who is authorized by a principal to perform a single act or transaction; a real estate broker is usually a special agent authorized to find a ready, willing and able buyer for a particular property.

special assessment A tax or levy customarily imposed against only those specific parcels of real estate that will benefit from a proposed public improvement such as a street or sewer.

special warranty deed A deed in which the grantor warrants, or guarantees, the title only against defects arising during the period of his or her ownership of the property and not against defects existing before that time, generally using the language, "by, through or under the grantor but not otherwise."

specific lien A lien affecting or attaching only to a certain, specific parcel of land or piece of property.

specific performance A legal action to compel a party to carry out the terms of a contract.

square-foot method The appraisal method of estimating building costs by multiplying the number of square feet in the improvements being appraised by the cost per square foot for recently constructed similar improvements.

State Real Estate Commission The agency established by the Pennsylvania Real Estate Licensing and Registration Act to administer this law and supervise the activities of licensees.

Statute of Frauds That part of a state law that requires certain instruments, such as deeds, real estate sales contracts and certain leases, to be in writing to be legally enforceable.

statute of limitations That law pertaining to the period of time within which certain actions must be brought to court.

statutory lien A lien imposed on property by statute—a tax lien, for example—in contrast to an *equitable lien,* which arises out of common law.

statutory redemption The right of a defaulted property owner to recover the property after its sale by paying the appropriate fees and charges.

steering The illegal practice of channeling home seekers to particular areas to maintain the homogeneity of an area or to change the character of an area in order to create a speculative situation.

straight-line method A method of calculating depreciation for tax purposes, computed by dividing the adjusted basis of a property by the estimated number of years of remaining useful life.

straight (term) loan A loan in which only interest is paid during the term of the loan, with the entire principal amount due with the final interest payment.

subagent One who is employed by a person already acting as an agent. Typically a reference to a salesperson licensed under a broker (agent) who is employed under the terms of a listing agreement.

subdivider One who buys undeveloped land, divides it into smaller, usable lots and sells the lots to potential users.

subdivision A tract of land divided by the owner, known as the *subdivider,* into blocks, building lots and streets according to a recorded subdivision plat, which must comply with local ordinances and regulations.

subdivision and development ordinances Municipal ordinances that establish requirements for subdivisions and development.

subdivision plat *See* plat map.

sublease *See* subletting.

subletting The leasing of premises by a lessee to a third party for part of the lessee's remaining term. *See also* assignment.

subordination Relegation to a lesser position, usually in respect to a right or security.

subordination agreement A written agreement between holders of liens on a property that changes the priority of mortgage, judgment and other liens under certain circumstances.

subrogation The substitution of one creditor for another, with the substituted person succeeding to the legal rights and claims of the original claimant. Subrogation is used by title insurers to acquire from the injured party rights to sue in order to recover any claims they have paid.

substitution An appraisal principle that states that the maximum value of a property tends to be set by the cost of purchasing an equally desirable and valuable substitute property, assuming that no costly delay is encountered in making the substitution.

subsurface rights Ownership rights in a parcel of real estate to the water, minerals, gas, oil and so forth that lie beneath the surface of the property.

suit for possession A court suit initiated by a landlord to evict a tenant from leased premises after the tenant has breached one of the terms of the lease or has held possession of the property after the lease's expiration.

suit for specific performance *See* specific performance.

suit to quiet title A court action intended to establish or settle the title to a particular property, especially when there is a cloud on the title.

supply The amount of goods available in the market to be sold at a given price. The term is often coupled with *demand*.

supply and demand The appraisal principle that follows the interrelationship of the supply of and demand for real estate. As appraising is based on economic concepts, this principle recognizes that real property is subject to the influences of the marketplace just as is any other commodity.

surface rights Ownership rights in a parcel of real estate that are limited to the surface of the property and do not include the air above it (*air rights*) or the minerals below the surface (*sub-surface rights*).

survey The process by which boundaries are measured and land areas are determined; the on-site measurement of lot lines, dimensions and position of a house on a lot, including the determination of any existing encroachments or easements.

syndicate A combination of people or firms formed to accomplish a business venture of mutual interest by pooling resources. In a *real estate investment syndicate,* the parties own and/or develop property, with the main profit generally arising from the sale of the property.

tacking Adding or combining successive periods of continuous occupation of real property by adverse possessors. This concept enables someone who has not been in possession for the entire statutory period to establish a claim of adverse possession.

taxation The process by which a government or municipal quasi-public body raises monies to fund its operation.

tax credit An amount by which tax owed is reduced directly.

tax deed An instrument, similar to a certificate of sale, given to a purchaser at a tax sale. *See also* certificate of sale.

tax lien A charge against property created by operation of law. Tax liens and assessments take priority over all other liens.

tax sale A court-ordered sale of real property to raise money to cover delinquent taxes.

tenancy by the entirety The joint ownership, recognized in some states, of property acquired by husband and wife during marriage. Upon the death of one spouse, the survivor becomes the owner of the property.

tenancy in common A form of co-ownership by which each owner holds an undivided interest in real property as if he or she were sole owner. Each individual owner has the right to partition. Unlike joint tenants, tenants in common have right of inheritance.

tenant One who holds or possesses lands or tenements by any kind of right or title.

tenant improvements Alterations to the interior of a building to meet the functional demands of the tenant.

testate Having made and left a valid will.

testator A person who has made a valid will. A woman often is referred to as a testatrix, although testator can be used for either gender.

time is of the essence A phrase in a contract that requires the performance of a certain act within a stated period of time.

time-share A form of ownership interest that may include an estate interest in property or a contract for use, which allows use of the property for a fixed or variable time period.

time-share salesperson A licensee who, either as an employee or independent contractor, sells time shares under the supervision of a broker.

title (1) The right to or ownership of land. (2) The evidence of ownership of land.

title insurance A policy insuring the owner or mortgagee against loss by reason of defects in the title to a parcel of real estate, other than encumbrances, defects and matters specifically excluded by the policy.

title search The examination of public records relating to real estate to determine the current state of the ownership.

title theory Some states interpret a mortgage to mean that the lender is the owner of mortgaged land. Upon full payment of the mortgage debt the borrower becomes the landowner.

Torrens system A method of evidencing title by registration with the proper public authority, generally called the *registrar,* named for its founder, Sir Robert Torrens.

township The principal unit of the rectangular (government) survey system. A township is a square with 6-mile sides and an area of 36 square miles.

trade fixture An article installed by a tenant under the terms of a lease and removable by the tenant before the lease expires.

transactional licensee A licensee who provides unbundled services to the public without an agency relationship.

transfer tax Tax stamps required to be affixed to a deed by state and/or local law.

trust A fiduciary arrangement whereby property is conveyed to a person or institution, called a *trustee,* to be held and administered on behalf of another person, called a *beneficiary*. The one who conveys the trust is called the *trustor*.

trust deed An instrument used to create a mortgage lien by which the borrower conveys title to a trustee, who holds it as security for the benefit of the note holder (the lender); also called a *deed of trust*.

trustee The holder of bare legal title in a deed of trust loan transaction.

trustor A borrower in a deed of trust loan transaction.

undivided interest *See* tenancy in common.

unenforceable contract A contract that has all the elements of a valid contract, yet neither party can sue the other to force performance of it. For example, an unsigned contract is generally unenforceable.

Uniform Commercial Code A codification of commercial law, adopted in most states, that attempts to make uniform all laws relating to commercial transactions, including chattel mortgages and bulk transfers. Security interests in chattels are created by an instrument known as a *security agreement*. To give notice of the security interest, a *financing statement* must be recorded. Article 6 of the code regulates *bulk transfers*—the sale of a business as a whole, including all fixtures, chattels, and merchandise.

unilateral contract A one-sided contract wherein one party makes a promise so as to induce a second party to do something. The second party is not legally bound to perform; however, if the second party does comply, the first party is obligated to keep the promise.

unit-in-place method The appraisal method of estimating building costs by calculating the costs of all of the physical components in the structure, with the cost of each item including its proper installation, connection, etc.; also called the *segregated cost method*.

unity of ownership The four unities that are traditionally needed to create a joint tenancy—unity of title, time, interest and possession.

usury Charging interest at a higher rate than the maximum rate established by state law.

valid contract A contract that complies with all the essentials of a contract and is binding and enforceable on all parties to it.

VA loan A mortgage loan on approved property made to a qualified veteran by an authorized lender and guaranteed by the Department of Veterans Affairs in order to limit the lender's possible loss.

value The power of a good or service to command other goods in exchange for the present worth of future rights to its income or amenities.

variance Permission obtained from zoning authorities to build a structure or conduct a use that is expressly prohibited by the current zoning laws; an exception from the zoning ordinances.

vendee A buyer, usually under the terms of a land contract.

vendor A seller, usually under the terms of a land contract.

void contract A contract that has no legal force or effect because it does not meet the essential elements of a contract.

voidable contract A contract that seems to be valid on the surface but may be rejected or disaffirmed by one or both of the parties.

voluntary alienation *See* alienation.

voluntary lien A lien placed on property with the knowledge and consent of the property owner.

warranty of habitability *See* implied warranty of habitability.

waste An improper use or an abuse of a property by a possessor who holds less than fee ownership, such as a tenant, life tenant, mortgagor or vendee. Such waste ordinarily impairs the value of the land or the interest of the person holding the title or the reversionary rights.

will A written document, properly witnessed, providing for the transfer of title to property owned by the deceased, called the *testator*.

wraparound loan A method of refinancing in which the new mortgage is placed in a secondary, or subordinate, position; the new mortgage includes both the unpaid principal balance of the first mortgage and whatever additional sums are advanced by the lender. In essence it is an additional mortgage in which another lender refinances a borrower by lending an amount over the existing first mortgage amount without disturbing the existence of the first mortgage.

zoning ordinance An exercise of police power by a municipality to regulate and control the character and use of property.

Answer Key

Following are the correct answers to the questions found at the end of each chapter of the text, and at the end of Appendices A, B and C.

Chapter 1:
Real Property
and the Law
1. c
2. c
3. c
4. d
5. d
6. a
7. a
8. a
9. c
10. c

Chapter 2:
Land-Use Controls
and Development
1. a
2. a
3. b
4. c
5. c
6. d
7. b
8. a
9. b
10. a
11. d
12. b
13. a
14. b
15. c

Chapter 2:
(continued)
16. d
17. d
18. a

Chapter 3:
Environmental Issues
in Real Estate
1. b
2. d
3. a
4. c
5. c
6. a
7. b
8. d
9. d
10. a

Chapter 4:
Legal Descriptions
1. b
2. c
3. b
4. a
5. b
6. b
7. b
8. c
9. d
10. c

Chapter 4:
(continued)
11. c
12. c
13. d

Chapter 5:
Interests in Real
Estate
1. b
2. a
3. c
4. d
5. c
6. a
7. d
8. c
9. a
10. d
11. b
12. b
13. b
14. d
15. a
16. d

Chapter 6:
Landlord and Tenant
Interests
1. c
2. c
3. d

Chapter 6:
(continued)
4. a
5. c
6. b
7. d
8. c
9. b
10. b
11. b
12. a
13. b
14. c
15. d

Chapter 7:
Forms of Real
Estate Ownership
1. d
2. b
3. a
4. c
5. b
6. b
7. a
8. b
9. c
10. d
11. d
12. d
13. d

Chapter 7:
(continued)
14. b
15. b
16. c
17. b
18. b
19. d
20. a
21. c

Chapter 8:
Transfer of Title
1. a
2. a
3. d
4. a
5. b
6. c
7. d
8. d
9. b
10. c
11. b
12. b
13. b
14. c
15. b
16. d
17. a
18. a
19. b
20. d
21. c

Chapter 9:
Real Estate Taxes
and Other Liens
1. d
2. b
3. b
4. c
5. b
6. c
7. c
8. c
9. b
10. c
11. d
12. d
13. c
14. b
15. b
16. d

Chapter 9:
(continued)
17. b
18. d

Chapter 10:
Title Records
1. a
2. a
3. c
4. a
5. a
6. d
7. d
8. c
9. a
10. c
11. b
12. d
13. c
14. a
15. b

Chapter 11:
Principles of Real
Estate Contracts
1. c
2. b
3. d
4. b
5. c
6. a
7. d
8. d
9. d
10. d
11. c
12. a
13. b
14. b

Chapter 12:
Principles of Real
Estate Financing
1. c
2. a
3. a
4. d
5. b
6. d
7. c
8. a
9. b
10. a

Chapter 12:
(continued)
11. b
12. b
13. c

Chapter 13:
Pennsylvannia Real
Estate License Laws
1. d
2. a
3. b
4. c
5. d
6. d
7. d
8. a
9. d
10. d
11. d
12. b
13. d
14. a
15. d

Chapter 14:
The Real Estate
Business
1. b
2. b
3. d
4. b
5. d
6. b
7. a
8. b
9. c
10. b
11. b
12. d

Chapter 15:
Real Estate
Brokerage and
Agency
1. a
2. d
3. a
4. a
5. b
6. c
7. b
8. d
9. b

Chapter 15:
(continued)
10. d
11. b
12. a
13. d
14. a
15. c
16. d
17. c

Chapter 16:
Ethical Practices
and Fair Housing
1. c
2. a
3. d
4. b
5. c
6. a
7. b
8. c
9. c
10. b
11. a
12. c
13. d
14. d

Chapter 17:
Agency Contracts
1. a
2. c
3. c
4. a
5. c
6. d
7. b
8. c
9. a
10. c
11. b
12. a
13. b
14. b
15. a
16. d
17. d

Chapter 18:
Sales Contracts
1. a
2. a
3. d

Chapter 18:
(continued)
  4. b
  5. d
  6. d
  7. b
  8. b
  9. c
10. b
11. d
12. d

Chapter 19:
Appraising Real
Estate
  1. c
  2. b
  3. b
  4. b
  5. d
  6. a
  7. d
  8. c

Chapter 19:
(continued)
  9. b
10. d
11. c
12. c
13. c
14. b
15. c
16. b
17. d
18. b
19. a
20. b

Chapter 20:
Financing the Real
Estate Transaction
  1. b
  2. d
  3. c
  4. a

Chapter 20:
(continued)
  5. c
  6. b
  7. c
  8. b
  9. b
10. c
11. d
12. b

Chapter 21:
Closing the Real
Estate Transaction
  1. d
  2. b
  3. d
  4. a
  5. b
  6. c
  7. c
  8. b

Chapter 21:
(continued)
  9. d
10. c
11. a
12. b
13. b
14. b
15. d
16. d

Chapter 22:
Property Management
  1. a
  2. d
  3. c
  4. b
  5. b
  6. c
  7. a
  8. c
  9. b

Appendix A: Pennsylvania Real Estate Licensing Examination

1. **B.** The Real Estate Licensing and Registration Act was passed to protect the public interest. The duties and powers of the Commission are to administer the act, including promulgating its Rules and Regulations.

2. **D.** The Department of State issues licenses and contracts with a testing agency. The Commission has the authority to prescribe the subjects to be tested (not conduct the tests) and promulgate Rules and Regulations. The Governor appoints Commissioners.

3. **B.** By Section 604 of the Act, owners, attorneys-in-fact and licensed auctioneers are exempt from licensure. The Commission has authority to take disciplinary actions against licensees, including campground membership salespersons.

4. **C.** Criminal penalties apply to unlicensed practice. Awards from the Recovery Fund apply to individuals who have an uncollectable judgment from a civil action against a licensee for fraud, deceit and misrepresentation. The Commission is not connected with any real estate organization. The Commission has the authority to fine a licensee and to suspend or revoke a license for violations under Section 604 of the Act.

5. **D.** An individual cannot perform any activities for which licensure is required until the license is *issued*. Attending a training program is not a licensed activity.

6. **A.** All of the named licenses have an education requirement except a builder-owner salesperson.

7. **D.** The broker is responsible for all activities conducted by licensees employed by the broker in all of the broker's offices.

8. **C.** There is no citizenship requirement for any real estate licenses.

9. **B.** The act applies to licensees when dealing with their own properties. The licensee is responsible for disclosing that she or he is licensed. The act does not prohibit an individual from dealing with self-owned property or from collecting a commission in those transactions.

10. **B.** The Commission has no jurisdiction over this situation. The salesperson should seek recovery of the money due through civil court action.

11. **D.** The broker is always responsible for the activities, even if a branch office is managed by an associate broker. A branch office license can only be issued if the broker's license is currently renewed and not subject to disciplinary action; there is nothing in the Regulations that limits the number of branch offices.

12. **C.** The bonus can only be accepted by the salesperson's broker; the salesperson can receive compensation only from the employing broker.

13. **A.** The salesperson must work from the office address on the license. The broker keeps records, not the licenses, at the main office.

14. **C.** Estimated statements of closing costs are *estimates*. There is no requirement that they be signed. The disclosure of whom the broker represents is made in agreements of sale.

15. **C.** The employment of a salesperson by a broker does not automatically implicate the broker in the case of a violation. For the broker to be in violation, the broker must have had actual knowledge of the event, directed a course of action or allowed a course of action to continue.

16. **D.** The broker is responsible for depositing the check. Interest is suggested to be paid if the money is to be held for more than six months. The broker's duty to escrow is nonwaivable.

17. **B.** The Commission requires that ads include the business name. If a salesperson's name or phone number is included in the ad, the broker name and phone number must appear in greater prominence.

18. **C.** All of the other statements are requirements by the Commission's Regulations.

19. **A.** All of the other statements are requirements by the Commission's Regulations.

20. **D.** Necessary disclosures prior to the seller's signing a listing contract include whether the broker is an agent for the seller or for the buyer; that the commission and term of listing are negotiable; the existence of the Recovery Fund; and the requirement that an agreement of sale contain the zoning classification of the property, unless zoned primarily for single-family use.

21. **D.** In the other cases, the seller may sell his or her own property without being liable for a commission. A multiple-listing is not a kind of listing, but a multiple listing clause could exist in a listing agreement.

22. **C.** The agreement of sale for a time share must disclose the purchaser's right to cancel the contract by midnight of the fifth day after the signing of the contract. The purchaser may keep any gifts awarded prior to purchase and is entitled to recovery of any hand money without further action. The Recovery Fund serves a different purpose.

23. **C.** This is the only situation in which broker and client funds can be mixed.

24. **C.** Families with children are protected by the fair housing laws. These laws apply to both owners and licensees. The licensee is obligated to follow only *lawful* instructions of the principal.

25. **B.** The disclosure that commissions have been determined as a result of negotiations appears in a listing contract.

26. **D.** Individuals who have a disability are protected under the fair housing laws. A guide animal is not a pet. Individuals in the protected classes cannot be charged different amounts or be subjected to different conditions than are others.

27. **A.** Licensees are not to practice law. Any concern about the provisions in a contract should be referred to legal counsel.

28. **C.** The Commission's Regulations specify that such claims must be based on *closed* transactions.

29. **A.** An automatic renewal clause is prohibited in exclusive listing contracts.

30. **B.** The Commission's Regulations prohibit giving assurances that the licensee knows or should be expected to know are inaccurate or improbable. There is no way a licensee could assure such a claim; only historical information is verifiable.

31. **C.** Protecting the public is the law's primary purpose. It does not intend to restrict people from getting into the business, but rather ensure that people who are licensed meet certain standards. The Real Estate Commission exists to administer and enforce the law.

32. **A.** Holding an open house, listing properties and negotiating listings are all activities for which a license is required. The only way you can help the neighbor is to suggest he contact someone, your prospective broker is fine, to get the property marketed quickly.

33. **B.** Section 604 (11) of the Act prohibits a licensee from inducing any party to a contract to substitute a new contract where the substitution is motivated by personal gain. Neither the salesperson nor the salesperson's broker can do this. The buyer and seller are innocent victims of the salesperson's behavior.

34. **D.** The salesperson, not the broker, is responsible for notifying the *Commission* within 10 days of the change of employment.

35. **B.** Any license that is not renewed is considered inactive and the person is not permitted to practice until it is properly renewed. Licensed brokers and salespeople must satisfy the continuing education requirement during the two years *prior to* the renewal date, regardless of their length of practice.

36. **C.** Only a licensed broker can manage a real estate office. Working to qualify for a broker license, lengthy sales experience and titles do not alter this requirement.

37. **D.** To qualify for a salesperson license the individual must be at least 18 years of age (21 for a broker) and satisfy a 60-hour education requirement (30 hours for time-share salespeople). Time-share and campground membership salespeople are required to complete on-site training.

38. **A.** According to Section 803 of the Act, any aggrieved person who obtains a final judgment against a licensee for fraud, misrepresentation or deceit and is unsuccessful collecting it from the licensee can recover the money from the Recovery Fund. The fund does not exist for any other purpose.

39. **C.** The act and the Regulations require the hand money to be deposited by the end of business following the day of receipt. The only way it can be held until there is a contract is if both the buyer and seller agree in writing. The duty of the broker to escrow is nonwaivable, which means that once money is tendered to the licensee it must be escrowed.

40. **B.** The broker to whom the check is made payable has the responsibility for escrowing. Only when the buyer has been informed in accordance with the Regulations is the broker permitted to endorse the check over to the other broker. The same rules apply as cited in the previous question regarding the timing of the deposit.

Appendix B: Review Examination

1. b	25. b	49. b	73. c
2. a	26. b	50. c	74. d
3. a	27. b	51. d	75. b
4. c	28. b	52. b	76. d
5. c	29. d	53. c	77. d
6. b	30. d	54. a	78. d
7. a	31. b	55. b	79. c
8. a	32. b	56. d	80. c
9. a	33. b	57. b	81. b
10. d	34. a	58. c	82. c
11. a	35. a	59. a	83. d
12. b	36. b	60. d	84. d
13. a	37. a	61. d	85. d
14. a	38. a	62. b	86. b
15. c	39. d	63. d	87. b
16. d	40. b	64. b	88. a
17. a	41. c	65. d	89. d
18. b	42. b	66. a	90. c
19. a	43. d	67. a	91. d
20. d	44. d	68. d	92. b
21. b	45. c	69. d	93. b
22. b	46. b	70. a	94. c
23. c	47. b	71. d	95. a
24. d	48. b	72. b	

Index